The Leviathan's Choice

The Leviathan's Choice

Capital Punishment in the Twenty-First Century

J. Michael Martinez,
William D. Richardson,
D. Brandon Hornsby,
Editors

ROWMAN & LITTLEFIELD PUBLISHERS, INC.
Lanham • Boulder • New York • Oxford

ROWMAN & LITTLEFIELD PUBLISHERS, INC.

Published in the United States of America
by Rowman & Littlefield Publishers, Inc.
A Member of the Rowman & Littlefield Publishing Group
4720 Boston Way, Lanham, Maryland 20706
www.rowmanlittlefield.com

12 Hid's Copse Road
Cumnor Hill, Oxford OX2 9JJ, England

British Library Cataloguing in Publication Information Available

Library of Congress Cataloging-in-Publication Data

The Leviathan's choice : capital punishment in the twenty-first century / edited by J. Michael Martinez, William D. Richardson, D. Brandon Hornsby.
    p. cm.
    Includes index.
    ISBN 0-8476-9730-4 (cloth : alk. paper)—ISBN 0-8476-9731-2 (pbk. : alk. paper)
    1. Capital punishment. I. Martinez, J. Michael (James Michael) II. Richardson, William D. III. Hornsby, D. Brandon, 1968–

HV8694 .L475 2002
364.66—dc21

2002005055

Printed in the United States of America

∞™ The paper used in this publication meets the minimum requirements of American National Standard for Information Sciences—Permanence of Paper for Printed Library Materials, ANSI/NISO Z39.48-1992.

For Paula R. Carter, who originally sparked my interest in the topic and encouraged me along every step of the journey.

—J. Michael Martinez

For Richard H. Cox, who so ably introduced students to the great works of political philosophy.

—William D. Richardson

For my father.

—D. Brandon Hornsby

Contents

Preface and Acknowledgments

After all that has been written about capital punishment, a wary reader might ask what a new collection could possibly add to the many fine works written on this topic throughout the years. The rejoinder to this healthy dose of skepticism is to say that as long as the state deems it necessary to execute citizens, the topic requires continual reexamination. One of the editors of this collection exclaimed at the outset of the project, "Let's make this the definitive book on the death penalty." Experience has shown that no book can make such a claim. Changing social norms, new directions in philosophical and theological thinking, technological advances, and additional historical experience with state-sanctioned executions constantly challenge our preconceived notions of capital punishment.

Nonetheless, the organization of this work offers a new perspective on an old subject. Most books and secondary sources on the topic present information in a point–counterpoint format, which works well enough, but distinctions among and between academic disciplines help to clarify points further, even when some overlap occurs. Accordingly, parts 1 to 4 of the book lay out four positions—two in favor of capital punishment and two against it—from theological, philosophical, social science, and legal perspectives—that is, from the most general to the most specific disciplines. Part 5 then offers two concluding essays on the future directions of the debate.

Experience also has taught the editors that no one writes a book or compiles a collection of essays without incurring numerous debts along the way. This is the place where we acknowledge those debts, express our gratitude to all who made this book possible, and attempt to pay down the account as best we can.

First and foremost, we wish to thank the contributors for their efforts. Much ink has been spilled on the subject of capital punishment, but we believe that this collection stands above the crowd, in no small measure owing to the labors of the fine writers and thinkers whose words grace these pages. Moreover, we appreciate the efforts of Mary Carpenter, our acquisitions editor, and the excellent editorial staff at Rowman & Littlefield, especially Ginger Strader and Laura Roberts. They have been extremely patient and kind as we struggled through the many inevitable delays that occurred as we received the contributions and edited them for publication.

Even the best writers and thinkers in the world would accomplish nothing without assistance from the people who attend to the burdensome administrative details required of a book-length project. Several individuals, in particular, labored above and beyond the call of duty. Meghan Hoppe, Justin Kopetsky, Leslie Medema, Stana Donnelly, and Vanessa J. Gorden, students at the University of South Dakota, provided invaluable research assistance on several chapters, as did M. Christine Cagle, coauthor of chapter 9. Carol Nigro performed the difficult task of formatting parts of the book, no small feat for a work of this length. Cheryl Hovorka, an administrative assistant in the Department of Political Science at the University of South Dakota, assisted in the mechanics of preparing the manuscript as well. Laura M. Martinez and Paula R. Carter were generous with their time, reading many chapters and offering suggestions for improvement. Paula was especially helpful in tracking down last-minute citations and other missing information.

Several chapters have been published previously, and we express our appreciation for permission to reprint them here. They are chapter 2, Austin Sarat, "Bearing Witness and Writing History in the Struggle against Capital Punishment," *Yale Journal of Law & the Humanities* 8, no. 1 (1996): 451–63, reprinted by permission of the editors of the *Yale Journal of Law & the Humanities*; chapter 3, Ernest van den Haag, "Why Capital Punishment?" *Albany Law Review* 54, nos. 3–4 (1990): 501–14, reprinted by permission of the editorial staff of the *Albany Law Review*; chapter 5, Robert L. Young, "Religious Orientation, Race, and Support for the Death Penalty," *Journal for the Scientific Study of Religion* 31, no. 1 (March 1992): 76–87, reprinted by permission of the Society for the Scientific Study of Religion at Alfred University; chapter 7, Jacob J. Vellenga, "Is Capital Punishment Wrong?" *Christianity Today* 4, no. 1 (October 12, 1959): 7–9, reprinted by permission of the editors of *Christianity Today*; and chapter 16, Chris Hutton, "Flaws in Capital Sentencing: Skewing the Reasoned Moral Response," originally published as "Legitimizing Capital Punishment: Rationality Collides with Moral Judgment," *South Dakota Law Review* 42, no. 3 (1997): 399–433, reprinted by permission of the editorial staff of the *South Dakota Law Review*. The Library of Congress provided permission to reprint the photograph of the electric chair at Sing Sing Prison that appears on the cover of the paperback edition of this book.

The question of whether capital punishment should be imposed in a democratic regime is as old as the regime itself. Although no one work can profess to resolve the issue to the satisfaction of everyone, the editors trust that these essays will advance the debate as we enter the twenty-first century. If readers can explore these pages and come away from the work with an improved understanding of the arguments—pro and con—this collection will have served its purpose.

Introduction

PERSPECTIVES ON THE DEATH PENALTY

*J. Michael Martinez, William D. Richardson,
and D. Brandon Hornsby*

> Ritual human sacrifice was no more a horror long ago in
> our society than capital punishment is to us today, and
> there are periods in our history when a man was given high
> honors only through acts of what we today call murders
> and suicides. A man who killed his father was looked upon
> with awe at one time.
>
> —Jack Henry Abbott,
> *In the Belly of the Beast: Letters from Prison*[1]

We live in a violent world. This assertion requires no secondary references to buttress its logic or to convince even the most skeptical reader of its veracity. The twentieth century bore witness to acts of violence and cruelty almost unimaginable in an earlier time. As the twenty-first century dawns, the world is not poised to reverse its unenviable record. Consider a few examples. A wholesome-looking American man who blew up a federal building for vague and mostly amorphous reasons met his death through lethal injection for perpetrating one of the worst mass murders in U.S. history. An exiled Saudi Arabian religious fanatic apparently masterminded an ongoing conspiracy to murder all infidels—especially those in the United States—who disagreed with his apocalyptic worldview. On a less dramatic scale, almost every day American citizens take up arms against their fellow citizens and slaughter them for base human motives: jealousy, anger, revenge, greed, or because of mental illness.

It is little wonder that capital punishment remains popular among citizens who must interact with the world at the risk of suffering physical harm. The question, of course, is whether the imposition of capital punishment is an appropriate response to threats, real and imagined, from a hostile world. Setting aside the visceral reaction, thoughtful people must continually ask themselves if their government and their society should resort to state-sanctioned executions in lieu of some other response. This is precisely the question the commentators address in this book.

"That great Leviathan," wrote the seventeenth-century English philosopher Thomas Hobbes, exists as a "mortal god" to which "we owe, under the *immortal God*, our peace and defense."[2] Because the Leviathan—the state—is the most rational instrument developed by human beings for protecting individuals from violent death at the hands of their fellow men, in Hobbes's view, it must be infused with sufficient power and authority to control the dark excesses of human nature. Individuals covenant with each other to create the state and agree as part of their bargain to surrender some natural liberty in exchange for a measure of order and security. If the state indulges in abuses upon occasion, that is a small price to pay to escape the horrors of existing in an unbridled state of nature. His defense of a strong state was a hallmark of the Enlightenment's emphasis on creating rational governmental institutions to perfect—or at least circumvent the deficiencies of—the individual.[3]

The difficulty with Hobbes's perspective is that it assumes that the state should exercise supreme power over its citizens without adequately addressing the question of whether abuses perpetrated by the state will occur and, if so, how abuses will be corrected. Throughout his master work *Leviathan*, he contends that the state must be strong enough to prevent a return to a prestate existence, which he finds too terrible to contemplate. Hobbes's fear of the state of nature leads him to reject attacks on the state's authority as too dangerous. Nonetheless, we have traveled a long way since Hobbes's day. No longer do we argue for state supremacy over and above considerations of individual rights and civil liberties. Exploring the question of the state's power over life and death is an important line of inquiry for anyone who desires to understand fundamental issues—such as capital punishment—concerning the relationship between the individual and the collectivity.

Building on Hobbes's thesis that the state is a metaphorical Leviathan, this collection addresses the question of whether an entity outside the individual should exercise the power to decide questions of life and death and, if so, how far that power extends. Every question about capital punishment ultimately comes back to an inquiry into the relationship between individual citizens and the Leviathan that governs them. Implicit in this inquiry is a debate about the appropriate balance between liberty and equality.

If liberty is defined as "absence of constraints"—that is, the ability of an individual to act without being limited by anything other than the dictates of his reason—then it seems logical than human beings would desire the maximum amount of liberty possible. With the exception of classical anarchists and extreme libertarians, however, most mainstream Western thinkers have argued that a state of absolute liberty is a utopian dream unworthy of serious consideration. Instead, mainstream thinkers—at least those schooled in the social contract tradition—agree that the nature of man requires that some limitations be placed on individuals by some entity in exchange for a measure of liberty.

If equality is defined in the American sense of "equality of opportunity," the debate shifts to a question of how much liberty the citizens of a regime are prepared to surrender in exchange for state-enforced equality of opportunity. Clearly, a person who commits a capital crime must be punished to ensure that he will not repeat the offense, but beyond that simple precept the issues are far from clear. A state that takes human life cannot escape inquiries into its decision-making processes, its rationale for sanctioning executions, the repercussions of executions for the regime, and the necessity for safeguards to reduce or eliminate errors, accidents, and biases.

As many of these chapters vividly illustrate, the debate over capital punishment is as old as the concept of government itself. Indeed, the arguments are as old as the Western intellectual tradition itself. Aside from the familiar biblical refrain of "an eye for an eye," discussed by many authors herein, questions of whether capital punishment should be exercised by the state over its citizens extend back at least as far as the sixteenth century. "What *right*, I ask, have men to cut the throats of their fellow-creatures," the Italian criminologist Cesare Beccaria inquired in 1764.[4] Similarly, the issue came before the English parliament in 1701. "I am sensible," wrote one anonymous sage in a paper presented to that august body, "[t]hat the *English* Clemency and Mildness appear eminently in our Laws and Constitutions; but since it is found that *Ill* Men are grown so much more incorrigible, than in our fore-fathers Days, is it not fit that *Good Men* should grow less merciful to them, since gentler Methods are ineffectual?"[5]

Despite the persistence of the capital punishment debate throughout the years, the twentieth century presented a new set of problems. With advances in technology, on one hand, and our increased understanding of human psychology, on the other, we began to view the issue in a different light. Because this question has been posed in many different guises across many disciplines, the present collection is divided into four distinct parts, from the broad metaphysical questions posed by philosophers and theologians to the precise, contextual issues raised by social scientists and lawyers.

In part 1, "Philosophical Perspectives," the contributors discuss arguments for and against capital punishment based on philosophical ideas and concepts. Three academicians, J. Michael Martinez of Kennesaw State University, William D. Richardson of the University of South Dakota, and Cheryl A. Brown of Marshall University, lead off the section in chapter 1 by reviewing philosophical arguments in favor of capital punishment. Titled "Low Deeds and High Goods: Philosophical Foundations of the Death Penalty in the American Regime," the chapter focuses on the pro–death penalty arguments advanced by influential political thinkers such as Hobbes, John Locke, Thomas Jefferson, and the drafters of the U.S. Constitution. The authors also contend that John Stuart Mill's and Immanuel Kant's support for capital punishment created a firm foundation for the death penalty throughout American history. "Legislatures may have the power to abolish the death penalty, but generally they have not done so," the authors conclude. "Moreover, many Americans now and throughout our history have preferred to accept low deeds undertaken by the state as a method—and a powerful one, at that—to ensure that the high goods of the American political system come to fruition."

In chapter 2, "Bearing Witness and Writing History in the Struggle against Capital Punishment," a well-known death penalty opponent, Professor Austin Sarat of Amherst University, discusses the reasons why, in his view, capital punishment is barbaric and must be eliminated. He argues that although the law currently allows states to execute capital offenders, abolitionists can still push to mitigate, and perhaps eventually eliminate, capital punishment. In myriad ways, anti–death penalty lawyers can act so that future lawyers, judges, and political activists recognize the brutality of state-sanctioned executions. Even in cases where a lawyer knows he will lose and his client will be put to death, he must struggle to protect the record for the sake of history. In Sarat's opinion, "one of the tasks of lawyering in a losing cause is to find legal devices that address the future while continuing, however fruitlessly, the struggle against the present reality of law's violence."

A far different perspective follows in chapter 3. Ernest van den Haag, another well-known commentator, directly or indirectly addresses many of the issues raised by Sarat. In "Why Capital Punishment?" a reprint from a 1990 *Albany Law Review* article, van den Haag reviews the state of capital punishment at the beginning of the 1990s, when he wrote his chapter. Despite the continued popularity of capital punishment, he observes that judges are reluctant to impose such a harsh punishment. It may be that they have adopted sociological views on the "barbaric" nature of the death penalty, or they may interpret the Eighth Amendment's well-known prohibition on "cruel and unusual" punishment as a ban on such practices. Whatever the reason, van den Haag is not persuaded by arguments that capital punishment somehow is different than other punishments and therefore must be avoided at all costs. "Actually," he writes, "capital punishment makes some persons uneasy, not so much because of rational doubts about its constitutionality, but because it is irrevocable, not just irreversible as most punishments are. Our age seems allergic to irrevocability. However, death irrevocably will happen to us all."

The real issue in justifying the death penalty, in van den Haag's opinion, is to discern why the state chooses this type of punishment. If the reason is retribution—sometimes incorrectly labeled "revenge"—this is an acceptable rationale because it is a penalty imposed by law to "enforce and vindicate the social order." Such a *lex talionis*—the law of retaliation—has been recognized since Roman times as a permissible goal of the state. Even a venerable American statesman like Thomas Jefferson argued in favor of such purposes.

Could capital offenders be restrained by sentencing them to life in prison without the possibility of parole? If so, death penalty critics would be correct that state-sanctioned executions are excessive. Van den Haag contends, however, that convicted murderers still commit crimes behind bars; in fact, many violent crimes occur among and between inmates. "Even if it were completely incapacitative, a life sentence in prison could not replace the death penalty," he suggests. "Justice demands that murderers be excluded from the human community, including even the prison community."

Ultimately, then, the death penalty is a question of justice—that is, of giving what is owed. Arguments against capital punishment that stray from considerations of justice mistake the fundamental issue. This is especially true on the question of whether the death penalty serves as an effective deterrent for would-be capital offenders. "If the death penalty were morally wrong, no deterrent effect would make it right, unless deterrence constitutes a moral argument that trumps the moral arguments against the death penalty. For most deontologists, deterrence cannot do so. On the other hand, if the death penalty is morally right, it remains so, even if it is not deterrent."

As for arguments that the death penalty is applied inequitably, van den Haag observes that the best way to avoid being sentenced to die is to avoid committing capital crimes. More to the point, he observes that guilt is individual. Whether other offenders receive the same sentence has no direct effect on an individual's situation. Despite arguments that certain disparities exist in the American regime—racial discrimination, poverty, mental retardation, or youth—the fact remains that "the justice of a sentence does not depend on other sentences, just or unjust, but only on whether the convict's guilt justifies it."

Van den Haag concludes his chapter by reiterating that moral justifications and sound public policy support the imposition of the death penalty on capital offenders. The state owes its citizens a duty to protect their safety and welfare, to the extent possible. Capital punishment is one weapon that the state can—and should be able to—use in its efforts. To outlaw the death penalty is to restrict the state and unnecessarily endanger the populace.

The last chapter of this section, "'Woe to the Hand That Shed This Costly Blood': Philosophical Arguments against the Death Penalty," changes the emphasis and considers Western philosophical ideals on capital punishment from a much different perspective. According to J. Michael Martinez, a legal system in a democratic regime is predicated on a concept of fundamental fairness. Although this is a highly contested concept, Martinez suggests that most people in highly industrialized, Westernized nations probably would agree that fundamental fairness requires a moral presumption against killing human beings. If this is the case, a state that decides to sentence offenders to death has to rebut this presumption through persuasive, credible evidence. In Martinez's view, this burden is too difficult for the state to bear.

After reviewing the works of many Western philosophers and writers—including Thomas Hobbes, John Locke, Fyodor Dostoyevsky, Michel Foucault, Plato, John Stuart Mill, George Orwell, Clarence Darrow, Immanuel Kant, Albert Camus, and Jesus, among others—he concludes that arguments in support of "just executions" are not as logically compelling as arguments that portray the state as an entity interested primarily in retribution and revenge. "A nation that purports to live in accordance with the rule of law coupled with a notion of fundamental fairness can—and must—do better," he writes.

Moving from philosophical to theological arguments in part 2 of the book, chapter 5, "Religious Orientation, Race, and Support for the Death Penalty," examines the relationship between religion and social attitudes on capital punishment. Because race often is intertwined with the level and type of an individual's religious beliefs, author Robert L. Young performs a logistic regression analysis to determine the nature of the relationship between religious beliefs (the independent variable) and support for the death penalty (the dependent variable). Using data gathered from the 1988 General Social Survey, Young finds "a relatively clear and concise image of the role of religious orientation in influencing attitudes toward the death penalty." Not surprisingly, he finds that persons who support fundamentalism tended to support the death penalty to a greater extent than persons who adhere to other religious beliefs, probably because the fundamentalist orientation resolves much of the uncertainty that plagues other religious perspectives. Moreover, fundamentalists generally believe in the primacy of individual free will and responsibility, which means that they are not as likely to accept mitigating factors that convince other religious adherents to temper their support for state-sanctioned executions. Young also finds that evangelism showed the largest single impact on the dependent variable, perhaps because evangelicals demonstrate compassion for others as an integral part of their faith.

As for race, Young concludes that affiliation with fundamentalist churches does not seem to affect black attitudes toward the death penalty, unlike the case with white respondents. This may be the result of several factors. First, support for the death penalty remains consistently low in the African American community because blacks often view the American criminal justice system with deep mistrust. As a consequence, their opposition to the death penalty often antedates the development of their mature religious attitudes, despite the centrality of religion in African American life. In addition, even in cases where black religious attitudes affect perspectives on the death penalty, in Young's words, "the individualism associated with white Protestantism might be tempered by a more collectivist orientation that is deeply rooted in Afro-American history." In other words, whatever else he concludes from his study, Young acknowledges that religious attitudes toward the death penalty are not identical between white and black respondents.

Young cautious against applying the results of the study to situations not supported by the research without further refining the variables. "The results of this study also suggest the need for theoretical clarification of certain concepts in the sociology of religion," he writes. "Until this is accomplished, the empirical association between such variables as fundamentalism and evangelicalism should not blind us to the necessity of maintaining clear conceptual distinctions."

In chapter 6, Professor Mark Douglas of Columbia Theological Seminary argues for several conceptual distinctions in a chapter titled "Theological Arguments and the Case against Capital Punishment." At the outset, he contends that a "Christian theologian writing in opposition to capital punishment ought to have a fairly easy time of things." Yet, owing to support for the death penalty in the American regime, theological opposition is not as obvious as one might think. To correct what Douglas believes is a misguided popular perspective, he attempts to develop a theological argument against capital punishment while also encouraging readers to ask themselves whether their theological views are consistent with their views on capital punishment.

In developing a consistent theological perspective, a Christian generally adheres to at least one central idea—"namely, that the God above whose will is expressed through the graceful action of Jesus Christ is sovereign over and through the universe." To explore the implications of this insight, Douglas examines the work of several death penalty supporters. Ernest van den Haag, author of chapter 3 in this collection, receives special attention owing to his well-known arguments in favor of the death penalty. According to van den Haag, many death penalty opponents mix practical concerns with philosophical objections. "It follows, then, that a genuine theological opposition to the death penalty begins with the position that *nobody* deserves to be executed by the state regardless of their actions," Douglas suggests. This is the only theological position that allows the writer to maintain a logically consistent, defensible argument against state-sanctioned executions.

Douglas also examines the writings of Walter Berns, a capital punishment supporter who contends that society kills capital offenders as retribution for their crimes. In a sense, collective retribution allows us to restore the bonds that unite persons because it allows society to express its collective anger at capital offenders.

Douglas also examines the work of two historically prominent theologians, the thirteenth-century Catholic theologian St. Thomas Aquinas and the twentieth-century Protestant theologian Karl Barth, each of whom represents a broad tradition within the Christian church. In the former's view, when people violate the social order, they are subject to punishment by society, thereby allowing justice to be restored and deterring future criminal activity. As for Barth, he is less insistent than Aquinas that the death penalty can be justified, but he recognizes that in some instances life can be taken when it is the only means of preserving life.

Although these highly respected theologians present many good, well-reasoned arguments, Douglas argues that the capital punishment is rarely about rationality. "To the extent that religious language and ideologies may be close to or at the heart of the debate over capital punishment," he writes, "it may not be resolvable at the level of rational argument, since such language and ideology typically involve extra-rational belief structures and 'largely unspoken of and perhaps even subconscious' categories and modes of and motives for behavior." Capital punishment can be viewed as a ritual with certain customs and traditions that extend beyond the realm of reason alone. This may partially explain its continued popularity among many Americans.

The vision of Jesus Christ as savior and Lord, however, offers a different perspective. The reasons generally stated for executing capital offenders do not square with Jesus's teachings on redemption and the power of mercy. Rituals, a quest for justice, deterrence, and any other justifications simply fail to comport with Christianity. Douglas concludes that "I would hope . . . that Christian theologians would enter this discourse not only to help us all make sense of capital punishment, but to work for its abolition as well. That seems to me to be the only conclusion that the gospel of Jesus Christ will allow."

Standing in direct contrast to Douglas's approach is chapter 7, "Is Capital Punishment Wrong?" by Jacob J. Vellenga. The chapter is a reprint of a well-known article first published in *Christianity Today* in 1959. According to Vellenga, "[t]hose favoring capital punishment are not to be stigmatized as heartless, vengeful, and lacking in mercy, but are to be respected as advocating that which is the best for society as a whole." Reasonable minds can differ, and even biblical passages on the issue are not always clear.

Vellenga reviews passages from both the Old and New Testaments and argues that questions involving capital punishment involve violations of human law and therefore are best left to the government of man. Although Jesus may have spoken of loving one's enemies and turning the other cheek, he did not advocate establishing a permissive government where offenders are absolved of responsibility for their actions. Offenders may still receive God's mercy, but this may or may not affect their need to answer for violations of human law. God's mercy depends on the offender opening himself to forgiveness by forgiving others. For convicted murderers who seek mercy for themselves when they showed none to their victims, they are not ready to receive mercy. Love and mercy require an acceptance of basic justice and fair play that many capital offenders refuse to acknowledge.

In Vellenga's view, capital punishment is not vindictive if it is applied in accordance with "the careful and exact administering of justice by society's government." Moreover, despite the arguments set forth by some critics, capital punishment allows for repentance. A capital offender always has an opportunity between the time he is convicted and the time he is executed to make peace with God. This is part of the natural order of things, for "wherever and whenever God's love and mercy are rejected, as in crime, natural law and order must prevail, not as extraneous to redemption but as part of the whole scope of God's dealings with man."

At the conclusion of Vellenga's chapter, Glen H. Stassen of Fuller Theological Seminary returns to many of the themes raised by Professor Douglas earlier in the book. In chapter 8, "Deliverance from the Vicious Cycles of Murder," Stassen suggests that if we understand the true meaning of Jesus Christ, we will change our perspective on capital punishment. "I seek to do theological ethics from the perspective of the Lordship of Jesus Christ," he writes. "I believe Jesus teaches directly on the question of murder, and his way is the way of transforming initiatives that prevent murder, not the way of retaliation." In short, although Jesus does not specifically discuss the death penalty—at least not as we think of it in a modern context—he "points to initiatives that deliver us from our culture of violence." Consequently, from a Christian theological perspective, the argument is not whether a person supports or opposes the death penalty, but the issue is to explore "effective preventive initiatives." If we work to develop these initiatives, we cannot help but conclude that the death penalty is anathema.

Much of chapter 8 reviews and interprets Jesus' teachings throughout the New Testament as Stassen places various biblical passages into theological and historical context. He concludes that these passages, like passages from the Old Testament, can and should be interpreted as condemning the "cycles of murder" that give rise to the question of capital punishment. "What we have seen so far must not be understood as setting the New Testament versus the Old Testament, or the Hebrew Scriptures," he observes. "The direction of the Old Testament moves from the ancient practice of the death penalty toward its abolition." The New Testament then advances this perspective to an even greater extent by focusing on Jesus' life and work.

In Stassen's opinion, only persons who view the issue as a question of state authority instead of examining capital punishment as the right to life as expressed through Jesus' teaching can support the death penalty. "Church leaders and Christian ethicists who have studied the question widely agree that the death penalty contradicts justice, violates the sacredness of human life, and diverts us from effective ways of preventing murder," he concludes. "I add: it contradicts the Lordship of Jesus Christ."

Part 3 of the collection shifts to another discipline by offering social science perspectives for and against capital punishment. In chapter 9, M. Christine Cagle and J. Michael Martinez examine arguments about capital punishment based on social science data, especially a study conducted by researchers at Columbia University in 2000. Titled "Social Science Data and the Death Penalty: Understanding the Debate over 'A Broken System,'" the chapter examines a debate that has raged about whether the American capital punishment system is seriously, irreversibly flawed or whether it is amenable to relatively minor corrections to reduce or eliminate mistakes.

The Columbia University study, "A Broken System," was conducted by James S. Liebman, a law professor at Columbia University, Jeffrey Fagan, a visiting professor at Columbia University, and Valerie West, a doctoral candidate in sociology at New York University. The authors announced the study results in 2000, but they initiated the study in 1991 when Senator Joseph Biden (D-Delaware), chairman of the U.S. Senate Judiciary Committee, asked Professor Liebman to provide the committee with data on capital cases. Much to his astonishment, Liebman discovered that no reliable data existed on the frequency of errors in federal capital cases. As a result, the professor pieced together data from the National Association for the Advancement of Colored People (NAACP) Legal Defense Fund's quarterly death row census, but he remained unsatisfied. Realizing that more data were needed, he and his colleagues embarked on an ambitious research project. They examined 5,760 death penalty sentences imposed in the United States between 1973 and 1995. To understand the data, the researchers reviewed cases at three stages: direct appeals in state courts, postconviction review, and federal habeas corpus appeals. In their view, the data led to one inescapable conclusion: that "serious error—error substantially undermining the reliability of capital verdicts—has reached epidemic proportions throughout our death penalty system." Over all states, the study found an average rate of serious error of 68 percent.

"A Broken System" ignited a firestorm of criticism. Researchers Barry Latzer and James N. G. Cauthen argued that the Columbia researchers failed to distinguish between conviction rates and sentence reversal rates. Jaime Sneider of the *Columbia Daily Spectator* concluded that Liebman's study highlighted some flaws in America's criminal justice system, but its conclusions were hyperbolic and based on faulty data. Michael Rushford of the conservative Criminal Justice Legal Foundation called the study a "political document, timed to impact the congressional hearings." Echoing this criticism, David Horowitz, president of the

Center for the Study of Popular Culture, characterized Liebman and his colleagues as part of the liberal vanguard typified by "the left-wing media, namely the *New York Times* and the *L.A. Times.*" In Horowitz's opinion, Liebman is an anti–death penalty political activist intent on using his supposedly neutral study to advance his political agenda. "The corruption of our academic and press institutions by the political left has been going on for so long and has reached a point of such magnitude where abysmal disregard for the normal standards of academic inquiry and journalistic reportage is normal, that it is hard to take . . . each institution seriously anymore," Horowitz wrote.

The authors of "A Broken System" have responded to these attacks by defending the validity of their study in follow-up articles and interviews. Whatever the study's virtues and vices, it has provided fodder for debate and, in some cases, has pushed state governors and legislators to reexamine their statutes and capital punishment procedures. Most notably, Illinois governor George Ryan has called for a temporary moratorium on executions in his state. Although Governor Ryan's decision to review death penalty procedures in Illinois antedated the announcement of the Columbia study results, "A Broken System" certainly gave the governor more support in his quest to determine whether capital punishment could be administered fairly. According to a spokesman for the governor, "The study conclusions were not surprising, but only added fuel to the administration's belief that the death penalty system in Illinois had serious problems that were already known."

In a similar vein, Elizabeth Theiss Smith of the University of South Dakota questions whether states can implement the death penalty fairly in light of flaws and biases incorporated into state judicial systems. In chapter 10, "Fatal Flaws: The Implementation of the Death Penalty in the States," she reviews errors such as police and prosecutorial misconduct, ineffective assistance of counsel, political pressure applied to judges as they decide whether to impose capital punishment, and errors in jury instructions. In her view, even proposed reforms—assuming they could be implemented after undergoing legislative compromises and the lack of adequate resources in many states—would not necessarily ensure that fundamental fairness would result. "It is the nature of human institutions to be fallible and prone to error," she observes. With the multitude of errors that can, and often do, occur, capital punishment must be rejected out of hand. "This is unacceptable in a society that professes devotion to the democratic virtues of freedom, fairness, and equality."

In chapter 11, "Race and the Death Penalty," John C. McAdams examines one of the most sensitive and controversial areas of capital punishment—namely, the question of whether the argument against executions owing to "racial disparity" is "illogical in its form and mistaken in its normative and empirical premises." In his view, this is exactly the case. Arguments about the death penalty often are predicated on antiquated notions or mistaken impressions of the available legal and social science data. As a result, participants in the debate generally defend an ideological position that may not be based on accurate factual information.

According to McAdams, one of the most often cited and least effective arguments used by death penalty opponents is the contention that the death penalty is selectively applied. In particular, the argument generally suggests that African Americans are sentenced to death substantially more often than white defendants, even in cases where the circumstances of the crime were similar. McAdams contends that this argument is fallacious. As long as government treats individuals fairly—that is, it treats like cases alike—group disparity is not a justifiable argument for selective application of the death penalty. If some guilty murderers receive the death penalty and others do not, this does not allow the individual murderer who received a death sentence to argue that he was treated unfairly.

Guilt is assigned on an individual basis, which means that a murderer must examine whether he was treated fairly. Did he receive a fair trial from an impartial jury with the effective assistance of counsel? If so, he loses his right to contend that someone else from the group of convicted offenders received a different result. The U.S. Constitution promises a fair means—due process—but a particular end in an individual case is not guaranteed. If this were not the case, an individual defendant could simply search around for the most lenient punishment assigned and argue that he should not receive a sentence in excess of that sentence. By this logic, a motorist who was stopped for speeding could argue that he should not receive a traffic citation because the patrolman did not stop everyone who was speeding. Unconstitutional disparities exist only if an individual defendant is assigned a sentence in excess of other sentences solely because of his race and he can demonstrate that this racial animus existed *in his particular case*, not across a group of cases.

Even if disparities exist in some cases—and McAdams concedes that they might—this does not necessarily serve as legitimate ground for abolishing the death penalty. The death penalty may not be perfectly applied, but it may still be preferable to alternative forms of punishment if it achieves constitutionally permissible goals of the states. Moreover, if alternative methods of punishment also perpetuate disparities or fail to be effective, the death penalty cannot be rejected summarily because it may or may not affect different groups of people disproportionately. "The striking thing about the death penalty," he concludes, "is the extent to which it is an outcropping of the 'culture wars.' It seems to distill fundamental cultural values—about personal responsibility, guilt, the place of government, the therapeutic role of middle class professionals, and claims of victimhood."

A contrary, anti–death penalty perspective is presented in the next chapter. "'The Executioner's Face Is Always Well-Hidden': Social Science Arguments against Capital Punishment" recounts the misadventures of the Isaacs gang, a group of young men that slaughtered an entire family in rural south Georgia in 1973. Carl Isaacs, the acknowledged ringleader of the gang, never showed remorse for his horrific crime. In a 1977 television interview, he spoke of his victims dispassionately. "They don't mean a damn thing to me," he said when asked about the Alday family. "The only thing the Aldays ever did that stood out was getting killed by me."

When confronted with the Carl Issacs of the world, society understandably seeks to find a means of preventing future occurrences as well as protecting citizens from current perpetrators and expressing a collective sense of justice. The question is whether the use of the death penalty accomplishes these three societal goals. According to author J. Michael Martinez, the available social science data on these points are inconclusive at best. At worst, the death penalty cannot be shown to accomplish any of the three.

The deterrence argument assumes that offenders are rational maximizers who alter their behavior according to calculations of costs and benefits. If this hypothesis were accurate, data ought to demonstrate that states with capital punishment statutes have lower murder and nonnegligent homicide rates than states without such statutes because offenders have decided that the costs of perpetrating these crimes outweigh the "benefits," all other things being equal. Nonetheless, the data do not support this hypothesis; in some cases, the murder and nonnegligent homicide rate is lower in non–death penalty states. A capital punishment proponent might argue that this anomaly is the result of other variables, such as the demographics of the states being compared, the nature of the particular crimes under consideration, and the like, but the relationship among and between these variables is anything but clear.

The second question of whether the death penalty protects society from offenders who might strike again is difficult to assess because it assumes future behavior that may or may not occur. Although Carl Isaacs claimed that the death penalty did not bother him because "if I get away, I'll kill 1,000 more people," in most instances it is almost impossible to predict the behavior of persons convicted of heinous crimes. Even if one could say with a reasonable degree of certainty that the offender probably would act again, he or she can be confined for life, thereby effectively preventing the offender from harming society again. Death row inmates may escape from time to time in dramatic, well-publicized instances, but these are comparatively rare events. For a society that seeks to establish a criminal justice system that appropriately responds to criminal behavior, the question of whether the incapacitation of an offender justifies the imposition of the death penalty remains contentious.

As for the third question of whether capital punishment is an expression of society's collective sense of justice, Martinez observes that the public favors this approach, especially in cases involving unsympathetic criminals such as the Issacs gang. But is this genuinely a reflection of society's collective sense of justice or a visceral response to dramatic horror stories? According to several commentators, the public might choose alternatives to capital punishment if they were presented with a range of choices, such as life without the possibility of parole plus restitution to the families of the victim. Because traditional public opinion polls do not always present a range of alternatives, it is difficult to conclude that the public favors capital punishment or that society's collective sense of justice is offended. In light of these difficulties, according to Martinez, social science data generally do not support the use of the death penalty to accomplish societal goals. If this is the case, the imposition of the death penalty must be directed toward other goals.

Douglas Clouatre of Kennesaw State University argues in chapter 13, "Massive Resistance: Capital Punishment, the Abolitionist Movement, and the Supreme Court," that "the abolitionist movement abused the appeals process and was eventually defeated." In Clouatre's view, the abolitionists engaged a series of complex legal maneuvers in a deliberate effort to obfuscate the death penalty issue. As a result, "judges ensnared themselves in a legal thicket of contradictory and complex rulings." By the 1990s, the need for reform was readily apparent. An increasingly conservative Rehnquist Court was only too happy to lead reform efforts by streamlining the federal habeas corpus process, granting grand juries more discretion, and allowing the execution of underage offenders.

The inevitable result of the Rehnquist Court's reforms of death penalty jurisprudence has been to stop federal courts from micromanaging the death penalty process. This allows state legislators and judges more discretion in fulfilling their duties. In a federal system that appears to be revitalizing state authority after many decades of federal intervention into many issues originally deemed to be within the states' purview, the movement away from micromanaging death penalty questions is a healthy change, in Clouatre's opinion. "With its reforms in place," he concludes, "the Rehnquist Court, with aid from Congress, has ensured the enforcement of death sentences while protecting the safeguards for defendants challenging their sentences. In doing so they have protected the rule of law and dealt a serious blow to the abolitionist movement."

Chapter 14 moves from a discussion of the death penalty in general to the issue of sentencing disparities as the penalty is applied. In "'Freakishly Imposed' or 'Fundamentally Fair'? Legal Arguments against the Death Penalty," J. Michael Martinez asks whether it is possible to impose the death penalty in a fair and equitable manner. The U.S. Supreme Court has answered in the affirmative—as long as state statutes set forth standards and guidelines for capital cases. Many commentators have taken issue with the high court's reasoning, and Martinez explores their arguments in some detail.

A number of potential factors affect equity in sentencing, among them race, poverty, mental retardation, and youth. Martinez explores each issue in detail, offering a synopsis and analysis of the leading U.S. Supreme Court cases on the issue. In each instance, the court has concluded that these special factors, absent evidence of bias in specific cases, do not preclude imposition of capital punishment. At the conclusion of the chapter, Martinez suggests that the problem with capital punishment—and the reason that it remains so controversial—is that it seems to fall between two extremes. The courts and state legislatures have attempted to set forth standards that guide judges and juries on how to apply the punishment in a way that makes it not "freakishly imposed." This has been difficult because the standards must be uniform and consistent yet not so mechanistic that they prevent decision makers from considering the effects of special circumstances. By and large, judges and legislatures have done a credible job, even if the standards still leave some room for ambiguity and confusion.

Nonetheless, because so many factors and variables are present in each capital case, the death penalty seems to fall short of many definitions of "fundamental fairness." From the perspective of a nation that professes to treat its citizens more or less equitably, the death penalty always presents nagging doubts about how fairly it is applied to persons of color, the poor, the mentally retarded, and juveniles. In short, Martinez argues that capital punishment, in most cases, is neither freakishly imposed nor fundamentally fair. It is a hybrid sentence. Such a sentence will remain endlessly controversial because citizens will never agree on its virtues and vices.

In chapter 15, "Legal Arguments in Favor of the Death Penalty," Martinez considers the opposite argument by reviewing the major case law on capital punishment in the United States. According to Martinez, *Furman v. Georgia* was the first major opinion handed down by the U.S. Supreme Court in the modern era. In that landmark 1972 case, three African American defendants challenged death penalty statutes in Georgia and Texas. A deeply divided Supreme Court reversed the defendants' convictions and remanded the cases for further adjudication. Although the effect of the per curiam decision was to proclaim the death penalty cruel and unusual punishment in contravention of the Eighth and Fourteenth Amendments, each of the nine justices wrote a separate opinion that expressed a confusing range of perspectives.

Four years later, the U.S. Supreme Court announced another landmark opinion, *Gregg v. Georgia.* The *Gregg* case arose from another Georgia murder conviction. As with *Furman,* the justices were divided on the appropriate disposition, although seven of the nine concluded that the Georgia statute did not violate the Eighth Amendment. The practical effect of this conclusion was to overturn *Furman,* although the court did not expressly overrule the earlier case. In Martinez's view, "*Gregg* served notice to states that the Supreme Court was willing to examine state statutes closely to determine whether specific provisions and the application of statutory standards in specific cases were constitutionally permissible."

After *Gregg*, legal challenges to the death penalty generally shifted from questions of whether the punishment was constitutionally permissible (it was) to questions of how offenders were arrested, tried, and sentenced. This new direction served as the impetus for state legislators to revise their statutes and thereby explicitly provide guidelines for handling death penalty cases. As long as the statutes meet the U.S. Supreme Court's guidelines, the lower federal courts have been reluctant to intervene. Consequently, death penalty challenges since the mid-1970s generally have focused on whether states have adequately provided clear, consistent, fundamentally fair guidelines for executing certain offenders.

In chapter 16, "Flaws in Capital Sentencing: Skewing the Reasoned Moral Response," Chris Hutton, a law professor at the University of South Dakota, argues that the focus on applying the death penalty cannot be divorced from concerns about society's "reasoned moral response." Thus, questions about capital punishment are not strictly matters that should be considered from a narrow, legalistic perspective. Instead, we must always begin with a basic inquiry: *Should* the regime impose the ultimate penalty? The answer must be rooted in religious beliefs with full consideration of issues such as retribution or deterrence, as many of the chapters on this collection suggest. Next, assuming that capital punishment should be imposed, the focus shifts to the question of whether we *may* impose capital punishment under certain circumstances. In light of the U.S. Supreme Court's jurisprudence on this issue, the answer is an emphatic yes. As long as the requirements set forth in a series of cases, most notably *Gregg v. Georgia*, are met, states may impose the death penalty on duly convicted offenders. Finally, this leads to the final question: whether we *can* impose capital punishment. Hutton writes that the "answer depends in large part on what we demand of the legal system if it purports to be able to implement a capital punishment process."

Much of Hutton's chapter is a survey of capital punishment jurisprudence aimed at addressing each of these three questions. She concludes that the very act of a state imposing death on any of its citizens is an exercise fraught with peril. The potential for grievous error, bias, ineffective counsel, and irrational application is so great that it may be unrealistic to expect mortal man, with all his frailties and faults, to use this mighty weapon in a civilized, humane manner. "Thus, perhaps the most honest answer from the legal system is that it has tried but failed in the realm of capital punishment. The answer to the question 'Can we impose death sentences fairly, rationally, and accurately?' is no."

In the final section of the book, "Future Directions of Capital Punishment," Timothy J. Schorn discusses the perception of the death penalty in the international community. In chapter 17, "The Death Penalty and the International Community: Evolving Norms or Persistent Differences?" he observes that a movement is afoot in many industrialized nations to abolish capital punishment as inconsistent with the dictates of a just, civilized society. Generally, with the notable exception of the United States, only developing and underdeveloped countries retain this form of punishment. Nonetheless, despite a general movement away from state-sponsored executions, nations have not reached consensus on the issue. "While the right to life is universally accepted, that right is apparently not an absolute," he writes. "While the death penalty is a consistent pattern in some countries, it is not universally accepted to be a violation of an internationally recognized right."

This general movement, albeit without a consensus on the issue, raises a question that is directly addressed in the final chapter: What is the future of the death penalty? Reflecting on the question, the Honorable Robert A. Miller, a retired chief justice of the South Dakota Supreme Court, observes that public support for the death penalty in the United States remains high. This is especially true in the wake of the terrorist attacks of September 11, 2001. In Justice Miller's opinion, the likelihood of the United States abandoning capital punishment in the near future is extremely remote. Accordingly, it is incumbent upon scholars and practitioners to understand the challenges associated with applying the penalty in an equitable manner.

Constitutional protections must not be abrogated in the race to judgment. The desire to ensure that all rules of constitutional procedure are followed and individuals are protected means that the state and federal judiciaries must bear a heavy burden. The costs of implementing capital punishment are high, but in Justice Miller's view the criminal justice system must pay those costs. To turn a blind eye to the possibility of abuse presents an even higher cost to society. "I strongly support a constant and ongoing debate and scrutiny of it," he concludes. "Our citizens deserve no less."

As each of the chapters in this collection concludes, explicitly or implicitly, the death penalty remains a highly contested concept open to varying interpretations and opinions. Although this collection is unlikely to resolve the issue to anyone's satisfaction, the authors and editors trust that the discussions will add new perspectives to the ongoing national debate as we enter a new century and a new millennium. As long as the state executes its citizens, such periodic reevaluations will be necessary and, ultimately, healthy for the regime.

Part 1

PHILOSOPHICAL PERSPECTIVES

CHAPTER 1

Low Deeds and High Goods

PHILOSOPHICAL FOUNDATIONS OF THE
DEATH PENALTY IN THE AMERICAN REGIME

*J. Michael Martinez, William D. Richardson,
and Cheryl A. Brown*

Opponents of capital punishment often contend that state-sanctioned executions are antithetical to the high ideals of the American republic. In their view, the American tradition is predicated, at least in part, on the right of individuals to be protected from the tyrannical impulses of consolidated government. It is only through accidents of history and constitutional misinterpretation that state-sanctioned killing developed. Sooner or later—so the argument goes—a government that sentences its citizens to death will become overbearing and oppressive, subordinating the desire for justice to the quest for expediency. In effect, this is a slippery slope argument; government must not be imbued with authority to impose the ultimate penalty, for this inevitably leads to abuses that have no place in a republic founded on principles of individual liberty and freedom of thought.[1]

Although even a cursory examination of the patterns of history lends support for the argument that the American regime originally embraced a principle that might be expressed as the fear of too much power in too few hands, this insight should not be extended too far. The desire to control the power of a centralized government was not necessarily equivalent to limiting its effectiveness once its legitimacy had been established. The Founders of the American regime rejected the Articles of Confederation because the document could not reliably secure the peaceable enjoyment of citizens' rights. In its stead, the U.S. Constitution became a monument to the Goldilocks Principle. A tyrannical government such as the regime that existed in England under King George III was metaphorically too hard; the government that existed under the Articles of Confederation was too soft. The new regime created by the fifty-five men in Philadelphia was, more or less, about right. After the Constitution was ratified by the states, the decisions made by officials in the new government generally were afforded legitimacy—even if particular decisions were objectionable to much of the populace. This principle of majority rule, tempered by antidemocratic controls of "mixed" government (such as an unelected federal judiciary designed to control the "tyranny of the majority") became the cornerstone of the fledgling nation.[2]

Historians and political scientists have debated the implications of this attempt to balance competing interests since the Constitution was ratified; yet, inevitably, questions persist. In this context, the salient inquiry is to what extent the American regime should allow for capital punishment as an instrument of the state. In the words of one commentator, a "basic problem with the death penalty is justifying the government's authority to impose it. Pointing to the Constitution merely begs the question: it is like saying that the government has the power to impose the death penalty because the government has given itself that power."[3]

Modern anti–death penalty activists contend that the state-sanctioned executions have no place in a political system administered by fallible human beings who are subject to biases, mistaken impressions, and malicious behavior. Death penalty supporters, by contrast, argue that safeguards can be established that eliminate most, if not all, egregious errors and biases. From a philosophical perspective, we should explore two lines of inquiry to address this crucial difference of opinion. First, we must examine the historical record to deduce what we can about the theoretical presuppositions of the Founders concerning capital punishment. Second, apart from what we might deduce from the Founders' intent, we must explore philosophical justifications for retaining capital punishment in the modern American regime.

I. The Founders' Perspectives on Capital Punishment

As we shall make clear within these pages, whatever else one can conclude about the progenitors of the American tradition, it seems likely that they accepted capital punishment as a legitimate penalty. It is little wonder that they embraced state-sanctioned executions. The world of the eighteenth century was a brutal place, and, to the extent possible, the law developed as a means of protecting citizens from that brutality. Indeed, the colonial experience bore witness to a multitude of capital offenses, including property crimes, blasphemy, and worshipping false gods, among others.[4] Moreover, most of the philosophical ideas available to the revolutionary generation concluded that some crimes deserved the ultimate penalty. The question for the Founders was not whether capital punishment was justified but under what circumstances and in what manner it ought to be applied.

Any attempt to understand the Founders requires some basic familiarity with Enlightenment thinking. Simply put, the sixteenth and seventeenth centuries witnessed the decline of feudalism and the manorial system as the bases for medieval economic and political structures, and, with their demise, the authority of the church shrank as men began to question the source of economic and political power. In this new world of uncertainty, intellectuals seized the high ground by arguing in favor of a new, more rigorous method of understanding phenomena. In theory, this new method assumed that "objectivity" and "realism" were synonymous. Science was to be a tool—actually, *the* tool—by which mankind would peer through the social, political, cultural, religious, and historical fog to see things not as they might wish them to be but as they really exist. As a result, the scientific method had to be clear, logical, intellectually rigorous, verifiable, and ultimately replicable. Owing to its "objective" features, the method would be immune to the myths and contextual influences that infected other, lesser disciplines. Moreover, it would root out the biases and cronyism that had governed social intercourse since time immemorial. If the scientific method could be perfected, eventually mankind would solve the great problems that had always plagued human beings because man would know the unvarnished truth when he saw it.[5]

This emphasis on developing a scientific method assumed that problems associated with self-government could be overcome through science as well. In Federalist 9, Founding Father Alexander Hamilton explains the Enlightenment view of politics and government succinctly. "The science of politics," he writes, "like most other sciences, has received great improvement. The efficacy of various principles is now well understood, which were either not known or imperfectly known to the ancients. The regular distribution of power into distinct departments; the introduction of legislative balances and checks; the institution of courts composed of judges holding their offices during good behavior; the representation of the people in the legislature by deputies of their own election: these are wholly new discoveries or have made their principal progress toward perfection in modern times. They are means, and powerful means, by which the excellencies of republican government may be retained and its imperfections lessened or avoided."[6] Later, in Federalist 15, Hamilton inquires, "[w]hy has government been instituted at all?" The answer to this rhetorical question should be obvious to anyone steeped in the Enlightenment tradition. "Because the passions of men will not conform to the dictates of reason and justice without constraint."[7] Similarly, in *Common Sense*, Thomas Paine argues that a man in a state of nature cannot rely on other men to follow the dictates of reason. Instead, he must look to the state as the enforcer of rationality. In short, "he finds it necessary to surrender up a part of his property to furnish means for the protection of the rest, and this he is induced to do by the same prudence which in every other case advises him out of two evils to choose the least."[8]

Hamilton and Paine did not develop their views on the connection between reason and justice in a vacuum. This Enlightenment quest for scientific rigor and rationality in government was personified by the Founders' intellectual predecessors, especially the seventeenth-century Englishman Thomas Hobbes, author of the influential tract *Leviathan*. This magnum opus greatly influenced the Founders' ideas on politics and government immensely, and no wonder.[9] Leo Strauss once referred to Hobbes as "that imprudent, impish, and iconoclastic extremist, that first plebeian philosopher, who is so enjoyable a writer because of his almost boyish straightforwardness, his never failing humanity, and his marvelous clarity and force."[10] Strauss's playful prose belies an important point. Unlike some theorists of the Enlightenment, whose views must be extrapolated on the basis of incomplete or contradictory evidence, Hobbes clearly and directly considers whether the sovereign can sentence citizens of the regime to death. He answers affirmatively. The death penalty is, in his view, a reasonable punishment employed by an entity—the sovereign—created to be the ultimate instrument of human reason.

According to Hobbes, men create a sovereign government precisely because they fear the consequences of existing in a pregovernment state of nature. More to the point, individuals fear that they will be killed by their fellow man. By rationally entering into a social contract to create a powerful sovereign, these individual rational maximizers deliberately trade away some of their natural liberty in exchange for a measure of security and order. Just as the scientific method will advance man's understanding of the natural world, a scientifically based justification for creating government will ensure that rationality is the foundation of political life.[11]

The difficulty arises when the metaphorical signatories to the social contract violate the terms of the covenant. On occasion, an individual who agreed to create the sovereign will violate the terms of the agreement by engaging in criminal behavior. In such a case, he has acted in a way—that is, irrationally—that creates a dilemma for those who must react to this behavior. If the sovereign fails to act swiftly and decisively, he appears weak and ineffectual and therefore loses power. A weak sovereign endangers everyone, for he brings citizens ever closer to the brink of reentering the dreaded state of nature. Because fear of a violent death in a pregovernment state of nature forms the predominant basis for the social contract, individuals have an unconditional obligation to obey the law. If they do not obey the law, they must be punished accordingly. Irrational elements cannot be allowed to exist, for they threaten the rational basis of civil government.[12]

A sovereign has little choice but to impose the ultimate penalty for the ultimate crime. He cannot allow weakness or sentimental pleas for mercy to dissuade him fulfilling his duty. If he does not execute justice swiftly and severely, he sends the wrong message to his subjects. "[I]t is the nature of punishment to have for [an] end the disposing of men to obey the law, which end, if it be less than the benefit of the transgression, it attains not, but works to contrary effect," Hobbes contends.[13] Capital punishment deters others from engaging in similar behavior because it puts the community on notice that crimes against individuals also are crimes against the state.

For Hobbes, therefore, the death penalty is no more or less than a proportional response. If an offender acts in a manner that takes a human life, the state must respond in kind. If it does not, the offender will rationally consider that he has received a punishment that is less severe than the crime he committed. Moreover, other would-be offenders realize that they can engage in similar behavior because the sovereign lacks the will to impose the ultimate punishment.

Alternatively, a sovereign who imposes the death penalty sends a powerful message to everyone. No longer will rational calculations of costs and benefits allow an offender to act with a feeling of personal security. Now he must realize that his punishment will be imposed with the same severity as his crime. The social contract, hence the regime, is secure for all.

Modern critics might view Hobbes as vulnerable because he places too much faith in the ability of people to act as rational maximizers. The ironic contradiction in Hobbes's conception of political theory is his belief that individuals, fearful of being murdered by their unscrupulous peers, will put their faith in those same scurrilous characters by figuratively signing a social contract with them. If these fellows cannot be trusted to act rationally in a state of nature, how can they be trusted to act rationally in a civil society? Hobbes's rejoinder is that irrational individuals will not suddenly act rationally in society, but at least after the sovereign has been created through the social contract, a larger, ultimately more rational entity exists to correct and, if necessary, punish the behavior of offenders. This surely is true, and kudos to Hobbes for justifying his thought experiment as a desirable creation of rational individuals *after* the rational and irrational alike have agreed to create the sovereign. Still, the notion that rational calculations drive human actions and serve as the logical basis for punishment is subject to serious scrutiny in the postmodern era.

Critics also charge that Hobbes's failure to insist on due process is a fundamental flaw in his thinking. One commentator, Steven H. Jupiter, observes, "Hobbes did not demand of the sovereign any guarantee of due process because he did not believe that political power could be exercised unjustly. The sovereign was the source of all authority and thus incapable of illegitimate conduct. Hobbesian theories, then, do not adequately address the problem of political authority in American society because of our rejection of absolute government power."[14] Jupiter's point is well taken. Hobbes assumes that the nature of sovereign power is not open to the abuses witnessed in subsequent centuries—a proposition that is not accepted by the Founders of the American political system and the "men of little faith" who drafted the Bill of Rights.[15]

How, then, do we rehabilitate the overly rational, power-hungry Hobbes? First, as with any justification for social or political theories, a defender might rightly ask critics to offer alternatives. If Hobbes fails to appreciate the possibility that offenders are not always acting rationally—one might suggest that they are irrational by virtue of engaging in a criminal act in the first place—the focus shifts to forms of punishment that take irrational behavior into account. Do we excuse offenders owing to their youth, incapacity, mental infirmities, or the like?

This is the crux of the issue in the capital punishment debate. Does a modern, civilized society punish irrational, nonmaximizing behavior that harms the regime? As the chapters in this book attest, the answer depends on the underlying perspective of the polemicist. In this context, however, it seems reasonably clear that Hobbes, an intellectual precursor to the American republic, would extend capital punishment to offenders *as though* they were rational maximizers. As long as the punishment is proportionate to the crime committed, Hobbes does not concern himself with the nuances of human motivations and incapacities. The modern legal system might focus on the reasons for certain behaviors, but Hobbes does not extend his analysis into this quagmire.

This leads to the second rejoinder on Hobbes's behalf. He is focusing on the necessity of establishing a powerful sovereign imbued with sufficient authority to administer the regime effectively. He assumes without arguing that offenders who are sentenced to die at the hand of the state will be found guilty through fair and legal means. He leaves the details of how those means will be employed to other thinkers. As a result, the argument that Hobbes's view of the relationship between the individual and the state is not appropriate in the modern American political system does nothing to diminish his contention that capital punishment is a necessary penalty in egregious cases. His central thesis can be read as an endorsement of capital punishment *after* due process has been provided and the offender has been found guilty.

John Locke, another intellectual forebear of the American regime, seizes Hobbes's point on proportionality and develops it further. In Locke's classic essay "The Second Treatise of Civil Government," he exhibits the same faith in rationality that characterizes Hobbes's work. Man in a pregovernment state of nature exists in a state of complete liberty, but this is not tantamount to "a state of licence." In other words, he cannot do exactly as he pleases. "The state of nature has a law of nature to govern it which obliges every one; and reason, which is that law, teaches all mankind who but will consult it that, being all equal and independent, no one ought to harm another in his life, health, liberty, or possessions."[16]

The problem is that men are insufficiently rational because of a failure to consult that law of nature regularly.[17] In the absence of a settled, known set of laws for the promotion of orderly relations, men cannot reliably predict the intentions of their fellow men. Under these circumstances they will all too frequently misreason and act under the influence of such powerful passions as fear, anger, envy, love, or even hate. It is thus human nature itself—its propensity to irrational behavior—that ultimately renders the state of nature a place where man's life, in Hobbes's words, is "solitary, poor, nasty, brutish and short."[18] According to Locke, those members of the state of nature who may be "rational and industrious" and apply their labor to acquire private property from that which was previously held in common are particularly vulnerable in the state of nature. The "quarrelsome and contentious" members of that state may well be rational enough to realize that they can enjoy unearned fruits of the earth simply by targeting what their more energetic peers have accumulated.[19] The owners of insecure private property soon come to see the state of nature as an uncertain, dangerous place. They and like-minded men soon realize the benefits of fleeing from the state of nature into the comparative oasis of security promised by a social contract that establishes a civil society and an attendant government having clear, settled laws. The latter provides the equivalent of "an appeal to heaven"—that is, a sovereign to whom one can turn for the settling of disputes and the restraining of the quarrelsome and contentious.

The powers exercised by the sovereign are identical to the ones possessed but unreliably exercised by individual members in the state of nature. As Locke states, "the execution of the law of nature is, in that state, put into every man's hands, whereby everyone has a right to punish the transgressors of the law to such a degree as may hinder its violation."[20] Men entering into the social contract agree to give up the exercise of many of these powers (e.g., the right to punish offenders in proportion to the grievousness of their crimes) in exchange for the assured order provided by a sovereign who retains the exercise of those powers in accordance with known laws. However, individuals within the resultant civil society can readily—though temporarily—reclaim the exercise of their state of nature powers whenever they perceive the necessity of doing so. (For example, no member of civil society is expected meekly to surrender his life to a thug simply because the sovereign's representatives—the cops on the beat—are currently occupied elsewhere.)

Locke presents the essential definition of political power as "a right of making laws with penalties of death and, consequently, all less penalties for the regulating of preserving of property, and of employing the force of the community in the execution of such laws."[21] If a sovereign has that power, then he clearly has all attendant lesser political powers. Individuals in the state of nature possessed that ultimate power as well, but their unreliable implementation of it contributed to the brutishness of that state of nature. (Consider, for a moment, the likely results if the victims of an injustice were immediately after the fact able to impose on their tormentors what they considered to be proportional punishment. The passions of the victims would readily overwhelm their reason and easily result in the application of a deadly force out of all proportion to the injuries. Our criminal justice system recognizes this powerful ingredient in human nature and appropriately provides for what are termed "crimes of passion.")

Individuals enter into a social contract, in Locke's view, generally for the reasons that Hobbes mentions. Rational maximizers see that it benefits them to cut a deal with their peers. Instead of negotiating the contract owing to the fear of violent death, however, Locke contends that men enter into civil society to take advantage of the benefits, especially the existence of a neutral arbiter of disputes, provided by the state. The state, therefore, becomes the instrument for ensuring that all members of a civil society honor the social contract and obey the laws of nature. Thus, "the execution of the law of nature is, in that state, put into every man's hands, whereby everyone has a right to punish the transgressors of the law to such a degree as may hinder its violation."[22]

Locke views the social contract as an agreement among all parties to behave rationally. When a man chooses to step beyond the boundaries of reason, "the offender declares himself to live by another rule than that of reason and common equity, which is that measure God has set to the actions of men for their mutual security."[23] In short, an offender in a capital crime has moved beyond the boundaries of reason that constrain most men. In doing so, he has rejected the one major feature that God has given man to better his life on Earth. In rejecting that feature, the offender has served notice to his peers that he is not fully human and, therefore, not deserving of human treatment. As the protector of individuals' natural rights, the state must act to ensure that the offender is punished appropriately.[24]

Like Hobbes, Locke does not suggest that leaders of the regime punish offenders without sufficient evidence of criminal behavior. Once that behavior has been established, however, the regime must act to the benefit of all persons affected by the offender's actions. Death is the appropriate punishment when the offender has taken a human life.

The "eye for an eye" proportionality argument has been attacked by some commentators, especially Christian theologians, as overly simplistic. According to this perspective, the famous Old Testament maxim echoed by Hobbes and Locke is taken out of context. In the time of the Aryan exodus, the death penalty was imposed for a variety of crimes that today would be considered comparatively minor or not criminal behavior. Engaging in sorcery, profaning the Sabbath, practicing homosexuality, and stealing some types of property are not capital offenses today, but they were terrible offenses for the children of Israel. Accordingly, when the Old Testament argues for proportionality in Exodus 21:22–25, it is trying to limit the occasions when death legitimately can be imposed. It is a supreme irony to think that this limitation is cited as justification for imposing the death penalty in the modern world. As society changes and its understanding of crime changes, so should its use of capital punishment, according to anti–death penalty advocates. For critics of Hobbes and Locke, capital punishment might have had a place in a predemocratic society of a bygone era, but it has no place in the United States in the twenty-first century.[25]

Whatever their shortcomings, Hobbes's and Locke's works influenced many of the American Founders. Thomas Jefferson, in particular, embraces their teachings about the social contract and contractual rights, and he generally seems to accept their views on capital punishment. In his only sustained work of political philosophy, *Notes on the State of Virginia*, Jefferson writes of punishments imposed on persons guilty of crimes against nature and against the state. He focuses special attention on crimes perpetuated by slaves against their masters. "When a master was murdered," he reports, speaking of the Roman Empire, "all his slaves, in the same house, or within hearing were condemned to death."[26]

Setting aside the difficult questions associated with slavery, Jefferson's acceptance of the legitimacy of capital punishment in *Notes on the State of Virginia* seems reasonably clear. As long as the punishment is in proportion to the crime, a state can impose the ultimate penalty on its citizens without violating the sanctity of the individual. In fact, Jefferson carefully lists various crimes and their punishments, cautioning that, "we lay it down as fundamental, that laws, to be just, must give a reciprocation of right: that, without this, they are mere arbitrary rules of conduct, founded in force, and not in conscience."[27]

This is the heart of the issue—namely, that legitimacy is grounded in the "reciprocation of right." As long as the laws are administered equitably—that is, by treating like cases alike—and crimes are punished in proportion to the offense, the state is justified in taking a citizen's life. Jefferson does not delve into what he sees as ancillary questions of morality or whether the state owes a higher duty to individuals. A proportional sentence ensures that a capital offender has paid his debt to society, and Jefferson suggests that the subject requires no further discussion.

Yet Jefferson's melodic prose often seems to invite differing interpretations. Most famously, his stirring insistence in the Declaration of Independence that "all men are created equal" and "endowed by their Creator with certain unalienable Rights, that among these are Life, Liberty, and the pursuit of Happiness" implicitly conveys a view at odds with his statements in *Notes on the State of Virginia*. If the right to life is an "unalienable" right grounded in a person's humanity, the death penalty is difficult to justify. (However, one must emphasize that Jefferson closely follows Hobbes and Locke in considering that governments—perhaps especially the just ones established by the "consent of the governed"—are necessary precisely because such "unalienable rights" as life remain massively insecure without them.) But if the state can demonstrate a method for preventing future criminal actions—such as incarcerating an offender—how, then, can it argue the necessity of executing individuals who possess an unalienable right to life? This logical inference suggests that Jefferson opposed the death penalty except, perhaps, in rare cases. According to Steven H. Jupiter, "[i]f there had been effective penal alternatives, such as life imprisonment, Jefferson would probably have opposed the death penalty altogether."[28]

Despite Jupiter's comment, it is difficult to determine precisely Jefferson's views on capital punishment. Throughout his life, the master of Monticello was famous for his unparalleled use of eloquent rhetoric that presented contradictory messages when carefully scrutinized. One biographer even titled his award-winning book on Jefferson's elusive character *American Sphinx*.[29] When removed from their historical context, Jefferson's words are similar to words found in the Bible; they can be interpreted to buttress almost any claim that one wishes to make.[30] Perhaps all that can be said about Jefferson's views on the subject is that he leaves room for imposing the death penalty because he does not explicitly condemn capital punishment.

And what do we say of the most venerable founding document—the Constitution itself? Much has been made of the prohibition against "cruel and unusual punishment" found in the Eighth Amendment. What does it mean to behave cruelly and unusually? In the words of two respected commentators on criminal law, Wayne R. LaFave and Austin W. Scott Jr., the "prohibition on cruel and unusual punishment would also appear to bar punishment authorized by statute which is excessive, that is, out of proportion to the offense committed, although this proposition has not been fully developed by the Supreme Court."[31] Again, this is a fundamental issue in the debate over capital punishment: What does it mean to impose a proportional sentence? Some opponents, such as former U.S. Supreme Court justices Thurgood Marshall and William Brennan, famously argue that any state-sanctioned killing is cruel and unusual because biases can never be accounted for completely. Given these omnipresent biases, every time an offender is sentenced to death, the punishment is tainted, at least partially, by a biased witness, lawyer, judge, or juror. Therefore, in the interest of fairness, the Eighth Amendment must be interpreted as containing an implicit prohibition on capital punishment.[32] This broad interpretation of a vague constitutional provision has been derided vehemently by critics. One need only peruse Douglas Clouatre's contribution to this collection (chapter 13) to realize that some scholars view abolitionists as little more than judicial activists anxious to substitute their views for the views of legislators.

A second interpretation suggests that the Eighth Amendment's prohibition on cruel and unusual punishment does not prohibit state-sanctioned executions. Instead, it prohibits state-sanctioned executions that are unnecessarily painful or torturous to the offender. The goal is to give to everyone what he deserves— *suum cuique tribue*—no better, and no worse. In the words of a famous death penalty proponent, Ernest van den Haag, "[t]here is no objective measure of the cardinal gravity of a crime; or of the cardinal severity of a punishment; nor, finally, do we have an objective indication of what punishment is deserved per se by each degree of gravity."[33] In short, the application of the Eighth Amendment requires judges to determine which punishments are constitutional and which are not through case-by-case adjudication.

If the language of the Eighth Amendment cannot definitively settle the issue, perhaps some other constitutional provision holds the key. The Fifth Amendment may be a more promising starting point. Yet, far from supporting the position advocated by death penalty opponents, the Fifth Amendment can be read as evidence that the Founders inherently supported the death penalty, despite the generally pro–civil libertarian nature of that provision. The Fifth Amendment states, in relevant part, that a person cannot "be deprived of life, liberty, or property, without due process of law." If a person can never be deprived of life by the state, why is the clause "without due process of law" necessary? Two conclusions spring to mind. Either the Founders—almost all of whom were lawyers and accomplished legislative draftsmen—expressed their purposes quite clearly if we accept the notion that they allowed room for the possibility of capital punishment, *or* they erred (or deliberately obfuscated the issue) in constructing this portion of the Fifth Amendment. In any case, they could have constructed the provision to say that citizens cannot be deprived of liberty or property without due process of law and, moreover, that citizens can never be deprived of life, period. Such a construction would have made the prohibition against capital punishment clear and unambiguous. Yet they expressed the idea in a different manner. By including a phrase that allowed for the *possibility* that citizens might be denied their life, liberty, or property if certain procedural safeguards were in place—"due process"—they implied that individual life might be taken by the state under the right circumstances. The right circumstances—that is, the meaning of "due process"—are, of course, a matter of great debate throughout our history; nonetheless, the amendment seems to allow capital punishment to be imposed because it does not expressly prohibit the imposition of the death penalty.

The issue is further complicated by the evolving meaning of "due process." The phrase generally is interpreted to refer to procedural fairness. To strict constructionists, this means that all parties are to be treated equally before the eyes of the law as dictated by the plain meaning of the words contained in the Bill of Rights.[34] Substantive due process, however, carries the due process analysis a step further by allowing courts not merely to determine whether procedural rights have been protected, but also to consider the substantive merits of a claim. Commentator Steven H. Jupiter quite rightly observes that substantive due process "has not been universally embraced as a valid exercise of the judiciary's power" and "is not relevant to the Court's capital jurisprudence."[35] Because the U.S. Supreme Court has declared the death penalty generally to be constitutional, only procedural claims in individual cases are relevant. As a matter of black letter law, the court already has decided the substantive issue—whether capital punishment comports with the Constitution—in the affirmative.[36]

II. Mill and Kant: Influences on the American Regime

In addition to the Founders and their philosophical predecessors, two major theorists—John Stuart Mill and Immanuel Kant—especially influenced the development of the modern conception of individual rights in the American regime and therefore require a brief discussion in this context. Both theorists support the death penalty, albeit for different reasons. Moreover, in both cases, this pro–death penalty stance may seem inconsistent with each thinker's perspective that individuals are worthy of the utmost respect and dignity; however, upon closer examination, their positions on capital punishment can be reconciled with their general theories on individual rights.

Although his most famous works first appeared in England almost a century after the American Founding, Mill is perhaps the most passionate apologist for democratic government and libertarian principles of the American variety. As a result, his ideas have influenced the development of the American political system for more than 140 years. "The only purpose for which power can rightfully be exercised over any member of a civilized society against his will is to prevent harm to others," he writes in his most famous work, *On Liberty*. In Mill's view, all actions can be divided into two categories: "self regarding actions" and "other-regarding actions." Government can legitimately exercise control over human beings only in the latter category.[37] This distinction is necessary to ensure that government control does not obliterate an individual's right to live his life as he sees fit. "But with regard to the merely contingent, or, as it may be called, constructive injury which a person causes to society, by conduct which neither violates any specific duty to the public, nor occasions perceptible hurt to any assignable individual except himself," Mill argues that "the inconvenience is one which society can afford to bear, for the sake of the greater good of human freedom."[38]

Yet, despite these strong words on behalf of liberty, even an ardent opponent of entrenched governmental power advocates the death penalty in extreme cases. In Mill's view, murder and other crimes against persons are no longer tantamount to a vague, "constructive injury," but they represent genuine, tangible threats to public safety and order. The offender's violation of his duty to live and let live transforms "self regarding actions" into "other-regarding actions," and the analysis changes as a result. The offender has crossed the boundary where individual liberty is almost sacrosanct to a place where his freedom must be curtailed by the state—even if that means that the offender's life must be forfeited. When the facts of the case make the offender's guilt virtually certain, the state must take action. Mill writes, "I confess it appears to me that to deprive the criminal of the life of which he has proved himself to be unworthy—solemnly to blot him out from the fellowship of mankind and from the catalogue of the living—is the most appropriate, as it is certainly the most impressive, mode in which society can attach to so great a crime the penal consequences which for the security of life it is indispensable to annex to it."[39]

Kant agrees with Mill that capital punishment is permissible, but his reasons differ markedly. In fact, Kant's view that individuals must not be used as the means to an end differs from Mill's Utilitarian conception of the "greatest good for the greatest number" to an extraordinary degree. Mill focuses on both the state and the offender. By executing a capital offender who has engaged in "other-regarding actions" such as murder, the state is ensuring the greatest good for the greatest number of society's members. As for a would-be offender, when he realizes that the state can resort to executions, he must take note of this awesome power if he hopes to survive. Capital punishment thus becomes a weapon for influencing a potential offender's Utilitarian calculations because the state seeks to make the cost or consequence of murdering another person too steep for a rational person to consider paying it under all but extraordinary circumstances. This is a classic defense of the deterrence rationale.[40]

By contrast, Kant examines capital punishment from the perspective of the state without directly considering the offender's point of view except to say that the offender must be treated as a rational, autonomous, moral agent. Whatever else it does, the state must respect the worth of each individual. The deterrence argument is spurious because it insists that costs and benefits must be weighed alongside the worth of the individual—a process that devalues the individual. Kant therefore dismisses Utilitarian calculations as "hypothetical imperatives"— that is, conditional requirements placed on human beings. A hypothetical imperative is a command such as "You shouldn't kill someone else, or else you will be punished." This command admonishes a would-be offender to calculate the consequences of his actions and behave accordingly.

Instead of the Utilitarian approach, Kant contends that capital punishment must be imposed on individuals, ironically, because we must respect an individual's personhood. To assign punishments based on a hypothetical imperative is to treat persons as the means to the ends promoted by the state. Instead of relying on a hypothetical imperative, Kant suggests that a universal law must exist that applies regardless of time, place, and circumstances. He calls this the "categorical imperative." The categorical imperative is not subject to a means–ends calculation, nor is it a calculation based on consequences. If men are to comport with the categorical imperative, certain actions always are "right" and must be undertaken regardless of the consequences. This is true for relations among and between persons. If we respect persons, we will treat them as rational, autonomous, moral agents. Similarly, a person must act as a rational, autonomous, moral agent free from excuses and justifications. "Act only on that maxim whereby thou canst at the same time will that it should become a universal law," Kant writes.[41] In other words, follow the Golden Rule: Do unto others as you would have them do unto you.

If we assume that persons act as rational, autonomous moral agents, then it follows that an individual must be held accountable for his actions in accordance with the categorical imperative. To do otherwise is to undermine his personhood. Thus, if an individual murders his fellow man, he is, in effect, saying that murder is an acceptable act. If we assume that he is a rational, autonomous moral agent, we know that he would not view himself as an exception to the categorical imperative, for that conclusion would be irrational. Furthermore, if we do unto others as we would have others do unto us, we must treat the offender as he has told us by his actions that people should be treated. If we try to rehabilitate him or subject his body to bargaining and negotiation as part of an elaborate calculation of social utility, we again are violating his worth as an individual. Instead, we must execute him because he has told us through his actions that executions are legitimate.[42]

III. Conclusion: Low Deeds and High Goods

It is a sad day when the state executes its citizens. Virtually anyone—death penalty proponents and anti–death penalty advocates alike—would agree that killing a human is a low deed, a regrettably desperate measure undertaken with great solemnity by an admittedly desperate government. The question is whether the low deed is undertaken in the pursuit of a higher purpose—a "high good," as it were. Can a noble purpose such as protecting the welfare of the state and its citizens be advanced by taking the life of an individual, whatever the specific rationale? This is the point at which battle lines are drawn between the two sides of the debate, with one side arguing that executions protect the safety of the citizens in a regime and the other side arguing that state-sanctioned executions allow an increasingly totalitarian state to perpetuate abuses against citizens.

Although some states have abolished the death penalty and the abolitionist movement has garnered support from many sources throughout the years, death penalty advocates generally have gotten the better of their foes in the debate—if not in the theoretical realm, then certainly in the practical application of the penalty. Despite the vociferous arguments propounded by anti–death penalty forces, the American regime has a long tradition of allowing the state to take the life of its citizens under some circumstances. Even seminal theorists like Thomas Hobbes and John Locke recognize the permissibility of state-sanctioned executions in egregious cases, and their arguments, grounded on social contract theories, have been afforded great weight.

Based in no small measure on the theoretical foundations constructed by Hobbes and Locke, the American Founders also support the death penalty by allowing for the ultimate punishment to be imposed. If the Founders do not exactly embrace capital punishment, neither do they specifically prohibit it even when they might have done so. No language in the Eighth or the Fifth Amendments to the Constitution expressly precludes the death penalty from being imposed as long as the method is not torturous and the offender has his day in court. The battle over these constitutional provisions has centered not on the words themselves but on an appropriate interpretation of the implicit meaning of the amendments. So far, death penalty advocates have carried the day by contending that a prohibition on executions would have to be explicitly stated in the Constitution. Because it was not explicitly stated, capital punishment is not constitutionally precluded.

John Stuart Mill and Immanuel Kant, two champions of the worth and dignity of the individual, also present forceful arguments in favor of the death penalty. Whether one accepts Mill's Utilitarian balancing of costs and benefits or Kant's insistence that respect for personhood requires that we treat offenders in accordance with their actions, their acceptance of capital punishment as philosophically defensible does much to bolster the arguments set forth by death penalty supporters.

Commentator Steven H. Jupiter, a self-professed opponent of capital punishment, admits that state-sanctioned executions have "textual authorization within the Constitution," although, in his opinion, "the death penalty is incompatible with the American system of constitutional democracy in which government derives its limited powers through express consent of the people and in which life is to be held 'unalienable.'"[43] Later, he writes that "[a]s the Constitution merely authorizes capital punishment rather than mandating it, legislatures have the power to abolish it completely. The American people must come to understand that capital punishment is in complete opposition to one of the most fundamental principles of American democracy: the supremacy of individual existence over collective government."[44]

This proposition that capital punishment violates the basic tenets of the American regime, much debated and discussed, is an open question. As a matter of normative political theory, Jupiter cites an impressive array of cases and arguments to defend this position, but as a matter of descriptive historical and legal analysis, he is on shakier ground. Legislatures may have the power to abolish the death penalty, but generally they have not done so. Moreover, many Americans now and throughout our history have preferred to accept low deeds undertaken by the state as a method—and a powerful one, at that—to ensure that the high goods of the American political system come to fruition.

CHAPTER 2

Bearing Witness and Writing History in the Struggle against Capital Punishment

Austin Sarat

I had no evil intent when I taught the tricks of pleading, for I never meant them to be used to get the innocent condemned but, if the occasion arose, to save the lives of the guilty.

—St. Augustine[1]

[L]awyers must . . . bear witness to the shameful injustices which are all too routine in capital cases. . . . It is only by the witness of those who observe the injustices in capital cases firsthand that others in society can be accurately informed.

—Stephen Bright[2]

I

The struggle against capital punishment goes on every day in courtrooms across the United States. On the front lines are criminal defense lawyers who try to prevent the initial imposition of death sentences by judges and juries.[3] When that effort fails, the struggle is carried on by a small cadre of lawyers who specialize in providing legal representation in appellate and postconviction proceedings for persons on death row.[4] For much of the criminal defense bar, the legal work of opposing capital punishment is neither ideological nor political. For most specialized appellate death penalty lawyers, however, their legal work is part of an ideologically motivated campaign against capital punishment.[5] They carry on that campaign by representing individual clients; sometimes they use an individual case to bring a broader challenge to some aspect of the capital sentencing system, or even to attack the constitutionality of the death penalty itself. More often, however, they studiously avoid such frontal assaults in the hope of saving one life at a time.[6]

Whether these lawyers pursue wholesale challenges to capital punishment or limit themselves to detailing the injustice of a particular death sentence, death penalty lawyers today find themselves engaged in what looks increasingly like a losing cause.[7] While they have the advantage of being able to invoke the formal rights and protections of liberal-legalism,[8] the legal system seems ever more inhospitable to them and their work.[9] To oppose the death penalty through the legal process in the United States in the 1990s is not unlike fighting Apartheid in the courts of South Africa in the 1970s or litigating on behalf of Palestinian rights in the occupied territories in the 1980s.[10] In the face of a legal system seemingly ever more intent on imposing the death penalty and ever more resistant to abolitionist arguments, one might then ask why and how anti–death penalty lawyers adapt and explain their lawyering in the prevailing hostile legal climate. Answering these questions is the subject of this essay.

II

The usual answer to the apparent paradox of combating a hostile legal regime on its own terms is that legal discourse, because it provides the legitimating ideology of the powerful, can be an important weapon in political struggle.[11] However, in the case of the death penalty in the contemporary United States, this answer seems increasingly problematic. The legitimating promises of the law, found in the recognition that "death is different"[12] and the promise of "super due process"[13] in death cases, have been gradually but openly stripped away.[14] There is now little room to hold law to its promises because so many of those promises seem to have been broken without embarrassment.[15]

Another answer to the question of why (and/or how) law can be used by lawyers in the struggle against capital punishment might be found in Drucilla Cornell's admonition that "[l]egal interpretation demands that we remember the future."[16] In that phrase, Cornell suggests that law fixes its gaze temporally, not on the possibilities (or impossibilities) of the present, but on a future promise of justice.[17] She reminds us that there are, in fact, two audiences for every legal act, the audience of the present (to which one might appeal for an end to law's violence), and the audience of the future (which stands as a figure of law's redeeming promise of justice). In this sense, law, as Robert Cover writes, is "a bridge to alternity."[18]

In Cornell's and Cover's understanding, death penalty lawyering in the United States is a form of "redemptive constitutionalism."[19] Through their activities, death penalty lawyers refuse to recognize the present moment as the defining totality of law. In their work they serve as the carriers of a vision of a future in which justice prevails and the death penalty is abolished. For them, as Cover argues, "[r]edemption takes place within an eschatalogical schema that postulates: (1) the unredeemed character of reality as we know it, (2) the fundamentally different reality that should take its place, and (3) the replacement of one with the other."[20]

Cover uses the example of an abolitionist struggle of another era, namely antislavery activism in the mid-nineteenth century, to suggest that the work of "redemptive constitutionalism" reveals "a creative pulse that proliferates principle and precept, commentary and justification, even in the face of a state legal order less likely to hold slavery unconstitutional than to declare the imminent kingship of Jesus Christ on Earth."[21] According to this view, death penalty lawyers must speak in a prophetic voice as they supply the argumentative and interpretive resources to bridge the gap between the present, with its insistent attachment to capital punishment,[22] and a future in which the state no longer executes any of its citizens.[23]

There is perhaps a third way of understanding the work of death penalty lawyers in the present hostile climate. This understanding reverses Cover's image; redemption gives way to judgment and the future is called upon to remember the injustices of the present.[24] Thus, death penalty lawyers serve as witnesses testifying against the injustices of capital punishment. They provide "the testimonial *bridge* which, mediating between narrative and history, guarantees their correspondence and adherence to each other. This bridging between narrative and history is possible since the narrator is both an *informed* and an *honest* witness. . . . All the witness has to do is to *efface* himself, and let the *literality of events* voice its own *self-evidence*. His business is only to say: *this is what happened*, when he knows that it actually did happen."[25]

For death penalty lawyers, then, knowing what brought their clients to death row is essential to the legal representation they provide. Their work is fact-intensive in postconviction proceedings, especially when those proceedings focus on one of two kinds of claims: ineffective assistance of counsel or prosecutorial misconduct. In both of these claims, the job of the death penalty lawyer is to unearth facts that were omitted due to the negligent incompetence of trial counsel or the violation of the prosecutor's obligation of disclosure. Death penalty lawyers reinvestigate the case from beginning to end, reconstructing the social history of their clients,[26] and carefully examining how the legal system processed their client's case. This fact-intensive work enables them to speak about the histories of poverty and abuse that are all too often associated with the violent lives that their clients have led. It also enables them to speak about the prejudice and racism,[27] the extreme political pressures,[28] and the inadequacies of representation[29] that pervade the system of capital punishment.

However, death penalty lawyers do more than give testimony. They also write history. They use legal processes to record a history of the present and to preserve the present's pained voice. The litigated case can be used to create a record,[30] and the court can become an archive in which that record serves as the materialization of memory.[31] Due process guarantees an opportunity to speak to and be heard by the future. In this manner, due process guarantees that legal institutions can be turned into museums of unnecessary, unjust, undeserved pain and death.[32]

The legal hearing provides an opportunity to write and record history by creating narratives of present injustices.[33] By constructing and recording such narratives, death penalty lawyers call on an imagined future to choose justice over the jurispathic tendencies of the moment.[34] They ensure that even when no one (including many judges) seems willing to listen, the voices of the "oppressed" will not be silenced.

The movement from giving testimony to writing history is a movement from the immediacy of the eyewitness report to the mediated narration of a self-consciously constructed story.[35] While the history that is written by these lawyers is framed in the abstract, impersonal idiom of the law, it is neither abstract nor impersonal. It is the biography of a person sentenced to die, a story made relevant by decisions that permit the broadest range of evidence in mitigation.[36] Many death penalty lawyers describe the most crucial part of their work as coming after direct appeals have been exhausted, in the process of relitigating the case in habeas review. For them, the process of making a convincing argument for habeas relief is not unlike trying a case, with its attention to the vivid details of lives lived and choices made. Making such an argument may also involve telling a story of incompetent defense counsel, corrupt prosecutors, and inattentive judges.

As they write histories of the present, death penalty lawyers may frame the injustices they seek to record in one of the three narrative styles that Robert Gordon has identified.[37] Gordon calls the first of these styles "legalist."[38] This narrative treats the injustices of the present as wrongs "done by specific perpetrators to specific victims."[39] For example, legalist narratives in the death penalty context would focus on police or prosecutorial misconduct in a particular case and against a particular defendant without raising any systemic issues. Legalist narratives describe present injustice in terms of individual cases and individual defendants, and seek remedies that law could easily supply.

The second narrative style stays within the legalist mode but expands to involve what Gordon calls "broad agency."[40] In these narratives the history of injustice is a history of collective action taken by one *group* against another. Here, the focus in death penalty cases shifts to claims of discrimination of the type raised in *McCleskey v. Kemp*.[41]

The third narrative entails what Gordon describes as "bad structures rather than bad agents. . . . This historical enterprise takes the form of a search for explanations rather than a search for villainous agents and attribution of blame."[42] In this third narrative style, death penalty lawyers broaden the scope of inquiry by linking particular injustices with broader patterns of injustice and institutional practice, with poverty and its effects, and with societal decay and its consequences.[43] In such narratives, as Stephen Carter has written, the criminal himself is often portrayed as a victim. "Now victimhood becomes a matter of the sweep of history, not the actions of individual transgressors, and the government's role is not to punish transgressors but to alleviate the suffering of the victims. . . . On this view, black people are victims not because any individual has done harm to any other individual, but because the society's history and structure have combined to make of them an apparently permanent underclass, deprived of their fair share of wealth, education, health care, and the like. In this vision of victimhood, the criminal behavior of so many black males is itself a mark of victimhood, a victimhood virtually determined from birth. . . . Violence—especially violence directed externally, at white people and property . . . but also violence that is, in the argot, 'black-on-black'—is a statement of frustration. Remove the sources of frustration—the racism, the 'structural' unemployment, the inadequate education—and you eliminate much of the violence."[44]

The ability of death penalty lawyers to speak to the future and memorialize the present, both to bear witness and write history, has been ignored by those who have worried too much about the impact of politically engaged lawyering on the possibilities of the present.[45] For them, the value of political lawyering resides exclusively in its most immediate effects. But, as Cornell reminds us, law is as much about the future as the present, and as much about the possibilities of memory as the current prospects of political success. Thus when death penalty lawyers persist in their use of law, they "posit the very ideal . . . [they] purportedly find 'there' in the legal text, and as [they] posit the ideal or the ethical [they] promise to remain true to it. [Their] promise of fidelity to the ethical or to the ideal is precisely what breathes life into the dead letter of the law and provides a barrier against the violence of the word. . . . To heed the call to responsibility within law is to remind [ourselves] of the disjuncture between law and the ideal and to affirm our responsibility to make the promise to the ideal, to aspire to counter the violence of our world in the name of universal justice."[46]

Death penalty lawyering is one way of "remembering the future" and of ensuring that the future remembers. It is both a kind of testimony and a way of recording a history of present injustice. It seeks to put the death penalty in a narrative context which juxtaposes it to the Good. It turns courthouses into memorials of injustice and uses the legal process to create memory in the face of an obliterating violence.[47]

III

By paying attention to how such lawyering ensures that the future will be remembered, and that the future itself remembers, we gain a crucial perspective on the way many death penalty lawyers sustain their legal work when the prospects of success seem so remote. Extensive interviews conducted with death penalty practitioners confirm that today's death penalty bar conceives of itself in part as fulfilling a future-oriented function.[48]

The work of bearing witness and writing history is referred to among death penalty lawyers as "making a record." This phrase describes something more than just the legal work of building a case on appeal. One experienced death penalty lawyer explained, "as a lawyer every single act or omission that I am doing is calculated to make a record, but not just the record on appeal. It is bigger than that. I think you are making a record above and beyond the immediate case. You are making a record that even after you ultimately fail to save your client's life that he was a worthy human being, that there was an explanation for what he did which the legal system could not, or would not, hear. I know that because I know him in ways no one else does. And that there are other young men and women out there who can be helped if we learn from this case. You see, what we do is we tell a story that would otherwise not be told or remembered. There are lessons in the stories we tell, lessons about poverty, abuse, and injustice. Maybe they can't be heard just yet, but maybe they will be heard sometime."

This lawyer speaks first as a witness whose work testifies to the humanity of those condemned to die. He speaks as someone who has first hand knowledge: "I know that," he says, "because I know him in ways no one else does." But this lawyer also insists that his work is "bigger than that." "Making a record" involves recording the history of the present and placing a particular instance of injustice into a narrative that ties his case to a larger picture of "poverty, abuse and injustice." This process of generalization involves telling a story about "other young men and women out there." Such a story addresses those in the future who may (and should) remember, but whose recollection can only be spoken about as the possibility of an indeterminate "sometime."

By making a record, these lawyers believe that they can surmount, if they cannot stop, the injustice of capital punishment and keep alive the possibility of a more just future. They remember the future and insist that the future, if it is to be more just, must remember.

Yet without assurance that that "sometime" will ever arrive, some death penalty lawyers who conceive of their role as creating a record for the future seem more frustrated than hopeful. "Sometimes we talk like we are making a record for posterity," one longtime practitioner told me. "I hate that. I hate the idea that we are making a record for history. You know people say that all the time. But who the hell is going to read it? Who are we making a record for, God?"

Despite such frustration, the belief among death penalty lawyers in the importance of making a record remains pervasive. This belief is grounded in remembering the future and hearing its call to justice. It is also the task of making the future remember that shapes the work of making a record. As one new death penalty lawyer said, "I think of what I do as sort of making a narrative. I'm telling a story with page after page of facts which are put together to show the richness and complexity of my client's life, of the crime, and of the injustices of his trial. I am trying to put it together in a way that people can understand, that pulls heartstrings by getting at what is really going on. This is the best way to win in court, and it is the best way to make sure that the story is not just pushed aside and forgotten. And if enough of these narratives get produced then maybe they won't be ignored when, say fifty years from now, people try to figure out why we were executing the people we were executing in the way we were doing it."

In his words, the work of trying to win in court and build a record that will compel the future to remember go hand in hand. The accumulation of such narrative accounts links lawyering for an individual client with the broader political goal of ending capital punishment in an imagined future.

Another death penalty lawyer talked about this work in similar terms. "The story you are trying to construct has a number of parts. As a narrative it could be told from any of several perspectives. There is the life story of the client. Where did he come from, who was he as a child, and that includes what are the influences on him. Then there is the story of the crime. And retelling the story of the crime is really important because once an inept defense lawyer and a malicious prosecutor are done, the story of the crime is always of a cold, calculating, deliberate person, delighting in people's suffering, while the truth is that the crime is a culmination of neglect and abuse which the client himself has suffered. . . . [These are stories] of social injustice. The third part of the story is what happened at trial. Did his lawyer even bother to interview any witnesses? Was the family contacted to find out about his background? Was the judge a racist who referred to all the black jurors as 'coloreds'? . . . [T]his is a story of legal injustice."

Such multiple-stranded narratives take on special significance because "they become part of the public record." Becoming part of the public record means that they have "staying power"; they "won't go away." Making such a record, this lawyer explained, "is our way of acting in the world, our way of struggling against the system. We create these papers that we write. They are not going anywhere. They will be in government document warehouses forever. And I think that someday somebody will look at this, maybe one hundred years from now, but someone will look and say 'Oh my God, it was true that the death penalty was really just an engine of discrimination.' Even if it seems fruitless now, it is worth doing because we are making a record of who is getting the death penalty, and it is just the people who were mentally ill and too poor for treatment and who come from unhappy, broken families. And we did nothing to help these people, until they did something horrible so we could then get rid of them. . . . I've talked with enough other people [and we] describe this work as a witnessing sort of function."

What seems "fruitless" takes on meaning when viewed in the long term. A society now unwilling to see the links between poverty, neglect, and the death penalty, may, "one hundred years from now" be more receptive. Lawyering in what is today a losing cause is like trying to put a crucial piece of evidence in a time capsule. And, while the language of "witnessing" is explicit in this account, it is nevertheless as much an account of the writing of history as of giving testimony. This lawyer does not merely say what happened, he constructs an explanation that will focus the attention of the future on mental illness and poverty, on social neglect and the desire to "get rid of" people with problems rather than fix those problems. He, and others like him, do history by claiming that they can give at least partial explanations of past events, and "that in *some sense* we may understand a particular event by locating it correctly in a narrative sequence."[49]

IV

As witnesses giving testimony and historians creating a narrative of the present, death penalty lawyers find meaning in their work even as they find it increasingly difficult to end capital punishment or, failing that, to save the lives of their clients. Their struggle against the present reality of law's violence is carried out in the name of a justice deferred.[50] By bearing witness and writing history they give content to justice even as they acknowledge that it is attainable, if at all, in an uncertain future. As witnesses and historians they remember the future and insist that the future remember.[51] In so doing, they establish a continuing political claim for their work.

Their political claim and their address to the future is based on what I would call a "democratic optimism," a belief that present support for the death penalty is rooted in ignorance rather than venality, misunderstanding rather than clear-headed commitment.[52] As one lawyer earnestly explained, "I do not think that the death penalty will exist X years from now. While I don't know what X is, I think at some point people are going to look back and think 'Holey, moley, look at what was going on back then.'" "Look at Blackmun," another death penalty lawyer said. "He is not so very different from the rest of the country. His evolution is very representative of what eventually this country will come to if we continue to do our work. We have to look a little longer down the road, beyond the present moment."[53]

Such sentiments connect law to the future and establish a different understanding of the work of lawyers for beleaguered causes like the death penalty. The history-writing and witness-bearing functions of death penalty lawyering give law a life in and through time and describe the multiple audiences to which law speaks. These functions expand the political dimensions of lawyering: Indeed, they suggest that one of the tasks of lawyering in a losing cause is to find legal devices that address the future while continuing, however fruitless the struggle against the present reality of law's violence.

CHAPTER 3

Why Capital Punishment?

Ernest van den Haag

Since 1976, when the moratorium on executions ended, thirty-six states have passed constitutionally acceptable capital punishment statutes.[1] However, only thirteen states have executed anyone so far,[2] although about twenty-two thousand nonvehicular homicides are committed per year.[3] An unknown number of these homicides are capital crimes, but fewer than three hundred lead to death sentences.[4] No more than twenty-five persons have been executed in any year since 1976.[5] Because of the yawning gap between death sentences and executions, about 2,250 convicts are on death row now.[6] The number will continue to rise, although, at the current rate of executions (sixteen in 1989),[7] almost all will die of old age.

I. Judicial Reluctance

Why do we sentence people to death but do not carry out the sentence? What goes on? According to polls, more than 80 percent of Americans favor the death penalty. Juries apparently do, too, but, obviously, many judges and lawyers do not. More or less intentionally, they sabotage executions, delaying them (the average wait of those actually executed is eight years) and enormously inflating the cost. Some state appeals courts make it impossible to execute anyone, no matter how heinous the murder. The death penalty was reintroduced in New Jersey in 1982. But the New Jersey Supreme Court refused to affirm any death sentence until January 1991 when, after overturning twenty-six, the court upheld one.[8] The California Supreme Court also refused to affirm death sentences until the voters fired some justices.[9] (New Jersey voters are stuck: their court is not elected.) Death penalty legislation in New York was vetoed by Governor Mario Cuomo and his predecessor. Proponents have almost, but never quite, mustered the two-thirds majority needed to override.

The federal courts abet abolitionists by permitting abuses of habeas corpus and routinely serving as additional appeals courts after state court appeals have been exhausted. There is no capital case in which a constitutional violation is not claimed. *Mirabile dictu*, a federal court can always be found that will allow such claims to be litigated.

Why does the judiciary's view of capital punishment differ so much from that of the people? Judges are less likely to be murdered than the usual victims, such as slum dwellers, young blacks, store clerks, taxi drivers, or tenants in public housing. No less important, judges are college graduates, and college courses often deal with the causes of human conduct, including murder. Some graduates improperly infer that a bad and disadvantaged childhood, perhaps simply a non-middle-class childhood, not only explains a murderer's crime but also exculpates him, at least in part, and should mitigate his punishment. Explanations are not justifications, and to be caused is not inevitably, not even frequently, to be forced: Compulsion is only one kind of causation. Furthermore, little evidence indicates that a bad or disadvantaged childhood is necessary, or sufficient, for murder or exculpates murderers. Finally, even if their childhood experiences were shown to incline some persons to murder, the threats of the law, including capital punishment, are addressed to just such persons. The law is meant to restrain those inclined to violate it, whatever causes the inclination. Were the law to threaten only those unlikely to violate it, it would be useless. Although we do not punish those who cannot avoid crime,[10] those merely inclined to crime, because of their upbringing or social condition, are held responsible for their conduct.

Two points about responsibility might be noted. First, anyone can avoid the death penalty by not committing murder. One who does murder volunteers for the risk of suffering capital punishment. Second, the competence of some murderers may be doubted, either because they are very young, or because they are very stupid. As for the young, competence should be decided on by the court, aided by experts presented by the prosecution and defense. Prior to the age of twelve, incompetence may be statutorily presumed. I can see no reason, however, to presume or deny the competence of fifteen-year-olds on general grounds. The court should decide the issue of competence in each case. Certainly our current practice of giving the young a license to kill, with no fear of more than some years in prison, is asinine. Nor can I see the rationale for listing youthfulness as a mitigating circumstance to be considered by the jury. Most murderers are young. Why encourage them when they need more restraints than older persons?

There is no evidence that they are more easily reformed than older murderers. Anyway, we punish for actual past behavior, not for possible future behavior.

As for the low IQs, it should be up to the jury, as it should be with high IQs, to determine whether the requirements of the M'Naghten's rules[11] are met. Otherwise, stupidity or intelligence does not matter.

Still, the long-ago sociology course (or any course in the less disciplined disciplines) continues to rattle around in many a judge's head, disposing him not to hold defendants fully responsible, however much he understands that legally they are. In college, the death penalty was sneered at as barbarous, useless, and cruel.

Doubts about the constitutionality of capital punishment, resting on the misinterpreted Eighth Amendment phrase prohibiting "cruel and unusual" punishment, linger on. To entertain such doubts, one must be willing to disregard the words of the Constitution in favor of one's own moral convictions, since the Fifth and Fourteenth Amendments explicitly authorize the death penalty.[12] Such doubts also rest on the "evolving standards of decency," which Chief Justice Warren postulated in an expatriation case,[13] without explaining why the standards and their evolution should not be decided on by lawgivers, rather than by the interpreters of the law. Incidentally, Chief Justice Warren added: "[T]he death penalty . . . cannot be said to violate the constitutional concept of cruelty."[14] At any rate, "cruel and unusual" means cruel and uncustomary (the Framers did not want judges to invent *new* cruel punishments but did not abolish customary ones), a description not applicable to the death penalty.

Actually, capital punishment makes some persons uneasy, not so much because of rational doubts about its constitutionality but because it is irrevocable, not just irreversible as most punishments are. Our age seems allergic to irrevocability. However, death irrevocably will happen to us all. In John Stuart Mill's words, capital punishment merely "hasten[s]" it.[15] This hastening is within our control; therefore, unlike natural death, capital punishment requires moral justification.

II. Justice Brennan and the Right to Life

As all punishments do, capital punishment retributes for past conduct. However, unlike other punishments, execution cuts off the future. This, too, bothers many of us. Despite the clearly retrospective nature of all punishments, we tend to justify them prospectively as well. It is felt that punishment ought to improve the character of the punished person—which would exclude the death penalty. Rehabilitation has long been logically and empirically discredited—although we still optimistically call punishment "corrections."[16] Nonetheless, capital punishment makes people uneasy because it precludes rehabilitation, suggesting that some persons cannot be salvaged or that, in view of what they have done, we don't care to try, preferring to discard them altogether. To do so, former Justice Brennan protests, "treat[s] members of the human race . . . as objects to be . . . discarded"[17] and therefore is inconsistent with "the sanctity of life."[18] Brennan appears to believe that all humans have an imprescriptible right to life, that a murderer has just as much right to continue living—not to be executed—as his victim, or anyone else does. At most, murderers might be confined, as we cage a tiger, to reduce the danger to the public. Brennan overlooks, or obscures, the difference between the tiger and the murderer. Unlike the tiger, the murderer, by virtue of being human, is responsible for his acts: if legally guilty, he could have avoided murdering. He volunteered and is rational to that extent. Therefore, while we merely protect ourselves from a tiger, we punish a murderer as deserved by the gravity of his crime. We do not want murderers to survive their victims.

Brennan does not argue his reiteratively asseverated opinion that the death penalty is "degrading to human dignity"[19] and involves a "denial of the executed person's humanity."[20] Immanuel Kant and G. W. F. Hegel stressed the difference between humans and nonrational animals. They felt that capital punishment is needed to acknowledge fully the original humanity of the murderer,[21] however much he is dehumanized by his crime—not, as Brennan suggests, by his punishment.

Brennan seems to derive the murderer's "right" to continue living from a belief in imprescriptible natural (moral) rights. I agree with Jeremy Bentham: these are "nonsense on stilts."[22] We do live for a while. What could it mean to assert that we have an imprescriptible "right to live"? If such a right comes from society (a secular society knows no other source of rights: nature does not prescribe and has no authority, unless it is a disguise for God), society can make it a right to *innocent* life, as our Constitution does. That right, by definition, is prescriptible and can be forfeited by murder.

III. Justice and Revenge

Capital punishment is social retribution deserved by the murderer in the opinion of his fellow citizens. Doing justice requires no less than death for heinous murder. When retributive, punishment is an end in itself, satisfying a moral requirement. It is not a means to any material end, as are rehabilitation and incapacitation. Retribution is justified on purely moral grounds, as is the justice of which retribution is part. Although often invoked, justice is not currently fashionable, except when confused with utility, equality, or compassion. Retributive justice is even disparaged as revenge. In turn, revenge is denigrated as contrary to religious or moral norms. Yet, were it not for justice (retribution), why should we not punish innocents and let the guilty go when convenient? The very people who disparage retributive punishment would not want to punish innocents, however useful it may be. They must believe, then, that punishment is unjust except as retribution (i.e., paying back). Their disparagement of justice is incoherent when combined with their opposition to punishing innocents.

Revenge differs from retributive justice. Revenge is the motivation of victims for punishing their victimizers. That motivation is irrelevant to punishments imposed by law for the sake of justice and deterrence. Such punishments are required to enforce and vindicate the social order, regardless of the motivations or feelings of specific victims. Still, why disparage revenge? In his epistle to the Romans, St. Paul quotes the Lord as saying "vengeance is mine."[23] Surely that means not that revenge is bad per se but that, reserved to the Lord, it is not to be practiced by human beings who are enjoined elsewhere to forgive one another, since they all are sinners. The epistle continues: The ruler "beareth not the sword in vain: for he is . . . a revenger to execute wrath upon him that doeth evil."[24] The apostle discourages the taking of private revenge and encourages public retribution—justice—done by the government. He was, after all, *civis Romanus*.

Until the twentieth century, capital punishment was endorsed by the major Christian denominations. Currently, it is opposed by trendy churchmen of all denominations. In western Europe, it has been abolished in the wake of monstrous abuses by Stalin and Hitler. (Some countries, with very low homicide rates, abolished capital punishment even before.) We have no reason to be swayed by ecclesiastical or political fashions abroad. Our democracy was not founded on imitation of European fashions. Resistant to Mussolini, Stalin, and Hitler, it should resist the reaction to their abuses as well.

IV. Capital Punishment and the *Lex Talionis*

Is the death penalty just? It differs in kind from any other punishment. It is final. So is the crime of murder, which it punishes. Similar to many (though by no means all) punishments, capital punishment does to the criminal what he did to his victim. In former times, this most intelligible and direct, though often impractical, form of justice was practiced in ways we would today repudiate because they are repulsive to us. Thus, Thomas Jefferson:

> Whosoever shall be guilty of Rape, Polygamy, or Sodomy with man or woman shall be punished, if a man, by castration, if a woman, by cutting thro' the cartilage of her nose a hole of one half inch diameter at the least. . . .

> Whosoever . . . shall maim another, or shall disfigure him . . . shall
> be maimed or disfigured in like sort; or if that cannot be for want of
> the same part, then as nearly as may be in some other part of at least
> equal value.[25]

The *lex talionis* invoked by Jefferson sometimes is understood to require that punishment be no more painful to the offender than his crime was to the victim. There is no way of measuring this. At any rate, the *lex talionis* was meant to limit revenge by private persons, when murder was a private harm to be privately avenged or, more often, for which compensation was owed to private parties. We now have criminal law. A crime is considered primarily a public harm, not a private tort. Prosecutors ask for punishment in the name of "the people," not of the victim (who may get compensation in civil proceedings and perhaps should be represented independently at the criminal trial). The prosecutor's task is to obtain vindication, by means of retributive punishment, of the legal order violated by the crime. The gravity of the crime depends on the gravity of that violation (which includes, but is in no way limited by, the harm suffered by the specific victim); given culpability, so does the punishment required. Hence, the argument of Albert Camus,[26] who believed the death penalty wrong because it causes more suffering to the condemned man than he caused his victim, would be beside the point, even if the excess suffering were demonstrable. The *lex talionis* determines maximum compensation (or revenge) for tort harm, but no maximum punishment for any crime.

On a more primitive level, it is sometimes argued that if we do to the criminal what he did to his victim, we are as wrong as he was. This argument, which sometimes oxymoronically refers to execution as "legalized murder," overlooks that murder is a crime, an unlawful taking of life, while punishment is lawful, and capital punishment a lawful taking of life. The same physical act, homicide, can be lawful in self-defense, or war, or as punishment, and unlawful in murder. The difference between a lawful and an unlawful act, between execution and murder, is social, not physical, as is, generally, the difference between crime and punishment.

Sometimes a "brutalization effect" is ascribed to executions. Murderers are said to imitate, or to be inspired by, the legal killing of their late colleagues. Yet, all punishments, by definition and intent, do something unpleasant to the person punished. One wonders why punishments other than execution are not expected to be imitated. Why are thieves not inspired by legal fines? Kidnappers by arrest and imprisonment? I know of no such allegation even though it would be as reasonable as the alleged brutalization effect is. We do have some empirical studies by David P. Phillips[27] and by Stephen Stack[28] that not only negate the brutalization effect but demonstrate that upon executions, particularly highly publicized ones, there is a reduction of murders in both the short and long run. These studies confirm the results obtained by Isaac Ehrlich.[29]

V. Incapacitation and Deterrence

Would life in prison, without parole, incapacitate murderers as well as execution? I don't think so. Prevented by imprisonment from committing crimes outside, convicts can (and do) commit crimes within prison, assaulting, raping, and even killing fellow inmates and guards. The frequency of crime in prison seems higher than outside. Without the disincentive of the death penalty and the restraining incentive of parole, life prisoners, since they have nothing to lose and can kill with impunity, are a danger to other inmates and to guards.

Even if it were completely incapacitative, a life sentence in prison could not replace the death penalty. Justice demands that murderers be excluded from the human community, including even the prison community. Furthermore, the threat of imprisonment cannot deter future murderers as much as the threat of death. Where there is life there is hope. Threatened by lifelong imprisonment, murderers believe, not without reason, that they will get furloughs, as Willie Horton did in Massachusetts,[30] with opportunities for new crimes and escapes; or that they will be pardoned; or that they will somehow manage to escape. They may be wrong. But it is the belief that matters. No threat can deter as much as the threat of death. Death is final. Prison is not, and it is not perceived to be.

Statistical evidence that the death penalty deters more than alternative sanctions is controversial. The first sophisticated and scientifically respectable investigation was published by Isaac Ehrlich.[31] He concluded that each execution reduces the murder rate by between seven and eight murders per year.[32] Ten years later, Stephen Layson[33] found that the murder rate is reduced by about eighteen murders. These studies have been attacked and defended by numerous writers.[34] No consensus has been reached.

However, common experience (as well as many experiments) suggests that human conduct is shaped by incentives and disincentives. The threat of punishment, when credible, serves as a disincentive to most people most of the time. The more severe the disincentive and the more credible—the greater the risk— the more likely people are to be deterred. The effect of disincentives does not depend on calculations by those to be deterred, any more than the trajectory of a physical body depends on calculations by that body. The trajectory can be calculated and manipulated by outsiders. So can the behavior of human beings, including prospective criminals. They are notoriously influenced by their environment. Legal disincentives are an important, if not always decisive, part of it. Such disincentives tend to influence habit formation more than habits already formed. Thus, most people are habitually law abiding, because of the legal and moral disincentives to law breaking. They do not calculate, or even contemplate, criminal opportunities. Habitual law abiding simply leads them to ignore such opportunities. Most people ignore the opportunity for murder, because the disincentives always have been strong and have strongly contributed to a morality that eschews murder.[35]

Note that arguments for or against capital punishment based on alleged deterrence, or nondeterrence, are logically inconclusive, or at least incomplete (with unstated premises). If the death penalty were morally wrong, no deterrent effect would make it right, unless deterrence constitutes a moral argument that trumps the moral arguments against the death penalty. For most deontologists, deterrence cannot do so. On the other hand, if the death penalty is morally right, it remains so, even if it is not deterrent. Obviously, deontologists can ignore deterrence (although they seldom do), while consequentialists cannot.

VI. Some Further Objections

It is often noted that states such as Florida, despite many executions, have higher homicide rates than states with fewer executions. This would argue against a deterrent effect of executions if they alone determined homicide rates. Nobody believes they do. Penalties are only one of the factors determining crime rates—the factor most readily subject to legal action. Actually, the Florida homicide rate increased as the Miami drug trade did. Drug dealers—apparently firm believers in the deterrent effect of the death penalty—often kill one another to deter intruders on their turf or those they feel cheat them.

Maldistribution of the death penalty among murderers is often urged as an argument against it. Distribution is alleged to be freakish, resembling a lottery (i.e., capricious), or it is alleged to be discriminatory: black and poor murderers are thought to be more likely to be executed than equally guilty whites. This last point is no longer true. In 1986, 2 percent of black and 2 percent of white murderers were sentenced to death.[36] Currently, twelve blacks are sent to death row for every thousand arrested for murder, whereas sixteen whites are (i.e., whites have a 33 percent higher probability of ending up on death row).[37] Of a total of 3,746 death row inmates between 1977 and 1989, 3.2 percent of the black inmates were actually executed compared to 3.3 percent of the white inmates[38] (i.e., whites were more likely to be executed). Generally, discrimination based on the criminal's race has been on the way out since the death penalty for rape was declared unconstitutional.

However, David Baldus has shown that, in the state of Georgia, blacks who murder whites are more likely to be executed, *ceteris paribus*, than blacks who murder blacks.[39] This discrimination favors black murderers, most of whom kill other blacks. Still, irrational discriminations are wrong and invidious.

At any rate, objections to the death penalty because of discriminatory distribution object to what is distributed when the objection is to its distribution.

It would be irrational to abolish any punishments or rewards because they are maldistributed, unless it could be shown that, by their nature, they must be improperly or irrationally distributed. Nothing in the nature of the death penalty, any more than of the Nobel Prize or of incarceration, requires maldistribution.

To regard the death penalty as unjust because it is unequally distributed also confuses inequality with injustice. The guilt of any one murderer (and the justice of imposing the death penalty on him) is not diminished if other, equally or more guilty, murderers are not convicted or executed, whether because of racial discrimination, accident, or sheer capriciousness.[40] Guilt is personal. That others were spared punishment is no reason to spare you the punishment your crime deserves. Others got away with murder; they were not caught, convicted, or executed, for whatever reason. If these were grounds for not punishing those caught and convicted, we could never punish.

To extend justice to all is to treat all equally. If Smith and Jones each are dealt with justly, they are treated equally. However, justice—punishments imposed by due process according to law, as deserved by the gravity of the crime and the guilt of the criminal—cannot be replaced by equality: equal injustice is quite possible. To be sure, unequal sentencing based on skin color differs in significant respects from inequalities not caused by racial discrimination. Still, the justice of a sentence does not depend on other sentences, just or unjust, but only on whether the convict's guilt justifies it. We may well succeed in eliminating racial discrimination. Still, in an imperfect world justice will never be as equal as we would like. Yet, unequal justice is better than no justice, let alone equal injustice.

The existence of the death penalty implies the possibility, and in the long run the statistical likelihood, that innocent people will be executed. Courts are not infallible. Therefore, miscarriages of justice will occur. Since no one ever contended that courts are infallible, Hugo Adam Bedau and Michael Radelet do not tell us anything unexpected when they elaborately suggest that of more than seven thousand persons executed in the United States between 1900 and 1985, twenty-three were innocent.[41] Subsequently, a refutation was published[42] arguing that Bedau and Radelet were wrong in most of their cases. They rejoined candidly: "we have not 'proved' these executed defendants to be innocent."[43]

In my opinion, less than half of those listed by Bedau and Radelet as executed, although innocent, actually were innocent. On the other hand, it is admittedly quite possible that Bedau and Radelet did not discover all the innocents executed between 1900 and 1985. I do not see how we can ever know the number of executed innocents if we do not accept the verdict of the courts, which we cannot do if we set out to discover miscarriages. Thus, the Bedau–Radelet enterprise leaves us little wiser than we were before. It strikes me as a quixotic contribution to the exhaustion of possibilities.

Miscarriages of justice actually would argue for abolition if they were so frequent as to make the death penalty counterproductive—that is, if the risk of suffering the penalty when innocent were perceived to rival that of suffering it when guilty. Twenty-three controversial cases, out of seven thousand (one-third of 1 percent), do not indicate as much.

Policing, war, or traffic, to name but a few instances, often cause persons who have not volunteered to take that risk, such as innocent bystanders, civilians, or pedestrians, to lose their lives. Yet, these activities are continued. Despite the statistically certain losses, they provide a net advantage. So does the death penalty. Those who believe in justice perceive the moral necessity of not allowing murderers to live. We also know that the deterrent effect is likely to save more innocent lives from murder than it destroys by the execution of innocents through unintended miscarriages.[44]

One can argue, on rather hazy deontological grounds, that it is morally wrong ever to take the risk of executing an innocent, however many other innocents are certain to be saved if one takes the risk. Such an argument leads to absurdity. Nobody could ever be punished, let alone executed. Even Blackstone's more moderate view, that we should risk letting ten guilty persons go for the sake of sparing one innocent, seems unsustainable to me.[45]

It seems immoral, as well as unwise, to promise prospective murderers that what they will do to their victims will never be done to them, that they will survive.

VII. The Death Penalty in New York

Governor Cuomo promised to veto any death penalty bill that the majority of the New York State Legislature sent him. His veto was likely to be sustained. What would happen if it were overridden? There is little chance of death sentences being carried out in New York in the foreseeable future, even if they should be authorized by law.

In neighboring New Jersey, by 1990 the supreme court had reviewed twenty-seven death sentences since capital punishment was authorized.[46] It overturned twenty-six, affirming the first one in January 1991.[47] One can only speculate on the likely behavior of the New York Court of Appeals, but there is little reason to believe that it will be more inclined to affirm death sentences than the New Jersey Supreme Court. Thus, it seems unlikely that, even if we had, once more, a valid death penalty statute in New York, it would lead to executions. Its significance would be largely symbolic. Under these circumstances, is the matter worth pursuing? I think so.

It is possible, though not established, that the risk of suffering the death penalty, however small, will deter some murderers not deterred by the risk of imprisonment. That possibility, even if it were not a probability, makes the death penalty a moral duty, in my opinion. It is better to execute a murderer risking that his execution will not deter others, than not to execute him, risking the lives of innocents who could have been spared had their murderer been deterred by execution. Furthermore, the possibility of capital punishment strengthens the prosecution in plea bargains, enabling it to obtain life imprisonment without the expense of a trial. Without the threat of the death penalty, no defendant will consent to life imprisonment.

Finally, consider the position of a criminal holding a hostage. He can tell the police that, unless his conditions are met, the hostage will die. The police cannot tell him that if the hostage dies, he will be executed. The most that currently can happen to the criminal, if he kills his hostage in New York, is time in prison. Even a slight risk of execution might restrain him more. One may also hope that, in time, that risk will increase and, finally, that the reintroduction of the death penalty will help produce changes in judicial practices in New York, making them more effective in protecting the public.

CHAPTER 4

"Woe to the Hand That Shed This Costly Blood"

PHILOSOPHICAL ARGUMENTS
AGAINST THE DEATH PENALTY

J. Michael Martinez

> Woe to the hand that shed this costly blood!
> Over thy wounds now do I prophesy,—
> Which, like dumb mouths, do ope their ruby lips,
> To beg the voice and utterance of my tongue,—
> A curse shall be upon the limbs of men.
>
> —William Shakespeare, *Julius Caesar*, Act III, scene 1[1]

Any discussion of the death penalty raises philosophical issues that cannot be ignored by a regime that professes to govern in accordance with the rule of law coupled with a concept of fundamental fairness. At its core, the rule of law is the generally accepted basis for legitimizing power in stable, ongoing democratic governments in Western, highly industrialized nations.[2] It operates through the existence of clearly defined, generally accepted rules characteristically found in bureaucratic states.[3] Legitimate authority attaches to the office, not to the whims of a particular individual—hence the famous maxim "a government of laws and not of men."[4] In the words of one commentator, the "rule of law depends upon courts deciding the legal issues before them based upon the Constitution and the law."[5]

Yet a discussion of the death penalty raises issues far more profound than questions of positivist law, despite the undeniable importance of understanding and applying the law as part of society's formal rules. The rule of law seems to be a necessary, but insufficient, cornerstone for a government grounded on notions of equity. The sovereign may decide as a matter of law that capital punishment is an appropriate remedy for a litany of heinous acts—and the public may applaud its use in egregious cases—but this begs the deeper philosophical question of whether a state-sanctioned death penalty is justified by any rationale other than the ability of a government to command allegiance through the use of force. Since time immemorial, political philosophers have sought to ground a regime in an ethic that rises above "might makes right." Otherwise, as Thomas Hobbes argued, the sovereign could, "upon sufficient sign of the will," relieve individuals of their responsibility for addressing moral questions because the sovereign himself will make "the distinction of right and wrong."[6] Surely a democratic regime requires something more of its citizens than a cramped notion of positivist law in which all deeper moral questions are, in fact, legal questions decided by the state. What of "higher law" considerations that embody, in the words of one commentator, "certain principles of right and justice which are entitled to prevail of their own intrinsic excellence" because they are "eternal and immutable"?[7] Could it be that the Nazis were punished illegitimately at Nuremberg, as they claimed, merely because they had the misfortune to lose on the battlefields of World War II?[8] To the victor belong the spoils! If so, we are squarely within the province of "might makes right."

Power exercised without being grounded on a concept of fundamental fairness—the definition of "might makes right"—risks abuses of the sort demonstrated over the course of centuries of human history. The difficulty lies in understanding the appropriate role and limitations on the power of the sovereign—first, absent a concept of fundamental fairness (apart from the sovereign's pronouncements) and, next, grounded on a concept of fundamental fairness. The final argument here is that coupling the rule of law with a notion of fundamental fairness provides a deeper, more nuanced understanding of citizen requirements for a democratic regime and its foundations than does an understanding that considers society's rules as but a reflection of the sovereign's power. Yet, in the final analysis, a notion of fundamental fairness severely weakens the philosophical argument on behalf of capital punishment because fairness is applied not just to abstract discussions of the death penalty but to the sentencing of offenders in the real world. As we shall see at the conclusion of this chapter, mitigating factors on the part of the offender and biases on the part of the state in imposing sentences erode the moral justification for capital punishment. Before examining practical considerations, however, it is instructive to explore the philosophical bases that justify the power of the sovereign to impose punishment on citizens.

I. The Power of the Sovereign

Because the American democratic regime was established in accordance with social contract theories that can be traced to seventeenth-century Enlightenment thinkers, this examination should commence with a discussion of the ideas propounded by Thomas Hobbes and John Locke. In many ways, these two theorists influenced the American Founders (and therefore the subsequent operation of the American regime) more than almost any other Western political thinkers of the Enlightenment, with the possible exception of David Hume and Montesquieu.[9]

In his great work *Leviathan*, Hobbes reacts against the metaphysical pretensions of the Greek and Scholastic philosophers who preceded him because he considered their "pie-in-the-sky" theoretical presuppositions absurd. In his view, the paramount consideration in a human life is the need for self-preservation. Men create a government and promulgate civil laws precisely because they fear the distinct possibility that they will be violently harmed or killed in a chaotic state of nature. Their covenant with each other is to create a strong sovereign who will rule with firmness so that individuals do not engage in behavior that will undermine or even destroy the sovereign's power and hence the regime itself.[10] Persons who engage in criminal behavior violate the terms of their covenant because their actions weaken the sovereign's power to protect citizens from harm.[11] Offenders, therefore, must be punished appropriately. Moreover, any action the sovereign undertakes to deter future criminal behavior is appropriate.

The question thus becomes an issue of how a punishment should be administered.[12] Hobbes acknowledges that the penalty must fit the crime, but proportionality is a difficult question. On one hand, "if the harm inflicted be less than the benefit or contentment that naturally follows the crime committed, that harm is not within the definition [of a punishment], and is rather the price of redemption than the punishment of a crime." In other words, excessive leniency should be avoided "because it is of the nature of punishment to have for end the disposing of men to obey the law, which end, if it be less than the benefit of the transgression, it attains not, but works to contrary effect."[13] On the other hand, a punishment that is too harsh also should be avoided. Hobbes contends that "if a punishment be determined and prescribed in the law itself, and after the crime committed there be a greater punishment inflicted, the excess is not punishment but an act of hostility." In short, the sovereign must not brutally oppress citizens of the regime in his quest to punish offenders. "For seeing the aim of punishment is not a revenge but terror, and the terror of a great punishment unknown is taken away by the declaration of a less, the unexpected addition is no part of the punishment."[14]

Hobbes recognizes that a sovereign possesses the authority to impose capital punishment for capital offenses. As long as the offender's identity is established in an open forum through what we would today call "due process," the sovereign can impose a variety of punishments, provided that they are proportionate to the crime. In Hobbes's view, types of punishment can be classified according to their nature: corporal (against the body, including capital punishment), pecuniary, ignominy, imprisonment, or exile. The sovereign legitimately imposes these penalties because all persons who covenanted to create the sovereign tacitly empowered him to decide questions of reward and punishment. In "laying down [their rights, they] strengthened him to use his own as he should think fit for the preservation of them all."[15]

To some extent, John Locke followed in Hobbes's footsteps. Writing at the end of the seventeenth century, Locke also supports the judicious use of the death penalty to ensure the safety of citizens in a regime. Like Hobbes, Locke urges that offenders be punished in proportion to their crimes. The penalty should be imposed "only retribute to him, so far as calm reason and conscience dictate, what is proportionate to his transgression, which is so much as may serve for reparation or restraint." Capital punishment may be justified as proportionate, in some instances, because "[I]n transgressing the law of nature, the offender declares himself to live by another rule than that of reason and common equity." Consequently, "he becomes dangerous to mankind." Anyone who is threatened by an offender has a natural right to protect himself against harm. "Which being a trespass against the whole species and the peace and safety of it provided for by the law of nature, every man upon this score, by the right he hath to preserve mankind in general, may restrain, or, where it is necessary, destroy things noxious to them, and so may bring such evil on any one who hath transgressed the law, as may make him repent the doing of it and thereby deter him, and by his example others, from doing like mischief. And in this case, and upon this ground *every man hath a right to punish the offender and be executioner of the law of nature.*"[16]

Because men in a state of nature legitimately can defend themselves—even to the point of killing someone who would kill them—when they enter into a social contract, they transfer this legitimacy to the state. Accordingly, the state can take human life, in some instances. Moreover, just as people in a state of nature can defend themselves in proportion to the threat posed by the offender, so, too, can the state punish "a criminal who, having renounced reason—the common rule and measure God hath given to mankind—hath, by the unjust violence and slaughter he hath committed upon one, declared war against all mankind; and therefore may be destroyed as a lion or a tiger, one of those wild savage beasts with whom men can have no society nor security." The state's authority to punish offenders, therefore, is an extension of an individual's natural right to life. In a restatement of the Old Testament credo, Locke observes that, "[a]nd upon this is grounded that great law of nature, 'Whoso sheddeth man's blood, by man shall his blood be shed.'"[17]

Locke goes a step further in justifying his support for the death penalty. He realizes that some critics might object to the severity of the punishment, but he believes that it is a necessary penalty for heinous offenses. "By the same reason may a man in the state of nature punish the lesser breaches of law. It will perhaps be demanded: with death? I answer: Each transgression may be punished to that degree and with so much severity as will suffice to make it an ill bargain to the offender, give him cause to repent, and terrify others from doing the like."[18]

Both Hobbes and Locke reflect the Enlightenment's belief in the rationality of mankind and the perfectibility of human nature through the judicious use of the institutions of government. According to this perspective, the death penalty is an appropriate punishment for a rogue figure that rejects rationality and, for whatever reason, commits a capital crime and thereby revels in the dark side of human nature. Notice the presuppositions built into the Enlightenment perspective: By taking the offender's life as punishment, the state ensures that the particular offender will not misbehave in the future and, in addition, deters would-be offenders from engaging in such behavior. In generating a feeling of terror in its citizens, the state is fulfilling its role as a human-created instrument for imposing rationality, security, and civic order on the populace. Whenever anyone within the populace rejects rationality, he steps beyond the accepted boundaries of human society. Because he threatens the established social and civic order, he is an unacceptable threat and must be handled appropriately.

Enlightenment thinkers such as Hobbes and Locke do not enjoy the advantages of examining social science data. They form their beliefs that capital punishment will segregate past offenders from the population of innocents and also deter potential offenders on faith. They also are not bothered by the element of revenge implicit in capital punishment. From a broader perspective, they also assume that the rationality of the state ultimately will ensure a higher quality of life for all citizens.

Before addressing the well-worn segregation, deterrence, and revenge arguments raised by Hobbes and Locke, it is instructive to consider the larger point about the power of the state to impose death under any circumstances. From the perspective of the twenty-first century—with the clarifying benefit of hindsight—we might rightly ask whether the Enlightenment thinkers were justified in tendering such faith in the wisdom of the state. Although Locke retains his famous right of revolution in situations where the state acted egregiously through "a long train of abuses, prevarications, and artifices, all tending the same way," he contends that the state seldom will engage in such wrongful behavior.[19] Instead, he contends that a powerful state generally would act on behalf of the public good. For his part, Hobbes argues that it was preferable to endure the abuses of a heavy-handed sovereign than return to a state of nature.

The weakness in Hobbes's and Locke's arguments on behalf of a powerful sovereign with authority to impose death on citizens is the question of what remedies exist when a state is too harsh in its treatment of a particular citizen. In other words, who determines whether the sovereign has imposed an appropriately proportionate punishment? A general right of revolution brings little comfort to a specific individual facing the death penalty. A state with such awesome power at its disposal may become a de facto totalitarian state, despite the citizens' general right of revolution for ongoing, long-term abuses (assuming that we accept Locke's view of rights). The possibilities of abuses perpetrated by a brutal sovereign with the power to impose the death penalty perhaps is best illustrated by the story of the Grand Inquisitor in Book V, chapter 5, of the great Russian novelist Fyodor Dostoyevsky's masterpiece, *The Brothers Karamazov*.[20] Admittedly, this is an extreme case, but it does underscore the need for coupling sovereign power with a concept of fundamental fairness that errs—if it errs at all—on the side of justice tempered with mercy.

Dostoyevsky's chapter opens in the sixteenth century during the Spanish Inquisition, a time when the sovereign persecuted non-Catholics without benefit of due process. As the tale begins, the Grand Inquisitor, an old man of ninety, "tall and erect, with a withered face and sunken eyes, in which there is still a gleam of light," confronts a solitary figure in a "gloomy vaulted prison in the ancient palace of the Holy Inquisition" during a "dark, burning 'breathless' night" in Seville. As he enters the chamber, the Inquisitor "sees everything." He knows the identity of the man with whom he speaks, for earlier the Inquisitor witnessed a crowd of people gathered around the mysterious figure. They kissed the stranger's feet. The masses regard him as Christ resurrected from the dead.

Although he is supposed to be an instrument of the church, the Grand Inquisitor—Dostoyevsky's symbol of the omnipotent, brutal sovereign—is not pleased when he learns of the Second Coming of the Messiah. The figure could be dangerous to organized religion if he chose to contravene long-established church doctrine. As a result, the Grand Inquisitor has ordered his men to take the figure into custody to ensure that his presence does not provoke a popular uprising. Dostoyevsky's description of the interlocutor's awesome power is telling. "And such is his power, so completely are the people cowed into submission and trembling obedience to him, that the crowd immediately make way for the guards, and in the midst of deathlike silence they lay hands on Him and lead him away."[21] Despite the masses' reverence for the Christ figure, they know that the state is too powerful to resist and the sovereign will not tolerate dissent.

The Grand Inquisitor comes face-to-face with the stranger within the walls of the dark prison. Their silence is awkward. Finally, the Inquisitor demands to know whether the solitary figure is Christ, as the crowd seems to believe. When the figure remains silent, the Grand Inquisitor tells his prisoner that he recognizes him as the savior. Yet, strangely, this confirmation of the Inquisitor's religious faith provides no comfort, for "Thou hast come to hinder us." Even if he is the Messiah arisen from the dead to bring a message of hope and a promise of salvation to mankind, this solitary figure threatens the authority of the established church. Thus, despite his identity as the resurrected Christ, he will be burned at the stake and denounced as a heretic. According to the Grand Inquisitor, "the very people who have today kissed Thy feet, tomorrow at the faintest sign from me will rush to heap up the embers of Thy fire."[22] Such is the awe-inspiring power of the state that people will turn their backs on Christ himself if the sovereign commands them to stand aside.

The remainder of the chapter explores the Grand Inquisitor's justification for his brutal actions during the Spanish Inquisition. It does not matter that the state has persecuted many people who probably were innocent of wrongdoing. Notions of equity and fairness are not essential to the operation of the well-ordered, "just" regime. He argues that a "just" regime is one where the state wields enormous power—the power to control virtually every aspect of citizens' lives. An all-powerful state can ensure order, hence tranquility, which is what people really want in their lives. They are willing to suffer through patently unfair proceedings in exchange for a strong, stable regime. Innocent individuals occasionally must be sacrificed on the altar of security in order to ensure the collective well-being of all other citizens.

In the face of this rationalization, the Christ figure remains silent. He represents the idea that the individual can be true to himself; he need not bow to the all-powerful state. Truth and freedom of conscience are important themes for Dostoyevsky because they suggest that an individual can legitimately resist the power of the sovereign in the name of a higher law—the law of justice or mercy.

The Grand Inquisitor dismisses this belief out of hand. People do not want the freedom to follow the dictates of conscience. The responsibilities inherent in a system in which individuals can accept individual freedom of choice are too great, and people are too weak. He contends that mankind values "bread"—order and security—above truth. Freedom for the masses, therefore, is not exploring an objective truth and making moral decisions. The masses exhibit a "craving for community of worship." They worship God not because they value the lessons of Christ. They seek to join a community with others who worship. They seek conformity. Freedom, according to the Grand Inquisitor, results from individuals entrusting a powerful sovereign with complete, unquestioned authority to decide right and wrong. "I tell Thee that man is tormented by no greater anxiety than to find someone quickly to whom he can hand over that gift of freedom with which the ill-fitted creature is born," he insists.[23]

The state steps in and fills the void in the human heart. It takes individual freedom as payment in exchange for security. Thus, the sovereign has "corrected

Thy work" by founding a regime based "upon miracle, mystery, and authority." Citizens—good Christians, all—are unperturbed; they have greeted the heavy-handedness of the state "and rejoiced that they were again led like sheep."[24] Even when the sovereign imposes harsh penalties, citizens will acquiesce in the face of the state's terrible power. According to the Grand Inquisitor, "We shall tell them that every sin will be expiated, if it is done with our permission, that we allow them to sin because we love them, and the punishment for these sins we take upon ourselves."[25] In effect, this is an argument in favor of the state as the basis of a civil religion that supersedes the original religious ideals propagated by Jesus Christ.

The Grand Inquisitor presents a strong case for an all-powerful sovereign who holds absolute power and brooks no dissent. "Fundamental fairness" is whatever the sovereign deems it to be. Because he protects his citizens from the vicissitudes of life, he has their eternal gratitude, no matter how much of their freedom he destroys. People are willing to subordinate their right to make all decisions, including decisions on morality, to the authority of the state.

At the conclusion of the tale, the Grand Inquisitor stands defiantly before the Christ figure, waiting for his reaction to the arguments in favor of the omnipotent power of the sovereign. In Dostoyevsky's words, the interrogator looked at the prisoner and "longed for him to say something, however bitter and terrible. But he suddenly approached the old man and softly kissed him on his bloodless, aged lips."[26]

Christ's actions at the culmination of the tale suggest that something is missing from the Grand Inquisitor's view of the state and his perspective on human freedom. The Grand Inquisitor has failed to provide for justice, mercy, and fairness. Without a sense of fundamental fairness, the state is but an instrument of unfettered power—the embodiment of "might makes right"—which brings us back to where we were at the beginning of our discussion. If the state is to be more than merely a repository of unbridled power, it must rest on a principle separate and apart from the series of positivist laws that are enacted and obeyed simply because the sovereign commands it. Dostoyevsky's point is exactly this: The state must rest on a deeper, embedded principle separate from positivist law; otherwise, it can and probably will become an instrument of citizen oppression.

A proponent of capital punishment might argue that the tale of the Grand Inquisitor presents a far different scenario than the prospect faced by a condemned man in a democratic regime. Unlike the resurrected Christ imprisoned in Seville, a death row defendant in the United States enjoys the benefits of due process, habeas corpus appeals, the services of lawyers, and numerous other procedural safeguards—a far cry from the Spanish Inquisition. The point is well taken, but the meaning of the Grand Inquisitor story is not that a democratic regime mirrors the totalitarian abuses of the Spanish Inquisition. Dostoyevsky's argument is that a regime with power to impose the death penalty on an offender based solely on the pronouncements of the sovereign risks being too heavy-handed, hence unjust. Mistakes can be made, or a sovereign who seeks to protect the power of the state over the individual may sacrifice innocent citizens. Thus, a sovereign who exercises absolute power over life and death risks sacrificing a few on the altar of the many. It is a difference of degree—not a difference in kind—from the Spanish Inquisition. In the words of the English Utilitarian John Stuart Mill, the "mischief begins when, instead of calling forth the activity and powers of individuals and bodies," a government presumes to dictate all the important questions of life itself. In short, a powerful sovereign harms everyone, even those persons not engaged in, or affected by, criminal activity. According to Mill, "a State which dwarfs its men, in order that they may be more docile instruments in its hands even for beneficial purposes—will find that with small men no great thing can really be accomplished."[27]

Many theorists have echoed this concern about the potential for abuses when a sovereign exercises too much power over questions of life and death. Perhaps the French postmodernist Michel Foucault propounds the most eloquent and incisive commentary in the twentieth century. Although he does not share Dostoyevsky's religious orientation, Foucault agrees with the Russian's concern about the sovereign's unlimited power to create mischief. Foucault also extends the analysis to consider not simply the effects of an all-powerful state but the subtle consequences of living in a society influenced by an array of social and political forces in meting out punishments. In *Discipline and Punish: The Birth of the Prison*, he examines historical changes in society's methods of defining crimes and punishing those persons labeled as "criminals."[28]

Before the twentieth century, according to Foucault, punishments were public spectacles designed to educate citizens on the consequences of committing certain crimes. The penalties were gruesome reminders that the sovereign would punish the body of the condemned man or woman by using instruments of torture. As the Enlightenment changed societal attitudes about crime and punishment, the sovereign changed the purpose, and therefore the nature, of punishment. No longer was it a public spectacle to be viewed by citizens in the town square. In fact, punishment became the most hidden component of the criminal justice system. Attention shifted to the trial and sentencing of the condemned. Legal codes, rules of procedure, and an emphasis on the rights of the accused displaced the idea that the public should bear witness to punishing an errant member of the polity. Offenders were no longer viewed as sinners or pariahs; instead, they and their lawyers became celebrities—sometimes, even folk heroes—as they jockeyed for position in the public consciousness. Book deals, movie rights, and public acclaim transformed the nature of punishment. In Foucault's words, "[a]t the beginning of the nineteenth century, then, the great spectacle of physical punishment disappeared; the tortured body was avoided; the theatrical representation of pain was excluded from punishment. The age of sobriety in punishment had begun."[29]

To many modern observers, this movement away from grisly public executions was a positive step in modern society, for it no longer encouraged a passionate crowd to wallow in theatrical displays of torture. In Foucault's view, however, this development holds other consequences as well. As executions move behind prison walls, away from the prying eyes of the average citizen, society's emphasis on capital punishment shifts from punishing the body to punishing the soul. "The expiation that once rained down upon the body must be replaced by a punishment that acts in depth on the heart, the thoughts, the will, the inclinations," he writes.[30] This holds enormous implications for society because it suggests that traditional defenses of capital punishment—especially the argument that executions deter would-be offenders from acting—no longer remain persuasive. If we hide executions from sight, this lessens the deterrent effect because it mutes the horrors associated with killing the body.

Moreover, the process of judging an offender's actions has become much more complicated. In previous centuries, the king or the prosecuting authority determined the particular crime that has been committed and how it should be punished. Over time, the analysis changed. In the twentieth century, the focus shifted to an inquiry about the nature of the offender's act. What were the parameters of the act? What was the offender thinking when he engaged in the act? Did heredity, peers, social institutions, or special circumstances influence his behavior? A multitude of experts is now employed to explore these questions: psychiatrists, psychologists, lawyers, police officers, jury consultants, and so forth.

As our understanding of crime and punishment evolves, we seem to embrace a "more humane manner" of punishing offenders. By moving executions behind the walls of the prison and focusing on the rights of the accused, we congratulate ourselves on our sense of fundamental decency because we are not as barbaric as our forbears were in doling out punishments. What we often fail to realize is how this gradual evolution increases the power of the state. No longer do citizens actively participate in punishing offenders, to the extent that they ever participated. Because punishments are out of sight, citizens lose their understanding of the brutal nature of capital punishment. In addition, the criminal justice system is far more complex than ever before. Only the most knowledgeable experts can fully appreciate the rules, procedures and standards necessary to punish offenders. In effect, all knowledge and power about capital punishment are vested in the state and its agents. Foucault argues that "[w]e must first rid ourselves of the illusion that penality is above all (if not exclusively) a means of reducing crime and that, in this role, according to social forms, the political beliefs, it may be severe or lenient, tend toward expiation of obtaining redress, toward the pursuit of individuals or the attribution of collective responsibility." He asks that we reformulate our understanding of punishment by changing the way we examine such issues. "We must analyze, rather, the 'concrete system of punishment,' study them as social phenomena that cannot be accounted for by the juridical structure of society alone, nor by its fundamental ethical choices," he contends.[31]

In short, much as Dostoyevsky is concerned that the state wields enormous power to impose capital punishment, Foucault expresses concern that the issue of capital punishment goes far beyond questions of whether a particular offender engaged in a given behavior in a given instance. Foucault even moves beyond Dostoyevsky in his analysis. The issue is not merely whether we wish to leave such fundamental questions in the hands of a possibly brutal sovereign, but whether we realize that issues of crime and punishment involve complex social and political forces. Neither Dostoyevsky nor Foucault explicitly presents an argument against capital punishment under all circumstances, but they do raise questions about the complex forces that influence the state's—and, by extension, society's—decisions about the legitimacy of imposing death on individual human beings.

II. The Concept of Fundamental Fairness

In light of Dostoyevsky's and Foucault's concerns about capital punishment as an expression of a powerful sovereign (and, in Foucault's view, an expression of other complex social forces), let us consider the second point. What does it mean to argue on behalf of fundamental fairness in imposing capital punishment—fair to whom? The argument is fraught with peril, for any movement beyond positivist law loses the benefit of its relatively clear, easily explicated characteristics. This journey requires the inquirer to step behind positivist laws and ask moral questions—that is, questions about an individual's responsibilities to the sovereign, to other persons within the state, and to himself. One must examine fundamental fairness from the standpoint both of fairness to an offender charged with a capital crime as well as fairness to the victims of that crime. Questions of fairness ultimately become ethical questions.[32]

Elsewhere, I have wrestled with the distinction between law and ethics in detail.[33] Suffice it to say here that ethical questions go to the core of the human condition. They are the context-specific, value-laden questions that confront individuals as they go about their daily lives. This definition distinguishes ethical questions from the rule-bound, codified, "known and knowable" characteristics of positivist laws promulgated by authoritative governmental bodies. To say that the death penalty fundamentally is an ethical question is to say that the "ethical or moral meaning" of capital punishment, in the words of one commentator, "must be derived from attending to the moral life in all its complexity, in its social context as well as in its expression in individual lives."[34]

Social context is an important component of any philosophical discussion of the death penalty because all questions of punishment with life and death in the balance are raised in relation to other people. Setting aside an offender's mental illness, low intelligence, youth, and other possibly mitigating factors for the time being, the often-cited deterrence argument suggests that when the sovereign executes a defendant, the execution serves the ends of justice. The argument is that it is fundamentally fair to the victim and it is fair to the offender. The deterrence argument is empirical, but it holds philosophical implications as well. The core question is whether capital punishment serves a major purpose for which it was instituted—that is, does it prevent future crimes from occurring?[35]

A. "JUST EXECUTION"

If capital punishment deters future crimes from occurring and protects innocent citizens from suffering harm, the killing of an offender may be deemed a "just execution." The concept is based on the rationale that a political authority has an obligation to ensure, to the extent possible, the well-being of citizens. Thus, the sovereign is not merely acting from a desire for revenge against an offender, according to this perspective. He is protecting law-abiding citizens within the state either from the possibility that a duly convicted offender will repeat his acts or that others will see the state's leniency as an invitation to engage in mayhem in the future. In this view, fairness is twofold. It is fair to from the perspective of the victim and the victim's family to rob the offender of his life because the offender initiated the sequence of actions that eventually robbed the victim of his life. Moreover, it is fair from the perspective of the offender because he gets his just deserts; his actions cause the state to wield the terrible swift sword of punishment against him. By imposing the most stringent penalty possible—state-sanctioned deprivation of life—the sovereign sends a powerful message to everyone in the regime. The offender is dead, and would-be offenders must take heed, lest they might face a similar fate as a result of their misdeeds.

The philosophical justification for a "just execution" is rooted in the biblical requirement of an "eye for an eye, a tooth for a tooth"—a maxim that initially sounds appealing because it seems to be an intuitive plea for proportionality.[36] If one accepts the argument that justice primarily is procedural—the result of "the basic structure of society, or more exactly, the way in which the major social institutions distribute fundamental rights and duties," in John Rawls's words[37]—justice would seem to be served as long as the offender is afforded the appropriate procedural rights. If the offender's guilt is established beyond a reasonable doubt, justice seems to demand that the offender pay the ultimate price.

Proponents of the just execution theory argue that symmetry exists between the actions of the offender and the punishment meted out by the sovereign. Because the offender has, in a sense, unbalanced the scales of justice by engaging in a capital offense, he is paying for his crime and thereby righting the scales of justice by offering up his life. One hesitates to extend the analogy too far, but it may be somewhat analogous to conversion theory in the law. When an offender destroys property, he has constructively "purchased" the property. His payment, plus applicable punitive damages, amounts to a righting of the scales of justice because he is, in effect, compensating the victim. Because a murder victim is dead and cannot be compensated, however, the offender in such cases must pay for his crime not in specie, but in blood. John Stuart Mill observes, "I confess it appears to me that to deprive the criminal of the life of which he has proved himself to be unworthy—solemnly to blot him out from the fellowship of mankind and from the catalogue of the living—is the most appropriate, as it is certainly the most impressive, mode in which society can attach to so great a crime the penal consequences which for the security of life it is indispensable to annex to it."[38] A just execution is giving back to the offender what he or she has given originally to the regime—*suum cuique tribue* (to give everyone what he deserves).

State-sanctioned executions have a long history in the Western tradition because this justification resonates with such authority. The Old Testament is replete with verses that extol the virtues of capital punishment for a variety of offenses, some of which do not strike modern ears as capital crimes.[39] The Code of Hammurabi listed numerous crimes for which death was an appropriate penalty.[40] In a paper presented before the English Parliament in 1701, an anonymous author stated that, "I must beg leave to say, that those who shew no mercy should find none; and if Hanging will not restrain them, Hanging them in Chains, and Starving them, or (if Murderers and Robbers at the same time, or Night Incendiaries) breaking them on the Wheel, or Whipping them to Death, a *Roman* Punishment should."[41]

The "eye for an eye" argument often is raised in criminal trials even in modern times. Sometimes democratic principles are added to the equation to justify the regime's actions and to mitigate the harsh authoritarian credo that stories such as the Grand Inquisitor's tale impute to the state. A good example of this appeal to democracy can be found in the Leopold and Loeb murder case in Chicago in the 1920s. The state's attorney for Cook County, Illinois, Robert E. Crowe, prosecuted the infamous case. Leopold and Loeb was a "crime of the century" that occurred when two wealthy, supremely intelligent young men killed a fourteen-year-old boy simply for the thrill of snuffing out the life of another human being. In his argument, Crowe contended that democratic government required the death penalty to be imposed if the people, speaking through the legislature, deemed it to be appropriate. "The law says in extreme cases death shall be the penalty," he observed. "If I were in the legislature I might vote against such a law. I don't know. But as a judge, I have no right to set aside the law. I have no right to defeat the will of the people, as expressed by the legislature of Illinois. I have no right to be a judicial anarchist."[42] Later in the argument, he explained his position in a more forthright manner. "I believe that the penalty for murder should be death. I urge capital punishment for murder not because I believe that society wishes to take the life of a murderer but because society does not wish to lose its own." In Crowe's view, the sovereign can justify capital punishment if it is meted out "in a properly constituted court over whose deliberations a properly elected judge has presided and in which, after hours and days and sometimes weeks of patient and deliberate inquiry, a jury of twelve men selected in the manner which the law provides" finds that the offender should pay the ultimate price.[43] We will return to the Leopold and Loeb case later as we consider defense attorney Clarence Darrow's argument against the death penalty.

Three decades later, in the infamous Rosenberg "atom spy case" during the early 1950s, two commentators remarked that the death penalty often was applied in a less than equitable manner. Although the defendant Julius Rosenberg probably was guilty of espionage for passing secrets of the atomic bomb to the Soviet Union, his wife Ethel "probably knew and supported her husband's endeavors," but "the FBI investigative files contain no hard information to show that Ethel's active participation in the spy ring extended beyond" communicating with her brother, David Greenglass, who also was involved in espionage. "The legal case against her, moreover, was based in large part on a last-minute change of testimony by the key witnesses against her and was relatively weak, even so."[44] Yet she was executed because public hysteria over communism during the Cold War demanded retribution. In short, democracy required the execution because the people needed to be reassured that their government would protect them from the evils of an expanding communist regime. The "people" spoke through government officials, who therefore carried out the sentence.

Opponents of the "just execution" theory cite a number of arguments to justify their opposition.[45] One of the most famous arguments against giving an offender what he has given to society can be found in Book I of Plato's *Republic*. As the dialogue opens, Plato's teacher, Socrates, goes down to the Piraeus to attend a festival. During his journey, a slave belonging to a prominent Athenian citizen, Polemarchus, stops him. The slave insists that Socrates accompany him to his master's house. Reluctantly, Socrates agrees to go. Later in the dialogue, as Socrates continues to be waylaid from his journey, he is surrounded by a group of citizens who ask the great philosopher to discuss the meaning of justice. In the course of a long conversation, Socrates refuses to tell his audience what justice requires, for he humbly acknowledges his own ignorance of the matter. Instead, he prefers to question their views. At one point, Polemarchus tells Socrates that "if Simonides should be believed at all," then justice "is just to give to each what is owed." In appealing to authority (Simonides), Polemarchus is articulating a variant of the "just execution" theory.[46] He represents a kind of conventional appeal to precedent. Let us look to the past and rely on society's views about justice, he suggests.

Polemarchus offers the argument that justice is giving back to the offender what the offender has given to the victim—a kind of reverse golden rule. In Polemarchus's words, "justice is doing good to friends and harm to enemies."[47] This argument has intuitive appeal. Most people would agree that we should be kind and good to our friends because they wish us well. Our enemies mean to do us harm; accordingly, we should harm them—if for no other reason than to protect ourselves from their spiteful actions. This is the logic behind what military strategists call a "preemptive strike."

Socrates eventually rejects Polemarchus's view of justice. Instead, he argues that the just man never intentionally harms anyone or anything, regardless of how others treat him. Justice requires something more than giving back mistreatment. Two wrongs do not make a right, in modern parlance. This insight sounds remarkably similar to the true Golden Rule: Do unto others as you would have them do unto you. "Then it is not the work of the just man to harm either a friend or anyone else, Polemarchus, but of his opposite, the unjust man," Socrates contends. "For it has become apparent to us that it is never just to injure anyone."[48]

Socrates' perspective foreshadows New Testament–based theological positions against the death penalty discussed by Mark Douglas and Glen H. Stassen elsewhere in this collection. If Socrates and adherents of the New Testament are correct, justice requires more than retribution. Executing people based on the eye-for-an-eye rationale leads only to more bloodshed. Mohandas Gandhi expressed it well when he observed, "[I]f everyone took an eye for an eye, the whole world would be blind."[49]

What of the argument that democracy requires executions when the people, acting through their duly elected representatives, demand that an offender get back what he has given to (or, more properly, taken from) society? As I wrote these words, Timothy McVeigh, the man who became the greatest American-born mass murderer in U.S. history when he bombed the Alfred P. Murrah Federal Building in Oklahoma City, Oklahoma, on April 19, 1995—killing 168 people, 19 of whom were children—was making headlines across the country owing to his execution for the crime. According to McVeigh, "I understand what they felt in Oklahoma City. I have no sympathy for them." Asked in an interview about his reaction when he learned that he had caused the deaths of innocent children, McVeigh was philosophically fatalistic. "That's a large amount of collateral damage," he said.[50]

If anyone deserves to be put to death, surely an amoral sociopath like Timothy McVeigh qualifies for the ultimate penalty—if for no other reason than to dissuade copycats (assuming that the deterrence argument is valid). Yet the problem with executing people owing to the popularity of capital punishment can be understood best by examining the writings of John Stuart Mill once again. Mill's view that capital punishment is morally defensible is not surprising in light of Utilitarian doctrine, which posits that the consequences of an action determine its value. Thus, if the death penalty can be shown to be an effective deterrent or simply a tool in reducing recidivism among offenders, then the greatest good of society arguably has been served. In other words, utility has been maximized.[51]

Of course, a problem occurs if the deterrence argument fails. According to commentator Lloyd Steffen, flaws in the deterrence argument undermine Mill's presuppositions about deterrence and the effect of "psychological arousal" that promotes fear in persons who might commit a capital crime.[52] "To make this case I would argue that in American society, Americans cannot be affected behaviorally by Mill's 'experience in terror' because in this society, the violent death visited upon persons by execution fails to stand out from a background of violence that is so much a part of common social experience," Steffen contends.[53] Ironically, to the extent that ordinary citizens experience terror at the prospect of suffering capital punishment, their feelings may be muted by background violence around them. Even if some ordinary citizens might be terrorized, offenders may be immune to such calculations of cause and effect.

A broader criticism of Utilitarianism's precepts can be found elsewhere. John Rawls objects to utilitarian arguments because classical Utilitarianism "fails to take seriously the distinction between persons."[54] That is, Utilitarianism assumes that all persons should be treated equally and, therefore, all preferences must be accorded the same or substantially similar weight. If all preferences are weighed the same, presumably they can be calculated with no small measure of precision. This sounds satisfactory until one attempts to calculate goods and discovers that, in some instances, preferences are unidentifiable, ever-changing, vague, ambiguous, or they risk alienating a substantial minority of persons.[55]

Furthermore, Utilitarianism may inadvertently result in a tyranny of the majority. When the ancient Athenians led a military expedition against the small island of Melos during the Peloponnesian War, the Melians argued that might does not make right. When a majority uses its superior force to subjugate a weaker force, "you have stopped us from speaking of justice and persuade[d] us to submit to your expedient interest."[56] The rights of a minority are sacrificed for the maximum utility of a majority. Justice is not served simply because an offender is executed owing to the wishes of a majority of the public; justice requires a greater rationale than simply an appeal to numbers.

Earlier in this chapter, we set aside a discussion of whether an offender has the capacity to understand the nature of his or her crime. We must take up the question here. If the purpose of capital punishment is to protect society from further acts committed by the offender, on one hand, and to deter others from engaging in similar acts, on the other hand, this argument breaks down when we consider persons of diminished capacity—minor children, persons under the influence of alcohol or drugs, and the mentally infirm. Persons who are incapacitated will not necessarily be deterred from engaging in further actions. They may or may not engage in future capital offenses when and if the conditions of their infirmity are removed. In any case, even if they might engage in such future acts, life imprisonment can, in most cases, protect society from possible future misdeeds.[57]

As an ethical matter, the question of diminished capacity strikes at the heart of the "just execution" theory. Despite Utilitarianism's requirement that all persons should be treated alike, persons with diminished capacity require special treatment because they present special circumstances. As with the general deterrence argument, the argument of diminished capacity or special circumstances quickly raises two empirical questions. Does the imposition of the death penalty on persons with low intelligence, impaired cognition, ethnic minority status, or persons of color prevent others (some of whom are similarly situated) from engaging in criminal acts? Also, does the imposition of the death penalty prevent offenders who have been sentenced to death from undertaking the same or similar acts in the future more effectively than the imposition of a lesser sentence? As before, the empirical argument depends on who is making the argument and how that person uses and interprets the available data. Thus, Nat Hentoff argues that the U.S. Supreme Court erred in its conclusion in *Penry v. Lynaugh* that it is not cruel and unusual punishment under the Eighth Amendment to execute mentally retarded offenders.[58] Similarly, Michael Ross contends that the death penalty is applied unfairly to African Americans,[59] and Nick DiSpoldo claims that poor offenders are disproportionately sentenced to death compared with more affluent offenders.[60] For each of these empirical arguments, commentators present counterarguments based on, among other things, social science data. I will leave the full explication of these arguments to the chapters that discuss social science data later in this collection.[61]

One of the most moving exhortations against the "just execution" concept is found not in a philosophical work but in literature, specifically in George Orwell's classic short tale, "A Hanging." Always a vociferous critic of any power that might suppress human freedom, Orwell tells the story, presumably true, of witnessing an execution in Burma. He does not discuss the details of the crime, the sentencing, or the victims' grief. Instead, he focuses on the impressions of the witnesses who gather to observe the offender as the man is led to the gallows. One small event leaves a deep impression on Orwell's psyche. As he marches toward his date with destiny on a platform high above the assembled throng, the prisoner steps around a mud puddle. Orwell finds the condemned man's desire to avoid the mud a curious and distinctly human reaction. Why did he avoid the mud? What would it matter if the offender's shoes were dirty when he met his death in mere seconds or, at most, minutes?

Orwell's language is poetic. "It is curious," he muses,

> but till that moment I had never realized what it means to destroy a healthy, conscious man. When I saw the prisoner step aside to avoid the puddle I saw the mystery, the unspeakable wrongness, of cutting a life short when it is in full tide. The man was not dying; he was alive just as we are alive. All the organs of his body were working—bowels digesting food, skin renewing itself, nails growing, tissues forming— all toiling away in solemn foolery. His nails would still be growing when he stood on the drop, when he was falling through the air with a tenth-of-a-second to live.[62]

The details of the crime are immaterial to those persons who witness an execution. Implicit in Orwell's story is the idea that capital punishment obviously deprives the condemned man of his life, but it deprives his executioner of something as well—his humanity. The old adage told to errant children by a parent administering corporal punishment—"This hurts me more than it hurts you"— apparently has a grain of truth to it, in Orwell's view.

The famous defense attorney, Clarence Darrow, champions a similar concept when he argues against the imposition of the death penalty in the Leopold and Loeb murder case. At the beginning of his summation, Darrow acknowledges that the crime had outraged the public, and the behavior of the defendants was anathema to civilized people. "And when the public is interested and demands a punishment in the eyes of the public, no matter what the offense, great or small, it thinks of only one punishment, and that is death," Darrow observes. Yet a judge must examine factors apart from the popularity of capital punishment in the eyes of the public, for the public often acts as a passion-inflamed mob. Justice requires something more than a mob mentality. "It may not be a question that involves the taking of human life; it may be a question of pure prejudice," Darrow argues. "But when the public speaks as one man it thinks only of killing."[63]

The theme of Darrow's argument is that capital punishment is a tool used by civilized people of an earlier age. Over time, as civilization grew more sophisticated, the state learned to handle offenders through more sophisticated measures. Methods of punishment evolved as society's understanding of crime and its antecedents evolved. At one time in the Western tradition, people did not realize that mental illness might push an offender to perpetrate a crime. Now that civilized people understand this cause better (although we still do not know with certainty what factors trigger mental illness in its various forms), it would be cruel for society to impose the death penalty, especially on offenders who are mentally ill, children, or acting under special circumstances.

In a final plea over the course of seven hours, Darrow reviews, among other things, the history of the death penalty, tracing its lineage back to antiquity, when capital punishment was meted out for a litany of crimes that did not necessarily include murder. In a rousing conclusion, perhaps one of the most eloquent anti–death penalty orations ever recorded, he says, "the easy thing and the popular thing to do is to hang my clients. I know it. Men and women who do not think will applaud. The cruel and thoughtless will approve." In Darrow's opinion, a court of justice must not yield to such base human impulses.

Instead, "I am pleading for life, understanding, charity, kindness, and the infinite mercy that considers all. I am pleading that we overcome cruelty with kindness and hatred with love. I know the future is on my side." Pointing to the judge, Darrow explains the significance of the case. "Your Honor stands between the past and the future. You may hang these boys; you may hang them by the neck until they are dead. But in doing it you are making it harder for every other boy who in ignorance and darkness must grope his way through the mazes which only childhood knows." Addressing the rest of the packed courtroom, Darrow finishes with a rhetorical flourish. "I am pleading for the future; I am pleading for a time when hatred and cruelty will not control the hearts of men. When we can learn by reason and judgment and understanding and faith that all life is worth saving, and mercy is the highest attribute of man."[64]

Darrow appeals to the American legal system not to succumb to passion and cruelty in judging Leopold and Loeb because to do so would be for society to embrace the offenders' view of the world. If a regime executes offenders based on the popularity of an eye-for-an-eye rationale, retribution becomes the foundation of society's system of justice. In primitive cultures, retribution might be a satisfactory basis for a moral code, but more advanced societies must have more advanced notions of justice, according to Darrow.[65]

B. RETRIBUTION

Darrow raises an intriguing point that should be explored in more detail. Can retribution ever be considered just? The eighteenth-century German Idealist

Immanuel Kant argues that "just retribution" is possible in some instances. Retribution need not be tantamount to state-sponsored revenge.

Kant is disturbed by the relativist conceptions of justice prevalent in his day. In particular, he believes that the "serpentine-windings of Utilitarianism" undermine human dignity because that philosophy does not respect the individuality of each person. The core of the Utilitarian endeavor is to calculate social goods; in Kant's view, this transforms persons into the means by which the state accomplishes its ends. Individuals sometimes must compromise their goals as individual human beings in the interests of others or in the interests of the state.[66] Utilitarian conceptions of justice, therefore, require that policymakers calculate the greatest good for the greatest number by comparing the value of some people's happiness against the value of others people's happiness. This reduces human dignity because it makes individuals pawns in an elaborate game played by the state. When people are treated as aggregate units to be measured and calculated as though their humanity were subject to mathematical functions as well as negotiation and compromise, they become little more than fixtures in the landscape.

Kant refers to conditional requirements imposed on human beings as "hypothetical imperatives." He contends that hypothetical imperatives have their place in human life, but they should not be the basis for addressing enduring moral questions that affect individuals. In the practical world, a hypothetical imperative is a calculation such as "If you want to lose weight, then you should diet and exercise to achieve this goal." The means (diet and exercise) presumably will lead to the desired end (losing weight). This kind of imperative is satisfactory for dieting, bartering for property, or engaging in many forms of social and economic intercourse because such activities do not directly affect human dignity or morality. A means–ends negotiation presents problems when human beings become the means by which the state achieves its ends, for it reduces eternal human questions to a series of relative, ever-changing propositions.[67]

It follows from this perspective that punishment based on a hypothetical imperative is morally indefensible. In the context of a capital crime, to lock away an offender for life to protect other citizens is to use the offender for the good of others. In other words, according to Utilitarian conceptions of justice, the ends (protecting innocent citizens from harm) justify the means (locking away the offender)—*exitus acta probat* (the ends justify the means). Kant argues that if the state can impose punishment based on calculations of social utility, ultimately totalitarianism may result as the state metes out increasingly harsh penalties in the interests of the collective good.

It also is morally indefensible for the state to rehabilitate an offender because an attempt to change a person's character is an attempt to manipulate his personality, hence his personhood, making him conform to rules established by others. Social engineering implies that external forces should shape a human being, not the internal choices he makes in his life. Citizens may applaud the ends (protection), but Kant argues that this approval does not legitimate the means (the state's attempts at rehabilitation). If all human beings are free, rational, moral agents, then rules governing the relationship between a state and its citizens cannot be predicated on bargaining and negotiation about moral requirements, even if the goal meets with popular approval.

Instead of a hypothetical imperative, Kant contends that a universal moral law must exist. Moreover, this law must establish a single, universal standard of conduct for all free, rational, moral agents, regardless of time, place, or circumstances. He called this law the "categorical imperative." It is distinguished from a hypothetical imperative because the categorical imperative is not subject to a means–ends analysis. A person does not act morally simply because he might achieve another goal. He acts morally because it is the right thing to do. In other words, a person tells the truth not because he calculates that it is in his best interests to tell the truth in this particular situation. He tells the truth because people should tell the truth. Even if it harms his interests, an individual must tell the truth to live a genuinely moral life.

"Act only on that maxim whereby thou canst at the same time will that it should become a universal law," Kant wrote.[68] A person should act with an understanding that his actions cannot be excused owing to the presence or absence of external stimuli. First and foremost, a human being is responsible for his actions. Relying on mitigating factors such as "The devil made me do it" or pleas for leniency do not entitle a free moral agent to escape the repercussions of his behavior. Therefore, if an offender has perpetrated a horrible crime, he must take his punishment. As a free, rational, moral agent, he—and he alone—is culpable.

Instead of the usual Utilitarian views of punishment, Kant grounded his theory of punishment on what he called "juridical" rights and duties. Because every person potentially will violate another person's rights and, conversely, every person may have his rights violated by another, the sovereign must punish an offender for no other reason than because he has committed a crime. The state should not try to restore a balance, pay back the offender (an eye for an eye), change his personality (rehabilitation), or use the offender as an object lesson for potential offenders (deterrence).[69] Kant observes that "[j]uridical punishment can never be administered merely as a means for promoting another good either with regard to the criminal himself or to civil society, but must in all cases be imposed only because the individual on whom it is inflicted has committed a crime."[70]

Kant endorses the use of capital punishment in situations where the severity of the offense warrants such a penalty. It may seem ironic that Kant considers the imposition of capital punishment as a reflection of the state's respect for the offender's personhood, but that is exactly his position. If a person truly is responsible for his actions, he must be punished in a manner commensurate with the character of his crime. One commentator, James Rachels, explains Kant's rationale succinctly: "[W]hen a rational being decides to treat people in a certain way, he decrees that in his judgment *this is the way people are to be treated.* Thus if we treat him the same way in return, we are doing nothing more than treating him *as he has decided* people are to be treated."[71] This is Kant's concept of juridical rights and duties interpreted with a vengeance.

C. REVENGE

The counterargument to Kant's idea that autonomous human beings should be treated in accordance with the world they fashioned—even if this means imposing the death penalty—is offered by the twentieth-century French existentialist and Nobel laureate Albert Camus. In his famous essay "Reflections on the Guillotine" from the collection *Resistance, Rebellion, and Death*, Camus argues that any regime that administers capital punishment ultimately is a regime based on revenge. The sovereign has become, in effect, a murderer when he puts his subjects to death, regardless of their crimes. In Camus's view, "this new murder, far from making amends for the harm done to the social body, adds a new blot to the first one."[72]

At the beginning of his essay, Camus recounts the tale of his own father, a proponent of capital punishment. The elder Camus was incensed on hearing the details of a heinous crime committed in the community. As a result, he wanted to witness the offender's decapitation. "What he saw that morning he never told anyone," Camus recalled years later. It must have been a terrible ordeal. When the father came home after the execution with "his face distorted," he promptly vomited. "He had just discovered the reality hidden under the noble phrases with which it was masked."[73] Camus uses this anecdote to tell us that "[w]hen the extreme penalty causes vomiting on the part of the respectable citizen it is supposed to protect, how can anyone maintain that it is likely, as it ought to be, to bring more peace and order to the community?"[74]

Camus attacks the deterrence argument used by capital punishment supporters. If the penalty is to be an effective deterrent, why not photograph or film the executions and distribute the images as widely as possible? Instead, society hides executions behind a cloak of secrecy as though the sovereign were ashamed of his actions on behalf of the populace. In Camus's view, however, if the state truly acts on behalf of the public good and the goal is to deter future capital offenses, heavy media promotion of executions is required for the sovereign to achieve the goal. Moreover, the grisly details should be publicized so that people could understand how terrible and frightening this punishment is for the condemned person.

The irony, of course, is that the death penalty already frightens most ordinary individuals even without further publicity. Widely publicized photographs of bloody executions no doubt would intimidate the average citizen to a greater extent, but the class of psychopaths or impassioned lovers that commits capital crimes probably would be undeterred by such gruesome displays of bloodlust. In fact, they might be stimulated by images that many people would find repellant. This class of deviants acts without rationally considering the consequences of their actions (or, if they consider them, they are cold, calculating killers who will not be dissuaded from acting). Thus, the argument that capital punishment is a deterrent is built on a faulty foundation. Its premises simply are not supported by common experience. "The guillotine exists, and so does the crime," Camus writes. "Between the two there is no other apparent connection than that of the law."[75]

Capital punishment continues to be enshrined in law and used by officers of the law because it is a tradition in many countries. When the state attempts to rationalize the tradition by arguing that capital punishment prevents future crimes, it merely invents an argument for an action that it already has decided to take. This is hypocrisy of the worst sort, and Camus argues that the sovereign should not be hypothetical. "A punishment that penalizes without forestalling is indeed called revenge."[76]

Revenge is a natural impulse. Who would not strike out at someone who has injured him? A fundamental law of nature is to protect oneself from harm. Yet, "[l]aw, by definition, cannot obey the same rules as nature," Camus concludes.[77] Law is an instrument designed by man to correct the deficiencies of nature, which is "red in tooth and claw." By contrast, law aims to lift mankind up from the muck and celebrate his distinctiveness, his dignity as a being separate and apart from nature and from other beings. Capital punishment, despite it supposed lawfulness in some regimes, has the opposite effect. When an execution occurs, "[s]ociety is suddenly reduced to a state of primitive terrors where nothing can be judged. All equity and all dignity have disappeared."[78] Instead of moving away from the dreaded Hobbesian state of nature by protecting the power of the state, capital punishment pulls mankind back down into the muck. He becomes less human and more animalistic. Worse, the state becomes an instrument for perpetuating this base impulse instead of a mechanism for improving the human condition. The promises of the Enlightenment—that rationality can be advanced and human institutions will support the spread of rational action—are abandoned in favor of little more than primitive blood lust.

Later in the essay, Camus reviews the major arguments generally set forth against capital punishment, such as whether even the most hardened criminals are beyond rehabilitation and whether innocent people have been executed. He argues that all convicted criminals have the potential to be rehabilitated. In any case, it is preferable to imprison many offenders who will never be rehabilitated than to execute someone later found to be innocent. This is a restatement of the old adage that it is better that one hundred guilty men go free than to allow one falsely accused man to be punished.

Camus concludes his essay with a plea for human freedom and dignity in abolishing capital punishment. He argues that the "excessive power of the State" is far more dangerous to the population than the dangers posed by a relatively few offenders who have crossed the boundaries of the law. Humanity requires a society based on reason, justice, and mercy. Yet, the state-sanctioned executions continue with alarming frequency. "There will be no lasting peace either in the heart of individuals or in social customs until death is outlawed," he writes.[79]

III. Conclusion: The Rule of Law and Fundamental Fairness

The maddeningly difficult problem in arguing that capital punishment is precluded in a political system founded on a rule of law coupled with a sense of fundamental fairness is that these terms remain contested. As an abstract proposition, virtually everyone would agree that a regime should be founded on a system of well-explicated rules that are applied more or less equally to everyone in the regime. Similarly, almost everyone would desire a sense of fundamental fairness exercised by a sovereign in implementing the law and imposing capital sentences. In concrete situations, however, the concepts are impossible to clarify to the satisfaction of everyone. Questions invariably arise about how the rule of law applies and what constitutes fundamental fairness when (or if) the death penalty is imposed on offenders. Is the rule of law equitably applied by a strong sovereign with the awesome power to impose capital punishment—as Hobbes and Locke suggest—or is this the quintessential example of too much power in too few hands and therefore potentially dangerous to the civil liberties of all citizens, not simply duly convicted offenders? Does the sovereign's power always degenerate into the kind of tyrannical regime envisioned by Dostoyevsky in the Grand Inquisitor's tale from *The Brothers Karamazov*, or can a powerful sovereign act with fairness as well as severity? In addition, does fundamental fairness require the state to forgo imposing capital punishment because such punishment is cruel and unmerciful, hence unfair—as Orwell, Darrow, and Camus seem to argue—or is Kant correct that it is fair to impose death on offenders who have killed their fellow human beings because the offenders must be respected as free, autonomous, moral agents? Is the ancient maxim of "an eye for an eye" morally defensible—assuming that we even understand and apply as it was meant to be applied—or is Socrates correct that justice requires giving to offenders better than they gave to their fellow citizens?

However one would define the dictates of the rule of law and fundamental fairness, most citizens living in Western, industrialized nations probably would embrace a moral presumption against killing based on a person's membership within the community of human beings. The state must overcome this moral presumption if it wishes to defend its actions in executing a person as consistent with the rule of law and with notions of fundamental fairness. Therein lies the most difficult problem for proponents of capital punishment to overcome. Rebutting the presumption against killing becomes morally indefensible when we move from abstract theories to concrete applications, if for no other reasons than because of the biases that exist in imposing capital punishment on offenders.

One commentator, Lloyd Steffen, has written on this problem in some detail. In his opinion, "a reasonable case cannot be made that execution is a last resort and that no comparable alternative to execution exists." Moreover, in Steffen's view, other philosophical arguments undermine the validity of capital punishment. "Proportionality seems to me to fail as well, since destroying the body to punish the moral personality seems extreme and violative of the person's fundamental right to possess the good of life so long as any threat the person might pose to others has been neutralized," Steffen contends. "And the claim that capital punishment is objectively the most extreme penalty for the most extreme crime seems ludicrous in light of the history of capital punishment, even that in the United States where only a few murderers are executed and the vast majority of murderers—the average murderer—serve a shorter sentence than do those sentenced for nonviolent drug offenses." The closer one examines the death penalty, the more problems emerge from the examination. "Lengthy waits for death and the prospect of botched executions fail the test prohibiting cruelty; the punishment continues to fall disproportionately on poor and minority and male persons; and everywhere—on every criterion—there is practical failure to meet the standards of justice. This failure robs the death penalty of moral justification."[80]

Proponents of the death penalty often fail to recognize that capital punishment is not merely an abstract question of law and ethics. Despite the discussions in this chapter—where an artificial distinction is made to explore applicable philosophical arguments—fundamental fairness cannot be divorced from practical, "real world" questions. Sometimes offenders suffer from mental incapacity, low intelligence, intoxication, the delusions of youth, or other mitigating factors. Sometimes death is imposed disproportionately on members of certain ethnic minority groups, the poor, the infirm, or other disenfranchised peoples.

Sometimes the question of whether an offender lives or dies depends on the jurisdiction involved, the identity of the judge, the identity of the victim or the offender, the biases of the jury, the media coverage, and so forth.[81] Can a regime that imposes the ultimate punishment call itself fundamentally fair when so many permutations and combinations can, and often do, affect the outcome?[82]

When the state seeks to kill one of its citizens, it must overcome the moral presumption against killing. This seems to be an insurmountable burden to bear. In every reasonable, philosophical defense of capital punishment—an eye for an eye, the concept of a "just execution," the necessity of deterrence, retribution, or revenge—an element of expediency exists. The state executes an offender ultimately because it wields awesome power; it acts because it can. This reasoning collapses back into the "might makes right" conundrum. If Socrates and Jesus were correct that justice requires giving back better than we get, capital punishment is philosophically and morally indefensible. A nation that purports to live in accordance with the rule of law coupled with a notion of fundamental fairness can—and must—do better.

Part 2

THEOLOGICAL
PERSPECTIVES

CHAPTER 5

Religious Orientation, Race, and Support for the Death Penalty

Robert L. Young

By virtually any definition, religion involves a central concern with making sense of life and death. The American legal system, rooted in Judeo-Christian ethics, routinely confronts issues that test our basic assumptions about the meaning and sanctity of life and about the role of the state in shaping and sustaining such meanings. The exact nature of the state's role in the taking of life remains at or near the center of this controversy. Contemporary debates over capital punishment represent the continuation of a historically rich struggle in which verbal assaults have tended to focus on moral and philosophical concerns even as many of the more consequential battles have been waged in the political arena. Indeed, a rise in political activism among certain fundamentalist religious groups has forged an even closer link between the moral-philosophical and political dimensions of this issue. However, researchers of public opinion have essentially ignored the role of religion in shaping attitudes toward capital punishment.

This research was inspired largely by an experience I had several years ago as a consultant to the court-appointed defense in a capital murder case. During the course of the jury selection, I was struck with the number of venire members who cited the Bible in unsolicited justification of their position on capital punishment. In fact, the Scriptures were cited almost equally by both supporters and opponents. This poses an interesting question for religious fundamentalists: With the Bible providing what is perceived to be un equivocal support for both sides of this debate, what is a sincere Christian fundamentalist to think? More generally, the central question of this research is: What is the role of individual religious orientations in shaping attitudes toward the death penalty?[1]

Religion and Social Attitudes

The idea that religion is of major significance in American civil life has been expressed unequivocally by Lenski, who concluded that "religion in various ways is constantly influencing the daily lives of the masses of men and women."[2] Although the influence of religion on attitudes toward the death penalty has been largely ignored, numerous studies have linked religious variables to a host of other social attitudes.

Among the earliest and best known are the works of Allport, Adorno et al., and others who showed that certain religious factors were associated with racial prejudice, ethnocentrism, and authoritarianism. Those initial findings were sufficiently provocative to have triggered a number of follow-up studies. For example, Allport and Allport and Ross found that such negative concomitants of religiosity applied only to those whose religious orientation is rooted in instrumental or utilitarian motives. Allport and Ross contrasted this extrinsic orientation [E] with the more intrinsically religious nature [I] of those who "live" their religion. They contended that the intrinsically religious are less prejudiced than are either the extrinsically or the "indiscriminately" religious. Although a number of studies have supported the Allport–Ross thesis; others have shown that the relationship between I-E orientation and prejudice is much more complex and variable than previously assumed. Moreover, Kirkpatrick and Hood have persuasively criticized the simple I-E framework on both methodological and theoretical grounds.[3]

The literature on the relationship of fundamentalism and related concepts (e.g., Batson's notion of "doctrinal orthodoxy") to prejudice is equally inconclusive.[4] After a thorough review of the literature up to the early 1970s, Gorsuch and Aleshire argued that "the more intrinsically religious, nonfundamentalistic, and theologically discriminating," the more tolerant the individual.[5] In a more recent review, however, Hood has contended that the consistency of such findings in early research was the result of a "pervasive bias" against fundamentalism.[6] He is especially critical of those who have explained the relationship between fundamentalism and prejudice in terms of authoritarianism, citing the works of Hoge and Carroll and Gilmore as counterevidence.[7]

Perhaps the most reasonable conclusion to be drawn from the literature is that religious orientation is a highly complex phenomenon that supports a variety of seemingly contradictory attitudes and behaviors. This has been supported by McFarland, for example, who has found that fundamentalism "cloaks a general closed minded, ethnocentric mindset," which supports a "general tendency to discriminate" while simultaneously producing a "contradictory tendency" toward nondiscrimination, based on the biblical admonition that all are equal in God's eyes.[8]

Indeed, it is the recognition of the complex and often seemingly contradictory nature of religious beliefs that informs the analysis presented here. Rather than relying on the somewhat questionable I-E distinction, or on a simple contrast between fundamentalists and others, this research has attempted to investigate the unique roles of certain key religious variables in determining support for or opposition to the death penalty. To that end, it is necessary to articulate clear conceptual distinctions between empirically related elements of religious life.

Fundamentalism, Evangelism, and the Death Penalty

Discussions of fundamentalism and evangelicalism often create more confusion than clarity. According to Kellstedt and Smidt, "fundamentalism does not have a widely shared meaning among journalists, scholars, or the general public."[9] Indeed, sociologists of religion have been inconsistent in their use of these terms, sometimes employing fundamentalism and evangelicalism interchangeably, and sometimes combining various elements of the two in order to describe a particular subgroup.

The term *fundamentalist* can be traced at least as far back as the publication of *The Fundamentals* in 1910. That very significant work promulgated a number of closely related doctrines that provided the intellectual thrust for the fundamentalist movement. Inasmuch as each of the four other primary doctrines discussed in *The Fundamentals* can be derived essentially from a literal interpretation of the scriptures, it is clear that the central tenet of this orientation is biblical literalism. However, many contemporary discussions of fundamentalism define the general orientation not only in terms of biblical literalism, but also include born-again experiences and the tendency to proselytize.[10] While these three factors might be positively correlated empirically, maintaining conceptual distinctions among them is critical to this research.

Evangelicalism and fundamentalism did indeed have common roots in the reaction of certain groups to what they perceived to be the perversions of the social gospel movement and the increased secularization of late nineteenth-century America.[11] Even today there is considerable empirical overlap, but a clarification of the difference between these two orientations will help us understand their impact on attitudes toward various social issues. Rather than the more general and ambiguous *evangelicalism*, I will employ the term *evangelism* to denote specifically a proselytizing orientation. While the essence of *fundamentalism* can be found in a central or closely related set of beliefs, *evangelism* is essentially defined as an active effort to convert others to the faith. Although Christian fundamentalists tend to be evangelists, many evangelists are not fundamentalists.[12]

More importantly for this research, however, the two terms suggest conceptually distinct orientations toward secular issues. Fundamentalists tend to deny the possibility of moral relativity. Such absolutism, whether a cause or a consequence of fundamentalist beliefs, is likely to be associated with the perception of considerable evil in the world, for the morality of human action is not to be judged relative to social context.

This rejection of moral relativity might be one of the conceptual links between fundamentalism and political conservatism, a link that has been noted by a number of authors.[13] It is clear that any analysis of the relationship between fundamentalism and death penalty attitudes (also empirically related to conservatism) should be carried out in such a way as to take political orientation also into consideration.

In contrast to fundamentalism, the evangelistic desire to convert, although in some cases rooted in absolutist beliefs, could be interpreted as an expression of compassion and concern for the souls of others. If so, such compassion might exert pressure in a more liberal direction with regard to certain social issues. Thus, we might expect support for the death penalty to be relatively low among those of an evangelistic orientation. Indeed, there is a certain logic to an evangelistic preference for life imprisonment over the death penalty, since the latter puts the lost soul beyond the reach of those who might be able to lead him or her to a state of grace. Alternatively, evangelism might reflect a selfish need to ensure one's own salvation through conformity to biblical and clerical directives.

Fundamentalism would seem to provide less ambiguous support for a punitive orientation. If there is a cognitive link between fundamentalism and support for extreme forms of punishment, it might be found in the ideology of individualism.[14] With their decentralized organizational structure and emphasis on individual salvation, fundamentalist denominations might encourage a tendency to hold individuals responsible for their crimes rather than blaming situational circumstances. Indeed, Lupfer et al. have provided evidence that fundamentalists are more inclined than others to favor personal over environmental attributions, even when the evidence does not support such attributions.[15] Their data, however, suggest that this tendency could be an indirect manifestation of greater authoritarianism among fundamentalists. Moreover, Wrightsman's data have shown that fundamentalist college students score low on the trustworthiness dimension of his "Philosophies of Human Nature Scale."[16] Finally, in at least one other related study, Vinney et al. found no link between the belief in free will, a correlate of fundamentalism, and either the rationale or the magnitude of punishment.[17] Thus, while there is a theoretical logic to the notion that fundamentalism produces a more punitive orientation, the empirical evidence is less than compelling.

However, if we assume fundamentalists conform to the positions of their leaders, there is clear evidence that support for capital punishment should be relatively high among members of fundamentalist churches. Numerous statements of support for the death penalty by prominent fundamentalist leaders can be found in such publications as the *Fundamentalist Journal.*[18] Such support is also reflected in the attitudes of fundamentalist seminary students, whom Hunter found to be significantly more supportive of capital punishment than were students at either evangelical colleges or public universities.[19]

Thus logic, and to some extent empirical research, both suggest that the empirically correlated orientations of evangelism and fundamentalism represent countervailing influences on death penalty attitudes. To the extent that fundamentalists tend to hold the individual solely responsible for his or her actions, they are likely to be more punitive than others. Moreover, those who attend church regularly are likely to hear such punitiveness legitimated from the pulpit. When controls for fundamentalist beliefs and church attendance are introduced, however, evangelicals might be less inclined than others to support the death penalty.

Devotionalism and the Death Penalty

For many individuals, fundamentalist or evangelistic orientations are the result of being socialized into a particular religious subculture. Race, region of the country, and social class significantly influence one's religious affiliation. However, the extent to which religion influences attitudes and behaviors depends largely upon the importance of religion in the daily life of the individual. Those for whom religion is not salient should not be expected to harbor social attitudes consistent with their religious beliefs.

Devotionalism is a clear indication of the salience of religion in daily life. Regular prayer, Bible reading, and attendance at worship services indicate more than a situational commitment to religion. Thus, any differences between the effects of fundamentalism and evangelism on support for capital punishment should be most prominent among those who are most devoted to their religion.

Race, Religion, and the Death Penalty

It is common knowledge that support for capital punishment varies substantially by race. For a variety of reasons, whites are much more likely than blacks to support the death penalty.[20] Moreover, the centrality and unique character of religion in Afro-American versus white American culture have been well documented by, for example, Frazier and Sernett.[21]

More recently, the importance of religion in Afro-American life was revealed during the civil rights movement of the 1950s and '60s. Not only did black ministers provide leadership to the movement, but the church itself was often the focal point of organizational efforts. Indeed, the role of black religion in civil affairs has been an accepted and important element in Afro-American social and political life. Although Euro-American religion has often involved itself indirectly in political and social issues, it has not often played such a central role. Thus, as a result of both historical and contemporary factors, we might expect religion to affect the social and political attitudes of black and white Americans somewhat differently.

Methods

DATA ANALYSIS

The data for this study were taken from the 1988 General Social Survey.[22] The full probability sample consisted of 1,481 English-speaking persons eighteen years of age or older. The loss of a few cases due to missing data and the elimination of members of other racial groups from the sample resulted in a final sample of 1,078 whites and 150 blacks. Respondents consisted of Protestants, Catholics, Jews, and those who expressed no religious preference. Other religious groups were excluded because (1) they were so few in number, and (2) it was assumed that many of the core questions would not be relevant for them.

Because the dependent variable is dichotomous, models were tested through the use of logistic regression analysis with the BMDP statistical software program.[23] Logit models may be interpreted in much the same way as the results of an ordinary least-squares analysis (OLS): The coefficients represent the relationship of each independent variable with the dependent variable, minus the effects of other variables in the model. The most notable exception to the OLS analogy is that in logistic regression what is modelled, in an additive form, is the natural log of the odds of the dependent variable. The distribution of the ratios of the coefficients to their standard errors is asymptotically normal.

VARIABLES

Literal biblical interpretation, evangelism, and the experience of being "born again" have been discussed by various authors as elements of a fundamentalist and/or evangelical orientation. As suggested earlier, although these three variables are empirically correlated, they appear in this analysis as separate variables. Fundamentalist church affiliation was coded from respondents' answers to the following questions: (1) What is your religious preference? and (2) What specific denomination is that, if any?[24] "Literal interpreters" were defined as those who believed that "the Bible is the actual word of God and is to be taken literally, word for word."[25] Evangelists were defined as those who answered yes to the question "Have you ever tried to encourage someone to believe in Jesus Christ or to accept Jesus Christ as his or her savior?"[26] The REBORN variable was defined by a positive response to the question "Would you say you have been 'born again' or have had a 'born again' experience—that is, a turning point in your life when you committed yourself to Christ?"[27] Finally, devotionalism was measured by questions regarding how often the respondent (1) attended religious services, (2) prayed, and (3) read the Bible at home. Although all of the religion variables were intercorrelated, the largest single bivariate correlation, between REBORN and EVANGELISM, was .58. Correlations among the three DEVOTIONAL-ISM items ranged from .40 to .42.

AGE, SEX, and EDUCATION (high school or less vs. beyond high school) were included as control variables since each has been shown in previous studies to correlate with race and with support for the death penalty. The CONSERVATISM variable (defined according to the respondent's location of self on a seven-point scale from extremely liberal to extremely conservative) was also included as a control because of its positive correlation with the dependent variable and with a number of the religious variables.

Finally, REGION of residence (other vs. South) was included because of the possibility of its interaction with race. Although recent survey data have indicated similar levels of support for capital punishment across regions, the unique history of the South with regard to both legal and illegal executions of blacks might make southern blacks especially averse to the death penalty. The use of region of residences, as opposed to region of socialization, was based on Stump's finding that religious commitment is related to region of current residence rather than to region of origin.[28]

RESULTS

Table 5.1 contains the results of the additive logistic regression model. As expected, whites and males were more supportive of capital punishment than were blacks and females. Although age, education, and region of residence did not affect level of support, conservatism had a significant positive influence. Of the five religious variables, having had a "born again" experience was the only one not related to death penalty support. Membership in a fundamentalist church and belief in biblical literalism increased support, while evangelism was associated with reduced support.

Table 5.1.   Additive Model of Support for the Death Penalty

Independent Variable	Coefficient	Standard Error	P Value	Mean Variation
Race	−.7301	.1007	<.01	.122
Sex	−.2039	.0754	<.01	.564
Age	.0015	.0043	.73	44.8
Education	−.0151	.0768	.84	.425
Region	.0111	.0794	.89	.346
Conservatism	.2201	.0809	<.01	.348
Fundamentalist Church	.1742	.0915	.06	.349
Literalism	.1964	.0871	.02	.345
Reborn	−.0220	.0972	.82	.371
Devotionalism	−.2125	.0849	.01	.366
Evangelism	−.2028	.0898	.02	.468

Although devotionalism was significantly related to opposition to the death penalty, it was also expected to have an interactive influence. As an indicator of the salience of religion in the everyday life of the individual, level of devotionalism was expected to affect the extent to which the other religious variables influenced support for capital punishment. In order to probe this idea, I dichotomized the sample according to level of devotionalism. The results of that analysis, though not reported here, suggested that devotionalism interacts only with evangelism, decreasing support for the death penalty primarily among evangelists who scored high on devotionalism. The appropriate interaction term, therefore, was included in the final interaction model.

The primary set of expected interactions involved the influence of race on the relationship between the religious variables and the dependent variables. As a preliminary step toward identifying the relevant interactions for the final model, separate models were run for blacks and whites (table 5.2). An examination of the variable means reveals substantial differences in the overall religious orientations of the two groups. The most obvious interactions suggested by table 5.2 are the joint impacts of (1) race and membership in a fundamentalist church, and (2) race and devotionalism. Also suggested are possible interactions between race and evangelism, and, least probably, between race and literal biblical interpretation.

The full interaction model appears in table 5.3. This formal specification of the relationships, suggested both by theoretical considerations and by the initial empirical analysis discussed earlier, presents a fairly clear picture. It is obvious from this analysis that the role of religion in shaping attitudes toward the death penalty is quite different for blacks and whites. In general, evangelism is associated with relatively less support, although its impact is strongest among blacks.

Table 5.2. Sample Model for Support for the Death Penalty by Race

Independent Variable	Coefficient	Standard Error	P Value	Mean Variation
White				
Sex	−.1777	.0833	.03	.554
Age	.0058	.0048	.23	45.4
Education	−.0459	.0849	.59	.430
Region	.0403	.0905	.66	.346
Conservatism	.2895	.0909	<.01	.367
Fundamentalist Church	.2672	.1065	.01	.300
Literalism	.1480	.0994	.14	.201
Reborn	−.0397	.1114	.72	.342
Devotionalism	−.3149	.0958	<.01	.347
Evangelism	−.1242	.1002	.22	.43
Black				
Sex	−.2664	.1965	.17	.633
Age	−.0235	.0117	.05	40.8
Education	.0240	.2001	.90	.397
Region	−.2106	.1903	.27	.337
Conservatism	−.1375	.2232	.53	.212
Fundamentalist Church	−.2302	.2144	.28	.702
Literalism	.4378	.2052	.04	.318
Reborn	.0623	.2228	.78	.573
Devotionalism	.1981	.2019	.33	.510
Evangelism	−.7256	.2368	<.01	.675

Table 5.3. Interaction Model for Support for the Death Penalty

Independent Variable	Coefficient	Standard Error	P Value
Race	−.5509	.1199	<.01
Education	−.0094	.0778	.90
Region	−.0061	.0805	.94
Conservatism	−.2245	.0821	<.01
Fundamentalist Church	.0007	.1164	.99
Literalism	.2651	.1083	.01
Reborn	.0085	.0998	.93
Devotionalism	.0667	.1105	.55
Evangelism	−.4248	.1239	<.01
Race × Fundamentalist Church	−.2875	.1142	.01
Race × Literal	.0984	.1063	.35
Race × Devotionalism	.2182	.1056	.04
Race × Evangelism	−.2657	.1153	.02
Devotion × Evangelism	−.1395	.0843	.10

In fact, among all the subgroups identified in this study, opposition to capital punishment was strongest among black evangelists. As expected, a fundamentalist orientation toward the Bible was associated with relatively strong support for the death penalty, and this influence held for both blacks and whites.

In contrast, attendance at fundamentalist churches and devotionalism led to different attitudes for the two races. Attending fundamentalist churches increased support only among whites, while devotionalism decreased support only among whites. Finally, although the results seen in table 5.3 are equivocal on this point, they suggest that the tendency of evangelists to oppose the death penalty is largely restricted to those who take their religion seriously enough to sustain regular devotional practices.

Of course, it is quite likely that a number of the religious variables are also associated with political conservatism and various social status variables. Thus, it is important to note that all these relationships held even when the influences of political conservatism, age, education, sex, and region of residence were considered.

Conclusions

The results of this study reveal a relatively clear and concise image of the role of religious orientation in influencing attitudes toward the death penalty. Of all the religious variables in the final model, EVANGELISM showed the single largest impact on the dependent variable. This finding supports an interpretation of evangelism as a manifestation of (or perhaps a demand for) compassion and concern for the fate of others. That such concern for prisoners is especially evident among black Americans is probably related to their tendency to make situational rather than personal attributions, and to the relative skepticism with which they view the American criminal justice system.[29]

The association of fundamentalism with high levels of support for the death penalty was also not surprising. The absolutism of a fundamentalist orientation appears to eliminate some of the uncertainty which others experience in considering the appropriateness of this punishment. Whether this association is a function of higher levels of authoritarianism, as some have suggested, or is the result of specific attributional tendencies of fundamentalists, is impossible to determine from this study. What does seem clear, however, is that support for the death penalty is likely to be increased by the belief in individual free will and responsibility that characterizes fundamentalism.

It is also important to note that these inclinations are apparently nurtured only in *white* fundamentalist churches, since affiliation with fundamentalist churches had no significant influence on the death penalty attitudes of blacks. In black churches, the individualism associated with white Protestantism might be tempered by a more collectivist orientation that is deeply rooted in Afro-American history. In fact, the *recent* emphasis among white fundamentalists on collective action as a way of promoting their vision of a just society contrasts with a *long-standing* concern for exactly that among America's black churches.[30]

The results of this study also suggest the need for a theoretical clarification of certain concepts in the sociology of religion. Until this is accomplished, the empirical association between such variables as fundamentalism and evangelism should not blind us to the necessity of maintaining clear conceptual distinctions. The melding of such distinctions into convenient monolithic images denies the inherent complexity of religion as both a psychological and a social force.

CHAPTER 6

Theological Arguments and the Case against Capital Punishment

Mark Douglas

A Christian theologian writing in opposition to capital punishment ought to have a fairly easy time of things. The witness of Scripture as read through the lens of the life, death, resurrection, and teachings of Jesus Christ seems not only to value human life in all forms (and particularly those lives that society views as having less worth) but generally to oppose taking life.[1] In spite of the tacit consent or explicit agreement the church has often given to capital punishment, the long theological history of the Christian church in almost all of its manifestations begins with a presumption against killing that may be overridden in particular cases but nevertheless generally reaffirms the value of life.[2] Moreover, almost all mainline denominations currently oppose the use of capital punishment in the United States.[3] Given the moral weight of Scripture, theological tradition, and contemporary church positions, one would think that at least a prima facie[4] opposition to capital punishment is normative and that those theologians who favor capital punishment bear the burden of explicitly and convincingly justifying their position over against that norm.

Yet in a country where roughly three-quarters of its citizens support the use of capital punishment, as do 72 percent of its Protestant pastors,[5] the *ought* within the above sentence "A Christian theologian . . . ought to have a fairly easy time of things" does not easily square with available evidence. In this chapter, I intend not only to develop a theological argument against capital punishment but to do so in such a way as to encourage others to think more carefully through the relation between their theological frameworks and their positions on the death penalty, and to suggest ways that theologians might better make their case in opposition to capital punishment among those who are not initially interested in theology.[6]

I. Developing Perspective

To say that I write as a theologian within the Christian tradition is deceptive. There is no single Christian tradition, and whatever normative claims various traditions might make about being the "one true faith," none denies the existence of other traditions within the Christian fold. Eastern versus Western church, Roman Catholic versus Protestant, Lutheran versus Calvinist: each distinction can be repeated at increasingly local levels. Making these distinctions does not necessarily invalidate the Christian witness. Indeed, I take the existence of so many traditions to be—in part—evidence that God's holy mystery cannot be exhaustively expressed within a single set of theological convictions or polity claims. Whether the question at hand concerns capital punishment, infant baptism, or the doctrine of the Trinity, perspectives vary and are enriched by that variance.

This does, however, point to the importance of clarifying my own theological orientation within the Christian witness. I stand within the Reformed tradition as traced back to John Calvin, the Protestant reformer of sixteenth-century Geneva. In brief, the message of the Reformed tradition is "All glory goes to God alone, who is authoritatively revealed by scripture alone, which proclaims salvation by grace alone, achieved by God through Christ alone, and received by believers through faith alone."[7]

Each of these "alones" points to a notable emphasis within this tradition—namely, that the God whose will is expressed through the graceful action of Jesus Christ is sovereign over and through the entire universe. Thus, to confess "Jesus is Lord"[8] is not only to appeal to a way things ought to be but to make a statement about the way things actually are. God's graceful actions are actually occurring and in Christ, God is working God's will out from creation to the consummation of all parts of God's creation as it is reunited in God.[9]

Many implications follow from this claim, but two are of special import for this paper. First, this emphasis on God's sovereignty means that Christians must constantly listen and watch for the way God is working and respond in a manner fitting to God's actions. That is, neither Christians nor the church are initiators of God's work but only participants in it as God uses them. Any claims about right or wrong actions and better or worse policies can only come after more fundamental questions about what God is commanding and enabling the church to do. If the church makes such claims without first seeking clarity about what God is doing in the world *at that point in time and space*, it attempts to usurp God's role. Within the context of debates about capital punishment, this first implication of God's sovereignty calls the church toward both purposefulness and humility and away from the types of detached, intransigent, and authoritative statements that so characterize many of the debates that surround the death penalty. Screaming "Vengeance is God's alone!" neither treats seriously the long history of God's call for the church to do justice nor moves forward disagreements about whether and when the death penalty might be appropriately invoked.

A second implication of the emphasis on God's sovereignty follows from the first; namely, the church—perhaps alone among all the institutions of the world—is in the peculiar spot of always listening for God to express God's will spoken through the persons and events of particular moments in time and space—even when it is spoken through those with whom it disagrees. If Jesus is Lord, his Lordship extends even through those who would not make that confession. Those persons and groups who seem to oppose God's will may, in fact, be instruments through which God works that will out. This is not to say that what such persons or groups say and do is what God commands and enables any more than it is to say that the church's position can simply be taken as God's position. Instead, this implication calls believers to listen even to the statements of those with whom they disagree and attempt to discern how God is speaking in the midst of and through those statements.[10]

In section III, I will attempt to illustrate how these implications come into play in the debates about capital punishment by analyzing two important positions taken by theologians that represent broad traditions within the Christian church. These are the positions of Roman Catholic theologian Thomas Aquinas and Reformed Protestant theologian Karl Barth. My point in analyzing these two positions on capital punishment is not so much to find points of overlap as to try to discern how God has spoken and might be speaking in the midst of them. Overlap is overrated; not only do these scholars disagree in important places, but ignoring those disagreements dismisses the very thoughts that make each theologian distinctive and important in the first place. Discernment, on the other hand, is often underemphasized. Nor is my point in analyzing these two positions to reach agreement with them. Indeed, both of them allow for capital punishment within their respective ethics, Thomas with apparent impunity and Barth in a much more reserved way. Instead, I will use their valuable insights on theology, punishment, and human life to attempt to discern why capital punishment is an incoherent practice within the Christian faith.

The task of discernment inevitably necessitates listening to how others have heard God speak as well; the listening Christian never listens alone. Thus, I will occasionally mention key features of various theological arguments advanced in light of their work. Obviously, if both support capital punishment, I will occasionally find myself in substantial disagreement with them. This does nothing to weaken my case. Indeed, I would argue that it is precisely my ability to use their own deepest theological and ethical arguments against their conclusions that make them both important and importantly wrong.

While I disagree with their conclusions, however, I find myself in broad agreement with many of their theological presuppositions. This is not the case for all of those with whom I disagree. Therefore, before engaging Thomas and

Barth, I will attempt to give fuller expression to the second implication of my emphasis on God's sovereignty in section II. That is, I will attempt to listen attentively to two voices with whom I strongly disagree, even at the level of their presuppositions: pro–capital punishment philosophers Ernest van den Haag and Walter Berns. Regardless of my disagreements with them, van den Haag and Berns have made important contributions to the debate, and their work needs to be taken seriously by both supporters and opponents of capital punishment—and perhaps by opponents more than supporters. Ultimately, I hope to show not only why I think they are wrong but places where I think they are correct and why those places matter for theologians involved in the debate and seeking its resolution. I begin with van den Haag.

II. God's Sovereignty

A. LEARNING FROM VAN DEN HAAG

Ernest van den Haag argues that the essential moral question surrounding the death penalty is "Is the death penalty morally just and/or useful?"[11] While this is a seemingly innocuous question, in van den Haag's hands it is freighted with moral implications. While the "and/or" juxtaposition in that sentence itself bears further thought (if the death penalty proved to be both useful and immoral, would we practice it?), I will set it aside in order to reflect on the justice question first, before engaging the usefulness question.

Theoretically, if the death penalty is not just, then it will remain unjust regardless of the fairness of its distribution or its success as a deterrent. That is, even if the death penalty were proven to be a successful deterrent and even if it could be distributed so as to avoid charges of racial, gender, or class bias, it would still be immoral. Provided we think that the state ought not knowingly to engage in immoral practices, it follows that no one—for any reason—ought to be sentenced to death. On the other hand, if the death penalty is just, then problems of distribution and efficacy are just that: problems not with the death penalty per se but with our failures to use it properly. It cannot be ruled out on grounds other than its own merits.

Yet to van den Haag's way of thinking, this is precisely what abolitionists are attempting to do. To use van den Haag's phrase, many of the arguments against the death penalty are "sham arguments." If justice consists in "punishing the guilty and sparing the innocent,"[12] as van den Haag suggests, then "nondeterrence" and "maldistribution among the guilty"[13] are arguments that will not ultimately help those who wish to abolish capital punishment, since they do not directly address the actual guilt of those individuals sentenced to death by the state. Presumably, if we are absolutely certain that an individual is guilty of a heinous crime, then abolitionists whose arguments turn on either maldistribution or nondeterrence are left without a reason to object to the state's killing that person.

Moreover, the possibility of accidentally executing an innocent person wrongly convicted can be treated not so much as a reason to abolish the death penalty as an in-house question among those who favor capital punishment, since the miscarriage of justice does not negate the demands of justice any more than drug abuse negates the need for pharmaceuticals. "If," in van den Haag's words, "the advantages sufficiently outweigh the disadvantages, human activities, including those of the penal system with all its punishments, are morally justified."[14]

Once he engages the question of deterrence, he begins to slide from questions about justice toward those about efficacy. He reads the contested evidence regarding deterrence as bearing sufficient weight to at least continue favoring the use of capital punishment until conclusive evidence to the contrary is established, and since the argument from deterrence is premised on capital punishment's ability to save the lives of innocent persons by taking the lives of guilty ones, then, by his own admission, van den Haag will continue to "value the life of innocents more than the life of murderers,"[15] even if, in the process of saving many innocent lives, a few innocent lives are lost. Moreover, since most abolitionists admit to opposing capital punishment even if it does have a deterrent value, van den Haag calls deterrence-based opposition a sham argument as well.

Barring the advent of conclusive evidence about the efficacy of capital punishment as a deterrent[16]—evidence that will almost certainly remain unavailable to us if we continue to live in a constitutional democracy that sets and maintains certain basic standards about how we administer justice—the argument from deterrence eventually turns on the question of how to weigh the actual lives of a few innocent persons against the possible lives of many innocent persons. I know of no convincing way to adjudicate such a question. I doubt one exists. And barring such adjudication, any such argument from deterrence—based as it is on efficacy—will fail to cohere with the demands of justice.

What can we learn from van den Haag? Several things. First, the arguments from arbitrariness, discrimination, and miscarriage of justice are not the strongest arguments that abolitionists can put forward. They function primarily as ad hominem arguments made by those who hope that stacking enough arguments against the death penalty on top of each other will suffice in causing it to founder, even if those arguments are individually too weak to collapse it. Problems with applying the death penalty arbitrarily or in a discriminatory fashion among persons or occasionally to innocent persons could, in theory, be ruled out by applying it more consistently or more carefully; in either case, the death penalty would stand.

Second, those of us who oppose capital punishment have the responsibility of presenting our cases and our motives as fully and openly as possible. If we believe that the death penalty is wrong *in theory*, then we ought not to hide behind practical arguments that do not necessarily reach that same conclusion, lest some thoughtful reader like Ernest van den Haag comes along and sees through our practical arguments to the theory that drives them. This does not mean that all persons oppose the death penalty for the same reason. It could be that some persons will oppose the death penalty until various weaknesses in its distribution are resolved, at which point they will favor its implementation. But that is not my argument, nor that of many of my colleagues.

It follows, then, that a genuine theological opposition to the death penalty begins with the position that *nobody* deserves to be executed by the state regardless of their actions and that the reason nobody deserves such an execution has something to do with what it means to be a human being in a specific type of relationship to God in the first place. Begin with the worst of cases—for example, an individual who has had a fair trial, has given an uncoerced confession about a heinous crime involving the murder of at least one innocent person, remains unrepentant over his actions in spite of the fact that he is capable of understanding them and their implications, and warns that, if freed, he will commit such crimes again—and then argue that *even this person* should not be executed. Anything less than this leaves the door theoretically open for the defenders of capital punishment.

B. LEARNING FROM BERNS

Another pro–capital punishment writer, Walter Berns, argues that there is only one fitting response to the instance I have just described—namely, the type of moral outrage that might only be satisfied by death. Therein, Berns calls us back to the possibility that capital punishment ought to be about retribution: "We punish criminals principally *in order to pay them back*, and we execute the worst of them out of moral necessity."[17] Using Nazi hunter Simon Wiesenthal's mission as an example, Berns argues that taking less than total revenge upon those who commit totally vicious acts not only devalues our memories of the victims but demeans the criminals as well. Inverting the logic of those opponents of capital punishment who argue that it treats criminals as less than fully human, Berns suggests that in some cases, capital punishment is the only way to affirm their full humanity. This suggestion warrants clarification but also serious consideration, for if Berns is correct, then the very values on which opponents build part of their case—namely, those associated with proclaiming that our willingness to execute the condemned marks them as somehow less than fully human—can also be used to knock that case down.

For Berns, retributive measures are appropriate because when criminals break laws, they break the very bonds that unite persons across communities and within nations. Some form of retribution must be necessary precisely because something must be done in order to restore those broken bonds, and the only thing that can restore such bonds is punishing those who break them. Moral outrage is, in part, a sign that we value these bonds. Any society that neither values nor expresses anger when such bonds are broken has lost an important part of its ability to form communities and affirm social relationships.

Not only ought we be angry when the bonds that hold us together are violated, we ought to respect what that anger points to: our need to restore those bonds. "Anger," writes Berns, "is expressed or manifested on those occasions when someone has acted in a manner that is thought to be unjust, and one of its origins is the opinion that men are responsible, and should be held responsible, for what they do."[18] Anger is an appropriate emotional expression—but there are also appropriate and inappropriate expressions of anger. We ought not to be angry—or at least we ought not to maintain our anger—at objects or persons who cannot be held responsible for their actions. Upon reflection, we feel foolish after acting in anger against an object (say, the rock on which a toe was stubbed) and sorrow or pity after acting in anger against someone who could not help him- or herself (say, a small child who has spilled juice on the rug). Instead, "anger acknowledges the humanity of its objects: it holds them accountable for what they do. And in holding particular men responsible, it pays them the respect that is due them as men."[19] Thus, to deny either our anger or the acts of revenge that it initiates is not only to act as something other than human ourselves but to deny that the objects of our anger are human.

Setting aside my disagreements about whether admitting the human quality of anger necessarily means we ought to kill criminals (a conclusion that does not necessarily follow, given the existence of other forms of punishment), whether the bonds that tie us to each other are best understood in terms of law and whether those bonds are best restored through acts of revenge (both of which I doubt), and whether we human beings are actually more likely to rationalize the appropriateness of our anger rather than feeling foolish, sorrowful, or pity after inappropriately expressing it (which I tend to think), I do believe that Berns reminds us of at least one important concern when thinking about capital punishment—namely, that those who oppose capital punishment must take the anger of those who feel victimized by serious criminal activity into account. Too few of us who oppose capital punishment pay attention to the deep, residual pain and anger with which the families and acquaintances of victims struggle every day, and almost none of us pay adequate attention to the social anger that induces citizens to stand outside federal penitentiaries yelling, "Fry, baby, fry!" If nothing else, Walter Berns turns our attention back to the important role human emotions—especially anger and the desire for revenge—play in shaping people's convictions about capital punishment. Indeed, it is precisely at the level of recognizing and naming social anger that I think religious thought may make a distinctive contribution to the death penalty debate. I will return to this concern about the human desire for retribution and suggest a religious explication of that desire in the last part of this chapter.

In the meantime, I turn to the heart of my argument, analyzing the two historically significant and theologically nuanced positions developed by Thomas Aquinas and Karl Barth, each of whom represents a broad tradition within the history of the Christian church. Just as I have done with van den Haag and Berns, I will seek to discern how God may be speaking through these positions in a way that is meaningful and helpful in developing a contemporary theological opposition to the death penalty.

III. Thomas Aquinas on Capital Punishment

Thomas Aquinas (1225–1274) was a Dominican monk whose thought—particularly as expressed in *Summa Theologica*—has provided the foundation for Roman Catholic theology and moral thought from his time to the present.[20] His work is marked by a thoughtful and deliberate attempt to incorporate Aristotelian moral philosophy with biblical teachings as read through an Augustinian emphasis on love. Taken as a whole, the *Summa* describes a path by which all things proceed from God at creation and then return to God, who is love, at the end of history; this is Thomas's *exitus-reditus* schema. All the various and rich aspects of his thought fit within this rubric, including his writings on morality, the purposes of punishment, and the taking of human life.[21] Thus, any attempt to separate out one aspect of his thought and discuss it apart from its larger whole risks misunderstanding its deeply entrenched relation to that whole.

Thomas argued that human beings are naturally inclined to move toward God and that all morally good actions promote movement toward that goal. Sin is the attempt to move in a different direction or the misunderstanding about how to move in the right direction, and it must be compensated for by moral actions that serve as correctives, goads, and guides. These moral actions are developed through habitually practicing intellectual, moral, and spiritual virtues and by promoting a just and properly ordered society in which to practice these virtues. Thus, Thomas's moral vision insists not only on the recognition of a natural order within the complex web of personal, social, and God–human relationships that constitutes creation but also on the gradual instilling of virtues in individual lives so that each person may move forward toward God. In this schema, criminal activity is sinful activity, and punishment is designed both to maintain and/or restore order and to redirect the criminal toward more virtuous modes of behavior.

Thomas is explicit that "man can be punished with a threefold punishment corresponding to the three orders to which the human will is subject."[22] That is, when individuals violate their own better sense of behavior, they are punished by their consciences. When they violate social laws, they are punished by their superiors. And when they violate God's laws, they are punished by God. Of these three orders, capital punishment pertains to the second, since conscience remains personal and God's punishment is eternal rather than temporal.

Thomas is also explicit in describing the three functions of punishment within the social order, which might be roughly labeled as retribution, rehabilitation, and deterrence. First, punishment can be inflicted as retribution or payment for a debt—that is, in direct response to an individual's actual sin, in which case "each one is punished for his own sin only, because the sinful act is something personal."[23] This function of punishment—what Thomas calls the "penal function"—is adequate to restore justice, but it neither addresses nor leaves room for the possibility that someone's punishment might satisfy a social need. Second, punishment can be inflicted as a form of rehabilitation or, to use Thomas's language, in a "medicinal way" to prevent sin, wherein a punishment guides the criminal toward better behavior in the future. Rehabilitation, however, plays no role in the death penalty, so this second function of punishment does not pertain in cases of capital punishment. Finally, punishment can be inflicted to deter future criminal activity. Thomas argues that this latter purpose of punishment is also medicinal, though it serves as a medicine for society rather than the individual per se since, in this instance, it serves as a warning to others.[24]

Having placed Thomas's conception of punishment within its theological context, the way is now open to take up the question of capital punishment explicitly. What does Thomas have to say about capital punishment? He favors it. In his *Summa Theologica* II–II, question 64, article 2, he answers the question "Whether It Is Lawful to Kill Sinners?" as follows:

> It is lawful to kill dumb animals, in so far as they are naturally directed to man's use, as the imperfect is directed to the perfect. Now every part is directed to the whole, as imperfect to perfect, wherefore every part is naturally for the sake of the whole. For this reason we observe that if the health of the whole body demands the excision of a member, through its being decayed or infectious to the other members, it will be both praiseworthy and advantageous to have it cut away. Now every individual person is compared to the whole community, as part to whole. Therefore if a man be dangerous and infectious to the community, on account of some sin, it is praiseworthy and advantageous that he be killed in order to safeguard the common good, since a little leaven corrupteth the whole lump. (1 Cor.:6)[25]

This is more than a single response to the question. It is two composite answers, either of which Thomas might have used alone and both of which he combined to strengthen his argument. These answers are the dumb animal analogy/imperfection–perfection relationship and the body analogy/part–whole relationship. While these answers are different and deserve the type of independent consideration I will not be able to supply here,[26] they do share two important similarities. First, in both cases Thomas reinforces the idea that there is a natural order to things such that humans are superior to animals, perfection is better than imperfection, and wholes are more important than parts. Second, even in regard to capital punishment, Thomas sees crime as disrupting order and punishment as an attempt to restore that order. These two similarities are at the core of Thomas's justification of capital punishment.

Yet these justifications for capital punishment are not, in themselves, satisfactory. Not only do they need to cohere with Thomas's larger moral schema—including his understanding of the purposes of punishment—but they need to be challenged where either they do not fit or they ignore important intermediate positions that cohere better with that moral schema. The question that remains, then, is whether capital punishment necessarily follows from the need to restore and maintain order. On this point, Thomas posits what he should have discussed: that removal from society means death. This supposition is the basis for Thomas's answer that order is maintained by taking a criminal's life. Perhaps in his time—marked as it was by the church killing heretics and engaging in armed battle against emperors—the conclusion that removing a criminal from society and killing a criminal are the same was self-apparent.

Yet this conclusion is not only less apparent now, but there are pieces of Thomas's own thought in the *Summa* that weigh against it. First, Thomas repeatedly favored using only as much force as was necessary on any given occasion to achieve a desired end as, for example, in the case of killing in self-defense.[27] The logic of this argument, when applied to removing criminals from society, would suggest that life imprisonment is adequate for serious offenses. This argument is undergirded by Thomas's explicit conclusion that though evildoers must be punished, the form of that punishment cannot be clearly derived from any particular divinely given moral law but must instead be discerned by human beings using their powers of reason to make human laws that accord with that intrinsic moral law.[28] Thus, capital punishment cannot be understood as a precise demand of the divine moral law in maintenance of moral order but must instead be viewed as one possible response to the demands of the divine moral law—a response that must be evaluated, in part, by its coherence within the larger moral framework of the universe.

Second—and in contrast to his dumb animal analogy—Thomas elsewhere recognizes that "[a] beast is by nature distinct from man . . . [and] a man who has sinned is not by nature distinct from good men."[29] This conclusion undermines the notion that killing a human being can be tantamount to killing a beast and underlines the value of human life such that the wild beast analogy can be no more than a rough and flawed analogy. In that light, killing a human being needs to be seen as a far more momentous and troublesome act than Thomas's casual reference to killing dumb animals within the context of capital punishment suggests.

Third, while Thomas would agree that religious leaders should participate in promoting the common good, he explicitly rejected the idea that they could become involved in killing: "It is unlawful for clerics to kill, for two reasons. First, because they are chosen for the ministry of the altar, whereon is represented the Passion of Christ slain *Who, when He was struck did not strike*. . . . [Second] because clerics are entrusted with the ministry of the New Law, wherein no punishment of death or of bodily maiming is appointed."[30] To the degree that Thomas believed in the growing and ultimate authority of "the New Law" over the lives of all beings—and not just clerics—this point might at least suggest that capital punishment should become less and less of an option as creation moves closer and closer to consummation. Or, said differently, Thomas may have viewed taking a criminal's life as a *necessary* act of punishment, but he would not have viewed it as an *ideal* act of punishment. If he could be convinced of an alternative, he would probably have chosen that alternative. Given these three pieces of evidence, we are at least in a position to conclude that Thomas's position on capital punishment ought to be treated as an anomaly within his thought rather than the norm.

This conclusion is reinforced by correcting a common misperception implicit in those who defend Thomas's position; namely, that Thomas's emphasis on the good of the community over against the good of the individual leads to a concurrent emphasis on maintaining current order as the greatest of social goods (and therein an emphasis on capital punishment as necessary for maintaining order). This misconception results from reading Thomas in such a way as to allow the static qualities of Aristotelian metaphysics to trump the dynamism of Augustinian theology, and it is visible in the thought of both those who defend Thomas's position on capital punishment and those who criticize it.[31] Undoubtedly, Thomas does emphasize right order in society. He does not, however, believe that social order is a static concept in which maintaining the status quo ought to be society's proper goal. Instead, social order is a dynamic good that must change as all beings move toward their proper end, which is God. Again, all of Thomas's thought—including that on capital punishment—must be read in light of his grand *exitus-reditus* schema. Thomas might say that capital punishment has been necessary and therefore must be allowed. He would never say that capital punishment ought to be an ideal or permanent fixture in society as creation moves toward consummation. Thus, we might well conclude, with Brian Calvert, that "it is difficult to believe an Aquinas brought back to earth could be anything other than an abolitionist."[32]

Recognizing the uncomfortable fit of Thomas's thought about capital punishment specifically within the context of his thoughts about punishment more generally allows us neither to dismiss him as hopelessly confused nor to argue that, in spite of the explicit statements, the logic of his position is actually to oppose capital punishment. Instead, it both highlights the degree to which Thomas's support of capital punishment is significantly more constrained than a cursory reading of II–II, question 64, suggests and also promotes the possibility that one can build a substantial case against capital punishment by using

Thomas's own arguments.[33] Having tempered Thomas's defense of capital punishment via a slightly closer reading of his work and opened it up in order to draw conclusions other than the one Thomas reached, we now have the way opened to take the next step—namely, to discern how God might be speaking through Thomas Aquinas and into our contemporary context.

The centuries between us certainly add complexity to this task, but there are parts of Thomas's thought from which we might learn. Primary among them are at least the following two conclusions: first, that those theological suppositions and dogmas that undergird any type of religious argument about capital punishment must, themselves, be embedded within a larger theological vision of the way God and world relate; and second, that within that context, what it means to be human must, itself, be understood through the systems of relationships that constitute human identity and interaction. Each of these conclusions deserves further consideration.

The first conclusion—that whatever we say theologically about capital punishment must, itself, be coherent with and embedded within a larger set of theologically informed beliefs and practices—follows from Thomas's own painstaking attempt to hold all the manifold parts of his work within the *exitus-reditus* framework. Not only does such a conclusion lead us to reject logical inconsistencies in moral thought (as, e.g., when persons oppose capital punishment because all life is sacred while favoring abortion without explaining why the sacredness of life is not of paramount importance when dealing with fetuses). It also pushes us to expand any ideas we might have about capital punishment so that they match with our deepest and most firmly held convictions about God's actions in creating, judging, and redeeming the world. If, for example, we understand God's will as uniquely and authoritatively expressed by Jesus Christ, who was sent into the world not to condemn it "but in order that the world might be saved through him,"[34] then somehow that more central conviction must have some bearing in the way we think about the death penalty. In that context, condemnation and punishment are not the ends toward which we strive but instead—and at best—correctives toward an end that is constituted by reconciliation and joy.

The second conclusion follows from the first and insists that embedding theological language about capital punishment within a larger theological context must also mean embedding it within questions of what it means to be a human in relationship to God and to other humans. While a detailed discussion of such questions would extend far beyond the reach of this chapter, the following classical Christian theological affirmations—all of which are affirmations that Thomas would share—at least bear mention:

1. To be created in the image of God[35] means at least two things: that human beings are creatures and, therefore, finite, and that we bear some resemblance to the God who created us such that this resemblance endows us with deep, if not infinite, worth.

2. Unless they further clarify what it means to be created by God, any other qualities by which humans might be theologically described (e.g., human beings are "sinners") do not pertain to what is essentially or intrinsically human about us. This is not to say that sinfulness is mere illusion but merely to reaffirm that humans are not created by God as sinners and that nothing and no one else is ultimately responsible for creating human beings.

3. Because God's image is intrinsic to human beings, no person can be separated from that image. Or, put positively, God's image remains in all persons, no matter how far their actions seem to separate them from God or cause them to lose that image.

4. Created in the image of a Triune God who wills that they fully participate in the joy of his existence, human beings are intrinsically relational creatures. They cannot fully make sense of their lives apart from their relations to other persons and to God.

5. As fully God and fully human, Jesus Christ serves as the goal for what we might become when we do fully participate in God's joy, and his life and teaching instruct us on how to behave right now.

6. As our creator, judge, and redeemer, God is the one true Lord of life. Denying that relationship or attempting to usurp it misunderstands the way humans relate with God.

7. As relational creatures, human beings ought not act in ways that ignore the welfare of others. That is, persons ought not to set their personal good over that of society because society is composed of other persons created in God's image.

8. From these, it follows that any actions that threaten to separate persons from one another must be viewed with gravity; any actions that lead to the death of someone created in the image of God must be viewed with profound gravity; and any actions that deny the image of God in the other, ignore the life Jesus models, or are expressions of the belief that someone or something else can properly exert ultimate control over human life are immoral.

While these eight affirmations do not necessarily mean that capital punishment is immoral, they do highlight both the reasons that capital punishment may seem necessary and the reasons that it should be so morally disquieting. For on the one hand, we are most likely to insist on the death penalty for those who have acted in ways contrary to the affirmations expressed in 1 through 7, and on the other hand, capital punishment seems, on its face, to be precisely the type of action described in 8 *and* contrary to 1 through 7.

These affirmations all receive expression in the work of Thomas Aquinas, who thoughtfully developed them in the *Summa Theologica*. Moreover, they are the basis for the current Roman Catholic opposition to capital punishment. While the Catholic Church recognizes that a believer can reach a different conclusion regarding capital punishment based on these same affirmations—much as Thomas did—it nevertheless urges all believers to attempt to base their respective positions on the death penalty upon these affirmations.[36]

So also, I would urge Christians to think through these affirmations in light of their own understandings of their faith and to consider the way the resultant convictions relate to their position on the death penalty. To do any less is to do violence to both the Christian faith and to fellow creatures created by God.

IV. Implications

A. KARL BARTH ON CAPITAL PUNISHMENT

If there is a Protestant equivalent to Thomas Aquinas, it is, perhaps, Karl Barth. Barth was a Swiss theologian writing in the middle of the twentieth century; his thirteen-volume *Church Dogmatics*[37] represents one of the most comprehensive Protestant systematic theologies in existence. Deep within it, Barth lays out his own position on capital punishment based on his theological convictions about God, the world, and ethics.

A cursory reading of Barth's conception of ethics might suggest that he would be hard-pressed to say much of anything about capital punishment in general because he is fairly suspicious of anything that looks like an ethical system. Ethics, Barth tells us, is what the serpent promised Adam and Eve when it told them that eating the fruit would give them the knowledge of good and evil; it is what got us into trouble in the first place. When we try to do ethics, we stop listening for God's command spoken to us about how to behave in each particular moment. Indeed, at first glance, the only "ought" in Barth's ethics is the *ought* in the sentence "We ought to listen for the command of God rather than trying to think systematically about ethics." This isn't especially helpful if we want to think about almost any of the normative issues with which we struggle every day, much less capital punishment. Thinking about how to fit ethical reflection on capital punishment into a larger theological system—something Thomas Aquinas teaches us to do—is inordinately difficult if that system rejects systematic ethical reflection.[38]

By the beginning of *Church Dogmatics* III.4, however, we may begin to get a better sense of how Barth could and does develop his theological ethics. The problem, he explains, isn't that there may be a system of ethics but that the systems we develop are closed. If we could maintain an open system—one that always begins in the attempt to hear God's specific word spoken to concrete situations and that always leaves room for God to command us in fresh ways—then we could use an ethical system as a way of helping us make sense of and structure those commands. Ethics can't determine what we ought to do, but it can serve as an aid to hearing what we ought to do. Ethics doesn't give answers; it helps us test the answers we think God might be giving us.

Over and against general ethics—what we might describe as a closed system in which decisions about what ought and ought not be done can be determined prior to the point at which those decisions may be necessary—Barth develops a notion of special ethics. These ethics are based on the attempt to hear God's command and obey it at each point in time and space. They begin in the assumption that God is still active in the world, continuing to express God's sovereign will over all that God has created. The assumption that God continues to speak to specific times and places means that those who would think about ethics must do so in specific terms via fairly concrete cases and contextually sensitive evaluations. Thus, in III.4, Barth enters into a lengthy set of discussions about the kind of concrete cases that aid our hearing when we listen for God to speak to us about matters of life and death. These are cases that reveal prominent lines of thought designed to help guide our theological ethics.

He begins by describing life as a loan from God.[39] The term *loan* highlights the degree to which life—like all other things—ultimately belongs to God but also the fact that each of us is responsible for our lives and what we do with them. Ultimately, this responsibility means at least two things for Barth. First, that we ought to treat life with respect. Of all the things that God has created, human life has a unique place because God created it in such a way as to enter freely into fellowship with its creator and with other creatures, therein glorifying the God who created them all. Second, though we ought to treat life with respect, we cannot treat it as having absolute worth. Life's value comes precisely in its relationship to God, through whom all worth is measured. Thus, we must express our respect for life by protecting it, but "the protection of life required of us is not unlimited or absolute. It is simply the protection which God wills to demand of man as the Creator of this life and the Giver of the future eternal life."[40] In Barth's ethic, life has only a proximate value, and it is therefore possible that the Lord of life may nevertheless command its surrender or sacrifice.

Barth describes these instances when God commands that life be surrendered or sacrificed as *grenzfall*, or limit, cases. This doesn't mean that there are a fixed or limited number of such cases so much as that *grenzfall* cases describe the extreme limits of God's command to people that they ought to live. They are the exceptions that reinforce the rule: "[W]e cannot deny the possibility that God as the Lord of life may further its protection even in the strange form of its conclusion and termination rather than its preservation and advancement."[41] In most of the examples Barth later gives to describe these *grenzfall* cases, life is taken only when not taking life could lead to more lives being taken. Even *grenzfall* cases, however, can only be recognized as such if all other avenues of action are exhausted. That is, the command to preserve and maintain the loan that is human life is so compelling that any action that appears to contradict it must only be a last resort—and only then where the command to preserve life somehow expresses itself through life's termination.

The idea that life can be taken in order to be preserved is counterintuitive. To help clarify how this can be the case—but even more to highlight the stringency of the command that life not be taken—Barth turns to the relation between his special ethics and the protection of life in extraordinary cases such as suicide, abortion, euthanasia, war, and capital punishment.

While Barth will eventually support the possibility of specific instances of capital punishment, it is important at the outset of this investigation to highlight the degree to which Barth opposes capital punishment in *Church Dogmatics*. From Barth's perspective, there is no way that capital punishment can be established as normatively acceptable. When the state allows for the establishment and practice of the death penalty, it usurps divine right. Regardless of the existence of exceptional cases, thoughtful Christians cannot defend legalizing capital punishment. Thus, those arguments that exist between Barth and those of us who cannot support capital punishment even in exceptional cases ought to be seen as arguments between abolitionists rather than between pro– and con–capital punishment positions.[42]

Barth prefaces his exploration into capital punishment with a warning and concludes it with an apology. First, the apology. In spite of the commands of its Lord, the church has historically allowed for and even promoted capital punishment. It ought to have led the cause to abolish capital punishment; it has not. Instead, "it is one of the disconcerting blessings of the divine overruling of history" that the abolitionist cause has been "adopted far more readily and energetically by the children of the world than by the children of light."[43] God's graceful actions in history, however, do not relieve the church of its responsibility or excuse it for its actions. The church has much to atone for, and in Barth's mind, that atonement must include working for the abolition of a legalized death penalty.

Second, the warning. Unlike most cases that involve taking or protecting human life, capital punishment implicates more than a few individuals or a specific category of citizens in its actions. In any modern, broadly democratic nation that practices capital punishment, it is ultimately that nation's citizens who carry out its executions rather than some abstract entity known as "the state" or a state employee known as "the executioner." His point is clear: No one in any such nation can say of capital punishment, "This does not concern me." Delegating the authority to take life to the state in no way diminishes individual responsibility; indeed, it increases it: "[D]elegation means that every individual who belongs to a lawfully constituted society has a share which he cannot delegate to others in the pronouncement and execution of a capital sentence. . . . We think responsibly only if we realize and accept the fact that it is we ourselves who do it all in the person of these others."[44] In this light, maintaining the anonymity of executioners by hiding them behind masks at the guillotine, blanks at the firing squad, or indeterminacy at the lethal injection only hides us from ourselves; the blood of the executed is always already on our hands as citizens who approve of such actions.

Having placed the responsibility for carrying out the death penalty squarely on the shoulders of those who would be reading his work, Barth attempts to draw out and theologically evaluate several prominent lines of thought regarding capital punishment. Toward that end, he describes three theories of punishment (deterrence, retribution/expiation, and rehabilitation), their respective approaches to capital punishment, and their problems.

He deals with the theory of punishment as rehabilitation in short order. While it has the advantage of being meaningful for the offender him- or herself—of treating the offender as fully human and a member of society—it cannot be coherently reconciled with the use of the death penalty. A society guided by the theory that persons can and ought to be rehabilitated can only take life by treating an offender as beyond the scope of possible improvement and therefore beyond personhood. That is, a society that attempts to rehabilitate all except those it kills tacitly claims that some are so evil that they are incapable of change or being changed; they are somehow inhuman. A society claiming that these people lack the very qualities that make us human in the first place—namely, that they have been created good and that this goodness cannot be utterly removed from them no matter how deeply it is hidden or how hard we or they try to pervert it—is not so much executing criminals as slaughtering animals. Yet this claim accords with neither the Christian vision of what it means to be human nor, more important, with Christianity's deepest beliefs about what God is capable of doing. Thus, Barth closes this section with the question "What right has society to let one of its members fall, to declare itself incapable of having further contact with him, and thus to maintain that it is justified in breaking off this contact once and for all and irrevocably?"[45] and the implicit answer to this rhetorical question: no right at all.

He is almost as short with the theory of punishment as retribution or expiation. While recognizing that this theory is "much favored by Christians who approve of the death penalty . . . [and] naturally quite right in the sense that all human punishment should be an earthly representation of the retributive justice of God both to the transgressor himself and to the rest of society,"[46] Barth nevertheless highlights two deeply troubling problems with the theological articulation of this theory. First, it lacks the proper humility to recognize that all human decisions are fallible, no matter what or whose image they are trying to mirror. Any human attempt to represent God's retributive justice must leave itself open to the possibility that it is wrong; thus, "other sentences which are not ultimate can and may [reflect divine retribution] because with their refusal to speak the final word, though less severe, they plainly reveal the limitation of all human understanding and therefore the humility required of man in relation both to God and to the fellow-man who is to be punished."[47] Capital punishment, as both an ultimate and an irrevocable form of punishment, lacks proper human humility.

Moreover—and more important for Barth—even if human punishment ought somehow to mirror divine retribution, the starting point for Christian reflection on this conception of punishment must begin in the recognition that Jesus' crucifixion completely satisfies God's demand for retribution. There is no need for any further expiatory death; in dying on the cross, Jesus fully pays the price for the sins that demand God's judgment. For "on the Christian view the retributive justice of God has already found full and final expression, the expiation demanded by Him for all human transgression has already been made. . . . God gave His only Son for this very purpose."[48]

Christians who approve of capital punishment as an earthly representation of God's retributive justice must also consider acts of forgiveness as earthly representations of God's mercy. After all, Jesus' death not only satisfies God's demands for retributive justice but also opens the way for God's forgiveness to all people. If Christians claim that Jesus died so that all persons might be forgiven, they cannot set aside a particular category of persons who are beyond forgiveness or redemption. Taking human life as an expression of retributive punishment denies the opportunity for Christians to participate in or mirror God's forgiveness, and Christians risk their own election by refusing to forgive others as God has forgiven them. This is not to say that punishment is rejected per se, but a criminal's punishment

> should not shorten the allotted time which still remains to him but afford him the opportunity of filling it better than he has done in the past. It must restrain him from further lapses, but also stimulate him positively to take his place in orderly human society. He must not go unpunished, but be punished in such a way that his life is affirmed and not denied as in capital punishment. Only thus can his punishment be a human reflection of the righteous action of God in His conflict with chaos.[49]

Barth's treatment of capital punishment-as-deterrent is longer and more complex than his arguments about reform or retribution, but no less critical. In his opinion, each argument from deterrence faces an internal contradiction that it cannot overcome and that ought to lead to capital punishment's abolition. Where society argues that it has an interest in its own protection, and "capital punishment is an infallibly effective means of preventing the criminal from continuing or repeating his outrages,"[50] Barth points out that the criminal stands inside that society; "indeed, he is its product, a result of the conditions [therein]. He has enjoyed the benefits of its order, but he has also suffered from its imperfections and contradictions, from the manifest or concealed injustice prevalent within it."[51] As a result, society bears at least partial blame for the criminal conduct of one of its members, whose own protection from injustice was usually inadequate in his or her upbringing. A just society cannot simultaneously argue for its own protection and deny extending that protection to all of its citizens. Where society argues that capital punishment provides an enormous amount of security to its members, Barth points out that this security comes at the cost of revealing a profound disorderliness within society's core structures, since by taking life, society reveals that it is acting out of a fright so deep that it believes it cannot achieve this security by any lesser means, including life imprisonment. And when a society reveals the tenuousness of its basic structures of order by taking lives, it can only promote an inchoate or half-felt insecurity within its members. Society undermines itself when it pays for its obvious attempt at promoting security only by revealing its own underlying insecurity. Where society argues that capital punishment serves as a warning to others about the dangers of imitating the criminal, Barth points out that capital punishment may only strengthen the conviction of a potential criminal that his or her society does not merit care because it does not express care for its members, that he or she "is dealing with a wild and very dangerous beast [i.e., society] which he must approach with the greatest care but against which its own example teaches him [sic] to make use of every possible means."[52] If a society attempts to deter crime by killing criminals, it undermines its proper authority and instead usurps and opposes divine authority. This can only have deleterious consequences for the citizens it purports to protect.

Thus, Barth concludes, "[i]f the command to protect life is accepted and asserted in some sense in a national community, then it is impossible to maintain capital punishment as an element in its normal and continuing order."[53] Moreover, "from the point of view of the Gospel there is nothing to be said for its institution, and everything against it."[54]

But what of a *grenzfall* case for capital punishment? In spite of his apparently unequivocal opposition to it, in *Church Dogmatics* Barth nevertheless suggests that such a case might exist. This case does not allow for capital punishment to be established as a practice, since practices are expressions of norms, rather than exceptions. However, it is not absolutely excluded and forbidden by the command of God in all forms and circumstances. Thus, "on the far edge of what can be commanded, there is certainly a place for the killing of those whose existence threatens the state and its stability in such a way that a choice has to be made between their existence and that of the state. When it is seen that this situation exists, it may be the will and command of God that they should be killed."[55]

Even here, however, Barth allows for such exceptions "only when the state exists in the abnormal situation in which God demands it [capital punishment] from one or more of its responsible leaders for its [the state's] preservation *in extremis*."[56] Capital punishment never plays a role within normal state functioning. Moreover, even if the state does exist in such an abnormal situation, Barth still sets out a series of conditions that must be met before taking such an action. First, those who would take life must determine that the continued existence of the state is worth more than that individual's life. Given the extreme abnormality of any situation in which one might have to choose between individual and state existence, this condition must be treated with a seriousness that calls into question the immediate utilitarian answer of sacrificing the one for the good of the many. In such an odd situation, an individual's life could be more meaningful than the state's existence.[57] Second, those who would take life must determine that this action is actually the will of God. Finally, they must conclude that taking life is the only available option in this instance. Even within Barth's *grenzfall* cases, there are restrictions.

Clarifying his argument, Barth raises two possible specific instances in which the continued existence of the state is threatened by the life of an individual and capital punishment might, therefore, be allowed by God. The first of these is as a penalty for high treason in the case of war: "If a man surrenders military secrets to an actual or potential enemy and thus violates his military oath and endangers his own country, the existence of the state, and the lives of possibly thousands of his comrades, he may be said to have forfeited his right to live in this community and therefore rightly be subject to death, assuming that the gravity of his action has been scrupulously weighed and proved."[58] The second example is that of tyrannicide. If an individual gains the ability to control the state, if he or she uses that control toward illegitimate ends, and if those who are able to remove this tyrant are either unable or unwilling to do so, then in defense of the state, then other members of the state may have to respond by taking that tyrant's life in defense of the state.

How concerned should an abolitionist be with Barth's *grenzfall* cases? Not very. First, Barth has so restricted his exceptional cases as to make them of no use for those who favor capital punishment as a practice. Not only can Barth's *grenzfall* cases not be used to defend the practice of capital punishment generally, but even where he does allow for an exceptional case, he still sets up a series of stringent conditions that must be met, the negative answer to any one of which would prohibit enforcing the death penalty.

Second, Barth's *grenzfall* cases are, themselves, caught in logical contradiction when held up against his earlier statements about capital punishment. That is, they only come into play where a state "exists in an abnormal situation." Yet Barth initiates his discussion of capital punishment by setting it within the context of "a society standardized by constitution and law,"[59] which is to say a stable state. Thus, the only cases in which Barth allows for capital punishment exist outside the very structures Barth designates as the necessary background for discussing capital punishment in the first place. As a result, neither of his two examples actually fall within the realm of his discussion of capital punishment. Indeed, as John Howard Yoder points out, the two examples—high treason and assassination of a tyrant—pertain more closely to Barth's discussion of war than his discussion of capital punishment.[60]

As if to reaffirm this point, Barth would later change his mind about the *grenzfall* cases he described. In a question-and-answer session several years after he wrote *Church Dogmatics* III.4, Barth was asked about his position on capital punishment. At that time, Barth rejected the exceptions he made in *Church Dogmatics*:

> I am asked now, what about exceptions concerning the death penalty for treachery in war? I am embarrassed, because I myself made an exception in *Church Dogmatics* III.4. . . . Today I probably would not write what I wrote there. . . . I wrote it rather soon after the end of World War II, under the pressure of a series of about twenty severe cases of treachery. . . . It is never good for a theologian to let himself be pressured by historic experiences.
>
> Actually, I did not want to legitimate the death penalty for treachery in war as punishment at all. . . . In what he did, the traitor joined the side of the enemy and now he has to risk it: as one shoots at the enemy, so now one shoots at him, too. . . . One does not punish the enemy in a war, but deals with him as enemy.[61]

Shorn of his *grenzfall* case and expressing his conviction in this question-and-answer session that the only theologically legitimate purpose for punishment must begin with a concern for the prisoner's welfare (*Fürsorge*, more literally, thoughtful concern), Barth can only conclude that "since *everything* depends on that, I would say—one can only say—'No' to the death penalty as a matter of principle, because the death penalty fails at this understanding of welfare."[62]

Finally, if Barth includes the existence of a *grenzfall* case only because he believes he must maintain the openness of his system, then he is caught in an ironic trap. Such a motivation actually induces him to close his system by creating a principle that there must be an exception to every rule. For Barth, a conclusion based on a logical principle would fail to cohere with the theological emphasis on openness within his dogmatics, since it is still posited on a belief that one can know ahead of time how God will act. Who can say definitively that God's command can always be expressed in a strange way? Barth certainly cannot.

If Barth's *grenzfall* cases do not hold, then we are left with only a prohibition against capital punishment—and a theologically driven one at that. Barth's position can, therefore, be briefly summarized in the following set of affirmations and rejections:

1. In a broadly democratic society, everyone bears the responsibility for the deaths of those who are executed by the state. This, alone, ought to induce religious persons to engage the issue.
2. There are only three broad purposes of punishment: rehabilitation, deterrence, and retribution. From a Christian theological perspective, capital punishment fails to serve any of these purposes because of points 3 through 5 here.

3. Any state that promotes rehabilitation as the proper purpose of punishment can only support the death penalty by setting up two categories of persons—namely, those who can be rehabilitated and those who cannot. Yet the belief that some persons cannot be rehabilitated is not only based on a non-Christian vision of what it means to be human but on a faulty vision of what and who God is capable of redeeming.

4. Any state that promotes deterrence as the proper purpose of punishment can only support the death penalty by explicitly denying its obligation to protect all its members, by implicitly revealing just how tenuous the security of its citizenry actually is, or by willingly admitting that it can usurp divine authority by practicing capital punishment. None of these should be attractive to the state, and the latter should be very problematic to Christians.

5. Any state that promotes retribution as the proper purpose of punishment cannot simultaneously claim to be guided by Christian values, since if it were, it would recognize that the only retributive price that can be paid for heinous crimes has already been paid by Jesus Christ, whose actions on the cross reveal the divine justice, compassion, and forgiveness that ought to be the exemplars of Christian moral action.[63]

These affirmations, when combined with the earlier set of affirmations arising out of Thomas's theology, express both the range and depth of theological reasoning that calls for Christians to oppose the death penalty. Having begun this chapter by suggesting that there is a basis for at least a prima facie opposition to capital punishment within the Christian tradition, I am now in a place to argue that these are the very affirmations that must be overcome by any Christian who favors using the death penalty. That is, until each of these affirmations can be undermined or made nonapplicable, then those who confess that Jesus is Lord over their lives and the world are left with no alternative but to oppose capital punishment. I believe this is an all but insurmountable task for those who attempt it.

Moreover, by presenting my case in this manner, I can defend it against any accusations made by Ernest van den Haag or those who follow him that I am engaging in a series of "sham arguments." These theological affirmations are premised neither on any confusions between the use and abuse of capital punishment nor any ad hoc arguments that can be resolved by distributing capital punishment more carefully. Nor, for that matter, do they rely on any secret or hidden arguments. Perhaps van den Haag or others may disagree with my use of theology to make my point, but that disagreement is of a different category than any disagreements about capital punishment per se.

Thus far, I have explained why I believe Christians ought to oppose the death penalty. Many of the convictions that drive this opposition are relatively unavailable to the larger public, however. I doubt, for example, that Christ's expiatory death on the cross has any special significance as an argument against capital punishment in a society that separates church and state. Thus, while I have given reasons for Christians to oppose capital punishment, I have not necessarily given any reasons for its abolition in a secular society. It is, after all, quite possible and increasingly probable for Christian convictions to have no special bearing on state practices. In the remaining section of this chapter, I turn to this concern.

V. Christian Convictions and State Practices

Innumerable books and journal articles have been penned in the attempt to make sense of the complex relationship between religious thought and public political positions in the United States. While some pertain specifically to church–state relations arising out of the First Amendment's statement that "Congress shall make no law respecting an establishment of religion, nor prohibiting the free exercise thereof," most are less interested in legal practices per se than the proper role of religious convictions in a broadly secular liberal state.[64] To even attempt to cover the range and depth of thought on these matters would take me far from my present task. Instead, I will begin with a series of disclaimers that will, hopefully, be of some comfort to those who worry about religious agendas manipulating public decisions, including those that concern capital punishment.

First, I do not believe that religious convictions are appropriate for or adequate to the task of undergirding state policies in a modern democratic secular state. Second, given the variety of possible state systems, I believe that a modern democratic secular state may be the best among current alternative forms of state. Third, I believe that the primary mode by which the church engages the state should not be an attempt to influence legislation but instead a process of giving witness to a different way of living in the world, a way that is marked less by contract, conflict, and violence than by covenant, community, and peace. Fourth, I believe that all individuals, including those with religious perspectives, have the right and responsibility to engage in public discourse about state matters in our shared attempt to continue the American democratic experiment. Finally, I believe that the most important public discourses about which we ought to concern ourselves involve the treatment of other persons, and especially the taking of human life. I doubt that nonreligious persons would raise any especially substantive disagreements with any of these disclaimers.

Having made these disclaimers, I want to describe how a Christian opposed to the death penalty might enter into public discourse about this public concern. I begin by returning to a point made early in the chapter: that I write not only as a Christian but as a particular type of Christian—that is, as one who stands within the Reformed tradition as initiated by John Calvin. For while Calvin and his associates in the Reformed tradition did have their faults—not the least of which were tendencies toward puritanical totalitarianism and moral severity— they also did a couple of things well. They suggested that for those who hold deep religious convictions, these convictions should matter in all aspects of human life—including the activities of the body politic. Moreover, their critical examination of religion extended past their antipathy toward the Roman Catholic Church into a close examination of the way religion was used and misused by other Protestants and by their fellow Calvinists. Add to this a willingness to draw from resources in the science, philosophy, and law of the day, and the Calvinists' ability to engage in public discourse over a variety of issues cannot be understated.

It can, however, be denied by any liberal democratic theorist who thinks that in order for the state to function, individuals within it must keep their religious convictions purely private since they grow out of and/or breed intolerance. The most common secular liberal response to religious discourse is "Your beliefs are fine for you in your life, but you cannot use them when you engage in public discourse because the rest of us don't share your religious sensibilities. If you want to talk in the public sphere, you have to use a language we all can recognize and use."[65] Following the nomenclature of political philosopher Michael Walzer, we might call the various languages we use in private "morally thick" and the language we can use in public "morally thin."[66] The basic liberal idea is that thin language carries fewer suppositions and less metaphysical baggage with it and therefore can be used by more different types of people. The standard liberal assumption is that this thin account of morality serves as the proper foundation on which liberal cultures build their ethical structures. Moreover, since more different types of people can use this morally thin language, it must contain the various moral injunctions that are most basic to human life and flourishing. Since Reformed Christians cannot even make sense of their position apart from its religious aspects, and since the U.S. espouses a generally liberal polity, then the demand for them to use morally thin language might simply cut these Christians out of public conversations.

There is, however, a different way of reading the relationship between thick and thin accounts of morality. In his book *Thick and Thin*, Walzer redescribes the two types of moral language and their relation to each other. "Thin" accounts of morality might be described as a set of very circumscribed universal attitudes toward which everyone (or almost everyone) feels sympathetic agreement—or, to use Walzer's language, moral attitudes that "resonate" with everyone. "Thick" accounts are those that incorporate the specific goods, goals, and practices of specific societies and groups, including religious groups.

However, Walzer's relations between thick and thin accounts of morality are considerably different from those of most liberal political theorists. Walzer argues that where philosophers have traditionally described morality in terms of thin accounts that act as the foundation for a set of beliefs on which individual cultures then build their own ethical superstructures, they instead ought to think of morality as "thick from the beginning, culturally integrated, fully resonant, and revealing itself thinly only on special occasions, when moral language is turned to specific purposes."[67] For Walzer, moral minimums do not exist alone, nor can maximal morality be pared down to just the minimums, since the very act of paring down is an expression of maximal morality. Moral minimums can serve a purpose—for example, as the consensus on a set of standards by which all societies should abide: "negative injunctions, most likely, rules against murder, deceit, torture, oppression, and tyranny"[68] derived from common responses to a number of issues by a wide variety of cultures. However, such standards will only be coherent and expressible in a morally maximal language.

As Walzer describes moral minimums, they provide a way of translating "common, garden variety justice"[69] so that one group of persons can identify with another group of persons who are fighting against injustice, albeit across two vocabularies that are only expressible in morally maximal terms. These groups do not identify with each other through appeals to a shared theory or epistemology from which each group might derive common morals. Instead, one group appeals directly to either the experiences or the sympathies of the other group. So understood, an appeal to moral minimums is not an act of derivation but an act of imagination.

Two points are worth reiterating here. First, Walzer explicitly refuses to isolate thick accounts of morality from the thin ones demanded by most liberal conceptions of publicly accessible moral language. As such, a thin account on its own cannot stand against a thick one as a basis for judgment. Second, and more important, Walzer can be read as arguing that thin accounts of morality are only useful *because* they arise out of thick ones. One might argue that only accounts that are sufficiently thick to cope with the moral complexity of our world— which is to say, quite thick accounts indeed—can give birth to helpful thin accounts. Read this way, religious traditions and their morally thick languages do not *inhibit* public discourse but are vital in helping *constitute* it.

If Walzer's description of the relation between thick and thin moral languages is compelling, it follows that religious languages, as thick moral languages, might provide important contributions to debates about public concerns. Moreover, they might do so precisely as *religious* languages. Therefore, persons who use these languages not only do not have to separate out their religious from their secular reasons but ought not to do so. Thus, a Reformed theologian ought to carry his or her Reformed perspective into debates about capital punishment and express that perspective in all its religious fullness. This certainly does not mandate that the state is compelled to make decisions based on that perspective, any more than it ought to make decisions about capital punishment based on the morally thick languages of any other group of persons. It does, however, suggest that a religious perspective like the one I have laid out is no less likely to prove valuable in discerning answers to the problems with capital punishment than any other perspective and that it cannot be dismissed simply because it is religious.

The foregoing reveals *how* and *why* a Reformed theological perspective can openly engage the debates about capital punishment. It does not, however, suggest *what* that perspective might helpfully contribute to those debates. In the concluding section of this chapter, I will suggest at least one area that a religious perspective may be especially well situated to address.

A. CAPITAL PUNISHMENT AS RITUAL SACRIFICE

Recall Walter Berns's argument that part of what it means to be human is to express anger over injustice and that the means by which we express that anger must, in some cases, involve executing those who perpetrate such injustices. Parting ways with death penalty advocates who continue to categorize capital punishment as a form of deterrence, Berns recognizes and applauds the retributive impetus specifically. In setting up his arguments around anger and desire for revenge, Berns therein touches on an often-overlooked piece of the capital punishment debate: that the broad public support the death penalty enjoys is driven, at least in part, by social anger at the condemned. Moreover, any attempt to abolish capital punishment must somehow account for that anger. In an age in which debates about the death penalty have tended to occur at theoretical and abstract levels, Berns brings us back to Earth, reminding us of our genuine motives and, in the process, that capital punishment is really about real people who are really being killed.

Recently, several studies have attempted to address capital punishment at precisely these levels. Rather than ignoring anger and revenge, they start with a recognition of the way anger and revenge actually function within the establishment of capital punishment. In 1995, James McBride used Stanford literary theorist Rene Girard's conception of originary violence and scapegoating to analyze the death penalty.[70] McBride argues that capital punishment as it is currently practiced in the United States cannot be understood apart from a theory of religion that begins with the premise that the desire for revenge is, at its core, deeply religious. This desire must be satisfied, lest it explode out of the general population in a frenzied religious rage. Therefore, the purpose of the death penalty is not that it "deters criminals from acts of violence . . . but that capital punishment deters law-abiding citizens from vigilantism."[71] If this is the case, argues McBride, then capital punishment actually functions as a religious activity and is therefore unconstitutional under the First Amendment's prohibition of establishing religion.

While McBride's analysis is thought-provoking, it will probably not prove convincing to anyone who does not subscribe to Girard's theory of the relation of violence and religion. Compelling as Girard's thought may be, many reasonable people might disagree with Girard and, therefore, with McBride.

In 2000, however, Brian K. Smith brought the relationship of religion and capital punishment to the fore again, in this instance shorn of the Girardian substructure that undergirds McBride's thought. Functioning as a sociologist of religion, Smith proposes to examine "whether, in the practice and ideology surrounding capital punishment, modern executions in the United States are comparable to the ideology and practice of those traditional religious rituals that have been deemed 'sacrifices.'"[72]

Smith compares modern executions to religious sacrifices at three levels. First, he highlights the degree to which modern executions are ritualized. Setting aside the question of whether these rituals are religious in some way, Smith traces out the formalized, rule-bound, and repeatable qualities of current state executions. "[T]he ceremonial last meal, the administration of last rites, the last words of the victim, the covering of the head of the prisoner before death, the protection of the identity of the executioner, and the dispersal of responsibility for the death [as well as] the concern to ritualize time, to mark it off and to heighten each and every moment of the process"[73] all mark the degree to which modern executions proceed along a ritualized pattern of actions. If ritual is "the creation of a controlled environment where the variables (i.e., the accidents) of ordinary life may be displaced,"[74] then executions are clearly rituals.

Second, Smith argues that "the selection, depiction, and role of the victim in both capital punishment cases and in traditional forms of religious sacrifice also seem comparable in several respects."[75] Like McBride, Smith turns to Girard at this point. Unlike McBride, however, he is more specifically interested in Girard's development of a cultural anthropological perspective than in Girard's theory of originary violence per se; indeed, other cultural anthropologists might have served Smith just as well (one thinks, e.g., of Mary Douglas's work in this regard).[76] By simultaneously moving Girard away from the center of his argument and relying on the less controversial aspects of Girard's theory, Smith avoids the difficulty that McBride faced—namely, convincing people of both the validity of Girard's theory and also his application of that theory to capital punishment. As a sociologist, Smith can first observe that "[c]apital punishment seems to be freighted with more symbolic than rational purport. The deterrence question, which is fundamentally about the functional utility of capital punishment and its rational effects, seems not to be the point among the populace at large"[77] and then ask why this might be the case without inextricably wedding himself to a single large theory.

Finally, Smith argues that "by comparing modern executions to sacrifice we can understand better why this issue is so hotly debated and contested in the United States."[78] To the extent that religious language and ideologies may be close to or at the heart of the debate over capital punishment, it may not be resolvable at the level of rational argument, since such language and ideology typically involve extrarational belief structures and "largely unspoken and perhaps even subconscious"[79] categories and modes of and motives for behavior.

As Smith explicitly states, his point in setting up the comparison between modern executions and human sacrifice is not to favor one side of the debate over another. Instead, it is to offer a way of viewing capital punishment that may explain not only its continued existence but its popularity within the American public as well as the vehemence and intransigence of the debates over it. If Smith's hypothesis is in any way compelling, it ought to lead us to further investigations about whether capital punishment actually functions as a religious ritual in the United States. Moreover, if Smith's hypothesis is correct, its answers to previously vexing questions may be vital for the public to address as it makes sense of the United States' involvement with the death penalty.

Regardless of whether one thinks Smith's hypothesis is compelling or correct, pursuing it mandates that we think about the way religion functions in society, in specific acts of capital punishment, and in popular support for the death penalty. Who better to pursue such thoughts than those persons who are most familiar with religion and ritual? Who better to pursue such thoughts than theologians and philosophers of religion? Smith's work suggests that those who can think in religious terms may be especially well placed—perhaps even uniquely placed—to make sense of what happens when the United States chooses to execute its prisoners. And given not only the importance of the moral questions that capital punishment raises but also the controversy that surrounds it, hearing from religious thinkers may turn out to be critical to move us out of the current set of impasses that characterize debates about capital punishment.

I certainly do not mean to say that only Christians can make such a contribution. Christians, Jews, Muslims, Buddhists—theologians of all faiths may make an important contribution to the debates. Nor do I mean to say that only those who oppose the death penalty can make such a contribution. Theologians of differing opinions might make contributions. It is simply to say that when the public engages in discourse over capital punishment, it might be important for religious thinkers to function as religious thinkers in those conversations. I would hope, though, that Christian theologians would enter this discourse not only to help us all make sense of capital punishment but to work for its abolition as well. That seems to me to be the only conclusion that the gospel of Jesus Christ will allow—which is sufficient reason for anyone who confesses that Jesus is Lord to act.

CHAPTER 7

Is Capital Punishment Wrong?

Jacob J. Vellenga

The church at large is giving serious thought to capital punishment. Church councils and denominational assemblies are making strong pronouncements against it. We are hearing such arguments as: "Capital punishment brutalizes society by cheapening life." "Capital punishment is morally indefensible." "Capital punishment is no deterrent to murder." "Capital punishment makes it impossible to rehabilitate the criminal."

But many of us are convinced that the church should not meddle with capital punishment. Church members should be strong in supporting good legislation, militant against wrong laws, opposed to weak and partial law enforcement. But we should be sure that what we endorse or what we oppose is intimately related to the common good, the benefit to society, the establishment of justice, and the upholding of high moral and ethical standards.

There is a good reason for saying that opposition to capital punishment is not for the common good but sides with evil; shows more regard for the criminal than the victim of the crime; weakens justice and encourages murder; is not based on Scripture but on a vague philosophical system that makes a fetish of the idea that the taking of life is wrong, under every circumstance; and fails to distinguish adequately between killing and murder, between punishment and crime.

Capital punishment is a controversial issue upon which good people are divided, both having high motives in their respective convictions. But capital punishment should not be classified with social evils like segregation, racketeering, liquor traffic, and gambling.

Those favoring capital punishment are not to be stigmatized as heartless, vengeful, and lacking in mercy, but are to be respected as advocating that which is the best for society as a whole. When we stand for the common good, we must of necessity be strongly opposed to that behavior which is contrary to the common good.

I. Old Testament on Capital Punishment

From time immemorial the conviction of good society has been that life is sacred, and he who violates the sacredness of life through murder must pay the supreme penalty. This ancient belief is well expressed in Scripture: "Only you shall not eat flesh with its life, that is, its blood. For your lifeblood I will surely require a reckoning; of every beast I will require it and of man; of every man's brother I will require the life of man. Whoever sheds the blood of man, by man shall his blood be shed; for God made man in his own image."[1] Life is sacred. He who violates the law must pay the supreme penalty, just because life is sacred. Life is sacred since God made man in His image. There is a distinction here between murder and penalty.

Many who oppose capital punishment make a strong argument out of the Sixth Commandment: "Thou shalt not kill."[2] But they fail to note the commentary on that Commandment which follows: "Whoever strikes a man so that he dies shall be put to death. . . . If a man willfully attacks another to kill him treacherously, you shall take him from my altar that he may die."[3] It is faulty exegesis to take a verse of Scripture out of its context and interpret it without regard to its qualifying words.

The Exodus reference is not the only one referring to capital punishment. In Leviticus 24:17 we read: "He who kills a man shall be put to death." Numbers 35:30–34 goes into more detail on the subject:

> If any one kills a person, the murderer shall be put to death on the evidence of witnesses; but no person shall put to death on the testimony of one witness. Moreover you shall accept no ransom for the life of a murderer who is guilty of death; but he shall be put to death. . . . You shall not thus pollute the land in which you live; for blood pollutes the land, and no expiation can be made for the land, for the blood that is shed in it, except by the blood of him who shed it. You shall not defile the land in which you live, in the midst of which I dwell; for I the Lord dwell in the midst of the people of Israel.[4]

Deuteronomy 19:4–6, 10, distinguishes between accidental killing and willfull murder:

> If any one kills his neighbor unintentionally without having been at enmity with him in time past . . . he may flee to one of these cities

[cities of refuge] and save his life; lest the avenger of blood in hot anger pursue the manslayer and overtake him, because the way is long, and wound him mortally, though the man did not deserve to die, since he was not at enmity with his neighbor in time past . . . lest innocent blood be shed in your land which the Lord your God gives you for an inheritance, and so the guilt of bloodshed be upon you.

The cry of the prophets against social evils was not only directed against discrimination of the poor, and the oppression of widows and orphans, but primarily against laxness in the administration of justice. They were opposed to the laws being flouted and criminals not being punished. A vivid expression of the prophet's attitude is recorded in Isaiah:

Justice is turned back, and righteousness stands afar off; for truth has fallen in the public squares, and uprightness cannot enter. . . . The Lord saw it and it displeased him that there was no justice. He saw that there was no man, and wondered that there was no one to intervene; then his own arm brought him victory, and his righteousness upheld him. He put on righteousness as a breastplate, and a helmet of salvation upon his head; he put on garments of vengeance for clothing and wrapped himself in a fury as a mantle. According to their deeds, so will he repay, wrath to his adversaries, requital to his enemies.[5]

II. New Testament on Capital Punishment

The teachings of the New Testament are in harmony with the Old Testament. Christ came to fulfill the law, not to destroy the basic principles of law and order, righteousness and justice. In Matthew 5:17–20, we read: "Think not that I have come to abolish the law and the prophets; I have come not to abolish them but to fulfill them. For truly, I say to you, till heaven and earth pass away, not an iota, not a dot, will pass from the law until all is accomplished. . . . For I tell you, unless your righteousness exceeds that of the scribes and Pharisees, you will never enter the kingdom of heaven."

Then Christ speaks of hate and murder: "You have heard that it was said to the men of old, 'You shall not kill; and whoever kills shall be liable to judgment [capital punishment].' But I say to you that everyone who is angry with his brother shall be liable to judgment [capital punishment]."[6] It is evident that Jesus was not condemning the established law of capital punishment, but was actually saying that hate deserved capital punishment. Jesus was not advocating doing away with capital punishment but urging his followers to live above the law so that law and punishment could not touch them. To live above the law is not the same as abrogating it.

The church, the Body of Christ, has enough to do to evangelize and educate society to live above the law and positively to influence society to high and noble living by maintaining a wide margin between right and wrong. The early Christians did not meddle with laws against wrongdoing. Paul expresses this attitude in his letter to the Romans: "Therefore, he who resists the authorities resists what God has appointed, and those who resist will incur judgment. For rulers are not a terror to good conduct, but to bad . . . for he is God's servant for your good. But if you do wrong, be afraid, for he does not bear the sword in vain; he is the servant of God to execute his wrath on the wrongdoer."[7]

The early Christians suffered many injustices and were victims of inhuman treatment. Many became martyrs because of their faith. Consequently, they were often tempted to take the law in their own hands. But Paul cautioned them: "Beloved, never avenge yourselves, but leave it to the wrath of God for it is written, 'Vengeance is mine, I will repay, says the Lord.' No, 'if your enemy is hungry, feed him; if he is thirsty, give him drink; for by so doing you will heap burning coals upon his head.'"[8]

There is not a hint of indication in the New Testament that laws should be changed to make it lenient for the wrongdoer. Rather, the whole trend is that the church leave matters of justice and law enforcement to the government in power. "Let every person be subject to the governing authorities. For there is no authority except from God, and those that exist have been instituted by God."[9] Note the juxtaposition of love to enemies with a healthy respect for government. The Christian fellowship is not to take law in its own hands, for God has government in his economy in order to take care of matters of justice.

Jesus' words on loving one's enemies, turning the other cheek, and walking the second mile were not propaganda to change jurisprudence, but they were meant to establish a new society not merely made up of law-abiding citizens but those who lived a life higher than the law, so that stealing, adultery, and murder would become inoperative, but not annulled. The law of love, also called the law of liberty, was not presented to do away with the natural laws of society, but to inaugurate a new concept of law written on the heart where the mainsprings of action are born. The church is ever to strive for superior law and order, not to advocate a lower order that makes wrongdoing less culpable.

Love and mercy have no stability without agreement on basic justice and fair play. Mercy always infers a tacit recognition that justice and rightness are to be expected. Lowering the standards of justice is never to be a substitute for the concept of mercy. The Holy God does not show mercy contrary to his righteousness but in harmony with it. This is why the awful Cross was necessary and righteous Christ had to hang on it. This is why God's redemption is always conditioned by one's heart attitude. There is no forgiveness for anyone who is unforgiving. "Forgive us our debts, as we forgive our debtors."[10] Here is no mercy for anyone who will not be merciful. "Blessed are the merciful for they shall obtain mercy."[11] There is striking similarity to these verses in Psalm 18:25–26: "With the loyal thou dost show thyself loyal; with the blameless man thou dost show thyself blameless; with the pure thou dost show thyself pure; and with the crooked thou dost show thyself perverse."

Professor C. S. Lewis in his book *Reflections on the Psalms* deals with the difficult subject of the spirit of hatred which is in some of the psalms. He points out that these hatreds had a good motivation.

> Such hatreds are the kind of thing that cruelty and injustice, by a sort of natural law, produce. . . . Not to receive it at all—not even to be tempted to resentment—to accept it as the most ordinary thing in the world—argues a terrifying insensibility. Thus the absence of anger, especially that sort of anger which we call indignation, can, in my opinon, be a most alarming symptom. . . . If the Jews cursed more bitterly than the Pagans this was, I think, at least in part because they took right and wrong more seriously.

Vindictiveness is a sin, but only because a sense of justice has gotten out of hand. The check on revenge must be in the careful and exact administering of justice by society's government. This is the clear teaching of Scripture in both the Old and New Testaments. The church and individual Christians should be active in their witness to the Gospel of love and forgiveness and ever lead people to the high law of love of God and our neighbors as ourselves; but meanwhile wherever and whenever God's love and mercy are rejected, as in crime, natural law and order must prevail, not as extraneous to redemption but as part of the whole scope of God's dealings with man.

The argument that capital punishment rules out the possibility of repentance for crime is unrealistic. If a wanton killer does not repent when the sentence of death is upon him, he certainly will not repent if he has twenty to fifty years of life imprisonment ahead of him.

We, who are supposed to be Christian, make too much of physical life. Jesus said, "And do not fear those who kill the body but cannot kill the soul; rather fear him who can destroy both soul and body in hell."[12] Laxness in law tends to send both soul and body to hell. It is more than a pious remark when a judge says to the condemned criminal: "And may God have mercy on your soul." The sentence of death on a killer is more redemptive than the tendency to excuse his crime as no worse than grand larceny.

It is significant that when Jesus voluntarily went the way of the Cross he chose the capital punishment of his day as his instrument to save the world. And when he gave redemption to the repentant thief he did not save him from capital punishment but gave him Paradise instead, which was far better. We see again that mercy and forgiveness are something different than being excused from wrongdoing.

No one can deny that the execution of a murderer is a horrible spectacle. But we must not forget that murder is more horrible. The supreme penalty should be exacted only after the guilt is established beyond the shadow of a doubt and only for wanton, willful, premeditated murder. But the law of capital punishment must stand, no matter how often a jury recommends mercy. The law of capital punishment must stand as a silent but powerful witness to the sacredness of God-given life. Words are not enough to show that life is sacred. Active justice must be administered when the sacredness of life is violated.

It is recognized that this essay will only impress those who are convinced that the Scriptures of the Old and New Testament are the supreme authority of faith and practice. If one accepts the authority of Scripture, then the issue of capital punishment must be decided on what Scripture actually teaches and not on the popular, naturalistic ideas of sociology and penology that prevail today. One generation's thinking is not enough to comprehend the implications of the age-old problem of murder. We need the best thinking of the ages on how best to deal with crime and punishment. We need the Word of God to guide us.

CHAPTER 8

Deliverance from the Vicious Cycles of Murder

Glen H. Stassen

More values shape our ethics of the death penalty than we often realize. To get hold of the variables that shape us, I want to employ a holistic method—a social theory model of ethics—with input from social theorist Talcott Parsons and ethicist Ralph Potter at Harvard, philosopher Stephen Toulmin at the University of California–Los Angeles, and my own research on the cognitive processing of foreign policy decision makers. This is not the place to discuss the model extensively.[1] Suffice it to say that its purpose is antireductionistic; it seeks to counter the reduction of ethics only to moral principles of "ought." People not only act ethically or unethically on the basis of the moral principles they hold but also are powerfully influenced by other dimensions of their character. An adequate ethical method needs a more holistic understanding of what is involved in our not only having an ethical position on an issue but actually putting it into practice. Following Parsons and Potter, the model has four dimensions: *style of reasoning* about moral oughts; the *basic convictions* that moral oughts are grounded on; the *basic passions, loyalties, and interests* that drive us; and the *perception grids* through which we understand our social context for being and acting.

Within each of those dimensions, the model identifies several key variables that most powerfully shape our ethics. Key variables shaping the ethics of the death penalty are *loyalties to victims*, perceptions of *threat to society* and of *means of social change*, basic convictions about *love and justice* and about *God's character*, and basic convictions about the *mission of the church or religious community* in distinction from the secular culture's ethic.

I. Loyalties to Victims and Their Families

When you talk with the families of victims of homicide, you discover complex and powerful emotions that pull people apart. The aunt and uncle of a friend of mine hoped to resolve their sense of shock and disbelief, grief, disempowerment, endangerment, anger, and resentment by going to the trial and, when that did not help, going to the execution. It, too, did not help. They are still being eaten up by those passions, especially the feeling of disempowered resentment. My friend says resentment is eating them alive. The murder is claiming these family members as victims also.

> Victimization usually triggers feelings of extreme fear and vulnerability. Guilt, self-blame, myriad questions come with it. So does tremendous anger—anger at the offender but also anger at oneself, at the system, at one's loved ones, even at God. A sense of isolation and disconnection from friends and families is common. One may come to doubt everything and everyone he or she has believed in. The experience affects most areas of life—work, play, sleep, marriage—leaving one isolated, full of doubt, questioning his or her own memories, perceptions, and interpretations. Unnerving dreams, unfathomable mood swings, overwhelming and seemingly unending grief, an oscillation between emotional numbness and emotional overload.[2]

For healing one dimension of the problem, I recommend five books on the process of forgiveness. Lewis Smedes's *Forgive and Forget: Healing the Hurts We Don't Deserve* is highly readable and has helped hundreds of thousands to be healed of deep hurts.[3] David Augsburger's *Caring Enough to Forgive* is equally readable and helpful.[4] Miroslav Volf's *Exclusion and Embrace* is a theologically profound discussion based in part on Volf's struggle as a Croatian to forgive Serbs in the deep historical struggle over identity.[5] Donald Shriver's *An Ethic for Enemies* is a beautifully written assessment of forgiveness as important not only for individual relations but for peace between nations and racial groups.[6] L. Gregory Jones's *Embodying Forgiveness* is a fairly dense theological discussion of the issues in the other books.[7]

II. Perceptions of Threat to Society and of Means of Social Change

Another dimension of the problem, however, is the sense of powerlessness. Many persons push for the death penalty because they hope it does something effective about murder or about what is wrong with our society. The problem, however, is that the death penalty is an empty solution. Many good statistical studies have been carried out to seek to determine the effectiveness of the death penalty to deter murder and reduce the murder rate. They find that the death penalty does not decrease the number of murders and may in fact increase them. This is because when the government puts someone to death, it teaches dramatically that sometimes it is right to put someone to death. Just as homicide rates increase inside a nation when that nation goes to war against another nation, so also when a state puts someone to death. The homicide rate tends to increase in that region in the next few months. Government's example of killing decreases respect for the value of life and is sometimes emulated. On the other hand, there may also be some deterrent effect. The net effect from these two factors is a slight increase in murders, but not enough to be statistically certain.[8]

Not only is the death penalty an empty solution, an ineffective effort. Worse, it diverts loyalties and passions away from solutions that are effective. It is like trying to cure pneumonia by bloodletting instead of antibiotics. Once people realize what does work to prevent homicides and reduce the murder rate, they can be empowered to work to support those actions. This may be the best cure for the sense of disempowerment that victims' families experience. Examples are Mothers against Drunk Driving and the Million Moms March against Gun Violence. Joining a group like this not only is effective in combating homicide but gives group support and thus helps cure the sense of isolation. Then the victim will not have died in vain; his or her death will have strengthened effective efforts to prevent more such violence.

Extensive social science literature exists on studies of what does work to reduce homicides. I can give only a brief summary of results here. (My website gives a more extensive summary and leads into further literature: www.fuller. edu/sot/faculty/stassen. There see "just peacemaking theory—Parkridge Bulletin.")

Social science research is convincing. I believe that the following actions are effective in reducing homicide. I base this opinion not simply on a few studies but on a broad survey of very many studies, many of which test the results of other studies so that the results are cumulative.

Boycotts of TV shows that portray violence favorably. In the words of one commentator, "according to the American Psychological Association task force report on television and American society . . . by the time the average child . . . who watches 2 to 4 hours of television each day finishes elementary school, he or she will have witnessed at least 8,000 murders and more than 100,000 other acts of violence on television."[9] This is powerful conditioning.

Studies indicate that "exposure to media violence at a young age can have lasting, long-life negative consequences. If aggressive habits are learned early in life, they may form the foundation for later antisocial behavior." One research team "concluded that early viewing of violence on television stimulates aggression and that early aggression is a statistical precursor to later criminal behavior. . . . Their analyses indicate that approximately 10 percent of the variability in later criminal behavior can be attributed to television violence."[10]

The most important initiative parents can take, and that they can teach children to take, is to boycott TV shows that especially influence people to be violent. These are shows in which violence or its perpetrators are portrayed favorably or its destructive effects are masked or hidden.

Early training in conflict resolution. Research results indicate that "most violent events are preceded by escalation from verbal conflict through insults and threats" and that teaching people to interrupt escalation by mediation and conflict resolution is effective and lasting if they are taught in the early grades. They are much less effective if not taught until high school, after habitual responses to conflict have been formed and reinforced by years of practice.[11] It is all the more effective to teach conflict resolution and talking things through even earlier in life, in the family, rather than parents relying on physical dominance and bodily punishment. "Research on maltreated children and adolescents clearly shows that in interactions with their parents, these children receive less verbal interaction, less approval, less instruction, less shared play . . . and less reasoning during conflict situations. Similarly research on violent adolescents shows" that their relationships have low amounts of positive emotional expression and communication. This parallels research on attachment, which indicates that *warmth and sensitivity by the mother* produces secure attachments and positive child behaviors and adjustment. Furthermore, "what young people value more than anything else are relationships. They want good interpersonal ties and they want to be loved. The contest isn't even close."[12]

Job training and job availability. Relative economic deprivation is a major cause of homicides. "The national homicide rate has peaked twice in this century; each peak was followed by a decline. The first peak was in the early 1930s," during the Great Depression. After 1934, as jobs and real income steadily improved, "the rate then fell for the next thirty years, to reach a low in the early 1960s." When the post-Vietnam stagnation hit, the homicide rate began to increase in 1973 until it hit something of a peak in 1980–83 and a higher one in about 1989, during the period when job-providing and job-training programs were being canceled, real income of workers and of the poor was declining, and income was being shifted to the wealthy, so that the ratio of income of the wealthy to worker income doubled. Then in the 1990s, as real wages and employment steadily improved, the homicide rate declined steadily each year.[13]

Coalitions to strengthen neighborhood and community organization. When middle- and working-class families move out of ghetto areas, community networks of informal social control break down. The remaining residents experience high levels of family disruption via divorce, desertion, female-headed families, and the breakdown of community networks of informal social control. Furthermore, "in studies of neighborhood rates of violent crime, measures of the density of multi-unit housing, residential mobility, and the prevalence of disrupted family structures generally accounted for more variation than did measures of poverty and income inequality."[14] The antidote is to strengthen neighborhood and community organization. In Boston, the Ten Point Coalition was organized by pastors of small community-based churches that committed themselves to do youth evangelism in the streets where the youth were; to establish mentoring and tutoring relationships; to help in preparing for jobs and finding jobs; to involve youth in church youth activities and community service. Churches adopted gangs and showed they cared. Besides the Ten Point Coalition, Operation Cease Fire tackles youth firearm violence with a wide range of coalition partners. The police introduced decentralized neighborhood policing to address local problems. In the Youth Service Providers Network, police officers refer at-risk youngsters to social workers hired by the Boys & Girls Clubs of Boston (under contract from the police). The social workers help youngsters and their families locate programs tailored to the needs of the youth, such as counseling and treatment, academic services, recreational programs, jobs, and other programs. The result: 1997 homicide victimization among those twenty-four years of age and younger has fallen 70 percent from the means of 1991–95; and among juveniles, firearm homicides were down 90 percent in 1997 compared to 1990.

Good police–community relations that help catch criminals efficiently. Again, consider the Boston example just noted. Better police–community relations, so police get more help and are more effective in catching criminals, does help decrease homicides. But punitive justice, as in increasing length of sentences and putting juveniles in adult prisons, does not help. Evidence suggests that putting juveniles in adult prisons results in a "much lower probability of any treatment while in custody, and an increased risk of subsequent offending when released."[15] Putting people in jail for longer sentences does not cure the widespread culture of violence, but a public health approach like the Los Angeles Coalition does work effectively to reduce violence.[16]

Reducing handgun availability. "The most thoroughly evaluated restriction on gun use is the 1974 Bartley–Fox Amendment, which expanded Massachusetts licensing procedures and mandated a one-year sentence for unlicensed carrying of firearms in public." An "extensive evaluation that compared statewide trends with trends in neighboring states demonstrated rather clearly that the law decreased gun use in assaults and robberies and also decreased gun homicides during the two-year evaluation period."[17] The 1977 Washington, D.C., law that prohibited handgun ownership by virtually everyone except police officers, security guards, and previous gun owners was evaluated in three studies. "During periods of vig-orous enforcement, the D.C. law did reduce the rates of gun robbery, assault, and homicide during the three years following implementation. The effect was espe-cially strong for homicides arising from disputes among family members and ac-quaintances." There were "decreases of about one-fourth in D.C. gun homicides and suicides immediately after passage of the law. The effect . . . was not mirrored by trends in D.C. nongun homicides or suicides, or in gun homicides or suicides in nearby suburban areas that were not subject to the law."[18]

Drug rehabilitation programs. Research indicates that investment in drug re-habilitation programs is effective, regardless of the different methods of rehabil-itation used.

Evangelism and spiritual support for youth. Recall the Ten Point Coalition de-scribed earlier. "[W]hat has been lacking in the professional discourse about vi-olence prevention . . . is an examination of the role of spirituality. . . . Adults who work with youth need to step away from attempting to be objective about value-laden issues. . . . When adults avoid mentioning their values by being objective about value-laden issues, they may inadvertently teach *valuelessness* as the pri-mary value. . . . An adolescent's understanding of his or her own spiritual belief system makes a unique contribution to that person's development on both per-sonal and societal levels."[19] Thomas and Carver's review of literature "shows that religious involvement and commitment are consistently related to increases in the abilities and skills required for adequate functioning in society and to de-creases in the likelihood of participating in activities that are devalued in soci-ety." They also show that a faith–mentor relationship can help the youth set prosocial goals. Williams of the Search Institute concludes that "when parents act in ways that are congruent with their stated beliefs and provide a warm, sup-portive atmosphere for their youth at home and in the church, youth are likely to develop values similar to those of their parents." He emphasizes that "both *dis-cussion* of values and *consistent demonstration* are necessary for this transfer to oc-cur."[20] (See the Search Institute research for a strong emphasis on spirituality and resilience.[21])

It may seem odd that in a theological chapter I should begin by emphasiz-ing what works to deliver us from homicides. But I think this approach is im-portant for families of victims and people who identify with victims. There is a second, more complex reason: I seek to do theological ethics from the perspec-tive of the Lordship of Jesus Christ. I believe Jesus teaches directly on the ques-tion of murder, and his way is the way of transforming initiatives that prevent murder, not the way of retaliation. Let me explain—though very succinctly in the short space I have.

Like many other Christian ethicists, I have been greatly influenced by his-tories of the enormous earthquake in the middle of the last century—the takeover of Germany by a racist and militarist dictator, Adolf Hitler, and the resulting Holocaust and world war that killed fifty-six million people. Many Christians in Germany had been taught to take their ethics from secular sources or general philosophical principles, and they were sucked in by the ideology of fascism. It was a powerful demonstration that that general way of doing ethics was a pernicious failure. The Christians who resisted the evil of the Nazis were those of the Confessing Church movement, which produced the Barmen Confession in 1934. It rejected approaches that take their bearing from some general ethic or some secular source, or some leader like Hitler. Its first two articles stated:

1. "Jesus Christ, as he is attested for us in Holy Scripture, is the one Word of God which we have to hear and which we have to trust and obey in life and in death.

    We reject the false doctrine, as though the Church could and would have to acknowledge as a source of its proclamation, apart from and besides this one Word of God, still other events and powers, figures and truths, as God's revelation.
2. As Jesus Christ is God's assurance of the forgiveness of all our sins, so in the same way and with the same seriousness he is also God's mighty claim upon our whole life . . . .

    We reject the false doctrine, as though there were areas of our life in which we would not belong to Jesus Christ, but to other lords.

David Gushee has written an incisive historical study of those Christians who rescued Jews from the Holocaust while most others did nothing or even cheered the Nazis on. He found that rescuers were likely to have an ethic of following Jesus concretely.[22] I believe I have seen analogous results in the civil rights movement, peacemaking struggles, and other tests of Christian ethics in the laboratory of history. So I advocate a theological ethic in the Barmen tradition. I begin with Jesus' teaching, concretely, and with Jesus' crucifixion, the cross.

But an erroneous assumption has crept into the thought of many that for some reason if one does ethics that pays attention to Jesus, one probably retreats from the world. This is odd, since Jesus was so clearly in the prophetic tradition, confronting the problems of his day and showing the way of repentance and deliverance. He went to Jerusalem to confront the powers and authorities, and they understood that well enough to plot to kill him. In this brief space, I want to begin to show that Jesus' teaching is highly relevant both to social science and to philosophical discussions of the death penalty.

In the Sermon on the Mount (especially Mt 5:21–48), Jesus names vicious cycles of anger, retaliation, and hate that lead to murder. He teaches transforming initiatives that deliver us from those vicious cycles—a way of deliverance and prevention. I shall show some of that later. I believe there is a clear connection between Jesus' way of transforming initiatives and the preventive initiatives that I have named earlier.[23] The way of Jesus is not simply to condemn the death penalty, and certainly not to affirm it, but to point us to initiatives that deliver us from our culture of violence. A Christian theological approach to the death penalty should be not simply to have a position pro or con but to take effective preventive initiatives. That is what I have pointed to so far.

III. Basic Convictions about Relating Love and Justice

A central question in debates about the death penalty is how to relate the Lordship of Jesus Christ and his teachings of love and compassion to one's view of justice in society. Some Christians fence them off from each other and systematically do not let Jesus influence their understanding of justice. Others begin with Jesus Christ as Lord, with a commitment to be followers of Jesus, and deny that there is some other Lord we should follow instead. Therefore, for Christian ethics, justice should not be defined without guidance from Jesus.

As I analyze the many theological-ethical essays on the death penalty, I am struck by how this distinction divides the opponents from the proponents, if and when they do pay attention to biblical teaching. Those who oppose the death penalty take the Lordship of Christ as key for their interpretation of scripture.

A. TAKING JESUS CHRIST AS KEY FOR INTERPRETING SCRIPTURE

Matthew 5:2ff. is about preventing murder. Jesus begins with the traditional teaching in the Ten Commandments, "Thou shall not murder" (Ex 20:13). The commandment does not prescribe any specific penalty, and neither does Jesus. He says, "You have heard that it was said . . . 'whoever murders will be subject to judgment,'" but avoids saying what the judgment will be. He avoids quoting Old Testament passages that prescribe the death penalty as Exodus 21:12 and Numbers 35:16ff. do—though in both passages providing sanctuary for the killer to which he may flee if it was not premeditated—or as Leviticus 24:17 does. We see here a thoroughly consistent pattern in Jesus' teaching: he often quotes part of an Old Testament teaching but always omits the parts of the teaching that teach violence or nationalistic triumph against enemies. He avoids the violent parts of the teaching so systematically that it cannot be happenstance.

Then Jesus points to vicious cycles that cause murder: continuing in anger and calling the brother fool (Mt 5:22). He is diagnosing, naming vicious cycles that lead to murder. As the way of deliverance from these causes of murder, he commands we make peace with the one who is angry with us, or is accusing us (5:23–26).

Similarly, Matthew 5:38*ff.* is about preventing violent retaliation. Notice what Jesus omits in citing the three Old Testament passages that speak of retaliation: Exodus 21:24 and Deuteronomy 19:21 both say "life for life, eye for eye, tooth for tooth." Leviticus 24:20*ff.* says "eye for eye, tooth for tooth . . . and he who kills a man shall be put to death." Jesus omits "life for life" and "shall be put to death." Again, we see the pattern: he quotes Old Testament passages but specifically omits the part that advocates the violent solution of taking the life of the murderer.

Then Jesus names the vicious cycle as violent or revengeful retaliation (5:39). The Greek here is usually translated simply as "resistance," but it means specifically violent, retaliating, revengeful resistance.[24] Jesus repeatedly resisted evil, but never by violent, revengeful retaliation. Revengeful retaliation leads to more killing. Rather than advocating the death penalty, Jesus names retaliation as a vicious cycle that leads to killing. He commands four transforming initiatives that deliver us from the vicious cycle of retaliation and instead into transforming initiatives that prevent killing (5:39–42). Jesus here opposes taking a life as retribution for a life. The Apostle Paul also refers to this teaching of Jesus in Romans 12:19: "Beloved, never avenge yourselves, but leave it to the wrath of God; for it is written, 'Vengeance is mine, I will repay, says the Lord.'"

The third teaching is Matthew 5:43*ff.* Here Jesus teaches that our response to our enemy is to be love, not hate. We are to give enemies love and prayer, not hate and vengeance, as God gives sun and rain to God's enemies.

If our only teaching on the death penalty were Jesus' teaching in the Sermon on the Mount, if we forgot about all other customs, habits, practices, and teachings, and sought to follow only Jesus as Lord, we would surely say followers of Jesus are not people who seek retaliation by taking life for life, but instead they seek ways of deliverance from such vicious cycles that add more killing to killing.

Jesus was confronted by the death penalty directly in John 8.[25] The scribes and Pharisees made a woman stand before him to be judged. "Teacher, this woman was caught in the very act of adultery. In the law Moses commanded us to stone such women. Now what do you say? . . . They said this to test him, so that they might have some charge to bring against him." If he had replied flatly, "God's mercy forbids the death penalty," they could charge him with the blasphemy of disagreeing with Moses and stone him. Jesus answered, "Let anyone among you who is without sin throw the first stone." When they heard this, they went away one by one, and Jesus was left with the woman standing before him.

He said to her, "Woman, where are they? Has no one condemned you?" She said, "No one, sir." Jesus said, "Neither do I condemn you. Go your way, and from now on do not sin again."

Raymond E. Brown, the widely respected scholar on the Gospel of John, praises the beauty of this story with "its succinct expression of the mercy of Jesus." He concludes, "The delicate balance between the justice of Jesus in not condoning the sin and his mercy in forgiving the sinner is one of the great gospel lessons."[26] Jesus releases the woman from the death penalty, but he admonishes her not to commit adultery again.

Bishop Lowell Erdahl says the accusers "were convicted of their own sins and accepted the fact that there is no justification for the vengeful execution of one sinner by another. If all Christians had followed their example, there would have been no blessing of capital punishment in Christian history." He points out that this fits Jesus' consistent character and teaching. "The woman's accusers knew enough about Jesus to expect that he might oppose her execution. We too are not surprised, . . . We would be shocked if Jesus had said, ' . . . Go ahead and kill this wretched sinner.'"[27]

B. TAKING GENESIS 9:6 AS KEY FOR INTERPRETING SCRIPTURE

Those who favor the death penalty and argue for it biblically regularly base their argument not on Jesus but on what is for them the key passage—Genesis 9:6: "Whoever sheds the blood of man, by man (shall or will) his blood be shed."[28] They take this verse to be a legal command, as part of God's covenant with Noah, and argue it is obligatory on all humankind. It is universal and not limited to Israel; all killers must be put to death—"whoever sheds the blood of man." Actually, they avoid what their own logic indicates: that this passage should be interpreted as universal law; that all killers—including accidental killing, manslaughter, defensive killing, killing with mitigating factors, or killing in war—should be put to death. Instead, they advocate only what would correspond with legal practice in the United States. Thus, U.S. secular practice shapes their biblical interpretation and their understanding of *justice* as obligatory retribution, and they do not let Jesus' teaching add or change anything in their understanding of justice.

They then interpret the rest of the Bible in terms of their interpretation of this passage. They usually overlook the examples of murderers whom God did not want killed: Cain is the father of all murderers. He murders his own brother, out of premeditated jealousy. "Then the Lord put a mark on Cain, so that no one who found him would kill him" (Gn 4:14–15). Similarly, Moses is seen in the act of murder and, instead of receiving the death penalty, is chosen by God to deliver his people from slavery (Ex 2:1*ff.*). David not only committed adultery with the beautiful Bathsheba while she was still having her period (twice deserving the death penalty by Mosaic law) but then had Bathsheba's husband killed (a third time deserving it). Nathan the prophet confronted him, saying, "You have smitten Uriah the Hittite with the sword, and have taken his wife to be your wife." David confessed, saying, "'I have sinned against the Lord.' And Nathan said to David, 'The Lord has put away your sin; you shall not die'" (2 Sm 11–12). Accused of adultery, Tamar admitted she had committed adultery with her father-in-law, an act specifically requiring the death penalty. She was allowed to live, and her adultery produced an ancestor of David and Jesus (Gn 38; Mt 1:3; Lk 3:33). The book of Hosea tells how Gomer committed adultery repeatedly, and Hosea, not without great pain, forgave her, welcoming her back into their covenant relationship. In this forgiveness Hosea saw the picture of God's will for forgiveness of his people for their whoring with other gods.

Proponents of the death penalty also bypass the fact that the first five books of the Bible also command the death penalty for ownership of an animal that kills people (Ex 21:14, 29); kidnapping (Ex 21:16; Dt 24:7); false witness against a defendant in a death penalty trial (Dt 18:18–21); a stubborn son's disobedience to his mother or father or a child's cursing or striking a parent (Ex 21:15, 17; Lv 20:9; Dt 21:18–21); incest, adultery, bestiality, homosexual practice, rape, and sex during a woman's menstrual period (Ex 22:19; Dt 22:21, 24, 25; Lv 20:10–14; 21:18); for witchcraft and sorcery (Ex 22:18; Lv 20:27); Sabbath breaking (Ex 31:14; Nm 15:32–36); child sacrifice (Lv 21:9); false claim to be a prophet (Dt 13:5, 10); blasphemy (Lv 24:15–16); and a non-Levite who enters the sacred place (Nm 1:51, 3:10, 38; 18:7). They either overlook these other crimes that require the death penalty or say that "Jesus freed believers from the judicial authority of the Law," but not from Genesis 9:6, which differs from all the other Old Testament law.[29]

Genesis 9:6 also dominates their interpretation of Jesus. In three ways they teach that Jesus adds nothing to the conclusion they have reached from Genesis 9:6. First, Jesus "said nothing specific about the death penalty."[30] In addition, Jesus "centers on personal responses . . . the attitude more than the act." Finally, Jesus' teachings are not "directed to the governmental authorities of his day." H. Wayne House then draws a threefold conclusion: Jesus "[a] accepted it [the death penalty] [b] as a valid exercise of governmental authority and [c] a proper part of the Mosaic Code."[31] The same author who two pages previously said Jesus said nothing specific about the death penalty draws this conclusion that Jesus accepted the death penalty. Moreover, the same author who one page earlier said Jesus did not direct his teachings to governmental authority draws the conclusion that Jesus accepted it "as a valid exercise of governmental authority."

The conclusion that Jesus affirmed the Mosaic Code is drawn by the same author who three pages earlier said Jesus freed believers from the Mosaic Code.

What surely appears thoroughly contradictory is explained by House's effort to maintain Genesis 9:6 as the universally valid law for present-day practice by governments. First he fences Jesus off from saying anything that might suggest a different insight or interpretation of Genesis 9:6. Then he turns Jesus into confirming Genesis 9:6 as law for governments. Jesus is not allowed to say anything that could differ from his interpretation of Genesis 9:6, but he is allowed to confirm that interpretation. Nothing positive is learned from Jesus. Thus, Jacob Vellenga establishes the Old Testament's teaching on the basis of Genesis 9:6 and the law of retaliation passages in the Old Testament, and then he states the New Testament adds nothing new: "The teachings of the New Testament are in harmony with the Old Testament." And Jesus' teachings "did not meddle with laws," did not say "that laws should be changed. . . . Rather, the whole trend is that the church leave matters of justice and law enforcement to the government in power. . . . Natural law and order must prevail." Thus, in two ways Vellenga fences Jesus off from saying anything new about the subject and says Christians must instead let the secular or natural government set our standards. Similarly, House fences off Jesus' teaching regarding the death penalty for the woman caught in adultery: he says it applies only to adultery, not murder. Furthermore, it is only about forgiveness, not about the death penalty. He concludes, "Capital punishment never became an issue for Jesus."[32]

By contrast, opponents of the death penalty take Jesus' teaching as the key and interpret Genesis through Jesus. Jesus echoes Genesis 9:6 when his disciple takes up his sword to cut off the ear of one of the soldiers coming to arrest Jesus. Jesus tells him to put up the sword: "All who take the sword, by the sword will die" (Mt 26:52, literal translation). Here Jesus gives the teaching not as a *command* that every sword user should be given the death penalty but as a *proverb* that predicts the likely consequence of relying on the sword: you are likely to end up getting killed.[33]

Indeed, careful examination of Genesis 9:6 by the best biblical scholars likewise indicates that it seems to be a proverb, not a command. Claus Westermann is the Old Testament scholar who has written what is widely recognized as the most authoritative commentary on Genesis. He explains that the embarrassment is that scholars do not agree whether this is a legal penalty, a prophetic admonition, or a proverb.[34] This is because it is based on ancient practices of revenge and still shows some influence from ancient traditional laws of revenge, but in Genesis it clearly has the form of a proverb and not a law. In other words, it does not command the death penalty but gives wise advice based on likely consequence of your action: if you kill someone, you will end up being killed, just as Jesus interpreted it (Mt 26:52). Both Westermann in his commentary on Genesis (467–68) and Hagner in his commentary on Matthew see Jesus as here interpreting the meaning of Genesis 9:6. And Jesus clearly interprets it as a proverb, teaching "the generally true principle that violence begets violence."[35] This fits the fact that nowhere in the Old Testament is there a case in which what seem like prescriptions of the death penalty for various offences were carried out by a criminal law system. They function like statements of ideals, saying, "These offences are really serious." They are taught in the priestly parts of the Bible that put things in sacrificial language and are never acted on as laws.[36]

John Howard Yoder also interprets Genesis 9:6 from the perspective of Jesus as Lord. He sees Genesis 9:6 as having its meaning both as a proverb and as a sacrificial expiation of sin. A very strong anthropological argument has also been made that the death penalty functions in U.S. society as a religious ritual of scapegoating or sacrificial expiation of sin.[37] And Yoder argues that Jesus' death is the once-for-all sacrifice for expiating sin. If we believe Jesus has paid the penalty of death for sin as representative of all of us, eternally, then it is pagan to insist that others pay the penalty of death as expiation for sin again, as if Jesus had not already done this once for all, for all of us. "Christians begin to deny their Lord when they admit that there are certain realms of life in which it would be inappropriate to bring Christ's rule to bear. Of course, non-Christians will insist that we should keep our *religion* out of the way of their *politics*. But the reason for that is not that Jesus has nothing to do with the public realm; it is that they want nothing to do with Jesus as Lord. . . . What we believe about Christ must apply to all our behavior, no matter how many of our neighbors remain unconvinced."[38] We should test "all things for whether they are compatible with Christ (1 Cor 12:1–3, 1 Jn 4:1–2)." "Our interest should . . . be to discern, *in the midst* of this complexity, what the Christian gospel has to say." The culmination of the gospel story "is that the Cross of Christ puts an end to sacrifice for sin. . . . The Epistle to the Hebrews takes as its central theme the way the death of Christ is the end of all sacrifice."[39]

IV. Jesus' Crucifixion Was Unjust

Jesus confronted the death penalty one other time. He himself was the victim of the death penalty. Crucifixion was state terrorism. It was given only to slaves and rebels. They were tortured and then killed in full public view to terrorize other slaves and potential rebels, to coerce them into docility in spite of unjust imperialism.

Proponents and opponents of the death penalty also interpret the cross differently. Opponents say Jesus' trial was unjust, and the plots by the authorities to have Jesus crucified were sinful. One part of the work of the cross in atoning for sin is its disclosure of the depth of sin in humankind: we killed God's Son. As Jesus himself taught:

> The tenants took his servants and beat one, killed another, and stoned another. Again he sent other servants, more than the first; and they did the same to them. Afterward he sent his son to them saying, "They will respect my son." But when the tenants saw the son, they said to themselves, "This is the heir; come, let us kill him and have the inheritance." And they took him and cast him out of the vineyard, and killed him.

Jesus then predicts judgment: "The chief priest and the Pharisees . . . perceived that he was speaking about them" (Mt 21:37ff). All are represented in the crucifixion—Christians, Jews, and Gentiles. Jesus was betrayed by a Christian disciple, denied by the chief disciple, and deserted by all the disciples. Jewish authorities demanded his crucifixion; Gentile Roman authority and soldiers crucified him. The gospel accounts make clear that Jesus was falsely accused and unjustly condemned (e.g., Jn 18:38). Ironically, Barabbas, who was actually guilty of the crime of insurrection that Jesus was falsely accused of, was freed in Jesus' place. This was clearly unjust. Jesus said from the cross, "Father, forgive them, for they know not what they do" (Lk 23:34). The reason they needed forgiveness is that they were doing terrible wrong. The New Testament witness is that God used their wrong to bring forgiveness and redemption, and this includes the disclosure of their sin, their injustice. The crucifixion was unjust. Christians who remember their Lord was unjustly and cruelly given the death penalty have a hard time being enthusiastic about imposing the death penalty on others. The cross on Christian churches signifies not that we should advocate more crosses for others, but that we all need mercy. We are not to seek vengeance (Rom 12:19). We are to love our enemies and seek to do mercy (Lk 6:35–36).

Proponents of the death penalty argue that the cross shows Jesus approved of the death penalty. Hence, they usually avoid mentioning that this death penalty was sinful, a terrible wrong, unjust. Surely if asked, they would agree that the cross discloses human sin, but when they seek to justify the death penalty, surprisingly, they argue that the cross discloses the death penalty was and is right. To make this argument, William H. Baker refers to a conversation in John 19 between Jesus and the Roman colonial government authority, Pilate, as Pilate is about to sentence Jesus to death. Pilate asserts he has authority to crucify Jesus. Jesus answers, "You would have no authority over me, unless it had been given you from above; for this reason he who delivered me up to you has the greater sin."[40]

Jesus is clearly saying that what Pilate is doing is wrong, a sin, and that delivering Jesus to Pilate to be crucified is a greater sin. Yet Baker argues this shows

God approves of the death penalty and governmental authority to order the death penalty. Baker and Pilate both *think* the conversation is about Pilate's secular authority. But read in context, John is clearly showing Pilate misunderstands the nature of the topic.

The theme of ironic misunderstanding runs throughout the Gospel of John, and this passage is a good example. Jesus is speaking of God's power to bring about the hour of redemption, when he will die so that we will live. Pilate plays a role in *this* death only because God is allowing it. And he misses the point, thinking the topic is his power to command legions and kill people. Jesus is speaking of God's gift of redemption, not engaging in a discussion of whether God approves of the death penalty.[41] As Raymond Brown says, "No one can take Jesus' life from him; he alone has power to lay it down. However, now Jesus has voluntarily entered 'the hour' appointed by his Father (12:37) when he will lay down his life. In the context of 'the hour' therefore, the Father has permitted men to have power over Jesus' life."[42]

The gospels make clear that the governmental authorities acted unjustly in sentencing Jesus to death. By no means do they teach that giving the death penalty to Jesus was justice. Baker himself admits "that Pilate allowed a miscarriage of justice to take place." To use this miscarriage of justice as an argument for the rightness of the death penalty suggests desperation to find a New Testament rationalization for a preconceived interest.

V. All Death Penalties in the New Testament Are Unjust

Baker makes a similar argument concerning Acts 25:11, although he admits the passage does not have "the express purpose of teaching anything about the subject of capital punishment."[43] The point of the passage is the Apostle Paul's defense against accusers who want to kill him. Paul says, "*[I]f* I . . . have committed anything worthy of death." He knows he does not deserve the death penalty. The authorities twice explicitly declare they have found that "he had done nothing deserving of death" (Acts 25:25; 26:31).

What Paul says is not that he approves of the death penalty but that he is not afraid to die. This is a point he makes elsewhere, writing, for example, "For me to live is Christ and to die is gain" (Phil 1:21). His defense tells how he had once voted for the death penalty for Christians as blasphemers and how he has now repented for his action (Acts 26:10*ff.*).

An individual passage should not be (mis)interpreted as an isolated prooftext. It should be understood in the context of the many instances of the death penalty mentioned in the New Testament. Otherwise it is too easy to read one's own bias into a single passage. The New Testament describes ten instances of the death penalty being threatened or imposed. Nowhere do the followers of Jesus advocate the death penalty. Every instance of the death penalty mentioned by the New Testament is clearly presented as an injustice: the beheading of John the Baptist (Mt 14:9*ff.*); the crucifixion of Jesus (Jn 18:38 and Lk 23:34); the stoning of Stephen (Acts 7); the stoning of other Christians (Mt 21:35; 23:37; Jn 10:31*f.*; Acts 14:5); Herod's killing of James (Acts 12:2); the threatened death penalty for Paul (Acts 25:11, 25:25, and 26:31); the persecution of Christians in the Book of Revelation. Furthermore, in the Letter to Philemon, Paul writes persuasively "to save the life of the escaped slave, Onesimus, who under Roman law was liable to execution."[44]

What we have seen so far must not be understood as setting the New Testament versus the Old Testament, or the Hebrew Scriptures. The direction of the Old Testament moves from the ancient practice of the death penalty toward its abolition. We have seen that Genesis 9:6 is a proverb, not a command. Even those who interpret it as a command agree that it is based on the creation of every human person in the image of God and that it strongly asserts God's command that we value the sacredness of the life of all human persons. This underlying sacredness of each human person based on God's creation of all persons in God's image works through the Old Testament to oppose actually carrying out a death penalty. This explains why what look like commands in the first five books of the Bible for giving death to great varieties of offenses actually do not function as commands to kill offenders but as commands that these offenses be taken with great seriousness. Not only is it true that there is no example of the death penalty being carried out for adultery in the whole Hebrew Scriptures, but not one of the books of the prophets or the later writings like Psalms, Proverbs, Ecclesiastes, or Job affirms the death penalty for any offense whatsoever.

The Mishnah is the record of authoritative oral interpretation of the written law of the Torah by the Jewish religious leaders from about 200 B.C.E. to about 200 C.E. It makes the death penalty almost impossible. It requires twenty-three judges to reach agreement in death penalty trials. It requires at least two eye witnesses to the commission of the crime (Dt 19:15), which "prevented many cases from being brought to trial at all, since such crimes are seldom committed with so much publicity." The testimony of near relatives, women, slaves, or people with a bad reputation is not admitted. "It is clear that with such a procedure conviction in capital cases was next to impossible, and that this was the intention of the framers of the rules is equally plain."[45] The Mishnah brands a court that executes one man in seven years as "ruinous" or "destructive." It summarizes the teaching of authoritative rabbis: "Rabbi Eliezar ben Azariah says: Or one in even seventy years. Rabbi Tarfon and Rabbi Akiba say: Had we been in the Sanhedrin none would ever have been put to death. Rabbi Simeon ben Gamaliel says: [for the Sanhedrin to put someone to death] would have multiplied the shedders of blood in Israel."[46] Modern Israel has never had capital punishment, which shows something of present-day Jewish understanding of the meaning of the tradition. The American Jewish Congress says, "[C]apital punishment degrades and brutalizes the society which practices it; and . . . is cruel, unjust, and incompatible with the dignity and self respect of men."

VI. Romans 13 Concerns the Authority to Tax, Not the Death Penalty

Some have argued that the authority of the Roman government to impose the death penalty is specifically endorsed in Romans 13: "Let every person be subject to the governing authorities. . . . For the authority does not bear the sword in vain. . . . For the same reason you also pay taxes, for the authorities are God's servants, busy with this very thing. Pay to all what is due them—taxes to whom taxes are due, revenue to whom revenue is due."

A team of well-known New Testament scholars in Germany wrote the authoritative study of this passage.[47] They point out that Paul is not teaching about the death penalty. Paul is urging his readers to pay their taxes and not to participate in a rebellion against Nero's new tax. An insurrection against taxes had recently occurred and had gotten Christians kicked out of Rome, including Priscilla and Aquilla. Another one was brewing. The Greek in Romans 13:4 translated *sword* (*machairan*) names the symbol of authority carried by the police who accompanied tax collectors. Paul was urging Christians to make peace, pay Nero's new tax, and not rebel. He was not arguing for the death penalty. He was arguing *against* the violence of insurrection.

Once again, those who oppose the death penalty see Jesus' way as the norm for interpreting this passage. They say its context is Romans 12:14–21 and 13:8–10, which are Jesus' teachings about love and peacemaking as reported by Paul. Jesus' way is the key to the interpretation. Romans 13:1–7 is about owing nothing but love to our enemies, including the Roman government, and making peace with them; it is not about approving of killing people.

Throughout the theological/biblical discussions, it is striking how the theological proponents of the death penalty consistently fence Jesus' teachings and cross off so we learn nothing new from him. The underlying question is whether Jesus really is Lord or whether Christians should compartmentalize his teachings where they do not apply to the real world and then in practice substitute some other loyalty.

VII. Justice and God's Character

Jesus cared greatly about injustice. How could he do otherwise, since as Christians maintain, he was the revelation of God in our midst, and the Scriptures are clear about God's caring for justice, mentioning the two Hebrew and two Greek words for justice 1,060 times? God's character is to care deeply about justice and mercy. Jesus said it: "Woe to you scribes and Pharisees! For you tithe mint and dill and cumin, and have neglected the weightier matters of the law, justice and mercy and faithfulness. . . . You blind guides, straining out a gnat and swallowing a camel!" (Mt 23:23). "You tithe mint and rue and every herb, and neglect justice and the love of God" (Lk 20:42).

I count forty-eight times in the gospels when Jesus confronts the powers and authorities of his day for their injustice. There were four dimensions to the injustice that Jesus focused on: the injustice of violence to persons, the injustice of excluding outcasts from community, injustice to the poor and powerless, and oppression by the powerful.

I count twenty-one times—not counting parallels—when Jesus confronts the authorities for the injustice of violence and makes clear his mission is nonviolent. For example, Matthew 23:3ff.: "You are sons of those who murdered the prophets. Therefore I send you prophets and wise men and scribes, some of whom you will kill and crucify, and some you will scourge in your synagogues and persecute from town to town, that upon you may come all the righteous blood shed on earth." In Luke 13:3ff., the Pharisees warn Jesus that Herod wants to kill him. He says, "Go and tell that fox, I cast out demons and perform cures today and tomorrow, and the third day I finish. Nevertheless, I must go on, for it cannot be that a prophet should perish away from Jerusalem." In Matthew 23:37ff., Jesus mourns, "O Jerusalem, Jerusalem, killing the prophets and stoning those who are sent to you! How often would I have gathered your children together as a hen gathers her brood under her wings, and you would not!"

Jesus' understanding of justice knew the crucial importance of being included in community and not being cast out. We think of the poignant story of the cripple at the Pool of Bethsaida, who had no one to move him into the water when it was troubled. He lacked community and so was powerless. Jesus healed him and restored him to community. Often Jesus healed outcasts and brought them back into society by touching those whom no one in that society would touch, such as lepers or women with a flow of blood or the dead, or their touching him, and he regularly instructed the healed person to submit to the priests, so as to be certified as includable in community or to go back to their community. Furthermore, he connected healing and forgiveness (Mk 2:5–9), where forgiveness meant not only wiping out past sins but embracing in community.

I count eighteen passages in which Jesus, in the tradition of the prophets, confronts the wealthy, and the religiopolitical powers and authorities who were in cahoots with the wealthy, for cheating the poor, for hoarding for themselves and committing injustice against the poor, and calls for justice for the poor. For example, Mark 7:9*ff*.: "You have a fine way of rejecting the commandment of God in order to keep your tradition. For Moses said, 'Honor your father and your mother. . . .' But you say that if anyone tells father or mother 'Whatever support you might have had from me is Corban,' . . . then you no longer permit doing anything for a father or a mother." Luke 12:21 speaks of the rich man who builds bigger barns to hoard all his grain and his goods—" So is he who lays up treasure for himself, and is not rich toward God." Consider also Luke 16:14*f*.: "The Pharisees, who were lovers of money, . . . scoffed at him. But he said to them, 'You are those who justify yourselves before men, but God knows your hearts.'" See also Mark 10:17–21: "Go sell what you own and give the money to the poor"; Mark 10:25: "It is easier for a camel to go through the eye of a needle than for someone who is rich to enter the kingdom of God"; and Mark 12:40: "Beware of the scribes . . . who devour widows' houses and for the sake of appearance say long prayers. They will receive the greater condemnation." Consider, too, Matthew 23:25: "Woe to you, scribes and Pharisees, hypocrites! For you clean the outside of the cup and the plate, but inside they are full of greed and self-indulgence." Also see Luke 7:24–30, where Jesus praised John the Baptist as God's prophet to warn them and said, by contrast, "those who are gorgeously apparelled and live in luxury are in kings' courts. . . . All the people who heard this . . . acknowledged the justice of God, because they had been baptized with John's baptism."[48]

Finally, Jesus repeatedly confronts those who dominate others. Some teachings fit in more than one category; I count nineteen passages in this category of domination and lording it over others—for example, Mark 10:42: "Those who are supposed to rule over the Gentiles lord it over them, and their great men exercise authority over them. But . . . whoever would be great among you must be your servant." In Luke 6:9*ff*., Jesus asks the scribes and Pharisees, Is it lawful on the Sabbath to do good or to do harm, to save life or to destroy it? And he healed the man with the withered arm. "But they were filled with fury and discussed with one another what they might do to Jesus." Matthew 5:10–11: Blessed are you when they revile you and persecute you and utter all kinds of evil against you falsely on my account, for so they persecuted the prophets who were before you." Matthew 23:1*ff*.: "The scribes and the Pharisees [Lk 20 says lawyers] . . . preach, but do not practice. They bind heavy burdens, hard to bear, and lay them on people's shoulders; but they themselves will not lift a finger to help them . . . and they love the place of honor at feasts." Mark 12:38: "Beware of the scribes, who like to walk around in long robes, and to be greeted with respect in the marketplaces, and to have the best seats in the synagogues and places of honor at Banquets. They devour widows' houses and for the sake of appearance say long prayers."[49]

The death penalty is certainly violence against the person who receives it. Even those writers who advocate it show their discomfort at its violence and seek to develop some rational justifying such violence. The death penalty is certainly given disproportionately to the poor. Even Walter Berns, in his book advocating the death penalty, admits that no affluent person has ever been given the death penalty in U.S. history.[50] The death penalty certainly embodies and enacts the injustice of excluding outcasts from community. It has been given disproportionately to African Americans and most disproportionately when their alleged victims were white. Its symbol is the exclusion of solitary confinement and the permanent exclusion from society of enforced death. It has been administered by the powers and authorities that have economic and political standing against those who lack it. In recent years, more people have been executed in Texas than in all other states combined. And more people have been executed in the county in which the city of Houston is located than in all other counties of Texas combined. Surely there is strong evidence of arbitrary imposition of this violent penalty by one or a few particular power structures. Once the death penalty has been administered, those powers and authorities cannot repent for errors and redeem those errors. Nor, once they have been executed, can those executed live to come to a time of repentance and redemption. Nothing redeems the death penalty from its violation of all four dimensions of justice that Jesus concentrated on in his confrontations of the powers and authorities in his day. As the gospels make clear, it was his confrontation of the powers of his day for this kind of injustice that brought about their decision to administer the death penalty to him. This is the epitome of injustice. It is sin.

Once we begin to see the richness of Jesus' teaching, we see how powerfully it connects with the sense of justice expressed in many other chapters in this book—and how clearly it rejects other understandings. This is why in public discourse, Christians may translate or express their Christian commitments in public language such as human rights, human dignity, justice for the powerless, preventive practices, opposition to scapegoating, and injustice that defends special privilege. I learn especially from the political theorist Michael Walzer, with his opposition to domination and his advocacy of mutual respect and the rights of life, liberty, and community. But the key is to be clear what loyalty to Jesus as Lord means, so the public language is as faithful a translation as possible and not the replacement of Jesus by an ideology that serves causes of authoritarianism, domination, special privilege, self-righteousness, and scapegoating.

VIII. How We Got This Way, and How We Can Find Our Way Again

James Megivern, professor of religion at the University of North Carolina–Wilmington, has written the history of the church's entanglement with the death penalty and then its recovery. Gradually one realizes the story is like a parable, a penetrating view into something much deeper. It reveals how the church departed from following Jesus and instead turned to other sources for its ethics. It also points the way for the church to recover its way and its life.[51]

As the church became entangled in the death penalty, it got entangled in other kinds of ethics besides following Jesus. It shifted from an ethics of arguing from Jesus' teachings to an ethics of arguing from secular analogies, Roman law, and philosophical principles—none of which took Jesus as normative or even mentioned Jesus' teachings.

The church started out opposing the death penalty and citing Jesus in its ethics. By contrast, Clement of Alexandria, notorious for accommodating the gospel to the culture, writing after 202 C.E., was "the first Christian writer to provide theoretical grounds for the justification of capital punishment. In this he . . . appealed to a rather questionable medical analogy [a doctor amputates a diseased organ if it threatens the body] rather than to anything of specifically Christian inspiration."[52] None of the passages Megivern quotes that justify the death penalty from the third century through the twelfth century even hints at any reference to the teachings of Jesus. The Bavarian Law, from the end of the seventh century, stands out brightly in contrast, citing Jesus in the Lord's Prayer: "For the Lord has said: 'The one who forgives will be forgiven.'" This beam of light from Jesus in the midst of the darkness led the Bavarian Law to be exceptional in clearly opposing the death penalty.[53]

Persecution of heretics was the main source of entanglement with the death penalty. After Constantine became the first pro-Christian emperor in 312, "emperors passed at least sixty-six decrees against Christian heretics, and another twenty-five laws 'against paganism in all its forms.' The violence of the age was extraordinary, and Christians were becoming more and more deeply involved in it. . . . Once Christianity had become the state religion, the imperial values articulated in Roman law tended to overwhelm gospel values." At first Augustine flatly rejected force against heretics. What caused him to change his mind by 408 was his persecution of the Donatists. The Theodosian Code, a decade after Augustine's death, has "120 laws that assign death as the proper penalty; they are the accumulation of all the earlier laws of the pagan empire plus the even stricter ones enacted over the previous century for the express purpose of 'Christianizing' the empire." In 785, a law prescribed death for eating meat during the Lenten season, burning a cadaver in pagan style instead of burying it in a Christian cemetery, and going into hiding rather than presenting oneself for baptism! "The whole issue of heresy thus continued to provoke the entanglement of churchmen ever more deeply in the use of the death penalty." Megivern gives bloody examples of horrible violence by popes and the Inquisition, giving the death penalty to thousands and thousands of Christians, including Jan Hus, Joan of Arc, Albigensians, Waldensians, Franciscans, Knights Templars, and Anabaptists. "This bizarre chapter in church history demonstrated that once the earlier tendencies were allowed to prevail, the trend toward diminished regard for human life led to the acceptance of violence and bloodshed as ordinary conduct . . . even at the heart of the church." In the witch craze of the seventeenth century, two hundred thousand to five hundred thousand or more were executed across Europe and the New World.[54]

In the fourth through eleventh centuries, the almost-uninterrupted waging of war, including the crusades, was the second source of entanglement, causing Christian values to be ignored. It was "a time of appalling ignorance and immorality among the clergy, who were thus unable to communicate much of the gospel to the masses." There were pogroms against Jews, crusades killing them. "And the brutality of the wars of religion from 1559 to 1648, climaxing in the Thirty Years War [which killed one-third of Europe's population]."[55]

Another way the topic was shifted away from Jesus' way was discussing the death penalty as a question of the authority of the state rather than of the right to life: German Lutheran theologians Paul Althaus and Walter Künneth epitomized this shift, arguing on the basis of the authority of the state as a God-given institution (Rom 13:4) to justify the death penalty.

Megivern credits the Waldensians six centuries before the Enlightenment, John Wycliff, numerous Anabaptist leaders, and others of the radical reformation, as well as the Quakers, as "motivated by their understanding of the gospel to criticize the death penalty as an ungodly abomination long before the abolitionist movements began." Their objections designated it a violation of "the 'hard sayings' of Christ, which gave priority to love and forgiveness and rejected all revenge-taking among his followers. . . . Reform movements desirous of translating and distributing the Bible to the common people were invariably the wellsprings. . . . There was no way to escape the impact of the Sermon on the Mount."[56]

Megivern also tells the story of the church's disentanglement from the death penalty since Pope John XXIII in *Pacem in Terris* insisted, "Every human being is a person. . . . By virtue of this he has rights and duties of his own . . . which are *universal, inviolable, and inalienable*." The right to life is given by the Creator and intrinsic to human personhood. Some may argue that in unusual cases it can be *overridden* by some greater need, such as saving the lives of others, but it can never be *forfeited*. "Is talk about the 'image of God' or the 'sanctity of life' anything more than rhetoric if it can be 'forfeited' and go up in smoke upon a person's misconduct?" The Italian Franciscan theologian Gino Concetti wrote in *L'Osservatore Romano*:

> In light of the word of God, and thus of faith, life—all human life—is sacred and untouchable. No matter how heinous the crimes . . . the criminal does not lose his fundamental right to life, for it is primordial, inviolable and inalienable, and thus comes under the power of no one whatsoever. If this right is so absolute, it is because of the image which, at creation, God impressed on human nature itself. No force, no violence, no passion can remove or destroy it. In virtue of this divine image, every human is a person with dignity and rights.

The other key to the church's recovery was its turning again to Jesus' teachings against revenge and violence. His teachings reappear regularly and repeatedly in the churches' ethics during and since the turning against the death penalty.[57]

Now almost all the major Christian denominations have declared their opposition to the death penalty.[58] The same is true of teachers of Christian ethics. Every Christian ethicist but one who responded to my essay "Biblical Teaching on Capital Punishment" at the annual meeting of the Society of Christian Ethics—the professional society of college, university, and seminary Christian ethicists—including the twelve most recent presidents of the society—signed and endorsed the essay.[59] Its argument has influenced the middle part of the present chapter. Church leaders and Christian ethicists who have studied the question widely agree that the death penalty contradicts justice, violates the sacredness of human life, and diverts us from effective ways of preventing murder. I add that it contradicts the Lordship of Jesus Christ.

Part 3

SOCIAL SCIENCE
PERSPECTIVES

CHAPTER 9

Social Science Data and the Death Penalty

UNDERSTANDING THE DEBATE
OVER "A BROKEN SYSTEM"

M. Christine Cagle and J. Michael Martinez

I. A Timeless and Timely Issue

On April 21, 1868, the eminent philosopher and politician John Stuart Mill rose to speak as a contentious bill came before the English Parliament for consideration. In typically eloquent fashion, Mill outlined reasons why Great Britain should not outlaw capital punishment. "Does fining a criminal show want of respect for property or imprisoning him, for personal freedom?" he asked with a rhetorical flourish. "Just as unreasonable is it to think that to take the life of a man who has taken the life of another is to show want regard for human life. We show, on the contrary, most emphatically our regard for it, by the adoption of a rule that he who violates that right in another forfeits it for himself."[1]

Mill's argument that respect for human life is demonstrated, ironically, by depriving capital offenders of their lives as payment for their crimes still resonates with capital punishment supporters more than a century later. Today, if anything, the debate about whether a liberal democracy can allow the state to execute its citizens is as relevant and contentious as it was in Mill's day, as the chapters in this book illustrate. Capital punishment divides policymakers perhaps more than any other public policy issue at the beginning of the twenty-first century. The arguments remain timeless and timely even as the situations change and sources of information and data proliferate.

Mill lived at a time when social science research still was in its infancy; accordingly, he did not have access to the statistical data available to debate participants in later years. One might assume that access to such data would clarify the debate and reveal the strengths and weaknesses in the arguments that have been

141

propounded since antiquity. Unfortunately, data are seldom clear and unequivocal. Depending on the presuppositions and methodologies employed by researchers, social science research on capital punishment can be used to support the arguments advanced by ideologues on both sides of the debate. To illustrate this point in some detail, this chapter will discuss one of the most significant statistical reports on capital punishment in recent years as well as the controversy surrounding its methodology and findings.

Before we turn to the report on flaws in America's capital punishment system, however, it is helpful to consider one highly publicized issue of recent years (and an issue raised in the report): the adequacy, or lack thereof, of defense counsel. According to much social science research, this is one of the most often-cited reasons that capital cases are reversed on appeal. The issue was especially evident in a controversial case that captured the public imagination. On June 22, 2000, at 8:49 P.M., a death row defendant named Gary Graham, alias Shaka Sankofa, became the 135th prisoner to be executed by the state of Texas. In criticizing Graham's execution, death penalty opponents raised the usual issues of morality and the awesome power of the state to impose the ultimate penalty on its citizens. They also raised the issue of the competency of Graham's court-appointed attorney, Ronald G. Mock.[2]

African American civil rights leaders, most notably the Reverend Jesse Jackson and the Reverend Al Sharpton, led the criticism of Mock's dismal performance. Texas Supreme Court Chief Justice Charles Baird captured the opponents' frustration with inadequate defense attorneys when he remarked that he "saw cases where the right to effective counsel was trampled down by lawyers sleeping through trials." In fact, among "Graham's last words before his execution, was that he was a victim of one of the nation's increasing fears: an unjust death penalty system."[3]

This is indeed a major fear shared by many Americans. To be falsely accused and convicted of a capital crime with only meager resources at one's disposal and therefore saddled with an inexperienced, overworked, unprepared attorney—probably a public defender—almost guarantees a conviction. Add to this possible racial prejudice against an African American defendant, and the debate is especially emotionally charged.

Capital punishment opponents found especially fertile ground for their arguments in Graham's case. According to the trial record, Mock failed to call two crucial witnesses and did not present ballistics evidence that might have exonerated the defendant. The defendant was convicted primarily based on the testimony of a single witness who supposedly saw him from thirty to forty feet away through a car windshield. Despite the difficulty in identifying someone under such conditions, Mock did not cast doubt on the witness's testimony, nor did he inform the jury of a defective lineup procedure that all but pointed out the defendant to the witness. Mock's previous record of defending capital offenders was no better, and perhaps a good deal worse. Seven of his twelve previous death row clients had been executed. In the words of one commentator, Mock enjoys "the dubious distinction of having a subsection of the Texas death row unofficially named for him: The Mock wing."[4]

II. The Columbia University Report: "A Broken System"

A. FINDINGS

If the charges leveled against Ronald G. Mock were a singular example of incompetent representation, the legal system might dismiss this tale as an aberration in an otherwise working, and workable, system. Unfortunately, a growing body of data suggests that Mock's performance may not be the rare exception but the standard. In fact, according to a major study published by Columbia University in June 2000, "A Broken System: Error Rates in Capital Cases, 1973–1995," the incompetence of court-appointed defense attorneys may be one of the most common serious errors in capital cases. These errors often are so egregious that the convictions are reversed on appeal. According to the study, the "most common errors prompting a majority of reversals at the state post-conviction state are egregiously incompetent defense lawyers who didn't even look for—and demonstrably missed—important evidence that the defendant was innocent or did not deserve to die (37 percent of state post-conviction reversals); and police or prosecutors (16–19 percent) who did not discover that kind of evidence but suppressed it, again keeping it from the jury."[5]

The study, conducted by James S. Liebman, a professor of law at Columbia University, with assistance from his colleagues Jeffrey Fagan, a visiting professor at Columbia, and Valerie West, a doctoral candidate in sociology at New York University, examined 5,760 death sentences imposed in the United States during the twenty-three years from 1973 to 1995. The authors examined all appeals in death penalty cases (4,578) included in the study at three stages: direct appeals in state court, postconviction review, and federal habeas corpus appeals. In undertaking this exhaustive review, the authors found that their research was the "first statistical study ever undertaken of modern American capital appeals." Moreover, based on their findings, they concluded that "serious error—error substantially undermining the reliability of capital verdicts—has reached epidemic proportions throughout our death penalty system. More than two out of every three capital judgments reversed by the courts during the twenty-three-year study period were found to be seriously flawed."[6]

The Columbia University study began in 1991 at the behest of Senator Joseph F. Biden, a Democrat from Delaware who was serving as chairman of the U.S. Senate Judiciary Committee at the time. Senator Biden asked Liebman to calculate the frequency of errors in federal death penalty appeals when the convictions later were reversed. To his astonishment, Liebman found that data collection was exceedingly difficult because no organization or central clearinghouse had systematically combined information on death penalty cases. He pieced together data from the National Association for the Advancement of Colored People (NAACP) Legal Defense Fund's quarterly death row census as well as traditional legal research through state and federal cases and codes and conversations with death penalty resource centers and local lawyers who handled capital cases. From this initial effort, Liebman began counting cases and compiling his own tally of capital cases containing serious errors.[7]

In 1995, the Columbia researchers expanded their study from simply counting cases and their outcomes to searching for background information that would allow them to delve into the facts and discover why serious errors seemed to be so pervasive. They especially focused on why federal habeas corpus procedures seemed to grant relief so frequently when state appellate courts had declined to do so. In 599 cases at the federal habeas corpus phase of the appeals process, 237—40 percent—were reversed owing to serious error.

The study immediately raised questions, among other things, about the pervasive lack of effective defense counsel in capital cases. Based on the statistical evidence, the authors argued that their findings "demanded some type of judicial reform in the American capital punishment system" because they "show a death penalty system collapsing under the weight of its own mistakes." Anticipating a barrage of criticism from capital punishment supporters, Liebman and his colleagues carefully explained their methodology. They derived a "success rate" by determining the proportion of capital judgments that underwent and passed a three-stage judicial inspection process. Conversely, the proportion of capital judgments overturned when inspected by judges during any of the three stages was the "error rate."[8]

Determining whether an error was "serious" was more problematic. In the authors' judgment, an error was defined as serious when it was prejudicial "either because the defendant has actually shown that it probably affected the outcome of his/her case or because it is the kind of error that almost always has that effect." Moreover, the error must have been properly preserved in the record. If the defendant failed to file appropriate motions in time, did not object to improperly admitted evidence at trial, or did not protect that record through subsequent trial motions, an appeals court generally will not overturn a lower court's rulings absent extenuating circumstances such as the discovery of compelling new evidence. In such cases, the error could not be brought before the appeals court because it was not preserved at trial; therefore, it could not serve as the basis for determining whether a "serious" error occurred. Finally, in the authors' words, "no matter how prejudicial the error, it is only reversible if it is discovered. If it is not discovered [or] the party responsible for it failed to disclose it, reversal will not occur and the error will not be deemed serious."[9]

Based on this definition of serious error, Liebman and his colleagues found numerous defects in the American criminal justice system. For example, state courts dismissed 47 percent of death sentences owing to serious error. Later federal court reviews uncovered serious error in 40 percent of the remaining cases. These high error rates put many defendants in jeopardy of receiving the death penalty in circumstances where death sentences generally have not been imposed in the past. When death penalty cases imposed by state courts were retried, 82 percent resulted in sentences less severe than death. Approximately 7 percent of capital offenders subsequently were found not guilty.

The researchers found that serious error rates were not an anomaly confined to a small time period. In twenty of the twenty-three years covered in the study, serious flaws, such as those found in the Graham case, were commonplace. In slightly more than half the years, the overall rate of serious errors was 60 percent or higher. The national average across all states was 68 percent.

The paramount problem with a high rate of serious errors is that it takes an average of nine years to correct errors in cases in which the error is discovered and subsequently rectified. The time and costs imposed on society—financial, social, political, and legal—are enormous, to say nothing of the terrible burdens borne by victims' families, the families of innocent defendants, the public's faith in the judicial system and, of course, the wrongly accused. Worst of all, in the authors' view, a system rife with serious errors undermines the fundamental purposes generally cited in support of capital punishment—closure, retribution, and deterrence.[10]

Despite the innumerable errors, Liebman also found that executions were rare. Of the 5,760 death sentences imposed in the United States from 1973 to 1995, only 313 (about 5 percent, or one in nineteen) resulted in an execution. State appeals courts reviewed 4,578 cases (79 percent) and dismissed 1,885 (41 percent) owing to serious error. Despite the relative rarity of executions, Liebman and his colleagues expressed concern that serious errors were so common and that 7 percent of defendants were found not guilty of capital crimes during subsequent retrials.[11] Moreover, "when the nation as a whole never executes more than 2.6 percent of its death population a year, the retributive and deterrent credibility of the death penalty is low."[12] An article in the *National Catholic Reporter* echoed this view, claiming that "the large percent of murder convictions being overturned on appeal is one of the most damning pieces of evidence pointing out the need for deep judicial reform."[13]

Although executions in the United States have increased since 1988, this does not mean that reversible errors have been corrected. Instead, the increasingly high execution rate suggests that more people are languishing on death row awaiting execution. "Instead of reflecting improvement in the quality of death sentences under review, the rising number of executions may simply reflect how many more sentences have piled up for review," the study reports. "Even consistently tiny proportions of people being executed because of consistently prodigious error and reversal rates are prompting the number of executions to rise."

Based on these data, the researchers concluded that the American criminal justice system is in serious need of repair. The lengthy time necessary to adjudicate cases, appeal, and ultimately decide the issue is difficult for all parties—victims and their families, the families of the accused, and taxpayers who must finance an increasingly inefficient legal system. In the authors' words, "Given that nearly seven in ten capital judgments have proven to be seriously flawed, and given that four out of five capital cases in which serious error is found turn out on retrial to be more appropriately handled as non-capital cases, it is hard to escape the conclusion that large amounts of resources are being wasted on cases that should never have been capital in the first place."[14]

Aside from efficiency, the inequities of potentially killing persons convicted on the basis of questionable evidence, represented by inadequate defense counsel, and forced to wait for years for exoneration suggest that policymakers should act soon to correct these numerous deficiencies. If they wait until more serious errors occur and the public grows more disillusioned and jaded, the American legal system will continue to suffer. "A Broken System" became not only a systematic study of capital punishment over a twenty-three-year period but a call to action.

B. REACTION

As other chapters in this book attest, the debate over capital punishment has continued across the life of the republic. During the last quarter of the twentieth century especially, researchers began to observe increased public support of the death penalty as citizens became more concerned about the effects of violent crime. A Fox News Survey reported in February 2001 that a substantial majority of the American public supported the death penalty, although the rate declined in the years immediately preceding the survey. Public support stood at 76 percent in May 1997, but it dropped to 67 percent by February 2000. Gallup researchers found the public almost evenly divided when offered the choice between the death penalty and life imprisonment without the possibility of parole as policy options.[15] In a nation like the United States, public attitudes are important in determining whether capital punishment should be used to punish capital offenders. As researcher Steven Stack has argued, "public opinion is frequently used in the debate over establishing and/or extending the deployment of execution in the war against street crime. In the policy debate, many actors contend that in a democratic society public opinion regarding punishment should be respected."[16]

Since they were released in 2000, the findings in the Columbia University study have figured prominently in the ongoing capital punishment debate and have helped shape public opinion and the actions of opinion leaders. Perhaps the most notable opinion leader to cite the Columbia study was Illinois governor George Ryan. In January 2000, Governor Ryan issued a temporary moratorium on executions in his state. Although the governor's actions occurred before the Columbia University study was released, the new information subsequently confirmed Ryan's insight that the state capital punishment system required substantial review. David Urbanek, a spokesman for the governor, remarked that "the study conclusions were not surprising, but only added fuel to the administration's belief that the death penalty system in Illinois had serious problems that were already known."[17]

At a press conference in Chicago, Governor Ryan, a Republican and staunch supporter of capital punishment, explained his reasons for placing the moratorium on executions. "Until I can be sure that everyone sentenced to death in Illinois is truly guilty, until I can be sure with moral certainty that no innocent man or woman is facing a lethal injection," he said, "no one will meet that fate." In addition to the moratorium, the Illinois legislature earmarked $20 million to improve the criminal justice system, and Governor Ryan appointed a committee to study flaws in the system and make recommendations to remedy them.[18]

Illinois became the first state to suspend the death penalty pending an examination of its application and essential fallibility.[19] Ryan did not arrive at his decision lightly. After thirteen high-profile Illinois death row prisoners were exonerated based on new evidence that revealed strong doubt about their convictions, he realized that it was possible that the state might have executed innocent people in the past.[20] Despite the governor's general support for capital punishment, he did not believe in good conscience that he could allow executions to continue if serious errors had been made and might continue to be made. According to one commentator, the governor was a man of high moral principles who saw that "the imposition of the death penalty in his state is so unreliable that it must be halted until the system can be reevaluated for fundamental fairness."[21]

Other death penalty advocates agreed that Governor Ryan had acted appropriately—at least in Illinois. One capital punishment proponent remarked that "the capital punishment system in the state was uniquely awful."[22] Even the governors of Florida and Texas—Jeb Bush and his brother, George W. Bush, respectively—claimed that Governor Ryan's decision was correct, although they were careful to conclude that their own states' records were not nearly as desultory as the Illinois record. They contended "that actions in Illinois are not relevant else-where, because high error rates are unique to Illinois."[23]

Despite the national attention given specifically to Illinois in the wake of Governor Ryan's moratorium, the Columbia University study did not find the state's error rate especially unusual and certainly not unique. The authors found that "Illinois did not produce atypically faulty death sentences. The overall rate of serious error found in Illinois capital sentences (66 percent) is very close—and slightly lower than—the national average of 68 percent."[24] The Columbia researchers cautioned that the low figure in Illinois, in the words of two re-porters from the *St. Louis–Post Dispatch*, "might merely reflect a streamlined ap-peals process that misses mistakes. '[A] lot of people have said Illinois is unique [in its high error rate]. This study shows Illinois right at the national average. What the study calls for is a close look at the death penalty in all states,'" ac-cording to Liebman.[25]

When the study was released, it was unclear whether the Columbia Univer-sity data would compel all states to review their death penalty systems, but the study (along with Governor Ryan's moratorium) certainly focused attention on Illinois. Between 1977, when Illinois reinstated the death penalty, and 2000, 262 capital offenders were executed. During the same time period, the state appellate courts reversed eighty-six capital cases, and other verdicts were overturned in state postconviction hearings or in federal court appeals.[26] Despite this record and Governor Ryan's moratorium, Illinois citizens expressed a desire to "get tough on crime." According to Illinois state senator Carl Hawkins, "[t]he gover-nor and many of us in the legislature and in the public still support the state's death penalty. The same citizens and members want to make sure the process has the integrity it should."[27]

Several states followed Illinois's lead and undertook a review of their death penalty laws after Governor Ryan called attention to the problems in his state.[28] Using the results of the Columbia University study as ammunition, death penalty opponents attacked the flawed bases of the states' capital punishment systems, thereby pushing states to examine their death penalty laws and policies. Anti–death penalty advocates especially objected to errors committed by incom-petent defense lawyers like Ronald Mock. They also voiced concerns about the withholding of "evidence by overzealous police officers and prosecutors."[29]

By late 2000 and early 2001, lawmakers in twenty-four states were debating proposals aimed at ensuring that death row inmates were not executed for crimes they did not commit. According to one commentator, "[t]he bills under consid-eration would create standards for routine DNA testing, ensure competent de-fense counsel in capital cases and impose moratoriums to stop executions of those already sentenced until top-to-bottom reviews of death penalty procedures are done."[30] Also in 2000, six other states joined Illinois in approving studies of their death penalty systems. Thirteen other states proposed halting executions while similar studies were conducted.[31] Both houses of the U.S. Congress, with support from the American Bar Association, began considering legislation to impose a national moratorium on federal and state executions, "pending a review of the reasons why the death business has failed so miserably."[32]

City leaders also began pressuring their state representatives to consider moratoriums on executions. In fact, immediately following Governor Ryan's announcement, the Philadelphia City Council urged the Pennsylvania legislature to issue an execution moratorium.[33] Since mid-1999, Charlotte, North Carolina, became the seventh largest municipality (and the largest in the Carolinas) to pass a resolution calling for a moratorium on executions. In October 2000, the Greensboro, North Carolina, City Council adopted a similar resolution. Twelve other cities around the country—including Atlanta, Baltimore, and San Francisco—adopted death penalty moratoriums around the same time. Although none of the city resolutions carried the force and effect of law, they seemed to represent changing public attitudes about capital punishment. According to one commentator, "[a] quarter-century after the Supreme Court allowed reinstatement of the death penalty, vast numbers of people, including elected officials, are expressing doubt [about] how it is administered."[34]

As one might imagine when a controversial issue takes center stage in a national policy debate, many capital punishment supporters have criticized the Columbia University study and the new trend in execution moratoriums it seems to have supported, if not triggered. Because James S. Liebman is a well-known opponent of capital punishment, his detractors suggest that he may have consciously or unconsciously manipulated the study results.[35] In one high-profile example, Ari Fleischer, a spokesperson for Republican presidential candidate George W. Bush (and later White House press secretary in the Bush administration), attacked the results of the Columbia study. In Fleischer's view, far from highlighting a defective criminal justice system, the report revealed how well the safeguards of the judicial inspection system work. "It is proof that there is an extra level of vigilance and caution in death penalty cases," he said.[36] Later, Fleischer remarked that "people who have their cases overturned are still guilty of something . . . 93 percent of inmates who are retried are convicted later, albeit of a lesser offense."[37]

Other criticisms appeared in periodicals immediately after the Columbia study was released. One common criticism suggested that the methodology that Liebman and company used to calculate the 68 percent national error rate was flawed. Researchers Barry Latzer and James N. G. Cauthen also have studied death penalty error rates over time, and they dispute the findings in the Columbia study. In particular, they claim that the Columbia study provides misleading conclusions because the authors fail to distinguish between conviction rates and sentence reversal rates. Highlighting their ten-year research into capital appeals in twenty-five states, Latzer and Cauthen contend that "a more accurate reversal rate before retrials and rehearings, assuming a significant undercount of the number of death sentences undergoing judicial inspection, was an effective reversal rate that was closer to 43 percent, not 68 percent." Moreover, they argue that the Columbia study's "error rate was based on cases actually reviewed at each of the three stages rather than on all cases available for review at each stage, which significantly overstated the error rate. . . . If the Columbia researchers had used this approach, the error rate would have been 52 percent, but 68 percent because the calculations would be based on error rates for state direct appeal, state post-conviction, and federal habeas corpus cases."[38]

The major deficiency in the Columbia study, according to Latzer and Cauthen, is its hyperbolic tone and overall reliance on inflated statistics.

> In other words, the total capital reversal rate is closer to one of two, not two out of three cases—a high, but substantially more acceptable ratio. Because the 68 percent error rate is inflated, the Columbia researchers were able to assert that their error rate accurately measures the risk that the capital punishment system mistakenly executes those who are not deathworthy. The findings infer that the courts found error in 68 percent of the cases they reviewed, then a 68 percent risk existed that those put to death are wrongfully executed.[39]

Without delving into the reasons for the flawed methodology used by the Columbia researchers in this initial critique—is it sloppy research, or have Liebman and his associates deliberately manipulated the data?—Latzer and Cauthen simply express skepticism in embracing the report's findings. "[A]ny proper assessment of the capital adjudication process must be based on an accurate measure of the appellate reversal rate as well as a full account of the many idiosyncratic features of that process," they conclude. "'A Broken System' provides neither."[40]

In Latzer and Cauthen's opinion, the Columbia researchers are justified in arguing that the nation's capital punishment system should undergo a thorough reexamination. Data that antedate the Columbia study suggest that many parts of the system are in desperate need of repair. Nonetheless, they object to the tone and hyperbolic language in the report, to say nothing of the dramatic title. Is a system genuinely broken when, "[a]fter all the retrials/hearings were complete, for every one hundred death sentences imposed at trial, forty-four death sentences survived the entire judicial gauntlet"?[41] This self-correcting feature seems to characterize a generally workable system that needs to be reformed slightly as opposed to an unworkable, patently biased, broken system that Liebman and his colleagues claim to find.

Another commentator, Jaime Sneider of the *Columbia Daily Spectator*, is not as veiled in his criticisms as Latzer and Cauthen are in their article. Sneider argues that the error rate cited by the Columbia study is deliberately and pointedly misleading. In Sneider's view, the Columbia researchers failed to find a single case in twenty-three years in which an innocent person had been executed. This failure undercuts virtually everything else they conclude about the error rate in death penalty cases.[42] He cites comments from other death penalty researchers— most notably law professor Paul G. Cassell and Massachusetts Institute of Technology management professor Arnold Barnett—who criticize the Liebman study. According to Sneider, these sources disagree with the almost every aspect of the Columbia findings. They especially find the error rate flawed, calling

> the ratio "meaningless" because it does not constitute an error rate as many people had ignorantly assumed. An error rate is computed by dividing the number of innocent persons executed by the total number executed. Reporting how many people were not executed "yields no insight," according to Barnett, simply because it does not necessarily represent a flaw in the system. It instead shows that the system corrected itself, not that any execution was or has been incorrectly performed.[43]

Sneider also argues that the death penalty system not only exhibits few of the flaws identified by Liebman and his associates, but it may have reduced incidents of violent crime in the United States. "During the last ten years, as the number of executions has increased, the number of murders has simultaneously dropped," he writes. Although this does not necessarily translate into a cause-and-effect relationship, it is powerful circumstantial evidence that executions deter would-be offenders from undertaking violent acts. "The most dramatic decline in murders over the last decade has been precisely in those regions that have the most executions. . . . Since 1990, Texas, Oklahoma, Louisiana, and Arkansas have performed half the nation's executions and murder rates in these four states have fallen faster than anywhere else in the country."[44]

Michael Rushford of the Criminal Justice Legal Foundation (CJLF) joins ranks with Sneider in contending that the Columbia study is fundamentally flawed in its methodology and findings. In Rushford's opinion, as in Sneider's, the flaws are not the result of sloppy calculations; they are deliberate, cynical manipulations of the data, stemming from Liebman's liberal political agenda. As a result, the study is a "political document, timed to impact the congressional hearings." After the report is boiled down to its essential elements, the findings— when divorced from the ludicrous "error rate"—do not uncover any new information on executions. Accordingly, the only purpose of the report is to advance the position propagated by anti–death penalty advocates. "It does not show an unreliable or broken system," Rushford argues. "It shows a system successfully obstructed by opponents of capital punishment. The reasons for the rate are far more complex than simplistic assertions that trials are unreasonable."[45]

Rushford categorizes his criticism of the study into five distinct areas. First, he contends that the Columbia researchers rely on archaic, unreliable data in formulating their conclusions. By focusing on cases beginning in 1973, Liebman intentionally skews the results. "The old data makes the study findings suspect because a great many cases were reversed in the 1970s because the Supreme Court was creating a new set of rules for capital punishment and applying them retroactively," Rushford observes. Consequently, the Columbia study classifies cases still undergoing Supreme Court review as containing errors when the errors, if they occurred at all, occurred at the trial stage. In many cases, however, the errors are corrected at the appellate level as reviewing courts remand cases and order retrials.[46]

Similarly, Rushford agrees with Latzer and Cauthen that Liebman's definition of "serious error" is misleading owing to the suspect methodology he uses to calculate the error rate. A "serious error" ought to be one in which the outcome of the case is proximately and materially affected by the error; however, the Columbia study does not confine its definition of "serious error" to this standard. Instead, it defines "serious error" as any error shown by a defendant to have been prejudicial or almost always prejudicial—whether or not that supposed prejudice influenced the verdict. In other words, it is possible that an error occurred in a case, but it did not lead to the imposition of the death penalty because the penalty would have been applied regardless of whether the error occurred. In Rushford's opinion, therefore, Liebman and his colleagues make a "blatantly false statement of the law because the general constitutional standard on appeal is that the prosecution must prove error harmless beyond a reasonable doubt, or else it results in reversal. This includes claims that have nothing whatever to do with the reliability of the verdict, such as Miranda claims and unlawful search claims. It was also the standard for most claims in federal courts for all but the last two years of the study period."[47] The study's failure to distinguish between types of errors is a fatal defect in the reliability of the study results because it mixes different errors and counts them as flaws in the death penalty system even when the error does not involve the death penalty.

The third problem with the Columbia study is far more insidious, in Rushford's view. The researchers deliberately omit data that do not support their anti-death penalty stance by ignoring evidence of erroneous reversals. "Instead of counting [a] reversal as the fault of the reversing court, the Columbia researchers accepted reversal as proof that the trial court was erroneous," Rushford writes. The implicit assumption that any reversal by definition means that an error has occurred is fallacious. The researchers ignore cases when the reviewing court makes an error in reversing the trial court, which correctly applied the law. "For example, in the mid-1980s, the California Supreme Court reversed eighteen sentences for error in instruction which is now known as correct. The study would count these cases as erroneous trials, when in reality they are erroneous reversals," he argues. The problem with this method of determining an error rate is that it counts cases in which a state supreme court and lower federal courts disagree on an open question that has not been decided definitively by the U.S. Supreme Court. How can something be an error when it is unclear which law applies under the circumstances?[48]

In a related issue, the Columbia study fails to control for evolving judicial standards. As the Court has announced expanded protections of civil liberties, especially beginning with the Warren Court in the 1950s and 1960s, cases that had been deemed constitutionally sufficient in previous years were found to be erroneous under the new standards. Judicial standards seldom exist as static pronouncements of the law; they constantly evolve as courts change personnel and as new cases are brought into the legal system. As a result, defendants, especially in capital cases, are afforded new and generally greater protections at all stages of the judicial process. This means that newly discovered "errors"—far from providing evidence of defendants' terrible plight—may actually demonstrate the opposite point. Because they enjoy an expanded scope of civil liberties protections as judicial standards change, defendants are helped, not harmed, by the determination that their cases do not meet new constitutional standards. "Since 1961," Rushford explains, "the Supreme Court has created various rules for protection of defendants extending beyond the requirements of the U.S. Constitution or fundamental fairness. Serious error as the study uses the term may involve a rule with little or no connection to the reliability of the result."[49]

Finally, Rushford questions the validity of "second guessing the trial lawyer." In retrospect, long after a trial has ended, it is comparatively easy to be a "Monday morning quarterback." This is a potentially dangerous development, however, because it places lawyers under an almost impossible standard, and it means that theoretically "serious error" occurs in virtually every trial. Without understanding the difficulties and choices facing defense counsel, we may find fault where even the most seasoned and skilled attorneys could not have corrected the errors at the time. Accordingly, this retrospective look at the trial does not necessarily mean that the defense attorney was incompetent or that the defendant was a victim of ineffective assistance of counsel. Trials are by nature unpredictable events. Witnesses often are missing, forgetful, lying, or inconsistent in their testimony. Evidence may be included or excluded based on a trial judge's discretion, and this can affect the outcome of the case. Lawyers have to juggle all these considerations, often on the spot, and discretion is a key ingredient of their defense. Years later, in reviewing the case, we may see with the benefit of hindsight that the defense attorney should have pursued a different line of questioning or emphasized a different aspect of the case and perhaps, as a result, his client would not have been found guilty or sentenced to death. In Rushford's view, "[s]econd guessing the tactical decisions of the defense lawyers is all too easy. Far from showing egregiously incompetent lawyers, this case shows egregiously intrusive judging."[50]

Rushford advances a number of persuasive arguments, but he is far from the last critic of "A Broken System." In addition to opinions expressed by reporters and academic commentators, some practitioners in the criminal justice system also have found the report to be fallacious. Bennett Barylan, deputy attorney general in the Division of Criminal Justice, Appellate Bureau, of the U.S. Department of Justice, criticized the study in a missive he wrote in November 2000. In Barylan's view, the Columbia study limits its scope by not including death penalty reversals in three key eastern states: New York, New Jersey, and Connecticut. Had the study included these states, the error rate probably would have been lower. The omission is hardly surprising, according to Barylan, in light of Liebman's anti–death penalty perspective. "Liebman could not possibly characterize himself as a neutral observer in the death-penalty debate," Barylan observes. "On the contrary, he is a zealous partisan, clearly committed to the abolition of capital punishment. Liebman is vehemently opposed to capital punishment in the lengthy discussions of recent developments in various states, including the Illinois moratorium. The authors of the study are confident that their study will intensify and galvanize opposition to capital punishment by broadly indicting a system which they allege is neither a success nor even minimally rational."[51]

David Horowitz, president of the Center for the Study of Popular Culture and an avid supporter of the death penalty, sees a larger trend in the Columbia study. In his opinion, Liebman and his supporters are part of the liberal vanguard typified by "the left-wing media, namely the *New York Times* and the *L.A. Times.*" In analyzing media coverage of Liebman's study, Horowitz finds that the results have garnered front-page coverage because they support the liberal agenda and portray anti–death penalty judges in a positive light.

"For example, the report records that 87 percent of the death penalty cases in California in the twenty-three-year study period were reversed," Horowitz writes. "The implication is that the death penalty sentences were wrongly imposed." Observers can draw a far different from the data. "These reversals instead represent a political campaign by the left to subvert the death penalty. No one was executed in California after 1973, when Governor Jerry Brown was elected in 1972, until the anti–death penalty chief justice of the California Supreme Court appointed by Brown was removed and a Republican governor was able to put in place justices who respect the law." The media does not report this information because it undercuts the implicit argument advanced by Liebman and his supporters that the "broken system" is responsible for an ever-increasing number of executions of possibly innocent people. "The corruption of our academic and press institutions by the political left has been going on for so long and has reached a point of such magnitude where abysmal disregard for the normal standards of academic inquiry and journalistic reportage is normal, that it is hard to take each . . . institution seriously anymore."[52]

Professor Liebman responded to the firestorm of criticism by defending his study in several public venues. For example, in an interview published by the *Tennessean*, a Tennessee-based newspaper, in 2000, he suggests that the methodology and findings in the study are defensible; however, his detractors often take the data out of context and thereby inflate the flaws in the study. Moreover, he cautions reporters against drawing wide-ranging inferences out of statistical information based on a small number of cases. In the final analysis, despite the barrage of criticism, Liebman suggests that the death penalty system in virtually every state is "broken." In Tennessee, he concludes, "[o]ne thing that stood out to me . . . was the large number of cases that were reversed due to ineffective assistance of counsel (poor lawyering at the trial level)."[53]

Along with his coauthors Jeffrey Fagan and Valerie West, Liebman also responded to critics of "A Broken System," especially Latzer and Cauthen, in the fall 2000 issue of *Judicature*, a journal of the American Judicature Society devoted to topics involving trials and the legal system. Just as Latzer and Cauthen criticize the methodology employed in "A Broken System," the Columbia researchers consider their critics' methodology. "Four methodological defects deprive Latzer and Cauthen's study of validity," Liebman and his associates write. "First, they are forced to use phrases like 'closer to 27 percent' when juxtaposing the number of 'conviction' reversals to our 68 percent figure for all capital reversals because the comparison they purport to make is classically one of apples and elephants." Instead of relying on the actual numbers, Latzer and Cauthen sample reversals between 1990 and 1999. Liebman, however, counts *all* reversals during the twenty-three-year study period, not simply a sampling of the population. "Because the numbers are based on different sets of cases, they are not comparable." In short, if Latzer and Cauthen choose to compare statistical inferences, they must use the same data set or the results will be skewed.[54]

In addition, Latzer and Cauthen's sampling method undercounts "conviction" reversals because it is not sufficiently precise to account for all cases that result in reversals but are not designated as "conviction" reversals. They also compound the methodological errors by mixing their sampling of direct appeal reversals and postconviction reversals, which results in a confused and confusing array of results and does not differentiate between types of reversals. Moreover, "Latzer and Cauthen assign cases to their two categories—'conviction' and 'sentence' reversals—based on an arbitrary distinction between *identical* reversals. The result is a meaningless count of reversals in each category."[55]

After the Columbia researchers published their rejoinder, Latzer and Cauthen were not satisfied to allow their attacks on the Columbia researchers to be attacked; thus, the war of words and methodologies continued in another issue of *Judicature*. In "The Meaning of Capital Appeals: A Rejoinder to Liebman, Fagan, and West," Latzer and Cauthen argue that "[n]othing they write changes the fact that most reversals simply negate—often temporarily—the death sentence of a guilty murderer." Even if one accepts the 68 percent error rate cited by Liebman and his colleagues—a dubious proposition in the first place—this does not mean that 68 percent of innocent persons convicted of a capital crime face execution. "Unless sentenced to death on retrial, the sixty-eight of one hundred capital defendants who win their appeals no longer face the risk of execution," Latzer and Cauthen observe. "Thus, their measure has nothing to do with the persons selected for execution; it only addresses the likelihood that a capital conviction or death sentence will be reversed."[56]

Furthermore, a reversal on appeal does not necessarily mean that an innocent person has been erroneously convicted. Appellate courts focus on whether the trial judge correctly applied the law to the facts of the case and not questions of guilt or innocence, although such questions often turn on procedural niceties. Still, the Columbia University study is misleading when it focuses on appellate reversals and infers that such reversals necessarily lead to the execution of innocent persons. "If success on appeal really connoted innocence," the authors wryly observe, "double jeopardy principles would preclude retrial."[57]

In fact, Liebman's astonishment at the enormous number of errors found in capital cases is relatively easy to explain. "In death cases, errors ordinarily considered harmless are treated more seriously because the defendant's life is on the line." Consequently, this heightened level of scrutiny means that even comparatively minor errors may result in an appellate reversal. This "means simply that the ground rules of review are different and the scrutiny more intensive. The sentencing phase of capital trials, unique to death penalty cases, offers particularly fertile soil for findings of reversible error." Ironically, according to Latzer and Cauthen, 61 percent of all reversible error occur at the sentencing phase. Because sentencing is a distinct part of a capital case, errors at this stage do not suggest that an innocent person faces execution.[58]

III. Conclusion

It is difficult to assess the multitude of data and interpretations that have proliferated in the wake of the reported findings in "A Broken System." The Columbia University study undoubtedly is one of the most significant studies ever undertaken on capital punishment in the United States. The doubt arises as to how a thoughtful person should interpret the data and their implications. Were Liebman and his colleagues fairly and accurately reporting the trends they observed, or were they, as their critics charged, ideologues masquerading as neutral social scientists but actually manipulating the data to advance their anti–death penalty views? As this chapter demonstrates, this is not an easy question to answer.

Social science research can provide researchers with insights into capital punishment rates and other quantitative information that were unavailable during earlier eras. In fact, most debates over the death penalty before the twentieth century required both sides to make enormous inferential leaps of faith that had little grounding in reliable empirical data. That situation changed in the modern era as social scientists developed more sophisticated methodologies and statistical tools to aid policymakers in their deliberations. Unfortunately, instead of clarifying the debate over capital punishment, these new tools may have obfuscated the arguments beneath a thin veneer of "scientific" respectability. Each side in the debate cites statistics indicating, on one hand, that America's death penalty system is a fundamentally flawed enterprise that perpetuates innumerable inequities or, on the other hand, that it works reasonably well despite occasional problems that can be rectified without abolishing capital punishment.

With or without the assistance of social science research, questions of state-sanctioned executions are impossible to answer to everyone's satisfaction. Because the controversy over the death penalty cannot be resolved solely on the basis of available data divorced from their underlying assumptions and biases, policymakers are forced to turn to other sources of information. Only by combining social science data with insights provided by other disciplines (as outlined in other chapters of this book)—philosophy, theology, and the law—can the thoughtful policymaker make informed decisions about this ongoing debate.

CHAPTER 10

Fatal Flaws

THE IMPLEMENTATION OF THE
DEATH PENALTY IN THE STATES

Elizabeth Theiss Smith

> From this day forward, I no longer shall tinker with the ma-
> chinery of death. For more than twenty years I have en-
> deavored . . . along with a majority of this Court, to de-
> velop procedural and substantive rules that would lend
> more than the mere appearance of fairness to the death
> penalty endeavor. Rather than continue to coddle the
> Court's delusion that the desired level of fairness has been
> achieved and the need for regulation eviscerated, I feel
> morally and intellectually obligated simply to concede that
> the death penalty experiment has failed. It is virtually self-
> evident to me now that no combination of procedural rules
> or substantive regulations ever can save the death penalty
> from its inherent constitutional deficiencies.
>
> —Justice Harry Blackmun, in dissent, *Callins v. Collins*[1]

In February 2000, Governor George Ryan of Illinois placed a moratorium on executions in the state after appeals courts ruled on the thirteenth of twenty-five
convicts on death row to have been convicted in error. A conservative state legislature supported the actions of the pro–death penalty governor.

Questions about the capacity of state judicial systems to administer state death
penalty policy fairly have assumed increased importance since the early eighties
when the Supreme Court deregulated death penalty trials. From 1976 until 1983,
the Court's major focus had been on identifying protections that must be afforded
to capital defendants.[2] However, in 1983 members of the Court, most notably
Rehnquist and Powell, began to express concern that defendants were delaying

execution through endless appeals that amounted to an abuse of the process.[3] The Court took the position that defendants should not be permitted to use federal habeas corpus to delay execution indefinitely and that the states have an interest in rapid executions.[4] Using a federalism framework for viewing death penalty questions, the Court increasingly has been reluctant to interfere with state administration of the death penalty.[5] A key rationale is that any residual shortcomings in the administration of the death penalty may be remedied by use of executive clemency at the state level to commute the sentences of the wrongfully convicted.[6] The net result of this new judicial policy has been a shift in the Court's major concern from insisting on uniform application of constitutional protections in capital cases to promoting expeditious executions.[7] Today, the Supreme Court is unlikely to intervene in capital cases, unless a state court has committed an egregious violation of a defendant's constitutional rights.[8] And while the Supreme Court began granting more stays of executions during the 1999–2000 term,[9] the Court continues to come down consistently on the side of the states.

This chapter explores the extent to which states have the capacity to implement the death penalty fairly within the framework of current state judicial systems. First, it evaluates existing evidence of the error rate in capital convictions. Second, it identifies and evaluates factors that appear to contribute toward error. Third, it examines the impact of diminished opportunities to correct wrongful convictions due to federal and state policies regarding habeas corpus review and appeals. Finally, it reviews reform proposals and argues along with Justice Blackmun that, given the existing structure of capital trials and appeals, the contemporary politics of crime, and the normal human propensity for mistakes, error appears likely to occur and remain uncorrected.

I. Error Rates in Capital Convictions

How likely is a state court to wrongfully convict an innocent defendant in a capital trial? Perhaps the criminal justice system in Illinois is in some way flawed, and state criminal justice systems in general are in fact able to fairly and reliably administer death penalty statutes. To administer the death penalty, courts must be able to distinguish guilt from innocence, conduct a fair and impartial trial, and weigh aggravating and mitigating circumstances that increase or diminish responsibility for capital crimes. If courts are unable to accomplish these tasks without undue error, then wrongful executions are unavoidable.

Evidence of flaws in the application of the death penalty in the states has been mounting. Of the 6,139 persons sentenced to death from 1973 to 1997, 33.1 percent have had sentences or convictions subsequently overturned. The average annual murder rate in recent years is twenty-four thousand. The death penalty is sought in about 280 cases, and capital convictions result in about 150 cases. Of cases that reach appeals courts, about 40 percent have either the conviction or the sentence overturned.[10]

Law school death penalty clinics have begun to obtain a significant number of reversals based on DNA and other evidence. The Innocence Project, a program headed by Attorney Barry Scheck of Cardozo University School of Law, provides pro bono legal assistance to inmates who challenge their convictions based on DNA evidence. The project worked on thirty-three of fifty-four cases in which convictions have been reversed or overturned. DNA testing has exonerated nine death row inmates awaiting execution.[11] Two hundred cases are now in process, with a backlog of a thousand cases. The Cornell University Death Penalty Project's capital punishment clinic, organized in 1997, created a capital punishment clinic. Research conducted at Cornell on jury instructions indicated that flawed jury instructions changed the outcome of at least one trial from life to death.[12]

University-sponsored teams of journalism students have also been taking a prominent role in death penalty reversals. Northwestern University students, under the leadership of journalism professor David Protess, conducted an investigation that led to the reversal of a death sentence because the state's chief witness changed his story.

A systematic way of arriving at an explanation for the error rate in capital convictions is to analyze cases in which death penalty convictions were reversed. Analyzing summaries[13] of 75 cases of wrongful capital convictions between 1972 and 1998 revealed the following frequencies and factors responsible for wrongful conviction:

Prosecutorial misconduct	35	34%
Eyewitness testimony	32	31%
Police error	14	14%
Jailhouse informant testimony	11	10%
Incompetent counsel	7	7%
Flawed jury instructions	2	2%

Note that more than one cause of error is often present. Thus, the factors responsible for wrongful conviction add up to more than the sum of the cases. Moreover, "interaction effects" often compound error.[14]

The hallmarks of wrongful convictions are a lack of physical evidence or eyewitnesses, reliance on the testimony of a jailed informant who may receive more favorable treatment in recompense, unsubstantiated claims of a confession, and use of weak or suspect science in the investigation. The defendant is most likely poor, minority, and criminal and had an ineffective attorney.[15]

Reversals typically result from new evidence identifying the real killer, witness recantations, and DNA testing.[16]

II. Fatal Flaws

The death penalty is imposed in only 250 of all homicides in the United States each year.[17] How reliably do the courts distinguish the innocent from the guilty, the heinous from the comprehensible, the degree of responsibility that the murderer should be assigned for his or her crime? What follows is a discussion of factors that are often implicated in wrongful convictions, including police misconduct, prosecutorial misconduct, incompetent counsel, political pressure on judges, death-qualified jury bias, and flawed jury instructions.

A major contributing factor in wrongful convictions has been police misconduct. Police do not have the same legal duty to report exculpatory evidence that prosecutors have, yet ethical imperatives would argue that police ought to do so. Nonetheless, evidence suggests that police reports sometimes are deliberately misleading because of omission of evidence, failure to pursue leads, or fabrication of evidence. Some departments have two different filing systems, one for "official" records that are subject to legal disclosure, and a second "street file" that is not.[18] In at least some cases in which wrongful convictions have been documented, police focused early in the investigation on a particular suspect and committed all resources toward establishing that suspect's guilt, rather than conducting a full and fair investigation. A recent investigation into the Los Angeles Police Department revealed that "officers shot an unarmed man in handcuffs, planted guns, drugs and other evidence on suspects, lied in court testimony to frame innocent people and stole drugs and money."[19] While it is difficult to determine how widespread such behavior may be, the percentage of wrongful convictions due to police misconduct suggests that it occurs often enough to constitute a significant source of error in the application of the death penalty.

A second major factor in wrongful convictions is prosecutorial misconduct. The role of a prosecutor in capital cases is critical: to see that the guilty are punished and the innocent set free. Prosecutorial responsibility with respect to evidence is clear: Prosecutors are required to disclose evidence that would tend to exonerate the defendant.[20] Yet, prosecutors have withheld critical evidence, permitted evidence and testimony known to be false, and made closing arguments tainted by conclusions without evidentiary support to win capital convictions.

How widespread is prosecutorial misconduct? Over the past thirty-six years, 381 homicide convictions, 67 of which resulted in a sentence of death, were reversed because "prosecutors knowingly used false evidence or withheld evidence suggesting the defendant's innocence."[21] Research into convictions set aside in

Cook County, Illinois, during the 1980s and 1990s found that, on average, a conviction was set aside once a month because of a judicial finding of improper conduct by prosecutors.[22] An examination of criminal cases from 1978 through 1998 found 326 state court convictions reversed because of prosecutor misconduct.[23] Finally, a review of seventy-two death penalty reversals indicates that prosecutorial misconduct was clearly responsible for wrongful conviction in 34 percent of the cases. The *Chicago Tribune*'s recent analysis of thousands of court records suggests that "it happens frequently and in nearly limitless ways."[24]

A retired Texas judge, who presided over more than fifty capital cases during his forty-one-year career, said, "It was a game for prosecutors to withhold material that would even exonerate the defendants. In most cases, they knew what they were doing."[25]

Two recent cases provide instructive examples: The South Dakota capital case of Robert Leroy Anderson, sentenced to death for murder, is back in court again because a volunteer witness, whose testimony was kept out of court to avoid "muddying the waters," contacted defense lawyers with information that implicates the prosecution's star witness against the defendant. The prosecution never contacted the defense with information that cast serious doubt on the guilt of the defendant.[26] In a second case, in New York City, prosecutors used the testimony of a notoriously unreliable, violent, addicted convict to try to implicate a detective in a murder. In tapes that were discovered later, investigators may be heard offering the witness a "very, very, very sweet deal" in exchange for his testimony. The *New York Times* editorialized, "That's what happens when there is no one to investigate the investigators."[27]

The rate of prosecutorial conduct may be increasing, though it is possible that the rate of discovery of misconduct is responsible for the appearance of an increase. The number of cases of prosecutorial misconduct tripled in the 1990s, perhaps as a reflection of the distinctively more conservative approach to crime taken by Congress, the Supreme Court, and many state legislatures. In 1995, the Justice Department's Office of Professional Responsibility investigated 196 new cases of alleged prosecutorial misconduct.

Equally difficult to address is the problem of prosecutor misconduct in jury argument. Unless opposing counsel objects to misstatements by the prosecution, the trial goes on. In Cook County, Illinois, improper closing arguments were the most frequent cause for reversal—108 times out of 207 cases over a twenty-year period.

Incentives for prosecutors to conceal evidence or commit other violations of professional ethics and the law are comprehensible within the context of the prosecutor's job situation. The will to win seems to be at the heart of the matter. Most prosecutors in the United States are elected every two, four, or six years and must pay attention to electoral considerations. A good win record is a valued campaign resource. A win allows the prosecutor to "clear the books." Prosecutors may also feel a responsibility to the victim's family. In addition, winning is rewarding in its own right. One study suggests that racism, public pressure for results, and a desire to hide prosecutors' mistakes are the major factors underlying prosecutorial misconduct.[28]

Few sanctions exist for prosecutorial misconduct. Even in the rare case when caught, prosecutors who conceal evidence are almost never prosecuted, and convictions are overturned only when the misconduct was likely to have altered the trial's final result.[29] Prosecutors enjoy either absolute or qualified immunity for misconduct and are therefore protected from the consequences of wrongful conviction, absent a showing of incompetence or a knowing violation of the law.[30] No misconduct charges were ever prosecuted until 1999.[31] The remedies offered by courts for serious misconduct are criminal punishment or professional sanctions,[32] but "the wrongdoer's fellow prosecutors and the local bar are not likely to provide an adequate remedy."[33] "Rarely are district attorneys monitored, corrected, or disciplined by anyone—not the Supreme Court, the Justice Department, federal and state politicians, and certainly not prosecutors themselves."[34]

Prosecutorial misconduct is difficult to discover and often surfaces as a result of serendipitous events—overheard conversations, newspaper lawsuits, anonymous tips.[35] In one instance, the case file of James Joseph Richardson, who had been on death row for five years, was stolen from an assistant prosecutor's office and made public. A subsequent investigation by the U.S. Justice Department revealed that the prosecutor knew that Richardson was innocent and had manufactured some of the evidence used to convict him.[36]

In summary, prosecutorial misconduct is a factor common to over one-third of wrongful convictions. It is difficult to detect and, when detected, is seldom sanctioned formally or informally. Therefore, the true prevalence of misconduct is unknown.

A third factor contributing to wrongful conviction is incompetent defense counsel. Defendants in capital trials have a constitutional right to effective assistance of counsel. The Supreme Court ruled in *Powell v. Alabama*[37] that the due process clause of the Fourteenth Amendment requires that defendants receive assistance of counsel in capital cases. *Strickland v. Washington*[38] interprets the Sixth Amendment right to counsel as the right to *effective* assistance of counsel but sets up the presumption that a wide range of reasonable professional assistance is acceptable. As a practical matter, this has not required that counsel be able or effective.

To what extent do capital defendants receive effective assistance of counsel? The evidence suggests that those accused of capital crimes are often defended by lawyers who lack the skills, resources, and commitment to provide effective representation.[39]

Whether defendants in capital cases receive adequate and effective assistance of counsel varies considerably depending on the jurisdiction in which the trial is held. While eleven states have statewide public defender programs, many other states with large death row populations, such as Texas, have no systematic means of providing adequate counsel.[40] Judges in such jurisdictions may appoint members of the bar to the defense, though the pay is often poor and the lawyers are often inexperienced.

Low pay in many jurisdictions makes it difficult to attract decent lawyers to capital defense work, and, when appointed, jurisdictions may not provide sufficient funds to allow a decent lawyer the time to mount an adequate defense. Caps are often placed on payments for out-of-court hours, and hourly rates are often very low. Because an investigation into "mitigating circumstances" often makes the difference between life and death, out-of-court hours are critical to death penalty defense counsel. In rural Texas, some jurisdictions pay no more than $800 for representation of an indigent in a capital case.[41] In Mississippi, a cap of $1,000 limits pay for capital defense.[42] Alabama has a $2,000 limit for out-of-court time spent on a death penalty case. If we accept an estimate of five hundred hours as adequate for investigation and preparation (about half of what Bright says is needed), the lawyer receives $4 an hour.[43]

As a result of low pay, appointed lawyers are often unwilling or unable to devote adequate time to capital cases that are unarguably a life-or-death matter. A *Newsday* survey of hundreds of death penalty cases found "court-appointed defense counsel often spent less than a week preparing cases that experts say would need four hundred to one thousand hours of investigation and research."[44] Experienced lawyers understandably avoid taking capital cases. Some counties retain law firms on a contract basis to represent the indigent. The incentive for the law firm is to provide minimal hours and services.

Many states have no minimum standards for capital counsel. A *National Law Journal* survey found that more than half of all defense counsel "were handling their first capital trials when their clients, now on death row, were convicted."[45] Capital defense lawyers in the "death belt"[46] have been disbarred or disciplined at rates three to forty-six times the rate for that state. One- to two-day capital trials are common and attorneys spend little time offering mitigating factors in the penalty phase of the trial, a key strategy in avoiding death. A third of those on death row have no appeals attorney at all.[47] It would appear that many state court judges appoint "inexperienced and incapable" lawyers to capital cases and deny sufficient funds for investigation.[48]

The Texas Court of Criminal Appeals refused to grant one death row convict a new trial despite the fact that his lawyer had slept through parts of the trial. A U.S. District Court judge subsequently granted a stay of execution in the case.

The conservative Fourth Circuit Court of Appeals' standard for ineffective assistance of counsel is that the defendant has to prove that the outcome of the case was "unfair or unreliable" and the outcome would have been different but for counsel. This is a much stricter standard than under *Strickland*.

In many cases, defendants lose the chance to appeal when an incompetent defense lawyer fails to bring up valid constitutional issues in the context of the trial. The lawyer may have been competent enough to pass muster under *Strickland*, but not competent enough to preserve the defendant's rights for appeal. Under the Court's procedural doctrines, appeals will not be considered under those circumstances.

The fact that the death penalty has enjoyed political popularity appears to have at least some influence on the likelihood of wrongful convictions. Electoral considerations force judges to a higher level of responsiveness to public opinion than procedural and substantive justice might require. In some jurisdictions, this has resulted in the appointment and retention of pro–death penalty judges, elected on platforms of increasing use of death penalty. This is especially noteworthy since thirty-two states both elect judges and sentence people to death.[49] Furthermore, the Supreme Court has "increasingly turned over the development of capital punishment policies and procedures to state legislatures and courts,"[50] a fact that allows state trial and appellate courts to be free of effective constitutional review. The political nature of decision making in capital cases has not escaped the notice of at least some Supreme Court justices:

> The "higher authority" to whom present-day capital judges may be too responsive is a political climate in which judges who covet higher office—or who merely wish to remain judges—must constantly profess their fealty to the death penalty. . . . The danger that they will bend to political pressures when pronouncing sentence in highly publicized capital cases is the same danger confronted by judges beholden to King George III.[51]

Appeals court judges, in particular, are often under intense political pressure to uphold death penalty convictions on appeal for fear of losing retention elections. In 1986, California governor George Deukmejian threatened Supreme Court justices with opposition during retention elections "unless they voted to uphold more death sentences."[52] He made good on his threat, and three justices lost seats in a campaign that hinged on the death penalty. After the replacement of the three justices, the new California Supreme Court affirmed nearly 97 percent of the cases it reviewed, making broad use of the harmless error doctrine. According to one law professor who studies the California court system, "One thing it shows is that when the voters speak loudly enough, even the judiciary listens."[53]

In Tennessee, Judge Penny White of the Tennessee Supreme Court lost a retention election after a bitter attack by pro–death penalty groups whose campaign advertisement suggested that voters "vote for capital punishment by voting No . . . for SC Justice Penny White."[54]

After Texas's high court reversed a capital conviction, a prominent Republican and former state party chair called for the party to take over the court in the 1994 election. Republicans fought for and won every position sought on a pro–death penalty, tough-on-crime platform. In Mississippi, two justices were voted off the court for being "soft on crime."[55]

Rates of affirming the death penalty on appeal over a ten-year period suggest a close correlation between the method of selection of state Supreme Court judges and the rate at which high courts affirm death sentences. The relationship is significant ($p < .01$) in the period following the high-profile battle over the California Supreme Court's position on the death penalty.[56]

Judges sometimes run on a pro–death penalty platform, often with the help of special interest groups that help fund such elections. However, Justice Stevens pointed out that "[a] campaign promise to . . . enforce the death penalty is evidence of bias that should disqualify a candidate from sitting in criminal cases."

Even in states with appointed judges, support for the death penalty has become the "ultimate litmus test" for proving to voters that the candidate is not soft on crime.[57] Governors who run for office on promises to appoint judges who will administer the death penalty are likely to do so, producing a judiciary that is tilted toward death.

Some may argue that criticisms of a politically responsive judiciary are invalid because such criticisms are antidemocratic as well as impractical. Radical changes to insulate state judiciaries entirely from public opinion would be unlikely, largely unwelcome, and almost certainly unsuccessful. However, the pressure on judges to be tough on crime in general creates unique issues when applied to capital cases. The death penalty is different because, unlike a lengthy term of imprisonment, it is irreversible. The judicial system must be held to higher standards of fairness in capital cases. When the capacity of courts to achieve impartial justice in death penalty cases is in doubt, it should prompt broader questions about the nature of capital trials and whether the odds of a fair trial under current rules are acceptable.

A fifth factor that may contribute to error rates in capital trials is the juror qualification process. Studies of jury decision making suggest that the process of qualifying jurors in capital trials may tilt jurors toward a verdict of death. Prosecutors and defense counsel in capital cases are permitted to question prospective jurors as to their attitudes toward capital punishment. The prosecution may exclude from the jury all who would automatically vote against the death penalty and those whose judgment as to guilt or innocence might be prejudiced by their attitude toward capital punishment.[58]

Is a jury that has been death qualified more apt to convict? Evidence from six conviction proneness studies suggests strongly that death-qualified juries may be prosecution prone.[59] In addition, research suggests that jurors "make life and death punishment decisions early in the trial, misunderstand sentencing guidelines, and often deny their responsibility for the punishment given to a defendant."[60] The rules for jury qualification in death penalty cases are unique to capital trials and appear to make conviction more likely through use of a screening mechanism that excludes any jurors who do not hold positive views on the use of the death penalty. These attitudes appear to affect not only the penalty phase of the trial but also the establishment of guilt or innocence.

Empirical evidence suggests that flawed jury instructions may also make a difference between life and death. "Jurors misunderstand how the capital sentencing decision should be made; which factors can and cannot be considered, what level of proof is needed, and what degree of concurrence is required for aggravating and mitigating factors."[61] Furthermore, three out of four jurors reported that the judge's instructions simply provided a framework for a decision they had already made.[62]

Standard jury instructions may not be sufficiently clear. In at least one study, clarification of jury instructions made the difference between sentences of life and death. In a simulation of the penalty phase of a capital trial, jurors who were read the standard jury instructions and denied clarification erroneously believed that a death sentence was mandatory when it was not. A decade-long study at Northeastern University's College of Criminal Justice suggests that "juries are not only confused by such instructions, but sometimes choose death as a result."[63] Interviews with more than nine hundred jurors from capital trials in eleven states demonstrated that jurors often choose death because they lack critical information about the option of imposing a lengthy or life sentence as an alternative.

During the penalty phase of the trial, jurors often do not understand the meaning of mitigating circumstances or procedurally how such information is to be applied. Since *Gregg v. Georgia*,[64] jurors are required to weigh mitigating circumstances against aggravating circumstances and decide whether, in the balance, mitigating factors outweigh aggravating factors. However, many jurors are confused about the meaning of mitigating factors. State and federal courts do not require that trial courts define the meaning of mitigating circumstances. Jury instructions may provide little guidance to genuinely confused jurors. Juries that request clarification are often referred back to the original instructions.[65]

In addition to the problem of definition, jurors often misapprehend the procedure by which mitigating factors are weighed. Juries must agree unanimously on a sentence of death if it is to be imposed. Any single juror who believes that mitigating factors are sufficient to preclude a death sentence effectively bars the imposition of the death penalty. However, many jurors think that belief in a mitigating factor must also be unanimous.[66] "There is no serious question that many individual jurors as well as entire juries do not understand the instructions that they must follow in reaching a verdict."[67]

III. Diminished Opportunities for Appeals Limit Chance to Prove Innocence

Efforts over the past decade to reduce the cost of administering the death penalty have focused on limiting opportunities for habeas corpus review and appeals. Between 1972 and 1980, federal courts invalidated about 60 percent of state death penalty convictions or sentences in response to habeas petitions.[68] However, the Supreme Court issued a series of decisions throughout the 1980s and early 1990s that limited access to federal court for state prisoners and lost interest in regulating state court imposition of the death penalty.

To further streamline the road to execution, in 1996 Congress passed the Antiterrorism and Effective Death Penalty Act that further forecloses federal review of state court proceedings. The act "bars habeas corpus review of issues that were not developed factually in state proceedings" and "bars federal habeas review of claims adjudicated in state court unless the state decision is contrary to clearly established law as determined by the Supreme Court." Habeas corpus proceedings and appeals provide valuable time and opportunities for the innocent to present additional proof. In Illinois, the average wait for execution on death row is thirteen years, during which time thirteen of twenty-five convicts were able to exonerate themselves.[69] The foreclosure of federal habeas corpus review increases the chances that a demonstrably innocent person will be executed.

An innocent person who is proven guilty in a state court often has no place at all to go with exculpatory evidence under the present system.[70] Actual innocence, even in cases in which new exculpatory evidence has come to light, is not a basis for federal habeas corpus review of a conviction. In *Herrera v. Collins,*[71] the Supreme Court granted certiorari to decide whether habeas corpus could be invoked to argue a claim of "actual innocence." The Court ruled that

> a death row prisoner convicted under state law has no right to a hearing in federal courts on grounds of newly discovered evidence purporting to show the defendant's innocence if the evidence is belated according to a state statute of limitations, unless the defendant can

> present a "truly persuasive show by clear and convincing evidence . . .
> that no reasonable juror would have found the defendant eligible for
> the death penalty."

According to Rehnquist's majority opinion, innocence is not a bar to execution so long as the trial was fair and the inmate had the opportunity to invoke executive clemency.[72] Once a defendant has had a fair trial, the presumption of innocence is erased.[73] Rehnquist reasoned that in cases in which innocence was manifest, Supreme Court review is unnecessary because the prisoner can request commutation of the death sentence.

On the state level, court review of exculpatory evidence may fare no better because the time period during which new evidence may be considered is sharply limited. In Texas, exculpatory evidence is inadmissible thirty days after conviction. In sixteen states, there is a sixty-day limit on new evidence. In eighteen states, time limits are between one and three years. Only in nine states are the wrongfully convicted able to present new evidence of innocence without time restrictions.[74] The net result is that, even when incontrovertible proof of innocence is available, the unjustly convicted may have no remedy available except executive clemency.

Unfortunately, executive clemency is likely to be a chimera for death row inmates, no matter how convincing the exculpatory evidence. Commutation of the death sentence of a convicted murderer whose trial was undoubtedly well publicized is a political act and one that may carry an awful price to be paid at the ballot box in the current "tough on crime" climate. Governors tend to take the role of "commander in chief of the execution."[75] The frequency with which clemency is granted has declined precipitously during the last twenty-five years, from one in four during the mid-1940s to one in forty in the mid-1990s.[76] In states such as Texas where public support for the death penalty is in the area of 90 percent, clemency had never been exercised as of the date of this writing.[77] When federal habeas corpus and state court review of new evidence are both dead ends for judicial correction of the wrongful conviction, and alternative relief in the form of executive clemency is unlikely, then claims of factual innocence have nowhere to go.

IV. Reform Proposals

What is to be done? While it would be impossible to end all wrongful convictions, analysis of the factors that contribute to wrongful death sentences suggests that certain policy changes on the state level could improve matters considerably.

At the very least, the right to death penalty appeals should be expanded generously through changes in state rules of court to permit the introduction of new evidence of factual innocence at any time after conviction in capital cases. New evidence should be welcomed in an effort to minimize the number of executions of the innocent. Today, a death-sentenced individual able to produce fresh evidence of innocence has two options: to appeal for executive clemency or to motion for a new trial based on new evidence.[78] However, many state courts have inflexible time limits on the introduction of new evidence. Because of these time limits, additional appeals based on claims of actual innocence are invalidated. Even where no time limit is imposed, the standard for a new trial is generally that the evidence must be new, unavailable at the time of trial, and point to probable acquittal.[79] The American Bar Association has called for the enhancement and streamlining of state and federal court authority and responsibility to adjudicate constitutional claims in state postconviction and habeas corpus actions.[80]

Police departments should be required by state statute to maintain evidence in capital cases for the duration of the convicted capital prisoner's life. The cost of doing so is minimal and the potential benefits to the cause of justice are substantial. In the majority of cases today, such evidence is destroyed after a verdict is reached, making additional testing of evidence using newly developed techniques such as DNA impossible.

DNA testing of biological evidence offers states an opportunity to reduce wrongful convictions, and some fourteen state legislatures and the U.S. Congress debated whether to provide DNA testing for inmates during the 2001 legislative session. More states should follow the lead of New York, Illinois, California, and Virginia that now have statutes allowing for postconviction DNA testing where it is probative. Ohio's attorney general initiated a program in 2000 to provide DNA testing for inmates who did not have access to such a test during trial. In addition, a federal Innocence Protection Act was introduced in the U.S. Senate in 2000 that would require states to allow DNA testing that could "produce new exculpatory evidence" and to consider the results of such testing. The proposal would also have required states to create procedures that preserve biological evidence and to make DNA testing available to inmates. While the federal statute appears unlikely to become law, it provides a model that states desirous of reducing wrongful convictions may follow.

States should adopt the ABA standards for qualifying defense lawyers to try capital cases. These standards include the following:

(a) establish organizations to recruit, train, select, monitor, support and assist attorneys representing capital clients; (b) appoint two experienced attorneys at each stage of a capital case; (c) ensure that attorneys receive "reasonable rate of hourly compensation which

reflects the extraordinary responsibilities inherent in capital litigation; (d) counsel should be provided with the time and necessary
funding for proper investigations, expert witnesses, and other support services.[81]

Many states such as Connecticut provide these services through a reasonably
well-funded public defender system. California also provides funds for the specialized legal services called for in death penalty cases through private nonprof-
its. States that rely on court-appointed attorneys for capital defendants have a
good deal more difficulty providing an adequate defense. In these states, adequate compensation and adherence to the ABA standards are critical. Where
statutory maximums for the payment of defense lawyers exist, they should be
abolished. In addition, reasonable funds must be provided through the courts for
investigative and support services, at both the guilt and penalty phases of trials.
These decisions are ultimately legislative and budgetary in nature, and the success of reform proposals will hinge on the ability of court leadership to convince
legislators of wisdom and necessity of reform. One model proposal developed by
Arizona attorney general Janet Napolitano would provide assistance to rural capital defense lawyers through a separate unit of public defenders staffed by experienced death penalty lawyers. Similar assistance would be available to prosecutors who requested it.[82]

Prosecutors who knowingly withhold exculpatory evidence, permit false testimony, or make misleading statements to the jury should be subject to professional and criminal sanctions.[83] To minimize unintentional errors that lead to
wrongful conviction, prosecutors should, as part of their regular training, learn
about the most common factors responsible for such convictions. The National
District Attorneys Association and statewide professional associations of prosecutors as well as judicial systems could take the lead in providing such training.

Eyewitness identification should be subject to a higher level of scrutiny especially in capital cases. To avoid biased line-ups, no identification procedures
should occur unless the suspect's attorney is present. Where no corroborating evidence is available, a pretrial session should be held for the purpose of carefully
evaluating eyewitness testimony. In addition, juries should be instructed to treat
eyewitness testimony with care.[84] Finally, it would be wise to ban the use of the
death penalty in all cases that rely strictly on eyewitness testimony where physical evidence is lacking.

Trial courts should provide capital juries with standardized "truth in sentencing" instructions that include accurate information about the minimum period of time that a convicted murderer would serve prior to parole eligibility. In
addition, courts should not suggest that the jurors' verdict or sentence might be
reconsidered or overturned.[85] Providing capital juries with clear and accurate in-

structions would help eliminate a common cause of error during the penalty phase of capital trials.

All states should allow governors to grant clemency without the recommendation of a board or commission. While the number of states that require board or commission recommendations is small, they are "death belt" states. For example, Texas, the state with the largest death row population, does not allow the governor to grant clemency without the recommendation of a board of pardons. The board has never made such a recommendation, and its members generally vote by fax rather than coming together to deliberate based on evidence. The U.S. Supreme Court has emphasized the importance of executive clemency as a remedy for wrongful convictions. When the power of clemency is delegated to an intermediate board or commission, executive responsibility is attenuated and diminished.

All states should compensate the victims of wrongful convictions to reflect lost wages, legal fees, and other damages suffered. Compensation programs now exist in California, Wisconsin, Illinois, New York, and Tennessee, though most awards are fairly minimal. This would have two positive effects: First, compensation would assist victims of long-term imprisonment with the transition from prison to employment. Second, expensive compensation awards would represent an incentive to the states to begin to correct intentional and unintentional abuses that result in wrongful convictions.

On the federal level, Congress should pass the Accuracy in Judicial Administration Act of 2000, introduced as HR 3623, which aims to protect the innocent by mandating a temporary moratorium on executions while the attorney general drafts standards to insure that the innocent will not be executed. The bill would expand pretrial discovery and guarantee the opportunity to those under sentence of death to introduce DNA evidence that might lead to exoneration.

If states do nothing else, they should appoint a commission to study the chances of wrongful conviction under existing state statutes and rules of court, with an eye toward proposing remedies where needed. Seven states and the federal system had appointed such commissions at the time of this writing.[86]

Yet even with safeguards such as these suggestions, the evidence cited here indicates that the system is flawed in ways that render guilt beyond a reasonable doubt difficult to establish. Witnesses are often unreliable. Police and prosecutors in their zeal for conviction may conduct biased investigations, coerce the innocent to confess, manufacture evidence, or overstep constitutional boundaries. Death-qualified juries appear to be tilted toward death. Unclear or incomplete sentencing instructions can lead juries to impose the death penalty in cases in which jurors would prefer a different result. Even when due diligence is exercised by participants who desire only that justice should be served, misconstructions of fact, misapplications of rules, and inaccurate personal perceptions can result in wrongful convictions.

Death penalty opponents argue that the problem of a flawed justice system and wrongful executions cannot be resolved by ad hoc reforms aimed at providing additional procedural protections. Given the human flaws that infect the system charged with the determination of guilt or innocence and life or death, it is important that the question of how much uncertainty is acceptable be addressed in the context of the death penalty debate. Is it acceptable to take a life in Illinois where the error rate in capital convictions and sentences is over 50 percent? What is our level of confidence that justice prevailed more frequently in the states such as Texas, California, and Florida where hundreds of prisoners await execution?

We have a collective moral responsibility to ensure that the innocent are not executed. Death is different. Execution is the only punishment for which no remedy is possible after the fact. States should consider a moratorium similar to that imposed by the U.S. attorney general and the state of Illinois, pending a comprehensive review of existing procedures and practices that may lead to error. Finally, states should review the use of the death penalty in light of available research on its flaws in practice.

CHAPTER 11

Race and the Death Penalty

John C. McAdams

The opponents of the death penalty often argue that, since the death penalty is administered in a racially biased way, it must be abandoned. This is one of those arguments that can't withstand the most basic critical scrutiny, yet it's widely bandied around. Is it perhaps the case that where race is an issue, critical thought isn't common? Is it perhaps the case that, in politically correct sectors of society—and that includes academia and the media, who dominate the debate—people routinely respond to claims of racial injustice by promptly conceding whatever arguments are made by the people who raise the issue?

The "racial disparity" argument against the death penalty is illogical in its form and mistaken in its normative and empirical premises. It starts with the idea that justice is something that applies only to groups; proceeds to argue that if a policy is found to have disparate impact, then it must be abandoned—notwithstanding that an alternative policy might have an equally disparate impact; and, worst of all, ignores the issue of whether fairness toward the accused or fairness toward the victim is the key issue.

In this chapter, I will argue, first, that government must treat individuals justly, and group disparity is not something that can justify treating individuals unjustly. Thus, if guilty murderers deserve the death penalty, they do so notwithstanding that other guilty murderers may be able to get off. Second, in the face of group disparity in the administration of a policy, *fixing* it will typically be the preferred response. Moreover, there is indeed a huge racial disparity in the way the death penalty is meted out, but the disparity is radically different from what most people suppose. Also, if an unfair group disparity cannot be fixed, an alternative policy should be adopted only if it promises less disparity. In addition, even an alternative policy that promises less disparity may not be preferable if it is ineffective or sacrifices too much in terms of either justice or utility. Finally, in deciding matters of justice, acting justly toward law-abiding members of the community—citizens who have a right to have their lives, liberty, and property protected by government—is the overriding priority.

I. Justice toward Individuals

The purpose of the criminal justice system is to mete out "just desserts" to individuals.[1] As Ernest van den Haag has noted:

> Guilt is individual. If guilty whites or wealthy people escape the gallows and guilty poor people do not, the poor or black do not become less guilty because the others escaped their deserved punishment. Whether due to willful discrimination, capriciousness, or unavoidable accidental circumstances, some people will always get away with murder. Is that a reason to deny the justice of the punishment of those guilty persons who did not get away? Their guilt is not diminished by the escape of the others, nor do they deserve less punishment because others did not get the punishment they deserve. Justice involves punishment according to what is deserved by the crime and the guilt of the criminal—regardless of whether others guilty of the same crime escape.[2]

Opponents of the death penalty would never think of denying this simple principle with regard to issues *other than executions*. It is not the case that, because some taxpayers find a way to cheat the Internal Revenue Service (IRS) and get away with it, everybody has the right to cheat. And it's certainly not required that the IRS be abolished. Uncounted thousands of criminals go free each year. Sometimes it's because they are careful not to leave incriminating evidence. Sometimes it's because witnesses are unwilling to cooperate with the cops. Sometimes the cops really didn't care a lot about a certain kind of offense or a certain class of victims. Sometimes it's because overburdened prosecutors lack the resources to bring a particular case to trial. Sometimes biased or merely stupid jurors acquit someone who was in fact guilty "beyond a reasonable doubt." None of this suggests that criminals who have had the misfortune to be caught, convicted, and sent to prison should be released.

Now someone might object to this line of logic by insisting that the real purpose of punishment is utilitarian. We punish criminals for the purpose of deterrence—both general deterrence and individual deterrence—and incapacitation.[3]

There is no doubt that, both among the general public and among public policy specialists, arguments about the utility of punishment carry great weight. Opponents of the death penalty often flatly claim that it has no deterrent effect. Unfortunately, they typically use simplistic analysis[4] and ignore several very well-done studies that show a deterrent effect of capital punishment.[5] Particularly important here are two new studies that examine the most recent data and find deterrent effects of executions.[6]

Note, however, that the same logic that we apply to just deserts also applies to utility. If government should do as much justice as it can do—notwithstanding that it will be far short of perfect justice—then it should seek to make the lives of citizens safer—notwithstanding that it can do this much better for some citizens that for others.

Consider government financial aid for college students. It only helps some young people, but not all. It does disproportionately help poor students, who would otherwise be unable to attend college and who can get larger financial aid packages because of low family incomes. But even among young people from poor families, it helps those who go to college and not those who don't. Should the government forgo the opportunity to aid some young people from poor families because it can't help all of them? Or should it seize the opportunity to help those it can help?

Opponents of capital punishment might reply to these arguments by saying that they believe the death penalty is neither just nor utilitarian. If they are right about this, then they have excellent reasons to oppose the death penalty, but these reasons have *nothing to do with racial disparity*. If capital punishment is neither just nor utilitarian, there is no reason to favor it. If it is just, or utilitarian, or both, then racial disparity is not a good reason to oppose it.

II. Dealing with Group Disparity

All of this is not to deny that unfair group disparities—most certainly including racial disparity—are a huge problem that government has to address. But opponents of the death penalty are making a most peculiar argument. They are arguing that, if the death penalty isn't administered with racial fairness, it must be abolished.

But suppose we find that black neighborhoods get less police protection than white neighborhoods? Would we advocate abolishing police protection entirely? If we found a particular mortgage lender discriminating against black applicants, would we demand that the lender cease lending to anybody at all?

III. The Nature of Racial Disparity

The foregoing discussion implies that the notion of racial disparity is of limited utility in deciding the merits of the death penalty. But we still want to know what the facts about racial disparity are, partly because racial disparity is an evil that needs correcting, and partly because as social scientists we want to know how the system works, independent of any policy consequences that might follow.

It is important to understand that there are two different notions about racial disparity in the death penalty, both frequently cited, and *they are flatly contradictory*: "mass market" and "specialist" (which we'll consider in a later section of this chapter).

A. THE "MASS MARKET" RACIAL DISPARITY ARGUMENT

The first theory I have labeled the "mass market" version of the racial disparity thesis.[7] It holds, quite simply, that black defendants are treated more harshly than white defendants. It follows quite directly from the notion that a criminal justice system dominated by whites—perhaps racist whites—and highly responsive to white fears about black crime will deal very roughly with blacks who fall into the maw of the system. Leigh Bienen has articulated the argument as follows:

> The criminal justice system is controlled and dominated by whites, although the recipients of punishment, including the death penalty, are disproportionately black. The death penalty is a symbol of state control and white control over blacks. Black males who present a threatening and defiant personae are the favorites of those administering the punishment, including the overwhelmingly middle-aged white, male prosecutors who—in running for election or reelection—find nothing gets them more votes than demonizing young black men.[8]

Likewise Jesse Jackson, never one to pass up an opportunity to promote a racial grievance, claims:

> Numerous researchers have shown conclusively that African American defendants are far more likely to receive the death penalty than are white defendants charged with the same crime. For instance, African Americans make up 25 percent of Alabama's population, yet of Alabama's 117 death row inmates, 43 percent are black. Indeed, 71

percent of the people executed there since the resumption of capital punishment have been black.[9]

It is common for writers dealing with the issue of racial disparity to put it in the historical context of the Slave Codes, which imposed particularly harsh punishments on blacks. Indeed, this genre of writings frequently discusses lynchings in an attempt to frame the issue in terms of historically severe treatment of blacks accused of crimes.[10]

The mass market version of the racial disparity thesis fits neatly with the politically correct notion that white racism is endemic and that whites can be expected, at best, to care little about fairness to black defendants or, at worst, to harbor an active animus toward blacks. It is also supported by casual empiricism. As Frank Chapman put this issue, "For 48 percent of the death row population in our country to be Black is clearly practicing genocide when you consider that Afro-Americans are only 12 per cent of the population." This, one is supposed to conclude, is because of racist prejudice on the part of prosecutors, or juries, or perhaps voters to whom judges and prosecutors are responsible.

It is indeed true that blacks are overrepresented among death row inmates. For example, the most recent data show 42.3 percent of prisoners on death row are black, and among people who have been executed since 1977, 34.3 percent have been black.[11] But what do we find when we look at the data in a bit more detail?

Table 11.1 shows that blacks comprise over half of those classified as offenders in murder and nonnegligent homicide cases. This is a clear disproportion. And there is a similar disproportion of victims—47.2 percent of victims are black. These similar disproportions make sense when we note that the vast majority of murders are *intra*racial and not *inter*racial. Among murders classified in table 11.1, 90 percent are intraracial.[12] Among interracial murders, three-quarters involve blacks killing whites, and only a few involve whites murdering blacks.

Table 11.1. Murders and Nonnegligent Manslaughters Known to Police, United States, 1998

Race of Victim	Race of Offender		Total
	White	Black	
White	3,205	449	3,654
Black	205	3,067	3,272
Total	3,410	3,516	6,926

Note: Omitted are cases in which either the victim or the offender was of the "other" racial classification, or was of unknown race, and cases that involved multiple victims or offenders.

In this context, the disproportion of blacks on death row looks reasonable. Blacks are disproportionately likely to be murderers. Barring a massive police conspiracy to frame blacks for the killing of black victims actually killed by whites, we have to conclude that, at least in broad and gross terms, there is fairness.

B. TESTING RACIAL DISPARITY

But suppose we want to get beyond a "broad and gross" assessment of the racial disparity thesis. To do this, we have to consider legitimate factors that might justify a harsher or a more lenient sentence in a homicide case. Death penalty opponents have given us come clear examples of how *not* to analyze the data, actually claiming racial disparity on the basis of the fact that blacks who kill whites are punished more harshly than blacks who kill blacks. This only makes sense if interracial murders and intraracial murders are similar in terms of circumstances, and there are no legitimate nonracial reasons—such as a prior conviction, the murder being connected with the commission of a felony, the presence of multiple victims, and so on—to consider the black-on-white murders "heinous."[13] In reality, black-on-black and black-on-white murders are likely to involve vastly different circumstances.

IV. Race and the Death Penalty

In any policy-relevant area of social science research, we usually find a raft of methodological problems and issues, and this area is no different. First, we have to face the fact that the application of the death penalty has changed over time. One particularly important watershed is the *Furman* decision, in the wake of which the Supreme Court imposed certain standards that purport to promote procedural fairness. Of course, there might or might not be greater procedural fairness since *Furman*. It might be that the main sources of unfairness are endemic and not subject to being remedied by procedural reforms. Indeed, it's quite possible that post-*Furman* reforms made the system less fair.[14] In criminal justice, as in all other areas of public policy, "unintended consequences" seem to be pervasive. Still, post-*Furman* data are the best data for assessing how the system operates today.

Then there is the issue of what our dependent variable is. In studying the death penalty, it might make sense to study executions. Unfortunately, executions are relatively few in number, so research in this area typically looks at death *sentences* (which may or may not have been carried out) or even the prosecutor's decision to ask for a death sentence (regardless of whether a death sentence is actually imposed). Ironically, the infrequency of executions, which makes it difficult to show that executions deter murders, also makes it difficult to assess racial disparity.[15]

Given that we are forced to study death sentences, rather than actual executions, we have to be a bit cautious interpreting the results. It's possible, for example, that racial bias leads to excessive harshness toward blacks in sentencing, but then blacks sentenced to death attract the support of capable political activist lawyers who represent them during the appeals process. If this is the case, then we risk finding a disparity in sentencing when in fact there is no disparity in executions.

V. A Statistical Model

To assess the nature of any racial disparity, we have constructed a statistical model of death sentences, using the published data of Gross and Mauro. The unit of analysis is homicides. The dependent variable is a dichotomy based on whether a particular homicide resulted in a death penalty or not.

In studying death sentences, we are aggregating over several decision points in the process that may ultimately lead to execution. A suspect may or may not be apprehended. Evidence may or may not be sufficient to bring a murder charge, and prosecutors may be more or less aggressive in bringing such a charge, refusing to plea-bargain, and asking for a death sentence. Judges may be more or less favorable to the defendant, and juries more or less willing to convict and impose a death sentence. So our dependent variable, a "death sentence," is a good "bottom line" assessment of the way the system works—with the important proviso that we are not studying actual executions.

Gross and Mauro's published data include all homicides reported to the Federal Bureau of Investigation (FBI) from 1976 through 1980 from eight states with a relatively large number of homicides.[16] We model death sentences as a function of the race of the victim, and race of the suspect, and the number of aggravating circumstances associated with the crime. Aggravating circumstances include (1) whether the murder was associated with another felony, (2) whether the victim was a stranger, and (3) whether there was more than one victim. This latter variable is an absolutely critical index of the "heinousness" of a murder. As we shall see, it is an exceedingly powerful predictor of whether a murder results in a death sentence.

To create our model, we use logistic regression, the method required by our dependent variable, which is a dichotomy and badly skewed.[17] This creates numbers that look rather arcane to readers without graduate courses in statistics. Such readers are asked to bear with us, for the numbers will eventually be interpreted in understandable terms. We use multivariate logistic regression to assess the independent effect of each variable *after* controlling for the other variables in our model (see table 11.2).

In model 1, we include only two independent variables: the race of the suspect and the number of aggravating circumstances. We find that black suspects are treated more leniently (i.e., less likely to get a death sentence) than white suspects. That's right, *more* leniently. While this might suggest a racist bias against whites, it's important that we also look at the race of the victim. Model 2 shows the effect of the victim's race on the likelihood of a death sentence, after con-

Table 11.2.   Death Sentences in Homicide Cases: Logistic Regression (Standard Errors in Parentheses)

Independent Variable	Model 1	2	3	4	5
Aggravating	1.75	1.60	1.59	1.58	1.66
circumstances	(.065)	(.066)	(.068)	(.069)	(.072)
Black suspect	−.714		.066		
	(.113)		(.134)		
Black victim		−1.56	−1.60	−1.61	−1.49
		(.154)	(.176)	(.169)	(.173)
Black-on-white				.144	.174
murder				(.136)	(.141)
White-on-black				.937	.730
murder				(.419)	(.427)
Arkansas					.384
					(.374)
Florida					.920
					(.267)
Georgia					1.41
					(.279)
Illinois					−.218
					(.294)
Mississippi					1.17
					(.352)
Oklahoma					1.42
					(.309)
North Carolina					.192
					(.330)
Constant	−4.80	−4.54	−4.54	−4.55	−5.36
−2 log likelihood	3,469.8	3,469.9	3,469.9	3,469.8	2,391.7

trolling for the number of aggravating circumstances. The model shows a powerful effect of victim's race. People who murder blacks get vastly more lenient treatment than people who murder whites. Looking at the size of the coefficients, it seems that having a black victim can counterbalance one aggravating factor. In other words, someone who kills a black stranger is about as likely to draw a death penalty as someone who kills a white whom he knows. Someone who kills multiple black victims is about as likely to draw a death penalty as someone who kills a single white.

Since the race of the suspect and the race of the victim are highly correlated, we estimate model 3 to assess the independent effects of the suspect's race and the victim's race. It seems that the race of the suspect has essentially zero effect. The estimated effect is very small, and it is smaller than its associated standard error, which means that so far as we can determine statistically, it is nonexistent. The race of the victim continues to have a very large effect.

The next question to be addressed with this data concerns interracial murders. Given that people who murder blacks are treated more leniently than people who murder whites, are whites who murder blacks treated more leniently than are blacks who murder blacks? Are blacks that murder whites treated especially harshly?

Model 4 addresses this issue. It shows that a black-on-white murder is no more likely to draw a death sentence than a white-on-white murder. The numbers, widely used by opponents of the death penalty showing that blacks who murder whites are treated unusually harshly, are apparently biased by a failure to take into account aggravating factors. The typical black-on-white murder is likely to be between strangers, or perhaps incident to a felony (e.g., the robbery of a convenience store), and would get tougher treatment independent of racial factors.

It may come as a surprise that white-on-black murders are significantly more likely to result in a death sentence than are black-on-black murders. It's a bit of a puzzle figuring out why this might be the case, but it's important to remember that white-on-black murders are exceedingly rare (see table 11.1). Perhaps the circumstances of the typical white-on-black murder are heinous in ways that our index of aggravating factors doesn't pick up. Perhaps the typical white-on-black murder is likely to be considered a "hate crime" and thus punished severely. Perhaps the black community is better mobilized politically to demand that "hate crimes" against blacks be harshly punished. And perhaps the simple rarity of such murders causes them to seem more heinous. The much-publicized dragging death of James Byrd in Texas in 1998[18] supports several of these speculations.

Model 5 inserts dummy variables to pick up state-to-state variation in severity (Virginia is the excluded reference category). A key point here is methodological: the estimates of our other parameters are affected only trivially by the inclusion of state effects in our model. It seems that Florida, Georgia, Mississippi, and Oklahoma are more likely to sentence people to death. The magnitude of these effects is large. It seems, for example, that someone who murders a black in Georgia is treated about as harshly as someone who murders a white in Illinois.

Whether these state variations are yet another unfair "inequity" in the way the death penalty is administered or are rather a legitimate consequence of a federal system in which policies vary among states is beyond the scope of this essay.

Readers who are a bit put off by the "logistic regression coefficients" in table 11.2 will find refuge in table 11.3. Here the regression coefficients from table 11.2 are translated into probabilities. The table shows the probability a suspect will get the death penalty under different circumstances. For example, where the suspect is black, the victim is black, and there are no aggravating factors (or at least none that fit within our index), the probability that the suspect will be convicted and get a death sentence is .0021. In other words, about two out of a thousand such murders result in a death sentence. Aggravating circumstances certainly matter, since a single such circumstance will increase the likelihood that a black who kills a black will get a death sentence to about one in a hundred.

At all levels of aggravation, suspects who murder whites are treated more harshly. A white-on-white murder with zero aggravating factors is about five times as likely to draw a death sentence as a similar black-on-black murder.

This rather simplistic model is hardly the last word on this issue, but it does have very real virtues. It includes data on over fourteen thousand murders, separates race-of-victim and race-of-suspect effects, and uses a robust measure of the severity of the crime for a control.

Table 11.3.   Probability That a Homicide Will Result in a Death Sentence

Race of Victim	Race of Suspect	Number of Aggravating Factors	Probability of a Death Sentence
Black	Black	0	.0021
Black	Black	1	.0102
Black	Black	2	.0476
Black	Black	3	.1955
Black	White	0	.0054
White	White	0	.0105
White	White	2	.1996

Note: Estimates are based on model 4, table 11.2.

VI. Other Studies

There have been numerous previous studies of racial disparity in the application of the death penalty. We will bypass many of these, since they are deficient in some key respect compared to the more recent and better studies. We won't, for example, review studies that fail to control for the heinousness of each murder or that look at the race of prisoners incarcerated for murder without considering the race of the victim.[19]

The best studies on this issue are single-state studies. Using data from only a single state has huge advantages in terms of data collection, although it limits the number of cases that can be studied and precludes getting any solid estimates of how interracial murders are treated. The best studies have a long list of "control" variables. These elaborate controls limit the possibility that the relationships discovered are artifacts of the failure to consider some important factor.[20]

A. RACE-OF-VICTIM EFFECTS

All of the best studies of racial disparity show strong race-of-victim effects. For example, Sheldon Ekland-Olson used data from Texas on cases brought between 1974 and 1983.[21] He showed that offenders who had killed a white were over-represented and those who killed a black or a Hispanic were underrepresented on death row.[22] Paternoster, using data from South Carolina on the probability that prosecutors will *seek* the death penalty in a homicide case, likewise found, even after the imposition of a fairly complete set of control variables, that cases in which whites killed whites were much more likely to result in a death penalty request than cases of a black killing a black.[23] Using Florida data, William J. Bowers found that blacks who killed whites and whites who killed whites were substantially more likely to be indicted for first-degree murder and substantially more likely to be convicted for first-degree murder than blacks who killed blacks.[24] Michael Radelet likewise used Florida data, examining 637 homicide indictments. He looked for racial disparity both in indictments (was the defendant indicted for first-degree murder as opposed to a lesser charge?) and in sentencing (was a death sentence handed down). He divided his cases into "primary murder cases" (in which the victim and defendant were acquainted) and "other" cases (in which they were not). Since the death penalty is so rarely imposed in murders in which victim and offender knew each other, Radelet looked for racial disparity among the "other" cases and found robust race-of-victim effects for both indictments and sentences.[25]

The data of Vito and Keil included all defendants indicted for murder in Kentucky between December 22, 1976, and October 1, 1986. The issue was whether there was racial disparity in prosecutors' decisions to ask for a "death-qualified" jury, which would be able to impose the death penalty. They found that there was. Defendants who were accused of killing whites were more likely to face such a "death-qualified" jury than those accused of killing blacks.[26]

Using data on Missouri cases from 1977 through 1991, Sorensen and Wallace found a robust race-of-victim effect in capital murder convictions with, as expected, cases in which a white was killed being more likely to draw such a conviction.[27]

In one of the few studies to come from a nonsouthern state, Leigh Bienen and her colleagues compiled data on 703 homicides—all those that occurred in New Jersey between 1982 and 1986. The dependent variable was the prosecutor's decision to seek a death sentence. Forty-three percent of defendants who had killed a black were charged with capital murder, as opposed to 28 percent who killed a black victim and 19 percent of those who killed a Hispanic victim. These racial disparities held up in the presence of elaborate statistical controls.[28]

Likewise, an analysis of data from Georgia done by David Baldus and his colleagues showed clear race-of-victim effects, which were robust in the fact of elaborate statistical controls.[29] Baldus and his colleagues looked at the prosecutor's decision to seek a death penalty. This study added one interesting wrinkle: the race-of-victim effects were most apparent in the middle levels of "aggravation." In cases in which there were no aggravating factors, no racial disparity was found, apparently because it is so extremely rare for prosecutors to ask for a death sentence in such cases.[30]

The single partial exception to this impressive consistency of findings is a study by Foley and Powell. Based on Florida data, it included many of the same cases that Radelet analyzed. It included a better set of controls for the heinousness of the murder in question and showed no significant race-of-victim effects either for prosecutors' decisions (seeking the death penalty) or for juries' decisions (to assess a death penalty). However, they did show such significant racial disparities in the behavior of trial judges, who were harsher with defendants who had murdered whites.

B. RACE-OF-OFFENDER EFFECTS

In contrast to the findings regarding the race of the victim, the data on racial disparity in the treatment of suspects fail to show any robust effects. The best studies rarely turn up significant race-of-suspect effects, and when such effects show up, they lack statistical robustness. Among the studies we discussed earlier, Bowers reported no race-of-defendant effects.[31] Radelet looked for race-of-defendant effects and found none either for first-degree murder indictments or for death sentences.[32] Likewise, Foley and Powell found none for prosecutors' decisions to seek the death penalty or for juries' decisions to levy the death penalty, or for the actual sentences imposed by trial judges.[33] Paternoster, likewise, found no significant race-of-suspect effects.[34]

Bienen et al. found no race-of-defendant effects with regard to the prosecutor's decision to plea-bargain rather than go to trial. Where the prosecutors decision to "serve a notice of factors" (i.e., to claim aggravating factors that might justify a death sentence), the pattern was more complicated, but there seemed to be no net race-of-defendant effect.[35] Gross and Mauro found statistically significant race-of-suspect effects in Illinois, but not in any of the other seven states in their study.[36] Since they had no reason to believe that Illinois—and not any of the other states—would be biased against black defendants, we should pretty much ignore this "finding." Sorensen and Wallace also found race-of-offender effects in their Missouri data, although the magnitude of the effect was much smaller than their race-of-victim effects.[37] Thus, while we cannot absolutely rule out a bias against black defendants, the statistical findings supporting this notion are few, scattered, and not robust. It seems to be the case that, if you go mushing in the data enough, you will quite likely find "effects" that are mere statistical phantoms.

VII. The "Specialist" Argument about Racial Disparity

Thus, the mass market version of the racial disparity thesis is simply wrong. The system is not tougher on black suspects, others things being equal. Indeed, it is more lenient with black suspects—but only because they likely killed other blacks. Now let's consider the "specialist" version of the racial disparity argument: that the criminal justice system discriminates against blacks by its lack of concern for black victims. As Anthony Amsterdam has claimed, "Although less than 40 percent of Georgia homicide cases involve white victims, in 87 percent of the cases in which a death sentence is imposed, the victim is white. White-victim cases are almost eleven times more likely to produce a death sentence than are black-victim cases."[38] Randall L. Kennedy, likewise describing the Baldus study we have cited, laments what he describes as the fact that "*in Georgia's marketplace of emotion the lives of blacks simply count for less that the lives of whites.*"[39]

I call this the "specialist" version because it is the one propounded by specialists who have actually analyzed the data. It should not escape our notice that it flatly contradicts the "mass market" version. It also should not escape our notice that it follows from radically different philosophical premises compared to the mass market version. In the mass market version, all the concern is for the accused. The issue is whether *accused* blacks get tougher treatment than whites. When a superficial data analysis shows this to be so, the opponents of the death penalty rail about "racism in the criminal justice system."

But then when better data analysis shows that black suspects are treated too leniently, the emphasis suddenly shifts to the victim. Were the death penalty opponents philosophically consistent, they might laud the finding of leniency toward black suspects as a kind of affirmative action. Against a backdrop of historically rough treatment of blacks accused of crime, black suspects are now getting a break. But no, they decide that they care about victims after all. Thus, an offender-centered view is replaced, in no time flat, with a convenient victim-centered view.

A. THE PUZZLE OF "RACISM" AND THE DEATH PENALTY

Politically correct people who like to rail against "racism" can certainly do so with regard to the death penalty—although they might be a bit uncomfortable having to adopt a victim-centered approach. After all, many are the people who have been especially concerned with the rights of the accused, have ridiculed notions of personal responsibility (society is really at fault, they have told us), made excuses for criminals, and demanded rehabilitation rather than punishment.

But are they right in condemning the system as "racist"? Absolutely. But the warm feeling of righteousness that flows from condemning racism should not be allowed to obscure the fact that we have a major intellectual puzzle here. Why *not* a bias against black defendants? Why, rather, a bias against protecting the lives of potential black victims and against retribution for the deaths of blacks that have been killed?

The key attraction of the mass market view of racial disparity is the ease of seeing how it works. Racist cops, racist prosecutors, racist juries, and racist judges deal harshly with hapless black suspects. But how do we explain the specialist version?

It's extremely hard to see how it could follow from any active ill will toward black people on the part of whites. It is the black suspect, after all, who is caught in the maw of the system. He (or more rarely she) is the one on whom racist whites can impose direct palpable harm. One might try imagining a jury consisting entirely of Klansmen. While such a jury would have far too little solicitude for the victim, it is hard to see why they would have any solicitude at all for the defendant. Why not convict him and sentence him to death?

Of course, we could posit shrewd, insightful, malevolent Klansmen who know that they can do the black community more harm by treating black criminals leniently. I find this implausible. If they were capable of that level of so-phistication, they wouldn't be Klansmen.[40]

So if active ill will toward black people can't explain the racial disparity in the system, what does? One possibility is that we have something akin to what President George W. Bush has called the "soft bigotry of low expectations."[41] Bush was talking about education, but the principle may well apply to criminal justice. Perhaps we deal leniently with black defendants because we expect large numbers of blacks to be criminals. Perhaps we have come to expect black neigh-borhoods to be unsafe and therefore consider crime in those neighborhoods to be pretty much a routine matter. Perhaps we view murders as "heinous" when the circumstances are rare and shocking, and we have ceased to view murders of black people as rare and shocking.

If this is the case, then people who are convinced of their own racial good-will and their own righteousness in opposing racism in all its forms need to do a little soul searching. Where education is concerned, they have told us that black children can't learn until there is a massive increase in federal spending on edu-cation, or until there is racial balance in the schools, or until the proper sort of curriculum reform. Where criminal justice is concerned, they have told us that crime can't be reduced until societal racism is ended, or until there is a massive increase in social welfare spending, or until we replace of philosophy of punish-ment with one of rehabilitation.

VIII. Black Public Opinion

Clearly, black people are victims of an unfairly administered system of punish-ment. Given this fact, how do we deal with it? Interestingly, polls of black peo-ple show a clear majority favoring the death penalty. The most recent Gallup Poll for which demographic breakdowns are available found 54 percent of blacks fa-voring the death penalty and only 46 percent opposed.[42] Linda Lichter commis-sioned a nationwide poll that went to considerable expense to oversample blacks—something that is highly desirable if we want a statistically reliable mea-surement of black opinion—and questioned over six hundred black respondents. Among those respondents with an opinion, 55 percent favored the death penalty and 45 percent opposed it. Another approach to getting a good number of black respondents is to look at surveys that have been asked over repeated years. For example, the General Social Survey of the National Opinion Research Center shows that for the years 1991–96, 57.7 percent of blacks who had an opinion on the issue favored capital punishment, while only 42.3 percent opposed it.[43] Even 60 percent of the upscale readers of *Ebony* said capital punishment is "the only just punishment" for murder.[44]

Of course, the fact that a majority of blacks favor a policy no more makes it a good policy than the fact that a majority of whites does. But it does underline the fact that concern with racial disparity doesn't require opposition to the death penalty.

IX. Reform the Death Penalty?

One simple response to the racial inequities in the death penalty is to reform the administration of criminal justice to eliminate the inequities. Unfortunately, it's not at all clear how to do that. If juries are disinclined to convict a defendant who murdered a black, it's hard to see a constitutional remedy. If they are disinclined to assess a death penalty in a case in which the victim is black, the decision could be given back to the judge, but this would require the admission that the "reform" that followed the *Furman* decision was ill conceived. If prosecutors are more inclined to plea-bargain in cases in which the victim is black, that discretion in theory could be taken from them, but only at a very high cost.

Probably the long-term solution lies in a change of attitudes. Simply *knowing* that the problem is not harshness toward black suspects but leniency toward black suspects would be a huge help. If prosecutors feared charges of "racism" not because they sought tough punishment of black defendants but because they failed to seek tough punishment, things might be very different. Likewise, if the media paid less attention to cases in which a supposedly innocent black defendant was convicted of murder and more attention to cases in which someone who murdered a black got off lightly, that would also help.

Thus, we can offer no short-term remedy for racial disparity. Note, however, that if the racial disparity in the way death sentences are meted out can't be fixed any time soon, neither can the death penalty be abolished any time soon, given the overwhelming support it has among the American people. This was shown in the 2000 presidential election, when liberal supporters of Vice President Al Gore attacked George W. Bush for the supposedly large number of executions he had presided over in Texas. Not only did the attack fall flat, but by the third presidential debate, Gore reiterated his longtime support for capital punishment.[45] So neither the supporters nor the opponents of the death penalty have any plausible short-term solutions.

X. Would Abolition Lead to Fairness?

At this point, we must ask whether abolition of the death penalty would in fact do away with racial disparity. In one sense it would. If nobody is being executed, then it cannot be the case that any particular racial group is being disproportionately executed. The problem with this argument is that while we can, in theory, end executions, we aren't going to end punishments for murder. Most likely, the abolition of the death penalty would lead to a general ratcheting down of punishments, with the inequities remaining. Prosecutors would still face the fact that bringing a case to trial requires a large commitment of resources and would still have an incentive to plea-bargain. Judges who currently assess harsher punishments against those who murder whites would likely continue to do so, but at a lower level of severity.

Indeed, there is quite a lot of evidence of racial disparity in the way we punish murderers below the level of execution. One interesting study dealt with 245 persons arrested for homicide in Philadelphia in 1970.[46] Of these, 170 were eventually convicted of some charge. Sixty-five percent of defendants who killed a white got either life imprisonment or a death sentence, while only 25 percent of those who killed a black did.[47] Since these murders produced only three death sentences (all imposed on blacks who killed whites), most of the apparent racial unfairness involved life imprisonment, not execution.

Alfred Blumstein studied racial disproportionality of prison populations and found that in 1991 blacks were *underrepresented* among prisoners convicted of murder.[48] Given the data we have seen thus far, it seems overwhelmingly likely that this is because suspects accused of murdering blacks (who are themselves overwhelmingly likely to be black) are treated leniently. In spite of some methodological problems,[49] his results strongly suggest that the same racial bias that affects death sentences also affects imprisonment: those who kill blacks are underpunished.

William J. Bowers, in a study we have already discussed, found that defendants who killed whites were more likely to be indicted for first-degree murder— rather than a lesser charge—and more likely to be convicted for first-degree murder than defendants who killed blacks.[50] Along similar lines Radelet, in a study of indictments for murder in Florida, found that 85 percent of the killers of white victims were indicted for first-degree murder, while only 53.6 percent of the killers of black victims were.[51]

Leigh Bienen and her colleagues, in their study of New Jersey homicides (also discussed earlier) examined the issue of whether a particular case is plea-bargained or whether it goes to trial. Cases involving white victims were found to go to trial more often that cases involving either black or Hispanic victims.[52]

One particularly interesting study involved prosecutors' decisions to "upgrade" or "downgrade" a homicide. An "upgrade" involved a prosecutor making a charge of a felony connected with the homicide when no such felony was mentioned in the police report. On the other hand, cases were said to be "downgraded" when the police report indicated the commission of a felony, but the prosecutor's charge did not mention it. A statistical model that controlled for the circumstances of the crime and the characteristics of the offender showed that white victim murders were more likely to be upgraded than black victim murders.[53]

What we find here, in sum, is a system that consistently undervalues the lives of black victims. It does so when the issue is who will be given a death sentence. And it also does so when the issue is whether a case will be plea-bargained as opposed to being brought to trial. It does so when the issue is who will go to prison for murder. It does so when the issue is who will be indicted for first-degree murder, as opposed to a lesser charge. It does so when the issue is who will be convicted of first-degree murder.

This all makes perfect sense; indeed, it would be almost shocking to find otherwise. If the system undervalues the lives of black victims, it's vastly implausible to think it does so only when execution is the issue, and not in other circumstances. If prosecutors are less willing to devote resources to prosecuting those who murder blacks, and if judges and juries are less likely to view the murder of a black as deserving of severe punishment, it's hard to see how simply abolishing the death penalty would change any of that. Merely doing away with the death penalty doesn't guarantee that everybody will be treated fairly. It merely guarantees that they cannot be executed.

Note that even if a system without capital punishment had less racial disparity, it wouldn't necessarily follow that the death penalty should be abolished. If the costs, both in terms of deterrence and in terms of doing justice, were very high we might decide that racial disparity is tolerable, relative to the alternative.[54] Indeed, having the death penalty might be "Pareto optimal," causing both blacks and whites to be better off, notwithstanding that it helped whites more than it helped blacks. But this whole discussion is academic, since there is no reason at all to believe that a system without the death penalty would have less racial disparity.

XI. Conclusion

We are thus stuck with a system of criminal justice that discriminates against black victims, and we are stuck with it for the foreseeable future, regardless of whether we abolish the death penalty or not. Long-term change for the better will require fundamental changes in attitude and will especially require them among sectors of the population who think themselves to be enlightened and opposed to racism.

The striking thing about the death penalty is the extent to which it is an outcropping of the "culture wars." It seems to distill fundamental cultural values—

about personal responsibility, guilt, the place of government, the therapeutic role of middle-class professionals, and claims of victimhood. It seems to pit people who would legalize gay marriage and outlaw sport utility vehicles against people who would legalize school prayer and outlaw abortion.

But unfortunately, fighting the culture wars has little to do with making people who need protection safer. As we come to terms with the reality of racial disparity, we should remember that abolition of the death penalty would in no way make black people (with the exception of a tiny minority of black murderers sentenced to death) any better off.

CHAPTER 12

"The Executioner's Face Is Always Well Hidden"

SOCIAL SCIENCE ARGUMENTS AGAINST CAPITAL PUNISHMENT

J. Michael Martinez

I

Early in the morning of May 14, 1973, twenty-one-year-old Carl Isaacs and three members of his "gang" left a seedy motel in Flagler Beach, Florida, north of Daytona, driving a stolen car. They traveled up through the Florida panhandle and into rural southwest Georgia. Even to the casual observer, Isaacs and his confederates—his older half-brother, Wayne Carl Coleman, twenty-eight; Isaac's fifteen-year-old brother, Billy; and a friend, George "Snail" Dungee, thirty-five—were trouble waiting to happen. Throughout the day, Carl drove the car, as usual, and Billy sat beside him, riding "shotgun." Wayne and his slow-witted friend, Snail, occupied the rear. They looked exactly like what they were: four deeply disturbed young men—career criminals—hell-bent on wreaking havoc on anything and anyone in their path. Earlier in the week, the young men had escaped from a Maryland prison camp and headed into McConnellsburg, Pennsylvania. There, on May 10, they kidnapped nineteen-year-old Richard Wayne Miller and stole his 1968 Chevrolet Chevelle. After shooting Miller in the head and leaving his lifeless body in the woods of Allegany County, Maryland, the gang drove south to Florida in search of good times. They later confessed they wanted to reach Florida and "show Wayne the ocean."[1]

By all accounts, they enjoyed their time at the beach. Four days later, tanned and rested, the gang departed from Daytona and headed north. Bored with the interstate, the young men eventually exited and traveled the back roads of south Georgia looking for a place to burglarize. They had blown their last $10 on a twelve-pack of beer and desperately needed cash to continue their misadventures.

As luck would have it, around 4:00 P.M. that afternoon, they stumbled onto a mobile home owned by Jerry Alday, thirty-five, and his wife, Mary, twenty-six. The trailer was parked on River Road in rural Seminole County near the sleepy hamlet of Donalsonville, Georgia. Donalsonville was a quiet little town of seven thousand far removed from the hustle and bustle of metropolitan Atlanta to the north and the sunny shores of Florida to the southeast. It was the kind of place where nothing remarkable or newsworthy ever happened. Neighbors knew each other and never felt the need to lock their doors. It was a close-knit community filled with friends and relatives. They had a saying that "If you aren't an Alday or a Johnson, you're married to one." All that changed during a long, violent afternoon in May 1973.

The gang initially was attracted to Jerry Alday's mobile home because they thought they saw a gas pump around back; they soon found they were mistaken. Because they had already stopped to investigate, however, the young men decided to take advantage of the opportunity to break into the mobile home. The plan they hatched that afternoon was as ill conceived as it was fortuitous. Fifteen-year-old Billy Isaacs served as a lookout while Carl Isaacs and Wayne Coleman entered the mobile home in search of cash, clothing, and firearms. Carl instructed Snail Dungee to sit in the car with the engine running to ensure a smooth, quick getaway, if necessary.[2] In case the plan went awry, the burglars were prepared for any contingency: Carl Isaacs was armed with a .32 pistol, and Wayne Coleman carried a .380.[3]

Within a few minutes after the would-be burglars entered the premises, the original plan was foiled. The owner of the mobile home, Jerry Alday, and his father, Ned, sixty-two, drove into the yard in a jeep. Ned Alday had been slowed by arthritis in recent years, but he could look back on a reasonably successful life, especially for a man who came of age in modest Seminole County during the Great Depression. After he lost all his land in the 1930s, he had taken a job in a sawmill. Gradually over the years, he had saved enough money to buy back his land and transform the fallow fields into a 525-acre farm that supported his large, close-knit family.

The Aldays had lived in Seminole County for more than a hundred years, at least since the days of the Civil War. Because family members lived within a few miles of each other, they often dropped in unannounced, a practice that would lead to tragic consequences on this long, bloody afternoon. They were religious people, leaders in the local Spring Creek Baptist Church, which their great-grandfather had founded during the nineteenth century. Everyone in the clan was a teetotaler who believed that strict discipline and hard work were keys to a successful life. No one exemplified this belief more than Ned Alday.

Apparently without realizing that intruders were inside the mobile home that afternoon, Ned and Jerry pulled up behind the house and stepped from their vehicle. Some commentators have speculated that the Alday men may have been investigating the strange car with out-of-state license plates parked in front of the trailer, but their impressions are lost to history; their intentions remain unclear to this day. Whatever their motivations, when the two men approached the front door of the mobile home, their family changed forever.[4]

Deciding that the best defense is a good offense, Carl Isaacs and Wayne Coleman burst from the trailer and told the two men to put up their hands. The Aldays were shocked but did as they had been ordered. After the intruders ordered their prisoners inside the mobile home, Carl took Jerry into one bedroom while Wayne escorted Ned into another.

The routine burglary escalated into murder, although it remains unclear how or why this occurred. Without warning, Wayne pointed his gun and shot the family patriarch in the head at point-blank range. The perpetrators' accounts often conflict on the details, but Carl and Wayne agree they were startled when Ned Alday, bleeding profusely from his head wound, struggled to his feet and somehow staggered into the hall. He was already mortally wounded. Undaunted, Carl pushed him back into the bedroom. According to Billy Isaacs, who later testified against his brother, "there were several shots and Carl came back out and asked where Wayne was. Carl walked into the other bedroom. I followed behind and stuck my head in. The oldest of the two men was kind of half way lying on the bed, kneeling on the floor, his body jerking. Wayne and Carl were standing at the foot of the bed. They pointed their pistols at the man and both fired at him until he finally quit moving." According to Larry Howard, director of the state crime lab, Ned Alday was shot seven times in the head, and Jerry Alday was shot four times.[5]

The Alday family slaughter was far from over. Not long after Carl and Wayne killed Jerry and Ned, Jimmy Alday, twenty-five—Jerry's brother and Ned's son—drove into the yard on a tractor. As he approached the mobile home, Jimmy was surprised when the door flew open and Wayne Coleman pointed a gun at him. According to Billy Isaacs, Carl and Wayne ordered Jimmy inside and asked him whether he had heard shots. When he said he had heard nothing, Carl brandished his pistol and told Jimmy with as much bravado as he could muster, "You're going to hear something now." He ordered the young man to lie down on the couch and then shot Jimmy twice at close range. Afterward, Carl put on Jimmy's cowboy hat and walked outside to move the tractor.[6]

Fate intervened once again. As Carl Isaacs was moving the tractor, Jerry Alday's wife, Mary, drove her 1970 Chevrolet Impala into the yard. She must not have seen Isaacs because she stepped from the car and began carrying groceries into the mobile home as though nothing out of the ordinary had occurred. As she entered the front door with an armload of packages, Carl came up behind her, knocked the bags from her hands, and spun her against the wall. Frightened into tears, Mary became hysterical, screaming and begging not to be hurt. "Carl told her to shut up but she couldn't," Billy later testified.

Events quickly moved to a climax. As the killers confronted the sobbing Mary, two more Alday family members arrived on the scene. Chester (Shugie), thirty-two, and his uncle, fifty-seven-year-old Aubrey, drove up in a pickup truck. They were laughing as they sat inside the cab. For some reason, their good mood infuriated Carl Isaacs. He marched out of the trailer, snatched open the door to the truck, waved his pistol in their faces, and ordered the men inside. Surprised and alarmed by the sight of the gun, they complied. Once inside, Carl made them sit on the kitchen floor. The scene grew somber when they saw Mary's tear-drenched face. Years later, Billy Isaacs recalled that, "Carl asked why they were laughing, if they thought he was funny. Mary Alday said to the men that Jimmy was hurt."

No longer outside awaiting the getaway, Snail Dungee escorted Mary into the bathroom while Carl took Aubrey into one bedroom and Wayne took Chester into another. Wayne shot and killed his prey instantly—with no hesitation or remorse. As for Aubrey, his death was delayed briefly. "I heard clicking noises from the bedroom," Billy said. "Carl came running out to me and said, 'My gun's empty.'" Grabbing a .38-caliber pistol, Carl charged back into the bedroom. Shots rang out. Seconds later, Carl stepped from the room, laughing. According to Billy Isaacs, "I asked him what was so funny, and Carl said, 'That bastard begged for mercy.'"[7]

That left one victim. No doubt Mary realized her predicament, but she was powerless to act. While Billy Isaacs took some items from the gang's stolen car to Mary's Impala, Carl, Wayne, and Snail brutally raped the woman on the kitchen floor of the mobile home. Afterward, they blindfolded and gagged her. Rough hands raked and clawed at her skin as they forced her into the car.

They drove Mary to a secluded dirt road about six miles away from the mobile home. As soon as they arrived at the spot, Wayne Coleman announced that he had left his wallet in the trailer. Although the men were frustrated, they quickly returned to the trailer to retrieve it before returning to the dirt road. Afterward, they raped Mary again. Carl later bragged that he had sodomized the frightened young woman as well, although the medical examiner found no such indications on the body. It was only one of many inconsistencies in the stories told that day.

Finally, when the gang was finished, Carl handed the .22 pistol to Wayne. He said nothing, but it was obvious that he wanted to claim one more victim before they ended the killing spree. Snail Dungee unexpectedly spoke up. Apparently feeling left out, he whined, "What about me?" Carl and Wayne looked at each other, shrugged, and handed the pistol to Snail. They watched as he marched Mary fifty or sixty feet away. In the toughest voice he could muster,

Snail ordered her to lie down. She did, and he shot her twice. "When we last saw Mary," Billy Isaacs said, "she was lying face down."[8]

Their business in Georgia was done. Leaving six dead victims in their wake, the gang fled into Alabama in Mary's Impala, but they did not get far. The car was old and needed work. Eventually, pushed beyond its limits, it overheated. The gang abandoned it and stole another vehicle. Not long after that, they were captured by Alabama police.

Over the years, observers have been astounded that not one of the men seemed to feel any remorse for his actions that day until years later, when the death penalty became an option. In a 1977 television documentary, Carl Isaacs recounted the events of that afternoon in a matter-of-fact voice. Referring to his victims, he said, "They ran up on us when we were robbing the place and we killed them. That's all there is to it. They don't mean a damn thing to me. . . . The only thing the Aldays ever did that stood out was getting killed by me."[9]

A psychologist testifying at one of Carl Isaacs's later trials attempted to put the crime into perspective. According to Dr. William A. Dickinson, Carl was a "self-hating, antisocial manipulator" who pushed his gang into committing the acts. "A combination of drugs and alcohol abuse, combined with mental illness, in my opinion, resulted in transient psychotic symptoms, and, in my opinion, explain what happened that afternoon," Dr. Dickinson concluded.[10]

II

Confronted with the facts of a brutal crime, the public cries out for the forces of law and order to do something. The public safety has been compromised, and the offenders must pay—preferably with their lives. And who can blame the public when confronted with defendants as unsympathetic as the Isaacs gang? Surely these men deserve the harshest punishment possible for their senseless, brutal crimes. Perhaps death is the only appropriate punishment for actions of this magnitude.

The question always arises at this point whether capital punishment is an appropriate penalty for heinous crimes. "Appropriate" means that the punishment achieves the objectives it was designed to accomplish. To answer this question, the objectives must be identified, and three readily spring to mind. First, the death penalty often is touted as an effective deterrent. In addition, imposition of the death penalty generally is lauded as a means of protecting society from future crimes perpetrated by an offender who will be forever dangerous, now and in the future. Finally, the death penalty is justified as an expression of society's collective sense of justice; it is not merely retribution but a thoughtful, proportionate response to the offender's outrageous actions. These objectives initially appear sound and reasonable, but it remains to be seen whether social science data support their efficacy.

The first objective, deterrence, is conceptually simple. It assumes that individuals rationally calculate the costs and benefits of engaging in certain activities. Consequently, an offender who is not mentally ill or acting under another sort of diminished capacity (intoxication, the heat of passion, or mistaken impressions) can be viewed as a rational maximizer who will seek to maximize benefits while minimizing costs. Theoretically, in a society where offenders believe that their activities confer greater benefits than costs, criminal activity should increase as rational maximizers weigh the pros and cons of engaging in crime (assuming that other, nonutilitarian considerations such as moral compunction are subtracted from the equation). To prevent crime, therefore, society must enact laws with harsh penalties that will alter the offender's calculations. In the context of the death penalty, the offender must view the possibility of being apprehended, tried, convicted, and executed for his crimes as so high that the costs outweigh the burdens.

The problem with the deterrence argument is that many offenders are not rational maximizers at the time they commit their crimes. Their offenses are crimes of passion or outrage undertaken with minimal, if any, forethought. These offenders will not be deterred because they cannot or will not calculate consequences in a rational manner. In such cases, capital punishment must be justified—if it is justified at all—on some other grounds.[11]

The empirical research on whether capital punishment deters any offenders from their activities is varied and difficult to assess. The research generally can be grouped according to the methodologies used to develop the conclusions. Some studies adopt a comparative approach by examining homicide rates for states that impose capital punishment and comparing them with homicide rates in neighboring states that do not impose capital punishment. Other studies compare homicide rates in the same state before and after capital punishment was instituted. In each case, the studies are inconclusive, at best. They depend on the assumptions incorporated into the studies and the means of coding the relevant variables. When some variables are controlled for in the studies, a causal connection between capital punishment and imposition of the death penalty is not demonstrated. This is persuasive—but not definitive—evidence that capital punishment does not deter offenders from committing crimes in all cases. It does not mean that deterrence fails in every case. It may be that one or more offenders are deterred from acting, but the data do not lend themselves to analyses of individual cases, especially cases in which crimes did not occur. More to the point from a broader perspective of crafting efficacious public policy, if deterrence fails generally, then capital punishment must be justified on some other grounds.[12]

Consider the data summarized in table 12.1. Using mean rates for murder and nonnegligent manslaughter and comparing them across time in death penalty and non–death penalty states, the deterrence argument can be tested. If the hypothesis holds true that the death penalty deters offenders from engaging in capital crimes, the data should indicate a lower rate of capital crimes in death penalty states. Contrary to what one would expect to find according to the deterrence hypothesis, however, the murder and nonnegligent manslaughter rate sometimes is lower in non–death penalty states. If deterrence were a major consideration of rational maximizers, one would assume that murders would occur more frequently in non–death penalty states, but this is not always the case.

Researchers must be careful not to take the analysis too far. These data do not explain why differences exist between death penalty and non–death penalty states. Other variables may explain the differences. For example, death penalty states may include cities with large urban, black, young, and poor populations, which are demographic characteristics associated with increases in the murder and nonnegligent manslaughter rate. In such cases, the murder rate probably would be higher than the rate in other states regardless of whether imposition of the death penalty was a strong possibility. The question is whether the rate would be higher in a state housing such populations if the death penalty were unavailable.

Some capital punishment studies have addressed this question by examining the death penalty over time in a single jurisdiction, especially by comparing the

Table 12.1.   Mean Rates of Murder and Nonnegligent Manslaughter in Death Penalty and Non–Death Penalty States (per 100,000 Population)[13]

Year	Death Penalty States	Non–Death Penalty States
1980	9.4	5.2
1981	9.2	5.3
1982	8.5	5.2
1983	7.3	4.8
1984	6.9	4.4
1985	7.0	4.6
1986	7.6	4.7
1987	7.1	4.9
1988	7.2	4.5
1989	7.1	5.1
1990	7.9	5.0
1991	8.2	5.1
1992	7.8	4.9
1993	8.1	5.3
1994	8.0	4.4
1995	7.5	4.1

murder and nonnegligent manslaughter rates in a state before the death penalty was provided for in the law and later, after it was provided for in the law. The data have been inconclusive. In some cases, the murder rate declined when the death penalty was reinstated; in others, it increased after reinstatement. When other variables were accounted for in the data, probably the best that could be said was that the murder rate either was unaffected or was affected in ways that were not immediately clear from the available statistics.[14]

Some critics have argued that the death penalty could be an effective deterrent, but the full force of this punishment is muted by numerous procedural delays interposed by a society that has no stomach for killing all but the most unsympathetic criminals. The "interminable appeals process" that allows death row inmates to languish in jails for an average of nine to fourteen years "has made the death penalty more a hollow threat than an effective deterrent," in the words of one commentator.[15] The stated concern for protecting innocent men wrongly convicted of capital crimes is misplaced, according to this view. Given the sophisticated tools available to defense attorneys to establish the innocence of their clients as well as the onerous burden of proof ("beyond a reasonable doubt") for convicting persons accused of crimes, the likelihood that an innocent man will be executed in a rush to judgment is minuscule, at best. The solution to this problem of convicted killers who populate death row for decades is to eliminate "trivial procedural delays" and reform habeas corpus appeals. If criminals knew they would face execution in a relatively short time after conviction, the deterrent effect of capital punishment would be patently obvious.

This argument extends further to suggest that the days when habeas corpus appeals were essential tools in ensuring that certain ethnic minorities, especially African Americans, were provided with appropriate procedural safeguards under discriminatory state laws are over. Only when a state court blatantly ignores or defies U.S. Supreme Court precedents or when compelling new evidence exonerates a death row defendant should federal habeas corpus review be used. Both cases, however, are exceedingly rare. Habeas corpus is abused by offenders and clog the federal court system, even though "[n]early half the total delay" occurs in cases "with no doubt whatever concerning the identity of the killer."[16]

The opposite argument is that habeas corpus appeals are necessary to the equitable administration of justice. Because imposing capital punishment is the most important and terrible decision a regime can make, it is preferable to err on the side of caution. It is better that delays occur in certain individual cases than to rush forward in a misguided attempt to extract justice without providing death row defendants with every opportunity to present a vigorous defense. In recent years, however, an increasingly conservative U.S. Supreme Court has narrowed access to habeas corpus appeals and federal procedural reviews because it wants to "send a message" to criminals that law and order will be observed in the

United States. The message that it actually sends, however, may be far different. By denying offenders a full opportunity to avail themselves of due process, the court has weakened the Bill of Rights.[17]

Would deterrence be more effective if its harshness were not muted by procedural delays? Perhaps, but again the available data do not support this hypothesis. If the offenders are not rational maximizers in the first place, the question of whether they will be put to death does not arise in their calculations. A 90 percent chance of receiving the death penalty or a 10 percent chance makes little, if any, difference to an offender who engages in a capital crime if he never considers the consequences. Perhaps future studies will focus on this question in more detail.

Moving on from the deterrence argument, the second question is whether the imposition of the death penalty protects society from the subsequent violent actions of an offender. The incapacitation argument, as it is sometimes called, goes to the heart of society's fears about recidivism, especially when career criminals are turned lose on the streets to commit future crimes. In the words of a Texas criminal statute, the question is whether there is "a probability that the defendant would commit criminal acts of violence that would constitute a continuing threat to society."[18]

Setting aside the broader philosophical question of whether it is equitable to execute an offender because of what he or she may do in the future, the inquiry focuses on the available social science data. The problem is that most of the data are derived from the opinions and conclusions of psychiatrists, psychologists, and mental health care professionals who are called on to make subjective professional judgments. Predictions of whether an offender will be dangerous in the future are speculative at best, and health care professionals may overstate the threat.[19]

Clinical testimony by medical doctors and other such attempts to predict future dangerousness stretches back as far as the eighteenth century. The most notorious examples occurred in witchcraft trials, but the use of medical professionals as experts in capital cases continued well into the nineteenth century. An Italian physician and university professor, Cesare Lombroso, once claimed that he could determine a person's criminal proclivities by examining certain atavistic characteristics—for example, protruding lips and a low, sloping forehead—that indicate whether that person has completed the necessary evolutionary processes. Lombroso did not subscribe to notions of rehabilitation or deterrence; accordingly, in his expert opinion, the only solution to the problem of persons who exhibited these characteristics was to put them to death before any overt acts were committed.[20]

By today's standards, Lombroso was an extreme case. No mainstream medical professional would argue for punishing an offender solely based on predictions of what that person might do in the future. Nonetheless, even in the twentieth century, abuses have occurred in the name of "medical judgment." In the first half of the twentieth century, some clinicians argued that criminality and feeblemindedness were hereditary. These conclusions fit in nicely with the eugenics movement, which led U.S. doctors in the early 1900s to sterilize more than seventy thousand people thought to be mentally inferior.[21] In the 1930s, Charles Hooton, an American anthropologist teaching at Harvard University, contended that the only means of eradicating crime was to eradicate inferior organisms (i.e., criminals) before they could infect society. This conclusion comes dangerously close to the pseudoscientific theories propounded by some of the more infamous medical doctors of the modern era—say, the Third Reich—in an effort to cleanse society of racial and ethnic impurities.[22]

Modern attempts to assess future violent actions are more sensitive to the characteristics of individuals than were past efforts to focus on crimes committed by groups of people possessing certain undesirable, inherited traits. Still, although medical judgments made today are not nearly as dramatic or salacious as some made in the past, the results of recent studies have been conflicting. Even mental health professionals admit that their diagnoses rely in no small measure on qualitative judgments of questionable reliability. Any subjective assessment of recidivism necessarily requires the medical professional who makes judgments to use past behavior as a key component in predicting anticipated future behavior. Faith in such qualitative assessments strikes critics as retrograde determinism that is but a thinly disguised dogma, unsupported by social science data.[23]

If qualitative data contain subjective judgments of questionable reliability, perhaps quantitative data may provide an answer. The most obvious source for quantitative data can be found in actuarial tables. Insurance companies often use actuarial data to make predictions about risk assessment to assist them in setting premiums for persons in certain categories based on age, income, smoking, and other lifestyle preferences and habits involving general health. As with subjective judgments made by health care professionals, however, these data are not necessarily accurate in predicting rates of violent recidivism. In the words of one commentator, "[a]s with clinical predictions, actuarial methods overpredict, resulting in large numbers of false positives for those who have been predicted to be dangerous but in reality pose no threat. As such, actuarial prediction, although vastly superior to clinical prediction, is still of little utility in predicting dangerousness in capital trials."[24]

The question naturally arises: Is this concern for the future dangerousness of capital offenders overblown? What is the likelihood that someone convicted of a heinous crime will be back on the streets and menacing society? Although one might find comfort in the statistical data suggesting that offenders convicted of heinous crimes seldom escape and return to the streets, the story of the Isaacs gang again provides food for thought.

III

None of the eight court-appointed defense lawyers from southwest Georgia wanted the burden of representing the defendants in the Alday murder trial. When told that he had been appointed to represent Carl Isaacs, Bainbridge attorney Willis Conger did not disguise his reluctance. "I despise it. I'd rather take a whipping," he said. "But the judge appointed me, and I have to do my job." Fortunately for Conger, he was relieved from the case when a noted Savannah attorney, Bobby Hill, agreed to take over Isaacs's defense. A leader of the black caucus in the Georgia House of Representatives, Hill had argued the landmark U.S. Supreme Court case, *Furman v. Georgia*, that temporarily ended capital punishment in the United States.[25] In that case, the high court ruled that many state statutes discriminated against ethnic minorities, especially blacks, which led to disproportionate application of the death penalty. In the aftermath of the *Furman* case, Georgia was among many states that redrafted their criminal codes to satisfy the Supreme Court's objections. Governor Jimmy Carter signed the new statutory provisions into law on March 28, 1973—forty-seven days before the Alday murders. Hill viewed the Isaacs case as an opportunity to challenge the new statute.

The circumstances of Carl Isaacs's trial were controversial from the beginning and laid the groundwork for appeals that stretched across two decades. Under Georgia law at the time, victims' families were allowed to hire a special prosecutor to handle the case on the state's (and the family's) behalf. The surviving Alday family members paid $5,000 to hire Peter Zack Geer to prosecute the case. Geer had served as lieutenant governor of Georgia in the early 1960s. Since his return to private practice, he had lived and worked in Albany. He also had been hunting and fishing with Ned and Aubrey Alday, and, in one instance, he had handled an insurance suit for Aubrey. The capital case was tried before Superior Court Judge Walter Idus Geer of Cuthbert, the special prosecutor's uncle. When defense attorneys asked Judge Geer to recuse himself, he refused. Georgia attorney general Arthur Bolton said that he saw no conflict of interest in the arrangement because Judge Geer "won't decide the case; he's merely a referee."

Defense attorney Bobby Hill presented no witnesses on his client's behalf, and the jury lost no time in rendering a verdict. After little more than an hour of deliberations, they found Carl Isaacs guilty of first-degree murder. Georgia law required that the jury deliberate a second time to determine whether the accused should be executed. Arguing against the notion of deterrence, the defense attorney contended that the death penalty relieved Isaacs of responsibility for his crime and placed the burden of state-sanctioned murder squarely on the shoulders of the jurors. Isaacs would pay with his life, thereby restoring a kind of balance to the accounts, but the jury would have to carry the guilt of what it had done for a long time. "There's something unfair about a system that takes the burden off Carl Isaacs and puts it on you," Hill said. "It won't stop this kind of thing from happening again. It will only cheapen human life."

As one might expect, psychological testimony introduced at the trial relied on qualitative judgments and subjective medical conclusions. Because Carl Isaacs was beaten as a child by hard-drinking parents, rejected by his mother, and gang-raped in a Maryland prison when he was nineteen years old, he had been transformed into an antisocial personality. Although he agreed that no one—not even Isaacs—is "born bad," Dr. William A. Dickinson, a defense psychologist, testified that Isaacs had been transformed into a monster by the circumstances of his life. The defendant harbored a low self-image and a compulsive need to "manipulate people, put them down and be abusive to them." Moreover, Isaacs had "little or no interaction with women, indeed, has a tremendous fear of females." In Dickinson's opinion, Isaacs should be spared the death penalty but locked away from society forever.[26]

The jury was unpersuaded by defense pleas to spare the killer's life. After deliberating for a mere thirty-eight minutes, jurors sentenced Carl Isaacs to die in Georgia's electric chair. For his part, Isaacs seemed unperturbed. "Death makes no difference to me," he said with a shrug after he was sentenced to die. "If I get away, I'll kill one thousand more people."[27]

His words proved to be eerily prescient. A decade later, on July 28, 1980, after numerous appeals and procedural delays, prison guards came to escort Carl Isaacs from the Georgia State Prison in southeast Georgia's Reidsville—a notoriously brutal facility located in rural Tattnall County—to another prison, the Georgia Diagnostic and Classification Center, an hour south of Atlanta. If the guards had not been in such a hurry to transport the prisoner to the new facility, they might have noticed the bars in his old cell. Isaacs had been diligently using a smuggled hacksaw blade to saw through the bars. He was almost finished with his work. Much to his chagrin, he was hustled out of the cell before he could complete the task.[28]

Isaacs's prison buddies were more successful. Wearing guard uniforms made from blue mail-order pajamas, complete with U.S. flag patches, name tags, and fake badges fashioned from cardboard and a soft drink can, four inmates walked out the front gate and drove off in a car that had been left in the parking lot by a relative of one of the escapees. Had he not been moved that day, Isaacs might well have joined them, for investigators discovered later that Isaacs had been the mastermind behind the plot. Three of the four escaped felons were captured several days later in North Carolina. The fourth prisoner was killed in a vicious barroom brawl.[29]

Disappointed but not dissuaded, Isaacs immediately set to work sawing through a ventilation grate in his new cell near Atlanta. He concealed the hacksaw blades in a special pocket he had sewn into his boxer shorts so that he could elude detection. For many months, he worked on the project until he was discovered by authorities on November 26, 1982. Two weeks later, the Eleventh Circuit Court of Appeals overturned Isaacs's 1974 conviction owing to the prejudicial nature of the publicity during the original trial.[30]

As Isaacs was retried, reconvicted, and filed numerous appeals, he continued trying to escape. He made another attempt in 1985. In 1995, an Ohio woman, fifty-year-old Mary Popp, was arrested and indicted for mailing a twelve-inch hacksaw blade to Isaacs. She had hidden the blade inside a box of Little Debbie angel food snack cakes included in a Christmas package. After arresting Popp, agents from the Georgia Bureau of Investigation called Isaacs a "brilliant manipulator" who used his charm to persuade the woman to send him the package. Jerry Thomas, the warden at the prison where Isaacs received the package, said, "He told her that when he escaped he would rendezvous with her. And then I suppose they were going to ride off into the sunset."[31] For her part, Popp, facing up to five years in prison, said, "I think I was a little naive. I'm devastated." She told investigators that she had never broken the law—she had never even gotten a speeding ticket—before she began corresponding with the charismatic Carl Isaacs.[32]

IV

Once again, Carl Isaacs presents critics of the death penalty with a difficult case. He shows no remorse and never changes his behavior. As long as he lives and breathes, he will be a problem for society, for he probably will never give up trying to escape his cell or manipulate others into assisting him. Despite the availability of statistics showing that deterrence is ineffective and that future dangerousness cannot be predicted with any reasonable degree of accuracy supported by hard social science data, the Carl Isaacs of the world convince the public that the death penalty is the only satisfactory means of handling an ongoing, never-ending problem. In every deed he performs and every statement he makes, he seems to assault society's collective sense of justice.

This brings us to the third and final objective in determining whether the death penalty should be deemed an appropriate societal response to capital offenses: Does it serve as an expression of society's collective sense of justice? Initially, the answer appears to be yes. The death penalty is overwhelmingly popular in the United States.[33] According to one commentator, approximately 80 percent of Americans indicate their support for capital punishment—the highest percentage in more than sixty years of public opinion polling. Since 1966, when public support reached its lowest point—42 percent—the approval rating has steadily climbed at least one percentage point a year.[34] This overwhelming public support for capital punishment suggests that the collective sense of justice is so outraged by the behavior of capital offenders that death is the only appropriate punishment for crimes that shock the conscience and endanger the well-being of the community.

Using public opinion polls to gauge society's collective sense of justice is not a new enterprise. The American Institute of Public Opinion, the same pollsters who produce the Gallup polls, conducted the first polls on the death penalty in 1936. In the wake of the highly publicized Lindbergh baby kidnapping case, in which Bruno Richard Hauptmann was executed for killing the child of famed aviator Charles Lindbergh, 61 percent of the 2,201 adults interviewed in 1936 responded that they believed the death penalty was appropriate, while 39 percent did not. The categories "no opinion" and "don't know" were conspicuously absent from those early polls.[35]

By 1994, the number of adults supporting the death penalty had risen by nearly nineteen percentage points, and the number of adults who opposed it had fallen from 39 percent to 16 percent. Four percent had no opinion.[36] The trends in the data initially suggest that the death penalty has become more popular over time as more and more Americans have grown weary of the increased rate of capital crimes and the need to "get tough" with capital offenders.

One difficulty with the questions posed by traditional public opinion polls, however, is that they do not present a set of alternatives. Respondents are forced to select either death or no death. Some citizens might choose a lesser penalty if it were presented among a choice of alternatives. This is exactly the issue explored by two researchers, William J. Bowers and Benjamin D. Steiner, in a 1998 essay.[37]

Bowers and Steiner constructed a survey that posed a series of options, including a sentence of life in prison without parole (LWOP) and a sentence of life without parole plus restitution to the victims' families (LWOP+R). The researchers administered the poll to 500 New York residents, 506 Nebraska residents, 411 Kansas residents, and 603 Massachusetts residents. They chose these states to compare public opinion in two regions of the country: the Northeast and the Midwest. According to Bowers and Steiner, the first alternative, LWOP, tests public reaction to the question of whether convicted capital offenders should be segregated from society without the "violence and degradation of executions." The LWOP question was phrased this way: "If convicted first-degree murderers in this state could be sentenced to life in prison with absolutely no chance of ever being considered for parole, would you prefer this as an alternative to the death penalty?" The results are summarized in table 12.2.

These data suggest that more people prefer to sentence capital offenders to life in prison without the possibility of parole in lieu of the death penalty in two

Table 12.2. Response Rates for Citizens of Four States on the Question of LWOP in Lieu of the Death Penalty

Responses	New York	Nebraska	Kansas	Massachusetts
Yes	55%	46%	47%	54%
No	36%	43%	49%	38%
Not sure	10%	11%	4%	8%

states—New York and Massachusetts—and the data are virtually even in Nebraska and Kansas. Because the question assures respondents that parole is not an option, one major argument in favor of capital punishment—fear of putting violent criminals back on the street—is eliminated. Society can feel relatively safe against the possible future dangerousness of a capital offender, despite the occasional aberration of a Carl Isaacs who might try to escape from prison. In the face of such responses, the argument that society's collective sense of justice cries out for the death penalty is no longer as obvious as it initially appeared to be.

Bowers and Steiner were not satisfied to leave the issue at the possibility of life without parole. Instead, they modified the question to include a statement about providing restitution for victims' families. They asked the following question: "If convicted first-degree murderers in this state could be sentenced to life in prison with no chance of parole and also be required to work in prison industries for money that would go to the family of their victims, would you prefer this as an alternative to the death penalty?" The responses to this question are summarized in table 12.3.

These data suggest that when restitution is coupled with no possibility of parole, respondents overwhelmingly disfavor the death penalty. Bowers and Steiner surmise that this opinion may result from respondents' belief that LWOP+R "was seen as the greatest good for all concerned." In questions of capital punishment, in their view, "people's personal ideals of justice closely mirrored what they saw as the greatest good for all concerned and eschewed harshness."[38]

The Bowers and Steiner data are by no means conclusive, for it is obvious in the phrasing of their questions that they disfavor the death penalty. Their study is therefore hardly free of bias. Nonetheless, their conclusions challenge the arguments of capital punishment proponents that the public overwhelmingly favors

Table 12.3. Response Rates for Citizens of Four States on the Question of LWOP+R in Lieu of the Death Penalty

Responses	New York	Nebraska	Kansas	Massachusetts
Yes	73%	64%	66%	67%
No	19%	26%	30%	23%
Not sure	8%	10%	4%	10%

the death penalty. Thus, social science arguments about whether the death penalty is effective quickly degenerate into a battle of experts who wield their statistics as swords and shields in an ongoing battle.

Whatever else the data indicate, they underscore the difficulty in clearly and convincingly arguing that capital punishment achieves the three objectives set forth at the beginning of this chapter. The possibility of receiving the death penalty does not dissuade all capital offenders from committing crimes, although it may dissuade some. Because capital offenders may be segregated from society by means other than execution, it is not necessarily the only method of preventing future dangerousness—assuming future dangerousness is always a problem. Finally, the death penalty does not necessarily satisfy society's collective sense of justice, especially when other alternatives are available. In short, proponents of capital punishment who seek to buttress their arguments by relying on social science data face a difficult chore. The data in favor of the death penalty are anything but clear and convincing. As the Bob Dylan song lyric (from "A Hard Rain's A-Gonna Fall[17]) in the title of this chapter suggests, there is much about capital punishment that remains hidden from view.

Part 4

LEGAL
PERSPECTIVES

CHAPTER 13

Massive Resistance

CAPITAL PUNISHMENT, THE ABOLITIONIST
MOVEMENT, AND THE SUPREME COURT

Douglas Clouatre

Capital punishment is one of the most complex areas of United States constitutional law. The Supreme Court has driven the development of death penalty law during a period of thirty years, during which time the Court moved from an abolitionist majority to five justices seeking to streamline the process for speeding the pace of execution. This change has produced a tangle of law involving mitigating and aggravating factors, Eighth Amendment claims against specific methods of inflicting capital punishment, challenges based on racial disparities in death sentences, and the availability of federal habeas corpus relief for death row inmates.

Amid all of the litigation of capital crimes is the underlying abolitionist movement seeking to overturn scores of Court decisions supporting the constitutionality of capital punishment. This movement's singular purpose developed after the Court's decision in *Gregg v. Georgia*.[1] In *Gregg*, seven justices upheld the death penalty from an Eighth Amendment challenge. For the abolitionists, Gregg was greeted in a similar fashion as some people greeted *Brown v. Board of Education*[2] with a defiant cry of "Never!"

After the 1976 decision, the abolitionists filed volleys of appeals with the intention of delaying death sentences. With each new appeal, another layer of rules, frequently contradictory in nature, were added leading to further litigation and delay. Hence, a decade after *Gregg* the death penalty remained a rarely enforced punishment.

Two justices, William Brennan and Thurgood Marshall—assisted in their crusade by a host of law clerks—aided the abolitionists. The attitude of the abolitionists can be found in the writing of the former Court clerk, Edward Lazarus who sneeringly contended that clerks supporting the death penalty deliberately slanted memos to hurry along executions. At the same time, Lazarus expressed his view that abolitionist clerks were innocent of any attempt to use their position to slant memos for their cause.[3]

These tactics, including the tendency of Justices Brennan and Marshall to vote to strike down every death sentence appealed to the Court, undermined established law and entangled their colleagues in an ever-growing thicket of complex rules. Their fellow justices responded with a series of decisions that produced a degree of finality opposed by the abolitionist movement.

This chapter will focus on the law created by the clash between capital punishment abolitionists and those favoring an effective death penalty. This clash between those favoring and those opposing the death penalty as government policy has marked much of the legal debate over capital punishment. The tactics of the abolitionists favored using delay to prevent the timely enforcement of death sentences while undermining their arguments. This chapter will relate how the abolitionist movement abused the appeals process and was eventually defeated.

I. Cruel and Unusual

During the Warren Court of the 1960s and the Burger Court of the 1970s, capital punishment was attacked mainly on Eighth Amendment grounds. Opponents of capital punishment argued it was cruel and unusual punishment. Yet such an argument ignored the other constitutional clauses that recognized the death penalty as within the power of Congress and the states to impose as a punishment.

The Fifth Amendment mentions capital punishment in three clauses. The amendment requires that a person tried for a capital crime must first be indicted by a grand jury. In addition, the amendment forbids double jeopardy in cases in which an individual is threatened with punishment involving life or limb. Finally, the Due Process Clause of the same amendment requires due process where people are threatened with losing their life, liberty, or property. All three recognize that capital punishment is part of the constitutional powers of government and places restrictions on its use.

The Fifth Amendment was ratified at the same time as the Eighth Amendment, and each became a part of the Bill of Rights. Because the same Congress composed the two amendments and the same members debated their effects, it seems unlikely that the Eighth Amendment was intended to prohibit the very punishments outlined in the Fifth Amendment. The framers of both amendments would have been engaged in needless redundancy, recognizing capital punishment then prohibiting it in a simultaneous enactment. Hence, arguments that capital punishment violates the Eighth Amendment founders on the shoals of the precise phrasing of the Fifth Amendment.

With neither the clear wording nor the all but certain intent of the framers on their side, the abolitionists turned to a more ambiguous and subjective interpretation of cruel and unusual punishment. This "evolving standards" argument focuses on the changing mores of society. It is based on such cases as *Trop v. Dulles*,[4] in which the Court ruled that the loss of citizenship was cruel and unusual punishment based on an evolving understanding of the meaning of cruel and unusual punishment.

In arguing for evolving standards, abolitionists adopted the noninterpretivist view of constitutional interpretation. This approach placed limited importance on the text of the Constitution. Instead, it focused on the overall theme of the words in that text and attempted to modify them in order to meet what was seen as the changing needs of society. The evolving standards doctrine ignored the clear constitutional text recognizing capital punishment and instead argued that modern society's view of cruel and unusual punishment included capital punishment.[5]

The difficulty with such an argument is the discretion given the justices in determining the mores of society. By not basing their decisions on clear constitutional text, judges are adopting a legislative role, codifying the desires of the community. Yet judges are specifically placed so as to be insulated from such political pressures.

Another argument against using the evolving standards argument to challenge the death penalty was society's increasingly strong support for capital punishment. After the *Furman* decision, public opinion spiked in favor of the death penalty and over thirty-five states passed new death penalty statutes. The major barometers of public beliefs—public opinion polls and the laws passed by their duly elected legislators—showed that society was evolving toward strong support of capital punishment.

With standards evolving against their view of capital punishment, abolitionists were forced to take a different line. One of their spokesmen, Justice Marshall, weakly claimed that if the American public had the same information he had about capital punishment, they would support its abolition. This truism that those who agreed with Justice Marshall would support his views convinced few of the rightness of his constitutional views.

The height of the evolving standards argument came with the *Furman* decision, which was based on the Eighth Amendment's prohibition against cruel and unusual punishment. Five justices found some element of a constitutional violation in the method of reaching the execution decision or the death statutes themselves. But seven justices in *Gregg* rejected the evolving standards argument. This forced abolitionists to offer additional arguments including that the death penalty was excessive when applied against rapists and that certain methods of death were to be considered cruel and unusual. In some cases, the abolitionists could find five justices who agreed with them, in others they could not construct a majority around their views.

The Supreme Court agreed in *Coker v. Georgia*[6] that the death penalty used in rape cases was disproportionate to the crime being punished. With *Coker*, the Court limited capital punishment to homicides. With success in *Coker*, the abolitionist movement continued its challenges with a focus on the execution of juveniles and the mentally retarded.

In *Thompson v. Oklahoma*,[7] the Court overturned a death sentence imposed on a defendant who was fifteen years old when committing a murder. The Court found that states imposed restrictions on the acts of juveniles including the right to vote, the right of marriage, and the right to serve on a jury. Based on these restrictions, the Court found that the state could not impose an adult penalty on a juvenile. The justices found a consensus that juveniles below the age of sixteen should not be executed. Once again they used the evolving standards argument to note that society would be repulsed by the execution of a convicted killer who was under sixteen when committing the act.

Even though the death sentence was overturned, the decision was not joined by a majority of the Court. Instead, Justice O'Connor concurred with the statement that because Oklahoma law did not specifically allow for the execution of juveniles it could not do so. This judicial aside prompted a different result in the later case of *Stanford v. Kentucky*.[8]

The *Stanford* case involved the death penalty used against defendants who were sixteen and seventeen years old when they committed a murder. Convicted and sentenced to death, the death row inmates claimed that under the *Thompson* decision, the state could impose a death sentence on a minor.

The Court disagreed. In his opinion for a five-member majority, Justice Scalia noted that during trial juries and judges make individualized decisions on the maturity of each defendant. Scalia noted that age did not denote maturity but rather that some individuals are able to make adult decisions before reaching the legal age of adulthood. He also noted that a majority of the states with capital punishment allow the execution of minors who committed crimes at the ages of sixteen or seventeen.

The Court also allowed the execution of convicted killers who were found to have an intelligence quotient (IQ) that placed them within the definition of mentally retarded. In *Penry v. Lynaugh*,[9] the Court considered the case of Penry, who was convicted of murder and sentenced to death. Penry was found to have an IQ in the fifties and hence diagnosed as mildly mentally retarded. Penry's counsel claimed that because of his mental deficiencies, he should not have been sentenced to death. The Court disagreed. In her opinion, Justice O'Connor drew upon the common law prohibition against executing the insane or the mentally retarded. She found that because Penry was considered competent to stand trial and had unsuccessfully filed an insanity plea, he was capable of understanding both his actions and his punishment. In addition, O'Connor found that there was no consensus in the states against executing those found to be mildly mentally retarded. Without any proof of evolving standards, the Court upheld Penry's death sentence.

The Court's rulings in *Penry* and *Stanford* exhibited how the evolving standards doctrine has become a counting game. In each of the opinions, the justices cite little constitutional text and instead appear to rely on the number of state laws that allow certain types of people to be executed. Evolving standards have relegated the Court to taking the public pulse and arguing whether there is a majority of states that support or oppose a certain use of capital punishment. This is the primary weakness of the evolving standards doctrine. If a majority of states approves of a punishment, then the Court can reason that the punishment is constitutional. Yet constitutional rights are not to be decided by a majority vote of the state legislatures. Only when state government has turned against a particular form of punishment can the Court summon enough evidence to prove that society's standards have evolved against a particular law. Evolving standards have left much of the Court's Eighth Amendment law up in the air, dependent on the ever-changing views of state legislators and their constituents.

II. Race and Capital Punishment

One of the more direct attacks on capital punishment has been the claim that juries assess based on the racial characteristics of the defendant and the victim. Abolitionists have utilized studies showing disparities in the frequency of death sentences handed down to black and white defendants. The most notorious of these studies was conducted by a University of Georgia professor, Dr. David Baldus. The Baldus studies examined Georgia death sentences during the late 1970s and early 1980s and found a correlation between the race of the victim and the race of the murderer. Blacks who killed whites were more likely to be sentenced to death than any other racial combination of killer and victim.

The Baldus findings were introduced to the Supreme Court through the case of *McCleskey v. Kemp*.[10] McCleskey, who was black, was convicted of murdering a white police officer and sentenced to death. His defense counsel argued the sentence was racially discriminatory and leaned heavily on the Baldus study, which included McCleskey's case in its data. The Supreme Court turned back McCleskey's appeal, focusing on the individualized aspect of jury trials rather than the Baldus data.

The Court found that overturning McCleskey's sentence on the basis of aggregate data in the analysis of capital cases would undermine the entire criminal justice system. The majority also recognized that juries were granted discretion that might lead to decisions based on a variety of factors. The Court noted there was no specific proof of racial discrimination in McCleskey's case and that without such proof, statistical analysis was insufficient to show an Eighth Amendment violation. McCleskey's counsel had stumbled into the well-known ecological fallacy of applying aggregate data findings to individual cases. The data collected for the Baldus study applied to all capital cases during a certain period. While it might exhibit a correlation between race and sentencing, it does not specifically show it existed in McCleskey's case. In improperly using statistical data to make a constitutional argument, McCleskey's counsel confused the issue of racial disparities in sentencing defendants to death.

Since *McCleskey*, the Court has not considered any capital punishment challenge based on race. Instead, it has focused more on the sentencing portion of the trial and the standards used by juries and judges in determining whether a convicted killer should receive the death penalty.

III. Micromanaging Capital Punishment

With the decision in *Furman*, the judiciary adopted a paternalistic approach to capital punishment, resembling its approach to schools after *Brown v. Board* and to women's health issues after *Roe v. Wade*.[11] Since 1972, the justices have approached death penalty statutes like legislators, fine-tuning and making incremental changes to state laws and courtroom procedures. With the Court acting on a case by case basis, the result has been a tangle of rulings that are contradictory and tend to produce a flood of litigation from death row inmates. The decision to place the rules of capital punishment under the control of the courts has forced the justices to make minute adjustments to law, a task usually reserved for legislators. It has also heightened the tension in the Supreme Court between those favoring the death penalty and those seeking to increase the already heavy burden imposed on the state to execute the guilty. The technical aspects of capital punishment include such issues as the sentencing hearing, the introduction of mitigating and aggravating circumstances, and the discretion granted the jury in determining the factors they would use.

With the *Gregg* format of a sentencing hearing separate from the trial, the courts have been forced to rule on the extent of aggravating and mitigating circumstances. During the hearing that will determine sentencing in a capital case, the prosecutor can present aggravating circumstances that would make the defendant a proper candidate for a death sentence. The prosecutor can argue for only those aggravating circumstances identified in the capital punishment legislation.

The Court has looked carefully at these statutes, determining whether they are overly vague or whether they provide too little guidance to the jurors in making a decision and violate due process guarantees of the Constitution. The justices have struck down laws allowing death to be imposed in cases in which a murder was "outrageously or wantonly vile, horrible and inhuman"[12] or in which the killing was "especially heinous, atrocious or cruel."[13] In both cases, the Court ruled juries were granted too much discretion in determining whether the defendant was to be sentenced to death. Such discretion, according to the Court, produced arbitrary decisions in support of the death penalty. The state would have to explicitly spell out the circumstances necessary for a jury to sentence a defendant to death. With these decisions, the Court became intimately involved with the wording of death penalty statutes and determined their constitutionality based on a changing interpretation of words.

But by the 1990s, and with the advent of a pro–capital punishment majority on the Rehnquist Court, the justices changed their views on the vagueness of aggravating factors for sentencing. In *Arave v. Creech*,[14] the justices considered an Idaho law that allowed judges or juries to sentence a defendant to death if his crime showed an "utter disregard for human life." Creech was implicated in almost two dozen murders and convicted in a murder of a fellow prisoner. The judge sentenced him to death using the "utter disregard" aggravating factor. On appeal, the Supreme Court agreed that such a standard provided the judge with sufficient guidance so that he could make an informed decision on sentencing Creech. In her opinion, Justice O'Connor laid out the argument that most juries and judges could define such terms as *pitiless, utter disregard,* and *coldblooded* in determining whether a particular defendant deserved the death penalty. *Creech* exemplified the Court's new tendency to grant juries greater discretion in their sentencing.

While juries and judges must be given constitutional guidelines on which to base their decision, the Court has also at times limited the information granted them in sentencing hearings. One controversial limitation imposed by the justices was a temporary ban on victim impact statements. These statements are given by the family members of the murder victim in which they describe the physical, psychological, and emotional effect the murder had on them. Such statements were used by prosecutors to show how heinous, cruel, or coldblooded a killing was to aid the jurors in reaching a sentencing decision. Two Supreme Court cases highlighted the differing views of abolitionists and those favoring capital punishment.

In *Booth v. Maryland*,[15] Booth was convicted of a double murder. As part of the sentencing hearing, the children of the victims recounted the emotional toll on them after finding their elderly parents bodies riddled with multiple stab wounds. Booth was sentenced to death. On appeal, a five-member Court majority overturned the sentence with the argument that the impact of the murders on the surviving family members was irrelevant to the sentencing and tended to produce emotional or arbitrary decisions on the death penalty.

Booth was dispatched to the constitutional ash heap four years later in *Payne v. Tennessee*.[16] Payne was convicted of killing a woman and her daughter and plunging a knife through her three-year-old son and pinning him to the linoleum floor. He was sentenced to death after the woman's mother described her suffering and the suffering of the little boy who survived the attack. In a six-to-three decision, the Court upheld the sentence, noting that the impact on the victim's family was relevant in determining the type of crime and the punishment for the killer. The justices dismissed the reasoning in *Booth*, noting that it was not based on precedent and had little grounding in Eighth Amendment law.

The effect of *Booth* and other decisions on the sentencing phase of capital crimes exhibits the Rehnquist Court's view that the more information and discretion granted a jury the more informed decision they can make. The decisions follow the general thrust of the original *Gregg* decision in which the Court recognized that juries and judges, with proper legislative guidance and with arguments presented by both sides, could reach a proper and defensible decision on whether to impose the death penalty. The decisions also produced a response representing the last gasp of the abolitionist movement within the Court. In *Callins v. Collins*,[17] the Supreme Court refused to hear Callins's appeal of his death sentence. While no formal opinion was written, two justices composed concurring and dissenting opinions debating the death penalty.

In his dissent, Justice Blackmun criticized what he perceived as the inability of the Supreme Court to agree to consistent standards on the implementation of capital punishment. He noted the disagreements on the various standards used by juries, the reforms of the habeas corpus process, and the continuing battles between prosecutors and the abolitionist movement. Concluding that fairness was not possible and that the state could never properly execute anyone without the possibility of killing an innocent man, Blackmun called for the abolition of the death penalty.

His arguments were answered in a short but fiery rejoinder from Justice Scalia. Scalia noted that the text of the Constitution provided for capital punishment and that the justices were expected to interpret that text rather than imposing their own political views. He also noted the difference between lethal injection of convicted killers and the suffering of their victims. He criticized Blackmun's misplaced sympathies and seemed to state the view of a majority of justices and the public in his support of capital punishment. Scalia's opinion reflects the Court's impatience with the dithering of federal judges to uphold the law. The Rehnquist Court has removed some of the discretion initially delegated to federal judges. In return, they have granted greater power to state judges in adjudicating state death penalty statutes. An issue involving state enforcement of their death penalty statutes involved the degree of deference granted to state courts and officials in enforcing their capital punishment statutes. The Court took the state's side in disputes involving the power of federal courts to grant habeas corpus relief to state death row inmates.

IV. Habeas Corpus and Capital Punishment

The Rehnquist Court's emphasis on federalism and respecting the decisions of state courts extended to issues of capital punishment. The justices have attempted to reform the habeas corpus reviews of state cases adhering to Justice O'Connor's call for finality and comity in *Teague v. Lane*.[18] In cases that followed the *Teague* decision, the Court challenged attempts by lower federal district and appellate courts to overrule state courts and delay the enforcement of death sentences.

The right to habeas corpus dates back to the British common law in which judges were given the power to free prisoners of the Crown if the government was found to be illegally holding a prisoner. Habeas corpus, or "Produce the body," provided a buffer and protection for individuals against the state. In the United States, federal habeas corpus law has expanded from its original creation in 1789. Prior to the Civil War, the federal courts only had the power to grant habeas corpus to federal prisoners held in violation of federal law or the federal constitution. After the Civil War and the period of political reconstruction, Congress passed the 1867 Habeas Corpus Act. Under this law, federal district court judges could hear petitions from state prisoners and grant federal habeas corpus relief if the judge believed the prisoner was being held in violation of the federal Constitution. The reasons for this dramatic expansion of federal judicial power was Congress's belief that southern state judges were unwilling to protect the constitutional rights of the newly freed slaves. In passing the Habeas Corpus Act, Congress allowed defendants to have their rights defended in federal courts where it was believed federal judges would be less swayed by the politics of the region. The ultimate result, though, was granting power to the federal judiciary to oversee the actions of state judges. This weakened the independence of the state judiciaries and federalized much of the criminal law in the states. Expansion of federal habeas corpus also allowed federal judges to impose policy choices on state judges by granting state defendants new trials.

But it was not until the 1960s that federal habeas corpus law became a tool for state defendants to challenge state convictions by appealing to federal courts.

In the case of *Fay v. Noia*,[19] the justices expanded federal habeas jurisdiction by sweeping away many of the state procedural barriers to federal habeas review. With the *Fay* ruling, federal courts were empowered to consider state prisoner claims after their state appeals were exhausted. The result was federal judges creating new constitutional rights and ignoring the state procedural concerns. What had originally been created as a federal check on the power of state courts instead became a federal weapon used to bludgeon state courts and to eliminate many of the state procedures intended to bring closure to the criminal justice system.

With the death penalty debate heating up during the 1970s and 1980s, state death row inmates used habeas corpus filings less as a method for defending their rights and more as a delaying tactic that allowed them to prolong the appellate process to over a decade. The usual approach to federal habeas corpus relief involved single appeals of issues to federal courts and the raising of new issues not considered by state courts. Years usually passed by the time each of the single issues work their way through the federal appellate system. Most appeals failed but resulted in a frustration with the criminal justice system. People saw that the government was not enforcing the punishments handed down at trial. With few constitutional arguments against the death penalty, foes of capital punishment relied on the habeas corpus process to advance the policy they could not pass in the legislature.

The delaying tactics of the abolitionist movement reached a crescendo with the successive habeas petitions filed by the convicted murderer, Robert Alton Harris. After he spent twelve years on death row, Harris's attorneys argued that his planned execution in the California gas chamber constituted cruel and unusual punishment. The Ninth Circuit Court of Appeals heard his petition, and Harris was granted a stay of execution. The state appealed to Justice O'Connor, who served as the Supreme Court justice overseeing the Ninth Circuit. O'Connor, taking note that Harris had been on death row throughout the eighties and had not raised the issue until 1992, overturned the stay and ordered that no further stays could be granted by anyone other than the Supreme Court itself.[20] This was a blow to the judges of the Ninth Circuit, who had been conducting a guerrilla-like war against executions within their jurisdiction.

In addition to granting stays of execution, the Ninth Circuit ignored some cases, refusing to issue decisions that could be appealed to and overturned by the U.S. Supreme Court. The state of Washington had convicted Charles Campbell of murder. After Campbell's death sentence was handed down and the state courts upheld it, he sought federal habeas relief. When his case came before the Ninth Circuit Court of Appeals, the justices delayed issuing a ruling for several months. It was only when Washington appealed to the Supreme Court and the justices warned the appeals court against delay that the circuit court issued a ruling. With abuses of the habeas corpus process by prisoners and federal judges, it was inevitable that reform efforts would be made to streamline the process.

With the appointment of politically conservative Supreme Court justices, habeas corpus reform became a major political and legal issue. The Rehnquist Court's emphasis on federalism and the respecting the decisions of state courts and laws was extended to federal review of state death sentences.

In a series of cases, the Court reinstated the primacy of state procedural rules. In doing so, the justices ended the circuslike atmosphere that had begun to pervade capital punishment jurisprudence. In *Coleman v. Thompson*,[21] the Court considered whether federal habeas protection could be provided when state courts dismissed a prisoner's appeal based on missing a state-imposed deadline for appeal.

Coleman was convicted of murder in Virginia and sentenced to death. Coleman's attorney filed the appeal claiming several constitutional violations in his trial. The state appeal, though, was filed after the thirty-day statutory limit established by Virginia. The state supreme court dismissed the appeal, noting the missed deadline.

Thompson sought federal habeas corpus relief. His counsel argued the state courts had dismissed his appeal involving federal constitutional rights and that the federal courts could intervene. The state argued the appeal was rejected purely on a matter of state law and could not be reached by the federal court. Coleman was granted habeas relief, and Virginia appealed to the United States Supreme Court.

In her opinion for the Court, Justice O'Connor set the tone of the decision by noting the case was based on principles of federalism and the respect owed state courts by the federal judiciary. As a former state judge, O'Connor was familiar with the difficulties presented by federal habeas decisions. She reiterated the need for federal comity or acceptance of state court decisions based on state law. Because the state court in Coleman based its rejection of his appeal on missing the state deadline, the federal courts could not grant habeas relief on that issue.

In addition to placing greater restrictions on habeas corpus filings by death row inmates, the Rehnquist Court also took aim at death row inmates who abused the habeas corpus process by filing repeated petitions to the federal courts. In *McCleskey v. Zant*,[22] the Court heard another appeal from Warren McCleskey and considered his petition for a new trial. This petition was filed six years after his first petition and nine years after his original conviction. In asking for a new trial, McCleskey raised constitutional issues in 1987 that he did not raise in his original petition in 1981. The result of these new claims was the further delaying of his execution as the federal courts considered his arguments.

When McCleskey's case reached the Supreme Court in 1991, he had been on death row for a dozen years, prompting the justices to express dismay at the process. In the second *McCleskey* case, the Court closed another avenue in what it saw as an abuse of the habeas process. In his opinion, Justice Kennedy noted the delays and costs imposed on the state by successive habeas petitions. He emphasized finality in judicial decisions and the sovereign rights of the states to maintain order within their borders. He also noted that some defendants utilize habeas corpus to manipulate the process, hence delaying their sentence. According to Kennedy, this leads to a disrespect of the system of justice as the public sees the law being flaunted. Finally, Kennedy warned that multiple and frivolous habeas corpus petitions can flood the courts and make them miss more meritorious appeals.

To combat this, Kennedy developed a new test. Once a prisoner filed a second habeas corpus petition, the burden of proof fell on him to prove that the second claim was not frivolous. If the petition was found to be without merit, then the federal courts could dismiss it.

The second *McCleskey* decision was an additional step in streamlining the Habeas process. Instead of filing individual petitions with different claims, thus clogging the judicial system and delaying the execution date, the death row inmate would have to file a single habeas petition, making all his constitutional claims in that filing. A second petition would have to surmount a sizable obstacle before the Court would hear it.

The Court's efforts to streamline the habeas corpus process were aided by the Republican Congress. In 1996, Congress passed the Antiterrorism and Effective Death Penalty Act.[23] The law utilized the reasoning and the procedures established in the Rehnquist Court's habeas corpus decisions. It limited the number of federal habeas corpus petitions that could be filed by a state prisoner. The law stated that prisoners could not file a second petition that reiterated the same arguments used in a previous petition. In addition, a second petition would be accepted only if it included clear and convincing evidence of the defendant's innocence or involved a right created by the Court in a recent case.

The legislation was challenged in *Felker v. Turpin*,[24] and a unanimous Court upheld the law. In his opinion, Chief Justice Rehnquist noted that Congress enacted the law as part of its power to ensure the proper and timely enforcement of the law. In addition, Congress was not suspending the writ of habeas corpus but rather following in the Court's footsteps by legislating in order to prevent an abuse of the writ. Congress had established clear guidelines that protected the rights of the death row inmate while ensuring finality in verdicts.

With the federal law in place, the Court's reform of the habeas corpus process came to an end. Since 1996, the justices have interpreted the law, weakening its provisions in some cases, strengthening it in others. Yet the result of the

Rehnquist Court's reform efforts is a streamlined process that ensures a death row inmate's appeals are heard and considered while shutting down the avenue for baseless delays intended to prevent the execution of the law.

V. Conclusion

Capital punishment has been a political and legal controversy for several decades. The Supreme Court has recognized the constitutionality and popular appeal of the death penalty. But in upholding capital punishment, the justices ensnared themselves in a legal thicket of contradictory and complex rulings. Their decisions were made even more complex by the delaying tactics of those favoring abolition of the death penalty. With judges and lawyers ever more involved in the minutia of capital punishment legislation, the death penalty was rarely enforced during the decade following it reinstatement by the Court.

By the 1990s, it was clear that the capital punishment process was in desperate need of reform. Supporters of the death penalty formed a majority on the Rehnquist Court and issued a series of decisions streamlining the federal habeas corpus process, granted juries more discretion and evidence to mull in deciding on a death sentence, and allowed the execution of underage defendants. The result of those decisions were the lifting of much of the judicial micromanagement of the process in favor of deference to state judges and officials in carrying out their legal duties. At the same time, the Court preserved the federal process for protecting rights while limiting the opportunities for delaying tactics. With its reforms in place, the Rehnquist Court, with aid from Congress, has ensured the enforcement of death sentences while protecting the safeguards for defendants challenging their sentences. In doing so, they have protected the rule of law and dealt a serious blow to the abolitionist movement.

CHAPTER 14

"Freakishly Imposed" or "Fundamentally Fair"?

LEGAL ARGUMENTS AGAINST
THE DEATH PENALTY

J. Michael Martinez

The death penalty has been applied in the United States for most of the nation's history; during that time, two questions about its justification have persisted. The first is primarily a philosophical query: Should the penalty ever be applied, or does state-sanctioned killing violate a fundamental precept of the American republic? If the answer is "No, it should not be applied," the discussion becomes a philosophical debate on the reasons why certain precepts prohibit the imposition of death under all circumstances. This is precisely the philosophical/theological debate that occupies parts 1 and 2 of this book.

A second question—a more narrowly tailored legal query—naturally follows on the heels of the first: If the death penalty on its face does not violate a fundamental American precept, can it be administered so that its application in individual cases comports with those same precepts? Because the range of responses to the first question is reflected elsewhere in this collection, this chapter will focus on the second question—that is, on whether the death penalty can be applied in a manner that is consistent with the tenets of the American regime. This exercise is much more difficult than merely prohibiting capital punishment as a philosophical question because it primarily necessitates an exploration of the legal issues to determine the appropriate standards for applying the penalty.[1] The assumption here is that the U.S. Supreme Court's decision in *Gregg v. Georgia*,[2] which held that capital punishment is constitutional if applied in accordance with clearly discernable, identifiable standards that are fitted to individual cases, will not be successfully challenged in the foreseeable future. Therefore, as a matter of positivist, black-letter law, capital punishment is legally permissible. Whether it can be applied in accordance with legal standards set forth by the U.S. Supreme Court is another matter and the subject of this chapter.

I. Beyond Human Ability?

The heart of the legal debate concerns whether fallible human beings are capable of setting aside their prejudices, biases, mistaken impressions, and misconceptions and applying the death penalty in a fair and equitable manner. In short, the question is whether constitutionally permissible standards can ever be developed and equitably applied. Because the legal system depends on many sometimes self-interested participants—law enforcement officials, lawyers, judges, juries, and eyewitnesses, among others—it is virtually impossible to establish with certainty the facts in a particular case. In almost every instance in which the legal system might impose a death sentence, a nagging doubt lingers long after the trial has ended. Could the eyewitnesses have been mistaken or, more ominously, vengeful in their recollections? Did law enforcement officials arrest the true offender, or has an innocent man been wrongly convicted? Did the prosecutor knowingly or unknowingly produce all exculpatory evidence to the defense? In most criminal cases, mistakes can be rectified in a subsequent proceeding if an innocent man has been convicted and imprisoned. In capital cases, however, the possibility that the state might kill an innocent defendant always exists.

This lingering doubt is cited by many anti–death penalty commentators as the reason that the state should not execute its citizens. For example, in *McGautha v. California*,[3] a 1971 capital case, Justice John Marshall Harlan succinctly expresses the concern about whether people can fairly apply the death penalty in a passage that would become famous among opponents of capital punishment. "Those who have come to grips with the hard task of actually attempting to draft means of channeling capital sentencing discretion have confirmed the lesson taught by the history recounted above," he writes. "To identify before the fact those characteristics of criminal homicides and their perpetrators which call for the death penalty, and to express these characteristics in language which can be fairly understood and applied by the sentencing authority, appear to be tasks which are beyond present human ability."[4]

James R. Acker and Charles S. Lanier, in an essay aptly titled "Beyond Human Ability"—an obvious reference to Justice Harlan's famous comment—contend that it is not possible to construct a legal system that roots out all biases so that we can confidently protect the innocent from the hangman's noose. Nor can we develop suitable standards for applying the penalty. Accordingly, regardless of its philosophical or historical merits, capital punishment cannot be applied in an equitable manner and should be abandoned. In their view, post-*Gregg* death-penalty statutes have offered little more than false promises. Serious and perhaps inexorable problems linger in their administration. These problems strike at the heart of procedural fairness. They involve such issues as race discrimination, the erroneous conviction and execution of innocent people, and unequal justice, where the kind of lawyer and the amount of resources an accused has can make a difference between life and death, or even guilt and innocence.[5]

Similarly, University of South Dakota law professor Chris Hutton argues in chapter 16 of this collection that so many inequities exist that the death penalty is never devoid of arbitrary and capricious elements. Despite the standards articulated in statutes passed after *Gregg v. Georgia*, the race of the defendant, the quality of one's attorney, the character of the jury, and the rulings of the judge, among other factors, combine to influence the verdict. If a regime cannot control for these inequities, it must reject a penalty that cannot be undone. "Thus, perhaps the most honest answer from the legal system is that it has tried, but failed in the realm of capital punishment," Hutton concludes. "The answer to the question 'Can we impose death sentences fairly, rationally, and accurately?' is 'no.'"[6]

The list of opponents of capital punishment is too numerous to mention here; suffice it to say that most anti–death penalty commentators have argued that sufficient guarantees cannot be afforded the wrongly convicted defendant. Accordingly, such a punishment must be rejected. No legal standards, regardless of how well they are crafted, can satisfactorily protect individuals from the awesome and terrible power of the state.[7]

By contrast, a well-known supporter of capital punishment, Ernest van den Haag, argues that justice demands that we give to someone what is owed. In his opinion, if capital punishment is morally acceptable as a means of giving someone what is owed, the inconsistent legal application is not sufficient grounds for rejecting the penalty. "Guilt is personal," he explains. "No murderer's guilt is diminished because other murderers escape punishment. . . . Justice demands that those deserving it suffer the death penalty, even if others, who deserve it no less, escape because of discrimination, prosecutorial incompetence, insufficient evidence or for any other reason."[8] (Van den Haag's views also are expressed in chapter 3 of this book.)

Aside from the nexus between moral justification and legal application of the penalty, Associate Supreme Court Justice Antonin Scalia repeatedly has contended that the U.S. Constitution allows for capital punishment as a legal principle; otherwise, the Founders would have prohibited it. "Convictions in opposition to the death penalty are passionate and deeply held," he has acknowledged. Nonetheless, as a matter of law, the ultimate punishment is permissible if it is a proportionate response to the crime committed and it is applied more or less fairly. In his view, "the creation of false, untextual and unhistorical contradictions within 'the Court's Eighth Amendment jurisprudence' should not prevent them."[9]

The dilemma, of course, is in articulating a standard to ensure equitable application of the standard in individual cases, assuming that such a standard can be developed in the first place. Accordingly, to explore these arguments further, it is helpful to examine cases in which biases, if they exist, are most readily apparent. This exploration should reveal much about whether capital punishment can be applied in a manner consistent with American ideals and values or whether it is merely subject to the arbitrariness of fate and the prejudices of imperfect human beings.[10]

II. Factors Potentially Affecting Equity in Sentencing

A. RACE

Racial prejudice probably is the most often cited cause of inequity in the American criminal justice system. Time and again, many studies have demonstrated that African Americans are convicted of, and executed for, capital crimes at far higher rates than their white counterparts. Moreover, statistics also reveal that death sentences are meted out in far fewer cases when African Americans are murder victims. In short, the race of the defendant and the victim matters. African American offenders are more likely than others to be punished and offenders who kill African American victims are less likely than others to be punished. This sends a powerful, if unintended, message: Black lives matter less than white lives in the United States.[11]

Assuming that these conclusions are warranted by the data—which by no means is an uncontested assumption—we must ask whether racial disparities in the criminal justice system are enough to condemn the death penalty to obsolescence as a barbaric form of punishment. Perhaps, as McAdams argues in chapter 11 of this collection, the issue of whether African Americans as a group receive death sentences more often than whites as a group receive them is irrelevant. Similarly, racial disparities in sentences imposed on groups of defendants who are convicted of murdering African Americans are not prime considerations. Instead, McAdams contends that individual juries act in individual cases. Reforming a system that deals with many people is not justified when each case differs owing to specific circumstances and possibly mitigating factors. "As we come to terms with the reality of racial disparity," he writes, "we should remember that abolition of the death penalty would in no way make black people (with the exception of a tiny minority of black murderers sentenced to death) any better off."[12]

The U.S. Supreme Court rejected the notion that racial disparity is necessarily tantamount to racial discrimination in a landmark decision in 1987, *McCleskey v. Kemp*.[13] *McCleskey* was a challenge to Georgia's capital punishment system based on the Fourteenth Amendment's Equal Protection Clause. By a 5–4 majority, the court held that an African American defendant had failed to demonstrate a denial of equal protection because he failed to show that either racial discrimination had occurred in his specific case or that the Georgia General Assembly had deliberately designed the statute to have a racially discriminatory effect.[14] According to Justice Lewis Powell's opinion, statistical evidence alone did not show "a constitutionally significant risk" that racial discrimination occurred absent specific proof of discriminatory actions.[15]

The procedural history in *McCleskey* is convoluted, but it is important to review the case to understand how the court reached its decision. It began on October 12, 1978, when four armed men entered a furniture store in Fulton County, Georgia, intent on robbing the proprietor. As the robbers were subduing the store manager and patrons, a police officer, answering a silent alarm, entered the premises through the front door. He was shot twice. One shot hit the officer in the face and killed him.

Several weeks later, McCleskey, a black man, was arrested for an unrelated offense. During his interrogation, he admitted that he had been one of the robbers in the furniture store on October 12, but he denied that he had shot the police officer. At trial, however, police ballistics experts testified that the bullet that had killed the policeman was fired from a .38-caliber revolver that matched the description of a gun that McCleskey carried during the robbery. Two prosecution witnesses also testified that they heard McCleskey confess to the killing.[16]

The jury convicted McCleskey of murder. Because McCleskey offered no evidence of mitigating circumstances, the jury also could recommend the death penalty under Georgia law. The jurors did exactly that, finding that McCleskey should receive two consecutive life sentences on the armed robbery charges and the death penalty for the murder of the police officer. The Georgia Supreme Court affirmed the convictions and the sentences, and the U.S. Supreme Court denied the defendant's petition for a writ of *certiorari*.[17]

McCleskey then filed a petition for a writ of habeas corpus in the Federal District Court for the Northern District of Georgia. Of the eighteen claims raised in the petition, one challenged the Georgia capital sentencing process as a violation of the Eighth and Fourteenth Amendments to the U.S. Constitution because McCleskey allegedly was sentenced in a racially discriminatory manner. To support this claim, McCleskey proffered a statistical study performed by three professors, David C. Baldus, Charles Pulaski, and George Woodworth, that purported to demonstrate a disparity in imposing the death sentence in Georgia based on the race of the murder victim and, to a lesser extent, the race of the defendant.[18]

After considering the Baldus study at length, the district court concluded that "statistics do not demonstrate a prima facie case in support of the contention that the death penalty was imposed upon him because of his race, because of the race of the victim, or because of any Eighth Amendment concern."[19] The Eleventh Circuit of Appeals, sitting en banc, affirmed the district court's denial of the habeas corpus petition, observing that statistics alone are "insufficient to demonstrate discriminatory intent or unconstitutional discrimination in the Fourteenth Amendment context, [and] insufficient to show irrationality, arbitrariness, and capriciousness under any kind of Eighth Amendment analysis."[20] The U.S. Supreme Court granted *certiorari* to consider, among other things, whether the use of statistical evidence, absent other factors, is sufficient to demonstrate racial discrimination in Georgia's system of capital sentencing.[21]

Justice Lewis Powell delivered the opinion of the court. In his view, "to prevail under the Equal Protection Clause, McCleskey must prove that the decision makers in his case acted with discriminatory purpose. He offers no evidence specific to his own case that would support an inference that racial considerations played a part in his sentence. Instead, he relies solely on the Baldus study."[22] Absent a showing of discrimination in his specific case, the defendant might yet prevail on an equal protection claim if he could show that the state legislature enacted the capital sentencing statute with an anticipated discriminatory effect in mind, but McCleskey failed to accomplish this goal as well. "As legislatures have wide discretion in the choice of criminal laws and penalties, and as there were legitimate reasons for the Georgia Legislature to adopt and maintain capital punishment . . . we will not infer a discriminatory purpose on the part of the State of Georgia. Accordingly, we reject McCleskey's equal protection claims," Powell explained.[23]

Justice William Brennan, a well-known opponent of capital punishment, dissented in an opinion joined by Justice Thurgood Marshall and partly joined by Justices Harry Blackmun and John Paul Stevens. Among other arguments, Brennan accepted the conclusions in the Baldus study that found a strong likelihood of racial discrimination in capital sentencing even if the particular circumstances could not be articulated in a given case. "The statistical evidence in this case thus relentlessly documents the risk that McCleskey's sentence was influenced by racial considerations. The evidence shows that there is a better than even chance in Georgia that race will influence the decision to impose the death penalty: a majority of defendants in white-victim crimes would not have been sentenced to die if their victims had been black."[24]

As for the argument propounded by capital punishment supporters like Ernest van den Haag who argue that guilt is inherently individual, Justice Brennan suggested that the fairness of the American criminal justice system must be examined from a broader perspective. In an eloquent passage, he writes that "[i]t is tempting to pretend that minorities on death row share a fate in no way connected to our own, that our treatment of them sounds no echoes beyond the chambers in which they die. Such an illusion is ultimately corrosive, for the reverberations of injustice are not so easily confined."[25]

Justice Blackmun also filed a dissent in *McCleskey*. In an opinion joined by Justices Marshall and Stevens and partly joined by Justice Brennan, Blackmun said that, in his view, McCleskey's statistics established the existence of an unconstitutional pattern of racial discrimination. "The court today sanctions the execution of a man despite his presentation of evidence that establishes a constitutionally intolerable level of discrimination leading to the imposition of his death sentence," he wrote. "Justice Brennan has thoroughly demonstrated, ante, that, if one assumes that the statistical evidence presented by petitioner McCleskey is valid, as we must in light of the Court of Appeals' assumption, there exists in the Georgia capital sentencing scheme a risk of racially based discrimination that is so acute that it violates the Eighth Amendment."[26] Moreover, Blackmun contended that the defendant had been denied equal protection of the laws under the Fourteenth Amendment. "Analysis of his case in terms of the Fourteenth Amendment is consistent with this Court's recognition that racial discrimination is fundamentally at odds with our constitutional guarantee of equal protection."[27]

As for the concern expressed by prosecutors and law enforcement personnel that allowing defendants to escape capital sentencing by arguing that it was racially biased will open a Pandora's box of constitutional challenges to the death penalty, Blackmun contended that such challenges would be healthy for the criminal justice system. "If a grant of relief to [McCleskey] were to lead to a closer examination of the effects of racial considerations throughout the criminal justice system, the system, hence society, might benefit."[28] All African American defendants would not escape the death penalty owing to charges of racial bias because not all defendants could point to statistics demonstrating discrimination in their respective jurisdictions. Moreover, discrimination would be muted in cases in which the evidence overwhelmingly pointed to the defendant's guilt or where aggravated circumstances existed.[29]

Justice Stevens, joined by Justice Blackmun, filed the final opinion in *McCleskey*. In a short dissent, Stevens argued that the court was placing its concern about whether the use of statistics demonstrating racial discrimination would undermine the criminal justice system above the merits of McCleskey's case. "In this case it is claimed—and the claim is supported by elaborate studies which the

Court properly assumes to be valid—that the jury's sentencing process was likely distorted by racial prejudice."[30] Yet the majority of the Supreme Court seemed to believe that statistics alone failed to demonstrate sufficient evidence of discrimination. "The Court's decision appears to be based on a fear that the acceptance of McCleskey's claim would sound the death knell for capital punishment in Georgia. If society were indeed forced to choose between a racially discriminatory death penalty (one that provides heightened protection against murder 'for whites only') and no death penalty at all, the choice mandated by the Constitution would be plain."[31]

Stevens did not believe that such a choice was necessary, however; the court could preserve the death penalty by providing further guidance to prosecutors on who is eligible for the death penalty and who is not eligible:

> One of the lessons of the Baldus study is that there exist certain categories of extremely serious crimes for which prosecutors consistently seek, and juries consistently impose, the death penalty without regard to the race of the victim or the race of the offender. If Georgia were to narrow the class of death-eligible defendants to these categories, the danger of arbitrary and discriminatory imposition of the death penalty would be significantly decreased, if not eradicated.[32]

In retrospect, it is clear that the Supreme Court in *McCleskey v. Kemp* deliberately made it difficult for a defendant alleging racial discrimination in a capital case to meet his burden of proof. Despite Justice Blackmun's and Stevens's assertions to the contrary, if the Court had concluded that statistics alone were sufficient to show racial discrimination, virtually every African American defendant in the United States probably could have escaped capital punishment by citing data showing disparate effects between black and white victims and offenders. By extension, if African Americans could never be executed for capital crimes because they were victims of general patterns of discrimination, other groups could argue that they were being denied equal protection. After all, why should a member of a non–African American group be executed when an African American convicted of the same crime would not meet the hangman or when the race of the victim tipped the scales? Had the majority decided to consider statistics alone as evidence of racial discrimination, *McCleskey* probably would have sounded the death knell for capital punishment in the American regime as a practical matter. Narrowing the class of death-eligible defendants to exclude certain defendants in situations involving various black–white combinations seems to raise fundamental equal protection issues however those issues are considered.[33]

Not surprisingly, *McCleskey* may have closed the door to federal judicial intervention in cases that lack specific, demonstrable allegations of racial discrimination in capital cases, but it triggered intense debate and a multitude of new academic studies. Most studies after *McCleskey* coupled statistics with other research methods, including postconviction interviews with jurors in capital cases. In this new era of death penalty research, both sides of the debate pushed for different interpretations of the data. For example, Stanley Rothman and Stephen Powers argue in "The Death Penalty Is Not Applied Unfairly to Blacks" that African Americans actually receive more lenient treatment than other groups. According to statistics prepared by analysts at the Bureau of Justice Statistics, the percentage of black inmates on death row (42 percent) is lower than the percentage of black defendants charged with murder or nonnegligent manslaughter (48 percent).[34] In their view, the Supreme Court was correct in its assessment of the role of race in *McCleskey*. Statistical evidence does not meet the Court's evidentiary standards, especially when other available statistics reveal the opposite conclusion. According to Rothman and Powers, the persistent view that blacks somehow find themselves condemned to death more often than whites is a myth based on abuse of sociological data and statistics as well as the political opportunism of anti–death penalty advocates and politically liberal individuals and groups.[35]

The rejoinder to these arguments is not only to focus on the race of a defendant or a victim but to consider what racial bias in capital sentencing does to the promise of fundamental fairness set forth by the regime. For example, in Texas, a state well known for the frequency of its executions, one academic study indicated that the state's capital punishment system is an outgrowth of a racist "legacy of slavery." An individual African American defendant on death row in Texas may not be able to point to a specific instance of racial bias in his case— and the statute itself may not reflect an overt discriminatory intent—but the authors of the Texas study suggested that the bias permeates the thinking of Texas citizens who serve on juries as well as the state's criminal justice institutions. If this conclusion is accurate, it is naïve to assume that blacks accused of a capital crime are afforded constitutional protections in a fundamentally fair manner. They are presumed to be guilty by virtue of their skin color before the trial ever begins.[36]

As for statistics on black defendants across the nation, anti–death penalty advocates argue that it is misleading to conclude that the lower percentage of blacks sentenced to death is less than the percentage of blacks charged with murder or nonnegligent manslaughter. The correct statistic is the percentage of blacks on death row compared to the percentage of blacks as a total percentage of the American population. Moreover, by comparing data during the twentieth century, a pattern emerges: African Americans generally have been executed for what were considered less than capital offenses more often than whites were executed. This is especially true for black juveniles.[37]

As with any statistics, however, the data are anything but uncontested, even among capital punishment opponents. Comparing the percentage of blacks on death row and the percentage of blacks in the population can be misleading, according to two well-known anti–death penalty commentators, David C. Baldus and George Woodworth. (Baldus, of course, was the lead author of the study cited in the *McCleskey* case.) In Baldus and Woodworth's opinion:

> [E]vidence that blacks constitute 12 percent of the national population, but 40 percent of the nationwide death row population, is sometimes offered as evidence of systemic race of defendant discrimination. Thus unadjusted disparity is highly misleading because it fails to control for the disproportionately high proportion of blacks (about 55 percent) among citizens arrested for homicide nationally. As a result, the comparison fails to control for the differential rates at which black and non-black citizens commit death eligible homicides.[38]

Instead, they suggest that other information must be examined to determine whether race plays a role in capital convictions. "Like many important issues, this question cannot be authoritatively answered through statistical analyses," Baldus and Woodworth conclude.[39] A large body of psychological, sociological, and political literature exists showing patterns of discrimination that may be invisible in individual cases—hence, they do not meet the Supreme Court's *McCleskey* standards—but they do not influence capital sentencing for persons of color.[40] If the courts and legislatures hope to develop equitable legal standards for imposing capital punishment—again, assuming that such a thing is possible—they must look beyond statistics for guidance. Thus, the majority in *McCleskey* was correct in its judgment that statistics will not suffice to meet legal standards, but the conclusion that the majority drew— namely, that racial discrimination does not exist if it cannot be proved in specific cases—was myopic and a denial of fundamental fairness in the criminal justice system.

The difficulty in developing suitable legal standards to ameliorate racial discrimination in applying the death penalty has not prevented legislative action. Congress waded into the fray by considering two measures: the Racial Justice Act and the Fairness in Death Sentencing Act. The former measure was designed to end "racially disproportionate capital sentencing" by striking down a capital sentence that was influenced by a racially discriminatory pattern of sentencing. The state could rebut the presumption of racial discrimination by showing through a preponderance of the evidence that nonracial factors, such as aggravating circumstances, led to the sentence. The U.S. Senate eventually rejected the Racial

Justice Act by a margin of fifty-two to thirty-five when it was debated in October 1988.[41]

The U.S. House of Representatives passed a measure titled the "Fairness in Death Sentencing Act" in 1990 and again in 1994, but in each instance it failed to win Senate approval. State attorneys general and law enforcement personnel took exception to the bill's conclusion that racial discrimination exists at the state level (absent specific proof of such discrimination), and they lobbied vociferously to defeat the measure. They reasoned that acknowledgment of racial discrimination in capital sentencing, absent a showing in specific cases, would lead to exactly the conundrum that the Supreme Court avoided when it rejected the use of statistics alone in *McCleskey*. Ultimately, this logic won the day.[42]

The result of this ongoing debate is that the American legal system generally turns a blind eye to general, unsupported allegations of racial discrimination. Depending on one's point of view, this may be a welcomed development or it may be a travesty of justice. However the data are interpreted, as commentators David C. Baldus, George A. Woodworth, and Charles A. Pulaski have pointed out, it seems likely that black defendants receive a death sentence more often than whites. Moreover, "the average odds of receiving a death sentence among all indicated cases were 4.3 times higher in cases with white victims."[43]

B. POVERTY

Justice Hugo Black once observed that, in his view, "[t]here can be no equal justice when the kind of trial a man gets depends on how much money he has."[44] In his famously inimitable way, Justice Black was raising a point that has plagued the capital punishment system throughout American history. Some commentators have argued that the death penalty is applied in an economically discriminatory manner. The rich can afford to hire savvy lawyers and thoroughly investigate all aspects of the case in presenting a defense. The poor, however, are forced to rely on overworked, underpaid, often ill-prepared public defenders, according to this perspective.[45] Two commentators have wryly remarked that, "the cases following *Gideon* [*v. Wainwright*, which provided the right to counsel for indigent defendants,] have made it increasingly clear that the 'right to counsel' doesn't mean the right to an attorney who is any good."[46]

As a result of wealth inequities and the quality (or lack thereof) of defense attorneys, a defendant's liberty (or even his life) is at the mercy of his wealth. "We employ a strategy that might be called an 'argument from contingent realities,'" Jeffrey L. Johnson and Colleen F. Johnson explain in a 2001 journal article on poverty and the death penalty.

> We grant that moral, legal, or constitutional rules might sanction some practice in a more perfect (just, fair, equitable, etc.) world, but argue that given the contingent realities of the actual world, the practice in question is not to be permitted. That is, in the abstract capital punishment may not be unconstitutional, but in fact the way in which it is dispensed, we believe, puts it at odds with the Eighth Amendment and the Equal Protection Clause.[47]

In the authors' view, the nation's death penalty jurisprudence is "an embarrassing constitutional failure."[48] Punishments for criminal acts are supposed to be assigned equitably—that is, by treating like cases alike; defendants charged with similar crimes should not receive disparate sentences. Although this may not result in inequity from the perspective of the defendant who must be judged as an individual (because guilt is an individual characteristic),[49] it raises disturbing questions from the perspective of the regime that professes to treat its citizens—even those judged guilty of a crime—in a nondiscriminatory manner.[50]

Even death penalty supporters agree that disparities in wealth among capital defendants may result in a less spirited defense on behalf of the indigent offender. The question is whether this difference is sufficient to curtail or eliminate application of the death penalty in individual cases. It is a truism to say that a capitalist society always results in the unequal distribution of wealth and property. In Ernest van den Haag's view, the issue is not whether a defendant can marshal enough resources to escape successful prosecution but whether he or she is guilty. If the argument is that a rich guilty man goes free while a poor guilty man is sentenced to death, this is not an argument in favor of providing more resources to the poor guilty man. The argument about disparities in wealth would be logically compelling only if opponents of the death penalty could show data that innocent people received the death penalty and would not have done so if they had possessed additional resources.[51] In the absence of such data, a guilty man should receive no security by arguing that he might have escaped his punishment if only he could have afforded to hire a better lawyer.[52]

C. MENTAL RETARDATION

One of the hallmarks of a regime that seeks to administer criminal law in an equitable manner is that the law is known and knowable beforehand. This is a necessary requirement to ensure that defendants are not punished for actions they did not know to be prohibited. For men and women of average intelligence and capacity, it is not difficult to discern whether the law prohibits a particular act, especially if the act involves a homicide. Accordingly, sentencing these men and women to death for their action clearly meets the "state of mind" condition needed to ensure equity in the application of general criminal law to individual circumstances.

Mentally retarded defendants present a far more difficult problem because it is questionable whether they understand and appreciate the consequences of their actions, much less the prohibitions of the criminal law. If a defendant is too mentally impaired to understand his or her actions, he or she cannot understand the proceedings, much less participate in an active defense. This means, in effect, that the legal requirements necessary for imposing penalties may be absent when mentally retarded persons are charged with a capital crime.[53]

The U.S. Supreme Court addressed these issues in a landmark Texas case, *Penry v. Lynaugh*, that came before the court in 1989.[54] In *Penry*, a twenty-two-year-old defendant, Johnny Paul Penry, was arrested and accused of brutally raping, beating, and repeatedly stabbing a young woman with a pair of scissors. Before she died, the victim regained consciousness enough to describe her assailant. The physical description and the aggravated circumstances of the crime led local sheriffs to suspect Penry, who recently had been released on parole after having been convicted of another rape.[55]

The defense attorney pursued an insanity defense. During Penry's competency hearing before trial, a clinical psychologist who examined the defendant testified that in his expert opinion the young man's intelligence quotient (IQ) was 56. In previous tests, his IQ had been tested at between 50 and 63, indicating mild to moderate mental retardation. The psychologist concluded that Penry's mental age was approximately six and a half, while his social maturity—that is, his ability to function in the world—was that of a nine- or ten-year-old child.[56]

Predictably, the state presented contradictory evidence. To rebut the psychologist's testimony offered on behalf of the defense, two prosecution psychiatrists testified that although Penry was a person of limited mental capacity who had suffered a horrendous childhood in an abusive household, his impairment and tragic personal history did not impair his sanity. Because he knew right from wrong, the state argued, he should not escape punishment just because he was mentally retarded. In short, the appropriate legal standard is whether the defendant was rational and knew what he was doing was wrong at the time he committed a crime, not whether he fully appreciated all the legal niceties in presenting a defense at trial. Insanity, according to this perspective, means that the defendant acted under the influence of delusion (irrationality) and did not understand the character of the act. By contrast, mental retardation means that the person is rational but diminished in his rational capacity. Diminished rationality, however, does not necessarily equal irrationality or insanity.[57]

The jury accepted the prosecution's arguments and found Penry competent to stand trial for murder. Later, after Penry had been found guilty and sentenced to death, the defense appealed, arguing that the defendant's low IQ should have precluded a death sentence. The Texas Court of Criminal Appeals affirmed the conviction, specifically holding that Penry's mental retardation did not prohibit the imposition of the death penalty. The U.S. Supreme Court denied *certiorari* to review the conviction.[58]

Penry's attorneys then filed a habeas corpus action claiming, among other things, that it was cruel and unusual punishment under the Eighth Amendment to the U.S. Constitution to sentence a mentally retarded defendant to death. The district court denied Penry's petition, as did the Fifth Circuit Court of Appeals. The U.S. Supreme Court agreed to hear the case to address several issues, including whether the Eighth Amendment categorically prohibits the execution of mentally retarded capital murderers.[59]

Writing for the Court, Justice Sandra Day O'Connor rejected Penry's claim that the Eighth Amendment leaves no room to impose the death penalty on a mentally retarded defendant. "He argues that because of their mental disabilities, mentally retarded people do not possess the level of moral culpability to justify imposing the death sentence," she wrote, succinctly summarizing his argument. "He also argues that there is an emerging national consensus against executing the retarded."[60]

In O'Connor's view, these arguments were fallacious. She admitted that the common law prohibition against punishing "idiots" was well established, but she did not view Penry's case in that light. "Penry was found competent to stand trial. In other words, he was found to have the ability to consult with his lawyer with a reasonable degree of rational understanding, and was found to have a rational as well as factual understanding of the proceedings against him," she wrote. "In addition, the jury rejected his insanity defense, which reflected their conclusion that Penry knew that his conduct was wrong and was capable of conforming his conduct to the requirements of the law."[61]

Justice O'Connor also rejected the broader argument that it is cruel and unusual punishment pursuant to the Eighth Amendment to execute *any* mentally retarded defendant, regardless of the circumstances. "I cannot conclude that all mentally retarded people of Penry's ability—by virtue of their mental retardation alone, and apart from any individualized consideration of their personal responsibility—inevitably lack the cognitive, volitional, and moral capacity to act with the degree of culpability associated with the death penalty."[62] As with any case, all the circumstances must be considered by the jury, including the level of a defendant's retardation. Thus, another mentally retarded person might escape punishment because he was far more impaired than Penry, but a blanket prohibition on executing mentally retarded people would be perverse, in O'Connor's view. "[W]e cannot conclude today that the Eighth Amendment precludes the execution of any mentally retarded person of Penry's ability convicted of a capital offense simply by virtue of his or her mental retardation alone. . . . While a national consensus against execution of the mentally retarded may some day emerge reflecting the 'evolving standards of decency that mark the progress of a maturing society,' there is insufficient evidence of such a consensus today."[63]

Justice William Brennan, joined by Justice Thurgood Marshall, concurred in part and dissented in part. Insofar as executing mentally retarded persons was concerned, he registered an emphatic dissent based on several factors. First, in Brennan's opinion, juries cannot adequately assess the capacity of mentally retarded persons to understand the nature of their crimes or the punishment awaiting them. As a result, an individualized consideration at sentencing, required by the U.S. Supreme Court as a necessary prerequisite for imposing capital punishment, is not present for mentally retarded defendants. "Lack of culpability as a result of mental retardation is simply not isolated at the sentencing stage as a factor that determinatively bars a death sentence; for individualized consideration at sentencing is not designed to ensure that mentally retarded offenders are not sentenced to death if they are not culpable to the degree necessary to render execution a proportionate response to their crimes."[64]

In addition, Brennan contended that executing the mentally retarded does not further the goals of retribution or deterrence. In the case of retribution, it is difficult to argue that a mentally retarded person got his or her "just deserts" when he or she did not understand the nature of the criminal act. Deterrence, in the meantime, assumes that a defendant will calculate and rationally decide not to perpetrate future crimes owing to the possibility of being captured and punished. A mentally retarded offender, however, may not be capable of such rational calculations. Consequently, Brennan explained that he could see no reason to execute mentally retarded capital offenders when they could be imprisoned instead, thereby ensuring the safety of society without stooping to barbarism in killing a mentally infirm individual. "Because I believe that the Eighth Amendment to the United States Constitution stands in the way of a State killing a mentally retarded person for a crime which, as a result of his or her disability, he or she if not fully culpable, I would reverse the judgment of the Court of Appeals in its entirety," he concluded.[65]

Similarly, Justice Stevens, joined by Justice Blackmun, also argued that executing mentally retarded defendants was, in his view, unconstitutional. For Stevens, the medical and scientific arguments set forth in the *amicus curiae* brief filed by the American Medical Association were especially persuasive. Executing persons with diminished rational capacity violates the Eighth Amendment because it treats them like any other individual, when clearly they are different. Like cases should be treated alike, it is true, but mentally retarded offenders are different cases. "I would therefore reverse the judgment of the Court of Appeals in its entirety."[66]

Justice Antonin Scalia, joined by Chief Justice William Rehnquist, Justice Byron White, and Justice Anthony Kennedy, filed the final opinion in *Penry v. Lynaugh*. In his usual erudite manner, Scalia explained why he concurred in part and dissented in part with the majority opinion. As for the question of whether mentally retarded persons can be executed in accordance with the Eighth Amendment, Scalia contended that Justice O'Connor's opinion went too far. "Part IV-C of her opinion goes on to examine whether application of the death penalty to mentally retarded offenders 'violates the Eighth Amendment because it makes no measurable contribution to acceptable goals of punishment and hence is nothing more than the purposeless and needless imposition of pain and suffering' or because it is 'grossly out of proportion to the severity of the crime.'"[67] Scalia disagreed with this analysis because he believed that it was unnecessary to consider such issues. A punishment is cruel and unusual, or it is not. "If it is not unusual, that is, if an objective examination of laws and jury determinations fails to demonstrate society's disapproval of it, the punishment is not unconstitutional even if out of accord with the theories of penology favored by the Justices of this Court."[68] Because society had not condemned the execution of mentally retarded persons, the Supreme Court did not need to analyze the matter any further.

As a result of the *Penry* case, mentally retarded people could be executed in the United States, depending on the circumstances in the case. In light of the controversial nature of this decision, however, it was only a matter of time before the court revisited the issue. A regime that allows the mentally impaired to die at the hands of the state is a regime that invites skepticism about the equitable application of capital punishment. Accordingly, as this book was in press, the high court announced its decision in a 2002 case, *Atkins v. Virginia*. By a 6–3 vote, the Justices held that executing mentally retarded persons (defined as anyone with an IQ of 70 or less) violates the Eighth Amendment's prohibition of cruel and unusual punishment. The repercussions of this ruling remain to be seen.[69]

D. YOUTH

In recent years, much has been written about whether juveniles (i.e., persons under eighteen years of age) should be subject to the death penalty.[70] Just as in the case of mentally retarded defendants, if the goal in the criminal justice system is to administer punishments in an equitable manner, it is important to punish defendants who possessed the capacity to appreciate the nature of their actions. Juveniles, however, may or may not possess such a capacity. Much depends on an individual defendant's age, home life, and social development. The courts have grappled with whether juveniles should be subject to the death penalty, and, predictably, they have concluded that the sentence depends on the circumstances in the case. To illustrate this point, consider the U.S. Supreme Court opinion in *Stanford v. Kentucky*,[71] which held that imposing capital punishment on a person who was sixteen or seventeen years old at the time he perpetrated the crime does not necessarily constitute cruel and unusual punishment under the Eighth Amendment.

Stanford involved two consolidated cases of juveniles who committed murders. In the first case, the defendant, Kevin Stanford, was seventeen years, four months old when he and an accomplice robbed a gas station. They kidnapped twenty-year-old Barbara Poore, repeatedly raped and sodomized her, drove her to a secluded location, and then Stanford shot her point-blank in the face and in the back of the head.

After Stanford's arrest, a Kentucky juvenile court conducted hearings to determine whether he should be tried as an adult. Under the applicable Kentucky criminal statute, a juvenile defendant could be tried as an adult if he was charged with a Class A felony or capital crime or if the defendant was at least sixteen years of age and charged with a felony. Owing to the aggravated nature of the crime as well as his age, Stanford fell within the statutory guidelines, so he was tried as an adult.[72]

The jury found him guilty of murder, first-degree sodomy, first-degree robbery, and receiving stolen property. As a result, he was sentenced to forty-five years in prison as well as given the death penalty. Despite the defendant's arguments that he should not have been sentenced to death because he was still considered a juvenile under the law, the court found that Stanford's "age and the possibility that he might be rehabilitated were mitigating factors appropriately left to the consideration of the jury that tried him." The jury considered the defendant's age and nonetheless sentenced him to die. The jurors apparently were unconvinced that Stanford would be rehabilitated or that he deserved leniency owing to his age.[73]

The second consolidated case involved Heath Wilkins, a defendant who was sixteen years, six months old when he robbed a convenience store in Avondale, Missouri, on July 27, 1985. During the robbery, Wilkins and an accomplice, Patrick Stevens, grabbed twenty-six-year-old Nancy Allen, a mother of two young children, and stabbed her repeatedly. The record reflected that Wilkins intended to rob the store and murder "whoever was behind the counter" because "a dead person can't talk." After stabbing the victim numerous times and eventually penetrating her carotid artery, Wilkins and Stevens fled the premises with liquor, cigarettes, rolling papers and approximately $450 in cash and checks in their possession.[74]

Under the applicable Missouri criminal statute, Wilkins was too young to receive the death penalty automatically; however, the juvenile court was permitted to hold a hearing for defendants fourteen to seventeen years of age and possibly certify a juvenile as an adult for purposes of a criminal trial. Owing to the viciousness of the crime and Wilkins's maturity, the juvenile court certified him as competent to be tried as an adult. Later, he was convicted of first-degree murder, armed criminal action, and carrying a concealed weapon. On mandatory review of the conviction, the Missouri Supreme Court rejected Wilkins's argument that it is cruel and unusual punishment to impose the death penalty on a juvenile and affirmed his conviction.[75]

The U.S. Supreme Court granted *certiorari* in the two cases to determine whether the Eighth Amendment absolutely prohibits imposing the death penalty on juvenile defendants. In a plurality opinion, Justice Antonin Scalia rejected the argument that "evolving standards of decency that mark the progress of a maturing society" necessarily preclude sentencing juvenile defendants to death for capital crimes. "In determining what standards have 'evolved,' however, we have looked not to our conceptions of decency, but to those of modern American society as a whole," he wrote. In Scalia's view, Americans are willing to impose the ultimate punishment on juvenile defendants, judging by the large number of criminal statutes enacted by state legislatures in a majority of states that allow juveniles to be tried as adults. In light of these legislative enactments, the justices of the U.S. Supreme Court should not substitute their judgment on what passes as "evolving standards of decency" when the standards already have been set in the states.[76]

Scalia also rejected the argument that juveniles should not be sentenced to death because they possess fewer cognitive skills than adults do, and therefore juveniles are less blameworthy. If scientific evidence demonstrated that juveniles were not as rational as adults—and therefore less culpable in their actions—then the Equal Protection Clause of the Fourteenth Amendment would apply because such evidence would undermine the rational basis for state statutes allowing capital punishment to apply to underage defendants. In Scalia's opinion, however, cases involving juveniles sentenced to death do not involve the Fourteenth Amendment because scientific evidence does not support the defendants' contentions. "The battle must be fought, then, on the field of the Eighth Amendment; and in that struggle socioscientific, ethioscientific, or even purely scientific evidence is not an available weapon," he concluded. "The punishment is either 'cruel and unusual' (i.e., society has set its face against it) or it is not." In this case, Scalia held that the punishment was not cruel and unusual.[77] In his concluding remarks, he wrote that "[w]e discern neither a historical nor a modern societal consensus forbidding the imposition of capital punishment on any person who murders at sixteen or seventeen years of age. Accordingly, we conclude that such punishment does not offend the Eighth Amendment's prohibition against cruel and unusual punishment."[78]

In a concurring opinion, Justice Sandra Day O'Connor wrote that she agreed with Justice Scalia that nothing in the Eighth Amendment prohibited the execution of juvenile defendants such as Stanford and Wilkins. Nonetheless, O'Connor argued that the Supreme Court had an obligation to conduct a "proportionality analysis." Such an analysis would require the high court to determine whether the punishment imposed was proportionate to the defendants' blameworthiness. Moreover, the court would have to determine whether the state statute under consideration furthered the acceptable goals of punishment. Scalia found such an analysis unnecessary because the Supreme Court has "never invalidated a punishment on this basis alone. All of our cases condemning a punishment under this mode of analysis also found that the objective indicators of state laws or jury determinations evidenced a societal consensus against that penalty."[79] O'Connor disagreed with Scalia on this point. "In my view, this Court does have a constitutional obligation to conduct proportionality analysis." Nonetheless, she agreed with the result in *Stanford* because she did not think it would change the result in the case. "Thus, although I do not believe that these particular cases can be resolved through proportionality analysis . . . I reject the suggestion that the use of such analysis is improper as a matter of Eighth Amendment jurisprudence."[80]

Justice Brennan, joined by Justices Marshall, Blackmun, and Stevens, dissented. "I believe that to take the life of a person as punishment for a crime committed when below the age of eighteen is cruel and unusual and hence is prohibited by the Eighth Amendment," he wrote at the outset.[81] In Brennan's opinion, the Supreme Court has an obligation to review "ethicoscientific" evidence in capital cases because such data provide the court with information necessary to make an informed judgment. He also contended that Justice Scalia's decision to determine "contemporary standards of decency" by reviewing legislative enactments alone does not go far enough to discern the relevant standards. "Our cases recognize that objective indicators of contemporary standards of decency in the form of legislation in other countries is also of relevance to Eighth Amendment analysis." It also is relevant to examine the opinions of respected organizations such as the American Bar Association, the National Council of Juvenile Court Judges, the American Law Institute's Model Penal Code, and the National Commission on Reform of the Federal Criminal Laws. When judges review information from these sources, the notion of common decency changes significantly. According to Brennan, "[s]ince 1979, Amnesty International has recorded only eight executions of offenders under eighteen throughout the world, three of these in the United States." This statistic places the American capital punishment system on par with the capital punishment systems in nations such as Pakistan, Bangladesh,

Rwanda, and Barbados—hardly esteemed company when it comes to issues of crime, punishment, or equal protection of the laws.[82]

Brennan argued vehemently against Scalia's "positivist approach" to death penalty jurisprudence when the latter examined what the majority of states chose to do in implementing capital punishment statutes. "This Court abandons its proven and proper role in our constitutional system when it hands back to the very majorities the Framers distrusted the power to define the precise scope of protection afforded by the Bill of Rights, rather than bringing its own judgment to bear on that question, after complete analysis," Brennan observed.[83] Instead, the Court is obligated to consider whether the punishment is out of proportion to the crime, which he must answer affirmatively. "In my view, juveniles so generally lack the degree of responsibility for their crimes that is a predicate for the constitutional imposition of the death penalty that the Eighth Amendment forbids that they receive that punishment."[84]

Justice Brennan concluded his dissent with an impassioned plea to consider the need for judging juveniles differently than adults. Because a majority of states decline to execute juveniles (regardless of whether their statutes allow juveniles to be tried as adults), respected organizations discourage such executions, and most other civilized nations abhor the practice, capital punishment for juveniles ought to be held unconstitutional. "These indicators serve to confirm in my view my conclusion that the Eighth Amendment prohibits the execution of persons for offenses they committed while below the age of eighteen, because the death penalty is disproportionate when applied to such young offenders and fails measurably to serve the goals of capital punishment. I dissent."[85]

III. Conclusion

As a black-letter legal rule, capital punishment is constitutional on its face in the United States; however, as this chapter has attempted to illustrate, many issues arise when the death penalty is applied in specific cases. Several factors potentially affect equity in sentencing, especially the race, poverty, mental capacity, or youth of the offender. As the cases discussed herein have indicated, the U.S. Supreme Court has determined that these general factors, absent evidence of specific bias in a particular case, do not automatically render the application of capital punishment unconstitutional.

In his concurrence in *Furman v. Georgia*,[86] Justice Potter Stewart remarked that the death penalty in the United States all too often has been "wantonly and freakishly imposed."[87] For abolitionists, this deficiency can never be corrected because so many biases and prejudices exist that human beings can never ensure a "fundamentally fair" system of capital punishment. Consequently, whether one is philosophically opposed to the concept of capital punishment owing to moral considerations or whether one believes that it is beyond human ability to impose the ultimate penalty in an equitable manner, state-sanctioned executions have no place within the fabric of American life. As the dissenters have pointed out in the leading cases discussed in this chapter, a legal system that professes to treat its citizens fairly ultimately must reject capital punishment. An enlightened nation has no choice but to turn its back on punishments that violate its fundamental tenets.

CHAPTER 15

Legal Arguments in Favor of the Death Penalty

J. Michael Martinez

Few topics invite more debate and rancor than the issue of capital punishment. This is hardly surprising, for the issue has been debated by Western nations since antiquity. America's common law heritage extending back five hundred years in English history finds numerous examples. In the sixteenth century, British law provided for the imposition of capital punishment for eight types of crimes: treason, petty treason (i.e., the killing of a husband by his wife), murder, larceny, robbery, burglary, rape, and arson. During the next two hundred years, the kings of England added more crimes to the list of capital offenses, making the total number fifty by the end of the seventeenth century. King George II added thirty-five more, and George III approved another sixty.

By the end of the eighteenth century, more than two hundred crimes were punishable by death, including pickpocketing and petty theft. Eventually, the English Parliament reformed the law and narrowed the list, but the death penalty remained intact for brutal crimes as long as the punishment fit the crime. In the words of one commentator, the purpose of capital punishment was to give back to perpetrators what they first gave to society. "Those who shew no mercy should have none," for if they cannot be controlled through lesser measures, "a *Roman* punishment [death] should" control them.[1]

On the other hand, many commentators have asked whether the "eye for an eye" rationale is a sufficient justification for capital punishment. "Is it not absurd, that the laws, which detest and punish homicide, should, in order to prevent murder, publicly commit murder themselves?" asked an eighteenth-century critic of the death penalty.[2] The battle lines for the capital punishment controversy were drawn before the United States even became a nation.

Despite centuries of debate, only in recent years has the death penalty issue assumed a prominent place in the history of American jurisprudence. In the early years of American colonial history, capital punishment was left to the discretion of individual states. "The Capitall Lawes of New-England," drafted in 1636, provided the first list of capital crimes in the American colonies and included a quotation from the Old Testament accompanying each crime listed. The crimes were as follows: idolatry, witchcraft, blasphemy, murder, assault in sudden anger, sodomy, buggery, adultery, statutory rape, rape, manstealing, perjury in a capital trial, and rebellion. Gradually, by the eighteenth century, lists of crimes in the colonies took on a more secular character. Moreover, the average number of capital offenses had narrowed to twelve.[3]

During this era, exceptions and extenuating circumstances abounded. It was not uncommon to see an offender escape the gallows because he could read, which meant that he must be a member of the clerical order and was therefore subject only to the jurisdiction of ecclesiastical courts. Executives could pardon offenders, generally for a fee. In addition, juries often stubbornly refused to apply the penalty to one of their own kind. It became clear over time that inequities had crept into the system of capital punishment.

States responded by attempting to draft statutes that more closely regulated when death could be sentenced and when it could not. They also attempted to differentiate among and between types of crimes; first-degree murder was worse than second-degree murder, which was worse than manslaughter or other crimes against persons that did not result in a homicide. Eventually, states began to revise their statutes to reserve capital punishment for only the most heinous crimes—crimes that by their unusual circumstances were horrific and shocked the sensibilities of the community.

As thinking about capital punishment evolved, states also began to search for more humane methods of executing offenders. Hangings were moved from the town square to inside the prison walls to avoid the public spectacles that had been commonplace in years past. Nonetheless, as late as 1936, the good citizens of Owensboro, Kentucky, turned out to watch an offender, Rainey Bethea, hanged for rape. A year later, the last public hanging in the United States occurred in Galena, Missouri, as some five hundred people witnessed the condemned man's trip to the gallows.

Anti–capital punishment sentiment increased in the nineteenth century as the abolitionist movement to end slavery took hold in some parts of the country. During the antebellum period, many abolitionists viewed slavery and capital punishment together as barbarous treatment that had no place in the life of an enlightened nation. Much of the activity aimed at reforming the American legal and political tradition at this time occurred at the state and not the federal level, for the state was the locus of political life for much of that era.

Even after the Civil War, the federal government had a small role in the death penalty debate because crime and punishment remained primarily issues of state criminal law. In 1847, the Michigan legislature abolished capital punishment, followed by Rhode Island in 1852 and Wisconsin in 1853. By 1917, twelve states had abolished capital punishment, and this was the situation in the United States well into the twentieth century. The trend continued throughout the decades; by 1969, fourteen states had either abolished capital punishment or made it so difficult to impose that it was all but abolished.[4] In 1967, the U.S. Senate Judiciary Committee debated a bill that would have abolished capital punishment for all federal crimes, but the measure died before it could reach the Senate floor.[5]

Before the United States Supreme Court decided the two seminal death penalty cases in the 1970s—*Furman v. Georgia*[6] and *Gregg v. Georgia*[7]—the federal courts were only minimally involved in capital cases. The Eighth Amendment to the Constitution, which prohibits "cruel and unusual punishment," was not interpreted by the Supreme Court until late in the nineteenth century, and even then the Court focused on the method of punishment, not the broader question of whether death was a constitutionally permissible penalty.[8] Aside from decisions requiring defendants to have access to court-appointed counsel, the federal courts were on the sidelines of the debate until the prevailing perspective on the appropriate balance of federalism gradually began to change during the 1950s and 1960s. Reflecting changing social mores, the growth of federal authority, the decisions of the politically liberal Warren Court, and the increasingly broad interpretation of the Due Process Clause of the Fourteenth Amendment, the federal courts became more actively involved in state issues after the 1930s. By the late 1960s, the death penalty issue was ripe for federal judicial intervention.[9]

I. *Furman v. Georgia*

The first important U.S. Supreme Court case involving the death penalty in the modern era was *Furman v. Georgia*, a 1972 case in which three African American defendants challenged state death penalty statutes in Georgia and Texas. In the first Georgia case, the defendant was convicted of murder. In the other two cases, the defendants were sentenced to death for rape. The question presented to the Supreme Court on appeal was, in the words of the Court's per curiam decision, "Does the imposition and carrying out of the death penalty in [these cases] constitute cruel and unusual punishment in violation of the Eighth and Fourteenth Amendment?"[10]

The Court was deeply divided on this question, ultimately reversing the judgment and remanding the case for further consideration. Although the Court struck down the death penalty statutes under review in *Furman*, the range of views made for confusing jurisprudence. The Court's per curiam decision held that the imposition and carrying out of the death penalty was cruel and unusual punishment, and therefore prohibited by the Constitution, but each of the nine justices wrote at least one separate opinion explaining his views; in some cases, one or more justices joined together to write a second opinion.[11]

In his concurrence, Justice William O. Douglas expressed concern that the death penalty was applied selectively to ethnic minorities who were unpopular and could not afford to defend themselves to the extent that more privileged defendants could defend themselves. This disparity between rich and poor created a de facto caste system that Justice Douglas found to be inconsistent with the dictates of the Constitution. "[W]e know that the discretion of judges and juries in imposing the death penalty enables the penalty to be selectively applied, feeding prejudices against the accused if he is poor and despised, lacking political clout, or if he is a member of a suspect or unpopular minority, and saving those who by social position may be in a more protected position," Justice Douglas observed. Thus, without rejecting the death penalty under all circumstances, he concluded that even facially neutral state statutes that allow judges and juries to apply capital punishment selectively "are pregnant with discrimination and discrimination is an ingredient not compatible with the idea of equal protection of the laws that is implicit in the ban on 'cruel and unusual' punishments."[12] In Douglas's opinion, the death penalty might be constitutionally permissible if the biases inherent in selective application of the punishment could be overcome.

Like Justice Douglas, Justice William Brennan's concurrence also focused on the Eighth Amendment's prohibition against cruel and unusual punishment; however, he went further than Douglas in exploring the historical context of the amendment. He argued that the Eighth Amendment should not be narrowly interpreted only to prohibit torturous punishments, but it should be understood to define "cruel and unusual" as any punishment that is "so severe as to be degrading to the dignity of human beings."[13] The problem with the treatment afforded the defendants in the *Furman* case was that their dignity was undermined, in Brennan's view. "The true significance of these punishments is that they treat members of the human race as nonhumans, as objects to be toyed with and discarded," he wrote. "They are thus inconsistent with the fundamental premise of the Clause that even the vilest criminal remains a human being possessed of common human dignity."[14] In short, Justice Brennan took Douglas's concern about the selective application of the death penalty to poor, disadvantaged offenders a step further by arguing that capital punishment destroys all human dignity, not simply those persons historically disenfranchised.

Echoing the comments of his brethren to some extent, Justice Potter Stewart recognized that the death penalty was selectively applied. He argued that his opinion specifically did not address the issue of whether the death penalty is inappropriate in all cases, but he believed it was inappropriate in the *Furman* case. Setting aside the question of whether race was involved in *Furman* (because, according to Stewart, it had not been proved), he concluded that the imposition of the penalty nonetheless had been "wantonly and freakishly imposed."[15] As was the case with Douglas, Stewart left open the possibility that the death penalty could be used if it were applied in a less arbitrary and capricious manner.

Justice Byron White was concerned that the state statutes challenged in *Furman* were drafted so that the legislature did not mandate the death penalty but delegated the decision to judges and juries. In his view, this poorly devised statutory scheme led to the freakish imposition of the death penalty that Justices Douglas and Stewart decried. Because it was applied in such a haphazard manner, according to Justice White, most state statutes provided for a constitutionally impermissible application of the punishment. Moreover, the imposition of the death penalty was applied so infrequently that "the threat of execution is too attenuated to be of substantial service to criminal justice."[16] Ironically, the death penalty was constitutionally suspect not because it ended human life but because it was not applied often enough to serve as a deterrent. If the death penalty is supposed to serve the legislative purpose of deterring would-be criminals, then it must be applied in such a way that it fulfills the legislative purpose; otherwise, it runs afoul of the Eighth Amendment.

A well-known opponent of the death penalty, Justice Thurgood Marshall followed in Brennan's footsteps by considering the much broader issue of whether capital punishment can ever be constitutional under the Eighth Amendment. After reviewing constitutional jurisprudence on the issue in detail, Justice Marshall concluded that the average citizen would not favor capital punishment if he knew the realities of inflicting death on his fellow man. He would "find it shocking to his conscience and sense of justice." In Marshall's opinion, an enlightened society must reject the death penalty because it is a remnant of an earlier age when people did not understand the causes of crime or the tools available to the criminal justice system to control offenders without using capital punishment. "In recognizing the humanity of our fellow beings, we pay ourselves the highest tribute," Justice Marshall argued. "We achieve 'a major milestone in the long road up from barbarism' and join approximately seventy other jurisdictions in the world which celebrate their regard for civilization and humanity by shunning capital punishment."[17]

The dissenting opinions were every bit as vociferous as the opinions of their brethren. Chief Justice Warren Burger, joined by Justices Blackmun, Powell, and Rehnquist, dissented on the grounds that the concurring opinions misconstrued the nature of the Court's Eighth Amendment jurisprudence. In the chief justice's view, the prohibition on cruel and unusual punishment should be interpreted as a prohibition on torture and other forms of barbaric treatment. Issues such as whether the death penalty is applied infrequently or whether it would be shocking to individual citizens miss the point. A penalty is not judged on how often it is applied or whether particular individuals would be upset by the details of an execution; either it passes constitutional muster, or it does not. As for the question of whether the death penalty is consistent with the Constitution, Chief Justice Burger examined past Supreme Court decisions, especially those recently announced. "In the 181 years since the enactment of the Eighth Amendment," he wrote, "not a single decision of this Court has cast the slightest shadow of a doubt on the constitutionality of capital punishment."[18]

Burger was mystified as to why several of his colleagues were concerned that the statutes under review in *Furman* allowed judges and juries to apply the standards selectively. In his opinion, this application of general standards to specific cases is the appropriate role of judges and juries. A judge examines broad, general legal principles articulated in statutes and prior case law and applies them to the facts that the jury determines in each individual case. "The motive or lack of motive of the perpetrator, the degree of injury or suffering of the victim or victims, and the degree of brutality in the commission of the crime would seem to be" permissible factors to consider.[19]

Moreover, a decent respect for federalism requires the federal courts to respect the decisions of state legislatures. In a case such as *Furman*, the Supreme Court should not interpose itself into the legislative process in the absence of clearly articulable reasons for interfering with the authority of states to determine appropriate penalties for criminal acts. It smacks of judicial activism when judges impose detailed standards on the states for determining when the death penalty is appropriate and when it is not. "The highest judicial duty is to recognize limits on judicial power and to permit the democratic processes to deal with matters falling outside of those limits," Burger concluded.[20]

In a separate dissent, Justice Harry Blackmun added "somewhat personal comments" owing to his "distaste, antipathy, and, indeed, abhorrence, for the death penalty." Justice Blackmun argued that he did not believe that the death penalty accomplished the legislative goals of deterrence but instead existed as an instrument of state retribution. Nonetheless, despite his professed hostility to the death penalty, Blackmun was even more disturbed regarding the Court's predilection to substitute its judgment for the judgment of state legislatures on matters of public policy. "I do not sit on these cases, however, as a legislator, responsive, at least in part, to the will of constituents," he observed, echoing Burger's concern. "Our task here, as must so frequently be emphasized and reemphasized, is to pass upon the constitutionality of legislation that has been enacted and that is challenged. This is the sole task for judges. We should not allow our personal preferences as to the wisdom of legislative and congressional action, or our distaste for such action, to guide our judicial decision in cases such as these."[21]

Justice Lewis Powell, joined by Chief Justice Burger and Justices Blackmun and Rehnquist, also dissented. In Powell's view, the plurality opinion filed by the majority of the Court failed to provide an adequate constitutional basis for striking down the death penalty. Despite the lack of an adequate constitutional basis, however, the practical effect of the Court's decision was that it invalidated hundreds of state and federal laws and provided confusing guidelines for states to redraft their death penalty statutes. The broad reach of the Court's actions and the lack of flexibility provided to the states dismayed Powell. "The sobering disadvantage of constitutional adjudication of this magnitude is the universality and permanence of the judgment," he wrote. "The enduring merit of legislative action is its responsiveness to the democratic process, and to revision and change: mistaken judgments may be corrected and refinements perfected."[22]

The final opinion filed in the *Furman* case was a dissent written by Justice Rehnquist, joined by the chief justice as well as Justices Blackmun and Powell. After briefly reviewing the intentions of the Founders and early court opinions, Rehnquist contended that the appropriate role of the Supreme Court is to exercise judicial restraint in deciding matters of broad public policy. He was especially concerned with what he saw as the willingness of the politically liberal, activist branch of the Court—notably, Douglas, Brennan, and Marshall—to act as superlegislators in rewriting the meaning of the Eighth Amendment in accordance with their own political views. In Rehnquist's opinion, this kind of judicial policymaking goes against the Madisonian concept of checks and balances discussed in the Federalist Papers. "The very nature of judicial review, as pointed out by Justice Stone in his dissent in the *Butler* case, makes the courts the least subject to Madisonian check in the event that they shall, for the best of motives, expand judicial authority beyond the limits contemplated by the Founders," Rehnquist wrote. "It is for this reason that judicial self-restraint is surely an implied, if not an expressed, condition of the grant of authority of judicial review. The Court's holding in these cases has been reached, I believe, in complete disregard of that implied condition."[23]

Despite the confusing set of permutations and combinations in the opinions, *Furman* proved to be a pivotal case. After the decision was handed down, the sentences of all 633 defendants on death row, including two women, were overturned. It also proved to be a controversial case, as the justices knew it would be. Abolitionist groups such as the National Association for the Advancement of

Colored People (NAACP) Legal Defense and Education Fund hailed the Court's conclusion as the first step toward invalidating capital punishment under all circumstances. Although only two justices—Brennan and Marshall—had expressed support for completely abolishing the death penalty, the NAACP and many other groups saw this as but an incremental step in an evolving jurisprudence that eventually would outlaw capital punishment in the United States.[24]

Pro–death penalty commentators expressed outrage that the Supreme Court had been "soft on crime," and state legislators expressed frustration at the Court's "guidance" on redrafting their death penalty statutes. Given the murkiness of the Court's plurality opinion, it seemed difficult to know how a statute could be worded so that clear standards were set forth while also allowing judges and juries to consider the individual factors in a case. Demonstrating his well-known penchant for hyperbole, Georgia lieutenant governor Lester Maddox, for example, reacted in an inimitable, blunt style, remarking that the *Furman* decision was a "license for anarchy, rape, [and] murder."[25]

Despite the murky conclusions in *Furman*, the case was an important step in the evolution of the Supreme Court's constitutional jurisprudence on capital punishment. Just as some of the dissenters predicted, the practical effect was to invalidate death penalty statutes not only in the states involved in the case but in thirty-eight others as well. Although it was the longest Supreme Court opinion on record at the time, *Furman* provided little concrete guidance on the future of capital punishment in the United States. Justices Brennan and Marshall were the only members of the Court who argued expressly that the death penalty was a per se violation of the Eighth Amendment. Justices Douglas, Stewart, and White suggested that capital punishment might be constitutionally permissible in some instances, although they did not fully address the issue. Despite the euphoria evident in the statements of some abolitionists at the time, *Furman* did not sound the death knell for capital punishment in the United States. As commentator Lloyd Steffen observed, "That the American judiciary has attended—however unconsciously or even unwittingly—to a theory of just execution . . . can be demonstrated by examining the particulars of various post–*Furman v. Georgia* Supreme Court decisions."[26]

II. *Gregg v. Georgia*

In the wake of the *Furman* decision, states began revising their capital punishment statutes to conform to the Supreme Court's requirements. Unfortunately, the per curiam opinion did not explicitly provide legislative drafters with definitive instructions on how to revise the statutes so they would pass constitutional muster. This lack of guidance led to another series of cases that eventually reached the Court in 1976. Of those challenges, *Gregg v. Georgia* was the landmark case.

The case arose from another Georgia murder conviction. On November 21, 1973, Troy Leon Gregg and a companion, Floyd Allen, were hitchhiking in Florida when two men, Fred Simmons and Bob Moore, picked them up in an automobile. The car later broke down, but Simmons purchased another one, and the four men continued their journey into Georgia. Along the way, they picked up another hitchhiker, Dennis Weaver. The quartet dropped Weaver in Atlanta before parking at a rest stop along the highway, where they spent the night.

The next morning, several motorists discovered the bodies of Simmons and Moore in a nearby ditch. Two days later, Dennis Weaver was reading the Atlanta paper when he saw an article about the killings. Recalling his time with the men, Weaver contacted police in Gwinnett County, Georgia, and described Gregg and Allen as well as the car. On the basis of Weaver's identification, police arrested the defendants in Asheville, North Carolina, the next afternoon. In a search incident to the arrest, they found a .25-caliber pistol that later was confirmed as the weapon that killed Simmons and Moore.

After receiving the warnings required by *Miranda v. Arizona*,[27] Gregg signed a written waiver of his rights and admitted shooting Simmons and Moore before he robbed them. He claimed, however, that the shootings were justified by self-defense. The police doubted his story; accordingly, they charged him under Georgia criminal law with committing armed robbery and murder.

Under the newly revised Georgia death penalty statute—drafted after the *Furman* case—the guilt or innocence of the defendant was determined in an initial trial. If the trial was by a jury, the judge was required to list lesser-included offenses in his jury charge. After a guilty verdict was returned, the statute required that a presentencing hearing must be held to determine whether any additional evidence existed concerning extenuating, mitigating, or aggravating circumstances. Defendants were afforded considerable latitude in introducing evidence of extenuating or mitigating circumstances during the penalty phase. Before sentencing a convicted capital defendant to death, the judge also had to find beyond a reasonable doubt that at least one of the ten statutorily prescribed aggravating circumstances existed.

The jury convicted Gregg of two counts of murder, and the judge sentenced him to death pursuant to the statutory provisions. On appeal, the Georgia Supreme Court upheld the convictions.[28] The U.S. Supreme Court then granted *certiorari* to consider the question of whether the death sentences that Gregg received in the case constituted cruel and unusual punishment under the Eighth Amendment.[29]

As in the *Furman* case, *Gregg* found a deeply divided Supreme Court. Although the Court could not agree on a majority opinion, seven justices agreed with the conclusion that the imposition of the death penalty for the crime of murder under the Georgia statute did not violate the Eighth Amendment. The practical effect of this conclusion was to overturn *Furman*, although the Court did not expressly do so. Instead, *Gregg* served notice to states that the Supreme Court was willing to examine state statutes closely to determine whether specific provisions and the application of statutory standards in specific cases were constitutionally permissible. Despite the optimistic assessments of abolitionists that capital punishment was moving toward extinction in the wake of the *Furman* case, it was clear that the Court would allow states to impose the death penalty in some instances.[30]

Justice Lewis Powell announced the opinion of the Court in a decision joined by Justice John Paul Stevens. According to Powell, the death penalty does not constitute cruel and unusual punishment in all instances. In fact, evolving standards of decency in society allow for changes in the interpretation of the Eighth Amendment over time. In distinguishing the Court's decision in *Furman*, decided only four years earlier, Powell explained that

> the petitioners in *Furman* and its companion cases predicated their argument primarily upon the asserted proposition that standards of decency had evolved to the point where capital punishment no longer could be tolerated. The petitioners in those cases said, in effect, that the evolutionary process had come to an end, and that standards of decency required that the Eighth Amendment be construed finally as prohibiting capital punishment for any crime regardless of its depravity and impact on society.

In Powell's opinion, this line of reasoning was never embraced by a majority of the Supreme Court. "This view was accepted by two Justices. The other Justices were unwilling to go so far; focusing on the procedures by which convicted defendants were selected for the death penalty rather than on the actual punishment inflicted, they joined the conclusion that the statutes before the Court were constitutionally invalid."[31]

In Powell's view, a legislature need not select the least severe penalty possible, provided that the punishment is commensurate with the crime. Based on prior decisions by the Court, the true meaning of the Eighth Amendment is to ensure that the state does not torture its citizens. For more than two hundred years, the courts have allowed the death penalty to stand as an acceptable means of accomplishing a number of valid social goals, primarily retribution and deterrence. According to Powell:

In sum, we cannot say that the judgment of the Georgia legislature that capital punishment may be necessary in some cases is clearly wrong. Considerations of federalism, as well as respect for the ability of a legislature to evaluate, in terms of its particular state, the moral consensus concerning the death penalty and its social utility as a sanction, require us to conclude, in the absence of more convincing evidence, that the infliction of death as a punishment for murder is not without justification and thus not unconstitutionally severe.[32]

Justice Powell concluded his lengthy opinion by reviewing the Georgia statute challenged in the *Gregg* case. In addition to upholding the state's constitutional authority to determine an appropriate punishment, he found that the Georgia provision allowing an automatic appellate review of all capital convictions served as a check against the "arbitrary imposition of the death penalty." In contrast to the circumstances in *Furman*, the Georgia statute in *Gregg* was appropriately drafted. "The new Georgia sentencing procedures, by contrast, focus the jury's attention on the particularized nature of the crime and the particularized characteristics of the individual defendant," Powell observed. "While the jury is permitted to consider any aggravating or mitigating circumstances, it must find and identify at least one statutory aggravating factor before it may impose a penalty of death. In this way, the jury's discretion is channeled. No longer can a jury wantonly and freakishly impose the death sentence; it is always circumscribed by the legislative guidelines." For these reasons, the Court concluded that the Georgia statute was constitutional as written and applied; therefore, Gregg's conviction and sentencing were upheld.[33]

In a separate concurrence, Justice Byron White, joined by Chief Justice Burger and Justice Rehnquist, agreed that the statute under consideration in the case could be carried out in a constitutionally permissible way. A statute that gives the jury discretion to decide the facts of the case but also allows the courts to determine whether the penalty was administered in a discriminatory, arbitrary, or rare fashion conforms to the dictates of the Eighth Amendment. In *Gregg*, the Georgia statute met the requirements set forth by the Supreme Court in *Furman v. Georgia*; consequently, the statute must be allowed to stand.

In White's view, "Petitioner has argued, in effect, that no matter how effective the death penalty may be as a punishment, government, created and run as it must be by humans, is inevitably incompetent to administer it. This cannot be accepted as a proposition of constitutional law." To argue that the death penalty is unconstitutional per se because human beings cannot root out all biases and inconsistencies in their decisions is to undermine the criminal justice system.

White did not deny that problems can, and probably do, occur, but the legal system, on the whole, can accommodate the needs of the states with the needs of citizens. "Mistakes will be made and discriminations will occur which will be difficult to explain," he wrote.

> However, one of society's most basic tasks is that of protecting the lives of its citizens and one of the basic ways in which it achieves this task is through criminal laws against murder. I decline to interfere with the manner in which Georgia has chosen to enforce such laws on what is simply an assertion of lack of faith in the ability of the system of justice to operate in a fundamentally fair manner.[34]

Chief Justice Burger and Justice Rehnquist filed a separate concurrence agreeing that "Georgia's system of capital punishment comports with the Court's holding in *Furman v. Georgia*." In another concurrence, Justice Blackmun also agreed with Justice White's decision.[35]

In a dissenting opinion, Justice William Brennan argued that several members of the Court misapplied "evolving standards of decency" in their determination. Instead of interpreting these standards by focusing on the procedures for applying the death penalty, Brennan suggested that the considerations should be reversed. "I read 'evolving standards of decency' as requiring focus upon the essence of the death penalty itself and not primarily or solely upon the procedures under which the determination to inflict the penalty upon a particular person was made."[36] When this is done, in Brennan's opinion, it becomes clear that the death penalty serves no legitimate purpose because the goals it seeks to achieve can be accomplished by less severe means. Reiterating his view from the *Furman* case, Brennan concluded by contending that society has evolved to the point where it need not rely on such a barbaric practice as state-sanctioned executions.[37]

Justice Thurgood Marshall filed the final opinion in *Gregg v. Georgia*. Despite the changes made by a majority of states to revise their statutes in the wake of the *Furman* case, he remained convinced that the death penalty violated the Eighth Amendment's prohibition against cruel and unusual punishment. It does not deter capital crimes, nor does it serve as a constitutionally permissible means of retribution that prevents citizens from extracting vigilante justice. In Marshall's view, these arguments are ridiculous. "It simply defies belief to suggest that the death penalty is necessary to prevent the American people from taking the law into their own hands." The arguments propagated by capital punishment proponents are not persuasive because they are excessive and fail to promote the legitimate goals of the criminal justice system. "They are essentially utilitarian in that they portray the death penalty as valuable because of its beneficial results," he observed. "These justifications for the death penalty are inadequate because the penalty is, quite clearly I think, not necessary to the accomplishment of those results."[38]

III. Capital Punishment after *Gregg v. Georgia*

The *Gregg* case was decided at the same time as four other cases: *Jurek v. Texas*,[39] *Proffitt v. Florida*,[40] *Woodson v. North Carolina*,[41] and *Roberts v. Louisiana*.[42] In the first two cases, the Court upheld the state statutes in question, while it struck down the statutes in *Woodson* and *Roberts*. In each case, the Court did not provide good general guidelines to the states; instead, it determined whether the statutes in question complied with the *Furman* instructions that the legislature must channel the death penalty in such a way as to ensure, to the extent possible, minimal bias and discrimination. These cases served notice to states that the federal courts would henceforth be active participants in reviewing the application of death penalty procedural safeguards contained in state statutes.

These cases also introduced the two schools of thought on the death penalty. The abolitionist school, represented by Brennan and Marshall, held that "death is different." Capital punishment is barbaric and should never be used by a society that professes to be enlightened, merciful, and just. Moreover, the possibility of the state mistakenly executing the wrong person is too great to allow death to be imposed, no matter how many safeguards are in place. The proponents' school of thought contended that capital punishment can be imposed on duly convicted capital offenders, provided that the procedures followed in reaching the decision and the means used to execute them are equitable.

A. DEATH PENALTY LEGISLATION SINCE THE 1970s

After *Gregg*, the focus of death penalty cases shifted from questions of whether it was a constitutional punishment to questions of how offenders were arrested, tried, and sentenced. States responded to the judicial "guidelines" contained in *Furman* and *Gregg*; thereafter, the courts closely scrutinized state legislation to determine whether it followed the guidelines. In many ways, however, legislative attempts to apply the death penalty have been as muddled as judicial attempts.

In *Furman* and *Gregg*, the Supreme Court left room for a variety of statutory schemes. Generally, the death penalty is reserved for crimes involving the loss of human life,[43] although some states impose the penalty for espionage, treason, or trafficking in large quantities of drugs. Whatever crimes are covered by a particular state's death penalty statute, the legislature must specify clearly the minimum requirements for death penalty eligibility.

Under the Model Penal Code, murder is broadly defined, but the "aggravating circumstances" necessary to narrow the class of offenders to an eligible class is far more specific.[44] For example, the Georgia criminal statute upheld by the Supreme Court in *Gregg v. Georgia* follows this rule closely. Under the Official Code of Georgia, Annotated (OCGA) §11-5-1 (1996), *murder* is defined as unlawfully causing the death of a human being "with malice aforethought, either express or implied." In an initial trial, the jury determines whether the defendant has committed the crime. If the defendant is convicted, he is given a separate hearing to determine whether he was involved in one or more of the ten aggravating circumstances listed in OCGA §17-10-30(b) (1996). In other states, aggravating circumstances are included as elements of capital murder; therefore, statutes in these states do not provide for a bifurcated trial to decide the penalty apart from the defendant's guilt. Instead, during the trial, the aggravating circumstances are weighed against mitigating circumstances to determine whether the defendant should be sentenced to death.[45]

State statutes sometimes differ on what they mean by "aggravating circumstances." In some states, the focus is on the characteristics of the defendant. Common questions include the defendant's past criminal record, his psychological condition, or the likelihood that he will continue to endanger others if he is allowed to live. In other states, the focus is on the circumstances of the crime. This analysis turns on the manner in which the defendant perpetrated the crime: Was he engaged in a felony at the time? Did he act in an especially cruel or vicious way? Did he perform more than one crime at the time, say, kidnapping coupled with aggravated assault and battery, rape, murder, and so forth?

Just as state statutes prescribe the necessary conditions for imposing the death penalty, they also provide certain exclusions. In several controversial opinions, the U.S. Supreme Court has allowed capital punishment to be imposed on defendants who were convicted of murder as young as age sixteen or defendants who are mentally retarded,[46] but states often develop their own standards. Thus, as of 1996, fourteen states and the federal government had enacted legislation prohibiting the imposition of the death penalty on defendants under the age of eighteen.[47] Two other states set the minimum age at seventeen. Eleven states and federal law provide an exemption for mentally retarded defendants.[48]

State sentencing statutes are considerably more complex in the wake of *Furman* and *Gregg* than they were in the 1960s and earlier. In an attempt to ensure that the proper standards are applied, statutes often contain verbose and confusing standards that require elaborate, often convoluted, jury charges prior to sentencing. Although judges retain their historically important role in guiding the conduct of the proceedings, in twenty-nine states and under federal law, the jury makes the final sentencing determination in capital cases. Critics argue, therefore, that leaving decisions that literally involve life and death in the hands of a jury is unconscionable because the possibilities for bias, discrimination, or simple mistakes are too great. Despite criticism that jurors cannot understand the complexities of death penalty law, however, the courts have upheld these statutory arrangements.[49]

The paramount problem with state sentencing statutes lies in providing jurors with intelligible guidelines to assist them in rendering a verdict and imposing a sentence appropriate to the circumstances of the case, however they are defined in the statute. Accordingly, some states require that juries be presented with reasonable alternatives at the same time that they are instructed on capital punishment. Other states provide guidelines to ensure, to the extent possible, that bias and discrimination are eliminated, or at least minimized. Still others incorporate a balancing scheme whereby jurors are allowed to weigh aggravating circumstances against mitigating factors in reaching a decision. Finally, some states provide for "threshold schemes" that require proof of at least one aggravating circumstance before the jury can impose a death sentence.[50]

B. DEATH PENALTY JURISPRUDENCE SINCE THE 1970s

According to two commentators, Carol S. Steiker and Jordan M. Steiker, judicial developments in capital punishment law since states revised their statutes in the aftermath of *Furman* and *Gregg* have focused on four distinct themes: desert, fairness, individualization, and heightened procedural reliability. *Desert* is the idea that capital punishment should not be imposed on defendants for crimes that by their nature fail to be capital offenses. As many of the other chapters in this book demonstrate, proportionality has been a concern for policymakers since the death penalty was first imposed. Some statutes originally proposed the death penalty for crimes that fell short of homicide; thus, these statutes were suspect because they seemed to require overly harsh punishments for some categories of crimes. The Court's concern for providing statutory standards for judges and juries in capital cases reflects this concern that the punishment should fit the crime.

Fairness, or treating like cases alike, is a similar consideration. Instead of the problem of overinclusion that occurs in discussions of desert, fairness is the question of underinclusion. Is it fair, one might ask, that a certain class or race of defendants is sentenced to death more often than other classes or races? When Justice Douglas wrote in his *Furman* concurrence that an equal protection theme is implicit in the Eighth Amendment, he was expressing exactly this concern.[51] Although not every commentator might agree that fairness should be a core issue in judicial review of state death penalty statutes, many courts have scrutinized statutory schemes with an eye toward ensuring a threshold level of fundamental fairness.[52]

State statutes also must be directed toward individualization of punishment. Legislative standards that automatically impose mandatory capital punishment for certain crimes do not allow judges and juries to consider individual mitigating circumstances. Ironically, in the wake of the *Furman* case, many states decided to take to heart the Supreme Court's admonition against arbitrary and capricious death penalty statutes and overly discretionary legislative guidelines by going too far in the opposite direction. They simply prescribed mandatory capital punishment for some crimes. This solution seemed to take care of the problem of too much discretion in the hands of the jury, but it raised another problem. In striking down mandatory capital punishment statutes in Louisiana and North Carolina, for example, the Supreme Court explained that these statutes placed the states' criminal justice system on a formulaic basis—a kind of automatic pilot and did not consider individual circumstances in a case-by-case framework. In effect, "every offense in a like legal category calls for identical punishment without regard to the past life and habits of a particular offender."[53] Just as too few standards are constitutionally impermissible, too many rigid, impersonalized standards are impermissible as well.

As Justice Brennan wrote in his *Furman* concurrence, the death penalty is not merely another punishment marked by a difference in degree; it is different in kind from other punishments. For that reason, it must be approached with a heightened degree of procedural reliability. If an offender in a noncapital case is inadvertently sentenced to a lengthy prison term, that mistake, as regrettable as it is, can be rectified if it is discovered before the offender's term ends. Even if he is imprisoned for many years, he can be compensated or made reasonably whole by other measures, even if they serve as poor substitutes for lost liberty. An offender who is executed and later exonerated cannot be made whole. The decision is irreversible. For that reason, courts historically have insisted that procedures were in place to ensure that the sentence was imposed fairly, accurately, and with a fundamental respect for human dignity. Although mistakes may be made, the interests of justice require that every reasonable safeguard be put into place to ensure that the mistakes will be minimized.[54]

Despite difficulties in ensuring that the death penalty is equitably imposed, it remains popular among the American public. As a result, abolitionists generally have been unsuccessful in their efforts to remove capital punishment as an option in most American states. They generally have recognized this reality and have pursued court cases to equalize the application of capital punishment. Technical issues such as race, the intellectual abilities of the defendant, the type and method of execution imposed, and similar issues have dominated capital punishment jurisprudence since the 1970s.

One important case that came before the Court at the end of the 1990s is a good example of this new focus on the constitutionality of death penalty methods. The case arose as a challenge to the use of the Florida electric chair. The case, *Bryan v. Moore*, came to the U.S. Supreme Court from the Eleventh Circuit Court of Appeals.[55] The petitioner, Anthony Bryan, brought the case in 1999 after being convicted of killing a man who had let him borrow tools to work on a boat. Bryan waited on death row in Florida for thirteen years before the Supreme Court agreed to hear his appeal.

In July 1999, as Bryan was facing an October 27 execution date, a fellow death row inmate, Allen Lee Davis, was executed in "Ol' Sparky," Florida's electric chair. The chair had been replaced in 1998, but its wiring and circuitry dated back to 1923, the year that Florida began executing capital offenders by electrocution. Ol' Sparky malfunctioned in an especially grisly fashion on several occasions. In 1990, flames leapt from the headpiece worn by an offender named Jesse Tafero. Seven years later, the same thing happened when Pedro Medina was executed. In both cases, smoke and the pungent smell of burning flesh filled the execution chamber. After Medina's death, Florida attorney general Robert Butterworth seemed unperturbed, commenting that the gruesome execution was not a negative occurrence; in fact, it would deter would-be offenders.

When Allen Lee Davis was executed in July 1999, he suffered a nosebleed during his execution. Although the cause was unclear, it could have resulted from having the leather strap buckled too tightly over the lower part of his face, or it may have been caused because the strap, which prevented the blood from flowing freely, asphyxiated him. In any event, the postmortem photographs taken of Davis's body were especially grotesque. Florida Supreme Court Justice Leander Shaw posted the photographs of Davis's body on his website as part of his dissent in another case challenging Florida's use of the electric chair, *Provenzano v. Moore*. In that case, the Florida Supreme Court upheld the constitutionality of using electrocution as a method of execution.

In his petition to the Florida Supreme Court, Bryan argued that Florida officials seemed unconcerned with Ol' Sparky's numerous malfunctions, especially after Davis's grotesque death. "Inmates do not routinely catch fire, bleed, continue to breathe, scream, moan, try to speak or otherwise attempt to react to execution-related pain in other states employing judicial electrocution," Bryan's attorney wrote in his petition for *certiorari*. "Although these things need not occur in Florida, officials of the state of Florida are deliberately indifferent to their occurrence."

The day before Bryan's scheduled execution, the U.S. Supreme Court granted him a stay to review his case. The Court eventually granted *certiorari* to consider whether electrocution in Florida's electric chair constitutes cruel and unusual punishment under the Eighth Amendment. The Supreme Court last considered the constitutionality of electrocution in 1890, when it held that New York's electric chair could be used in lieu of hanging.[56] As of 2000, thirty-four of thirty-eight states with death penalty statutes had elected to rely on lethal injection instead of the electric chair. In 1998, Florida enacted a statute that authorized the use of lethal injection as an alternative to the electric chair. Along with Alabama, Georgia, and Nebraska, Florida was the only state that still authorized electrocution for capital offenders in the last year of the old millennium.

Although the Supreme Court initially agreed to hear Bryan's petition, it dismissed his case on January 24, 2000, after the Florida attorney general indicated that the execution would be carried out using lethal injection instead of electrocution unless Bryan chose to die by electrocution. On that basis, the Supreme Court decided that granting *certiorari* to hear the petition was "improvidently granted," and it chose to wait until another challenge reached the Court to make a determination of the constitutionality of the electric chair.[57]

IV. Conclusion: Arguments in Favor of the Death Penalty

Given the evolving history of death penalty jurisprudence that has occurred in the United States, especially after *Furman* and *Gregg*, many commentators have argued that the punishment should be outlawed under all circumstances. This solution certainly would clear up the confusion and myriad court decisions that make up the body of law on the death penalty in the United States at the dawn of the twenty-first century. As other chapters in this book have argued, one might argue that the death penalty suffers from numerous defects that make it a suspect punishment in a society that professes to respect individual dignity and human worth. Yet this conclusion that human dignity necessitates rejecting capital punishment begs the underlying question. What is it about capital punishment that is so objectionable? One might ask why the courts continually uphold the constitutionality of this punishment and why the death penalty remains popular among average citizens if it demonstrates a lack of respect for human dignity.

For their part, federal courts often have expressed their reluctance to interfere into the legislative affairs of the states unless the circumstances are so egregious that no other action is warranted by the U.S. Constitution. Historically, criminal law has been within the purview of the states. Each time that a court strikes down a state statute as impermissible, it deals a blow to federalism—perhaps small and barely imperceptible, but a blow, nonetheless. The willingness of the federal courts to consider death penalty appeals and closely scrutinize states in this area has increased the power of the federal system to regulate state matters. Moreover, in a nation built on democratic principles, a danger always exists when a group of unelected officials—in this case, federal judges—decides questions that affect the polity on the basis of principles that countermand a democratic majority. Even commentators who argue that the federal court system was specifically designed to ensure that judges would not be directly affected by democratic majorities—hence possibly be subject to the tyranny of the majority—recognize that the judiciary wields enormous power. Absent a clearly articulable reason for striking down state statutes, restraintist judges argue that the judiciary should exercise power with maximal caution and minimal legislative intrusion.

The continuing citizen support for the death penalty is a more complicated issue. Clearly, the perception that violent crime has increased in recent years leads the populace toward public policy that "gets tough on crime." The first step in tough anticrime programs requires society to identify criminals and assign blame accordingly. In the words of one well-known proponent of capital punishment, Ernest van den Haag, "Capital punishment, a deliberate expulsion from human society, is meant to add deserved moral ignominy to death. This irks some abolitionists, who feel that nobody should be blamed for whatever he does. But murder deserves blame."[58] According to this perspective, the imposition of capital punishment is designed to assign legal responsibility to offenders who have committed the ultimate act of destruction against the mores of civil society.

Most serious crimes are perpetrated by a relatively small number of predatory offenders who could be controlled—or their activities severely curtailed—by punishing them in accordance with harsh penalties that fall short of capital punishment. In cases in which these offenders engage in capital crimes, they should receive the death penalty when they meet the relevant statutory requirements. This strategy requires a two-tiered approach. First, the criminal justice system must focus on reducing crime among repeat offenders. Next, it must apply the death penalty in cases where it is warranted by outrageous circumstances.

In an article that originally appeared in the July/August 1997 issue of *Policy Review* and was widely reprinted by the politically conservative Heritage Foundation, commentator Eugene H. Methvin set forth an argument for controlling crime in the United States.[59] According to Methvin, the most effective way to reduce the number of offenses is to identify families that are likely to be "cradles of crime." By providing enhanced educational opportunities, parenting advice to at-risk families, and training in what he calls "disciplined behavior," society can work on reducing criminal behavior in youngsters before it occurs. In the early phases of grammar school, at-risk children can be screened and given opportunities to participate in educational programs that may move them away from gangs and other external stimuli that cause crime. Without focusing on factors that contribute to social ills in the first place, any program that seeks to reduce the crime rate will enjoy only limited effectiveness.

Despite efforts to control crime before it occurs, undoubtedly some at-risk members of the population will break the law. When a youngster first comes into contact with police, Methvin argues that permanent records should be kept. Efforts to expunge juvenile records or provide lenient treatment at a first encounter will only encourage offenders to view the justice system as weak and ineffective. If the punishment is harsh—but equitably applied—some offenders will get the message that criminal behavior will not be tolerated. In many cases, offenders will not participate in a second offense.

In some cases, however, the offender will commit another crime. At the second contact with police, the young recidivist defendant becomes a candidate for intensive supervision and family intervention. To be effective, Methvin argues, the intervention must be intensive and ongoing. The casual visits by an overworked, underpaid social worker that occurs now for at-risk families is insufficient. He recognizes that such intensive supervision of youthful offenders and their families will require a significant allocation of resources, but Methvin argues that such a program will be well worth the investment if it can prevent even a few two-time offenders from engaging in a continuing pattern of criminal activity that may have far more serious consequences in the future.

In Methvin's view, the line of demarcation is the third offense. At this point, an offender has demonstrated a clear, unequivocal pattern of criminal behavior that is unlikely to be broken or controlled except through harsh measures. "Jailing serious three-time offenders would be a prudent alternative to suffering the millions of crimes habitual criminals perpetrate each year," he argues.[60] Underlying this approach is Methvin's contention that "[t]he rehabilitation ideal of the juvenile-court system leads to costly coddling of serious and persistent offenders."[61] Only when repeat offenders realize that they will face increasingly serious consequences for their behaviors can the possibility exist for reducing the crime rate among habitual criminals.

For that small number of offenders who cannot be controlled no matter how harsh the penalty, society must have the ultimate penalty at its disposal. Even if an offender is not engaging in a rational calculation of costs and benefits when he engages in a particular capital crime, society must establish a justice system that makes it generally clear that capital punishment is a distinct possibility. In van den Haag's view, this is essential to ensure that society does not fall prey to vicious predators who will always present a problem to the civilized world. "We protect ourselves from ferocious beasts," he notes, "but we do not punish them, because, unlike criminals, they cannot tell right from wrong or restrain themselves accordingly. Animals therefore are not, but criminals are responsible for their actions because they are human. Their punishment acknowledges rather than denies their responsibility and, thereby, their humanity."[62]

Arguments in favor of the death penalty are necessarily grounded in a clear conception of individual responsibility. When society makes excuses for an offender's behavior—he was raised in a broken home; he was pushed into joining a gang at a young age; he never had adequate educational opportunities, and so forth—it undermines the notion of an individual's culpability for his behavior. If Methvin's recommendations for reforming the criminal justice system are adopted, arguments that place responsibility on society in lieu of the individual lose whatever marginal moral force they might have. When society makes a concerted effort to assist those at-risk individuals who nonetheless turn to crime, the blame must be assigned where it belongs—on the shoulders of the individual who engaged in the prohibited behavior.

It is difficult to know whether capital punishment deters some criminals from engaging in capital crimes because the data are inconclusive. Depending on how one conducts the studies, the results suggest that deterrence may be a consideration, but it is unclear how many crimes have *not* occurred owing to the possibility that an offender might receive the death penalty. A decline in the capital crimes may be attributable to many interrelated (or unrelated) factors, none of which is more important than the other. Consequently, empirical studies of capital punishment quickly degenerate into a fruitless battle of the experts.[63]

Some abolitionists argue that the death penalty is morally unjustifiable because it reduces society to the level of the criminal. This is a kind of perversion of the Golden Rule. Society should not do unto the criminal as he does unto society because it reduces the moral worth of society to the level of the criminal. The counterargument is that unlike the criminal, society operates according to the dictates of social, political, and legal rules that are designed to safeguard the rights of offenders through substantive and procedural protections. In van den Haag's view, "The difference between a crime and a punishment is social, not physical. There is no need for physical dissimilarity. A crime is an unlawful act, legal punishment is a lawful act."[64]

Finally, the concern that innocent people, wrongly accused and convicted, will be executed is largely overwrought. While it is true that no system of punishment administered by human beings over human beings can be entirely foolproof, the American judicial system minimizes abuses to a great extent. The difficult burden of proof (beyond a reasonable doubt) and the requirement of unanimity in jury verdicts create a tremendous hurdle for prosecutors to overcome before a defendant can be convicted. Procedural safeguards as well as habeas corpus petitions further protect a duly convicted offender from being sentenced to death without overwhelming proof that he perpetrated the crime.[65]

The challenge for the future is to ensure that the death penalty is applied equitably. According to the NAACP Legal Defense Education Fund's publication *Death Row*, approximately 40 percent of the defendants on death row in 1994 were African American, even though African Americans comprise only about 12 percent of the U.S. population. Despite the U.S. Supreme Court's contrary opinion in *McCleskey v. Kemp*,[66] other studies suggest that African Americans are much more likely than members of other races to receive the death penalty for capital crimes.[67] Some evidence exists suggesting that the poor and the mentally infirm also are unfairly sentenced to death in some instances.[68]

Despite these challenges—as important as they are—the death penalty retains its viability as a form of punishment because, to put it crudely, it works. No other punishment ensures that society will be protected to the same extent as an execution. In van den Haag's words, "Abolition of the death penalty would promise prospective murderers that we will never do to them what they do to their victims. Such a promise seems unwise as well as immoral."[69]

CHAPTER 16

Flaws in Capital Sentencing
SKEWING THE REASONED MORAL RESPONSE

Chris Hutton

Horrifying events give rise to this country's death penalty jurisprudence. It is a daunting task to comprehend the murders of our daughters, brothers, parents, and friends.[1] The impulse is to respond immediately, in kind. Yet, the picture changes substantially when we consider the nightmare of those wrongfully accused and wrongfully convicted.[2] Reserving judgment, exercising caution and refusing to act on impulse become paramount as the legal system is called upon to assist society in reacting to brutal murders. As Justice O'Connor has reminded us, society must have a "reasoned moral response" to the crime and offender.[3] Legislatures, courts, and attorneys have accepted the challenge and assured the public that justice can be done in these cases—that capital punishment is appropriate and can be imposed on guilty offenders in a reasoned way with minimal risk of error.[4] The debate over the appropriateness of capital punishment continues.[5] Although institutions such as the Catholic Church have become vocal opponents of capital punishment in recent years,[6] the trend away from capital punishment is far from universal.[7] Philosophers and religious leaders will debate whether it is morally acceptable in this era.[8] How the legal system responds to capital cases, however, is a crucial question in light of the system is the seeming assurance that it can handle them fairly and accurately. This chapter addresses some of the areas of concern, first by sketching the legal background of capital punishment, and second by pinpointing weaknesses in the existing death penalty system.

I. A Survey of Capital Punishment in the United States Supreme Court[9]

In 1971, the United States Supreme Court reviewed the imposition of the death penalty in *McGautha v. California*.[10] In his memorable rejoinder to the defendants' plea to the Court to curb the discretion of juries dealing with capital punishment, Justice Harlan responded for the majority that it was virtually impossible to do so. He explained:

> Those who have come to grips with the hard task of actually attempting to draft means of channeling capital sentencing discretion have confirmed the lesson taught by the history recounted above. To identify before the fact those characteristics of criminal homicides and their perpetrators which call for the death penalty, and to express these characteristics in language which can be fairly understood and applied by the sentencing authority, appear to be tasks which are beyond present human ability.[11]

Yet a year later, in *Furman v. Georgia*,[12] the Court overturned the death penalty as it existed in thirty-nine states and the District of Columbia.[13] The Court adopted a range of theories to justify its action; however, one recurring theme in the separate opinions of the justices[14] was the need to circumscribe the discretion of jurors. Otherwise, arbitrary imposition of the death penalty was the predictable result.

While *Furman* appeared to signal the end of the death penalty in the United States,[15] the states proved themselves resourceful in responding to the concerns expressed by the *Furman* Court. Several states enacted new death penalties, and in 1976 the Court held in *Gregg v. Georgia,*[16] *Jurek v. Texas,*[17] and *Proffitt v. Florida*[18] that the statutory schemes adopted by the respective state legislatures were not facially unconstitutional. At the same time, in *Woodson v. North Carolina*[19] and *Roberts v. Louisiana,*[20] the Court invalidated mandatory death penalties, which had been enacted to overcome the problem of arbitrariness. Professor Robert Weisberg has characterized the Court's attitude toward capital punishment in this era as "romantic."[21] "Under the romantic account, the crucial plurality in the 1976 decisions viewed *McGautha* as a challenge to the powers of due process doctrine making, and *Furman* as a moral injunction to try to meet that challenge. Harlan had warned that no rule of law could identify those criminals who deserved to die. In the romantic view, the Court's motto might be, 'Harlan said it couldn't be done, but good old American know-how will prove him wrong."[22]

Thus, in *Gregg, Proffitt,* and *Jurek,* the Court held that the statutory schemes at issue sufficiently narrowed the class of persons upon whom a sentence of death could be imposed and, at least superficially, appeared to eliminate the arbitrariness that troubled the *Furman* Court. They did so in different ways. Georgia narrowed the class by providing that a person convicted of murder could receive a death sentence only if one of the ten enumerated aggravating circumstances were found.[23] Florida adopted a similar approach, but asked the jury to make only a nonbinding recommendation, with the trial judge determining the sentence.[24] Texas, on the other hand, categorized certain murders as "capital" because of their aggravating circumstances. If found guilty of capital murder, a defendant would be considered for a death sentence.[25] The jury was told to answer three questions about the crime and the defendant;[26] if the answers to all three were affirmative, automatically the defendant was sentenced to death. Using Professor Weisberg's formulation, one could say that the Court had decreed that the death penalty could be imposed with properly developed rules and that these states had succeeded in formulating such rules.

Two years later, however, a significant defect was found in death penalty schemes similar to those upheld in *Gregg* and its companion cases. In *Lockett v. Ohio*,[27] and later, in *Eddings v. Oklahoma*,[28] 5–4 majorities of the Court held that the death penalties imposed on the defendants were invalid. The deficiency in the sentencing statutes was the failure to permit the defendants to present evidence of mitigating circumstances in a way that enabled their juries to give the evidence meaningful consideration and to impose an appropriate sentence. Thus, the Court held that states needed not just to curb arbitrariness in selecting candidates for the death penalty, but also had to allow juries flexibility in choosing *not* to allow the execution of defendants who might facially fall within that narrowed class.

For almost thirty years, these two strands—narrowing the class and individualizing the decision to impose a death sentence—have permeated the Court's death penalty cases, with one or the other capturing a majority of the Court at varying times. From the first strand—eliminating arbitrariness by narrowing the class of those on whom capital punishment could be imposed—emerged restrictions on the states' power to execute. Along that line, several rules dealt with the categories of people on whom the death penalty could not be imposed. For example, the Court prohibited the execution of the insane[29] and of children under the age of sixteen at the time of the offense.[30] The Court overturned the death sentence of an individual whose offense was rape of an adult woman, stating the penalty was excessive in the absence of a killing.[31] The Court also placed restrictions on the circumstances in which the death penalty could be given even if there had been a murder. The justices decreed that an individual must have killed, attempted to kill, or intended that a killing take place.[32] The Court subsequently amended the standard, declaring that an individual who acted in reckless disregard of whether a killing occurred could receive a death sentence.[33]

The Court also curbed some of the states' efforts to maximize the number of offenses for which capital punishment was available. Although the *Gregg* Court had upheld the constitutionality of the Georgia capital sentencing scheme, the Justices subsequently revisited the statute's authorization of death for a murder that was "especially heinous, atrocious, and cruel."[34] The Court ruled that death could not be imposed under such a standard unless the terms were defined by statute or by an appellate court,[35] and the jury was instructed accordingly.

Procedural restrictions also appeared. For example, the Court held an individual given a life sentence instead of the death penalty couldn't be sentenced to death in a retrial under double jeopardy principles.[36] A defendant must be given notice that a death sentence is possible,[37] and the jury may not be misinformed about the role it plays in the sentencing process.[38] The defendant is entitled to view a presentence report relied on by the judge in imposing a death sentence.[39]

In recent years the Court has placed a slightly different impediment in the path of states desiring to impose capital punishment. The Court has examined the facts of several cases to determine whether the state process has resulted in a possibly innocent person being sentenced to death. Whether couched as substantive,[40] procedural,[41] or both,[42] the error at issue has prompted the Court to intervene and force the states to take another look. How much "error correction" the Supreme Court will pursue remains an open question.[43]

Despite this lengthy list of requirements, however, a great deal of flexibility has been made available to the states. The issues of racism, jury selection, and aggravating circumstances are indicative. Thus, in what may be its most important decision in this regard, the Court ruled in *McCleskey v. Kemp* that although race may be a factor in choosing to impose a death sentence, the potential role of race in sentencing is not sufficient to invalidate death penalty schemes per se.[44] The Court acknowledged that race can influence the sentencer's decision but required the defendant to show purposeful discrimination in his own case. The Court deemed statistical evidence inadequate to establish a "constitutionally significant risk of racial bias" affecting the sentencing process.[45] The difficulty of meeting the purposeful discrimination as standard means that a death sentence animated by racial bias ordinarily will be upheld.[46] But, not only has the Court maximized states' flexibility by allowing race to remain a factor in capital sentencing; it also has permitted prosecutors to select juries inclined to impose a death sentence. It did so by affirming that people who oppose the death penalty may be excluded for cause in a capital case,[47] even if that makes the jury more conviction prone.[48] Having thus treated the problems of racism and jury selection, the Court bolstered the states' death penalty enterprises in another way. It rejected a vagueness challenge to capital sentencing statutes that merely point the jury in a certain direction without dictating how to weigh aggravating and mitigating factors and that encompass as many as twenty "special circumstances" coupled with eleven "aggravating factors" that make the defendant a candidate for a death sentence.[49]

The Court also has approved a variety of procedures states use to impose capital punishment. For example, "double counting" of aggravating circumstances is permissible; therefore, one circumstance may be both an element of the offense and a factor for a death sentence.[50] Also, proof relevant to one aggravator may be considered for others as well.[51] Victim-impact evidence, which had been prohibited in capital cases,[52] now is permitted.[53] Juries may be told that a sentence to "life without parole" might not mean the person would be imprisoned for his or her entire life, if state law provides the opportunity for sentence reduction.[54] A sentencing judge may employ both statutory and nonstatutory aggravating circumstances, if state law permits.[55] Absent a statutory requirement, a judge may reject a jury's decision to impose a life sentence and may impose death without having given "great weight" to the jury's decision.[56] A state may even mandate the imposition of the death penalty if aggravating circumstances are proven and no mitigating circumstances exist[57] without running afoul of *Woodson's* prohibition of mandatory death sentences.[58] Finally, states are not constitutionally required to provide counsel for a habeas proceeding in a capital case,[59] although Congress recently has provided for the possibility of appointment of counsel for federal proceedings.[60]

The Court's effort to enhance the role of state courts in the death penalty scheme is most evident in its decisions concerning state appeals and the reach of federal habeas. The appellate court can be given an extremely powerful role: If the jury has imposed a death sentence based on more than one aggravating circumstance, an appellate court may invalidate an aggravating factor, reweigh the evidence, and uphold the death sentence based on the remaining aggravators.[61] The appellate court also may determine that errors made during the sentencing phase before a jury were harmless.[62] Consistent with its decisions restricting the scope of federal habeas in the noncapital setting, the Supreme Court has imposed stringent limitations on the prisoner who seeks relief from a capital sentence.[63] And, those limitations have been reinforced by statute.[64]

While the rules endeavoring to impose rationality were being developed, the competing strand of cases emerged—those compelling the states to treat the defendant as an individual. Thus, under *Lockett* and *Eddings*, the Court invalidated a variety of legislative and judicial actions that failed to give the jury the opportunity to refuse to impose a death sentence.[65] The Court ruled that a capital defendant is entitled to present mitigating evidence of his or her choice,[66] whether such evidence is statutory or nonstatutory.[67] The jury cannot be required to find proof of mitigation unanimously.[68] It must be instructed properly about future dangerousness if that is an issue.[69] Mandatory sentences are infirm because they preclude consideration of the defendant's mitigating evidence, which is designed to provide for individualization.[70] The sentencing statute may not be applied so narrowly that the jury is forced to impose a death sentence,[71] when the defendant's circumstances likely would have led it to the opposite result.

While these decisions provided capital defendants a number of important rights, they did not entirely prevent states from restricting the use and effect of mitigation. For example, the Court upheld a state statute requiring that the defendant prove mitigation by a preponderance of the evidence.[72] It permitted an instruction directing the jury not to be "swayed by mere sentiment, conjecture, sympathy, passion, prejudice, public opinion or public feeling" over the defendant's objection that he *did* want the jury to sympathize with him and decline to impose a death sentence.[73] Similarly, the Court upheld an instruction that the jury consider any evidence that "extenuates the gravity of the crime" as a sufficient indication that the jury consider the mitigating evidence presented.[74] The Court also determined that sufficient definition had occurred under *Godfrey v. Georgia* when the standard for conduct punishable by death, "exhibiting utter disregard for human life," was defined merely to mean the conduct was in "the highest, the utmost, callous disregard for human life, i.e., the cold-blooded, pitiless slayer."[75]

As is evident, both the substantive and procedural restraints imposed by the Court purported to control the potentially irrational behavior of the sentencer. But two major flaws quickly become apparent. First, close scrutiny reveals the controls are minimal. The Court has not implemented a strict regime of rules. Rather, the portrait that has emerged in the decades after *Furman* is one of a few guidelines and considerable flexibility for the states in devising a scheme for capital punishment. Second, that there might be difficulty in implementing both the guided discretion and individualization strands of authority escaped neither Court members nor commentators. Indeed, the *Lockett* dissenters[76] predicted the conflict. Noteworthy is Justice Scalia's denunciation of the *Lockett* line of authority as a reinsertion of arbitrariness into the capital sentencing process.[77] His objection is that one never knows what factor in a defendant's life will persuade the jury arbitrarily to refrain from imposing the death penalty.[78] He has said that this defeats the purpose of *Furman* so he will no longer abide by those precedents. His provocative conclusion is examined more fully in the next section.

II. Faultlines in Capital Punishment

A. RULES VERSUS INDIVIDUALIZATION: ARBITRARINESS CREEPS BACK INTO THE SYSTEM

As noted above,[79] once *Furman* decreed that arbitrary imposition of the death penalty violates the Constitution, the states endeavored to rationalize their capital punishment schemes. Primarily they did so by identifying the aggravating factors of a murder that would mark a defendant as a potential recipient of a death sentence.[80] Some states also identified the mitigating circumstances that would preclude imposition of the death penalty.[81] Yet, as it rapidly appeared, not every perpetrator of a murder classified as aggravated, whose mitigation did not fit into the statutory list, was a person who necessarily should receive a death sentence. While the legislative scheme might insist on it, the jury might think the penalty excessive. As a result, the Supreme Court declared that juries must be able to consider any mitigation and in turn spare a life where appropriate. That power to show mercy—albeit exercised without strictures and inconsistently— seems essential to capital punishment. Despite this, the resulting inconsistency has been the grist for extensive criticism of the Supreme Court's handling of capital punishment.

For example, in his characteristically caustic tone,[82] Justice Scalia has accused his fellow justices of inconsistency, and therefore incoherence, in developing the rules governing aggravation and mitigation. In his view, the death penalty decision is "a unitary one—the choice between death and imprisonment."[83] Therefore, to permit a defendant to argue, on the one hand, that the jury "had unconstitutionally *broad* discretion to sentence him to death instead of imprisonment," while on the other hand, to claim the jury "had unconstitutionally *narrow* discretion to sentence him to imprisonment instead of death" is nonsensical.[84] The proper course, according to the justice, is to abandon the requirement of *Woodson-Lockett* that the defendant be permitted to present mitigating evidence.

Justice Scalia has chosen this option in lieu of rejecting the guided discretion requirement of *Furman* and its progeny. His rationale is that the Eighth Amendment's prohibition against cruel and unusual punishment can be read to mean that a punishment would violate the Amendment only if its imposition were "freakish," as described by Justice Stewart in *Furman*.[85] He disapproves of "unfettered discretion" in the sentencer, and agrees it must be curbed. "I am therefore willing . . . to hold that when a State adopts capital punishment for a given crime but does not make it mandatory, the Eighth Amendment bars it from giving the sentencer unfettered discretion to select the recipients, but requires it to establish in advance, and convey to the sentencer, a governing standard."[86]

In contrast to his toleration of *Furman*, Justice Scalia has only ridicule for the *Woodson-Lockett* cases. Under his approach, the Eighth Amendment presents no obstacle to mandatory imposition of the death penalty, as *Woodson* prohibits.[87] Likewise, he has asserted that *Lockett's* prohibition against constraining the sentencer's discretion to decline to impose the death penalty "exploded" the concept of guided discretion[88] and "destroys whatever rationality and predictability the former requirement was designed to achieve."[89]

At first blush, Justice Scalia's denunciation is both startling and disturbing. To the extent society endorses capital punishment, must it not also demand that the sentencer consider individual deserts and have the option of dispensing mercy?[90] Justice Scalia would say no.[91] And, perhaps surprisingly, he is not alone in challenging the individualization facet of the Court's capital punishment jurisprudence. Shortly before his retirement from the bench, Justice Blackmun denounced the operation of capital punishment in this country. In a remarkable opinion, he declared that he no longer would vote to uphold any death sentence.[92] His reasons were varied. He thought *Furman* was correct in endeavoring to guarantee that the death penalty "be imposed fairly, and with reasonable consistency, or not at all."[93] Yet, like Justice Scalia, he was persuaded that, despite the attempt to "devise legal formulas and procedural rules to meet this daunting challenge,"[94] the undertaking had failed. In his view, "the death penalty remains fraught with arbitrariness, discrimination, caprice and mistake."[95] As Justice Blackmun demonstrated, the problems are intractable: "Experience has taught us that the constitutional goal of eliminating arbitrariness and discrimination from the administration of death [citation omitted] can never be achieved without compromising an equally essential component of fundamental fairness—individualized sentencing."[96] The justice feared that racial discrimination, which he felt was pervasive in capital sentencing, had not been and would not be abolished. And, he decried the restrictions on federal habeas that make it almost impossible for a federal court to intervene to overturn a death sentence.[97] From his perspective, capital punishment was an experiment the Court had approved in 1976 in *Gregg*. But the system had proved itself fatally flawed.

The justices' critiques raise a provocative question: Is the Court's individualization requirement irreconcilably inconsistent with the guided discretion imperative? Can they exist in harmony? Admittedly, reconciling them is difficult. To do so requires an acceptance of flexibility in juries, which necessarily yields unequal treatment of defendants. The Supreme Court has accepted this result, apparently being satisfied with making the best of a tough situation rather than achieving perfect justice and equality. Analytically, the Court accomplishes this goal by emphasizing that the imposition of a death sentence requires the sentencer to make two determinations: first, whether the defendant is "eligible" to receive it and, second, whether the jury ought to impose it.[98] As one scholar notes, dividing the inquiry into these two parts enables us to treat aggravating and mitigating circumstances differently because they are relevant to different issues.[99] Furthermore, the Eighth Amendment requires individualization since omitting individualization leads to mandatory death sentences. Such sentences contravene the Eighth Amendment because it is impossible for the states to define in advance the factors that properly authorize death in every circumstance,[100] and a serious problem of disproportionality results.[101]

Granting that the Eighth Amendment may require individualization, the dilemma is whether it can be harmonized with the guided discretion mandate. It is possible if the two are viewed as "complementary"[102] efforts to determine who is most deserving of a death sentence.[103] Conflict arises only if the discretion left in capital sentencing for individualization yields arbitrary and capricious results.[104] That emerges, for example, if the sentencer uses "random factors not rationally bearing on whether the defendant deserves death."[105] or if the standards are so flexible that sentencers do not consistently agree on which factors justify the death penalty.[106] Absent these concerns, jurors are asked to have their sentence "reflect a reasoned moral response"[107] which weaves together the rational and individual aspects of the decision.[108]

As one scholar has noted, the discretion mandated by *Lockett* is not the culprit in a system in which the death penalty is applied inconsistently.[109] Irrationality and inconsistency can creep into the system in many other ways: prosecutors choosing whether to seek the death penalty; legislators failing to define aggravating circumstances adequately; judges giving vague sentencing instructions;[110] appellate courts failing to give meaningful proportionality review;[111] sentencers discriminating on the basis of race; and defense counsel failing to perform adequately. Further, consistent treatment of unlike defendants is arbitrary.[112] Thus, the choice is between "competing risks"—whether an undeserving person receives a death sentence or a deserving person does not.[113] *Lockett's* emphasis on mitigation is necessary and appropriate. Any "tension" with *Furman* should be subsumed by their shared goal of determining who should be executed.[114]

Another way of capturing the rationality–individualization argument is to focus on Justice Scalia's view of the death penalty decision as a unitary one, in which either discretion exists or it does not.[115] As one critic has charged, in characterizing the issue as unitary—that is, choosing death or life—Justice Scalia conflates "the effect of a decision with the process leading to it."[116] The proper course is to recognize that "different parts of a process can be, and in some instances must be, structured in different ways."[117] The rationale for structuring the aggravation stage with rules, and leaving the mitigation facet unstructured, is compelling: "Suppose, however, that mitigation is not designed to achieve rationality and predictability; suppose instead it is designed to implement judgment. . . . Judgment cannot be captured in rules; if it could be, judgment would not be required."[118] Thus, the "vocabulary of rationality" makes sense[119] in employing a list of aggravating circumstances to determine whether a person should be excluded as a candidate for a death sentence because the penalty would be "inappropriate."[120] Mitigation, on the other hand, purports to draw distinctions among those who have been found to fit the criteria for a death sentence. These distinctions must be made on an individual basis because they "cannot be made by categorical rule. . . . [T]hey can only be made by judgment." To judge wisely the decision maker must be "free from rules and allowed to consider whatever is advanced."[121] This enables the sentencer to focus not on individual facts but upon a "web of facts"; that is, the sentencer views the entirety of the defendant's evidence to determine whether there is a case for mercy.[122] Certainly not all sentencers think alike, so the decision to impose capital punishment will not be consistent.[123] The resulting political problem is that, because certitude is preferred over unconstrained judgment, it appears the use of untrammeled mitigation coupled with judgment yields arbitrary results. Acknowledging that arbitrariness is the appearance, individualized decision making remains essential,[124] since "any effort to cabin such a process by rules will likely lead to unnecessary and counterproductive artificiality."[125]

Who has the better of the rationality–individualization dispute? Justice Scalia's point has merit. Indeed, Justice Blackmun agreed with him that rationality and individualization are oxymoronic in the capital punishment context. Yet, Justice Scalia appears to be a solitary proponent of scrapping the individualization mandate. Most observers agree that without individualization, capital punishment cannot exist in this country. But the arbitrariness in such a system is troubling. For Justice Blackmun, the irrationality (coupled with other factors)[126] was sufficient to eliminate his earlier endorsement of the capital punishment process. Others, recognizing the tension, accept it grudgingly.[127] To do otherwise leaves the politically unrealistic option of abolishing the death penalty altogether or, in the alternative, sending greater numbers to the gallows from the lack of individualization. This Hobson's Choice is inescapable and ensures that the legal system cannot and will not resolve the problem of arbitrariness in capital sentencing.

B. FALLIBILITY AND HUBRIS: DEFENSE COUNSEL ERROR AND PROSECUTORIAL DISCRETION

1. Defense Counsel

In capital cases, as in other criminal cases, defense counsel's performance is measured in terms of ineffective assistance of counsel.[128] The applicable standard establishes the minimum requirements for counsel but does not purport to describe a model for good, much less excellent, representation. The context for ineffective assistance is whether the defendant's conviction should be reversed because of counsel's mistakes; that is a far cry from a guarantee of a good attorney.[129] Recognizing that condemning counsel's errors mandates reversal of a possibly guilty defendant's conviction means courts may be reluctant to find ineffective assistance, even in the capital setting. Consequently, relatively few cases are reversed because of ineffective assistance. In fact, it is not uncommon for a reviewing court to note the existence of several serious errors by counsel and yet uphold the conviction. There is a huge gap between what is ineffective and what is good; only the worst representation is found ineffective. If counsel's performance were graded, ineffective counsel would receive an "F." Passing grades— a finding counsel was not ineffective—would be given both to the "D" and "A" performances, despite the tremendous difference in quality. In capital cases, then, defense counsel may make serious mistakes, but not enough to have been ineffective. Or, counsel may render generally excellent performance, with a few mistakes (as expected in all trials), and obviously not be ineffective. The system tolerates both in upholding convictions.

What prompts such mistakes? Lack of preparation or skill, overwhelming caseloads, and lack of experience are obvious explanations.[130] But sometimes, there may be an intangible present, as illustrated by the South Dakota case of *State v. Moeller*.[131] During the penalty phase of *Moeller*, the judge informed the jury that it was required to find at least one aggravating circumstance beyond a reasonable doubt if it were to sentence the defendant to die. The judge failed to define "reasonable doubt" for the jury at sentencing, however, although he had done so in the guilt phase.[132] In context, this is striking. Counsel for both sides and the judge made a mistake—a serious mistake that might have affected the outcome of the case. Those who practice law in the state are well aware that the judge and counsel in the *Moeller* case are recognized as among the most competent and talented members of the bar. How could such an error occur with the best attorneys on the case? An explanation offered by one of the attorneys for Donald Moeller is the exhaustion and emotional toll that an "arduous" capital case takes on all participants.[133] The explanation was not intended to be an excuse for counsels' and the judge's error, but was a reminder that even the best, most competent counsel can make mistakes in capital cases.[134] Relying on counsel to ensure the proper functioning of the process makes immeasurable demands on the fallible participants.[135]

If this anecdote is indicative, placing the heavy burden of responsibility for proper functioning of the death process on defense counsel is misguided, for mistakes are inevitable. Even more problematic is that although appointed counsel in the *Moeller* case were top-notch, there is no requirement that the best attorneys be appointed in capital cases. Nationwide, there are no minimum standards of experience or competence for counsel in death cases,[136] so we cannot necessarily expect superlative performance. And, when this fallibility is coupled with the minimal standard for competence set in *Strickland*, it is evident that defense counsel cannot guarantee a flawless capital process.

2. Prosecutors

While the quality of defense counsel's performance is crucial in a capital case, the prosecutor's role is as important. The prosecutor decides if a case will be brought as capital, selects the government's theory, gauges what evidence must be released to the defense, and tries the case as the government's representative. Choices are made throughout the process, with strategy and tactics playing an important role.[137] Creating or stumbling into error not egregious enough for reversal is typical. Less common—but a potential problem in every case—is the fabrication of a case against an innocent person. Misconduct, discretion, and error by the prosecutor are the subject of this section of the chapter.

Prosecutorial misconduct in a capital case is a shocking prospect. Nevertheless, such incidents occur, as the following sampling demonstrates. The most egregious misconduct by a prosecutor in a capital case is the manipulation of evidence to convict someone who is innocent. This occurs through the fabrication of evidence to make a case, or by concealing evidence which would exonerate someone.[138] Shocking incidents of this type of misconduct have been documented by a number of scholars. More than a decade ago, Professors Bedau and Radelet canvassed the convictions over eighty-five years of 350 people wrongfully convicted of capital murder; of these 23 were executed.[139] Anecdotal evidence of the conviction and execution of innocent people abounds.[140] Recent research and developments lead to the unfortunate conclusion that these kinds of errors and abuse have not been eliminated. To the contrary, as Professor Gershman establishes in discussing "the new prosecutors," the "accretion of prosecutorial power"[141] in capital and other cases has resulted in prosecutorial abuses involving the manufacture of crucial testimony and suppression of exculpatory evidence in obtaining convictions.[142] Equally shocking are the recent revelations about prosecutorial misconduct in Chicago,[143] in which the prosecutors allegedly constructed a sham case against an individual for the murder of a young girl.[144] The accused was sentenced to death and served ten years on death row before being acquitted. In an unusual development, the prosecutors in the case were themselves prosecuted (and acquitted) for their role in conspiring to contrive the case against the defendant.[145] A survey of additional instances of exoneration of death-sentenced prisoners[146] reveals that approximately forty people have been released from death row in this decade.[147] Their wrongful convictions involved the full spectrum of error and misconduct that occur in criminal cases, including ineffective assistance of counsel, prosecutorial misconduct in withholding evidence, and police pressure on individuals to implicate others regardless of their guilt.[148] Human fallibility and venality play an obvious role in these tragedies.

Prosecutorial misconduct is but one facet of prosecutorial behavior which should be examined. Discretion in charging a case as capital,[149] in choosing how to prove the case, and in accepting or refusing a guilty plea also present the opportunity for a prosecutor to make decisions which are unfair. Under most capital punishment regimes, there are few restrictions on a prosecutor's decision to bring a murder case as capital.[150] The proliferation of aggravating circumstances offers the prosecutor the death penalty option in most murder cases. Statutory restrictions on prosecutors' charging decisions are minimal,[151] with administrative constraints on federal practice worthy of note.[152] The result of this untrammeled discretion was described ably by one commentator as follows:

> The broad view is that the exercise of prosecutorial discretion in the selection of cases for capital prosecution within a single local jurisdiction is unlimited, unchecked, and unreviewed and unreviewable. This necessarily introduces arbitrariness because the local districts differ. Some are urban, and some are suburban; some local jurisdictions have few death-eligible homicides, and some have over a hundred each year. A related but distinct analysis is that prosecutors have different attitudes toward the death penalty; some are more zealous than others. Some prosecutors may charge every death-eligible case as a capital case, while others will select only a subset of death-eligible cases for capital prosecution. The individuality of the prosecutors necessarily introduces caprice and disparities. Therefore, whether a case is prosecuted as a capital case is a matter of chance depending upon the characteristics of the legal jurisdiction where the crime was committed.[153]

This amount of intrajurisdictional discretion highlights the accompanying issue of interjurisdictional disparity in treatment.[154] Obviously there is ultimate interjurisdictional disparity between states which do and those which do not have the death penalty.[155] And, among those which do, states have the prerogative to make the penalty widely or narrowly available subject only to conformance to the minimal requirements established by the Supreme Court. Thus, the choice to initiate a case as capital rests primarily in the hands of the individual who serves as prosecutor.

Once the judgment is made to proceed with a capital case, the prosecutor chooses the strategy for winning. For example, as described below in the context of habeas corpus, the government chose in Thomas Thompson's case to proceed against him as the perpetrator.[156] Later, the government switched tactics and pursued the codefendant in the same case as the perpetrator. It then did another turnabout and alleged the defendant was the perpetrator. While this utilitarian, unethical stance is indefensible, the reviewing court found no error worthy of its attention prior to Thompson's execution.

The prosecutor makes other tactical choices throughout the process. For example, the prosecutor selects what evidence to release to the defense, subject to the restrictions of *Brady v. Maryland.*[157] An illustration of prosecutors' bad choices in this regard is *Kyles v. Whitley,*[158] where the government withheld exculpatory evidence and obtained a conviction and death sentence. In a highly unusual move, the Supreme Court analyzed the facts in depth and reversed the conviction, perhaps persuaded by Fifth Circuit Judge King's comment that the government may have convicted an innocent man.[159] Another example of a tactical choice for the prosecutor is how to participate in jury selection. The prosecutor decides whether to try to exclude jurors who have any scruples about the death penalty, or in the alternative, allow those jurors to remain on a case because they may bring a note of caution or restraint to the facts and penalty. Prosecutors also choose how to prove the case—what witnesses to call and what information to release about them. A witness' motivation to lie may be crucial in a case, but remain undisclosed to the jury[160] Having been misled about the reliability of the witness, the jury may convict when reasonable disclosure would have caused it to be skeptical of the testimony. The prosecutor may use fraudulent or unreliable evidence—bogus autopsy results,[161] and false or coerced confessions[162] are examples. The prosecutor can manipulate this evidence to obtain a conviction and death sentence, abandoning ethical and moral restraints in the process. Misuse of the process may go undetected, with (obviously) fatal results.[163]

Finally, apart from purposeful misconduct or simply choosing one tactic over another, the prosecutor in a capital case may stumble into error. Admittedly, distinguishing between an honest mistake and purposeful misconduct can be difficult. Nevertheless, examples of error are presented here in the light most favorable to the government, that is, as blunders rather than calculated violations of the law. One of the most glaring prosecutorial mistakes is error in argument. Some prosecutors err by referring to the Bible or other religious sources. The California court described one such case:

> Toward the end of closing argument, the prosecutor referred to the Penal Code and then continued: "There is another book, written long ago, that mentions the crime of murder, and mentions what is the appropriate penalty for the crime of murder, and that book says a couple of different things. It says, 'Thou shalt not steal.' It says, 'Thou shalt not kill.' It says 'And if he smite with an instrument of iron so that he die, he is a murderer. The murderer shall surely be put to death.' It says, moreover, 'Ye shall take no satisfaction for the life of a murderer which is guilty of death, but shall be surely put to death.'" Defendant did not object.[164]

The court acknowledged that the defendant's failure to object waived the error but went on to explain:

> The prosecutor's reference to biblical authority was clear misconduct. There could be no purpose for this portion of the argument other

than to invite the jury to find support for a death verdict in the religious text. Although we condemn the prosecutor's biblical references as misconduct, we also conclude that the misconduct was not prejudicial under the circumstances of this case. The prosecution's argument focused primarily, and at great length, on the brutal circumstances of the crime. His brief allusions to biblical law amounted to little more than commonplaces, to emphasize his point that the jurors should instead judge defendant primarily by his acts.[165]

The *Roybal* prosecutor was certainly not alone in his misuse of biblical references in a capital case. In *People v. Wash*[166] the prosecutor's mistake was equally egregious. Despite the California Supreme Court's having addressed the impropriety of such conduct in a prior case,[167] the *Wash* prosecutor argued at length with biblical quotations, keeping the Bible at hand for the closing argument.[168] The majority rejected the state's assertion that the prosecutor had merely recounted a "biblical history" of the death penalty,[169] and characterized his remarks as a message that the Bible sanctions capital punishment[170] "precisely the sort of appeal to religious principles that we have repeatedly held to be improper."[171] Yet in affirming, the court did not find the prosecutor's comments prejudicial, because while they demonstrated the legitimacy of capital punishment, they did not endeavor to diminish the jury's sense of responsibility in imposing it or substitute religion for the court's instructions.[172] Although the dissenting justices appeared incredulous that the prosecutor's actions did not warrant reversal,[173] the majority affirmed the conviction.

Arguments grounded in the biblical text are just one type of prosecutorial error. Another illustration of error in argument is the prosecutor's misstating the applicable law, and arguing death is appropriate because the defendant will be paroled. In *State v. Hammond*, for example, the court cited the prosecutor's argument that the defendant should not be given a life sentence because "there is no life without parole in Georgia. So one day he will be a free man."[174] Previously, the court had ruled that such argument was error, and grounds for mistrial. Nevertheless the prosecutor made the argument. From inexperience or ignorance, defense counsel was unaware a mistrial was automatic, so he moved only for a curative instruction.[175] The prosecutor compounded his error with improper use of a religious argument.[176] Despite the court's having "condemned" remarks of this nature as an "inflammatory appeal to the jurors' private religious beliefs"[177] and "improper,"[178] the court ruled that, without defense objection, any error was harmless. Mr. Hammond's death sentence was affirmed.

As is evident, prosecutors' misconduct, unfair choices, and mistakes can shape cases to an alarming degree. Like defense counsel, prosecutors may be inexperienced and lack the required skills. But the prosecutor may also be motivated by personal gain, the prospect of reelection, or hubris. The latter exists when the prosecutor is sure he or she is right (i.e., has the guilty perpetrator on trial) and therefore should win at any cost. Whether this attitude is from arrogance or sincerity, it can lead to the temptation to falsify the case to procure a conviction. But the prosecutor can be wrong, and if the systemic and individual brakes fail, an innocent person or one not properly proved guilty may be convicted, sentenced, and executed. Fear of this halts many prosecutors—but not all—in their tracks. Human fallibility and hubris remain wild cards in the death penalty process that purports to be rational.

C. THE PROLIFERATION OF AGGRAVATING CIRCUMSTANCES

As was mentioned above, one way to impose a guided discretion regime on the state capital process is for the legislature to identify circumstances that "aggravate" a killing and make a defendant a potential recipient of a death sentence. Possible aggravators can be very comprehensive. As one state Supreme Court justice quipped: "This . . . presumes, of course, that the death penalty was desired by the legislature in most murder cases."[179] Although the justice intended his remark to be ironical, he is absolutely correct: in this time and place it appears that legislators, prosecutors, or the public think most murders should be punished—or punishable—by death. Perhaps the view is that discretion will operate on the system to ensure only the worst killings result in the death penalty; or perhaps the view is that nowadays, all murders are the worst. In any event, legislatures have enacted statutes with aggravating circumstances that encompass virtually every murder.

The benchmark for aggravating circumstances has been stated by the United States Supreme Court as follows: "If the sentencer fairly could conclude that an aggravating circumstance applies to every defendant eligible for the death penalty, the circumstance is constitutionally infirm."[180] Certainly, the Court is reasonable in proscribing any such all-encompassing aggravator.[181] Yet the concern is not simply that a single aggravator applies to all killings; equally troubling is that aggravators are vague, or that in combination, two or three aggravators comprehend every murder. In reality, of course, every murder is not prosecuted capitally. But under the schemes in effect in most states they could be—and the prosecutor exercises the discretion to treat a murder as capital or not. The facts of a case may barely bring it within the parameters of the aggravator[182] or aggravators, but if the case is referred capital it will be prosecuted and defended as such[183] with the life-or-death decision the culmination of the process.

Does genuine narrowing occur when either a single aggravator or a combination of two or three aggravators comprehends almost all murders? The state legislatures, state courts, and Supreme Court seem to think so, as is evident from the number and type of aggravating circumstances legislatures have enacted and which have been approved by the courts. Thus, Justice Kennedy describes the California death penalty scheme as follows: "In California, to sentence a defendant to death for first-degree murder the trier of fact must find the defendant guilty and also find one or more of nineteen special circumstances listed in California Penal Code Ann. §190.2," he observed. "The case then proceeds to the penalty phase, where the trier of fact must consider a number of specified factors in deciding whether to sentence the defendant to death. §190.3."[184]

The Court's review of the selected factors is "quite deferential,"[185] as is illustrated by Justice Kennedy's examples.[186] Justice Souter concurs that, "factors adequate to perform the function of genuine narrowing, as well as factors that otherwise guide the jury in selecting which defendants receive the death penalty, are not susceptible to mathematical precision; they must depend for their requisite clarity on embodying a 'common-sense core of meaning.'"[187]

Justice Blackmun disputes that a process resting on common sense performs the narrowing role sufficiently,[188] because the statutory factors have "been exploited to convince jurors that just about anything is aggravating."[189] After presenting the antinomic use of factors to justify a death sentence,[190] he concludes the California aggravators "embrace the entire spectrum of facts present in virtually every homicide—something this Court condemned in *Godfrey v. Georgia* (citation omitted)."[191] The Justice notes that, for example, the California court has dealt with the disparate treatment of age in capital cases[192] by remarking that age is a "metonym for any age-related matter suggested by the evidence or by common experience or morality that might reasonably inform the choice of penalty."[193] This description captures the issue regarding aggravating circumstances: if there are many, covering virtually every murder, and the cabining of discretion is guided only as "common experience" or "morality" indicate are reasonable, the jury's discretion is virtually unbounded.

In most states, the approach is similar. For example, in South Dakota the death penalty statute was enacted in 1979 with nine aggravating factors; it has been amended to encompass even more, including murders during drug dealing.[194] The state's homicide rate is very low, and there are three people who have received death sentences since 1977. Yet the statute encompasses virtually every murder committed in the state.[195] So, too, in Illinois, the death penalty statute has broad and narrow aggravators, and the list has been lengthened in recent years.[196] Texas takes a different approach: it classifies certain murders as capital,[197] then addresses whether the death penalty should be imposed.[198] This approach yields identical results with respect to the number of factors that "aggravate" a murder.

There have been calls to narrow the aggravators. For example, a common aggravator is that the killing was done for "pecuniary gain."[199] On its face, this covers every felony-murder involving robbery or theft.[200] Considering the vast number of such cases, some courts have called for elimination of the pecuniary gain factor as the sole aggravator, or have cautioned that it must be interpreted narrowly.[201] Judge Heaney briefly addressed this issue in *Singleton v. Norris*. "Sadly, I am compelled to concur in the result of this case," the judge wrote. "I believe that the Eighth Amendment's narrowing requirement prohibits the use of a pecuniary-gain motive as the sole aggravating circumstance to justify a death sentence in a robbery–murder case. Absent further review of this issue by either our court en banc or the United States Supreme Court, however, my hands are tied." [202] The United States Supreme Court has rebuffed the invitation to further narrow aggravating circumstances.[203] Congress,[204] state legislatures, and state courts likewise have declined for the most part. In fact, the trend seems to be in the other direction: expanding the list to encompass all killings. With that accomplished, the list of aggravators is meaningless as a narrowing tool.

D. HARMLESS ERROR

The public may assume erroneously that capital cases are free from error and that if error occurs, the case will be reversed. Those misconceptions are inconsistent with the harmless error rules applied on appellate review.

As Professor Davis noted in her colorful introduction to the topic of harmless error:

> Like Judge Roy Bean, the "Law West of the Pecos," the court of appeals keeps a six-gun lying on the bench. It may lie unused in any given case, or it may be the "holding" of last resort. Reams of meticulous analysis, scholarly application of intricate standards, pages of the most insightful logic—all potentially come to naught when, in the last few paragraphs of its opinion, a court picks up its six-gun and settles the issue: "But in any event, considering the record as a whole and the overwhelming evidence of guilt, such error was harmless beyond a reasonable doubt" [citations omitted] . . . the doctrine of harmless error disposes [citations omitted] of more appellate issues than any other single judicial application [citations omitted]. Thus, in any discussion of review, particularly in criminal cases, one must be mindful of the appellate six-gun: not only must the appellant show the error, he also must make a strong showing of prejudice [citations omitted].[205]

The "appellate six-gun" is available in both capital and noncapital cases, as the Court made clear in *Zant v. Stephens*,[206] where Justice Stevens commented, "[N]ot every imperfection in the deliberative process is sufficient, even in a capital case, to set aside a state court judgment."[207] Thus, if the reviewing court is satisfied the jury would have imposed the death penalty regardless of the error, the sentence will be affirmed.[208]

Error of some kind occurs in virtually every trial and in almost limitless forms. In capital cases, error potentially appears in opening statements, presentation of evidence, closing arguments, and instructions. Illustrations of error in capital cases are legion. Professor Gershman describes both the errors and the outcome in *Darden v. Wainwright*[209] as follows:

> In *Darden*, the prosecutor in argument to the jury characterized the defendant as an animal; told the jury that the only guarantee against his committing future crimes would be to execute him; that he should "have a leash on him"; and that he should have "his face blown away by a shotgun." The Supreme Court split 5–4 on whether these comments were harmless, echoing familiar language used to preserve convictions: "Darden's trial was not perfect—few are—but neither was it fundamentally unfair."[210]

Errors in other cases may be less offensive, but equally troubling. Along these lines, error in argument occurred when the prosecutor referred to the Bible to justify the death sentence.[211] Although improper, the error was harmless.[212] Error in sentencing argument occurred when the prosecutor mischaracterized a sentence of life in prison without parole.[213] That error, too, was deemed harmless.[214] Error in failing to clarify for the jury a vague sentencing standard was harmless,[215] as was error in admitting autopsy photos[216] and wrongfully shackling the defendant at trial.[217] Misstatements of law may be harmless error.[218]

Despite the possibility the harmless error doctrine may encourage sloppiness or unethical behavior from attorneys and judges in capital cases,[219] it appears entrenched. The upshot is that error will be a part of many capital cases. And fortunately, in many cases the error will have been trivial. But in others, where harmlessness is a "close call," we should be uneasy about upholding the conviction or death sentence. At the very least we must confront the fact that error in these cases exists. Ignoring mistakes, or deluding the profession and public about them, cannot be countenanced if we demand an honest assessment of whether and how well the legal system can deliver on its promise to provide an acceptable process for imposing capital punishment.

E. CURBING HABEAS CORPUS[220]

In withdrawing his endorsement of the procedural scheme for capital punishment in the United States,[221] Justice Blackmun explained that the newly defined role of federal habeas was a factor provoking his response. In his view, the capital sentencing process had "always rested on an understanding that certain procedural safeguards, chief among them the Federal Judiciary's power to reach and correct claims of constitutional error on federal habeas review, would ensure that death sentences are fairly imposed."[222] But by the time of Justice Blackmun's lament, habeas corpus had evolved into a far different remedy from its heyday following *Fay v. Noia*[223] when federal courts were viewed as having the "power and the duty"[224] to intervene in state criminal cases to ensure the vindication of federal constitutional rights. Finality, comity, federalism, and the avoidance of friction between the federal and state governments[225] had prevailed over the dual goals of insuring an accurate decision on federal constitutional claims[226] and of having the federal courts ready to intervene "to the extent federal law is erroneously applied by the state courts."[227]

Likewise, in the capital punishment context, a restricted role for habeas triumphed. In this vein, the Supreme Court has determined that the obstacles in applying "new rules" generally in habeas cases[228] also should pertain to habeas cases from death row prisoners.[229] The Court has enforced both the bar on successive habeas petitions[230] and the cause and prejudice standard for procedural defaults[231] developed in noncapital cases. The Court has decreed that a person with a successive, abusive or procedurally defaulted claim must show "actual innocence," by proving with clear and convincing evidence that but for a constitutional error, no reasonable juror would have found the person subject to the death penalty.[232] In a striking decision, three justices have stated that actual innocence is not grounds for habeas relief absent a distinct constitutional violation.[233] These prudential limitations on habeas developed by the Court have now been codified, along with more stringent measures,[234] and applied to death-sentenced persons through the Antiterrorism and Effective Death Penalty Act of 1996.[235]

The ramifications of this altered approach to federal habeas are of paramount importance to those sentenced to death. In a riveting account, Judge Reinhardt recently described how the new rules for federal habeas hamstrung the Ninth Circuit as it considered whether to provide relief in a capital case.[236] As indicated by the title of Judge Reinhardt's commentary, the case raised issues both of fairness and procedure. The fairness problem was that the murder for which the defendant was convicted and sentenced to death may have been committed by an accomplice—a person with a motive for the killing—with defendant as an aider, but not the instigator. *May* is the appropriate term in this context, because in the defendant's trial, the government argued he was the perpetrator, and thus, worthy of death. Yet, in the accompanying proceedings and in the codefendant's trial (subsequent to defendant's) the government's theory was that the codefendant, not the defendant, was the instigator and perpetrator. Thus, the fairness of the defendant's conviction and sentence was in issue, but the procedures available to pursue his claims were limited.[237] With no relief provided by the state or federal courts, the defendant, Thomas Thompson, was executed shortly after his federal remedy was eliminated.[238]

The *Thompson* case and the others cited earlier in this section raise serious questions about the process used in capital cases. Troubled by a time-consuming review of state convictions, proponents of streamlined federal review cite finality, comity, federalism, and scarce resources—certainly, not trivial concerns.[239] When those concerns predominate, the "intrusive" federal look or second federal look disappears.[240] That has a number of repercussions: less care from state courts which realize their decisions are insulated from review, or, perhaps, more care by state courts which realize their decisions are insulated from review. Conceivably, there will be less assurance of a correct application of federal constitutional rights. The consequences of restricted federal review may not be quantifiable and likely differ significantly from state to state. Yet, federal review on habeas generally was seen at one time as a mechanism to ensure "basic justice" through "procedural safeguards."[241] As Justice Brennan described it:

> Enforcement of *federal* constitutional rights that redress constitutional violations directed against the "guilty" is a particular function of *federal* habeas review, lest judges trying the "morally unworthy" be tempted not to execute the supreme law of the land. State judges popularly elected may have difficulty resisting popular pressures not experienced by federal judges given lifetime tenure designed to immunize them from such influences.[242]

The justice added that review by the lower federal courts is the only realistic way to ensure any federal review at all since the Supreme Court is unable to tackle such a monumental task.[243]

Concerns about elected state judges, limited Supreme Court resources, and vindication of federal constitutional rights have waned in the face of the efficiency–finality–comity–federalism arguments. The prevalent views now seem to be that the Supreme Court has done enough to state criminal procedure, and should intervene no more; the federal courts intervened to too great an extent on habeas; the states are the proper forums to handle criminal cases, including the federal rights implicated by those cases; or state processes have improved to such an extent that the country should have full confidence in each state's ability to dispense justice. Whatever the rationale, the reality is that the federal courts are no longer the backup or "enforcer" of federal constitutional rights in state criminal cases, whether capital or noncapital. The federal abdication leaves the responsibility for the federal constitution in state courts' hands. Yet state postconviction review may pose insurmountable barriers to adjudication of the merits of a convicted person's constitutional claims. As I have noted elsewhere:

> [S]tates have incorporated into their appeal and postconviction processes many federal standards which limit their ability to correct constitutional errors. Refusal of a state court to hear a convicted person's claim on habeas unless he or she meets the cause and prejudice standard for failure to raise it previously is an example. Refusal to apply new rules retroactively is another. Some states have adopted these approaches in an effort to bring themselves into accord with the federal standard or to modernize their state systems, apparently without reflecting on the unique role states must play in a process in which the federal backup has virtually disappeared. Acknowledging and accepting this revised role should be the impetus for states to reconsider the procedural hurdles they have erected for convicted persons. If they do not, the promise of careful review and reversal of a conviction obtained in violation of the constitution cannot be fulfilled, and the states will be unable to comply with their obligations to enforce the United States Constitution as the "supreme Law of the Land" by which "the Judges in every State shall be bound."[244]

And the problematic role for state judges who face election after dealing with capital cases has been documented.[245]

F. THE JURIES SELECTED

"Death-qualifying" the jury—approving only those jurors who indicate they are willing to consider imposition of a death sentence—is an integral part of the trial of a capital case. In fact, it may be as important as the presentation of evidence because it allows the government to eliminate opponents of capital punishment. The rationale is that only those who would be willing to consider any penalty the legislature has authorized ought to be able to sit on a case.[246]

This rule developed in a series of cases in which the Supreme Court acted first to curb the power of the government to exclude potential jurors who merely expressed "scruples" about the imposition of capital punishment.[247] The Court required instead a finding that the juror was unable or unwilling to follow the law in deciding guilt or punishment.[248] But the curb was modest. Subsequently, the Court clarified that the government could exclude a potential juror, even if the person equivocates about the inability to follow the law.[249] Thus, if the government seeks to strike the juror for cause, the trial judge will grant the challenge if "left with the definite impression" that the person could not apply the law.[250] A juror's uncertainty may be sufficient to sustain a prosecution challenge for cause.[251] The selection process can have a decisive impact: as the Court explained in *Witherspoon*, excluding potential jurors because of their scruples against capital punishment yields a jury not only more willing to convict but to impose a death sentence as well.[252]

A corollary to the "death qualification" of jurors[253] is that voir dire will include an exploration of the juror's attitudes toward capital punishment. That may involve an explanation of the facts of the case to be tried[254] and an assurance by the prospective juror that the death penalty could be an option. The process likely accomplishes what the trial practice experts suggest it should, which is to educate the jury about the theory of the case, familiarize jurors with the evidence to be presented, and ferret out the biases of those who have been called to sit on the jury.[255] It likely has another consequence as well: desensitizing jurors to the awesome task of imposing capital punishment.

Scholars in other fields have addressed this more pernicious effect of jury selection. As Professors Allen, Mabry, and McKelton noted recently, the literature encompasses a number of psychological studies of jury selection in capital cases. Important contributions have been made by Professor Haney,[256] whose studies have been incorporated into the meta-analysis conducted by Allen, Mabry and McKelton. They highlight some of Professor Haney's pellucid findings:

> According to Haney (1984), inclusion of death qualification in voir dire produces a paradox. Prospective jurors are immediately confronted with issues of guilt related to the penalty phase of the trial during the pretrial phase of jury selection. Haney views this as a "structural" problem in the logical sequence of a capital trial. Moreover, he notes five potentially deleterious consequences associated with the priming effects of death qualification procedures: (1) implication of defendant's guilt, (2) projecting penalty phase, (3) desensitizing to capital punishment, (4) public affirmation to using death penalty, and (5) personal censure implication of disqualification.[257]

These criticisms of the jury selection process evoke the concerns articulated by the Supreme Court to justify the *Witherspoon* decision.[258] In essence, Haney's suggestion is that capital case jury selection "repositions"[259] the question of guilt, which in turn taints the trial. The commentators summarize this problem as follows:

> Haney argues that asking venire persons to project themselves into a penalty phase of the trial, and estimate the likelihood of endorsing the death penalty in the event of finding the defendant guilty creates

an "availability heuristic" that disposes jurors to reconstruct experiences and events in the context of meanings assigned to the cognitive category. Thus, asking prospective jurors to consider hypothetically a guilty verdict forms a category of experience about the trial that labels the defendant guilty even before the trial begins. The consequence is to poison the well (juror's mind) as a precondition of jury service.[260]

And, Allen, Mabry, and McKelton conclude, the problem has persisted since Haney published his results. Having conducted meta-analysis of Haney's and other studies of the issue,[261] the authors offer the following insight:

A total of 14 studies were included in the analysis. The average effect indicates that persons favoring the death penalty were more likely to favor conviction of a defendant.

The results indicate that the use of a voir dire process increases the impact of attitudes toward the death penalty on attitudes toward guilt and punishment of the defendant.[262]

Attitudes of jurors who have served on capital juries toward the process used to convict and sentence a defendant are being explored by the Capital Jury Project.[263] Interviews with such jurors reveal both the personal struggle involved in imposing guilt and sentence, and an unfortunate amount of confusion over the jurors' roles.[264] Trial and appellate courts grapple with jury selection issues continuously. Some of the cases do little more on the issue than reiterate the rules, for example, that jurors who "state a strong preference for a death sentence when presented with a hypothetical situation are not subject to being stricken for cause [by the defense] in a capital case."[265] Yet, a challenge for cause by the state is properly granted if a prospective juror states it would violate his or her religious beliefs to consider imposing capital punishment and the person could not vote to impose it in any case.[266] The flavor of jury selection is lost if these rules are recited mechanistically. More revealing is the description of voir dire of individual jurors. Indicative is *State v. Greene*,[267] where the defendant was convicted of an armed robbery and murder, and sentenced to death. He challenged the exclusion of five potential jurors. The first stated she did not know if she could vote for the death penalty, then conceded there were circumstances in which she could, then followed up by saying she was "90 percent" opposed to the death penalty and opined that "only God should take a life."[268] The "conflicting and equivocal answers" revealed an inability to articulate her attitude, and thus, the trial court's judgment that she was disqualified was upheld.[269] A second potential juror in the same case expressed "serious concerns" about the death penalty and revealed such punishment conflicted with her religious beliefs. She then stated she would try to follow the court's orders and would "try to be fair," but then referred to her semistrong leaning against capital punishment.[270] The Supreme Court held it was not an abuse of discretion for the trial judge to conclude the juror's religious beliefs would prevent her from serving.[271] Yet another juror stated she was not conscientiously opposed to the death penalty but did not know if she could vote for it. She then said she would "hate to be involved in putting a man to death."[272] The state's challenge for cause was upheld.[273] Still another prospective juror stated she did not feel one should take the life of another but could vote for the death penalty in some circumstances. She then equivocated about whether or not she could impose a death sentence and expressed her strongly held belief that she would rather impose a life sentence.[274] At this point, she announced her beliefs were so strong she could not be convinced otherwise, and the challenge for cause was granted and upheld on appeal.[275] Finally, the fifth prospective juror asserted she was not conscientiously opposed to the death penalty but probably could not vote to put a person in the electric chair. Then she said she probably could do so in some circumstances, but then admitted she probably would always vote for a life sentence over the death penalty.[276] Again, the challenge for cause was upheld.

Three justices dissented in *Greene*, taking issue with the majority's adoption of a deferential standard of review of the exclusion of these jurors.[277] But equally disturbing to the justices was the trial court's conclusion that the jurors could be challenged for cause based on their equivocation during voir dire, for "the fact that a juror expresses a variety of opinions regarding the death penalty is not an unusual situation."[278] The justices quoted extensively from a former chief justice of their court:[279] "prospective jurors rarely come into court with precisely defined opinions relative to the death penalty. Instead, most carry with them contradictions arising from a deep-seated human need to avenge outrageous cruelty, a quasi-religious tendency toward forgiveness, and a sense of the worth of every human life."[280] Having canvassed the complexity of values and attitudes a single juror could have, Chief Justice Weltner offered an explanation for the equivocation a person called to serve on a jury might express:

> Few have been called upon to formulate and express their thoughts with any degree of clarity or precision. In reality, then, voir dire becomes an exercise in the shaping of opinions, more so than their expression. Again and again, the record in death cases will contain answers which are ambiguous, equivocal, and contradictory. That is not because the juror is attempting to dissimulate. . . . The fact that a juror may arrive at a posture which varies from his initial expressions should be understood as exactly what it is—a final distillation, after substantial questioning by contending counsel and often by the judge, of theretofore unarticulated, amorphous, and casual thoughts upon capital punishment.[281]

The justice's sensitivity to prospective jurors' thought processes and their ability to articulate was shared by the dissenting justices in *Greene*, who disagreed with the majority that the equivocation was sufficient to demonstrate the unambiguous and unequivocal automatic vote against the death penalty that *Witherspoon* demands.[282] The justices do not emphasize it, but it is evident from the opinion that the five people excluded were women. The race of the defendant and jurors also is not revealed, so we do not know from the opinion whether those excluded were the same race as each other and the defendant. At any rate, the community and defendant lost five women who had strong reservations about capital punishment—reservations that might well have been dispositive in the defendant's case.[283] Had these jurors been permitted to serve and had they viewed this felony-murder by the defendant as something other than the worst of the worst murder cases, the defendant would have received a life term. Not only would his life have been spared, but also it is conceivable that the voice of the community would have been better represented in imposing sentence.[284] As it was, the voices of restraint were eliminated.[285]

III. Conclusion

The struggle over capital punishment takes many forms. First, we must ask ourselves if we *should* impose capital punishment—whether we ought to subject another human being to such treatment. To answer, we might rely on religious beliefs[286] or more worldly assessments of appropriate retribution or deterrence.[287] Second, assuming we answer the *should* question in the affirmative, the next question is whether as a matter of legality, we *may* impose capital punishment. In *Gregg v. Georgia* and its companion cases, the United States Supreme Court resolved that we may. Our final question, then, must be whether we *can* impose capital punishment. The answer depends in large part on what we demand of the legal system if it purports to be able to implement a capital punishment process.

In our imperfect capital punishment system, abuses occur. The rationality for which we strive may elude us. As we seek to make an individualized decision about whether a particular defendant deserves to be executed, we see disparate treatment as juries rely on anything from religious beliefs to whim in giving or refraining from giving a death sentence. Human error and deceit by defense counsel and prosecutors may be interposed in the process, reducing its reliability and fairness. An assortment of aggravating factors, continuously expanding, makes virtually every murder punishable by death and offers little in the way of guidance to the jury, which must exercise its discretion. Error is accepted and perhaps encouraged in capital cases by bountiful application of harmless error rules. And few avenues of relief remain for a death-sentenced person who seeks federal review, since obtaining federal habeas relief has been foreclosed in all but a handful of cases. Finally, allowing the state to remove for cause jurors who are predisposed against a death sentence, and permitting a voir dire process which not only exposes this attitude but allows reinforcement of proconviction and pro–death penalty bias, skews the imposition of death sentences. Acknowledging these flaws in the handling of capital punishment not only should make us hesitant but should raise serious questions about the legal system's ability to deliver a system of capital punishment which is fair, rational and accurate.

In a provocative article written a number of years ago, Professor Weisberg argued that the Supreme Court had struggled to impose order on the death penalty process by forcing a regime of rules on the states. He posited:

> One side of the debate says that despite confusing signals and the appearance of contradiction, the Court has shown a steady commitment to formally disciplining the conduct of the state penalty trial. . . . The contending view is that the Court has never purported to do more than nudge the states into eliminating the most prejudicial injustices of the old lawless penalty scheme, while always acknowledging the impotence of constitutional law to make the penalty trial formally rational.[288]

He explained the dilemma posed by these contrasting views of the function of "rules" governing capital punishment:

> Capital punishment is at once the best and worst subject for legal rules. The state's decision to kill is so serious, and the cost of error so high, that we feel impelled to discipline the human power of the death sentence with rational legal rules. Yet a judge or jury's decision to kill is an intensely moral, subjective matter that seems to defy the designers of general formulas for legal decision.[289]

He criticized the Supreme Court's death penalty jurisprudence, arguing that the Court's "manufacture of legal doctrine mitigates moral ambivalence and intellectual instability."[290] In essence, he suggested, we have fooled ourselves into thinking we have a rational, operable capital punishment system.

If Weisberg's critique is correct, the legal profession and society as a whole must confront the fact that we have misled ourselves—the death penalty process is not the rational endeavor we have assumed. Rather, our elaborate procedures eliminate only the most egregious abuses. Weisberg concurred with Justice Harlan's assessment that rulemaking in the capital punishment context is "beyond present human ability."[291] He was careful to note that Justice Harlan's view does not mean the jury's decision is necessarily arbitrary or irrational, but only that imposing a death sentence is one type of legal decision which cannot be framed in legal rules. Other commentators agree. Professors Steiker and Steiker conclude that "the death penalty is, perversely both over- and under-regulated and the result has been to substantially reproduce the pre-*Furman* world of capital sentencing."[292] In their opinion, the Court's efforts to reform capital punishment have been abysmal failures. They suggest that the Court could have embraced effective reforms of capital punishment—"real" narrowing so that only "the worst" of the worst would be sentenced to death,[293] "real" proportionality review which would expand the categorical exclusions for death sentences,[294] and, finally, examining the actual outcomes of capital cases to determine whether, for example, race has played an improper and decisive role.[295] Calling the Court's regulation of capital sentencing a "disaster,"[296] Steiker and Steiker suggest the Court's failure to really control the process in favor of only appearing to do so has had a pernicious effect. They explain: "The Court's doctrine can be said to work as a facade to the extent that it is successful—and we argue below that it is—at making participants in the criminal justice system and the public at large more comfortable with the death penalty than they otherwise would be or should be."[297]

The effect, in their view, has been to legitimize capital punishment by assuring the participants in the legal system and the public that the system of capital punishment works well.[298] The sense of personal responsibility for a death sentence diminishes as people perceive the process as scientific and rational, and appreciate that other actors in the system are responsible for the actual approval and infliction of a death sentence. Legitimization also occurs as "the pubic develops a strong but false sense that many levels of safeguards protect against unjust or arbitrary executions."[299] In a disheartening conclusion, Steiker and Steiker lament, "We are left with the worst of all possible worlds: The Supreme Court's detailed attention to death penalty law has generated negligible improvements over the pre-*Furman* era, but has helped people to accept without second thoughts—much less "sober" ones—our profoundly failed system of capital punishment."[300]

Thus, perhaps the most honest answer from the legal system is that it has tried but failed in the realm of capital punishment. The answer to the question "Can we impose death sentences fairly, rationally, and accurately?" is no.

Part 5

FUTURE DIRECTIONS OF CAPITAL PUNISHMENT

CHAPTER 17

The Death Penalty and the International Community

EVOLVING NORMS OR PERSISTENT DIFFERENCES?

Timothy J. Schorn

Few issues are discussed at the subnational, national, and international level, but one such issue is the death penalty. Recently, at the subnational level, both Illinois and Nebraska discussed the possibility of enacting a death penalty moratorium.[1] At the national level, the federal death penalty is returning to the fore in the fight against terrorism. At the international level, Amnesty International publishes an annual report on the status of the death penalty in the international community. This chapter will focus on the status of the death penalty in the international arena, specifically the status of the death penalty under international law.

A movement in the international community to abolish the death penalty does exist, though the community members are far from a consensus. While the number of abolitionist states continues to grow, the death penalty is quite operational in many other states—the retentionist states. It might be a bit of an overstatement then to declare that "the international community is hurtling toward the abolition of the death penalty as a matter of law and in practice."[2]

The discussion of where the death penalty is going must be approached from two directions. First, we must examine international trends regarding the death penalty. Second, we must have an understanding of how law evolves and "where it comes from" internationally. Since there is no explicit, universal, conventional international law that prohibits the death penalty, the issue is whether there is customary law that outlaws capital punishment. To frame the discussion, a single question is posed: Is the death penalty prohibited under customary international law?

I. International Agreements and the Death Penalty

Most of the major human rights instruments are silent on the issue of the death penalty. Major international human rights agreements such as the Universal Declaration of Human Rights (UDHR) and the International Covenant on Civil and Political Rights (ICCPR) do protect the right to life, but they do not preclude the use of the death penalty.[3] The language of the ICCPR seemingly protects the use of the death penalty by its language, which states that "[n]o one shall be arbitrarily deprived of his life."[4] The use of the death penalty is qualified however; Article 6 explains that the death penalty may only be used in cases that involve "the most serious crimes."[5] Additionally, the "sentence of death shall not be imposed for crimes committed by persons below eighteen years of age and shall not be carried out on pregnant women."[6] More recently, the Second Optional Protocol to the ICCPR, which entered into force in 1991, does outlaw the death penalty; nearly forty states have become parties to that instrument.

Article 6 of the ICCPR does not clearly state what constitutes the "most serious crimes." State practice would seem to argue that treason and murder committed with aggravating circumstances are the most serious crimes. However, many other crimes are punishable by death in one or more states, including corruption, apostasy, drug trafficking, and kidnapping.[7] The Human Rights Committee did state that the phrase "most serious crimes" was to be read "restrictively" and was to be used only as a "quite exceptional measure."[8]

In 1968, the United Nations General Assembly (UNGA) stated that it would work to limit the application of the death penalty, not necessarily abolishing the practice altogether but certainly decreasing the offenses that resulted in the application of the death penalty in the member states.[9] Twenty years later it also requested its members to become parties to the Second Optional Protocol in December 1989.[10] This was followed in February 1993 by a call from the UN Commission on Human Rights to states to consider ratifying the Second Optional Protocol as well.[11] The Commission called for a worldwide moratorium in 1999, but the vote—30–10–12—was quite telling: An end to the death penalty is not a universal goal.[12]

Attempts by the UNGA to pass a resolution calling for a worldwide moratorium failed in 1999 because of the introduction of unfriendly amendments by retentionist countries led by Egypt and Singapore. Despite the urging by some retentionist states, the majority of the assembly refused to view the death penalty as a criminal justice issue rather than a human rights issue—criminal justice issues are considered to be local issues as opposed to the universal application of human rights. By viewing the death penalty as a criminal justice matter, it would have placed the issue under the notion of national sovereignty, essentially ending international comment on the use of the death penalty.[13]

II. Regional Organizations and the Death Penalty

More work to ban the death penalty has been accomplished at the regional level, primarily in Europe. The Sixth Protocol to the European Convention for the Protection of Human Rights and Fundamental Freedoms was quite clear and succinct when it addressed the capital punishment. "The death penalty shall be abolished. No one shall be condemned to such penalty or executed."[14] However, Article 2 of the protocol did permit countries to utilize the death penalty during times of war.[15] The protocol also made it clear that no reservations would be permissible, under Article 4.[16] The European Parliament has also taken steps to end the death penalty. In a resolution, it declared that "no state, and in particular no democratic state, may dispose of the lives of its citizens or other persons on its territory by having its law impose the death penalty."[17] The resolution called on all members of the Council of Europe and the then–Conference on Security and Cooperation in Europe (now Organization for Security and Cooperation in Europe) to end capital punishment. The language was clear; members were

> [t]o exert all possible political and diplomatic pressure in all quarters until the death penalty is entirely abolished in all countries in which it still exists and to conduct their foreign policy, especially the sector of economic and cooperation agreements, in such a way as to ensure that human rights are fully respected and, in particular, that the abolition of the death penalty becomes a factor of crucial importance.[18]

Following the actions of the European organization, one former Amnesty International worker commented that "it may not be too much to say that abolition of the death penalty has become an implicit condition of membership of the European Community."[19]

The European Parliament followed that action with a 1999 resolution calling for a universal death penalty moratorium. Another resolution addressed a number of death sentences handed down in the United States.[20] The European Union remains active in other ways to end the death penalty.

Abolishing the death penalty in Latin America has also become a multistep process. The American Convention on Human Rights stressed that the death penalty was to be imposed only for the most serious of crimes.[21] By allowing the death penalty to be used in certain circumstances, the convention clearly stayed away from the abolitionist line. It did state that the death penalty was not to be imposed on anyone under eighteen or over seventy or on pregnant women. The convention also stated that the death penalty is not to be used for political offenses or common crimes; the former is an important step in Latin America. However, some members of the Organization of American States were willing to go further.

The General Assembly of the Organization of American States approved the Inter-America Commission on Human Rights draft Protocol to the American Convention on Human Rights to Abolish the Death Penalty. The preamble to the protocol explained the reasons for calling for an end to the death penalty:

> The American Convention on Human Rights recognizes the right to life and restricts the application of the death penalty; That everyone has the inalienable right to respect for his life, a right that cannot be suspended for any reason; That the tendency among the American States is to be in favor of abolition of the death penalty; That application of the death penalty has irrevocable consequences, forecloses the correction of judicial error, and precludes any possibility of changing or rehabilitating those convicted; That the abolition of the death penalty helps to ensure more effective protection of the right to life.[22]

Article 1 stated that signatories agreed "not to apply the death penalty in their territory to any person subject to their jurisdiction."[23] The Inter-American Protocol included the same provisions regarding the death penalty in times of war and reservations to the agreement that the European Protocol did.[24] The American community has also taken an extra step through its Inter-American Convention on Extradition, which prohibited extradition from states without the death penalty to states that were retentionist unless "sufficient assurances" could be given that the death penalty would not be used.[25]

While the European and Inter-American attempts have been bold, the former have been much better received among countries in its respective region than the latter. Only a handful of countries have ratified the Inter-American protocol, while over two dozen have ratified the European protocol.

In Africa, steps that have been made are primarily due to the actions of individual countries. Despite the fact that almost all of the African states have ratified the Banjul Charter on Peoples' Rights, the majority continue to impose the ultimate sanction. Recently, the African Commission on Human and People's Rights passed a resolution that called on African states to consider a moratorium.[26] The response was not what the commission had hoped for, however.

III. Individual States

Some countries have begun to outlaw the death penalty through domestic legislation, constitutional changes, or court decisions. As an example of the latter, the Constitutional Court of South Africa deemed the death penalty to be "cruel, inhuman or degrading treatment or punishment" which is outlawed under the country's constitution.[27] The court's holding declared South Africa's death penalty statutes to be invalid on the grounds that such inhumane treatment denied the executed person's humanity.[28]

One author has discussed in detail the steps that southern African countries have taken to end the death penalty.[29] Along with South Africa, Namibia, Angola, and Mozambique have joined the abolitionist ranks. Hatchard noted that in Namibia, the constitutional provision that ended the death penalty in that country "was heavily influenced by the arbitrary use of the death sentence during the colonial period and a resultant determination that such activity should have no place in the new nation."[30] It may not be coincidental that the death penalty has been abolished in some countries that have been visited by war, death, and violence for too long.

Despite the fact that the death penalty has been abolished in a handful of countries in southern Africa, it has been retained in many more. It is doubtful then that an abolitionist norm is evolving. Hatchard however may reach a different conclusion, stating that his research "has shown that there is now a distinct trend towards the abolition of the death sentence in southern African States."[31]

European countries continue to join the ranks of the abolitionists. The Ukraine Constitutional Court ruled that the death penalty was inconsistent with the right to life enshrined in the Ukrainian constitution and called for the legislature to enact the necessary changes to domestic law.[32] The use of the death penalty in Europe has been all but eliminated.

IV. Summary Execution

While the international community has not prohibited the death penalty per se, it is fairly safe to say that summary and arbitrary executions have been prohibited. The language of some of the aforementioned international agreements prohibited the arbitrary deprivation of life. The UNGA has also been seized of this particular matter. In 1980, it issued a resolution on arbitrary and summary executions, and followed that a year later with an additional resolution.[33] Politically motivated, arbitrary and summary executions are probably prohibited under customary law,[34] having achieved that standard necessary to bind all states.[35]

V. Other Limitations on the Use of the Death Penalty

Norms have been evolving that limit the use of the death penalty. People who are juveniles at the time of the commission of the crime[36] and people who are mentally disabled are often excluded from the imposition of the death penalty.[37] As far as juveniles are concerned, one author put it in this context:

> Although the prohibition of the death penalty appears to resist the formulation of a tangible prohibition, its *non*-application to juveniles, those under the age of eighteen at the time of their offenses, is clearly emerging as customary international law. Of particular importance is a series of international instruments explicitly forbidding the use of capital punishment for juveniles. . . . The movement toward abolition of the death penalty for offenders under eighteen is further embodied in a series of United Nations resolutions and safeguards enacted throughout the 1980s. Even the United States may arguably bound by this customary rule of law, despite its recent reservation to its ratification of the International Covenant on Civil and Political Rights.[38]

Clearly, then, at least one author argues that the prohibition against executing juvenile offenders has achieved the status of customary international law. Whether it has reached the status of *jus cogens* remains questionable. Even countries that have retained the death penalty under other circumstances have restricted its use in the case of juveniles, essentially prohibiting the death penalty in such cases. Despite the general agreement that the death penalty should not be used against juvenile offenders, during 1999 such executions were carried out in Iran, Pakistan, the United States, and elsewhere.[39]

There is also consistent movement to abolish the death penalty in cases that involve the insane or mentally disabled. One author puts it succinctly in relation to the former: "Virtually all societies refuse to execute an insane person."[40] Schabas discusses the groups that are excluded from the death penalty by treaty language, such as juveniles, the elderly, and pregnant women, as well as the concern by many states that a list of exclusions may risk becoming cumbersome.[41] Excluded from these explicit exceptions were the insane and mentally disabled, although the United Nations Economic and Social Council did include the insane in a 1984 resolution.[42] However, as Schabas notes, "[t]he ECOSOC safeguards are only a resolution and do not create a binding norm of international law."[43]

The Committee on Crime Prevention and Control, part of the Economic and Social Council apparatus, discussed in 1988 the application of the death penalty in the international community. It focused on the mentally disabled rather than the insane however, due probably, according to Schabas, to the fact that "execution of the insane was *de facto* prohibited throughout the world."[44] The committee's draft resolution called upon countries to eliminate "the death penalty for persons suffering from mental retardation or extremely limited mental competence, whether at the stage of sentence or execution."[45]

Schabas argues that "the prohibition on execution of the insane is a customary norm of international human rights law."[46] He bases this conclusion on the fact that there is "no empirical evidence that any state actually executes the insane, even though many have no legislative provisions to this effect."[47] This is reinforced by the fact that even most retentionist states fail to execute the insane, including the United States. Some states have gone so far as to prohibit the death penalty in such cases.

VI. The Death Penalty as Practiced

There are a number of ways the death penalty in the international community can be examined when looking at states collectively: the growth in the number of "abolitionist" states, the number of states that retain capital punishment, the geographical location of both categories of states, or the limitations on the death penalty in states that still retain it. Additionally, we might look at trends in the international community and the international attempts to curb capital punishment.

Comparisons will be drawn between countries and regions that are considered developed and those that are considered less developed. If there are clear differences between the two groups, can we expect that as those lesser-developed countries progress, they will be less likely to utilize capital punishment? Or are the differences that exist now between the two groups of countries cosmetic?

While eight countries abolished the death penalty during 1999, there were still thirty-one countries carrying out executions—1,813 executions recorded. Since 1980, the number of countries using the death penalty has varied from 26 to 44, and the number of executions recorded has ranged from 743 in 1986 to 4,272 in 1996.[48] Of the executions performed in 1999, 85 percent of them were carried out in China, Iran, Saudi Arabia, the Democratic Republic of Congo, and the United States, with well over half in China alone.[49]

Forty-three countries have become parties to the Second Optional Protocol to the ICCPR; three more have signed but not yet ratified.[50] Thirty-six countries have become parties to the Sixth Optional Protocol to the European Convention; four more have signed but not ratified.[51] Only seven countries have ratified the Protocol to the American Convention while one has signed but not yet ratified.[52]

Amnesty International lists 108 countries that have abolished the death penalty in law or practice—73 abolitionist for all crimes, 13 abolitionist for ordinary crimes only, and 22 abolitionist in practice.[53] Of the 86 retentionist countries, most are located in Africa and the Middle East, over a dozen in Asia, and about a dozen more in the Americas.[54] Some of the retentionist countries do not actually utilize the practice though they do keep it available under their domestic law.

Clearly, most of the Western world has abolished the death penalty, either de jure or de facto. The most glaring exception is the United States. Europe has nearly eliminated the use of the death penalty. Limited strides have been made in Asia, Africa, and South America. While many in the developing world retain the death penalty, its use is most marked in China and a few Muslim countries in the Middle East.

At the end of the day, where does the death penalty stand under international law? Clearly, countries and regions differ on where the death penalty stands. Is it possible to find a conclusive source of law on the status of the death penalty internationally? In the United States, public international law is not widely known and understood, which makes taking a step back necessary. While custom and *jus cogens* have been mentioned earlier, they are not terms found in the everyday lexicon of Americans, even American lawyers and officials.

VII. International Law

Under Article 38 of the Statute of the International Court of Justice (ICJ), there are a number of "sources" of international law. To some extent, the term *source*, while popularly used, is a misnomer. Not all of the items mentioned by the statute create law; some serve as evidence of what the law is. Under the statute, the ICJ will look at conventions/treaties, custom, general principles, judicial decisions, and treatises.[55] Some of the sources are easily understandable and applied. Some, however, are not.

Conventions represent the treaties and agreements that make up the everyday life of international legal relationships. General principles are those principles of domestic law that are applicable at the international level. Judicial decisions lack the authority of precedence at the international level, certainly in the ICJ, but they do serve as evidence of what the law is. Treatises serve as evidence of what the law is, at least in the minds of the most learned and authoritative writers on the topic. Customary law may be the more complicated of the sources.

For something to become part of customary international law, two elements must exist. First, there must be a general practice in the international community—the objective requirement. Second, the practice must be adhered to because a state believes it to be an obligation, something known as *opinio juris*—the subjective requirement. This two-part requirement was confirmed by the ICJ in both the *Nicaragua Case* and the *Continental Shelf Case (Libya v. Malta)*.

As part of the discussion on customary international law, a number of questions arise. How prevalent must the practice be—that is, must it be universal? Do the practices of some states count more than the practices of others? Can a convention evolve into customary law, thus binding states that refused to become a party? Can regional customary law evolve, applying only to a group of states? All of these questions are pertinent to the discussion on the death penalty.

The existence of customary international law may be confirmed by looking at a number of sources, including statements made by governments, their participation in certain international organizational activities, national laws and legal decisions, or even in treatises. Additionally, treaties can be evidence of custom as well. "If the treaty claims to be declaratory of customary law, or is intended to codify customary law, it can be quoted as evidence of customary law even against a state which is not a party to the treaty."[56]

It is important to remember that customary law applies to the members of the international community, including the United States. As far as the United States is concerned, the Supreme Court settled that issue over a century ago. In *The Paquette Habana*, the Court stated:

> International law is part of our law, and must be ascertained and administered by the courts of justice of appropriate jurisdiction as often as questions of right depending upon it are duly presented for their determination. For this purpose, where there is no treaty and no controlling executive or legislative act or judicial decision, resort must be had to the customs and usages of civilized nations, and as evidence of these to the works of jurists and commentators who by years of labor, research, and experience have made themselves peculiarly well acquainted with the subjects of which they treat.[57]

Customary law and American domestic law could potentially conflict were customary law to develop in the area of the death penalty.

To inform further our discussion on custom, we turn to *The Case of the S.S. Lotus (France v. Turkey)*. The Permanent Court of International Justice explained that there must be evidence that a state has acquiesced to the customary rule or has taken steps to prevent such a rule from evolving.[58] The actions of a state are very pertinent to the discussion on the death penalty. In other words, has a state acquiesced to the customary rule on the death penalty or tired to prevent adoption of it?

A practice need not be universal for it to become customary international law. The practice must be consistent, however, and that may depend to some extent on the number of countries involved in the practice, or omission of a practice. Which countries abide by a certain norm may also determine the evolution of a particular custom.[59] Minor inconsistencies do not prevent a practice from becoming custom.[60] The practice must be rather habitual, though.

In the *Asylum Case (Colombia v. Peru)*, the International Court of Justice addressed the issue of whether a regional custom existed (i.e., an inter-American customary international law). The government of Colombia contended that a body of law somewhat peculiar to Latin America existed. The ICJ stated:

> The Party which relies on a custom of this kind must prove that this custom is established in such a manner that it has become binding on the other Party. The Colombian Government must prove that the rule invoked by it is in accordance with a constant and uniform usage practised by the States in question, and that this usage is the expression of a right appertaining to the State.[61]

The Court ultimately held that no such regional custom existed. Moreover, even if Colombia had proven such a custom existed, Peru would not have been bound by it because its government had repudiated the treaty on which the custom was based.

In a dissenting opinion in the *Asylum Case*, Judge Alavarez suggested that there were "systems of law . . . not subordinate to universal international law, but correlated to it."[62] Alvarez also believed that principles could be binding on a state even if that state had not ratified a particular treaty, if there was evidence that the principle in question had evolved into a regional custom.[63] If this is true, then regions and groupings of states may be able to argue that there is such a thing as regional customary law. The question becomes, How many regions must agree on the custom before it becomes part of customary international law (i.e., law that is universally binding)?

It is important to examine what states do, what they refrain from doing, and what they say. There is a "doctrine of acquiescence" that states that if a country fails to protest against another's actions or statement of law, the former accepts the latter's activities or statements as fitting within international law.[64] The discussion moves from a state's practice to *opinio juris*, in which the belief on the part of states that certain conduct, or the refraining from certain conduct, is required by law. The opinion of a state is ascertained both by what it does and does not do, and how it responds to what other states do. The issue can be approached through two basic questions. Is certain activity required under law? Or, conversely, is certain activity prohibited under law? States must avoid the activity because they believe that activity to be prohibited—their frame of mind is vitally important.[65]

Much of this discussion has taken place since the end of World War II, though it certainly began before that. Some of the norms that have evolved into customary international law have done so rather recently. How fast can custom evolve then? "An indispensable requirement would be that within the period in question, short though it might be, State practice, including that of States whose interests are specially affected, should have been both extensive and uniform."[66] Custom, according to the ICJ, could evolve quite rapidly if the conditions were correct. One problem that remains is that of the "persistent objector." If a state makes its objections to an evolving norm known repeatedly and consistently, the particular norm may not apply to that state.[67] However, if a custom becomes a peremptory norm, it applies to all states.[68] Very few peremptory norms exist; those accepted include prohibitions of genocide, aggression, torture, and racial discrimination. Most of those norms are applicable to state because the behavior threatens international security, not because of the effect of such practices on an individual.

While a state's treatment of an individual is governed by international human rights law, the international community takes note only when abuses become egregious. This partially explains why human rights norms as applied to individuals have not reached the status of *jus cogens*. Clearly, executions fit within the context of human rights, but, again, the use of the death penalty has not reached the point where a critical mass of states consider such practice to be an egregious human rights violation. Therefore, capital punishment is not a violation of a norm that has reached the status of *jus cogens*.

VIII. Custom and Human Rights

Human rights law has arguably flowed from customary international law and custom has been influenced by human rights agreements. Therefore, it is reasonable to examine the role that custom plays in human rights law. One author raises just that issue: "a juristic debate has taken place for some years on whether human right in whole or in part has become part of general customary international law."[69] What are the expectations of states in this context? Schachter explains that "[s]tates do not usually make claims on other States or protest violations that do not affect their nationals."[70] This makes it difficult to ascertain the extent to which nations believe human rights to be part of customary international law since rarely do they make extensive protests over particular issues of human rights. That being said, when countries prepare to carry out executions, there is often international attention, if not uproar.

Schachter explains that there are many types of evidence advanced in support of the argument that human rights constitute custom. He includes "the incorporation of human rights provisions in many national constitutions and laws," references to UN resolutions and declarations, resolutions by the UN and other organizations that condemn human rights violations, "statements by national officials criticizing other States," and decisions by the ICJ and national courts.[71] He argues that despite this evidence, and despite arguments made by many legal scholars, human rights have not reached the level of acceptance to be considered part of customary international law.

That being said, some particular rights have risen to the level of peremptory norms under customary international law and represent *jus cogens*—a norm that is binding on all nations—as discussed earlier. Whether or not a state is party to the particular agreement outlawing such practices, the state is still obligated to refrain from such practices. The question arises, Has the death penalty reached the point where it is prohibited by customary international law? Schachter suggests an answer: "Present tendencies also suggest that other human rights may be on their way to acceptance as general international law, especially in virtue of their widespread inclusion in national law plus general recognition of their international significance."[72] This is an attitude that is seemingly shared by Thomas Buergenthal.[73]

Rosalyn Higgins, a British jurist, offers this reminder: "New norms require both practice and *opinio juris* before they can be said to represent customary international law."[74] Louis Henkin argues that "[c]ustomary law was not *made*, it *resulted*, from an accretion of practices, though often the practice of individual States was intended to conform to what others had done, and often it was thought to be required by law."[75]

It may be time for the international community to apply a doctrine found in the United States. The rights promulgated by the U.S. Constitution as interpreted by the U.S. Supreme Court serve as a minimum standard. States are permitted to put in place standards that are more stringent (i.e., more rights may be granted but not fewer). By analogy, the international community would be bound by the minimum standards set forth by such documents as the ICCPR or ICESCR; thus, there would exist a universal measuring stick. However, *regions and states* may go further and have a more stringent standard (i.e., more rights may exist within a grouping of states but not fewer).

IX. Religious Perspectives

While religious leaders, groups, and denominations do not make international law, leaders' calls to the faithful can have an impact on public opinion. Additionally, one of the world's major monotheistic faiths is represented by a state—the Holy See. Pope John Paul II has been consistent in his desire to end the death penalty. Cardinals and bishops around the world have also been active in their respective countries, arguably assisting in building a grassroots movement in states. The Dalai Lama has also spoken against the use of the death penalty, and he, too, has the ability to mobilize millions.[76]

Unlike their Buddhist or Christian counterparts, Muslim leaders have not worked for an end to the death penalty. In fact, many advocate its use; both civil and religious crimes may result in capital punishment. Often, but not always, culture and religion may reinforce the presence of the death penalty. Abolishing capital punishment might be especially difficult in some regions. International law, or at least the adherence to it, sometimes meets its match when confronted by a particular culture or religion.[77]

X. Conclusion

Gilbert Guillaume, judge at the International Court of Justice, states, "The *Sixth Protocol* to the [European Convention on Human Rights] abolished, in 1982, the death penalty, except in time of war or imminent danger of war."[78]

In fact, the protocol did not abolish the death penalty. Without the ratification by individual countries, the Sixth Protocol had no effect whatsoever; and as it was ratified by states it applied only to each individual country that became a party. It eliminated capital punishment as an option only for those countries that became a party to it. While the protocol represents a significant number of countries today, it is limited to a collection that is relatively homogeneous when it comes to values, cultures, and ideologies, as well as being confined to a single continent. Furthermore, while the Sixth Protocol is an important step, that is all that it is. The protocol is abolitionist in intent but not yet in fact.

The European protocol shares this status with the *Additional Protocol to the American Convention on Human Rights to abolish the Death Penalty*, which has yet to attain the reach that its European counterpart has. Additionally, while Latin America can strive to eliminate judicial executions, it still has far to go to eliminate extrajudicial killings. Regional groups are in the forefront of eliminating the death penalty. Seemingly, those steps are evidence to at least one author that

> [i]nternational human rights law clearly contemplates abolition of the death penalty. To some extent, it has succeeded in promoting universal and imperative norms, as in the case of the prohibitions on torture and slavery. With respect to the death penalty, results have been more gradual and the effort has met with more opposition. Although international norms now exist prohibiting the death penalty, they are not yet widely ratified. This is why international organizations dedicated to the promotion of human rights have insisted upon strict limitation of the death penalty, including its total exclusion for certain categories, such as juveniles, pregnant women, the elderly, and the insane.

No treaty provision exists to exclude the insane from the death penalty. The conclusion that this prohibition represents a customary norm is an important one, with consequences not only in international law but also in domestic law since many states consider customary international law to be a part of their domestic law.[79]

If a state retains the use of the death penalty, is it in violation of international law? A state violates international law if it is engaged in "consistent patterns of gross violations of internationally recognized human rights." "A violation is gross if it is particularly shocking because of the importance of the right or the gravity of the violation." While the right to life is universally accepted, that right is apparently not absolute. The use of the death penalty is a consistent pattern in some countries; its use is not universally accepted to be a violation of an internationally recognized human right.

Some of the optimism displayed by those who believe that abolitionism is becoming a universal trend must be tempered by the fact that there are contrary developments. That is evidenced by occasional attempts to reintroduce the death penalty by states, resume the use of the death penalty after a period of nonuse, and expand the scope of the death penalty in countries where it is permitted.

The death penalty writ large has clearly not been outlawed by customary international law. It has not met the two requirements of custom: state practice, in this case refraining from such practice, and *opinio juris*, the belief on the part of the state that it is prohibited from carrying out executions under international law. In some regions, however, the death penalty has been effectively outlawed. Therefore, if a regional custom can exist, one that outlaws the death penalty in Europe does exist. Additionally, customary law does seemingly prohibit summary or arbitrary executions and the use of the death penalty against juvenile offenders, the mentally disabled, and insane, and in response to any but the most serious offenses.

CHAPTER 18

Reflections on the Future of the Death Penalty

Robert A. Miller

The editors have asked that I provide final comments on the death penalty as a capstone to this collection. I am a recently retired chief justice of the South Dakota Supreme Court, and, although I cannot profess to be an expert on capital punishment, I have given some thought to the matter. Accordingly, I am pleased to offer my reflections on this important and timely subject.

The citizens of my state, speaking through the legislature, have decided that the death penalty is an appropriate sentence for those who commit the most serious crimes. Although it is surely debated in many circles, particularly within the religious communities, capital punishment is not a pressing issue among the majority of our people. We live in a small and generally safe society where the last person was executed in the late 1940s. There are only five people (all of whom are white males) on death row.

Even though during sixteen years as a trial judge (from 1971 to 1986) I presided over a large number of murder trials, none resulted in the imposition of the death penalty. During my fifteen-year tenure on the South Dakota Supreme Court, we reviewed only three death penalty cases. I authored the majority opinion in all of them. Putting aside my personal and religious considerations, as judges must do, I have taken the law as propounded by the legislative authorities and reviewed it with particular close scrutiny to be assured that the defendants' constitutional rights have been fully protected.

In my association and conversations with numerous state court trial and appellate judges and chief justices from across the nation, most of whom have been routinely confronted with capital punishment issues, I am convinced that a majority of them share many of the sentiments I am about to express in this chapter.

315

Interestingly, I am also well acquainted with many jurists from jurisdictions that do not have the death penalty in their states. Most of them are pleased about that and are relieved that they do not have to deal with all of the difficult legal and emotional issues that flow from capital punishment. However, I should note that some of them express regret that capital punishment is not a viable alternative for them to impose, especially for the most heinous crimes.

I. Impact of Events on September 11, 2001

I am personally convinced that the tragic events on September 11, 2001, at the World Trade Center in New York City and the Pentagon, coupled with the events that have followed and continue to affect our country and the world, will put the entire focus and debate of the varied capital punishment arguments in an entirely new perspective. At the time of this writing, the events of that day are fresh in the minds of all of our citizens, lawmakers, and government leaders. People are frustrated and angry; many want to see blood and revenge, especially against those people who had any connection with the deaths of the thousands of people who lost their lives in New York and the nation's capital. Anyone with terrorist ties, or who is remotely involved in terrorist activities, is definitely at high risk.

Since those horrific events are so close in time to the writing of this article, it is difficult to place myself back into a pre–September 11 state of mind. However, I will attempt to do so. Certainly, only history will tell us what direct or indirect impact and effect that terrible day will have on the future of our nation's jurisprudence, especially as it pertains to the death penalty. It surely will be interesting to watch.

II. General Observations

As earlier chapters in this book have noted, the death penalty is constantly under attack. Along with a great number of other criticisms, a major concern in many areas seems to be that the death penalty has become a symbol of racial division in many areas of the country.

For several years, I have perceived significant momentum in the movement toward the abolition of capital punishment in several states. (At the very least there has been a more serious examination of the possibility of a moratorium in certain states.) Many well-respected authors on the subject seriously predict a future total abolition of the death penalty.

It appears to me that abolitionist thought exists both within and outside the legal community, and it crosses the broad spectrum of political, religious and racial lines. However, my personal belief is that, in many people's minds, the principal motive for abolition has little or nothing to do with the moral or religious arguments being propounded by several commentators. Rather, I suggest the most significant opposition has been fueled and generated by a number of well-founded frustrations with the legal system, especially as it relates to the speed (or lack thereof) and high cost of the death penalty process. In fact, a number of people whose intelligence and judgment I highly respect would repeal the death penalty for exclusively utilitarian reasons. In short, I believe that many persons who object to the death penalty do not object on philosophical grounds. The death penalty should not be abandoned, in their view; however, they are concerned that it is not applied effectively.

There is also a great deal of concern as it relates to the different methods of executing offenders. Although a majority of the states provide for lethal injection, some permit electrocution, gas chamber, hanging, and firing squad. The majority of states that do not provide for lethal injection impose the death penalty by electrocution. U.S. Supreme Court Justice William Brennan Jr., in his writing in *Glass v. Louisiana*, characterized it as "extremely violent" and asserted that it inflicted "pain and indignities far beyond the mere extinguishment of life."[1] Justice Brennan likened electrocution to "nothing less than the contemporary technological equivalent of burning people at the stake."[2] Because of a number of botched executions, coupled with detailed media coverage of them, it seems that even the most ardent supporters of the death penalty share Justice Brennan's sentiments and believe that lethal injection should be exclusively used because it is more humane and much less likely to violate the Eighth Amendment's ban on cruel and unusual punishment.

Furthermore, as some scholars have noted, unless there are tremendous increases in executions or significant decreases in death sentences, there will be unmanageable backlog, causing delays and wreaking havoc within the judicial and corrections systems of our nation. Clearly, the state courts have major control of death row populations, although the federal courts certainly affect the delays that occur in the process. Some authors suggest that irrespective of which court system is considered, there is a perception among many people that the logjams or backlogs are the result of judicial interference with the majority will of the legislators and citizens. That is an unfair and unfortunate blame shifting. It belies reality and the recognition of the important principles of our constitutional form of government—namely, that each citizen is entitled to his or her day in court. Assuredly, even the most ardent supporter of capital punishment would not want it imposed on any innocent person or even one whose constitutional rights have been trampled.

However, despite significant claims that it was being unfairly imposed, especially against minorities, political leaders do not seem to be interested in taking a lead for such repeals. They often appear to take a great deal of comfort in the belief that the courts will ensure that capital punishment is properly imposed. They also believe that new developments in scientific evidence—for example, DNA testing—will guarantee that only the guilty will be executed.

We in the judiciary appreciate the confidence expressed when citizens and lawmakers put such great reliance and trust in the criminal justice system, particularly the courts, to make certain that the death penalty is not unfairly or inappropriately applied. Despite that awesome trust, we jurists recognize that there is a legitimate frustration with the judicial system that affects its credibility in many quarters.

It is difficult to explain to our citizenry why it takes many years for the appeals, state and federal, to wind their way through the judicial system. Understandably, lay people do not comprehend the state and federal appellate structure or the complexities of the appeals process. Similarly, not everyone appreciates, or even cares about, the need for effective legal counsel, especially when considering the high cost of defense that flows from it.

It seems that among our citizens there is a great deal of ambivalence about the death penalty. Juries hesitate to impose it. Many citizens fear that discrimination, inequity, and error are an integral part of the system. They certainly want prompt and appropriate punishment, but few are willing to extend that through the imposition of the death penalty, except in the most egregious circumstances.

III. What Do I Foresee?

There is little doubt but that the debate of the varied capital punishment issues will continue. I believe that such debate is healthy. Some advocates will surely argue that, as the number of executions begins to rise, the impact of injustices will force itself into public consciousness. That assertion may have merit.

Clearly, for the foreseeable future, there is nothing to indicate that the United States Supreme Court will abolish or outlaw the death penalty. Congress and many state legislatures, frustrated by rising crime rates and pressured by a number of outraged citizen groups, will be loath to repeal their capital punishment laws. The events of September 11, 2001, in my view, make this a certainty. At the very least, because our citizens are so angry, I am convinced that they and their elected representatives will insist that the death penalty remain in place.

Thus, the increasing pace of executions and the public's concern about crime all indicate to me that the use of the death penalty will become commonplace. It will result in an increased number of persons on death row. However, because both sides of the debate are equally concerned about the moral implications of executing an innocent person, it is possible that a moratorium could result while task forces and concerned groups discuss its fairness and future.

The costs of the death penalty—be it for costs of defense, costs of special death row facilities, or whatever—will continue to put a strain on other crime fighting and prevention programs. Legislators and other policymakers will need to make very difficult and controversial choices between all of these important alternatives.

I see a time in the very near future where lethal injection will completely replace all other methods of execution. Even the most ardent supporters of capital punishment will demand that.

Procedures adopted to shorten the process must be closely scrutinized so that expediency does not destroy constitutional protections. Governments—federal, state, and local—must be prepared to pay all the costs, and those costs are, and will continue to be, significant. There will be a need to educate the public on the judicial process so that citizens can appreciate and understand the attendant delays. They must be made aware that the Constitution and general human rights requires that all appropriate steps must be taken to be assured that only the guilty are convicted and executed.

Continued reliance on the death penalty will enhance the burden on state and federal judiciaries to ensure, despite the cost, that all persons charged with capital crimes will be represented by only the most qualified lawyers. Scarcity of qualified counsel willing to take these cases will be a significant national problem. Special training must be made available, and mandatory, for all defense counsel doing death penalty work, at both the trial and appellate levels. Counsel must be appropriately compensated and governmental entities should be prepared to pay that cost. Citizens should be educated in this concept, too, so that if they persist in the demand to retain the death penalty in their states, they are prepared to pay the cost.

A proposal or concept that may have some appeal to many people on all sides of the capital punishment argument is to limit the death penalty to only serial or multiple killers. Supporters of that proposal note that nationally there would be savings of millions of dollars, and court time and resources would be freed up to do other important tasks. The risk of executing innocent persons would be dramatically reduced. Racial bias would be significantly reduced, since the vast majority of serial killers are not persons of a minority race. As one person put it, "only the worst of the worst" would be executed. Although such a proposal would not totally appease advocates at both ends of the spectrum, it would seem to be a reasonable compromise.

A judge that I highly respect believes that the events of September 11 may well have the effect of causing the demise of capital punishment. He predicts that should the United States and its allies get involved in an all-out war with terrorists, our citizens will become fed up with killings and insist that capital punishment be abolished. Although I do not agree with him or accept his theory, I believe it is interesting and certainly do not summarily discount it.

Of course, it is always possible, as time passes and the events of September 11 recede into memory, that the long-term reduction in violent crime likely to be associated with the aging of our population may reduce the fear of crime and support for capital punishment. That, naturally, is decades away.

In the meantime, although I agree with the conventional wisdom that capital punishment is here to stay, I strongly support a constant and ongoing debate and scrutiny of it. Our citizens deserve no less. On behalf of the editors and contributors to this collection, let me say that we hope this book will play at least a small part in that ongoing debate.

Notes

INTRODUCTION

1. Jack Henry Abbott, *In the Belly of the Beast: Letters from Prison* (New York: Vintage, 1981), 150.

2. Thomas Hobbes, *Leviathan*, ed. Herbert W. Schneider (Indianapolis: Bobbs-Merrill, 1958), 142–43.

3. See, for example, Laurence Berns, "Thomas Hobbes, 1588–1679," in *History of Political Philosophy*, 2d ed., ed. Leo Strauss and Joseph Cropsey (Chicago: University of Chicago Press, 1972), 370–94.

4. Cesare Beccaria, "The Death Penalty Will Not Discourage Crime (1764)," in *The Death Penalty: Opposing Viewpoints*, ed. Paul A. Winters (San Diego: Greenhaven, 1997), 22; emphasis in the original.

5. "The Death Penalty Will Discourage Crime (1701)," in *The Death Penalty*, ed. Winters, 18; emphasis in the original.

CHAPTER 1

1. Although many death penalty opponents have presented these arguments, perhaps the best-known commentator was the late associate justice of the U.S. Supreme Court Thurgood Marshall. In his concurring opinion in *Furman v. Georgia*, Justice Marshall contends that "[w]e achieve 'a major milestone in the long road up from barbarism' and join approximately seventy other jurisdictions in the world which celebrate their regard for civilization and humanity by shunning capital punishment." 408 U.S. 238, 371 (1972). Similarly, in *Gregg v. Georgia*, Justice Marshall argues that the death penalty cannot be justified "because the penalty is, quite clearly I think, not necessary to the accomplishment of those results" [i.e., deterrence]. 428 U.S. 153, 239 (1976). See also Hugo Adam Bedau, "Background and Developments," in

The Death Penalty in America, 3d ed., ed. Hugo Adam Bedau (New York: Oxford University Press, 1982), 3–28; and Stephen B. Bright, "The Politics of Capital Punishment: The Sacrifice of Fairness for Executions," in *America's Experiment with Capital Punishment*, ed. James R. Acker, Robert M. Bohm, and Charles S. Lanier (Durham, N.C.: Carolina Academic Press, 1998), 117–35.

2. See, for example: Vincent Ostrom, *The Political Theory of a Compound Republic: Designing the American Experiment*, 2d ed. (Lincoln: University of Nebraska Press, 1987); John P. Roche, "The Founding Fathers: A Reform Caucus in Action," in *American Government: Readings and Cases*, 3d ed., ed. Peter Woll (Boston: Little, Brown, 1969), 55–78; Clinton Rossiter, *1787: The Grand Convention* (New York: Macmillan, 1966); and Herbert J. Storing, "The Federal Convention of 1787: Politics, Principles, and Statesmanship," in *The American Founding: Politics, Statesmanship, and the Constitution*, ed. Ralph A. Rossum and Gary L. McDowell (Port Washington, N.Y.: Kennikat, 1981), 12–28.

3. Steven H. Jupiter, "Constitution Notwithstanding: The Political Illegitimacy of the Death Penalty in American Democracy," *Fordham Urban Law Journal* 23, no. 1 (1996): 464.

4. See, for example, George McKenna and Stanley Feingold, eds., *Taking Sides: Clashing Views on Controversial Political Issues*, 12th ed. (Guilford, Conn.: McGraw-Hill, 2001), 134. For a discussion of the movement away from capital punishment in many American states, see, for example, Norman Krivosha, Robert Copple, and Michael McDonough, "A Historical and Philosophical Look at the Death Penalty—Does It Serve Society's Needs?" *Creighton Law Review* 16, no. 1 (1982–83): 1–46, especially 22–30.

5. The Enlightenment view of science is discussed at length in Larry Laudan, *Progress and Its Problems: Towards a Theory of Scientific Growth* (Berkeley: University of California Press, 1977), especially 175–89. See also David E. Cooper, *World Philosophies: An Historical Introduction* (Cambridge, Mass.: Blackwell, 1996), 226–35; and J. Michael Martinez and Kerry R. Stewart, "Ethics, Virtue, and Character Development," in *Ethics and Character: The Pursuit of Democratic Virtues*, ed. William D. Richardson, J. Michael Martinez, and Kerry R. Stewart (Durham, N.C.: Carolina Academic Press, 1998), 28–29.

6. Alexander Hamilton, "Federalist Number 9," in Alexander Hamilton, James Madison, and John Jay, *The Federalist Papers*, ed. Clinton Rossiter (New York: Mentor, 1961), 72–73.

7. Hamilton, "Federalist 15," 110.

8. Thomas Paine, "On the Origin and Design of Government in General, with Concise Remarks on the English Constitution [excerpted from *Common Sense*]," in *American Political Thought*, ed. Kenneth M. Dolbeare (Chatham, N.J.: Chatham House, 1984), 43.

9. For more discussion on Hobbes's influence on the American Founders, see, for example: Edward S. Corwin, "The 'Higher Law' Background of American Constitutional Law," in *American Government: Readings and Cases*, 3d ed., ed. Peter Woll (Boston: Little, Brown, 1969), 37–54; Richard Hofstadter, *The American Political Tradition* (New York: Vintage, 1948); and Gary L. McDowell, "Private Conscience and Public Order: Hobbes & *The Federalist*," *Polity* 25, no. 3 (Spring 1993): 421–43.

10. Leo Strauss, *Natural Right and History* (Chicago: University of Chicago Press, 1953), 166.

11. For more on Hobbes's philosophy, see, for example, Laurence Berns, "Thomas Hobbes, 1588–1679," in *History of Political Philosophy*, 2d ed., ed. Leo Strauss and Joseph Cropsey (Chicago: University of Chicago Press, 1972), 370–94.

12. This point is discussed cogently in Lloyd Steffen, *Executing Justice: The Moral Meaning of the Death Penalty* (Cleveland, Ohio: Pilgrim, 1998), especially 89–90.

13. Thomas Hobbes, *Leviathan*, ed. Herbert W. Schneider (Indianapolis: Bobbs-Merrill, 1958), 245.

14. Jupiter, "Constitution Notwithstanding," 465.

15. For a more detailed discussion of the American Founders' movement away from the Hobbesian faith in the sovereign, see, for example, Martin Diamond, "Ethics and Politics: The American Way," in *Ethics and Character*, ed. Richardson et al., 171–201; and Christopher M. Duncan, "Men of a Different Faith: The Anti-Federalist Ideal in Early American Political Thought," *Polity* 26, no. 3 (Spring 1994): 387–415.

16. John Locke, "The Second Treatise of Civil Government: An Essay Concerning the True, Original, Extent, and End of Civil Government," in *Two Treatises of Civil Government*, ed. Thomas I. Cook (New York: Hafner, 1947), II, 123.

17. Locke, "The Second Treatise of Civil Government," II, 185.

18. Hobbes, *Leviathan*, 107.

19. See Locke's discussion of property in Chapter V in Locke, "The Second Treatise of Civil Government," II, 133–46. See also 184–94.

20. Locke, "The Second Treatise of Civil Government," II, 124.

21. Locke, "The Second Treatise of Civil Government," II, 122.

22. Locke, "The Second Treatise of Civil Government," II, 124.

23. Locke, "The Second Treatise of Civil Government," II, 124.

24. For more information on Locke's thinking, see, for example, Robert A. Goldwin, "John Locke, 1632–1704," in *History of Political Philosophy*, 2d ed., ed. Leo Strauss and Joseph Cropsey (Chicago: University of Chicago Press, 1972), 451–86.

25. For a detailed discussion of this argument, see, for example, Glen H. Stassen, "Biblical Teaching on Capital Punishment," in *Capital Punishment: A Reader*, ed. Glen H. Stassen (Cleveland, Ohio: Pilgrim, 1998), 121; and Helen Prejean, "The Death Penalty Is Morally Unjust," in *The Death Penalty: Opposing Viewpoints*, ed. Paul A. Winters (San Diego: Greenhaven, 1997), 57.

26. Thomas Jefferson, *Notes on the State of Virginia*, ed. William Peden (Chapel Hill: University of North Carolina Press, 1982), 142.

27. Jefferson, *Notes on the State of Virginia*, 142.

28. Jupiter, "Constitution Notwithstanding," 477.

29. Joseph J. Ellis, *American Sphinx: The Character of Thomas Jefferson* (New York: Vintage, 1996).

30. See, for example, Saul K. Padover, ed., *Thomas Jefferson on Democracy* (New York: Mentor, 1939).

31. Wayne R. LaFave and Austin W. Scott Jr., *Criminal Law* (St. Paul, Minn.: West, 1972), 164.

32. A good discussion of the debate about the ability (or inability) of the criminal justice system to root out biases can be found in James R. Acker and Charles S. Lanier, "Beyond Human Ability? The Rise and Fall of Death Penalty Legislation," in *America's Experiment with Capital Punishment*, ed. James R. Acker, Robert M. Bohm, and Charles S. Lanier (Durham, N.C.: Carolina Academic Press, 1998), 77–115; and Harry A. Blackmun, "The Death Penalty Is Legally Unjust," in *The Death Penalty*, ed. Winters, 66–71.

33. Ernest van den Haag, "Justice, Deterrence, and the Death Penalty," in *America's Experiment with Capital Punishment*, ed. Acker et al., 139.

34. See, for example, Martin Shapiro and Rocco J. Tresolini, *American Constitutional Law*, 6th ed. (New York: Macmillan, 1983), 292–94; and Ronald J. Allen and Richard B. Kuhns,

Constitutional Criminal Procedure: An Examination of the Fourth, Fifth and Sixth Amendments and Related Areas (Boston: Little, Brown, 1985), 925–26.

35. Jupiter, "Constitution Notwithstanding," 444. See also Shapiro and Tresolini, *American Constitutional Law*, 296–302.

36. *Gregg v. Georgia*, 428 U.S. 153 (1976).

37. The Mill quote and a discussion of the categories of action are found in Andrew Heywood, *Political Ideas and Concepts: An Introduction* (New York: St. Martin's, 1994), 113–15.

38. John Stuart Mill, *On Liberty* (Arlington Heights, Ill.: AHM, 1947), 82.

39. John Stuart Mill, "Society Must Retain the Death Penalty for Murder (1868)," in *The Death Penalty*, ed. Winters, 28.

40. See, for example, Cooper, *World Philosophies*, 303; Pierre Hassner, "Immanuel Kant, 1724–1804," in *History of Political Philosophy*, ed. Strauss and Cropsey, 554–93; and James Rachels, *The Elements of Moral Philosophy*, 3d ed. (Boston: McGraw Hill, 1999), 135–38.

41. Immanuel Kant, *Fundamental Principles of the Metaphysics of Morals*, trans. T. Abbott (New York: Prometheus, 1987), 49.

42. Rachels, *The Elements of Moral Philosophy*, 138.

43. Jupiter, "Constitution Notwithstanding," 480.

44. Jupiter, "Constitution Notwithstanding," 481.

CHAPTER 2

This chapter was previously published in the *Yale Journal of Law & the Humanities* 8 (1996): 451–63. Reprinted with permission.

1. St. Augustine, *Confessions*, trans. R. S. Pine-Coffin (New York: Penguin, 1961), 71–72.

2. Stephen Bright, "Counsel for the Poor: The Death Sentence Not for the Worst Crime but for the Worst Lawyer," *Yale Law Journal* 103, no. 7 (May 1994): 1879–80.

3. For a description of death penalty practice at the trial level, see Austin Sarat, "Speaking of Death: Narratives of Violence in Capital Trials," *Law & Society Review* 27, no. 1 (1993): 39. The tactics and competence of defense lawyers in capital trials are subjects of considerable controversy. See Bright, "Counsel for the Poor," and James M. Doyle, "The Lawyers' Art: 'Representation' in Capital Cases," *Yale Journal of Law & the Humanities* 8, no. 2 (Summer 1996): 417–49.

4. It is impossible to give a precise estimate of the number of people comprising the "death penalty bar" in the United States. Practitioners estimate that there are about two hundred such lawyers. Approximately that number regularly attends the annual Airlie Capital Punishment Conference sponsored by the National Association for the Advancement of Colored People (NAACP) Legal Defense Fund. Those who do appellate and postconviction work practice on a variety of settings. Some work for public interest organizations like the Southern Center for Human Rights, the Minnesota Advocates for Human Rights, the American Civil Liberties Union, or the NAACP Legal Defense Fund. Some are in private practice, and some worked until recently in agencies like the Federal Capital Defense Resource Centers funded by states or the federal government for the purpose of providing representation to persons sentenced to death. During a session of Congress in the mid-1990s, funding was cut off for the Resource Centers. See "Scrimping on the Court System," *Chicago Tribune*, April 12, 1996, 28; Saundra Torry, "Juggling the Issue of Representing Death-Row Inmates," *Washing-*

ton Post, February 5, 1996, F7. As a result, the current extent and organization of appellate and postconviction representation in capital cases is unclear.

5. For a discussion of the political views and commitments of death penalty lawyers, see Austin Sarat, "Between (the Presence of) Violence and (the Possibility of) Justice: Lawyering against Capital Punishment," in *Cause Lawyering: Political Commitments and Professional Responsibility*, ed. Austin Sarat and Stuart Scheingold (New York: Oxford University Press, 1997).

6. Michael Mello, "Outlaw Attorney: The 'Banality of Evil,'" in *The System of Capital Punishment and My Collaboration with that System* (1996), 180 (unpublished manuscript, on file with the author). Mello notes that "[c]apital postconviction representation today and for the foreseeable future involves not so much debates about the wisdom of the death penalty theory . . . but rather case-by-case constitutional attacks upon the legal system that selects which citizens have lost their moral entitlement to live."

7. See Louis Bilionis, "Legitimating Death," *Michigan Law Review* 91, no. 7 (June 1993): 1643–1702; Michael Oreskes, "The Political Stampede on Execution," *New York Times*, April 4, 1990, A16; Steven Goldstein, "Expediting the Federal Habeas Corpus Review Process in Capital Cases: An Examination of Recent Proposals," *Capital University Law Review* 19, no. 3 (1990): 599–647 (discussing various legislative proposals to restrict federal habeas petitions).

8. By "liberal-legalism," I mean a legal system committed to formalism and procedural justice. On the dangers of liberal-legalism, see Judith N. Shklar, *Liberalism without Illusions: Essays on Liberal Theory and the Political Vision of Judith N. Shklar* (Chicago: University of Chicago Press, 1996).

9. See Robert Weisberg, "Deregulating Death," *1983 Supreme Court Review* (1983): 305. See also Anthony G. Amsterdam, "In Favorem Mortis: The Supreme Court and Capital Punishment," *Human Rights* 14, no. 1 (Winter 1987): 14–17, 49–60.

10. See Richard Abel, *Politics by Other Means: Law in the Struggle against Apartheid, 1980–1995* (New York: Routledge, 1995); Ronen Shamir, "Litigation as Consummatory Action: The Instrumental Paradigm Reconsidered," *Studies in Law, Politics, and Society* 11, no. 1 (1991): 41–68. As Shamir argues, even in conditions of oppression, petitioners turn to courts because they "are able, for the first time, to express their grievances and to materialize their appeal for grace and abstract justice." See also Lisa Hajjar, "Authority, Resistance and the Law: A Study of the Israeli Military Court System in the Occupied Territories," Ph.D. diss., American University, 1995.

11. See E. P. Thompson, *Whigs and Hunters: The Origins of the Black Acts* (New York: Pantheon, 1976) (arguing that "'the law,' as a logic of equity, must always seek to transcend the inequalities of class power which, instrumentally, it is harnessed to serve").

12. *Woodson v. North Carolina*, 428 U.S. 280, 305 (1976).

13. Margaret Radin, "Cruel Punishment and Respect for Persons: Super Due Process for Death," *Southern California Law Review* 53, no. 2 (1980): 1143.

14. See, for example, *Herrera v. Collins*, 112 S. Ct. 2936 (1993) (holding that evidence of actual innocence may not be sufficient to justify habeas relief); *McCleskey v. Kemp*, 481 U.S. 279 (1987) (refusing to invalidate the death penalty even in the face of statistical evidence of systemic racial disparities in the administration of capital punishment).

15. My claim that these promises have been broken "without embarrassment" refers to the attitude seemingly displayed by the majority in *McCleskey* and *Herrera*. However, this is not to say that the gradual unwinding of "super due process" in death cases has been uncontentious. One example of contention is provided by the Robert Alton Harris case. See Evan

Caminker and Erwin Chemerinsky, "The Lawless Execution of Robert Alton Harris," *Yale Law Review* 102, no. 1 (October 1992): 225–54; Judge Stephen Reinhardt, "The Supreme Court, the Death Penalty, and the Harris Case," *Yale Law Journal* 102, no. 1 (October 1992): 205–23.

16. Drucilla Cornell, "From the Lighthouse: The Promise of Redemption and the Possibility of Legal Interpretation," *Cardozo Law Review* 11, nos. 5–6 (July–August 1990): 1709.

17. On the nature of this promise, see J. M. Balkin, "Being Just with Deconstruction," *Society & Legislative Studies International Journal* 3, no. 1 (1994): 401; Jacques Derrida, "Force of Law: The 'Mystical' Foundation of Authority," *Cardozo Law Review* 11, vols. 5–6 (July–August 1990): 963–73.

18. Robert Cover, "Supreme Court 1982 Term—Foreword: Nomos and Narrative," *Harvard Law Review* 97, no. 1 (November 1983): 9.

19. Cover, "Supreme Court 1982 Term," 34.

20. Cover, "Supreme Court 1982 Term," 34.

21. Cover, "Supreme Court 1982 Term," 39.

22. On the persistence of capital punishment in the United States, see Franklin Zimring and Gordon Hawkins, *Capital Punishment and the American Agenda* (Cambridge: Cambridge University Press, 1987), 3–49.

23. This possibility has been realized in South Africa. See *State v. T. Makwanyane and M. Mchunu*, case no. CCT/3/94 (Constitutional Court of the Republic of South Africa, 1995).

24. See Jacques Le Goff, *History and Memory*, trans. Steven Randall and Elizabeth Clamon (New York: Columbia University Press, 1996).

25. Shoshana Felman and Dori Laub, *Testimony: Crisis of Witnessing in Literature, Psychoanalysis, and History* (New York: Routledge, 1991). Treating the lawyer for a losing cause as a witness giving testimony suggests that he is addressing his work to the community of the future as much as to the law of the present. Feldman and Laub argue that "[t]o testify before a court of law or before the court of history and of the future . . . is more than simply to report a fact or an event or to relate what has been lived, recorded and remembered. Memory is conjured here essentially in order to address another, to impress upon a listener, to *appeal* to a community." Felman and Laub, *Testimony*, 204.

26. For an interesting discussion of what is involved in the construction of such a social history, see Craig Haney, "Psychological Secrecy and the Death Penalty: Observations on 'The Mere Extinguishment' of Human Life," *Studies in Law, Politics, and Society* 16, no. 1 (1997): 3–69.

27. See Samuel Gross and Robert Mauro, *Death and Discrimination: Racial Disparities in Capital Sentencing* (Boston: Northeastern University Press, 1989).

28. See Stephen Bright and Patrick Keenan, "Judges and the Politics of Death: Deciding between the Bill of Rights and the Next Election in Capital Cases," *Boston University Law Review* 75, no. 3 (May 1995): 769.

29. See Bright, "Counsel for the Poor."

30. "Even when I was writing legal briefs and petitions and stay applications, when the main audience was the judges and their law clerks, I remained fairly conscious of the fact that our litigation work products were also making a record for future students of state-sanctioned killings. We litigate for historians, anthropologists, and the sociologists. . . . [L]itigation [is] a means of leaving footprints in the historical sand." Mello, "Outlaw Attorney," 80.

31. See Pierre Nora, "Between Memory and History: Les Lieux de Memoire," *Representations* 7, no. 1 (1989): 15. ("Modern memory is, above all, archival. It relies entirely on the materiality of the trace, the immediacy of the recording, the visibility of the image.")

32. As Martha Minow suggests, legal rights matter not just because they provide dignity to the law's victims, or because they help to mobilize them to undertake political action, but because they provide an opportunity to tell a story that might not otherwise be told. See Minow, "Interpreting Rights: An Essay for Robert Cover," *Yale Law Journal* 96, no. 8 (July 1987): 1860–1915.

33. The work of lawyers in a losing cause is to construct narratives since "history is . . . the establishment of facts of the past through their narrativization." Felman and Laub, *Testimony*, 93. See also Hayden White, *The Content of the Form: Narrative Discourse and Historical Representation* (Baltimore: Johns Hopkins University Press, 1990). For a fuller elaboration of this argument in the context of death penalty lawyering, see Austin Sarat, "Narrative Strategy and Death Penalty Advocacy," *Harvard Civil Rights–Civil Liberties Law Review* 31, no. 2 (Summer 1996): 353–81.

34. Cover, "Supreme Court 1982 Term," 34.

35. See Felman and Laub, *Testimony*, 93. As James Wilkinson puts it, "The gap between the witness' initial intent and the historian's final discovery lies in the historian's ability to detect distortions, assumptions, discrepancies, and misperceptions through a critical reading of the evidence." James Wilkinson, "A Choice of Fictions: Historians, Memory, and Evidence," *PMLA* 111, no. 1 (1996): 85.

36. See, for example, *Lockett v. Ohio*, 438 U.S. 586, 605-05 (1978) (plurality opinion).

37. Robert Gordon, "Undoing Historical Injustice," in *Justice and Injustice in Law and Legal Theory*, ed. Austin Sarat and Thomas Kearns (Ann Arbor: University of Michigan Press, 1996), 1.

38. Gordon, "Undoing Historical Injustice," 1.

39. Gordon, "Undoing Historical Injustice," 1.

40. Gordon, "Undoing Historical Injustice," 2.

41. 481 U.S. 279 (1987). Patricia Ewick and Susan Silbey argue that *McCleskey* was a case in which the Supreme Court resisted a broad agency interpretation in favor of a "legalist" approach. Ewick and Silbey, "Subversive Stories and Hegemonic Tales: Toward a Sociology of Narrative," *Law & Society Review* 29, no. 2 (1995): 215–17.

42. Gordon, "Undoing Historical Injustice," 2–3.

43. Sarat, "Speaking of Death," 40.

44. Stephen L. Carter, "When Victims Happen to Be Black," *Yale Law Journal* 97, no. 3 (February 1988): 426–27.

45. See, for example, Stuart Scheingold, *The Politics of Rights: Lawyers, Public Policy, and Political Change* (New Haven, Conn.: Yale University Press, 1974). For criticism of those who focus solely on the immediate efficacy of politically engaged lawyering, see Michael McCann and Helena Silverstein, "The 'Lure of Litigation' and Other Myths about Movement Lawyers in the United States," in *Cause Lawyering*, ed. Sarat and Scheingold, n.p.

46. Drucilla Cornell, "Post-Structuralism, the Ethical Relation, and the Law," *Cardozo Law Review* 9, no. 6 (August 1988): 1587–1628.

47. For discussion of the linkage between the creation of memory and particular sites, see Wilkinson, "A Choice of Fictions," 87. As Wilkinson puts it, "while the site (defined in the broadest sense) remains constant, memory does not."

48. The quotations in this section are derived from in-person interviews I conducted with forty death penalty lawyers in ten states from all regions of the country. The interviews took place between 1993 and 1995. Some of the lawyers I interviewed practiced in practice firms or in public interest settings, but most were employed by federally funded Capital Defense

Resource Centers. Interviews were from one to three hours in length. In order to protect the confidentiality of my respondents, I provide only minimal descriptive information about them.

49. Louis O. Mink, "The Autonomy of Historical Understanding," *History & Theory* 5, no. 1 (1966): 24, 33.

50. See Balkin, "Being Just with Deconstruction," 398.

51. Concerning the work of death penalty lawyers, David Bruck suggests that "this phase in our history will not last forever. We will regain faith in our ability to address our problems as a society, and our sense of shared responsibility and of shared destiny as a people. And as we do, our country's enthusiasm for the death penalty will crest, subside, and disappear." Bruck, "Does the Death Penalty Matter?" *Reconstruction* 1, no. 1 (1991): 35, 39.

52. Here, they take instruction from the late Justice Thurgood Marshall, who, when confronted with evidence of widespread public endorsement of capital punishment, argued that "whether a punishment is cruel and unusual depends, not on whether its mere mention 'shocks the conscience and sense of justice of the people,' but on whether people who were fully informed as to the purposes of the penalty and its liabilities would find the penalty shocking, unjust, and unacceptable." *Furman v. Georgia*, 408 U.S. 238, 361 (1972) (Marshall, J., concurring). If they were given such information, Marshall believed, "the great mass of citizens would conclude . . . that the death penalty is immoral and therefore unconstitutional." 408 U.S. 238, 363.

53. The reference is to Justice Blackmun's change of heart on the death penalty. See *Callins v. Collins*, 114 S. Ct. 1127, 1128 (1994) (Blackmun, J., dissenting from denial of certiorari).

CHAPTER 3

This chapter was previously published in the *Albany Law Review* 54, no. 501 (1990). Reprinted with permission.

1. Bureau of Justice Statistics, U.S. Department of Justice, *Capital Punishment 1989* (Washington, D.C.: U.S. Government Printing Office, 1990), 4. The thirty-six states are Alabama, Arizona, Arkansas, California, Colorado, Connecticut, Delaware, Florida, Georgia, Idaho, Illinois, Indiana, Kentucky, Louisiana, Maryland, Mississippi, Missouri, Montana, Nebraska, Nevada, New Hampshire, New Jersey, New Mexico, North Carolina, Ohio, Oklahoma, Oregon, Pennsylvania, South Carolina, South Dakota, Tennessee, Texas, Utah, Virginia, Washington, and Wyoming.

2. *Capital Punishment 1989*, 8–9. The following states executed at least one person between 1976 and 1989: Alabama, Florida, Georgia, Indiana, Louisiana, Mississippi, Missouri, Nevada, North Carolina, South Carolina, Texas, Utah, and Virginia.

3. See Federal Bureau of Investigation, U.S. Department of Justice, *Uniform Crime Reports: Crime in the United States—1989* (Washington, D.C.: U.S. Government Printing Office, 1990). The total number of murders and non-negligent manslaughters in the United States in 1989 was 21,500.

4. See *Capital Punishment 1989*, 7. The number of convicts sentenced to death in 1989 was 250.

5. *Capital Punishment 1989*, 8.

6. *Capital Punishment 1989*, 7.

7. *Capital Punishment 1989*, 2. The sixteen executions were carried out by eight states: Alabama, Florida, Georgia, Mississippi, Missouri, Nevada, Texas, and Virginia.

8. Robert O. Marshall, whose death sentence was affirmed by the New Jersey Supreme Court, had his wife murdered by a contract killer for the sake of more than $1 million in insurance money. See *State v. Marshall*, 123 N.J. 1, 586 A.2d 85 (1990) and "New Jersey's High Court Upholds Death Sentence after Blocking," *New York Times*, January 25, 1991, A1. Marshall was exceptional among those sentenced to death in being a white middle-class person. Some of the death sentences overturned by the New Jersey Supreme Court concerned far more heinous murders by criminals who were not white middle-class persons.

9. California voters in 1986 refused to reelect state supreme court justice Rose Elizabeth Bird and two associate justices. "California: Top Judge Removed by Voters," *New York Times*, November 5, 1986, A27. The repeated failure of the Bird court to affirm death sentences was a major factor in the campaign to prevent reelection of justices Bird, Grodin, and Reynoso. See "Fear Stalks Death Row as the Inevitable Nears," *Los Angeles Times*, November 8, 1987, pt. 2, Metro, 1; and "Critics Try to Clip Wings of California's Justice Bird," *Chicago Tribune*, March 29, 1985, Tempo, 1.

10. For example, we do not punish those who are incapable of forming the requisite criminal intent by reason of mental disease or defect. See, for example, *N.Y. Penal Law* § 40.15 (1987).

11. These rules derive from *M'Naghten's Case*, 8 Eng. Rep. 718 (1843), and the subsequent statement in the House of Lords by Lord Chief Justice Tindall, who had presided over the case. See *M'Naghten's Case*, 59 Rev. Rep. 85, 90 (1843) (Tindall, JL.C.J.). According to Lord Justice Tindall, "[T]o establish a defense on the grounds of insanity, it must be clearly proved that, at the time of the committing of the act, the party accused was labouring under such a defect of reason, from disease of the mind, as not to know the nature and quality of the act he was doing; or, if he did know it, that he did not know he was doing what was wrong." 59 Rev. Rep. 912.

12. The Fifth Amendment, passed contemporaneously with the Eighth Amendment in 1791, authorizes depriving persons of "life, liberty, or property," if that deprivation occurs with "due process of law." U.S. Constitution, Amendment V. The Fourteenth Amendment, passed in 1868, applied an identical provision to the states. U.S. Constitution, Amendment XIV. "No state shall . . . deprive any person of life, liberty, or property, without due process of law."

13. *Trop v. Dulles*, 356 U.S. 86, 101 (1958).

14. 356 U.S. at 99.

15. Speech by John Stuart Mill on the "Capital Punishment within Prisons Bill" (April 21, 1868), reprinted in *Parliamentary Debates* 3, no. 1 (1868): 1050.

16. This idea lives on in New York, where the prison system is administered by the New York State Department of Correctional Services. See N.Y. Correctional Law § 5 (1987).

17. *Furman v. Georgia*, 408 U.S. 238, 272–73 (1972) (Brennan, J., concurring).

18. 408 U.S. at 286.

19. 408 U.S. at 291.

20. 408 U.S. at 290.

21. See G. W. F. Hegel, *Hegel's Philosophy of Right*, trans. T. M. Knox (New York: Oxford University Press, 1990), 70–71; and Immanuel Kant, *Philosophy of Law: An Exposition of the Fundamental Principles of Jurisprudence as the Science of Right*, trans. W. Hastie (New York: Kelley, 1974), 195–202.

22. Jeremy Bentham, *Works of Jeremy Bentham: Published under the Superintendence of His Executor, John Bowring*, ed. John Bowring (New York: Thoemmes, 1996), II, 501.

23. Romans 12:19.

24. Romans 13:4.

25. Thomas Jefferson, "A Bill Proportioning Crimes and Punishments in Cases Heretofore Capital," in *The Papers of Thomas Jefferson*, ed. J. P. Boyd (Princeton, N.J.: Princeton University Press, 1950), 497–98. Jefferson probably yielded to contemporary pressures. I am not certain about his personal views.

26. Albert Camus, "Reflections on the Guillotine," in *Resistance, Rebellion, and Death*, trans. Justin O'Brien (New York: Vintage, 1960), 151–53.

27. See David P. Philips, "The Deterrent Effect of Capital Punishment: New Evidence on an Old Controversy," *American Journal of Sociology* 86, no. 1 (July 1980): 139–48; David P. Phillips, "The Fluctuation of Homicides After Publicized Executions: Reply to Kobbervig, Inverarity, and Lauderdale," *American Journal of Sociology* 88, no. 1 (July 1982): 165–67; David P. Phillips and Kenneth A. Bollen, "Same Time, Last Year: Selective Data Dredging for Negative Findings," *American Sociological Review* 50, no. 3 (July 1985): 364–71.

28. See Stack, "Publicized Executions and Homicides, 1950–1980," *American Sociological Review* 52, no. 4 (August 1987): 532–40.

29. See Isaac Ehrlich, "The Deterrent Effect of Capital Punishment: A Question of Life and Death," *American Economic Review* 65, no. 3 (June 1975): 397–417.

30. Horton was convicted of first-degree murder and armed robbery in Massachusetts in 1978 and sentenced to life imprisonment without parole. See *Commonwealth v. Horton*, 376 Mass. 380, 381, 680 N.E.2d 687, 690 (1978); "Study Says 53,000 Got Prison Furloughs in '87, and Few Did Harm," *New York Times*, October 12, 1988, A23. He subsequently escaped from a work furlough program there and traveled to Maryland, where he attacked a couple and raped the wife. See "Willie Horton & The Making of an Election Issue," *Washington Post*, October 28, 1988, D1.

31. See Ehrlich, "The Deterrent Effect of Capital Punishment."

32. Ehrlich, "The Deterrent Effect of Capital Punishment," 414.

33. Stephen K. Layson, "Homicide and Deterrence: A Reexamination of the United States Time-Series Evidence," *Southern Economic Journal* 52, no. 1 (July 1985): 68–89, especially 80.

34. For a defense, see Isaac Ehrlich, "Deterrence: Evidence and Inference," *Yale Law Journal* 85, no. 1 (November 1975): 209–27; Isaac Ehrlich and Randall Mark, "Fear of Deterrence: A Critical Evaluation of the 'Report of the Panel on Research on Deterrent and Incapacitative Effects,'" *Journal of Legal Studies* 6, no. 1 (June 1977): 293–316.

35. The law of diminishing returns applies to more of the same disincentives (e.g., more years of prison) but not to a qualitatively different disincentive such as execution.

36. Approximately 2 percent of all persons convicted of murder in 1986 were sentenced to death, with those sentences divided equally between whites and blacks. Bureau of Justice Statistics, U.S. Department of Justice, *Profile of Felons Convicted in State Courts, 1986* (Washington, D.C.: U.S. Government Printing Office, 1990), 1.

37. There were 297 admissions to death row in 1986, of whom 55.2 percent were white and 41.4 percent were black. Bureau of Justice Statistics, U.S. Department of Justice, *Capital Punishment 1986* (Washington, D.C.: U.S. Government Printing Office, 1986), 6 (table 5).

38. *Capital Punishment 1989*, 9 (table 9).

39. See *McCleskey v. Kemp*, 481 U.S. 279, 286–87 (1987) (summarizing the conclusions of the Baldus study).

40. The "equal protection of the laws" is not denied a person suffering capital punishment by due process simply because equally guilty others do not suffer it. It is those others (and their victims) who are denied the equal protection that the Fourteenth Amendment promises.

41. Hugo Adam Bedau and Michael L. Radelet, "Miscarriages of Justice in Potentially Capital Cases," *Stanford Law Review* 40, no. 1 (1987): 21–179, especially 72–74.

42. See Stephen J. Markman and Paul G. Cassell, "Protecting the Innocent: A Response to the Bedau–Radelet Study," *Stanford Law Review* 41, no. 1 (1988): 121–60.

43. Hugo Adam Bedau and Michael L. Radelet, "The Myth of Infallibility: A Reply to Markman and Cassell," *Stanford Law Review* 41, no. 1 (1988): 161–70, especially 164.

44. The attitude of abolitionists to the marginal deterrent effect of capital punishment is puzzling. They go out of their way to deny it. Yet, when asked whether, if such an effect were shown—if each execution would reduce the homicide rate by one hundred cases annually— they would favor executions, prominent abolitionists, such as Hugo Adam Bedau and Ramsay Clark, answer with a resonant no. I conclude that, somehow, the life of a hundred innocents, who, *ex hypothesi*, would be spared by the execution of one murderer, is worth less to these abolitionists than the execution of that murderer.

45. See Jeffrey Reiman and Ernest van den Haag, "On the Common Saying That It Is Better That Ten Guilty Persons Escape Than That One Innocent Person Suffer: Pro and Con," *Social, Philosophy & Policy* 7, no. 2 (Spring 1990): 226–48, especially 240–48.

46. The New Jersey state legislature reinstated the death penalty for murder in 1982. *N.J. Stat. Ann.* § 2C: 11-3 (West 1982 & Supplement 1990); Leigh B. Bienen, Neil Alan Weiner, Deborah W. Denno, Paul D. Allison, and Douglas Lane Mills, "The Reimposition of Capital Punishment in New Jersey: The Role of Prosecutorial Discretion," *Rutgers Law Review* 41, no. 1 (Fall 1988): 27–372, especially 66; Leigh B. Bienen, Neil Alan Weiner, Paul D. Allison, and Douglas Lane Mills, "The Reimposition of Capital Punishment in New Jersey: Felony Murder Cases," *Albany Law Review* 54, nos. 3/4 (1990): 709–817 (discussing the New Jersey Supreme Court's review of death sentences in felony murder cases).

47. *State v. Marshall*, 123 N.J. at 1, 586 A.2d at 85.

CHAPTER 4

1. William Shakespeare, *Julius Caesar*, Act III, scene 1, ll. 254–62, in *The Works of William Shakespeare* (New York: Oxford University Press, 1904), 596.

2. Max Weber, "Selections from *Politics as a Vocation*," in *The Quest for Justice: Readings in Political Ethics*, 3d ed., ed. Leslie G. Rubin and Charles T. Rubin (Needham Heights, Mass.: Ginn Custom, 1992), 273–83.

3. For more on the rule of law, see, for example, H. L. A. Hart, *Law, Liberty, and Morality* (New York: Vintage, 1961), and H. L. A. Hart, *The Concept of Law* (Oxford: Oxford University Press, 1963).

4. Quoted in Andrew Heywood, *Political Ideas and Concepts: An Introduction* (New York: St. Martin's, 1994), 108.

5. Stephen B. Bright, "The Politics of Capital Punishment: The Sacrifice of Fairness for Executions," in *America's Experiment with Capital Punishment*, ed. James A. Acker, Robert M. Bohm, and Charles S. Lanier (Durham, N.C.: Carolina Academic Press, 1998), 122.

6. Thomas Hobbes, *The Leviathan*, ed. Herbert W. Schneider (Indianapolis: Bobbs-Merrill, 1958), 210.

7. Edward S. Corwin, "The 'Higher Law' Background of American Constitutional Law," in *Classic Readings in American Politics*, 3d ed., ed. Pietro S. Nivola and David H. Rosenbloom (New York: St. Martin's, 1999), 437.

8. For a detailed discussion of the Nazi argument that soldiers merely carried out the orders of the regime in accordance with the Fuhrer principle and therefore they should be relieved of responsibility for their individual actions (or at least their sentences should be mitigated), see Ann Tusa and John Tusa, *The Nuremberg Trial* (New York: Atheneum, 1986), 86–88.

9. Laurence Berns, "Thomas Hobbes, 1588–1679," in *History of Political Philosophy*, 2d ed., ed. Leo Strauss and Joseph Cropsey (Chicago: University of Chicago Press, 1972), 370–94, and Robert A. Goldwin, "John Locke, 1632–1704," in *History of Political Philosophy*, ed. Strauss and Cropsey, 451–86. Hobbes's and Locke's general influence on the Founders is well documented, although their influence on the colonials' death penalty views is not nearly as well known. Yet, for example, Thomas Jefferson's support for the death penalty sounds remarkably similar to Hobbes's and Locke's perspectives, although Jefferson also discussed the means for administering the penalty in some detail (including gibbeting and dissection for some crimes). Thomas Jefferson, *Notes on the State of Virginia*, ed. William Peden (Chapel Hill: University of North Carolina Press, 1982), 144–45.

10. In Hobbes's words, people create a regime, which he called a "commonwealth," when "one person, of whose acts a great multitude, by mutual covenants one with another, have made themselves every one the author, to the end he may use strength and means of them all as he shall think expedient for their peace and common defense. And he that carries this person is called 'sovereign' and said to have 'sovereign power'; and everyone besides, his 'subject'" (emphases omitted). Hobbes, *Leviathan*, 143.

11. In *Leviathan*, Hobbes defined a crime as "a sin consisting in the committing, by deed or word, of that which is judged by the same authority to be a transgression of the law; to that end that the will of men may thereby be better disposed to obedience." Hobbes, *Leviathan*, 230.

12. Hobbes defined a punishment as "an evil inflicted by public authority on him that has done or omitted that which is judged by the same authority to be a transgression of the law; to the end that the will of men may thereby the better be disposed to obedience." Hobbes, *Leviathan*, 243.

13. Hobbes, *Leviathan*, 245.

14. Hobbes, *Leviathan*, 245.

15. Hobbes, *Leviathan*, 244.

16. The quotations in this paragraph are found in John Locke, "The Second Treatise of Civil Government: An Essay Concerning the True Original, Extent, and End of Civil Government," in *Two Treatises of Government*, ed. Thomas I. Cook (New York: Hafner, 1947), II, 124–25; emphasis in original.

17. Locke, "The Second Treatise of Civil Government," II, 126.

18. Locke, "The Second Treatise of Civil Government," II, 126.

19. Locke, "The Second Treatise of Civil Government," XIX, 235.

20. Fyodor Dostoyevsky, *The Brothers Karamazov* (New York: Airmont, 1966), 223–39.

21. Dostoyevsky, *The Brothers Karamazov*, 226.

22. Dostoyevsky, *The Brothers Karamazov*, 226.

23. Dostoyevsky, *The Brothers Karamazov*, 230.

24. Dostoyevsky, *The Brothers Karamazov*, 232.

25. Dostoyevsky, *The Brothers Karamazov*, 234.

26. Dostoyevsky, *The Brothers Karamazov*, 237.

27. John Stuart Mill, *On Liberty*, ed. Alburey Castell (Arlington Heights, Ill.: AHM, 1947), 117–18.

28. Michel Foucault, *Discipline and Punish: The Birth of the Prison* (New York: Vintage, 1995).

29. Foucault, *Discipline and Punish*, 14.

30. Foucault, *Discipline and Punish*, 16.

31. Michel Foucault, "The Body of the Condemned (from *Discipline and Punish*)," in *The Foucault Reader*, ed. Paul Rabinow (New York: Pantheon, 1984), 171.

32. Questions about whether a person owes a duty to the sovereign first and foremost or whether a "higher" duty to conscience or God or "natural law" supersedes civic responsibility have existed since antiquity. See, for example, Sophocles, "Antigone," in *The Oedipus Cycle*, trans. and ed. Dudley Fitts and Robert Fitzgerald (New York: Harcourt Brace Jovanovich, 1977), 183–238; St. Augustine, *City of God*, trans. M. Dodd (Edinburgh: Clark, 1872); and Hobbes, *Leviathan*, discussed previously.

33. J. Michael Martinez, "Law versus Ethics: Reconciling Two Concepts of Public Service Ethics," *Administration & Society* 29, no. 6 (January 1998): 690–722, especially 691–94, reprinted in *Ethics and Character: The Pursuit of Democratic Virtues*, ed. William D. Richardson, J. Michael Martinez, and Kerry R. Stewart (Durham, N.C.: Carolina Academic Press, 1998), 107–39, especially 108–11.

34. Lloyd Steffen, *Executing Justice: The Moral Meaning of the Death Penalty* (Cleveland, Ohio: Pilgrim, 1998), 3.

35. Some proponents of capital punishment might argue that the effectiveness of the penalty cannot be separated from a discussion of "just executions" because an obviously ineffective capital punishment loses its moral force (and resembles little more than state-sanctioned murder) as a "just" act. Still, because the question of whether capital punishment serves as an effective deterrent as a matter of law and social science often degenerates into a "battle of the experts" who argue over the meaning of statistics on crime and recidivism, for the purposes of this discussion it will be helpful to make an artificial distinction, if for no other reason than to examine the question of whether the sovereign ought to have the power to impose the death penalty or not serves its intended purpose. We will return to the question of whether capital punishment can be imposed free of bias and whether deterrence is philosophically justifiable at the conclusion of this chapter.

36. The famous passage that contains this language is found in Exodus 21:22–25: "If, when men come to blows, they hurt a woman who is pregnant and she suffers a miscarriage, though she does not die of it, the man responsible must pay the compensation demanded of him by the woman's master; he shall hand it over after arbitration. But should she die, you shall give life for life, eye for eye, tooth for tooth, hand for hand, foot for foot, burn for burn, wound for wound, stroke for stroke." Sister Helen Prejean, the Catholic nun who wrote the popular book *Dead Man Walking*, argues that this passage often is misinterpreted by death penalty proponents because they take it out of context. The Old Testament was written at a time when women were considered property of their fathers and husbands. Moreover, the comparatively primitive societies of that time did not have a penal system with institutions and correctional facilities that might allow for a more humane treatment of offenders. Thus,

many crimes were punishable by death, including sorcery (Ex 22:18; Lev 20–27), contempt of parents (Ex 21:15, 17; Lev 24:17), profaning the Sabbath (Ex 31:14), and homosexuality (Lev 20:13), among others. The moral requirements of our society cannot be compared adequately with the needs of a different time because "no person with common sense would dream of appropriating such a moral code today." Society has evolved too much "over the three thousand or so years since biblical times and no longer consider such exaggerated and archaic punishments appropriate." Helen Prejean, "The Death Penalty Is Morally Unjust," in *The Death Penalty: Opposing Viewpoints*, ed. Paul A. Winters (San Diego: Greenhaven, 1997), 57. According to commentator Glen H. Stassen, people often confuse the purpose of the Old Testament passage because they consider it out of its historical context. "The Old Testament rule of retaliation—a life for a life, an eye for an eye, a tooth for a tooth (Ex 21:24, 25)—is intended not to require vengeance, but to limit it." In the context of antiquity, often a crime was paid for by a multi-fold punishment. If an offender caused someone to lose an eye or killed someone, a number of people in the offender's family or tribe was killed in retaliation. "By specifying a kind of reciprocity for crimes, Exodus is not approving of the harshness of capital punishment; it is limiting the harshness of other, more brutal criminal codes." Glen H. Stassen, "Biblical Teaching on Capital Punishment," in *Capital Punishment*, ed. Stassen, 121.

37. John Rawls, *A Theory of Justice* (Cambridge, Mass.: Belknap, 1971), 7.

38. John Stuart Mill, "Society Must Retain the Death Penalty for Murder," in *The Death Penalty*, ed. Winters, 28.

39. For example, the Code of the Covenant (Ex 20:22–23 to 23:19) provides a litany of capital offenses. The Code of Deuteronomy (Dt 12:1–26:19) lists numerous requirements for strict adherence to God's law. Otherwise, "The Lord will make the rain of your land powder and dust; from heaven it shall come down upon you until you are destroyed" (Dt 28:24). In Leviticus 24:17, the passage is explicit: "He who kills a man shall be put to death."

40. The code is discussed at length in Edwin M. Good, "Capital Punishment and Its Alternatives in Ancient Near Eastern Law," *Stanford Law Review* 19, no. 2 (May 1967): 947–77.

41. "The Death Penalty Will Discourage Crime (1701)," in *The Death Penalty*, ed. Winters, 18.

42. Robert E. Crowe, "The Argument of the State's Attorney," in Maureen McKernan, *The Amazing Crime and Trial of Leopold and Loeb* (Birmingham, Ala.: Notable Trials Library, 1989), 314.

43. Robert E. Crowe, "Capital Punishment is a safeguard for Society," in *The Death Penalty*, ed. Winters, 42.

44. Ronald Radosh and Joyce Milton, *The Rosenberg File: A Search for the Truth* (New York: Holt, Rinehart & Winston, 1983), 450–51.

45. For more detail than is possible here, see, for example, Hugo Adam Bedau, *The Case against the Death Penalty* (Washington, D.C.: American Civil Liberties Union, Capital Punishment Project, 1992); Death Penalty Information Center, *Killing Justice: Government Misconduct and the Death Penalty* (Washington, D.C.: Author, 1992); and Donald Thomas, *Hanged in Error?* (London: Hale, 1994).

46. Plato, *The Republic*, trans. Allan Bloom (New York: Basic Books, 1968), Book I, 7.

47. Plato, *The Republic*, Book I, 13.

48. Plato, *The Republic*, Book I, 13. If one disregards Plato's religious views, this partial definition of justice as never harming anyone sounds similar to the Christian idea of "turning the other cheek," as discussed in the New Testament.

49. Quoted in Prejean, "The Death Penalty Is Morally Unjust," 58.

50. The quote can be found in Carolyn Thompson, "McVeigh Admits Role in Attack to Authors; New Book Details Motive in Bombing," *Atlanta Journal & Constitution*, March 29, 2001, A3. The "new book" referred to in Thompson's article was Lou Michel and Dan Herbeck, *American Terrorist: Timothy McVeigh and the Oklahoma City Bombing* (New York: Regan, 2001), published in April 2001, approximately two months before McVeigh's execution by lethal injection in Terre Haute, Indiana, on June 11, 2001. See also Walter Berns, "Where Are the Death Penalty Critics Today?" *Wall Street Journal*, June 11, 2001, A22, and Dorothy Rabinowitz, "Finale in Terre Haute," *Wall Street Journal*, June 12, 2001, A22.

51. For a succinct discussion of Utilitarianism and theories of punishment, see also James Rachels, *The Elements of Moral Philosophy*, 3d ed. (Boston: McGraw-Hill 1999), 135–38.

52. Mill's argument is summarized in detail in Steffen, *Executing Justice*, 51–57.

53. Steffen, *Executing Justice*, 53.

54. Utilitarianism fails to recognize that although "like cases should be treated alike" in the sense that no one should enjoy favoritism before the law, individual circumstances may be so dire that justice requires unequal treatment so that the well-to-do cannot always triumph at the expense of the least-advantaged. In other words, justice sometimes requires that we recognize the moral distinction between persons and their preferences. Rawls, *A Theory of Justice*, 187. See also "Part I: Major Approaches," in *Justice and Economic Distribution*, 2d ed., ed. John Arthur and William H. Shaw (Englewood Cliffs, N.J.: Prentice Hall, 1991), 11–12.

55. See, for example, J. Michael Martinez and Kerry R. Stewart, "Ethics, Virtue, and Character Development," in *Ethics and Character: The Pursuit of Democratic Virtues*, ed. William D. Richardson, J. Michael Martinez, and Kerry R. Stewart (Durham, N.C.: Carolina Academic Press, 1998), 38–41.

56. Thucydides, "Selections from *The War of the Peloponnesians and the Athenians*," in *The Quest for Justice: Readings in Political Ethics*," 3d ed., ed. Leslie G. Rubin and Charles T. Rubin (Needham Heights, Mass.: Ginn Custom, 1992), 31.

57. Ernest van den Haag, whose reprinted article is found in chapter 3 of this collection, is a well-known supporter of capital punishment on philosophical grounds. He has taken issue with the argument against deterrence many times. First, he has argued that as an empirical question, deterrence can be tested, but such experiments "are seldom practical, feasible, or conclusive." As for the philosophical argument, he has written that "deterrence is not part of the moral aim of justice," but it can be justified "as an important instrumental purpose of punishment" because, although it obviously does not deter the current offender, it may deter a future one. This is difficult to test, of course, because we do not know directly—without making inferences—how many crimes were not committed that would have been committed if the death penalty were not a possible consequence. Still, the offender "is not punished merely to deter others, which would be inconsistent with justice, even if he is guilty. However, if his deserved punishment deters others, it helps to repay for the harm the crime did to the social order—to pay his 'debt to society.'" Ernest van den Haag, "Justice, Deterrence and the Death Penalty," in *America's Experiment with Capital Punishment*, ed. James R. Acker, Robert M. Bohm, and Charles S. Lanier (Durham, N.C.: Carolina Academic Press, 1998), 141. See also, for example, Ernest van den Haag, "The Death Penalty Is Not Unfair to the Guilty," in *The Death Penalty*, ed. Winters, 167–70.

The argument against deterrence often focuses on social science data. Ruth D. Peterson and William C. Bailey have argued that, "[i]n short, the empirical evidence does not support the belief that capital punishment was an effective deterrent for murder in years past. Nor is there any indication that returning to our past execution practices would have nay deterrent impact on the homicide problem." Peterson and Bailey, "Is Capital Punishment an Effective Deterrent for Murder? An Examination of the Social Science Data," in *America's Experiment with Capital Punishment*, ed. Acker et al., 177. See also James Alan Fox and Michael L. Radelet, "Persistent Flaws in Econometric Studies of the Deterrent Effect of the Death Penalty," *Loyola of Los Angeles Law Review* 23, no. 1 (Spring 1989): 29–44.

58. Nat Hentoff, "The Death Penalty Should Not Be Applied to the Retarded," in *The Death Penalty*, ed. Winters, 171–75.

59. Much ink has been spilled on this subject. See, for example, Michael Ross, "The Death Penalty Is Applied Unfairly to Blacks," in *The Death Penalty*, ed. Winters, 148–54; David Baldus, George Woolworth, David Zuckerman, and Barbara Broffitt, "In the Post-*Furman* Era: An Empirical and Legal Overview, with Recent Findings from Philadelphia," *Cornell Law Review* 83, no. 6 (1998): 1638–1770; David Baldus, George Woolworth, and Charles A. Pulaski Jr., "Reflections on the 'Inevitability' of Racial Discrimination in Capital Sentencing and the 'Impossibility' of Its Prevention, Detection, and Correction," *Washington and Lee Law Review* 51, no. 2 (Spring 1994): 359–430; David Baldus, Charles A. Pulaski Jr., and George Woolworth, "Arbitrariness and Discrimination in the Administration of the Death Penalty: A Challenge to State Supreme Courts," *Stetson Law Review* 15, no. 2 (Spring 1986): 133–261; John H. Blume, Theodore Eisenberg, and Sheri Lynn Johnson, "Post-*McCleskey* Racial Discrimination Claims in Capital Cases," *Cornell Law Review* 83, no. 6 (1998): 1771–1810; Stephen B. Bright, "Discrimination, Death, and Denial: The Tolerance of Racial Discrimination in the Infliction of the Death Penalty," *Santa Clara Law Review* 35, no. 2 (1995): 433–518; Erwin Chemerinsky, "Eliminating Discrimination in Administering the Death Penalty: The Need for the Racial Justice Act," *Santa Clara Law Review* 35, no. 2 (1995): 519–33; John C. McAdams, "Racial Disparity and the Death Penalty," *Law & Contemporary Problems* 61, no. 4 (1998): 153–70; Jeffrey J. Pokorak, "Probing the Capital Prosecutor's Perspective: Race of the Discretionary Actors," *Cornell Law Review* 83, no. 6 (1998): 1811–20; and Ronald J. Tabak, "Is Racism Irrelevant? Or Should the Fairness in Death Sentencing Act Be Enacted to Substantially Diminish Racial Discrimination in Capital Sentencing?" *New York University Review of Law and Social Change* 18, no. 3 (1990–91): 777–806.

60. Nick DiSpoldo, "The Death Penalty is Applied Unfairly to the Poor," in *The Death Penalty*, ed. Winters, 162–66.

61. Thus, Chris Gersten argues that mentally retarded persons should not be spared from the death penalty. Gersten, "The Retarded Should Not Be Exempt from the Death Penalty," in *The Death Penalty*, ed. Winters, 176–79. Stanley Rothman and Stephen Powers contend that African Americans are not unfairly sentenced to death for committing capital crimes. Rothman and Powers, "The Death Penalty is Not Unfairly Applied to Blacks," in *The Death Penalty*, ed. Winters, 155–61. As noted earlier, Ernest van den Haag argues that any offender—black or white, rich or poor—who commits a capital crime and is duly convicted has no moral basis for arguing that the imposition of the death penalty is unfair because it applied to him and not to someone else. Van den Haag's argument is along the lines of "don't do the crime if you can't do the time." Van den Haag, "The Death Penalty Is Not Unfair to the Guilty," 167–70.

62. George Orwell, "A Hanging," in *Strategies in Prose*, 4th ed., ed. Wilfred A. Ferrell and Nicholas A. Salerno (New York: Holt, Rinehart & Winston, 1978), 243.

63. Quoted in McKernan, *The Amazing Crime of Leopold and Loeb*, 213.

64. Quoted in McKernan, *The Amazing Crime of Leopold and Loeb*, 304.

65. This is Austin Sarat's point in his book *When the State Kills*. In Sarat's view, the death penalty harms the state as much as it harms the offender because executions promote feelings of vengeance and exacerbate racial divisions. Sarat, *When the State Kills: Capital Punishment and the American Condition* (Princeton, N.J.: Princeton University Press, 2001).

66. Rachels, *The Elements of Moral Philosophy*, 138.

67. In a famous passage, Kant writes that he was awakened from his "dogmatic slumbers" by reading the Utilitarian philosophy of the eighteenth century Scottish skeptic, David Hume. In Kant's view, the logical implications of Hume's hypothetical imperative were to transform ethical standards and notions of human dignity into a series of ever-changing rules with limited applicability. Martinez and Stewart, "Ethics, Virtue, and Character Development," 36–38. See also David E. Cooper, *World Philosophies: An Introduction* (Cambridge, Mass.: Blackwell, 1996), 303; and Pierre Hassner, "Immanuel Kant, 1724–1804," in *History of Political Philosophy*, 2d ed., ed. Leo Strauss and Joseph Cropsey (Chicago: University of Chicago Press, 1972), 554–93.

68. Immanuel Kant, *Fundamental Principles of the Metaphysics of Morals*, trans. T. Abbott (New York: Prometheus, 1987), 49. Sometimes the principle of the categorical imperative is misinterpreted to be a hidden consequentialist ethic, but it is not. In other words, sometimes commentators contend that Kant is asking people to think of the Golden Rule—"Do unto others as you would have them do unto you"—and consider the consequences of their actions. This misinterpretation is easy to understand because Kant stresses that people act as though their actions were universal; however, he stops short of asking individuals to consider anything beyond their duty to act. He does not ask them to calculate outcomes, as Utilitarianism would have them do.

69. This argument is summarized in Steffen, *Executing Justice*, 71.

70. Quoted in Rachels, *The Elements of Moral Philosophy*, 138.

71. Rachels, *The Elements of Moral Philosophy*, 141; emphases in original.

72. Albert Camus, "Reflections on the Guillotine," in *Resistance, Rebellion, and Death*, trans. Justin O'Brien (New York: Vintage, 1960), 176.

73. Camus, "Reflections on the Guillotine," 175.

74. Camus, "Reflections on the Guillotine," 176.

75. Camus, "Reflections on the Guillotine," 192.

76. Camus, "Reflections on the Guillotine," 197. Despite Hobbes's admonition in *Leviathan* that "the aim of punishment is not revenge but terror," Camus insists that both terror and revenge are the results when an omnipotent sovereign imposes the death penalty on citizens of the regime. Hobbes, *Leviathan*, 245.

77. Camus, "Reflections on the Guillotine," 198.

78. Camus, "Reflections on the Guillotine," 204.

79. Camus, "Reflections on the Guillotine," 234.

80. Steffen, *Executing Justice*, 139–40.

81. To this list we also might add that many other factors must be considered in capital cases. Executions increased dramatically at the end of the twentieth century as death row inmates exhausted the appeals process that had delayed their executions since the U.S. Supreme Court reinstated the death penalty in 1976. Consequently, timing becomes important in determining who lives or dies. In one highly publicized case in January 1999, Missouri governor Mel Carnahan granted executive clemency to a convicted triple-murderer, Darrell Mease, because Pope John Paul II was visiting St. Louis and asked the governor to show mercy. Two

months later, however, Governor Carnahan refused to halt the execution of another offender—a man who was convicted on questionable evidence and, based on the facts of the
case, seemed far more deserving than Mease. Not surprisingly, critics accused the governor of
playing politics with the death penalty. Carnahan, of course, denied the charge. Paul Duggan,
"To Kill or Not to Kill: Executions Are on the Rise—and So Is the Controversy Surrounding
Them," *Washington Post National Weekly Edition*, December 20–27, 1999, 31–32.

   82. As mentioned earlier, some commentators contend that "if you can't do the time, don't
do the crime." Thus, as Ernest van den Haag has argued, a guilty offender should not be allowed to take refuge in his or her race, ethnicity, or poverty as reasons to escape the death
penalty. "Their guilt is not diminished by the escape of others, nor do they deserve less punishment because others did not get the punishment they deserve. Justice involves punishment
according to what is deserved by the crime and the guilt of the criminal—regardless of
whether others guilty of the same crime escape." Van den Haag, "The Death Penalty Is Not
Unfair to the Guilty," 170. From the perspective of the guilty offender considering his punishment, van den Haag may have a point; however, from the perspective of a regime that professes to treat its citizens equitably, the unequal imposition of the death penalty owing to differences in race, ethnicity, wealth, and other factors presents a crucial moral and political
dilemma.

CHAPTER 5

This chapter was previously published in the *Journal for the Scientific Study of Religion* 31, no.
1 (1992). Reprinted with permission.

   1. Robert M. Bohm, "American Death Penalty Attitudes: A Critical Examination of Recent Evidence," *Criminal Justice and Behavior* 14, no. 3 (September 1987): 380–96.

   2. Gerhard Lenski, *The Religious Factor* (Garden City, N.Y.: Anchor, 1963), 320.

   3. Gordon W. Allport, *The Nature of Prejudice* (Cambridge, Mass.: Addison-Wesley,
1954); T. W. Adorno, Else Frankel-Brunswik, Daniel J. Levinson, and R. Nevitt Sanford, *The
Authoritarian Personality* (New York: Harper, 1950); Gordon W. Allport, "The Religious Context of Prejudice," *Journal for the Scientific Study of Religion* 5, no. 3 (Fall 1966): 447–57; Gordon W. Allport and Michael Ross, "Personal Religious Orientation and Prejudice," *Journal of
Personality and Social Psychology* 5, no. 4 (April 1967): 432–43; Richard C. Maddock and
Charles T. Kenny, "Philosophies of Human Nature and Personal Religious Orientation," *Jour-
nal for the Scientific Study of Religion* 11, no. 3 (September 1972): 277–81; Gregory M. Herek,
"Religious Orientation and Prejudice: A Comparison of Racial and Sexual Attitudes," *Person-
ality and Social Psychology Bulletin* 13, no. 1 (March 1987): 34–44; Marcel O. Ponton and
Richard L. Gorsuch, "Prejudice and Religion among Venezuelans," *Journal for the Scientific
Study of Religion* 27, no. 2 (June 1988): 260–71; C. Daniel Batson and W. Larry Ventis, *The
Religious Experience* (New York: Oxford University Press, 1982); C. Daniel Batson, "Religion
as Prosocial: Agent or Double Agent?" *Journal for the Scientific Study of Religion* 15, no. 1
(March 1976): 29–45; C. Daniel Batson and Janine Dyck Flory, "Goal-Relevant Cognitions
Associated with Helping Individuals High on Intrinsic, End Religion," *Journal for the Scien-
tific Study of Religion* 29, no. 3 (September 1990): 346–60; Sam G. McFarland, "Religious
Orientations and the Targets of Discrimination," *Journal for the Scientific Study of Religion* 28,
no. 3 (September 1989): 324–36; Lee A. Kirkpatrick and Ralph W. Hood Jr., "Intrinsic-

Extrinsic Religious Orientation: The Boon or Bane of Contemporary Psychology of Religion?" *Journal for the Scientific Study of Religion* 29, no. 4 (December 1990): 442–62.

4. Batson, "Religion as Prosocial."

5. Richard L. Gorsuch and Daniel Aleshire, "Christian Faith and Ethnic Prejudice: A Review and Interpretation of Research," *Journal for the Scientific Study of Religion* 13, no. 3 (September 1974): 281–307.

6. Ralph W. Hood Jr., "Social Psychology and Religious Fundamentalism," in *Rural Psychology*, ed. Alan W. Childs and Gary B. Milton (New York: Plenum, 1982), 169–98.

7. Dean R. Hoge and Jackson W. Carroll, "Religiosity and Prejudice in Northern and Southern Churches," *Journal for the Scientific Study of Religion* 12, no. 2 (June 1973): 181–97; Susan K. Gilmore, "Personality Differences between High and Low Dogmatism Groups of Pentecostal Believers," *Journal for the Scientific Study of Religion* 8, no. 1 (Spring 1969): 161–64.

8. McFarland, "Religious Orientations," 333.

9. Lyman Kellstedt and Corwin Smidt, "Measuring Fundamentalism: An Analysis of Different Operational Strategies," *Journal for the Scientific Study of Religion*" 30, no. 3 (September 1991): 259–78.

10. Kellstedt and Smidt, "Measuring Fundamentalism."

11. Ronald L. Johnstone, *Religion and Society in Interaction* (Englewood Cliffs, N.J.: Prentice Hall, 1975).

12. Kellstedt and Smidt, "Measuring Fundamentalism."

13. See, for example, Nancy Ammerman, *Bible Believers: Fundamentalists in the Modern World* (New Brunswick, N.J.: Rutgers University Press, 1987); Alan Peshkin, *God's Choice: The Total World of a Fundamentalist Christian School* (Chicago: University of Chicago Press, 1986); and Kellstedt and Smidt, "Measuring Fundamentalism."

14. Keith A. Roberts, *Religion in Sociological Perspective* (Belmont, Calif.: Wadsworth, 1990), 267.

15. Michael B. Lupfer, Patricia L. Hopkins, and Patricia Kelly, "An Exploration of the Attributional Styles of Christian Fundamentalists and of Authoritarians," *Journal for the Scientific Study of Religion* 27, no. 3 (1988): 389–98.

16. Lawrence S. Wrightsman, "Measurement of Philosophies of Human Nature," *Psychological Reports* 14, no. 3 (June 1964): 743–51.

17. Wayne Viney, Paula Parker-Martin, and Sandra D. H. Doten, "Beliefs in Free Will and Determinism and Lack of Relation to Punishment Rationale and Magnitude," *Journal of General Psychology* 115, no. 1 (January 1988): 15–23.

18. Jerry Falwell, "Capital Punishment for Capital Crimes," *Fundamentalist Journal* 1, no. 3 (March 1982): 8–9.

19. James Davidson Hunter, "Religion and Political Civility: The Coming Generation of American Evangelicals," *Journal for the Scientific Study of Religion* 23, no. 4 (December 1984): 364–80.

20. Robert L. Young, "Race, Conceptions of Crime and Justice, and Support for the Death Penalty," *Social Psychology Quarterly* 54, no. 1 (March 1991): 67–75.

21. E. Franklin Frazier, *The Negro Church in America* (New York: Schocken, 1974); *The Fundamental: A Testimony to the Truth*, 12 vols. (Chicago: Testimony, 1910); Milton C. Sernett, *Black Religion and American Evangelicalism* (Metuchen, N.J.: Scarecrow and the American Theological Library Association, 1975).

22. James Allan Davis and Tom W. Smith, *General Social Surveys, 1972–1989* (Storrs: Roper Center for Public Opinion Research, University of Connecticut, 1989).

23. Shelby J. Haberman, *Analysis of Qualitative Data* (New York: Academic Press, 1978); Robert S. Pindyck and Daniel L. Rubinfield, *Econometric Models and Economic Forecasts* (New York: McGraw-Hill, 1981); W. J. Dixon, *BMDP Statistical Software* (Berkeley: University of California Press, 1985).

24. Tom W. Smith, "Classifying Protestant Denomination," *GSS Technical Report No. 67* (Chicago: National Opinion Research Center, 1986).

25. Davis and Smith, *General Social Surveys*, 168.

26. Davis and Smith, *General Social Surveys*, 406.

27. Davis and Smith, *General Social Surveys*, 406.

28. Roger W. Stump, "Regional Migration and Religion Commitment in the U.S.A.," *Journal for the Scientific Study of Religion* 23, no. 3 (September 1984): 292–303.

29. Young, "Race, Conceptions of Crime and Justice, and Support for the Death Penalty."

30. Sernett, *Black Religion and Evangelicalism*.

CHAPTER 6

1. For a close and thoughtful reading of scriptural passages related to capital punishment and Jesus' teaching on social relations, see Glen H. Stassen's chapter, "Deliverance from the Vicious Cycles of Murder," later in this book (chapter 8). That chapter is, in my opinion, sufficient to answer any pro–capital punishment position that presumes to have the weight of scripture behind it. Rather than repeat the careful exegesis done there, I will explore theological arguments—each biblically based in its own way—that have been raised within the history of the Christian tradition. Stassen's analysis of Scripture, my analysis of several dominant threads of the Christian tradition, and the theological arguments we both raise should be understood as building upon each other, strengthening our case as a whole.

2. James J. Megivern's book *The Death Penalty: An Historical and Theological Survey* (New York: Paulist, 1997) is an excellent treatment of the history of capital punishment and the church, being especially strong in setting the historical context for the various positions taken by theologians throughout the ages. Its weakness, such as it has one, is not taking sufficient time to set those positions in their theological context. St. Thomas Aquinas, for example, sets questions about capital punishment within the context of a larger concern for the virtue of justice, which is, itself, only made coherent through Thomas's earlier and more foundational description of what it means to be human and in community. At that level, the value of human life among all embodied creatures is uniquely and strongly affirmed.

3. These statements are helpfully collected in Gardner C. Hanks, *Against the Death Penalty: Christian and Secular Arguments against Capital Punishment* (Scottdale, Pa.: Herald, 1997), 147–70.

4. *Prima facie norms* are those norms that apply all other things being equal but that may be overridden in exceptional cases. In such exceptional instances, prima facie norms still exert a pull toward their moral center. For example, if I believe in the prima facie norm of promise keeping and I promise to meet someone at 3:00, but on my way to that meeting I stop to assist a motorist injured in a car accident that I witness—in the process breaking my promise—the norm still exerts a moral pull such that I have the obligations to call ahead explaining and apologizing for my tardiness, to try to get to my meeting as soon as I can once I am not needed at the site of the accident, to reschedule that meeting as necessary, and so forth.

5. "Protestant Pastors Support Death Penalty," *The Christian Century* 117.26 (September 27–October 4, 2000): 948–49.

6. To say that I am developing a theological argument is to distinguish my argument from at least two other types of arguments—namely, those arguments that are principally philosophical, legal, or sociological (I leave it for other scholars in this book to make those arguments), and those that are often called "biblical arguments." By and large, biblical arguments turn around a particular set of texts and a particular interpretation of those texts. Where there are disagreements about which texts matter and how to read them, biblical arguments fail to do much more than reveal the variety of voices within scripture and contemporary interpreters. Indeed, shorn of a larger theological perspective, these disagreements manage to be simultaneously interminable and mind numbing.

This is not to say that the Bible is of peripheral importance to my argument or that all readings of this formative text are equal. It isn't and they aren't. It is simply to reaffirm the classic conviction that the Bible is sufficiently complex to warrant careful and thoughtful interpretation, and that such interpretation necessarily involves questions larger than "What does the Bible say?"

Nor is it to say that I will avoid reference to philosophy, law, or the social sciences. These disciplines are important and they make arguments that need to be taken seriously no matter who is reading them. It is, however, to say that I will incorporate them as they help me clarify a position that would be incomplete without reference to God and God's will and actions in the world.

7. William Stacy Johnson and John Leith, *Reformed Reader: A Sourcebook in Christian Theology,* vol. 1 (Louisville: Westminster/John Knox, 1993), xv.

8. Romans 10:9. I will rely on the New Revised Standard Version (NRSV) translation when I cite Scripture.

9. Romans 8:18–23.

10. For more extensive treatments of the notions of discernment, fit, response, and "command and enable" than I've sketched out here, see H. Richard Niebuhr's *The Responsible Self: An Essay in Christian Moral Philosophy* (San Francisco: HarperSanFrancisco, 1963); and James M. Gustafson, *Ethics from a Theocentric Perspective* (Chicago: University of Chicago Press, 1981).

11. Ernest van den Haag, "The Collapse of the Case against Capital Punishment," *Moral Issues and Christian Response,* 6th ed., ed. Paul T. Jersild et al. (Fort Worth, Tex.: Harcourt Brace College, 1998), 257.

12. Van den Haag, "Collapse," 258.

13. Van den Haag, "Collapse," 259, 258, respectively. Stephen Nathanson challenges van den Haag's assertion that arbitrary administration of the death penalty is irrelevant to questions about its justice. He argues that both arbitrariness and systematic discrimination in applying the death penalty unjustly favor those who are not executed, and that such an injustice is as bad as or worse than the injustice van den Haag sees in abolishing the death penalty, since it makes the severity of the punishment contingent on criteria that are immaterial to the acts for which the death penalty is sought. Van den Haag, in turn, responds that not punishing the guilty is less just than punishing only some of the guilty. Neither, however, moves much beyond the debate over where the greater injustice occurs. See Stephen Nathanson, "Does It Matter If the Death Penalty Is Arbitrarily Administered?" *Punishment: A Philosophy and Public Affairs Reader,* ed. A. John Simmons et al. (Princeton, N.J.: Princeton University Press, 1995), 308–23; and Ernest van den Haag, "Refuting Reiman and Nathanson," in *Punishment,* ed. Simmons et al., 324–35.

14. Van den Haag, "Collapse," 258.

15. Van den Haag, "Refuting Reiman and Nathanson," 329.

16. By "conclusive," I do not mean convincing, since both sides of the deterrence debate have evidence that is convincing to at least some. Instead, I mean evidence that is sufficiently compelling that all sides of the debate would agree with its conclusions.

17. Walter Berns, "The Morality of Anger," in *Punishment and the Death Penalty: The Current Debate*, ed. Robert M. Baird and Stuart E. Rosenbaum (Amherst, Mass.: Prometheus, 1995), 151; italics mine.

18. Berns, "The Morality of Anger," 152.

19. Berns, "The Morality of Anger," 152.

20. In his 1879 papal statement *Aeterni Patris*, Pope Leo XIII decreed that "the golden wisdom of St. Thomas" should be spread "far and wide in the defense and beauty of the Catholic faith," and, therefore, that all Roman Catholic seminaries should base their education on the writings of Thomas Aquinas. That statement would directly pertain to the Roman Catholic educational system up to the eve of the Second Vatican Council (1963–1965); it still indirectly pertains today. See Leo XIII, *Aeterni Patris, One Hundred Years of Thomism*, ed. Victor B. Brezik, C.S.B. (Houston: Center for Thomistic Studies, 1981), 195.

21. For more detailed analysis of Thomas's thought and its impact on the Roman Catholic moral tradition, see John Mahoney, *The Making of Moral Theology* (New York: Oxford University Press, 1987); and John A. Gallagher, *Time Past, Time Future* (New York: Paulist, 1990).

22. Thomas Aquinas, *Summa Theologica* I-II, question 87, art. 1, trans. the Fathers of the English Dominican Province (Westminster, Md.: Christian Classics, 1981), 973. The *Summa* is broken into four sections (I, I-II, II-II, and III), each consisting of a series of questions and articles within questions. I will refer to the section, question, and article as well as the page number within this translation.

23. Thomas Aquinas, I-II, question 87, art. 8, 979.

24. While this latter purpose opens up the possibility of using capital punishment in an expiatory way—that is, to satisfy the blood lust of a society that would otherwise release it through further criminal activity—it has seldom, if ever, been taken in that way. Indeed, once Thomas's thoughts on capital punishment are restricted only to those instances I have described, the way is clear to compare his conclusions to those of the contemporary Roman Catholic Church.

Since at least 1968's *Humanae Vitae*, the Catholic Church has emphasized persons and their rights, therein setting up a tension between the type of expiatory death Thomas allows and the refusal to treat any person as an object used toward some other end. Thus, when the U.S. Catholic bishops produced their 1980 "Statement on Capital Punishment," they walked a thin line between leaving open the possibility of capital punishment in theory and rejecting it in practice:

> We grant that the need for retribution does indeed justify punishment. . . But we maintain that *this need does not require nor does it justify* taking the life of the criminal, even in cases of murder. . . .
>
>   We believe that *in the conditions of contemporary American society,* the legitimate purposes of punishment do not justify the imposition of the death penalty.

See "U. S. Bishop's Statement on Capital Punishment" (Washington D.C.: United States Catholic Conference, 1980), 4, 5; emphasis mine.

This conclusion is especially pertinent, given Thomas's explicit emphasis on the good of the community over that of the individual in the case of capital punishment. Indeed, in spite of his argument that the community is more important than the individual, Thomas's language in regard to capital punishment emphasizes that the only legitimate danger to the community that might mandate capital punishment is from the individual who must be punished, not from any form of social upheaval within the community.

25. Thomas Aquinas, *Summa Theologica*, II-II, question 64, art. 2 (Westminster, Md.: Christian Classics, 1981), 1461.

26. Such detailed work has been done by, among others, Brian Calvert, "Aquinas and the Death Penalty," *American Journal of Jurisprudence* 37 (1992): 259–81, and Megivern, *The Death Penalty*, 111–21.

27. For Thomas's position on killing in self-defense, see Thomas Aquinas, II-II, question 64, art. 7, 1465.

28. See Thomas Aquinas, I-II, question 95, art. 2: 1014–15.

29. Thomas Aquinas, II-II, question 64, art. 3, 1462.

30. Thomas Aquinas, II-II, question 64, art. 4, 1462; italics taken from the text.

31. This distinction between Thomas the political philosopher and Thomas the theologian is the basis for the conclusion many commentators make that, at least in regard to capital punishment, "Thomas proceeds here more as an Aristotelian philosopher, drawing cold rationalist conclusions from a notion of natural law, than as a Christian theologian, dealing directly with the pastoral goals of the gospel." Megivern, *The Death Penalty*, 119.

32. Calvert, "Aquinas and the Death Penalty," 280.

33. Recognizing that Thomas's thought can be used to oppose capital punishment helps explain—at least in part—how the contemporary Roman Catholic Church can place Thomas's thought at the center of their theology and oppose capital punishment simultaneously.

34. John 3:17.

35. Genesis 1:27.

36. See, for example, the U.S. Catholic Bishops' Statement, 12:

> We recognize that many citizens may believe that capital punishment should be maintained as an integral part of our society's response to the evils of crime, nor is this position incompatible with Catholic tradition. We acknowledge the depth and the sincerity of their concern. We urge them to review the considerations we have offered which show both the evils associated with capital punishment and the harmony of the abolition of capital punishment with the values of the Gospel.

37. The *Church Dogmatics* is broken into four doctrines, each with several volumes, each volume with multiple sections, and each section with several subsections. Thus, for example, "*CD* III.4, § 55, 2" refers to the subsection "The Protection of Life" within section 55, "Freedom for Life," in the fourth volume of the third doctrine, "The Doctrine of Creation." I will refer to the doctrine, volume, and page number in my notes, but it may help the reader to know this nomenclature if I occasionally refer to a section or subsection.

38. See Karl Barth, *Church Dogmatics* II.2, § 36, ed. G. W. Bromiley and T. F. Torrance (Edinburgh: Clark, 1961).

39. See, for example, Barth, *CD* III.4, 335: "The freedom for life to which man is summoned by the command of God is the freedom to treat as a loan both the life of all men with his own and his own with that of all men."

40. Barth, *CD* III.4, 398.

41. Barth, *CD* III.4, 398.

42. This claim is similar to John Howard Yoder's argument that debates between Barth and those who absolutely oppose war must be understood as "in house" debates between types of pacifists, rather than between those who favor and those who oppose war. See Yoder, *Karl Barth and the Problem of War* (Nashville: Abingdon, 1970).

43. Barth, *CD* III.4, 445–46.

44. Barth, *CD* III.4, 439.

45. Barth, *CD* III.4, 441.

46. Barth, *CD* III.4, 442.

47. Barth, *CD* III.4, 442.

48. Barth, *CD* III.4, 442.

49. Barth, *CD* III.4, 443.

50. Barth, *CD* III.4, 444.

51. Barth, *CD* III.4, 444.

52. Barth, *CD* III.4, 445. In regard to capital punishment's effectiveness as a deterrent to other potential criminals, Barth also argues that there is no evidence that its presence makes for a more safe society or that its absence leads to a less safe society. He does not, however, cite any studies or statistics in defense of this argument, and I therefore raise it only in this note.

53. Barth, *CD* III.4, 445.

54. Barth, *CD* III.4, 446.

55. Barth, *CD* III.4, 446.

56. Barth, *CD* III.4, 447.

57. While the example falls short of any situation Barth might be considering, one might extrapolate toward such a situation by remembering Nelson Mandela's relationship to Apartheid South Africa while he was in prison. In this instance, one man's worth far exceeded the value of a brutal and dehumanizing racist regime. Obviously, this example differs from Barth's vision in the sense that South Africa's Apartheid leadership would have argued that my calculations are wrong when I say Mandela is worth more than that state. The point here is merely that any simple utilitarian process of weighing the worth of one against that of the many falls short of accounting for all the variables that may come into play in Barth's first condition for allowing capital punishment.

58. Barth, *CD* III.4, 448.

59. Barth, *CD* III.4, 438.

60. "[Both high treason and tyrannicide] belong in the field of warfare rather than in the field of normal judicial procedure" (Yoder, *Karl Barth and the Problem of War*, 34). For Barth's exploration of taking human life in war, see Barth, *CD* III.4, 450–70. See also Yoder, *Karl Barth*, for an extended analysis of this exploration.

61. Karl Barth, "*Barths Fragebeantwortung in Fulda,*" *Karl Barth: Gespräche, 1959–1962,* ed. Eberhard Busch (Zurich: Theologischer Verlag Zurich, *1995*), 73. My thanks to Eberhard Busch for alerting me to this text and to Margit Ernst for her assistance in helping me translate it. Any mistranslations are the result of my errors, however.

62. Barth, "*Barths Fragebeantoworyung in Fulda,*" 72.

63. The reader may have noticed that I have summarized what I believe we can learn from Barth before any discussion of listening for God through Barth. Unlike my earlier discussions of van den Haag, Berns, and Thomas Aquinas, I am in a decidedly more comfortable place in attempting to discern how God is speaking through Barth, mostly because I think he has done one of the most thoughtful jobs of placing capital punishment within a larger theological framework of any twentieth-century theologian, but partly because I agree with him. On the

one hand, this also leaves me in a more tenuous place, since it is much harder to critically examine one's own position than it is to do it to the position of someone with whom one disagrees. I hope my interrogation of his *grenzfall* cases at least reveals that I do not take Barth on face value. On the other hand, however, I continue to believe that anyone who wants to think about capital punishment theologically must contend with Barth and, in contending, will eventually be trained by his thought.

64. I use the word *liberal* here and in what follows not to describe a particular left-leaning political agenda traditionally associated with the Democratic Party and "big government" but to describe a long tradition of philosophical thought that is marked by its emphases on individual freedom, representative government, and tolerance for those whose opinions different from one's own. In this sense, *liberal* can be used to describe most, if not all, political parties in the United States.

65. Broadly speaking, John Rawls's influential books *A Theory of Justice* and *Political Liberalism* both describe such a position. See John Rawls, *A Theory of Justice* (Cambridge, Mass.: Belknap, 1971), and *Political Liberalism* (New York: Columbia University Press, 1993).

66. Michael Walzer, *Thick and Thin: Moral Argument at Home and Abroad* (Notre Dame, Ind.: University of Notre Dame Press, 1994).

67. Walzer, *Thick and Thin*, 4.

68. Walzer, *Thick and Thin*, 10.

69. Walzer, *Thick and Thin*, 2.

70. See, among others, René Girard, *Violence and the Sacred*, trans. Patrick Gregory (Baltimore: Johns Hopkins University Press, 1972).

71. James McBride, "Capital Punishment as the Unconstitutional Establishment of Religion: A Girardian Reading of the Death Penalty," *Journal of Church and State* 37 (Spring 1995): 269.

72. Brian K. Smith, "Capital Punishment and Human Sacrifice," *Journal of the American Academy of Religion* 68.1 (March 2000): 4.

73. Smith, "Capital Punishment and Human Sacrifice," 9–10.

74. Jonathan Z. Smith, quoted in Smith, "Capital Punishment and Human Sacrifice," 9.

75. Smith, "Capital Punishment and Human Sacrifice," 4.

76. See Mary Douglas, *Purity and Danger: An Analysis of the Concepts of Pollution and Taboo* (London: Routledge, 1966).

77. Smith, "Capital Punishment and Human Sacrifice," 15.

78. Smith, "Capital Punishment and Human Sacrifice," 4.

79. Smith, "Capital Punishment and Human Sacrifice," 4.

CHAPTER 7

This chapter was previously published in *Christianity Today* (October 1959). Reprinted with permission.

1. Genesis 9:4–6, Revised Standard Version.

2. Exodus 20:1–3.

3. Exodus 21:12, 14.

4. Compare Deuteronomy 17:6–7 and 19:11–13.

5. Isaiah 59:14–18.

6. Matthew 5:21–23.
7. Romans 13:2–4.
8. Romans 12:19–21.
9. Romans 13:1.
10. Matthew 6:12.
11. Matthew 5:7.
12. Matthew 10:28.

CHAPTER 8

1. David Gushee and Glen H. Stassen, *Christian Ethics as Following Jesus* (Downers Grove, Ill.: InterVarsity Press, forthcoming), especially chap. 2.

2. Howard Zehr, *Changing Lenses: A New Focus for Crime and Justice* (Scottdale, Pa.: Herald, 1980).

3. Lewis Smedes, *Mere Morality: What God Expects from Ordinary People* (Grand Rapids, Mich.: Eerdmans, 1983).

4. David Augsburger, *Caring Enough to Forgive* (Scottdale, Pa.: Herald, 1990).

5. Miroslav Volf, *Exclusion and Embrace: A Theological Exploration of Identity, Otherness, and Reconciliation* (Nashville: Abington, 1996).

6. Donald L. Shriver, *An Ethic for Enemies* (New York: Oxford University Press, 1995).

7. L. Gregory Jones, *Embodying Forgiveness* (Grand Rapids, Mich.: Eerdmans, 1995).

8. Glen H. Stassen, ed., *Capital Punishment: A Reader* (Cleveland, Ohio: Pilgrim, 1998), 62, 130, n. 21.

9. David A. Wolfe, Christine Wekerle, and Katreena Scott, *Alternatives to Violence: Empowering Youth to Develop Healthy Relationships* (Thousand Oaks, Calif.: Sage, 1997), 85.

10. Peter Benson, *A Fragile Foundation: The State of Developmental Assets among American Youth* (Minneapolis: Search Institute, 1999), 42; and Russell H. Geen and Edward Donnerstein, *Human Aggression: Theories, Research, and Implications for Social Policy* (San Diego: Academic Press, 1998), 177–78.

11. Albert J. Reiss Jr. and Jeffrey A. Roth, eds., *Understanding and Preventing Violence* (Washington, D.C.: National Academy Press, 1993), 8, 108–9.

12. Wolfe et al., *Alternatives to Violence*, 97–99.

13. Reiss and Roth, eds., *Understanding and Preventing Violence*, 3, 51, and 64. See also Ted Gurr, *Why Men Rebel* (Princeton, N.J.: Princeton University Press, 1970).

14. Reiss and Roth, eds., *Understanding and Preventing Violence*, 131–35.

15. Delbert S. Elliott, Beatrix A. Hamburg, and Kirk R. Williams, *Violence in America's Schools* (Cambridge: Cambridge University Press, 1998), 10–11, 171.

16. Robert L. Hampton, Pamela Jenkins, and Thomas P. Gullotta, eds., *Preventing Violence in America* (Thousand Oaks, Calif.: Sage, 1996), 197, 202–6.

17. Reiss and Roth, eds., *Understanding and Preventing Violence*, 275.

18. Reiss and Roth, eds., *Understanding and Preventing Violence*, 278.

19. Hampton et al., *Preventing Violence in America*, 117f.

20. Hampton et al., *Preventing Violence in America*, 122, 124.

21. See, for example, Benson, *A Fragile Foundation*.

22. David Gushee, *Righteous Gentiles of the Holocaust* (Minneapolis: Augsburg Fortress, 1994).

23. Gushee and Stassen, *Christian Ethics as Following Jesus*, chaps. 6–7.

24. Gushee and Stassen, *Christian Ethics as Following Jesus*, chap. 6.

25. In the section that follows, I am adapting parts of my "Biblical Teaching on Capital Punishment."

26. Raymond E. Brown, *The Gospel According to John*, Vol. I (Garden City, N.Y.: Doubleday, 1996), 336*ff.*

27. Lowell Erdahl, *Pro-Life/Pro-Peace* (Minneapolis: Augsburg, 1986), 114.

28. See, for example, H. Wayne House, "In Favor of the Death Penalty," in *The Death Penalty Debate*, ed. H. Wayne House and John Howard Yoder (Dallas: Word, 1991), 39–47; and Jacob J. Vellenga, "Is Capital Punishment Wrong?" in *Capital Punishment: A Reader*, ed. Glen H. Stassen (Cleveland, Ohio: Pilgrim, 1998), 131–36.

29. House, "In Favor of the Death Penalty," 61, 65.

30. House, "In Favor of the Death Penalty," 61, 65.

31. House, "In Favor of the Death Penalty," 62–63.

32. Vellenga, "Is Capital Punishment Wrong?" 132–35.

33. Smedes, *Mere Morality*, 119*f.*, and Stassen, ed., *Capital Punishment*, 129, n. 1.

34. Claus Westermann, *Genesis 1–11: A Commentary* (Minneapolis: Augsburg, 1984), 467.

35. Donald Hagner, *Matthew 14–28* (Dallas: Word, 1993), 789.

36. Henry McKeating, "The Development of the Law on Homicide in Ancient Israel," *Vetus Testamentum* 25 (1975): 61–67; and Henry McKeating, "Sanctions against Adultery in Ancient Israelite Society," *Journal for the Study of the Old Testament* 11 (1979): 58–59, 66–67.

37. James McBride, "Capital Punishment as the Unconstitutional Establishment of Religion: A Girardian Reading of the Death Penalty," in *Capital Punishment*, ed. Stassen, 182–202.

38. John Howard Yoder, "Against the Death Penalty," in *The Death Penalty Debate*, ed. House and Yoder, 144.

39. Yoder, "Against the Death Penalty," 159.

40. William H. Baker, *On Capital Punishment* (Chicago: Moody, 1973, 1985), 55*ff.*

41. Alan Culpepper, *Anatomy of the Fourth Gospel* (Philadelphia: Fortress, 1983), 161, 172.

42. Brown, *The Gospel According to John*, Vol. I, 892–93.

43. Baker, *On Capital Punishment*, 62*ff.*

44. Henlee Barnette, *Crucial Problems in Christian Perspective* (Philadelphia: Westminster, 1970), 129.

45. George Foot Moore, *Judaism in the First Centuries of the Christian Era*, Vol. II (New York: Shocken, 1971), 184–87. See also George Horowitz, *The Spirit of Jewish Law* (New York: Central Book, 1963), 165–70, 176.

46. Herbert Danby, trans., *The Mishnah* (London: Oxford University Press, 1993), 403.

47. Johannes Friedrich, Wolfgang Phlmann, and Peter Stuhlmacher, "Zur historischen Situation und Intention von rm," *Zeitschrift für Theologie und Kirche* 13 (1976): 131*ff.*

48. In addition, we might count the following passages: Matthew 5:42, 6:2, 6:19*ff.*, and 6:33; 12:7; Luke 1:52; 3:10*ff.*; 4:18; 6:20–21; 7:41*ff.*

49. Other passages include Matthew 13:24; 15:1*ff.*; 21:13; 23:23–25; 23:34; Mark 6:18; 8:15; 10:35*ff.*; 12:40; Luke 1:52; 3:5; 4:18; 13:10*ff.* Finally, Jesus' trial and crucifixion were his confrontation of massive injustice in the form of domination by religious and political authority, Jewish and Roman.

50. Walter Berns, *For Capital Punishment* (New York: Basic Books, 1979), 33*f.*

51. The following is an adaptation of Glen Stassen, "xxxx," *Sojourners* (December 2000).

52. James Megivern, *The Death Penalty: An Historical and Theological Survey* (New York: Paulist, 1997), 22.

53. Megivern, *The Death Penalty*, 46.

54. Megivern, *The Death Penalty*, 28, 45, 47, 50, 59, 138, 19*f.*

55. Megivern, *The Death Penalty*, 61, 67*f.*, 179.

56. Megivern, *The Death Penalty*, 193, 198, 271.

57. Megivern, *The Death Penalty*, 252, 289, 308, 356, 385, 392.

58. J. Gordon Melton, *The Churches Speak on Capital Punishment: Official Statements from Religious Bodies and Ecumenical Organizations* (Detroit: Gale Research, 1989).

59. Glen H. Stassen, "Biblical Teaching on Capital Punishment," in *Capital Punishment*, ed. Stassen, 119–30.

CHAPTER 9

1. John Stuart Mill, "Speech before the English Parliament in Favor of Capital Punishment," *Ethics Update*, http://ethics.acusd.edu/Mill.html, February 2001.

2. Shane Gil, "Who Was Shaka Sankofa and Why Did America Kill Him?" http://saveshaka.o-dec.com/newn/index.cfm?pID=8, March 2001. See also "Death Penalty Troubles in Texas" (editorial), *New York Times*, June 19, 2000, A18; "Due Process, Texas-Style" (editorial), *New York Times*, 21 June 2000, A22; Sara Rimer and Jim Yardley, "Pending Execution in Texas Spotlights a Powerful Board," *New York Times*, 21 June 2000, A1.

3. Jennifer L. Harry, "Death Penalty Disquiet Stirs Nations," *Corrections Today* 62, no. 7 (December 2000): 122–28, especially 126.

4. Jayson Blair, "The Nation: Death Penalty Defense; The Lawyers Live to Fight Again," *New York Times*, June 25, 2000, 4.3; and "Due Process, Texas-Style," A22. For more on the Graham case and defects in capital punishment laws owing to incompetent defense counsel, see also Frank Bruni, "Bush Stands Firm on Upholding Death Penalty," *New York Times*, June 22, 2000, A28; Frank Bruni and Jim Yardley, "With Bush Assent, Inmate is Executed," *New York Times*, June 23, 2000, A1; Dianne Clements and Dudley Sharp, "Guilty as Charged," *Wall Street Journal*, June 28, 2000, A22; Guillermo X. Garcia, "Inmate Fights Execution to the End; Courts Deny Last-Minute Civil Lawsuit," *USA Today*, June 23, 2000, 3A; David Gergen, "Death By Incompetence," *U.S. News & World Report* 128, no. 25 (June 26, 2000), 76; Kari Haskell, "One Step Farther from Death," *New York Times*, August 27, 2000, 4.3; "Irreversible Error in Texas" (editorial), *New York Times*, June 23, 2000, A22; "Letters to the Editor: The Gary Graham Defense," *Wall Street Journal*, July 19, 2000, 23.

5. James S. Liebman, Jeffrey Fagan, and Valerie West, "A Broken System: Error Rates in Capital Cases, 1973–1995" (New York: Columbia University, 2000), ii, 5; available at www.law.columbia.edu. The authors also reported the results in James Liebman, Jeffrey Fagan, Valerie West, and Jonathan Lloyd, "Capital Attrition: Error Rates in Capital Cases, 1973–1995," *Texas Law Review* 78, no. 7 (June 2000): 1839–65.

6. Liebman et al., "A Broken System," 1.

7. Liebman et al., "A Broken System," 24. See also Teresa Malcolm, "'Serious Error' Found in Death Penalty System," *National Catholic Reporter* 36, no. 33 (June 30, 2000), 8.

8. Liebman et al., "A Broken System," 25.

9. Liebman et al., "A Broken System," 129.

10. Liebman et al., "A Broken System," ii–iii.

11. Liebman et al., "A Broken System," 37.

12. Liebman et al., "A Broken System," 17.

13. "Damning Evidence Supports Deep Judicial Reform," *National Catholic Reporter* 36, no. 33 (June 30, 2000), 28.

14. Liebman et al., "A Broken System," 17.

15. "Crime and Punishment," *American Demographics* 23, no. 2 (February 2001): 24.

16. Steven Stack, "Support for the Death Penalty: A Gender Specific Model," *Sex Roles* 23, nos. 3 & 4 (August 2000): 163.

17. Kevin McDermott and Eric Stern, "Missouri Rates Well on Death Penalty Errors; Suspended Illinois System Is Average for the U.S., Study Finds," *St. Louis-Post Dispatch*, June 13, 2000, A1.

18. Donna Lyons and Michael Foote, "Capital Punishment on Trial," *State Legislatures* 26, no. 5 (May 2000): 14.

19. In 1999, the Nebraska legislature voted to place a two-year moratorium on executions, but Governor Mike Hohanns, a Republican, vetoed the measure. Afterward, the legislature decided to study the trends in state homicide cases even as the death penalty continued to be enforced. Lyons and Foote, "Capital Punishment on Trial," 14.

20. Perhaps the most famous Illinois case involved inmate Anthony Porter, who spent nearly sixteen years on death row for a double murder. He once came within two days of being executed. Porter was released when new evidence showed that he did not commit the crime for which he was convicted. The *Chicago Tribune* ran a series of articles about Porter and other death row inmates who later were found to have been wrongly convicted. Toni Locy, "Push to Reform Death Penalty Growing Advocates: Mistakes Could Shake Confidence in the System," *USA Today*, February 20, 2001, 5A.

21. David Lane, "Death Penalty Debate Touches State; Colorado's Process Every Bit as Flawed as Those in Other States," *Denver Rocky Mountain News*, July 2, 2000, 1B.

22. "United States: Murder One," *The Economist* 355, no. 8175 (June 17, 2000): 33.

23. Quoted in Liebman et al., "A Broken System," 74.

24. Liebman et al., "A Broken System," iii.

25. McDermott and Stern, "Missouri Rates Well on Death Penalty Errors," A1.

26. McDermott and Stern, "Missouri Rates Well on Death Penalty Errors," A1.

27. Lyons and Foot, "Capital Punishment on Trial," 21.

28. For more on this point, see especially Locy, "Push to Reform Death Penalty Growing Advocates," 5A.

29. Sara Rimer, "Support for a Moratorium in Execution Grows Stronger," *New York Times*, October 31, 2000, A18.

30. Early in 2001, Florida, Ohio, Utah, Virginia, and Texas were considering bills that would establish standards for routine testing of capital offenders' DNA. In the meantime, North Carolina, Alabama, and Arizona were implementing measures to improve the quality of court-appointed defense lawyers in capital cases. Arizona, Illinois, Indiana, Maryland, Nebraska, North Carolina, and Virginia were studying their capital punishment systems. Alabama, Connecticut, Kentucky, Maryland, Missouri, New Jersey, Ohio, Oklahoma, Pennsylvania, Tennessee, Texas, Virginia, and Washington were considering capital punishment moratoriums. Locy, "Push to Reform Death Penalty Growing Advocates," 5A.

31. McDermott and Stern, "Missouri Rates Well on Death Penalty Errors," A1.

32. Lane, "Death Penalty Debate Touches State," 1B.

33. "Death Penalty Moratoriums," *America Press* 182, no. 9 (March 18, 2000): 3.

34. Rimer, "Support for a Moratorium in Execution Gets Stronger," A18.

35. In addition to coauthoring the Columbia University study, Professor Liebman has written widely on the subject of crime and punishment, especially capital punishment. See, for example, James S. Liebman, "The Overproduction of Death," *Columbia Law Review* 100, no. 8 (December 2000): 2030–2156; James S. Liebman, "A Right of Citizens Abandoned," *Christian Science Monitor* 87, no. 59 (February 2, 1995), 20; and James S. Liebman and Randy Hertz, "*Brecht v. Abrahamson*: Harmful Errors in Habeas Corpus Law," *Journal of Criminal Law & Crimonology* 84, no. 4 (Winter/Spring 1994): 1109–56.

36. "Damning Evidence Supports Deep Judicial Reform," 28.

37. "United States: Murder One," 33.

38. Barry Latzer and James N. G. Cauthen, "Another Recount: Appeals in Capital Cases," *The Prosecutor* 35, no. 1 (January/February 2001): 26.

39. Latzer and Cauthen, "Another Recount," 26–27.

40. Latzer and Cauthen, "Another Recount," 28.

41. Latzer and Cauthen, "Another Recount," 25.

42. Jaime Sneider, "The Rationality Syndrome: Statistics Fail Activists," *Columbia Daily Spectator*, www.columbiaspectator.com/Opinion/article.asp?articleID=1649, February 6, 2001.

43. Sneider, "The Rationality Syndrome," 1–2.

44. Sneider, "The Rationality Syndrome," 2. The Columbia University study reported high rates of serious error in each of these states—Texas, 61 percent; Oklahoma, 100 percent; Louisiana, 77 percent; and Arkansas, 90 percent. Liebman et al., "A Broken System," 50, 57, 62.

45. Michael Rushford, "Death Penalty 'Error' Study Has Errors of Its Own," Criminal Justice Legal Foundation, www.prodeathpenalty.com/Liebman/LiebmanCJLF.htm, June 19, 2000.

46. Rushford, "Death Penalty 'Error' Study Has Errors of Its Own," 3.

47. Rushford, "Death Penalty 'Error' Study Has Errors of Its Own," 1.

48. Rushford, "Death Penalty 'Error' Study Has Errors of Its Own," 2.

49. Rushford, "Death Penalty 'Error' Study Has Errors of Its Own," 2.

50. Rushford, "Death Penalty 'Error' Study Has Errors of Its Own," 2. For more on the choices facing attorneys in capital trials, see, for example, John Gibeaut, "Deadly Choices," *ABA Journal* 87 (May 2001): 38–45.

51. Bennett A. Barylan, "A Response to Professor Liebman's 'A Broken System,'" Criminal Justice Legal Foundation, www.prodeathpenalty.com/Liebman/LIEBMAN2.htm, November 3–4, 2000.

52. David Horowitz, "Death Penalty Study: A Left-Wing Scam," Center for the Study of Popular Culture, Horowitz's Notepad, www.frontpagemag.com/horowitznotepad/2000/hn06-12-00.htm, June 12, 2000.

53. Kirk Loggins, "News Reports Misused Study's Data on Tennessee Death Penalty Appeals," *Tennessean*, www.tennessean.com/sii/00/06/13/deathdata13.shtml, June 13, 2000.

54. James S. Liebman, Jeffrey Fagan, and Valerie West, "Death Matters: A Reply to Latzer and Cauthen," *Judicature* 84, no. 2 (September–October 2000), www.lib.jjay.cuny/edu/docs/liebman.htm, 6.

55. Liebman et al., "Death Matters," 6–7.

56. Barry Latzer and James N.G. Cauthen, "The Meaning of Capital Appeals: A Rejoinder to Liebman, Fagan, and West," *Judicature* 84, no. 3 (November–December 2000): 142.

57. Latzer and Cauthen, "The Meaning of Capital Appeals," 142.

58. Latzer and Cauthen, "The Meaning of Capital Appeals," 142.

CHAPTER 10

1. *Callins v. Collins*, 510 U.S. (1994).

2. Welsh S. White, *The Death Penalty in the Nineties* (Ann Arbor: University of Michigan Press, 1991), 5.

3. White, *The Death Penalty in the Nineties*, 7–8.

4. White, *The Death Penalty in the Nineties*, 10.

5. White, *The Death Penalty in the Nineties*, 11.

6. Victoria J. Palacios, "Faith in Fantasy: The Supreme Court's Reliance on Commutation to Ensure Justice in Death Penalty Cases," *Vanderbilt University Law Review* 49, no. 1 (March 1996): 312.

7. White, *The Death Penalty in the Nineties*, 5.

8. White, *The Death Penalty in the Nineties*, 22.

9. The Supreme Court has granted six stays of execution during the current term from July 1999 to February 2000, while during its last term the Court granted only two. Ginsburg and Stevens dissent frequently when stays are denied. The Court continues to support the states over the defendants in death penalty cases by a 5–4 plurality with the majority including Rehnquist, Scalia, O'Connor, Kennedy, and Thomas. The dissenters are Stevens, Ginsburg, Souter, and Breyer.

10. Scott Pendleton, "When Innocence Gets Short Shrift," *Christian Science Monitor*, June 26, 1995.

11. Barry Scheck, Peter Neufeld, and Jim Dwyer, *Actual Innocence* (New York: Doubleday, 2000), xiv.

12. Stephen P. Garvey, Sheri Lynn Johnson, and Paul Marcus, "Correcting Deadly Confusion: Responding to Jury Inquiries in Capital Cases," *Cornell University Law School Working Paper*, www.law.cornell.edu/workingpapers/open/garvey/weeks.html, January 2000.

13. Case summaries were compiled by Northwestern University Legal Clinic's National Conference on Wrongful Convictions and the Death Penalty, www.ncwcdp.com/wrongly.html (n.d.).

14. Ronald C. Huff, Arye Rattner, and Edward Sagarin, *Convicted but Innocent: Wrongful Conviction and Public Policy* (Thousand Oaks, Calif.: Sage, 1996), 64.

15. Arlene Levinson, "Casualty of Death Row: A Survivor's Tale," *Topeka Capital Journal* 8, no. 1 (November 1998).

16. Levinson, "Casualty of Death Row."

17. Stephen B. Bright, "Counsel for the Poor: The Death Sentence Not for the Worst Crime but for the Worst Lawyer," *Yale Law Journal* 103, no. 1 (1994): 278.

18. Palacios, "Faith in Fantasy," 320.

19. James Sterngold, "Police Corruption Inquiry Expands in Los Angeles," *New York Times*, February 11, 2000.

20. *Brady v. Maryland*, 373 U.S. 83 (1963).

21. Maurice Possley and Ken Armstrong, "Prosecution on Trial in DuPage," *Chicago Tribune*, January 12, 1999.

22. Maurice Possley and Ken Armstrong, "The Flip Side of a Fair Trial," *Chicago Tribune*, January 11, 1999.

23. Possley and Armstrong, "The Flip Side of a Fair Trial."

24. Possley and Armstrong, "The Flip Side of a Fair Trial."

25. Pendleton, "When Innocence Gets Short Shrift."

26. Jennifer Gerrietts, "Anderson tries to get conviction tossed out," *Sioux Falls Argus Leader*, April 28, 2000.

27. Bob Herbert, "An Inquiry Out of Control," *New York Times*, April 24, 2000.

28. Pendleton, "When Innocence Gets Short Shrift," citing a Death Penalty Information Center study.

29. Ken Armstrong and Maurice Possley, "Break the Rules, Be Promoted," *Chicago Tribune*, January 14, 1999.

30. Anthony Meier, "Prosecutorial Immunity: Can Section 1983 Provide an Effective Deterrent to Prosecutorial Misconduct?" *Arizona State Law Journal* 30, no. 1 (Winter 1998): 1187.

31. Possley and Armstrong, "Prosecution on Trial in DuPage."

32. *Imbler v. Pachtman*, 424 U.S. 409 (1976).

33. Meier, "Prosecutorial Immunity," 1187.

34. Pendleton, "When Innocence Gets Short Shrift."

35. Ken Armstrong and Maurice Possley, "The Verdict: Dishonor," *Chicago Tribune*, January 10, 1999.

36. Pendleton, "When Innocence Gets Short Shrift."

37. *Powell v. Alabama*, 287 U.S. 45 (1932).

38. *Strickland v. Washington*, 466 U.S. 668 (1984).

39. Bright, "Counsel for the Poor," 275.

40. Bright, "Counsel for the Poor," 284.

41. Bright, "Counsel for the Poor," 285.

42. Bright, "Counsel for the Poor," 293.

43. Stephen B. Bright, "Conference: The Death Penalty in the Twenty-first Century," *American University Law Review* 45, no. 1 (December 1995).

44. Dick Thornburgh and Daniel Burton, "Incompetent Counsel Is a Significant Factor in Habeas Corpus Delay," Kentucky Department of Public Advocacy, www.dpa.state. kentucky.us/~rwheeler/thorn/thorn/archives/htm (n.d.).

45. Thornburgh and Burton, "Incompetent Counsel," n.p.

46. The "death belt" states are Alabama, Florida, Georgia, Louisiana, Mississippi, North Carolina, South Carolina, Texas, and Virginia.

47. Marcia Coyle, Fred Strasser, and Marianne Lavell, "Fatal Defense: Trial and Error in the Nation's Death Belt," *National Law Journal*, June 11, 1990, 30–34.

48. Bright, "Counsel for the Poor," 279.

49. Stephen B. Bright and Patrick J. Keenan, "Judges and the Politics of Death: Deciding Between the Bill of Rights and the Next Election in Capital Cases," *Boston University Law Review*, 75, no. 1 (May 1995): 760.

50. Lief Carter, "Capital Punishment" in *Oxford Companion to the Supreme Court*, ed. Kermit L. Hall (New York: Oxford University Press, 1992).

51. *Harris v. Alabama*, 115 S. Ct. 1031 (1995).

52. Bright and Keenan, "Judges and the Politics of Death," 760.

53. Bright and Keenan, "Judges and the Politics of Death," 761.

54. Stephen B. Bright, *Judicature* 169, no. 1 (January–February 1997): 80. See also Frances Kahn Zemans, "The Accountable Judge: Guardian of Judicial Independence," *Southern California Law Review* 72, no. 1 (January–March 1999): 625.

55. Bright and Keenan, "Judges and the Politics of Death," 763–65.

56. Bright and Keenan, Judges and the Politics of Death," 765.

57. Bright and Keenan, "Judges and the Politics of Death," 765.

58. White, *The Death Penalty in the Nineties*, 186.

59. White, *The Death Penalty in the Nineties*, 196–99.

60. William J. Bowers, "The Capital Jury: Is It Tilted toward Death?" *Judicature* 79, no. 1 (March–April 1996): 221–22.

61. Bowers, "The Capital Jury," 221.

62. Bowers, "The Capital Jury," 221.

63. Bowers, "The Capital Jury," 121.

64. *Gregg v. Georgia*, 428 U.S. 153 (1976).

65. Peter Meijes Tiersma, "Dictionaries and Death: Do Capital Jurors Understand Mitigation?" *Utah Law Review* 1, no. 1 (1995): 1.

66. Tiersma, "Dictionaries and Death," 25.

67. Tiersma, "Dictionaries and Death," 22–23.

68. Hugo A. Bedau, "Habeas Corpus and Other Constitutional Controversies," in *The Death Penalty in America*, ed. Hugo Adam Bedau (New York: Oxford University Press, 1997), 243.

69. "Death Row Exonerations Inspire Debate Over Death Penalty," CNN News, www.cnn.com/US/9908/15/death.row/index.html (n.d.).

70. Committee on the Judiciary Hearing, U.S. Senate, 103d Congress, First Session, *Innocence and the Death Penalty* (Washington, D.C.: U.S. Government Printing Office, 1994).

71. *Herrera v. Collins*, 506 U.S. 390 (1993).

72. Brent E. Newton, "A Case Study in System Unfairness: The Texas Death Penalty, 1973–1994," *Texas Forum on Civil Rights and Civil Liberties* 1, no. 1 (1994): 11.

73. Palacios, "Faith in Fantasy," 340.

74. *Innocence and the Death Penalty*.

75. Vivian Berger, "*Herrera v. Collins*: The Gateway of Innocence for Death-Sentenced Prisoners Leads Nowhere," *William and Mary Law Review* 35, no. 1 (Spring 1994): 969.

76. Palacios, "Faith in Fantasy," 347–48.

77. *Innocence and the Death Penalty*.

78. Berger, "*Herrera v. Collins*," 957.

79. Berger, "*Herrera v. Collins*," 960–63.

80. American Bar Association, *Individual Rights and Responsibilities, Section Report with Recommendations No. 107, Approved by the ABA House of Delegates on February 3, 1997* (Chicago: American Bar Association, 1997).

81. American Bar Associations, *Individual Rights and Responsibilities*.

82. A compendium of proposals to amend state death penalty law is available on the website of the Death Penalty Information Center, www.deathpenaltyinfo.org/changes/html [accessed April 24, 2001].

83. Huff et al., *Convicted but Innocent*, 152.

84. Huff et al., *Convicted but Innocent*, 156–57.

85. James S. Liebman, "The Overproduction of Death," *Columbia Law Review* 100, no. 8 (December 2000): 2030–2156.

86. The states that appointed commissions to review death penalty provisions and make recommendations to state legislatures included Arizona, Illinois, Indiana, Maryland, Nebraska, North Carolina, and Virginia as of early 2001.

CHAPTER 11

1. Andrew Von Hirsch, *Doing Justice* (New York: Hill & Wang, 1976).

2. Ernest van den Haag, "Murderers Deserve the Death Penalty," in *The World & I*, unpublished manuscript, November 1989.

3. *General deterrence* refers to the fact that the knowledge that offenders are punished may cause would-be criminals not to commit illegal acts. *Individual deterrence* refers to the fact that having been punished might cause the individual who has been punished to refrain from future illegal acts. Von Hirsch, *Doing Justice*, xxviii–xxix.

4. For example, opponents will point out that states with capital punishment often have higher murder rates than states that don't have capital punishment. Unfortunately, this ignores a host of demographic and cultural factors that may complicate the analysis. Even worse, it ignores the possibility that states have the death penalty precisely because the murder rate is high, and it might be higher still if the death penalty were abolished.

5. It's not the case that all, or even a majority of, studies show a deterrent effect of executions. But several studies, including some of the most sophisticated ones, do. See David Lester, "Executions as a Deterrent to Homicides," *Psychological Reports* 44, no. 1 (1979): 562; David Lester, "Deterring Effect of Executions on Murder as a Function of Number and Proportion of Executions," *Psychological Reports* 45, no. 1 (1979): 598; Stephen K. Layson, "Homicide and Deterrence: A Reexamination of the United States Time-Series Evidence," *Southern Economic Journal* 52, no. 1 (1985): 68–89; James A. Yunker, "Testing the Deterrent Effect of Capital Punishment: A Reduced Form Approach," *Criminology* 19, no. 4 (February 1982): 626–49; Dale O. Cloninger, "Capital Punishment and Deterrence: A Portfolio Approach," *Applied Economics* 24, no. 1 (1992): 635–45; Isaac Ehrlich, "The Deterrent Effect of Capital Punishment: A Question of Life and Death," *American Economic Review* 65, no. 1 (1975): 397–417; Isaac Ehrlich, "Capital Punishment and Deterrence: Some Further Thoughts and Additional Evidence," *Journal of Political Economy* 85, no. 1 (1977): 741–88.

6. Dale O. Cloninger, "Execution and Deterrence: A Quasi-Controlled Group Experiment," *Applied Economics* 33, no. 5 (April 2001): 569–76.

7. John McAdams, "Racial Disparity and the Death Penalty," *Law and Contemporary Problems* 61, no. 4 (Fall 1998).

8. "The Death Penalty: A Scholarly Forum," *Focus on Law Studies* 2, no. 1 (Spring 1997): 7.

9. Rev. Jesse Jackson, *Legal Lynching: Racism, Injustice, and the Death Penalty* (New York: Marlowe, 1996). In other passages, Jackson admits that the situation is more complex. As we shall see, the reality is not merely "more complex." The reality is precisely the opposite of what Jackson claims.

10. See, for example, Raymond Paternoster, *Capital Punishment in America* (New York: Lexington, 1991), 116–19.

11. United States Department of Justice, *Sourcebook of Criminal Justice Statistics* (Washington, D.C.: U.S. Government Printing Office, 1999), 549, 559.

12. Note that murders where either the victim or the offender was "unknown" or of an "other" racial category were omitted.

13. Samuel R. Gross and Robert Mauro, *Death and Discrimination* (Boston: Northeastern University Press, 1989), 12.

14. One reform that looks particularly suspect is the use of a bifurcated trial, with the jury deciding the sentence in what amounts to a second trial. These proceedings often degenerate into blatant attempts to manipulate the emotions of the jury.

15. Arnold Barnett, for example, examined one study that found no statistically significant deterrent effect: that of Passell. Barnett found that the model estimated by Passell had a prediction error—in terms of the number of homicides it predicted in forty-three states in 1960—of 1,635. But there were only forty-four persons executed for murder in 1960. If each of these executions had deterred 5 murders—which would be an excellent "return" in terms of deterrence—the reduction of 220 murders would not have been discernable, within accepted standards of statistical reliability, in Passell's data. Arnold Barnett, "The Deterrent Effect of Capital Punishment: A Test of Some Recent Studies," *Operations Research* 29, no. 2 (March–April 1981): 346–70.

16. Arkansas, Florida, Georgia, Illinois, Mississippi, North Carolina, Oklahoma, and Virginia. Given the attention the media devoted to executions in Texas during the governorship of George W. Bush, it is unfortunate that Texas data are unavailable.

17. Hanushek and Jackson, *Statistical Methods for Social Scientists* (New York: Academic Press, 1977), chap. 7.

18. Sue Anne Pressley, "Disabled Man Dragged to Death," *Washington Post*, June 10, 1998.

19. See for example Gary Kleck, "Racial Discrimination in Criminal Sentencing," *American Sociological Review* 46, no. 1 (1981): 783–805; Lawrence Greenfield and David Hinners, "Capital Punishment 1984," United States Department of Justice, *Bureau of Justice Statistics Bulletin* 1, no. 9 (1985).

20. The large number of "control variables" also has a downside: it tends to make the estimates less precise.

21. Sheldon Ekland-Olson, "Structured Discretion, Racial Bias, and the Death Penalty: The First Decade after *Furman* in Texas," *Social Science Quarterly* 69, no. 3 (1988): 851–73. It is important to note that Ekland-Olson studied death sentences, rather than actual executions.

22. Ekland-Olson, "Structured Discretion," 861. Ekland-Olson showed that the death row population overrepresented offenders who killed strangers and underrepresented offenders who killed acquaintances—consistent with our findings for "aggravating circumstances."

23. Raymond Paternoster, "Race of Victim and Location of Crime: The Decision to Seek the Death Penalty in South Carolina," *Journal of Criminal Law and Criminology* 74, no. 3 (Fall 1983): 754–85, especially 770.

24. William J. Bowers, "The Pervasiveness of Arbitrariness and Discrimination under Post-*Furman* Capital Statutes," *Journal of Criminal Law & Criminology* 74, no. 3 (1983): 1067. The data *tended* to show that blacks who killed whites and whites who killed whites were more likely to be sentenced to death, but Bowers could not establish this with the degree of statistical confidence that applied to the other two findings.

25. Michael L. Radelet, "Racial Characteristics and the Imposition of the Death Penalty," *American Sociological Review* 46, no. 3 (1981): 918–27.

26. Gennaro F. Vito and Thomas Keil, "Capital Sentencing in Kentucky: An Analysis of the Factors Influencing Decision Making in the Post-*Gregg* Period," *Journal of Criminal Law and Criminology* 79, no. 2 (1988): 483–503.

27. Jonathan R. Sorensen and Donald H. Wallace, "Capital Punishment in Missouri: Examining the Issue of Racial Disparity," *Behavioral Sciences and the Law* 13, no. 1 (1995): 61–80.

28. Leigh Bienen, Neil Alan Weiner, Deborah W. Denno, Paul D. Allison, and Douglas Lane Mills, "The Reimposition of Capital Punishment in New Jersey: The Role of Prosecutorial Discretion," *Rutgers Law Review* 41, no. 1 (1988): 27–372.

29. David C. Baldus, Charles Pulaski, and George Woodworth, "Comparative Review of Death Sentences: An Empirical Study of the Georgia Experience," *Journal of Criminal Law and Criminology* 74, no. 3 (Fall 1983): 708; David C. Baldus, George Woodworth, and Charles Pulaski Jr., *Equal Justice and the Death Penalty* (Boston: Northeastern University Press, 1990).

30. Baldus et al., "Comparative Review of Death Sentences," 709.

31. Baldus et al., "Comparative Review of Death Sentences,"1073, 1079, 1084.

32. Baldus et al., "Comparative Review of Death Sentences," 923–24.

33. Baldus et al., "Comparative Review of Death Sentences," 923–24.

34. Baldus et al., "Comparative Review of Death Sentences," 770.

35. Baldus et al., "Comparative Review of Death Sentences," 226, 235.

36. Baldus et al., "Comparative Review of Death Sentences," 68–69.

37. Baldus et al., "Comparative Review of Death Sentences," 70.

38. Anthony G. Amsterdam, "Race and the Death Penalty," *Criminal Justice Ethics* 7, no. 1 (Winter/Spring 1988): 84.

39. Randall L. Kennedy, "*McCleskey v. Kemp*: Race, Capital Punishment, and the Supreme Court," *Harvard Law Review* 101, no. 3 (1988): 1388–1443; emphasis in original.

40. I must note that this level of sophistication also seems to exceed that of many professors, political activists, and journalists.

41. "The 2000 Campaign; Exchanges between the Candidates in the Third Presidential Debate," *New York Times*, October 18, 2000.

42. *Gallup Poll of February 8–9, 1999*, in Lexis-Nexis® Academic Universe (online database), ca. 2001[accessed April 24, 2001], 1. Available from Reed Elsevier, Inc.

43. Tabulated by the author from online data, University of California, Berkeley, "Survey Documentation & Analysis (SDA) Archive," csa.berkeley.edu:7502/archive.htm. Whites are considerably more likely to favor the death penalty. In these data, 81.1 percent of whites favored capital punishment.

44. "Ebony's Annual Readers Poll," *Ebony* (September 1994): 43. This was far from being a scientific poll, but it is interesting both for the large number of respondents (9,657) and for the relatively affluent nature of the respondents.

45. "The 2000 Campaign."

46. Note that this is pre-*Furman*, but since only a tiny handful of the suspects was sentenced to death, there is no particular reason to believe that post-*Furman* changes much affect the results.

47. F. E. Zimring, J. Eigen, and S. O'Malley, "Punishing Homicide in Philadelphia: Perspectives on the Death Penalty," *University of Chicago Law Review* 43, no. 1 (1976): 227–52.

48. Alfred Blumstein, "Racial Disproportionality of U.S. Prison Populations Revisited," *University of Colorado Law Review* 64, no. 1 (1991): 743–60, especially 751. Note that Blumstein's 1979 data did not show this disproportionality.

49. These include failure to control for aggravating circumstances and a research design what leaves possible racial discrimination in arrests entirely out of account.

50. Blumstein, "Racial Disproportionality," 743–60.

51. Blumstein, "Racial Disproportionality," 743–60. This figure applies only to "nonprimary" homicide cases—those in which the victim and the defendant did not know each other.

52. Blumstein, "Racial Disproportionality," 743–60.

53. M. L. Radelet and G. L. Pierce, "Race and Prosecutorial Discretion in Homicide Cases," *Law and Society Review* 19, no. 2 (1985): 587–621.

54. See the earlier discussion of police protection.

CHAPTER 12

1. Bill Montgomery, "The Alday Family Murders: Aldays, the 'Isaacs Gang' from Two Different Worlds," *Atlanta Journal & Constitution*, October 19, 1986, A1.

2. Bill Montgomery, "The Alday Family Murders: The Burglary That Became a Massacre: As They Surprised Intruders, Aldays Were Slain One by One," *Atlanta Journal & Constitution*, October 20, 1986, A1.

3. Bill Montgomery, "Isaacs' Brother Recalls for Jurors Grim Final Hours of Alday Family," *Atlanta Journal & Constitution*, January 24, 1988, A1.

4. Montgomery, "The Alday Family Murders," A1.

5. Montgomery, "Isaac's Brother Recalls for Jurors Grim Final Hours of Alday Family," A1.

6. Montgomery, "Isaac's Brother Recalls for Jurors Grim Final Hours of Alday Family," A1.

7. Bill Montgomery, "First-Person Accounts of Alday Killings Heard," *Atlanta Journal & Constitution*, April 19, 1988, D4.

8. Montgomery, "Isaacs' Brother Recalls for Jurors Grim Final Hours of Alday Family," A1.

9. Quoted in Bill Montgomery, "The Alday Family Murders," *Atlanta Journal & Constitution*, October 22, 1986, A1.

10. Quoted in Bill Montgomery, "Isaacs a Self-Hating Manipulator Who Should Not Be Freed, Psychologist Says," *Atlanta Journal & Constitution*, January 29, 1988, A17.

11. This argument is summarized succinctly in Ruth D. Peterson and William C. Bailey, "Is Capital Punishment an Effective Deterrent for Murder? An Examination of the Social Science Research," in *America's Experiment with Capital Punishment*, ed. James R. Acker, Robert M. Bohm, and Charles S. Lanier (Durham, N.C.: Carolina Academic Press, 1998), 158–59.

12. Peterson and Bailey, "Is Capital Punishment an Effective Deterrent for Murder?" 158–59.

13. Adapted from Peterson and Bailey, "Is Capital Punishment an Effective Deterrent for Murder?" 160.

14. Peterson and Bailey, "Is Capital Punishment an Effective Deterrent for Murder?" 161.

15. Arlen Specter, "A Swifter Death Penalty Would Be an Effective Deterrent," in *The Death Penalty: Opposing Viewpoints*, ed. Paul A. Winter (San Diego: Greenhaven, 1997), 115.

16. Kent Scheidegger, "Habeas Corpus Is Abused by Convicts," in *The Death Penalty*, ed. Winter, 127.

17. Susan Blaustein, "Habeas Corpus Has Been Undermined by the Supreme Court," in *The Death Penalty*, ed. Winter, 130–33.

18. *Texas Code of Criminal Procedure*, Article 37.071 (1985).

19. H. J. Steadman, "Predicting Dangerousness among the Mentally Ill: Art, Magic, and Science," *International Journal of Law and Psychiatry* 6, no. 2 (1983), 381–90.

20. Jon Sorensen and James Marquart, "Future Dangerousness and Incapacitation," in *America's Experiment with Capital Punishment*, ed. Acker et al., 190.

21. Sorensen and Marquart, "Future Dangerousness and Incapacitation," 191.

22. Charles Hooton, *The American Criminal* (Cambridge, Mass.: Harvard University Press, 1939).

23. Sorensen and Marquart, "Future Dangerousness and Incapacitation," 195–97.

24. Sorensen and Marquart, "Future Dangerousness and Incapacitation," 188.

25. 408 U.S. 238 (1972).

26. Montgomery, "Isaacs a Self-Hating Manipulator Who Should Not Be Freed, Psychologist Says," A17.

27. Bill Montgomery, "The Alday Family Murders: From Start, Path to Justice Rocky for Alday Defendants," *Atlanta Journal & Constitution*, October 21, 1986, A1.

28. Bill Montgomery, "The Alday Family Murders: Move to a New Prison Foiled Escape Attempt by Isaacs," *Atlanta Journal & Constitution*, October 22, 1986, A1.

29. Montgomery, "The Alday Family Murders: Move to a New Prison Foiled Escape Attempt by Isaacs," A1.

30. Bill Montgomery, "On Tape, Isaacs Relates Story of Second Escape Try: State Seeking Electric Chair in Penalty Phase of Retrial," *Atlanta Journal & Constitution*, January 27, 1988, C1.

31. Bill Montgomery, "Saw Mailed to Isaacs on Death Row; Woman Held," *Atlanta Journal & Constitution*, February 9, 1995, A1.

32. Bill Montgomery, "'There's Not a Day I Don't Cry,' Says Woman Romanced by Killer," *Atlanta Journal & Constitution*, March 26, 2000, G6.

33. See, for example, Lloyd Steffen, *Executing Justice: The Moral Meaning of the Death Penalty* (Cleveland, Ohio: Pilgrim, 1998), 1–8.

34. Robert M. Bohm, "American Death Penalty Opinion: Past, Present, and Future," in *America's Experiment with Capital Punishment*, ed. Acker et al., 25.

35. Robert M. Bohm, "American Death Penalty Opinion, 1936–1986: A Critical Examination of the Gallup Polls," in *The Death Penalty in America: Current Research*, ed. Robert M. Bohm (Cincinnati, Ohio: Anderson, 1991), 115.

36. Bohm, "American Death Penalty Opinion: Past, Present, and Future," 27.

37. William J. Bowers and Benjamin D. Steiner, "The People Want an Alternative to the Death Penalty," in *Capital Punishment: A Reader*, ed. Glen H. Stassen (Cleveland: Pilgrim, 1998), 34–43.

38. Bowers and Steiner, "The People Wants an Alternative to the Death Penalty," 36–38.

CHAPTER 13

1. 482 U.S. 153 (1976). In *Gregg*, a divided Supreme Court upheld the new death penalty laws passed in several states while striking down others. In doing so, the justices established the rules necessary for a constitutional capital punishment.

2. 347 U.S. 483 (1954). In *Brown*, the Court struck down the state policy of segregated schools, overturning its decision in *Plessy v. Ferguson* 163 U.S. 537 (1896) and the fifty-eight-year-old doctrine of separate but equal public facilities. It would take nearly two decades before *Brown* was fully implemented in many school districts.

3. Edward Lazarus, *Closed Chambers* (New York: Penguin, 1998).

4. 356 U.S. 86 (1958).

5. An excellent discussion of the differences between interpretivism and noninterpretivism can be found in Robert Bork, *The Tempting of America* (New York: Free Press, 1990).

6. 433 U.S. 277 (1983).

7. 487 U.S. 815 (1988).

8. 492 U.S. 361 (1989).

9. 492 U.S. 302 (1989).

10. 481 U.S. 279 (1987).

11. 410 U.S. 113 (1973). In *Roe*, the Court created a right to an abortion from a right to privacy. After *Roe* the justices carefully studied each governmental attempt to regulate abortion using the three-trimester system created in *Roe*.

12. *Godfrey v. Georgia*, 446 U.S. 420 (1980).

13. *Clemons v. Georgia*, 494 U.S. 738 (1990).

14. 113 S. Ct. 1534 (1993).

15. 482 U.S. 496 (1987).

16. 111 S. Ct. 2597 (1991).

17. 510 U.S. 1141 (1994).

18. 489 U.S. 288 (1989). In *Teague*, the Court established new procedures in determining whether prisoners could raise new constitutional issues in their petitions for federal habeas corpus relief. In her opinion, Justice O'Connor raised the requirements for death row inmates, making it more difficult for them to raise those issues and have them heard by a federal judge.

19. 372 U.S. 391 (1963).

20. *Gomez v. United States District Court* 112 S. Ct. 1652 (1992). Harris's case was included among several California death row inmates filed by the American Civil Liberties Union.

21. 111 S. Ct. 2546 (1991).

22. 111 S. Ct. 1454 (1991).

23. 28 U.S.C. 2241.

24. 518 U.S. 1051 (1996). In *Felker*, the defendant, a convicted murderer and rapist was sentenced to death. He filed successive habeas petitions seeking a new trial and fell afoul of the new federal law on habeas petitions. He claimed the law violated the constitutional ban on Congress suspending habeas corpus rights except in cases of rebellion.

CHAPTER 14

1. In the wake of the 1996 passage of the federal Anti-Terrorism and Effective Death Penalty Act—which includes provisions to undermine a death row inmate's ability to use federal habeas corpus procedures to challenge the constitutionality of convictions and death sentences—the Individual Rights and Responsibilities section of the American Bar

Association revisited its policies on imposition of the death penalty. See, for example, "Whatever You Think about the Death Penalty, a System That Will Take Life Must First Give Justice," *Human Rights: Journal of the Section of Individual Rights & Responsibilities* 24, no. 1 (Winter 1997): 22–24.

2. 428 U.S. 153 (1976).

3. 402 U.S. 183 (1971).

4. 402 U.S. at 204.

5. James R. Acker and Charles S. Lanier, "Beyond Human Ability? The Rise and Fall of Death Penalty Legislation," in *America's Experiment with Capital Punishment*, ed. James R. Acker, Robert M. Bohm, and Charles S. Lanier (Durham, N.C.: Carolina Academic Press, 1998), 108–9. See also Charles Lund Black Jr., *Capital Punishment: The Inevitability of Caprice and Mistake*, 2d ed. (New York: Norton, 1982); Stephen B. Bright, "Will the Death Penalty Remain Alive in the Twenty-first Century? International Norms, Discrimination, Arbitrariness, and the Risk of Executing the Innocent," *Wisconsin Law Review* 2001, no. 1 (2001): 1–27; and Michael L. Radelet, Hugo Adam Bedau, and Constance Putnam, *In Spite of Innocence: Erroneous Convictions in Capital Cases* (Boston: Northeastern University Press, 1994).

6. See Chris Hutton, "Flaws in Capital Sentencing: Skewing the Reasoned Moral Response," chap. 16 in this volume.

7. Some of the best-known anti–death penalty commentators presented their central arguments succinctly in several readily available sources. See, for example, David C. Baldus, George Woodworth, and Charles A. Pulaski Jr., "Reflections on the 'Inevitability' of Racial Discrimination in Capital Sentencing and the 'Impossibility' of Its Prevention, Detection, and Correction," *Washington & Lee Law Review* 51, no. 2 (Spring 1994): 359–430; Stephen B. Bright, "The Death Penalty as the Answer to Crime: Costly, Counterproductive and Corrupting," *Santa Clara Law Review* 36, no. 4 (1996): 1069–96; James Liebman, Jeffrey Fagan, Valerie West, and Jonathan Lloyd, "Capital Attrition: Error Rates in Capital Cases, 1973–1995," *Texas Law Review* 78, no. 7 (2000): 1839–65; and Michael L. Radelet and Hugo Adam Bedau, "The Execution of the Innocent," *Law & Contemporary Problems* 61, no. 4 (Autumn 1998): 105–24.

8. Ernest van den Haag, "Justice, Deterrence and the Death Penalty," in *America's Experiment with Capital Punishment*, ed. Acker et al., 153.

9. Antonin Scalia, concurrence in *Callins v. Collins*, excerpted in "The Death Penalty Is Legally Just," in *The Death Penalty: Opposing Viewpoints*, ed. Paul A. Winters (San Diego: Greenhaven, 1997), 73, 75.

10. This argument is developed in detail in Barry Nakell and Kenneth A. Hardy, *The Arbitrariness of the Death Penalty* (Philadelphia: Temple University Press, 1986).

11. See, for example, Michael Ross, "The Death Penalty Is Applied Unfairly to Blacks," in *The Death Penalty*, ed. Winters, 148–54.

12. John C. McAdams, "Race and the Death Penalty," chap. 12 in this volume.

13. 481 U.S. 279 (1987).

14. 481 U.S. at 313.

15. 481 U.S. at 297.

16. 481 U.S. at 283.

17. 481 U.S. at 284–85.

18. 481 U.S. at 285–87.

19. *McCleskey v. Zant*, 580 F. Supp. 338, 379 (N.D. Ga. 1984).

20. *McCleskey v. Zant*, 753 F.2d 877, 891 (1985).

21. 481 U.S. at 291–92.

22. 481 U.S. at 292–93.

23. 481 U.S. at 298–99.

24. 481 U.S. at 328.

25. 481 U.S. at 344.

26. 481 U.S. at 345.

27. 481 U.S. at 346.

28. 481 U.S. at 365.

29. 481 U.S. at 365–66.

30. 481 U.S. at 366.

31. 481 U.S. at 367.

32. 481 U.S. at 367.

33. This logical inference is discussed in some detail in Ross, "The Death Penalty Is Applied Unfairly to Blacks," 153–54.

34. Stanley Rothman and Stephen Powers, "The Death Penalty Is Not Applied Unfairly to Blacks," in *The Death Penalty*, ed. Winters, 155–61.

35. Rothman and Powers, "The Death Penalty Is Not Applied Unfairly to Blacks," 160–61.

36. James W. Marquart, Sheldon Ekland-Olson, and Jonathan R. Sorensen, *The Rope, the Chair, and the Needle: Capital Punishment in Texas, 1923–1990* (Austin: University of Texas Press, 1998).

37. See, for example, William J. Bowers, *Legal Homicide: Death as Punishment in America, 1864–1982* (Boston: Northeastern University Press, 1984).

38. David C. Baldus and George Woodworth, "Race Discrimination and the Death Penalty: An Empirical and Legal Overview," in *America's Experiment with Capital Punishment*, ed. Acker et al., 395. The authors developed this point in some detail in David C. Baldus, George A. Woodworth, and Charles A. Pulaski, *Equal Justice and the Death Penalty: A Legal and Empirical Analysis* (Boston: Northeastern University Press, 1990).

39. Baldus and Woodworth, "Race Discrimination and the Death Penalty," 403.

40. This argument is developed in some detail in Samuel R. Gross and Robert Mauro, *Death and Discrimination: Racial Disparities in Capital Sentencing* (Boston: Northeastern University Press, 1989), especially 109–17.

41. This point is discussed in Ross, "The Death Penalty Is Applied Unfairly to Blacks," 153–54.

42. This point is discussed in Baldus and Woodworth, "Race Discrimination and the Death Penalty," 410–11.

43. Baldus et al., *Equal Justice and the Death Penalty*, 401. See also Mona Lynch and Craig Haney, "Discrimination and Instructional Comprehension: Guided Discretion, Racial Bias, and the Death Penalty," *Law and Human Behavior* 24, no. 3 (June 2000): 337–58.

44. *Griffin v. Illinois*, 351 U.S. 12, 19 (1956).

45. The argument linking the quality of a defendant's lawyer with the defendant's wealth is developed more fully in Stephen B. Bright, "Council for the Poor: The Death Penalty Not for the Worst Crime but for the Worst Lawyer," *Yale Law Journal* 103, no. 7 (May 1994): 1835–83. For more on ineffective assistance of counsel, see also David D. Langfitt and Billy H. Nolas, "Ineffective Assistance of Counsel in Death Penalty Cases," *Litigation* 26, no. 4 (Summer 2000): 6–13, 70–71.

46. Michael Mello and Paul Perkins, "Closing the Circle: The Illusion of Lawyers for People Litigating for Their Lives at the *Fin de Siecle*," in *America's Experiment with Capital Punishment*, ed. Acker et al., 281.

47. Jeffrey L. Johnson and Colleen F. Johnson, "Poverty and the Death Penalty," *Journal of Economic Issues* 35, no. 2 (June 2001): 517–18.

48. Johnson and Johnson, "Poverty and the Death Penalty," 518.

49. This is one of van den Haag's major points in "Justice, Deterrence and the Death Penalty," especially 152–53.

50. For information and data on the average income of death row defendants, see especially Michael Katz, *The Undeserving Poor* (New York: Pantheon, 1989), beginning at 24.

51. This is the same issue that M. Christine Cagle and J. Michael Martinez consider in chapter 10, "Social Science Data and the Death Penalty: Understanding the Debate over 'A Broken System,'" in this collection, especially in reference to the public defender Ronald G. Mock's abysmal performance in the Gary Graham (a.k.a. Shaka Sankofa) case.

52. Ernest van den Haag, "The Death Penalty Is Not Unfair to the Guilty," in *The Death Penalty*, ed. Winters (San Diego: Greenhaven, 1997), 168–69.

53. See, for example, "Putting the Mentally Retarded Criminal Defendant to Death: Charting the Development of a National Consensus to Exempt the Mentally Retarded from the Death Penalty," *Alabama Law Review* 52, no. 3 (Spring 2001): 911–41.

54. 492 U.S. 302 (1989). The American Bar Association has established a policy against executing persons who suffer from "mental retardation." See, for example, "Whatever You Think about the Death Penalty," 22–24.

55. 492 U.S. at 307.

56. 492 U.S. at 308.

57. 492 U.S. at 309–10.

58. 492 U.S. at 311–12.

59. 492 U.S. at 311–13.

60. 492 U.S. at 328–29.

61. 492 U.S. at 333.

62. 492 U.S. at 338.

63. 492 U.S. at 340.

64. 492 U.S. at 347.

65. 492 U.S. at 349.

66. 492 U.S. at 350.

67. 492 U.S. at 351.

68. 492 U.S. at 351.

69. *Atkins v. Virginia* (23435), Docket Number 00-8452 (certiorari granted September 25, 2001; order granting *in forma pauperis* motion and amending the certiorari order granted October 1, 2001). See also Stephen Krupin, "Execution Barred for Retarded Killers: Slew of Appeals Predicted after Landmark Ruling," *Atlanta Journal & Constitution*, June 21, 2002, B1.

70. See, for example, Mike Farrell, "On the Juvenile Death Penalty," *Whittier Law Review* 21, no. 1 (Fall 1999): 207–13; Victor L. Streib, "Emerging Issues in Juvenile Death Penalty Law," *Ohio Northern University Law Review* 26, no. 3 (2000): 725–39; Erica L. Templeton, "Killing Kids: The Impact of *Domingues v. Nevada* (961 P.2d 1279 [Nev. 1998]) on the Death Penalty as a Violation of International Law," *Boston College Law Review* 41, no. 5 (September 2000): 1175–1216. The American Bar Association has established a policy against executing anyone who was under eighteen years of age at the time that he or she committed the offenses for which they were convicted. See, for example, "Whatever You Think about the Death Penalty," 22–24.

71. 492 U.S. 361 (1989).
72. 492 U.S. at 365–66.
73. 492 U.S. at 366.
74. 492 U.S. at 366–67.
75. 492 U.S. at 367–68.
76. 492 U.S. at 369–70.
77. 492 U.S. at 378.
78. 492 U.S. at 380.
79. 492 U.S. at 379.
80. 492 U.S. at 382.
81. 492 U.S. at 382.
82. 492 U.S. at 388–89.
83. 492 U.S. at 392.
84. 492 U.S. at 394.
85. 492 U.S. at 405.
86. 408 U.S. 238 (1972).
87. 408 U.S. at 310.

CHAPTER 15

1. "The Death Penalty Will Discourage Crime (1701)," in *The Death Penalty: Opposing Viewpoints*, ed. Paul A. Winters (San Diego: Greenhaven, 1997), 18.

2. Cesare Beccaria, "The Death Penalty Will Not Discourage Crime," in *The Death Penalty*, ed. Winters, 26.

3. Discussed in *Furman v. Georgia*, 408 U.S. 238, 334–35 (1972) (Marshall, J., concurring).

4. This information about the history of early death penalty legislation was derived primarily from James R. Acker and Charles S. Lanier, "Beyond Human Ability? The Rise and Fall of Death Penalty Legislation" in *America's Experiment with Capital Punishment*, ed. James R. Acker, Robert M. Bohm, and Charles S. Lanier (Durham, N.C.: Carolina Academic Press, 1998), 81–85. See also Hugo Adam Bedau, "Background and Developments," in *The Death Penalty in America*, 3d ed., ed. Hugo Adam Bedau (New York: Oxford University Press, 1982), 328.

5. 408 U.S. 238, 339–340 (1972) (Marshall, J., concurring). See also Norman Krivosha, Robert Copple, and Michael McDonough, "A Historical and Philosophical Look at the Death Penalty: Does It Serve Society's Needs?" *Creighton Law Review* 16, no. 1 (1982–83): 1–46.

6. 408 U.S. 238 (1972).

7. 428 U.S. 153 (1976).

8. The Eighth Amendment states, "Excessive bail shall not be required, nor excessive fines imposed, nor cruel and unusual punishments inflicted." For earlier U.S. Supreme Court cases on what constitutes "cruel and unusual" punishment under the Eighth Amendment, see, for example, *Wilkerson v. Utah*, 99 U.S. 130 (1879); *In re Kemmler*, 136 U.S. 436 (1890); *O'Neil v. Vermont*, 144 U.S. 323 (1892); *Howard v. Fleming*, 191 U.S. 126 (1903); *Weems v. United States*, 217 U.S. 349 (1910); *Badders v. United States*, 240 U.S. 391 (1916); *United States ex rel. Milwaukee Social Democratic Publishing Company v. Burleson*, 255 U.S. 407 (1921); *Louisiana ex rel. Francis v. Resweber*, 329 U.S. 459 (1947); *Trop v. Dulles*, 356 U.S. 86 (1958); and *Robinson v. California*, 370 U.S. 660 (1962).

9. Hugo Adam Bedau, "The Courts, the Constitution, and Capital Punishment," *Utah Law Review* 1968, no. 1 (1968): 201–239.

10. 408 U.S. at 239. The relevant portion of §1 of the Fourteenth Amendment states, "[N]or shall any State deprive any person of life, liberty, or property, without due process of law."

11. 408 U.S. at 239–40.

12. 408 U.S. at 255–57.

13. 408 U.S. at 271.

14. 408 U.S. at 272–73.

15. 408 U.S. at 310.

16. 408 U.S. at 313.

17. 408 U.S. at 371.

18. 408 U.S. at 380.

19. 408 U.S. at 388.

20. 408 U.S. at 405.

21. 408 U.S. at 410–11.

22. 408 U.S. at 462.

23. 408 U.S. at 469. Ironically, Justice Rehnquist is arguing that judicial restraint is implied. Generally, implied conditions are associated with judicial activism, not with the restrainist position he advocates in the opinion.

24. The abolitionist debate continues to rage at the dawn of the twenty-first century. See, for example, Mark Hansen, "Death Knell for Death Row?" *ABA Journal* 86, no. 6 (June 2000): 40–48.

25. Quoted in James R. Acker, Robert M. Bohm, and Charles S. Lanier, "Introduction: America's Experiment with Capital Punishment," in *America's Experiment with Capital Punishment*, ed. Acker et al., 6.

26. Lloyd Steffen, *Executing Justice: The Moral Meaning of the Death Penalty* (Cleveland, Ohio: Pilgrim, 1998), 110.

27. 384 U.S. 436 (1966).

28. 233 Ga. 117, 210 S.E.2d 659 (1974).

29. 428 U.S. at 158–66.

30. For a more in-depth discussion of this point, see Carol S. Steiker and Jordan M. Steiker, "Judicial Developments in Capital Punishment Law," in *America's Experiment with Capital Punishment*, ed. Acker et al., 48–50.

31. 428 U.S. at 179.

32. 428 U.S. at 186–87.

33. 428 U.S. at 206–7.

34. 428 U.S. at 226.

35. 428 U.S. at 226–27.

36. 428 U.S. at 227–28.

37. 428 U.S. at 230–31.

38. 428 U.S. at 238–39.

39. 428 U.S. 262 (1976).

40. 428 U.S. 242 (1976).

41. 428 U.S. 280 (1976).

42. 428 U.S. 325 (1976).

43. In *Coker v. Georgia*, 433 U.S. 584 (1977), the Supreme Court held that the death penalty was excessive for rape. That same year, in *Eberheart v. Georgia*, 433 U.S. 917 (1977), the Court also determined that it was an impermissible penalty for kidnapping.

44. Acker and Lanier, "Beyond Human Ability," 89–90.

45. Acker and Lanier, "Beyond Human Ability," 90.

46. The leading case on the death penalty as it applies to youthful offenders is *Stanford v. Kentucky*, 492 U.S. 361 (1989). The leading case on applying the death penalty to mentally retarded defendants is *Penry v. Lynaugh*, 492 U.S. 302 (1989). For more on the issues surrounding imposition of the death penalty on the mentally retarded, see the exchange between Nat Hentoff and Chris Gersten in *The Death Penalty: Opposing Viewpoints.* Nat Hentoff, "The Death Penalty Should Not Be Applied to the Retarded," in *The Death Penalty: Opposing Viewpoints*, ed. Paul A. Winters (San Diego: Greenhaven, 1997), 171–75; and Chris Gersten, "The Retarded Should Not Be Exempt from the Death Penalty," in *The Death Penalty*, ed. Winters, 176–79.

47. James R. Acker, "When the Cheering Stopped: An Overview and Analysis of New York's Death Penalty Legislation," *Pace Law Review* 17, no. 1 (1996): 51, n. 36.

48. Acker and Lanier, "Beyond Human Ability," 97.

49. In one leading case, *Witherspoon v. Illinois*, 391 U.S. 510, 520, n. 15 (1968), quoting *Trop v. Dulles*, 356 U.S. 101 (1958), the Supreme Court referred to the jury as "a link between contemporary community values and the penal system—a link without which the determination of punishment could hardly reflect 'the evolving standards of decency that mark the progress of a maturing society.'"

50. Acker and Lanier, "Beyond Human Ability," 98–106.

51. 408 U.S. 238, 249–50.

52. For a contrary view along of the lines of "don't do the crime if you can't do the time," see, for example, Ernest van den Haag, "The Death Penalty Is Not Unfair to the Guilty," in *The Death Penalty*, ed. Winters, 167–70. Van den Haag's argument essentially is that a person who is guilty need not concern himself with whether someone else receives the death penalty. He forfeited the right to question his own treatment or his treatment in relation to others the moment he perpetrated the crime. If a person wants to ensure that he will be equitably treated and won't receive the death penalty himself, he should not commit the crime in the first place.

53. *Roberts v. Louisiana*, 428 U.S. 325 (1976).

54. These arguments are presented in Steiker and Steiker, "Judicial Developments in Capital Punishment Law," 50–56.

55. Case No. 99-6723 (2000).

56. *In re Kemmler*, 136 U.S. 436 (1890).

57. Case No. 99-6723.

58. Ernest van den Haag, "Justice, Deterrence and the Death Penalty," in *America's Experiment with Capital Punishment*, ed. Acker et al., 144.

59. Eugene H. Methvin, "Mugged By Reality: Eight Lessons We've Learned about the Epidemic of Crime—And What to Do about It," The Heritage Foundation, www.gppf.org/mugged.html (1997).

60. Methvin, "Mugged by Reality," 8.

61. Methvin, "Mugged by Reality," 4.

62. Van den Haag, "Justice, Deterrence and the Death Penalty," 143–44. This argument is similar to Immanuel Kant's view of the death penalty. For more information on Kant's perspective, see, for example, J. Michael Martinez, "'Woe to the Hand That Shed This Costly Blood': Philosophical Arguments against the Death Penalty," in chapter 4 of this collection.

63. This argument is set forth in van den Haag, "Justice, Deterrence and the Death Penalty," 145–46. See also Ernest van den Haag, "On Deterrence and the Death Penalty," in *Capital Punishment: A Reader*, ed. Glen H. Stassen (Cleveland, Ohio: Pilgrim, 1998), 47–58.

64. Van den Haag, "Justice, Deterrence and the Death Penalty," 146.

65. Van den Haag, "Justice, Deterrence and the Death Penalty," 147–49. For an alternative view, see, for example, Michael L. Radelet, Hugo Adam Bedau, and Constance E. Putnam, *In Spite of Innocence: Erroneous Convictions in Capital Cases* (Boston: Northeastern University Press, 1992).

66. 481 U.S. 279 (1987). By a 5–4 majority, the U.S. Supreme Court in *McCleskey v. Kemp* concluded that a statistical study showing that African American defendants who kill whites in Georgia have the greatest likelihood of receiving the death penalty does not prove that constitutionally impermissible racial discrimination necessarily occurred. The Court required that the defendant prove either that the decision makers in his case acted with a discriminatory purpose or intent or that the Georgia General Assembly enacted the state's death penalty statute knowing that it would have a discriminatory effect. Absent such a showing, the defendant could not argue that the state's capital punishment law violated the Equal Protection Clause of the Fourteenth Amendment.

67. See, for example, Michael Ross, "The Death Penalty Is Applied Unfairly to Blacks," in *The Death Penalty*, ed. Winters, 148–54; and Gerald Horne, "America's Justice System Discriminates against Blacks," quoted in *Race Relations*, ed. Paul A. Winters (San Diego: Greenhaven, 1996), 135. An alternative perspective is found in Stanley Rothman and Stephen Powers, "The Death Penalty Is Not Unfairly Applied to Blacks," in *The Death Penalty*, ed. Winters, 155–61.

68. See the exchange of perspectives in the book *The Death Penalty: Opposing Viewpoints*: Nick DiSpoldo, "The Death Penalty Is Applied Unfairly to the Poor," in *The Death Penalty*, ed. Winters, 162–66; Ernest van den Haag, "The Death Penalty Is Not Unfair to the Guilty," in *The Death Penalty*, ed. Winters, 167–70; Hentoff, "The Death Penalty Should Not Be Applied to the Retarded," 171–75; and Gersten, "The Retarded Should Not Be Exempt from the Death Penalty," 176–79.

69. Van den Haag, "Justice, Deterrence, and the Death Penalty," 156.

CHAPTER 16

This chapter was previously published in *South Dakota Law Review* 42, no. 399 (1997).

1. See, for example, *Wainwright v. Witt*, 469 U.S. 412 (1985); *Jones v. United States*, 119 S. Ct. 2090 (1999); *State v. Tucker*, 771 SW2d 523 (Tx. Ct. Crim. App. 1989); *Proctor v. California*, 512 U.S. 967 (1994). See also *State v. Anderson, Sioux Falls Argus Leader*, April 6, 7, 9, and 10, 1999, A1.

2. See, for example, James Liebman, Jeffrey Fagan, Valerie West, and Jonathan Lloyd, "Capital Attrition: Error Rates in Capital Cases, 1973–1995," *Texas Law Review* 78, no. 7 (2000): 1839–65; Michael L. Radelet and Hugo Adam Bedau, "The Execution of the Innocent," *Law & Contemporary Problems* 61, no. 4 (Autumn 1998): 105–24.

The popular press has discussed execution of innocent people extensively in recent months. See Caitlin Lovinger, "Life after Death Row," *New York Times,* August 22, 1999, 4; Sara Rimer and Raymond Bonner, "Fears on Fairness in Texas Death Penalty," *New York Times,* May 14, 2000, A1.

3. *California v. Brown,* 479 U.S. 538, 545 (1987) (O'Connor, J., concurring). See also Earl Martin, "Towards an Evolving Debate on the Decency of Capital Punishment," *George Washington Law Review* 66, no. 1 (November 1997): 84–134 (positing that capital case jurors should decide the "decency" of the sanction in each case).

4. See Carol Steiker and Jordan Steiker, "The Constitutional Regulation of Capital Punishment Since *Furman v. Georgia,*" *Saint Mary's Law Journal* 29, no. 4 (1998): 971–80.

5. See generally James J. Megivern, *The Death Penalty: An Historical and Theological Survey* (New York: Paulist, 1997). See also Samuel J. Levine, "Capital Punishment in Jewish Law and Its Application to the American Legal System: A Conceptual Overview," *Saint Mary's Law Journal* 29, no. 4 (1998): 1037–52; Irene Rosenberg and Yale Rosenberg, "Lone Star Liberal Musings on 'Eye for Eye' and the Death Penalty," *Utah Law Review* 1998, no. 5 (1998): 505–41.

6. Megivern, *The Death Penalty,* 381–454. See also Robert F. Drinan, S.J., "Will Religious Teachings and International Law End Capital Punishment?" *Saint Mary's Law Journal* 29, no. 4 (1998): 957–69; see also Pam Belluck, "Clemency for Killer Surprises Many Who Followed Case," *New York Times,* January 31, 1999, 12 (discussing the pope's plea for mercy for death sentenced prisoner).

7. Leonard Birdsong, "Is There a Rush to the Death Penalty in the Caribbean? Bahamas Say No," *Temple International & Comparative Law Journal* 13, no. 2 (Fall 1999): 285–309; Toni M. Fine, "Moratorium 2000: An International Dialogue toward a Ban on Capital Punishment," *Columbia Human Rights Law Review* 30, no. 2 (Spring 1999): 421–38 (comment); Ursula Bentele, "Back to an International Perspective on the Death Penalty as a Cruel Punishment: The Example of South Africa," *Tulane Law Review* 63, no. 1 (November 1998): 251–304. See also Mark Hansen, "Death Knell for Death Row?" *American Bar Association Journal* 86 (June 2000): 40–48.

8. The morality of capital punishment is not usually at the forefront of legal discussions of the issue. For example, in repudiating capital punishment, Justice Blackmun emphasized the procedural flaws in the system, not its moral weaknesses. *Callins v. Collins,* 510 U.S. 1141, 1143 (1994) (Blackmun, J., dissenting from denial of certiorari). Of course, that would be expected from a member of the judicial branch who is called on to interpret laws enacted by the legislature.

Some legal commentary does take a different approach. For example, Professor Louis Bilionis addresses the morality of capital punishment in his discussion of the American Bar Association's Resolution calling for a moratorium on imposition of death sentences. Louis Bilionis, "Eighth Amendment Meanings from the ABA's Moratorium Resolution," *Law & Contemporary Problems* 61, no. 4 (Autumn 1998): 29, 30. He also reminds readers of the many capital cases in which Justices Brennan and Marshall argued capital punishment is unconstitutional. See, for example, *Furman v. Georgia,* 408 U.S. 238, 273 (1972) (Brennan, J., concurring) (capital punishment violates the constitution by treating "members of the human race as nonhumans").

9. This survey is taken in substantial part from Chris Hutton, "Legitimizing Capital Punishment: Rationality Collides with Moral Judgment," *South Dakota Law Review* 42, no. 3 (1997): 399–433. Thanks to the editors of the *South Dakota Law Review* for permission to reprint an edited version here.

10. 402 U.S. 183 (1971). The defendants challenged the imposition of the death penalty on them, arguing the lack of standards to guide the jury violated due process. 402 U.S. at 196.

11. 402 U.S. at 204.

12. 408 U.S. 238 (1972).

13. *Furman*, 408 U.S. at 411 (Blackmun, J., dissenting).

14. *Furman* was a 5–4 opinion, per curiam. Each justice wrote an opinion, offering a somewhat divergent view on why the death penalty schemes at issue were invalid. Justices Marshall and Brennan agreed the penalty violates the Eighth Amendment (408 U.S. at 286). Justice Douglas argued the penalty was "selectively applied" (408 U.S. at 255) and that "the discretionary statutes are unconstitutional in their operation. They are pregnant with discrimination and discrimination is an ingredient not compatible with the idea of equal protection of the laws" (408 U.S. at 256–57). Justice Stewart found an Eighth Amendment violation stating, "these death sentences are cruel and unusual in the same way that being struck by lightning is cruel and unusual. . . . [T]he petitioners are among a capriciously selected random handful upon whom the sentence of death has in fact been imposed" (408 U.S. at 309–10). Justice White concurred, concluding the infrequency with which the death penalty was imposed rendered it inadequate as retribution or deterrence (408 U.S. at 311–13).

The four dissenting Justices joined Chief Justice Burger's opinion and would have approved the capital sentencing statutes before the Court. They disagreed that the Eighth Amendment prohibits standardless capital sentencing and adhered to the then-recent *McGautha* decision (408 U.S. at 387–88, Burger, C.J., dissenting). Justice Blackmun, while expressing his personal "abhorrence" for capital punishment (408 U.S. at 405), would have employed an analysis based on separation of powers and federalism to give federal and state legislatures the prerogative to enact it (408 U.S. at 400–11, Blackman, J., dissenting). Justice Powell, too, embraced "state decisions, federalism, judicial restraint and—most importantly-separation of powers," in arguing the statutes at issue should be approved (408 U.S. at 417, Powell, J., dissenting). Justice Rehnquist, too, emphasized the need for judicial restraint (408 U.S. at 466, Rehnquist, J., dissenting).

15. See, for example, Daniel D. Polsby, "The Death of Capital Punishment? *Furman v. Georgia*," *Supreme Court Review* 1972 (1972): 1–40. One commentator summarized the muddle created by *Furman*:

> Beyond a narrow proscription of standardless capital sentencing, *Furman* offered no clear guidance about how the Eighth Amendment regulated the use of the death penalty. The concurring opinions of the three Justices who voted to strike down the statutes on procedural grounds left major questions unanswered. None of these opinions addressed whether the death penalty always violated the Eighth Amendment, nor did they resolve what regulations would satisfy the Eighth Amendment if the death penalty were to be approved in limited circumstances. These opinions also did not clarify whether decisional standards were necessary at all phases of the selection process in capital cases— including the charging and plea-bargaining decisions by prosecutors—or only at the sentencing trial. Furthermore, *Furman* also left unclear how the Eighth Amendment regulates sentencing standards when they are required.

Scott W. Howe, "Resolving the Conflict in the Capital Sentencing Cases: A Desert-Oriented Theory of Regulation," *Georgia Law Review* 26, no. 2 (Winter 1992): 323, 331–32.

16. 428 U.S. 153 (1976).

17. 428 U.S. 262 (1976).

18. 428 U.S. 241 (1976).

19. 428 U.S. 280 (1976).

20. 428 U.S. 325 (1976). For an updated analysis of mandatory capital punishment, see Jeffrey Kirchmeier, "Aggravating and Mitigating Factors: The Paradox of Today's Arbitrary and Mandatory Capital Punishment Scheme," *William & Mary Bill of Rights Journal* 6, no. 2 (Spring 1998): 345–459.

21. Robert Weisberg, "Deregulating Death," *Supreme Court Review* (1983): 305–95.

22. Weisberg, "Deregulating Death," 318.

23. Ga. Code Ann. §27-2534.1 (Supp. 1975).

24. Fla. Stat. Ann. §921.141 (Supp. 1975–76).

25. Tex. Code Crim. Proc. Ann., art. 37.071 (West Supp. 1975–76).

26. The jury had to answer the following: (1) whether the conduct of the defendant that caused the death of the deceased was committed deliberately and with the reasonable expectation that the death of the deceased or another would result; (2) whether there is a probability that the defendant would commit criminal acts of violence that would constitute a continuing threat to society; and (3) if raised by the evidence, whether the conduct of the defendant in killing the decreased was unreasonable in response to the provocation, if any, by the deceased. Tex. Code Criminal. Proc. Ann. art. 37.071 (West Supp. 1975–76).

27. 438 U.S. 586 (1978). The defendant was a twenty-one-year-old woman without a serious criminal record. She had been the driver of a getaway car in a robbery. Although her prospects for rehabilitation were good, the judge could not consider it because the statutory mitigation did not encompass that factor.

28. 455 U.S. 104 (1982). Eddings was sixteen, and had a chaotic background that included an alcoholic mother and abusive father. He killed a trooper during a traffic stop.

29. *Ford v. Wainwright*, 477 U.S. 399 (1986).

30. *Thompson v. Oklahoma*, 487 U.S. 815 (1988). But see *Stanford v. Kentucky*, 492 U.S. 361 (1989) (holding there is no constitutional prohibition on executing those sixteen or seventeen at the time of the offense).

31. *Coker v. Georgia*, 433 U.S. 584 (1977).

32. *Enmund v. Florida*, 458 U.S. 782 (1982) (prohibiting death penalty for the getaway driver who was surprised by killing during robbery).

33. *Tison v. Arizona*, 481 U.S. 137 (1987).

34. *Godfrey v. Georgia*, 446 U.S. 420 (1980).

35. 446 U.S. at 420. See also *Maynard v. Cartwright*, 486 U.S. 356 (1988) (holding "especially heinous" is vague on its face and must be narrowed). But see *Lewis v. Jeffers*, 497 U.S. 764 (1990) (stating "heinous, depraved and cruel" has been narrowed by Arizona courts) and *Walton v. Arizona*, 497 U.S. 639 (1990) (holding "especially heinous, cruel or depraved" has been narrowed in Arizona appellate courts; trial judge is presumed to have been aware of proper standard).

36. *Bullington v. Missouri*, 451 U.S. 430 (1981).

37. *Lankford v. Idaho*, 500 U.S. 110 (1991).

38. *Caldwell v. Mississippi*, 422 U.S. 320 (1985) (holding it was reversible error to mislead capital sentencing jury into thinking the responsibility for the death sentence rested with the reviewing court). But see *Romano v. Oklahoma*, 512 U.S.1 (1994) (holding it was not error to introduce evidence that defendant already had been sentenced to death by another jury for another murder).

39. *Gardner v. Florida*, 430 U.S. 349 (1977).

40. *Kyles v. Whitley*, 514 U.S. 419 (1995) (holding government's failure to provide discovery to capital defendant denied him a fair trial on the merits).

41. *Schlup v. Delo*, 513 U.S. 298 (1995) (addressing defendant's claims that he was innocent of the crime and that counsel's ineffective performance caused his conviction; second federal habeas petition permitted if defendant can demonstrate a miscarriage of justice).

42. *Strickler v. Greene*, 427 U.S. 263, 119 S. Ct. 1936 (1999) (examining possible discovery violation in the context of a procedurally defaulted claim).

43. In *Kyles v. Whitley*, 514 U.S. 419 (1995), the chief justice and Justices Kennedy, Scalia, and Thomas dissented. Justice Scalia's opinion for the dissenting Justices captured their philosophy:

> In a sensible system of criminal justice, wrongful conviction is avoided by establishing, at the trial level, lines of procedural legality that leave ample margins of safety (for example, the requirement that guilt be proved beyond a reasonable doubt)—not by providing recurrent and repetitive appellate review of whether the facts in the record show those lines to have been narrowly crossed. (514 U.S. at 456)

He continued with the following caution:

> The greatest puzzle of today's decision is what could have caused this capital case to be singled out for favored treatment. Perhaps it has been randomly selected as a symbol, to reassure America that the United States Supreme Court is reviewing capital convictions to make sure no factual error has been made. If so, it is a false symbol, for we assuredly do not do that. (514 U.S. at 457)

He placed the burden of achieving accuracy elsewhere: "The reality is that responsibility for factual accuracy, in capital cases as in other cases, rests elsewhere—with trial judges and juries, state appellate courts, and the lower federal courts; we do nothing but encourage foolish reliance to pretend otherwise" (514 U.S. at 458). See also Joseph L. Hoffman, "Substance and Procedure in Capital Cases: Why Federal Habeas Courts Should Review the Merits of Every Death Sentence," *Texas Law Review* 78, no. 7 (June 2000): 1771–1803.

44. *McCleskey v. Kemp*, 481 U.S. 279 (1987) (holding defendant failed to prove purposeful discrimination in his own case and relying on statistics was insufficient as proof of discrimination).

45. *McCleskey*, 481 U.S. at 313.

46. See ABA House of Delegates Resolution of February 3, 1997 (describing racism in capital sentencing and calling for a moratorium on the death penalty until further progress is made in eliminating race as the basis for capital sentences). See also Stephen B. Bright, "Challenging Racial Discrimination in Capital Cases," *The Champion* (January/February 1997): 19. But see John C. McAdams, "Racial Disparity and the Death Penalty," *Law & Contemporary Problems* 16, no. 4 (Autumn 1998): 153–70 (describing racism in capital punishment as affecting black victims rather than black defendants).

47. *Wainwright v. Witt*, 469 U.S. 412 (1985). See also *State v. Rhines*, 1996 SD 55, &. 38, 548 NW2d at 429ñ33.

48. *Lockhart v. McCree*, 476 U.S. 162 (1986).

49. *Tuilaepa v. California*, 512 U.S. 1267 (1994).

50. *Lowenfield v. Phelps*, 484 U.S. 231 (1988).

51. *Jones v. United States*, 119 S. Ct. 2090 (1999). See also *Zant v. Stephens*, 462 U.S. 862, 885–88 (1993). For a state court application of this principle, see *State v. Rhines*, 1996 SD 55, 548 NW2d 415.

52. *Booth v. Maryland*, 482 U.S. 496 (1987) and *South Carolina v. Gathers*, 490 U.S. 805 (1989).

53. *Payne v. Tennessee*, 501 U.S. 808 (1991). But see Darcy Katzin, "The Relevance of Execution Impact: Testimony as Evidence of Capital Defendants' Character," *Fordham Law Review* 67, no. 3 (December 1998): 1193–1215 (note arguing for juries to consider such evidence).

54. *California v. Ramos*, 463 U.S. 992 (1983). See also *Jones v. United States*, 119 S. Ct. 2090 (1999) (addressing possible jury confusion over instruction on what penalty could be imposed on defendant in the federal system). See also *Simmons v. South Carolina*, 512 U.S. 154 (1994); *Ramdass v. Angelone*, 120 S. Ct. 2113 (2000).

55. *Barclay v. Florida*, 463 U.S. 939 (1983).

56. *Harris v. Alabama*, 513 U.S. 504 (1995).

57. *Blystone v. Pennsylvania*, 494 U.S. 299 (1990); *Boyde v. California*, 494 U.S. 370 (1990).

58. *Woodson*, 428 U.S. at 280; *Roberts*, 428 U.S. at 325.

59. *Murray v. Giarratano*, 492 U.S. 1 (1989).

60. 28 U.S.C. §2254(h).

61. *Clemons v. Mississippi*, 494 U.S. 738 (1990). See also *Sochor v. Florida*, 504 U.S. 527 (1992) (holding appellate court must provide statement of why reliance on invalid factor was harmless) and *Accord Richmond v. Lewis*, 506 U.S. 40 (1992).

62. *Zant v. Stephens*, 462 U.S. 862 (1983); *Satterwhite v. Texas*, 486 U.S. 249 (1988).

63. The specific limitations are discussed more fully in Part II. F., herein. It is noteworthy that Justice Blackman thought the restrictions so onerous, that capital punishment could no longer be approved. *Callins v. Collins*, 510 U.S. 1141, 1143 (1994) (Blackmun, J., dissenting).

64. The reinforcement was provided by the Antiterrorism and Effective Death Penalty Act of 1996 (AEDPA) Pub. L. 104–132, 110 Stat. 1214 (1996). The Conference Committee Report outlines the goals of AEDPA as follows:

> This title incorporates reforms to curb the abuse of the statutory writ of habeas corpus, and to address the acute problems of unnecessary delay and abuse in capital cases. It sets a one year limitation on an application for a habeas writ and revises the procedures for consideration of a writ in federal court. It provides for the exhaustion of state remedies and requires deference to the determinations of state courts that are neither "contrary to," nor an "unreasonable application of," clearly established federal law.
>
> The revision in capital habeas practice also sets a time limit within which the district court must act on a writ, and provides the government with the right to seek a writ of mandamus if the district court refuses to act within the allotted time period. Successive petitions must be approved by a panel of the court of appeals and are limited to those petitions that contain newly discovered evidence that would seriously undermine the jury's verdict or that involve new constitutional rights that have been retroactively applied by the Supreme Court.
>
> In capital cases, procedures are established for the appointment of counsel, conduct of evidentiary hearings, and the application of the procedures to state unitary review systems. Courts are directed to give habeas petitions in capital cases priority status and to decide those petitions within specified time periods. These procedures apply both to state and federal capital cases. (H. R. Conf. Rep. 104-518, 94th Cong., 2d Sess. 111 [1996])

See James Liebman and Randy Hertz, *Federal Habeas Corpus Practice and Procedure*, 3d ed. (1998), 107–80, discussing revisions wrought by AEDPA.

Selected portions of AEDPA have been interpreted by the United States Supreme Court. See, for example, *Williams v. Taylor*, 120 S. Ct. 1495 (2000); *Slack v. McDaniel*, 120 S. Ct. 1595 (2000); *Williams v. Taylor*, 120 S. Ct. 1479 (2000); *Hohn v. United States*, 524 U.S. 236 (1998); *Stewart v. Martinez-Villareal*, 523 U.S. 637 (1998); *Calderon v. Thompson*, 523 U.S. 538 (1998); *Lindh v. Murphy*, 521 U.S. 320 (1997).

65. In an interesting characterization of the sum total of this process, Professor Weisberg argues it results in "a penal arithmetic." Weisberg, "Deregulating Death," 376–77. The prosecutor can describe the aggravating circumstances, note the absence of specific mitigation, and thus "create a portrait of the hypothetical killer who deserves mercy," which the defendant does not. Weisberg, "Deregulating Death," 376–77. See also William S. Geimer, "Law and Reality in the Capital Penalty Trial," *Review of Law & Social Change* 18, no. 2 (1990–1991): 273–95 (setting forth strategy for "proving" an entitlement to a life sentence rather than death).

66. *Skipper v. South Carolina*, 476 U.S. 1 (1986).

67. *Hitchcock v. Dugger*, 481 U.S. 393 (1987).

68. *Mills v. Maryland*, 486 U.S. 393 (1988); *McKoy v. North Carolina*, 494 U.S. 433 (1990).

69. *Simmons v. South Carolina*, 512 U.S. 154 (1994).

70. *Sumner v. Shuman*, 483 U.S. 66 (1987).

71. *Penry v. Lynaugh*, 492 U.S. 302 (1989). In this regard, Penry's case was a classic: a defendant whose mental retardation and resulting likely future dangerousness might have elicited the "reasoned moral response" of a life sentence. However, the jury was forced to answer only a few narrow questions and not give greater consideration to the defendant's fate. The Supreme Court ruled the jury's discretion had been unconstitutionally circumscribed. Prior to *Penry*, as noted earlier, Texas sentencing juries were required to answer three questions and impose a death sentence if the three answers were affirmative. After *Penry*, the statute was amended to make the process less mechanical. The jury is now asked to exercise its judgment, and must decide as follows:

Whether, taking into consideration all of the evidence, including the circumstances of the offense, the defendant's character and background and the personal moral culpability of the defendant, there is a sufficient mitigating circumstance or circumstances to warrant that a sentence of life imprisonment rather than a death sentence be imposed. (Tex. Code Crim. Proc. Ann. art 37.071[2][e] [West Supp. 1992]

72. *Walton v. Arizona*, 497 U.S. 639 (1990).

73. *California v. Brown*, 479 U.S. 538 (1987).

74. *Boyde v. California*, 494 U.S. 370 (1990).

75. *Arave v. Creech*, 507 U.S. 463 (1993).

76. 438 U.S. 586, 625 (White, J., dissenting); 438 U.S. at 631 (Rehnquist, J., dissenting).

77. *Walton v. Arizona*, 497 U.S. 639, 656 (1990) (Scalia, J., concurring). Justice Scalia complained:

Our cases proudly announce that the Constitution effectively prohibits the States from excluding from the sentencing decision any aspect of a defendant's character or record, or any circumstance surrounding the crime: that the defendant had a poor and deprived childhood, or that he had a rich and spoiled childhood; that he had a great love for the victim's race, or that he had a pathological hatred for the victim's race; that he has limited mental capacity or that he has a brilliant mind which can make a great contribution to society; that he was kind to his mother, or that he despised his mother. Whatever evidence bearing on the crime or the criminal the defense wishes to introduce as rendering the defendant less deserving of the death penalty must be admitted into evidence and considered by the sentencer. (497 U.S. at 663 [Scalia, J., concurring])

78. 497 U.S. at 633–64.

79. See notes 13–14.

80. See, for example, Ga. Code Ann. §27-2534.1, approved in *Gregg v. Georgia*, 428 U.S. 153 (1976).

81. See, for example, Ohio Rev. Code Ann. §2929.04 (1975), at issue in *Lockett v. Ohio*, 438 U.S. 586 (1978) and 21 Okl. St. Ann. §701.12 (1976), at issue in *Eddings v. Oklahoma*, 455 U.S. 104 (1982).

82. "To acknowledge that 'there perhaps is an inherent tension' between this line of cases (*Woodson-Lockett*) and the line stemming from *Furman* . . . is rather like saying that there was perhaps an inherent tension between the Allies and the Axis Powers in World War II" (*Walton v. Arizona*, 497 U.S. at 664).

83. 497 U.S. at 656.

84. 497 U.S. at 656.

85. 408 U.S. at 309–10 (Stewart, J., concurring).

86. 497 U.S. at 671.

87. In his view, such a penalty would not be cruel or unusual. 497 U.S. at 671.

88. 497 U.S. at 661.

89. 497 U.S. at 664–65.

90. See, for example, Stephen P. Garvey, "'As the Gentle Rain from Heaven': Mercy in Capital Sentencing," *Cornell Law Review* 81, no. 5 (July 1996): 989–1048 (proposing a theory for how to incorporate mercy into the capital sentencing process on a formal basis); Eric L. Muller, "The Virtue of Mercy in Criminal Sentencing," *Seton Hall Law Review* 24, no. 1 (1993): 288–346. See also Phyllis L. Crocker, "Childhood Abuse and Adult Murder: Implications for the Death Penalty," *North Carolina Law Review* 77, no. 2 (1999): 1143–1222.

91. He has not read the Eighth Amendment in this manner. However, he has not interpreted the Eighth Amendment to prohibit juries from considering mercy, pursuant to legislative authorization.

92. *Callins v. Collins*, 510 U.S. 1141, 1147 (1994) (Blackmun, J., dissenting from denial of certiorari).

93. 510 U.S. at 1147. He was true to his word. See, for example, *Romano v. Oklahoma*, 512 U.S. 1 (1994); *Tuilaepa v. California*, 512 U.S. 1267 (1994).

94. *Callins v. Collins*, 510 U.S. at 1144.

95. 510 U.S. at 1144.

96. 510 U.S. at 1144.

97. 50 U.S. at 1157.

98. This process is described cogently in Scott E. Sundby, "The Lockett Paradox: Reconciling Guided Discretion and Unguided Mitigation in Capital Sentencing," *UCLA Law Review* 38, no. 5 (June 1991): 1147, 1162.

99. Sundby, "The Lockett Paradox," 1163–64. In contrast, Justice Scalia views this as a unitary choice (497 U.S. at 656).

100. Sundby, "The Lockett Paradox," at 1170. The facts of *Lockett v. Ohio* illustrate this point. See also *Woodson v. North Carolina*, 428 U.S. 280 (1976) and *Roberts v. Louisiana*, 428 U.S. 325 (1976).

101. Sundby, "The Lockett Paradox," 1170–72. He adds that on a practical level, the arbitrariness of the pre-*Furman* era could return as sentencers evade the stricture of mandatory death sentences by acquitting sympathetic defendants and convicting and sentencing to death disfavored ones. Or, in response to public outcry over excessive application in cases, states would implement discretionary systems at some point.

102. Sundby, "The Lockett Paradox," 1176.

103. Sundby, "The Lockett Paradox," 1176.

104. Sundby, "The Lockett Paradox," 1176.

105. Sundby, "The Lockett Paradox," 1778.

106. Sundby, "The Lockett Paradox," 1176. Professor Sundby suggests that perhaps the states should be permitted to define what factors are mitigating, so consistency would be achieved.

107. *California v. Brown*, 479 U.S. at 545; *Penry v. Lynaugh*, 492 U.S. at 319.

108. Sundby, "The Lockett Paradox," 1180. In *California v. Brown*, Justice O'Connor championed the "reasoned moral judgment" concept. 479 U.S. 538, 545 (1987).

109. Sundby, "The Lockett Paradox," 1184.

110. See, for example, *Jones v. United States*, 119 S. Ct. 2090 (1999).

111. For an example of a state's grappling with the mechanics of proportionality review see *State v. Rhines*, 1996 SD 55, 548 NW2d 415.

112. Sundby, "The Lockett Paradox," 1184.

113. Sundby, "The Lockett Paradox," 1185.

114. Sundby, "The Lockett Paradox," 1206.

115. Ronald J. Allen, "Evidence, Inference, Rules and Judgment in Constitutional Adjudication: The Intriguing Case of *Walton v. Arizona*," *Journal of Criminal Law & Criminology* 81, no. 4 (Winter 1991): 727, 738.

116. Allen, "Evidence, Inference, Rules and Judgment," 738.

117. Allen, "Evidence, Inference, Rules and Judgment," 739.

118. Allen, "Evidence, Inference, Rules and Judgment," 740.

119. Allen, "Evidence, Inference, Rules and Judgment," 740.

120. Allen, "Evidence, Inference, Rules and Judgment," 741.

121. Allen, "Evidence, Inference, Rules and Judgment," 742.

122. Allen, "Evidence, Inference, Rules and Judgment," 738.

123. Professor Allen disagreed with Justice Scalia that the differing results create "randomness" inconsistent with *Furman*. Allen, "Evidence, Inference, Rules and Judgment," 744.

124. Allen also noted that unconstrained judgment makes appellate review impossible. He suggested that is one reason appellate courts promote decision making by rules. Allen, "Evidence, Inference, Rules and Judgment," 746.

125. Allen, "Evidence, Inference, Rules and Judgment," 758.

126. *Callins v. Collins*, 510 U.S. at 1153–58 (discussing racism and curbs on habeas corpus in the capital sentencing context). See also David C. Baldus, George Woodworth and Charles A. Pulaski Jr., "Reflections on the 'Inevitability' of Racial Discrimination in Capital Sentencing and the 'Impossibility' of Its Prevention, Detection and Correction," *Washington & Lee Law Review* 51, no. 2 (Spring 1994): 359–430 (presenting strategies for addressing racial disparities in capital sentencing context).

127. For example, Professors Carol S. Steiker and Jordan M. Steiker concur that Justice Scalia errs in concluding individualization is not constitutionally required. They argue there is an individualization requirement in the Eighth Amendment and too narrow an appreciation of it would create a new Eighth Amendment problem of permitting death sentences "contrary to internal community consensus." Steiker and Steiker, "Let God Sort Them Out? Refining the Individualization Requirement in Capital Sentencing," *Yale Law Journal* 102, no. 3 (December 1992): 835, 840 (book review). The individualization requirement they discern, however, does not encompass unfettered use of mitigating evidence. They perceive the mitigation

required by the Eighth Amendment as limited to evidence of "reduced culpability"—that is, "evidence that suggests any impairment of a defendant's capacity to control his or her criminal behavior, or to appreciate its wrongfulness or likely consequences." Steiker and Steiker, "Let God Sort Them Out?" 846.

Having identified the core constitutional requirement that individualization addresses reduced culpability, Steiker and Steiker next focus on whether states must limit mitigation to that core. Their concern is that unconstrained mitigation undermines *Furman's* goal of rationality. And if rationality is constitutionally required, not only does it trump expansive individualization, but states would have to mark the limits of mitigation in advance. Steiker and Steiker reject this notion. They reason that forcing the states to define aggravation carefully is sensible because this provides guidance to the decision maker. However, reining in mitigation violates the Eighth Amendment because it results in overinclusiveness, meaning the death penalty is imposed on people the community thinks should not be executed. Steiker and Steiker, "Let God Sort Them Out?" 846.

Although they contend the *Woodson-Lockett* doctrine requires the mitigation described earlier, they understand those cases are inconsistent with *Furman*. In concluding so, they draw on the reasoning of Justice Harlan in *McGautha* that endeavoring to address the moral decision of capital sentencing through rules governing the process is futile. Thus, they reason that *Furman*, as it has been implemented, has added so little to the capital sentencing process that it is not constitutionally required. Steiker and Steiker, "Let God Sort Them Out?" 846.

Favoring individualization at the expense of *Furman's* purported rationality is a provocative approach. Yet, Steiker and Steiker retreat a bit and satisfy themselves that individualization and consistency, while in "tension," are compatible. The reasoned moral response championed by Justice O'Connor is achievable if we interpret the "reasoned" facet to encompass employing standards to enable sentencers to treat "like cases alike" and the "moral" facet to enable the consideration of "individual deserts." Steiker and Steiker, "Let God Sort Them Out?" 870. See also Carol S. Steiker and Jordan M. Steiker, "Sober Second Thoughts: Reflections on Two Decades of Constitutional Regulation of Capital Punishment," *Harvard Law Review* 109, no. 2 (December 1995): 355–438.

128. *Strickland v. Washington*, 466 U.S. 668 (1984) sets the federal standard:

> A convicted defendant's claim that counsel's assistance was so defective as to require reversal of a conviction or death sentence has two components. First, the defendant must show that counsel's performance was deficient. This requires showing that counsel made errors so serious that counsel was not functioning as the "counsel" guaranteed the defendant by the Sixth Amendment. Second, the defendant must show that the deficient performance prejudiced the defense. This requires showing that counsel's errors were so serious as to deprive the defendant of a fair trial, a trial whose result is reliable. Unless a defendant makes both showings, it cannot be said that the conviction or death sentence resulted from a breakdown in the adversary process that renders the result unreliable. (466 U.S. 668 at 687)

129. See, for example, Stephen B. Bright, "Death in Texas," *The Champion* (July 1999): 16 (discussing several Texas cases with incompetent counsel, including counsel who slept during proceedings; also describing election consequences for several justices who voted to overturn death sentences). See also John Spomer, "Scared to Death: The Separate Right to Counsel at Capital Sentencing," *Hastings Constitutional Law Quarterly* 26, no. 2 (Winter 1999): 505–32 (arguing for representation by a second attorney at capital sentencing).

130. Moral and ethical issues may pose challenges as well. See, for example, Phyllis L. Crocker, "Feminism and Defending Men on Death Row," *Saint Mary's Law Journal* 29, no. 4 (1998): 981–1007.

131. 1996 SD 60, & 94, 548 NW2d 465.

132. 1996 SD 60, & 94. The Supreme Court had already reversed the case on other grounds, so the court did not decide whether the failure to instruct would require automatic reversal. It intimated that would be necessary.

133. David R. Gienapp, remarks at the University of South Dakota School of Law's Gunderson Lecture, April 12, 1996.

134. The problem of competent counsel in capital cases has long been recognized. See Marcia Coyle, Fred Strasser, and Marianne Lavelle, "Fatal Defense," *National Law Journal,* June 11, 1990, 30; Marcia Coyle, Marianne Lavelle, and Fred Strasser, "Fatally Flawed," *National Law Journal,* November 19, 1990, 1. Both of these articles survey the performance of counsel, and include numerous anecdotes of incompetence.

See *McFarland v. Scott,* 512 U.S. 1256 (1994) (Blackmun, J., dissenting from denial of certiorari), discussing the "crisis" in representation at trial and postconviction proceedings. See also Stephen B. Bright, "The Death Penalty as the Answer to Crime: Costly, Counterproductive and Corrupting," *Santa Clara Law Review* 36, no. 4 (1996): 1069, 1078–84, describing incidents of incompetent counsel in several capital cases.

135. Gienapp remarks (noting that at least one defense attorney committed suicide after losing a capital case). Unfortunately, lawmakers have manifested inconsistent attitudes toward the role of defense counsel in capital cases. For example, the Antiterrorism and Effective Death Penalty Act of 1996 magnifies the role of counsel in the postconviction setting by streamlining review if certain standards concerning the "appointment, compensation, and payment of reasonable litigation expenses of competent counsel are met." 28 U.S.C. §2265 (1996). To date, no state's procedures have qualified for this "opt-in" process. Leah Prewitt and Renee McDonald, "A Brief Introduction: The Antiterrorism and Effective Death Penalty Act of 1996," *The Champion* (December 1996): 65.

At the same time, however, Congress eliminated funding for the death penalty resource centers. See Stephen Bright, "Capital Cases," *The Champion* (November 1996): 25.

136. See ABA Resolution No. 107, February 3, 1997 and accompanying report regarding a moratorium on the death penalty reprinted at *Law & Contemporary Problems* 61, no. 4 (Autumn 1998): 219–31. The issue of competent counsel, including guidelines for their appointment in capital cases, is discussed at *Law & Contemporary Problems* 61, no. 4 (Autumn 1998): 223–27.

137. For a cautionary note to prosecutors in charging cases as capital see E. Michael McCann, "Opposing Capital Punishment: A Prosecutor's Perspective," *Marquette Law Review* 79, no. 3 (Spring 1996): 649–706.

138. See, for example, *Kyles v. Whitley,* 514 U.S. 419 (1995). Both fabrication and concealment can be orchestrated by others in the process, such as pathologists and detectives. In those cases, the prosecutor is an unwitting participant in more general "government" misconduct. The focus here is on the prosecutor who is aware of the facts.

139. Adam Bedau and Michael Radelet, "Miscarriages of Justice in Potentially Capital Cases," *Stanford Law Review* 40, no. 1 (November 1987): 21–179.

140. For an in-depth account of the 1880 trial and botched execution of South Dakota's first victim of the death penalty—an Irish immigrant who denied his guilt and later was exonerated—see C. John Egan Jr., *Drop Him Til He Dies: The Twisted Tragedy of Immigrant Homesteader Thomas Egan* (New York: Ex Machina, 1994).

141. Bennett L. Gershman, "The New Prosecutors," *University of Pittsburgh Law Review* 53, no. 2 (Winter 1992): 393, 394.

142. Gershman, "The New Prosecutors," 384.

143. Ken Armstrong and Maurice Possley, "The Verdict: Dishonor," *Chicago Tribune,* Special Report, January 10–14, 1999.

144. Armstrong and Possley, "The Verdict: Dishonor," discussing conviction, sentence, retrials, and acquittal of Rolando Cruz.

145. Armstrong and Possley, "The Verdict: Dishonor."

146. Caitlin Lovinger, "Life after Death Row," *New York Times,* August 22, 1999, WK4.

147. Lovinger, "Life after Death Row."

148. Lovinger, "Life after Death Row."

149. See statistics cited in *McCleskey v. Kemp,* 481 U.S. 297 (1987) (noting prosecutors seek death penalty in 70 percent of cases involving black defendants and white victims, and in 19 percent of cases with white defendants and black victims). But see McAdams, "Racial Disparity," 162–66.

150. Challenges to a prosecutor's discretion to initiate capital proceedings typically fail. The argument usually focuses on the possibly arbitrary nature of the decision. But the California Supreme Court offered the usual rejoinder to such a claim:

> Defendant urges that the 1978 death penalty law violates the Eighth Amendment's proscription against cruel and unusual punishment because it allows prosecutors "standardless" discretion to decide when to seek the death penalty and thus leads to arbitrary and capricious imposition of the death penalty. He is mistaken. "[P]rosecutorial discretion to select those eligible cases in which the death penalty will actually be sought does not in and of itself evidence an arbitrary and capricious capital punishment system or offend principles of equal protection, due process, or cruel and/or unusual punishment." (*People v. Keenan, supra,* 46 Cal. 3d 478, 505, 250 Cal. Rptr. 550, 758 P.2d 1081; accord, *People v. Stanley,* 10 Cal. 4th, 764, 843, 42 Cal. Rptr. 2d 543, 897 P.2d 481; *People v. Visciotti* 2 Cal. 4th 1, 78, 5 Cal. Rptr. 2d 495, 825 P.2d 388)

People v. Arias, 13 Cal. 4th 92, 913 P.2d 980, 51 Cal. Rptr. 2d 770 (1996).

The *Arias* court also rejected defendant's claim that unfettered discretion violates the doctrine of separation of powers by allowing the executive branch, as opposed to legislative, determine the maximum penalty in a case (913 P.2d at 1042).

151. See, for example, 720 Ill. Comp. Stat. Ann. 5/9-1 (West 1993 & Supp. 1998). Although the substance of the statute is typical of capital punishment schemes, there is a procedural anomaly: the prosecutor may decide to charge a case as capital even after conviction. *People ex rel. Carey v. Cousins,* 397 N.E. 2d 809 (Ill. 1979). For a thorough discussion, see Leigh B. Bienen, "The Quality of Justice in Capital Cases: Illinois as a Case Study," *Law & Contemporary Problems* 61, no. 4 (Autumn 1998): 193, 197–207.

152. Bienen, "The Quality of Justice," 207, discussing the attorney general's constraints on practice under 18 U.S.C. §3593.

153. Bienen, "The Quality of Justice," 198–99.

154. Compare *State v. Rhines,* 1996 SD 55, 548 NW2d 415. See also Hugh O'Gara, "Death Penalty Wait," *Rapid City Journal,* September 16, 2000, discussing possible escalation of second-degree murder charge into capital case, based on habitual offender allegation from prior offense of vehicular homicide.

155. Raymond Bonner and Ford Fessenden, "States with No Death Penalty Share Lower Homicide Rates," *New York Times,* September 22, 2000, A1.

156. *Calderon v. Thompson,* 523 U.S. 538 (1998).

157. 373 U.S. 83 (1963). See also *United States v. Agurs,* 427 U.S. 97 (1976); *United States v. Bagley,* 473 U.S. 667 (1985).

158. 514 U.S. 419 (1995).

159. 5 F.3d 806, 820 (5th Cir. 1993) (King, J., dissenting). Kyles was retried and eventually freed.

160. See, for example, *Kyles v. Whitley*, 514 U.S. 419 (1995); *Jacobs v. Singletary*, 952 F.2d 1282 (11th Cir. 1992); *Carriger v. Stewart*, 132 F.3d 463 (9th Cir. 1997) (en banc); discussed in Samuel Gross, "Lost Lives: Miscarriages of Justice in Capital Cases," *Law & Contemporary Problems* 61, no. 4 (Autumn 1998): 125, 139.

161. See, for example, NACDL News, "Fred Zain Loses Appeal," *The Champion* (July 6, 2000): 13 (discussing trial for obtaining money by false pretenses by state police chemist for falsifying evidence in criminal cases); Geoffrey Campbell, "Erdmann Faces New Legal Woes: Pathologist Indicted for Perjury in Texas Murder," *American Bar Association Journal* (November 1995): 32.

162. See, for example, Gross, "Lost Lives," 140 (providing examples).

163. See generally Radelet and Bedau, "Execution of the Innocent," 105; Gross, "Lost Lives," 170.

164. *People v. Roybal*, 19 Cal. 4th 481, 519, 966 P.2d 521, 544–45, 79 Cal. Rptr. 2d 487, 510–11 (1998).

165. 19 Cal. 4th at 520–21.

166. 6 Cal. 4th 215, 861 P.2d 1107, 24 Cal. Rptr. 2d 421 (1994).

167. *People v. Sandoval*, 4 Cal. 4th 155, 200–1, 14 Cal. Rptr. 2d 342, 841 P.2d 862 (1992) (Mosk, J., concurring/dissenting).

168. *Wash*, 6 Cal. 4th 215, 272, 861 P.2d 1107, 1143 (1994) (quoting argument). The prosecutor then went further: he also "improperly urged the jury to sentence defendant to death based on a letter written by the father of a crime victim in an unrelated case." 6 Cal. 4th at 279.

169. 6 Cal. 4th at 260, 861 P.2d at 1135.

170. 6 Cal. 4th at 260, 861 P.2d at 1135.

171. 6 Cal. 4th at 260, 861 P.2d at 1135.

172. 6 Cal. 4th at 260, 861 P.2d at 1135.

173. 6 Cal. 4th at 279.

174. 264 Ga. 879, 891, 452 SE2d 745, 748 (1995).

175. The conviction was affirmed and counsel's performance was not deemed ineffective (264 Ga. at 891).

176. The prosecutor said that Hammond "violated the law of God. . . . Whoever sheds the blood of man by man shall his blood be shed" (264 Ga. at 886).

177. 264 Ga. at 886.

178. 264 Ga. at 886.

179. *State v. Rhines*, 1996 SD 55, 548 NW2d 415, 459 (Sabers, J., dissenting).

180. *Arave v. Creech*, 507 U.S. 463, 474 (1993).

181. Note that in *Godfrey v. Georgia*, 446 U.S. 420 (1980) the Court ruled that the "especially heinous, atrocious and cruel" standard was unconstitutionally vague if left undefined for the jury.

182. See, for example, *State v. Rhines*, 1996 SD 55, 548 NW2d 415 (upholding finding of torture).

183. For example, the jury will be "death qualified."

184. Citing eleven factors, including the circumstances of the crime, which presumably have been considered in finding the existence of at least one special circumstance. *Tuilaepa v. California*, 512 U.S. 967, 969 (1994).

185. *Tuilaepa*, 512 U.S. at 973 (citing *Walton*, 497 U.S. at 655 and *Gregg*, 428 U.S. at 193–94).

186. *Tuilaepa*, 512 U.S. at 977–78.

187. *Tuilaepa*, 512 U.S. at 980–81 (Souter, J., concurring) (quoting *Jurek v. Texas*, 428 U.S. 262, 279 (1976) [White, J., concurring]).

188. *Tuilaepa*, 512 U.S. at 984.

189. *Tuilaepa*, 512 U.S. at 986.

190. For example, killing in cold blood-hot blood, with motive—without motive. *Tuilaepa*, 512 U.S. at 986 and n. 2–14.

191. *Tuilaepa*, 512 U.S. at 988.

192. *Tuilaepa*, 512 U.S. at 988–99 and n. 16.

193. 512 U.S. at 989 (quoting *People v. Lucky*, 45 Cal. 3d 259, 302, 247 Cal. Rptr. 1, 28, 753 P.2d 1052, 1080 (1988), certiorari denied 488 U.S. 1034 (1989).

194. SDCL 23A-27A-1(10). The statute does not specify whether the drug-related killing must involve an undercover officer or innocent bystander, so it would encompass the killing of another drug dealer.

195. See *State v. Rhines*, 1996 SD 55, & 221, 548 NW2d 415, 458–461 (Sabers, J., dissenting) (canvassing murder cases in addressing proportionality of death penalty).

196. See 720 Ill. Comp. Stat. Ann. 5/9-1 (West 1993 and Supp. 1998). See also Bienen, "The Quality of Justice," 159.

197. Tex. Penal Code Ann. §19.03 (West 1994).

198. Tex. Code Crim. Proc. Ann. art. 37.071 (Supp. 1999).

199. See, for example, SDCL 23A-27A-1(3); OCGA. §17-10-30(b)(4); S.C. Code Ann. §16-3-20 (C)(a)(1)(e); N.J.S.A. 2C: 11-3c(4)(d).

200. See, for example, *State v. Rhines*, 1996 SD 55, 548 NW2d 415.

201. See *State v. Chew*, 695 A.2d 1301, 1311 (N.J. 1997); *State v. Wiley*, 484 So.2d 339 (Miss. 1986) overruled by *Willie v. State*, 585 So.2d 660 (Miss. 1991). But see *State v. Trostle*, 951 P.2d 869 (Az. 1997).

202. 108 F.3d 872, 874 (8th Cir. 1997) (Heaney, J., concurring).

203. *Tuilaepa v. California*, 512 U.S. 967 (1994) (approving California's aggravators and special circumstances); *Godfrey v. Georgia*, 446 U.S. 420 (1980) (disapproving of "heinous, atrocious and cruel" factor if terms are undefined).

204. See 18 U.S.C. 3591, *et seq* for the federal capital punishment scheme. The statute was enacted in 1994 and amended by the Antiterrorism and Effective Death Penalty Act of 1996. The federal death penalty was reinstituted by the Anti-Drug Abuse Act of 1988 (Pul. L. No. 100-690) with pertinent section codified at 21 U.S.C. 848(e). See generally David J. Novak, "Anatomy of a Federal Death Penalty Prosecution: A Primer for Prosecutors," *South Carolina Law Review* 50, no. 3 (Spring 1999): 645–77.

205. Steven Childress and Martha Davis, *Federal Standards of Review* 7-1 (3d ed., 1999).

206. 462 U.S. 862 (1983). The Court refused to grant relief to the convicted person despite error in the judge's instructions on one statutory aggravating circumstance.

207. 462 U.S. at 885. See also *Barclay v. Florida*, 463 U.S. 939 (1983); *Satterwhite v. Texas*, 486 U.S. 249 (1988).

208. *Satterwhite*, 486 U.S. at 258.

209. 477 U.S. 168 (1986).

210. Gershman, "The New Prosecutors," 427–28, quoting *Darden*, 477 U.S. at 180, 183.

211. *People v. Roybal*, 19 Cal. 4th 481, 966 P.2d 521, 79 Cal. Rptr. 2d 487 (1998).

212. *Roybal*, 19 Ca. 4th 4841.

213. *State v. Hammond*, 264 Ga. 879, 452 SE2d 745 (1995).

214. *State v. Hammond*, 264 Ga. at 879.

215. *State v. Rhines*, 1996 SD 55, 548 NW2d 415; *State v. Craig*, 699 So.2d 865 (La. 1997).

216. *Long v. State*, 823 SW2d 259 (Tx. Ct. Crim. App. 1992).

217. 823 SE2d at 259.

218. *State v. Roy*, 681 So.2d 1230 (La. 1996). See generally David McCord, "Is Death 'Different' for Purposes of Harmless Error Analysis? Should It Be? An Assessment of United States and Louisiana Supreme Court Case Law," *Louisiana Law Review* 59, no. 4 (Summer 1999): 1105–67.

219. Gershman, "The New Prosecutors," 428–29.

220. Larry W. Yackle, "The Figure in the Carpet," *Texas Law Review* 78, no. 7 (June 2000): 1731–70.

221. The Justice noted his "own deep moral reservations" about the death penalty, *Sawyer v. Whitley*, 505 U.S. 333, 358 (1992) (Blackmun, J., concurring in judgment); *Callins v. Collins*, 510 U.S. 1141, 1157 (1994) (Blackmun, J., dissenting from denial of certiorari).

222. *Sawyer v. Whitley*, 505 U.S. 333, 358 (1992). The justice reiterated this belief in *Callins v. Collins*, 510 U.S. 1141, 1157 (1994).

223. 372 U.S. 391 (1963).

224. *Whitley*, 505 U.S. at 441.

225. *Stone v. Powell*, 428 U.S. 465, 491 n. 31, and 493 n. 35 (1976).

226. *Powell*, 428 U.S. at 502 (Brennan, J., dissenting).

227. *Powell*, 428 U.S. at 530.

228. See *Lambrix v. Singletary*, 520 U.S. 518 (1997); *Teague v. Lane*, 489 U.S. 288 (1989). See also Larry W. Yackle, "The Habeas Hagioscope," *Southern California Law Review* 66, no. 6 (September 1993): 2331–2431; Joseph L. Hoffman, "The Supreme Court's New Vision of Federal Habeas Corpus for State Prisoners," *Supreme Court Review* 165 (1989): 165–93; Mary C. Hutton, "Retroactivity in the States: The Impact of *Teague v. Lane* on State Postconviction Remedies," *Alabama Law Review* 44, no. 2 (Winter 1993): 421–76.

229. *Saffle v. Parks*, 494 U.S. 484 (1990); *Butler v. McKellar*, 494 U.S. 407 (1990); *Sawyer v. Smith*, 497 U.S. 227 (1990); *Graham v. Collins*, 506 U.S. 461 (1993).

230. *McCleskey v. Zant*, 499 U.S. 467 (1991).

231. *Coleman v. Thompson*, 501 U.S. 722 (1991).

232. *Sawyer v. Whitley*, 505 U.S. 333 (1992).

233. *Herrera v. Collins*, 506 U.S. 390 (1993). Chief Justice Rehnquist and Justices Scalia and Thomas were in the plurality. The six other members of the Court stated that the execution of an innocent person would violate the Constitution. Justices O'Connor, Kennedy, and White joined the plurality to decide the prisoner had not presented sufficient evidence of actual innocence. Justices Blackmun, Stevens, and Souter dissented.

234. See, for example, 28 U.S.C. §2254(d), requiring that federal courts defer to state court applications of federal law, unless they are "contrary to, or involved an unreasonable application of clearly established Federal law, as determined by the Supreme Court of the United States." The Court had declined to adopt this standard of review in *Wright v. West*, 505 U.S. 277 (1992) but has acknowledged it is now bound by that standard, *Williams v. Taylor*, 120 S. Ct. 1495 (2000).

235. 28 U.S.C. §2241 (1994). See generally, Scott Moss, "An Appeal by Any Other Name: Congress's Empty Victory over Habeas Rights," *Harvard Civil Rights–Civil Liberties Law Review* 32, no. 1 (Winter 1997): 249–63.

236. Stephen Reinhardt, "The Anatomy of an Execution: Fairness vs. 'Process,'" *New York University Law Review* 74, no. 2 (May 1999): 313–53, discussing *Calderon v. Thompson*, 523 U.S. 538 (1998) reversing 120 F.3d 1045 (9th Cir. 1997) (en banc).

237. See Reinhardt, "The Anatomy of an Execution," 321–22 and 341–47.

238. Reinhardt, "The Anatomy of an Execution," 319 and n. 27.

239. *Stone v. Powell*, 428 U.S. at 491, n. 31, and 493, n. 35.

240. Successive petitions and abusive petitions were virtually eliminated by 28 U.S.C. 2254 through the habeas corpus amendments in the Antiterrorism and Effective Death Penalty Act of 1996. But see *Slack v. McDaniel*, 120 S. Ct. 1595 (2000).

241. *Stone v. Powell*, 428 U.S. 465, 523–24 (Brennan, J., dissenting).

242. *Powell*, 428 U.S. at 525. Ironically, the section quoted goes on to discuss the breadth of the federal habeas statute, encompassing expansive federal review of state cases. Congress has now aligned itself with those urging a decreased federal role in all habeas cases, including capital. See pertinent sections of the Antiterrorism and Effective Death Penalty Act of 1996, codified in various sections of 28 U.S.C. 2241, *et seq.*

243. *Powell*, 428 U.S. at 534.

244. Chris Hutton, "The 'New' Federal Habeas: Implications for State Standards of Review," *South Dakota Law Review* 40, no. 3 (1995): 442–77 (footnotes omitted).

245. See Stephen B. Bright, "Elected Judges and the Death Penalty in Texas: Why Full Habeas Corpus Review by Independent Federal Judges Is Indispensable to Protecting Constitutional Rights," *Texas Law Review* 78, no. 7 (June 2000): 1805–37; Stephen B. Bright, "Death in Texas," *The Champion* (July 1999): 16, 19 (noting that two judges on the Texas Court of Criminal Appeals who merely urged more care in capital cases did not win reelection to the court).

246. As the Court explained in *Wainwright v. Witt*, 469 U.S. 412, 423 (1985), "Exclusion of jurors opposed to capital punishment began with a recognition that certain of those jurors might frustrate the State's legitimate interest in administering constitutional capital sentencing schemes by not following their oaths."

It is interesting to note that when questioned, potential jurors may indicate opposition to the death penalty but be equally firm that their ability to judge guilt in the merits phase would be unaffected by potential punishment. Those jurors still may be challenged for cause. See, for example, *People v. Roybal*, 19 Cal. 4th 481, 518, 966 P.2d 521, 543, 79 Cal. Rptr. 487 (1998).

In addition, the defendant may seek to rehabilitate a prospective juror who expresses reservations about capital punishment and it may be error to refuse such a request. See, for example, *Willacy v. State*, 640 So.2d 1079 (Fla. 1994).

247. *Witherspoon v. Illinois*, 381 U.S. 510 (1968).

248. Witherspoon, 381 U.S. 510. The term "*Witherspoon*-excludables" developed to describe these people.

249. Recognizing the inconsistency between the standards for excluding jurors that it had announced in *Witherspoon v. Illinois*, 391 U.S. 510 (1968) and *Adams v. Texas*, 448 U.S. 38 (1980), the Court used *Wainwright v. Witt*, 469 U.S. 412 (1985) as the vehicle to make clear the pertinent test:

We therefore take this opportunity to clarify our decision in *Witherspoon*, and to reaffirm the above-quoted standard from *Adams* as the proper standard for determining when a prospective juror may be excluded for cause because of his or her views on capital punishment. That standard is whether the juror's views would "prevent or substantially impair the performance of his duties as a juror in accordance with his instructions and his oath." We note that, in addition to dispensing with *Witherspoon's* reference to "automatic" decision making, this standard likewise does not require that a juror's bias be proved with "unmistakable clarity." This is because determinations of juror bias cannot be reduced to question-and-answer sessions which obtain results in the manner of a catechism. What common sense should have realized experience has proved: many veniremen simply cannot be asked enough questions to reach the point where their bias has been made "unmistakably clear"; these veniremen may not know how they will react when faced with imposing the death sentence, or may be unable to articulate, or may wish to hide their true feelings. Despite this lack of clarity in the printed record, however, there will be situations where the trial judge is left with the definite impression that a prospective juror would be unable to faithfully and impartially apply the law. For reasons that will be developed more fully *infra*, this is why deference must be paid to the trial judge who sees and hears the juror. (*Wainwright v. Witt*, 469 U.S. at 424–25 [1985])

Whether states are required to follow *Wainwright v. Witt* was raised by the Georgia Supreme Court in *Greene v. State*, 268 Ga. 47, 485 SE2d 741, 742–43 (1997). States may choose to adopt the *Witt* standard regardless of whether they are required to do so. See *Foster v. State*, 614 So.2d 455 (Fla. 1992) certiorari denied 510 U.S. 951 (1993).

250. *Wainwright v. Witt*, 469 U.S. at 426.

251. See, for example, *People v. Wash*, 6 Cal. 4th 215, 861 P.2d 1107, 24 Cal. Rptr. 2d 421 (1993); *Castro v. State*, 644 So.2d 987 (Fl. 1994). Although a trial judge has great latitude in conducting voir dire, certain restrictive procedural rules may impinge on a defendant's right to a fair trial. In *State v. Erazo*, 126 N.J. 112, 594 A.2d 232 (N.J. 1991), the New Jersey Supreme Court reversed defendant's sentence because of insufficient evidence of an aggravating factor. While the majority focused on this deficiency, the concurring justice delved further into the trial record. The concurrence criticized the trial court's imposition of a "three-minute" rule for voir dire. Under this rule, counsel had a total of three minutes to "conduct a thorough examination" to inquire into potential juror bias. Moreover, the concurring justice blasted the trial court's refusal to ask defense counsel's questions during voir dire. In refusing to allow any of defense counsel's questions, the trial court unbelievably replied, "We're not interested in their opinions on the death penalty. This is not a philosophy class." Thus in refusing to permit an assessment of a prospective juror's views on the death penalty in voir dire, the trial judge failed to ensure a fair trial. 126 N.J. at 147 (Handler, J., concurring).

252. See, for example, *Van Poyck v. Singletary*, 715 So.2d 930, 936 (Fl. 1998) (examining voir dire of pro death penalty venire person). See also John Holdridge, "Selecting Capital Jurors Uncommonly Willing to Condemn a Man to Die: Lower Courts' Contradictory Readings of *Wainwright v. Witt* and *Morgan v. Illinois*," *Mississippi College Law Review* 19, no. 2 (Spring 1999): 283–303.

253. Some states incorporate these rules by statute. See, for example, La. C. Cr. P. art. 798(2) which provides that the state may challenge the following jurors for cause:

The juror tendered in a capital case who has conscientious scruples against the infliction of capital punishment without regard to any evidence that might be developed at the trial of the case before him;
    (a) That he would automatically vote against the imposition of capital punishment without regard to any evidence that might be developed at the trial of the case before him; (b) That his attitude toward the death penalty would prevent or substantially impair him from making an impartial decision as a juror in accordance with his instructions and his oath; or (c) That his attitude toward the death penalty would prevent him from making an impartial decision as to the defendant's guilt. . . .

In addition, a juror may be unqualified if he "is not impartial, whatever the cause [unless] he de-clares, and the court is satisfied, that he can render an impartial verdict according to the law and the evidence." (La.C.Cr.P. art. 797[2])
See *State v. Langley*, 711 So.2d 651, 672 (La. 1998).

254. *Langley*, 711 So.2d at 656–57.
255. Thomas A. Mauet, *Fundamentals of Trial Techniques*, 3d ed. (1992), 23.
256. Craig Haney, "Juries and the Death Penalty: Readdressing the Witherspoon Ques-tion," *Crime and Delinquency* 5, no. 1 (1980): 512–27; Craig Haney, "Examining Death Qualification: Further Analysis of the Process Effect," *Law and Human Behavior* 8, no. 5 1/2 (1984): 133–51; Craig Haney, "On the Selection of Capital Juries: The Biasing Effects of the Death-Qualification Process," *Law and Human Behavior* 8, no. 5 1/2 (1984): 121–32; Craig Haney, Aida Hurtado, and Luis Vega, "'Modern' Death Qualification: New Data on its Bias-ing Effect," *Law and Human Behavior* 18, no. 6 (1994): 619–33.
257. Mike Allen, Edward Mabry and Drue-Marie McKelton, "Impact of Juror Attitudes about the Death Penalty on Juror Evaluations of Guilt and Punishment: A Meta-Analysis," *Law and Human Behavior* 22, no. 6 (1998): 715, 716.
258. In *Witherspoon*, the Court expressed its concern that the jury selected under existing standards would be overly anxious to convict on the merits. The Court said:

If the State had excluded only those prospective jurors who stated in advance of trial that they would not even consider returning a verdict of death, it could argue that the resulting jury was simply "neu-tral" with respect to penalty. But when it swept from the jury all who expressed conscientious or re-ligious scruples against capital punishment and all who opposed it in principle, the State crossed the line of neutrality. In its quest for a jury capable of imposing the death penalty, the State produced a jury uncommonly willing to condemn a man to die. [Citations omitted]. (*Witherspoon*, 391 U.S. at 520–21)

259. Allen, Mabry and McKelton, "Impact of Juror Attitudes," 716.
260. Allen et al., "Impact of Juror Attitudes," 716.
261. The authors explain "meta-analysis" as follows:

Meta-analysis provides a method of systematically summarizing existing empirical literature. The goal of meta-analysis is to provide an average effect for a body of research. The process of meta-analysis involves (1) the collection of available studies, (2) the extraction of statistical information and conversion to a common metric, and then (3) the averaging of effects and the evaluation of the distribution of that information and possible moderating conditions.

Meta-analytic methodology uses a systematic form of literature review in which the individual studies are treated identically. The provision is that the effects of each study are weighted by sam-pling error. The weighting is based on the assumption that a study with a larger sample size is a bet-ter estimate of the effect than a study with a smaller sample size. This consideration permits the as-sessment of both Type I and Type II error in a compilation of literature.

The qualitative features that distinguish studies from one another, that is, methodological differ-ences, serve as possible sources of intervening influences. In other words, the methodological dis-tinction between studies could be the source of divergent effects. This possibility is considered by addressing whether the observed variability in effects could be the outcome of random sampling er-ror or the outcome of some other systematic influence that differs among the studies.

The goal of meta-analysis is to generate findings that represent an entire body of literature. The procedural process requires that researchers use explicit sets of rules. Explicit commitment to rules regarding the acquisition and analysis of data means the outcomes of the process can be replicated by other researchers. Nonquantitative reviews of the literature, often called narrative reviews, are difficult to compare because the basis of the literature search and the methods used by the investigator are not articulated in a manner that permits replication.

More importantly, meta-analytic findings can be compared to additional data sets not included in the original analysis and provide the basis for subsequent research efforts. Thus, future or newly uncovered research can be compared using the existing meta-analysis as a basis for comparison. Another important issue is that procedural variations as safeguards may be considered. The outcome from a different procedure can be compared to the current procedures to determine whether differences in outcomes occur. The explicitness of the method permits future reviewers to evaluate the adequacy and accuracy of any claim advanced. (Allen et al., "Impact of Juror Attitudes," 719–20)

262. Allen, Mabry and McKelton, "Impact of Juror Attitudes," 722–24.

263. See Stephen P. Garvey, "Aggravation and Mitigation in Capital Cases: What Do Jurors Think?" *Columbia Law Review* 98, no. 6 (October 1998): 1538–76 (describing results of survey of capital jurors who sat in forty-one capital cases in South Carolina between 1986 and 1993).

264. Beatrix Simon Zakhair and Rainey E. Ransom, "Jurors in Capital Cases: What Can One Maryland Jury Teach Us?" *Criminal Justice* 14, no. 2 (Summer 1999): 18–24. See also William J. Bowers and Benjamin Steiner, "Death by Default: An Empirical Demonstration of False and Forced Choices in Capital Sentencing," *Texas Law Review* 77, no. 3 (February 1999): 605–717.

265. *Crowe v. State*, 265 Ga. 582, 458 SE2d 799 (1995). See also *Pruitt v. State*, 258 Ga. 583, 373 SE2d 192 (1988). Rehabilitation of such jurors by the state is common.

266. *Pruitt v. State*, 258 Ga. 583, 373 SE2d 192 (1988). See also *Brice v. State*, 286 A.2d 132 (Md. Ct. App. 1972).

267. 268 Ga. 47, 485 SE2d 741 (1997).

268. 485 SE2d at 744.

269. 485 SE2d at 744.

270. 485 SE2d at 744.

271. 485 SE2d at 744.

272. 485 SE2d at 744.

273. 485 SE2d at 744.

274. 485 SE2d at 745–46.

275. 485 SE2d at 744.

276. 485 SE2d at 746.

277. 485 SE2d at 757.

278. 485 SE2d at 748.

279. 485 SE2d at 744, quoting Chief Justice Weltner in *Spivey v. State*, 253 Ga. 187, 197 n. 3, 319 SE2d 420 (1984).

280. 485 SE2d at 748.

281. 485 SE2d at 748, quoting *Spivey v. State*, 253 Ga. at 197, n. 3.

282. Jurors may not wish to serve on a capital case and may formulate their responses in voir dire to achieve this end. The court generally instructs jurors about what views would disqualify them; there exists a danger that the response would be fashioned accordingly. See, for example, *State v. Dixon*, 125 N.J. 223, 243, 493 A.2d 266, 276 (1991). See also *Morgan v. Illinois*, 504 U.S. 719, 726 (1992), concluding that "reverse-*Witherspoon*" questions are required to identify those prospective jurors who harbor convictions in support of the death penalty.

283. *Compare State v. Langley*, 711 So.2d 651, 673 (La. 1998) where the court stated:

> If the circumstances under which a prospective juror could vote for the death penalty are too narrowly limited, the prospective juror may be properly discharged for cause. This is similar to the issue we recently discussed in *Williams*, 96-1023; 708 So.2d 703. In our *Williams* opinion, we recognized that prospective jurors were properly excluded when their ability to decide on the death penalty would be substantially impaired by the presence of a mitigating factor—in that case the defendant's youth. *Williams*, 96-1023, pp. 9–10; 708 So.2d at 713.

The defendant in *Williams* was eighteen years old at the time of the offense. Perhaps jurors' unwillingness to impose capital punishment on a young defendant is an indication the community as a whole views it as excessive.

284. See *State v. Dixon*, 125 N.J. 223, 233, 593 A.2d 266, 271 (1991), discussing possible underrepresentation of minorities on capital case juries and presenting statistical analysis of race of members of jury pool.

285. See also *State v. Detrich*, 188 Ariz. 57, 65, 932 P.2d 1328, 1336 (1997) (disqualification of juror unable to be impartial about the death penalty is imperative). It is noteworthy that in Arizona, jurors are asked about their views on capital punishment during the voir dire in a capital case even though they do not impose sentence. That task is assigned to the trial judge. The inquiry in voir dire is to ascertain whether opposition to the death penalty would cause a juror to vote for acquittal, knowing death could result from a guilty verdict. See, for example, *State v. LaGrand*, 153 Ariz. 21, 31, 734 P.2d 563, 574 (1987); *State v. Martinez-Villareal*, 145 Ariz. 441, 449, 702 P.2d 670, 678 (1985) (citing cases).

A number of courts have held that *Batson v. Kentucky*, 476 U.S. 79 (1986), does not extend to views on the death penalty. See, for example, *State v. Detrich*, 188 Ariz. 57, 66, 932 P.2d 1328, 1337 (1997). However there may be some overlap in the *Batson* and death qualification issues. See, for example, *People v. Howard*, 1 Cal. 4th 1132, 824 P.2d 1315, 5 Cal. Rptr. 2d 268 (1992). And, there is no constitutional right to attorney-conducted voir dire in a capital case. *State v. Howard*, 192 N.J. Super. 571, 471 A.2d 796 (1983).

Improper exclusion of a juror for cause is not subject to harmless error review, although the penalty, and not the verdict, is subject to reversal in such a case. Courts have ruled that all peremptory challenges must be exercised to preserve the issue. *State v. Langley*, 711 So.2d 651, 671–72 (La. 1998) citing *Gray v. Mississippi*, 481 U.S. 648 (1987).

286. See, for example, Sister Monica Kostielney, "Understanding Justice with Clarity, Civility, and Compassion: Reflections on Selected Biblical Passages and Catholic Church Teaching on the Death Penalty," *Thomas M. Cooley Law Review* 13, no. 3 (Michaelmas Term 1996): 967–76; Thomas J. Walsh, "On the Abolition of Man: A Discussion of the Moral and Legal Issues Surrounding the Death Penalty," *Cleveland State Law Review* 44, no. 1 (1996): 23, 29–33; Walter Berns, "The Death Penalty: A Philosophical and Theological Perspective," *John Marshall Law Review* 30, no. 1 (Fall 1997): 463–506 (transcript of panel discussion).

287. The question may be viewed as a human rights issue. See, for example, Report by International Commission of Jurists, "Administration of the Death Penalty in the United States," *Human Rights Quarterly* 19, no. 1 (February 1997): 165–213, analyzing the death penalty in the United States under the International Covenant on Civil and Political Rights (ICCPR) ratified by the United States in 1992, and the International Convention on the Elimination of All Forms of Racial Discrimination (ICERD), ratified by the United States in 1994, and finding the capital punishment system lacking.

288. Weisberg, "Deregulating Death," 313.

289. Weisberg, "Deregulating Death," 313.

290. Weisberg, "Deregulating Death," 313.

291. *McGautha*, 402 U.S. 183, 204 (1971). Weisberg stressed that Justice Harlan did not say that a jury's decision to kill is inevitably irrational. He said with some confidence that as jurors face so obviously awesome a decision, they will naturally act with appropriate moral seriousness, guided by at least intuitive moral rationality. Harlan thought that we cannot mitigate our ambivalence about condemning people to death by dignifying our decision with the illusory language of legal science. Weisberg, "Deregulating Death," 312.

292. Steiker and Steiker, "Sober Second Thoughts," 349. For a resounding critique of Steiker and Steiker's article, see David McCord, "Judging the Effectiveness of the Supreme Court's Death Penalty Jurisprudence According to the Court's Own Goals: Mild Success or Major Disaster?" *Florida State University Law Review* 24, no. 3 (Spring 1997): 545–603.

293. Steiker and Steiker, "Sober Second Thoughts," 415.

294. Steiker and Steiker, "Sober Second Thoughts," 417–18.

295. Steiker and Steiker, "Sober Second Thoughts," 418–19. The authors note this would include consideration of statistical evidence, rejected as a possibility in *McCleskey v. Kemp*, 481 U.S. 279 (1987).

296. Steiker and Steiker, "Sober Second Thoughts," 426.

297. Steiker and Steiker, "Sober Second Thoughts," 431.

298. Steiker and Steiker, "Sober Second Thoughts," 429–34.

299. Steiker and Steiker, "Sober Second Thoughts," 436.

300. Steiker and Steiker, "Sober Second Thoughts," 438.

CHAPTER 17

1. Illinois governor George Ryan took the step of imposing a moratorium.

2. Sonia Rosen and Stephen Journey, "Abolition of the Death Penalty: An Emerging Norm of International Law," *Hamline Journal of Public Law and Policy* 14, no. 2 (Fall 1993): 163.

3. Universal Declaration of Human Rights (UDHR) Article 3, adopted December 10, 1948, G.A. Res. 217A (III), UN. Doc. A/810, at 71 (1948), and International Covenant on Civil and Political Rights (ICCPR) Article 6, adopted December 16, 1966, entered into force March 23, 1976, G.A. Res. 2200 (XXI), UN. Doc. A/6316 (1966).

4. ICCPR, Article 6.

5. ICCPR Article 6, para. 2.

6. ICCPR Article 6, para. 5. However, not all countries abide by this paragraph, see some minimum ages discussed in Dennis Wiechman, Jerry Kendall, and Ronald Bae, "International Use of the Death Penalty," *International Journal of Comparative and Applied Criminal Justice* 14, no. 2 (Winter 1990): 243.

7. See the discussion in Wiechman, Kendall, and Bae, "International Use of the Death Penalty," 242, and also Joseph E. Schumacher, "An International Look at the Death Penalty," *International Journal of Comparative and Applied Criminal Justice* 14, no. 2 (Winter 1990): 310–11.

8. Human Rights Committee, General Comment 6, U.N. Doc. HRI/GEN/1, 5.

9. Capital Punishment, U.N. GAOR 3d Committee, 23d Session, U.N. Doc. A/Res/2393 (1968).

10. UNGA Resolution 44/128, December 1989; discussed in John Hatchard, "Capital Punishment in Southern Africa: Some Recent Developments," *International and Comparative Law Quarterly* 43, no. 4 (October 1994): 923.

11. UN Commission on Human Rights, Resolution 1993/15, February 1993, in Hatchard, "Capital Punishment in Southern Africa: Some Recent Developments," 923.

12. Amnesty International, *The Death Penalty Worldwide: Developments in 1999* (Report ACT 50/04/00), 10.

13. Amnesty International, *The Death Penalty Worldwide: Developments in 1999*, 14.

14. The Sixth Protocol to the European Convention for the Protection of Human Rights and Fundamental Freedoms, Article 1, entered into force March 1, 1985. Protocol No. 6 to the European Convention for the Protection of Human Rights and Fundamental Freedom, adopted April 28, 1983, entered into force March 1, 1985, E.T.S. 114, reprinted in 22 I.L.M. 539 (1983). There are twenty-three states' parties.

15. The protocol states, "A State may make provision in its law for the death penalty in respect of acts committed in time of war or of imminent threat of war; such penalty shall be applied only in the instances laid down in the law and in accordance with its provisions" (Sixth Protocol, art. 2).

16. "No reservation may be made under Article 64 of the Convention in respect of the provisions of this Protocol" (art. 4).

17. Amnesty International Report 345 (1993) quoted in Rosen and Journey, "Abolition of the Death Penalty," 166.

18. Amnesty International Report 345 (1993) quoted in Rosen and Journey, "Abolition of the Death Penalty," 167.

19. Nigel Rodley, Amnesty International Report 345 (1993) quoted in Rosen and Journey, "Abolition of the Death Penalty," 167.

20. Amnesty International, *The Death Penalty Worldwide: Developments in 1999*, 9.

21. American Convention on Human Rights (pact of San Jose), signed November 22, 1969, entered into force July 18, 1978, O.A.S.T.S. 36, O.A.S. off Rec. OEA/Ser.L/II/II.23, doc. 21, rev., 6 (1979), reprinted in 9 I.L.M. 637 (1970). There are twenty-eight states' parties.

22. Protocol to the American Convention on Human Rights to Abolish the Death Penalty, adopted June 8, 1990, entered into force August 28, 1991, O.A.S.T.S. 73, reprinted in 29 I.L.M. 1447 (1990). There are three states' parties.

23. Article 1, O.A.S.T.S. No. 73.

24. Article 2.

25. Inter-American Convention on Extradition, 20 I.L.M. 723 (1981).

26. Amnesty International, *The Death Penalty Worldwide: Developments in 1999*, 9.

27. *State v. Makwanyane*, Constitutional Court of South Africa, 1995(3) South Africa Law Reports 391.

28. *State v. Makwanyane*, 26.

29. Hatchard, "Capital Punishment in Southern Africa," 923.

30. Hatchard, "Capital Punishment in Southern Africa: Some Recent Developments," 924.

31. Hatchard, "Capital Punishment in Southern Africa: Some Recent Developments," 934.

32. Amnesty International, *The Death Penalty Worldwide: Developments in 1999*, 16.

33. See A/RES/35/172, December 15, 1980, and Arbitrary and Summary Executions, G.A. Res. 36/22, U.N. G.A.O.R., 36th Sess., Supp. No. 51, at 168, U.N. Doc. A/36/645 (1981): November 9, 1981.

34. Further discussion on customary law can be found later.

35. See further discussion in William A. Schabas, "International Norms on Execution of the Insane and the Mentally Retarded," *Criminal Law Forum* 4, no. 1 (1993): 103–4.

36. See the discussion in Ved P. Nanda, "Recent Developments in the United States and Internationally Regarding Capital Punishment—An Appraisal," *St. John's Law Review* 67, no. 1 (Spring 1999): 546.

37. See the discussion in Hatchard, "Capital Punishment in South Africa: Some Recent Developments," 927. See also Schabas, "International Norms on Execution of the Insane and the Mentally Retarded," 95.

38. Nanda, "Recent Developments in the United States and Internationally," 523.

39. Amnesty International, *The Death Penalty Worldwide: Developments in 1999*, 21.

40. Schabas, "International Norms on Execution of the Insane and the Mentally Retarded," 96.

41. Schabas, "International Norms on Execution of the Insane and the Mentally Retarded," 98–100.

42. Safeguards Guaranteeing Protection of the Rights of Those Facing the Death Penalty, E.S.C. Res. 1984/50, U.N.E.S.C.O.R., Supp. No. 1, at 33, U.N. Doc. E/1984/92 (1984), cited in Schabas, "International Norms on Execution of the Insane and the Mentally Retarded," 101.

43. Schabas, "International Norms on Execution of the Insane and the Mentally Retarded," 101.

44. Schabas, "International Norms on Execution of the Insane and the Mentally Retarded," 107.

45. Report of the Committee on Crime Prevention and Control at Its Tenth Session, U.N. E.S.C.O.R., Supp. No. 10, at 28–29, U.N. Doc. E/1988/20 (1988), cited in Schabas, "International Norms on Execution of the Insane and the Mentally Retarded," 107–8.

46. Schabas, "International Norms on Execution of the Insane and the Mentally Retarded," 114.

47. Schabas, "International Norms on Execution of the Insane and the Mentally Retarded," 112–13.

48. Amnesty International, *The Death Penalty Worldwide: Developments in 1999*, 32–33.

49. Amnesty International, *Facts and Figures about the Death Penalty* (Report ACT 50/06/00), 2.

50. Amnesty International, *Facts and Figures about the Death Penalty*, 3.

51. Amnesty International, *Facts and Figures about the Death Penalty*, 3.

52. Amnesty International, *The Death Penalty Worldwide: Developments in 1999*, 32.

53. Amnesty International, *The Death Penalty: List of Abolitionist and Retentionist Countries* (Report ACT 50/05/00), 1.

54. Amnesty International, *The Death Penalty: List of Abolitionist and Retentionist Countries*, 5.

55. Statute of the International Court of Justice, Article 38, signed June 26, 1945.

56. Peter Malanczuk, *Akehurst's Modern Introduction to International Law* (New York: Routledge, 1997), 40.

57. *The Paquette Habana*, 175 U.S. 677 (1900).

58. *The Case of the S.S. Lotus* (France v. Turkey), Permanent Court of International Justice, P.C.I.J. Seer. A No. 10 (1927).

59. See Justice Stephen Schwebel's dissent in the *Advisory Opinion on the Legality of Nuclear Weapons*, 35 ILM 809 (1996), 836–37.

60. *Fisheries Case (United Kingdom v. Norway)*, I.C.J. 116 (1951), 138.

61. *Asylum Case (Colombia v. Peru)*, I.C.J. 266 (1950), 277.

62. *Colombia v. Peru*, 294.

63. *Colombia v. Peru*, 294.

64. Malanczuk, *Akehurst's Modern Introduction to International Law*, 43.

65. *France v. Turkey*, 28.

66. I.C.J. Decision in North Sea Continental Shelf Cases (Continental Shelf Boundaries: Relationship of Multilateral Treaties, Custom, and International Law) (*Federal Republic of Germany v. Denmark; Federal Republic of Germany v. Netherlands*), I.C.J. 3 (1969), 43.

67. *Colombia v. Peru*, 294.

68. "A peremptory norm of general international law is a norm accepted and recognized by the international community of States as a whole as a norm from which no derogation is permitted." Convention on the Law of Treaties (Vienna Convention), 1969, art. 53, I.L.M. vol. 8, 679.

69. Oscar Schachter, *International Law in Theory and Practice* (Dordrecht: Martinus Nijhoff, 1991), 335.

70. Schachter, *International Law*, 336.

71. Schachter, *International Law*, at 336.

72. Schachter, *International Law*, at 340.

73. Thomas Buergenthal, *International Human Rights in a Nutshell* (St. Paul, Minn.: West, 1988). This could be important in light of his election to the International Court of Justice.

74. Rosalyn Higgins, *Problems and Process: International Law and How We Use It* (Oxford: Clarendon, 1994), 19.

75. Louis Henkin, "International Law: Politics, Values and Functions: 216 Collected Courses of Hague Academy of International Law," *Recueil des Cours* 13, Vol. IV (1989): 54, quoted in Henry J. Steiner and Philip Alston, *International Human Rights in Context, Law, Politics, Morals* (Oxford: Oxford University Press, 1996).

76. See discussion of the role of religious groups in death penalty politics in Amnesty International, *The Death Penalty Worldwide: Developments in 1999*, 25.

77. This introduces the issue often discussed in the context of human rights—cultural relativism. This chapter obviously does not address cultural relativism in any depth.

78. Foreword in William Schabas, *The Abolition of the Death Penalty in International Law*, 2d ed. (Cambridge: Cambridge University Press, 1997), xi.

79. Schabas, "International Norms on Execution of the Insane and the Mentally Retarded," 116–17.

CHAPTER 18

1. 471 U.S. 1080, 1086 (1985).

2. 471 U.S. at 1094.

Index

Note: Entries in Italics refer to the table or chart on that page

About the Contributors

Cheryl A. Brown earned a Ph.D. in political science from Georgia State University in 1997. She currently teaches courses in political science and public administration as an assistant professor at Marshall University in Huntington, West Virginia, where she also serves as a graduate adviser. Her areas of expertise include public administration and all aspects of American politics, especially legislative affairs.

M. Christine Cagle works as a management analyst for the U.S. Centers for Disease Control and Prevention in Atlanta, Georgia, and also teaches political science as an adjunct professor at several universities in the Atlanta metropolitan area. She has published articles on American politics and public administration in a number of academic books and scholarly journals. Cagle earned a Ph.D. in political science from Georgia State University in 2000.

Douglas Clouatre is an assistant professor of political science at Kennesaw State University in Kennesaw, Georgia. He teaches courses in constitutional law and judicial politics and holds a Ph.D. in political science from the University of Tennessee.

Mark Douglas is an assistant professor of Christian ethics at Columbia Theological Seminary in Decatur, Georgia, and an ordained minister in the Presbyterian Church (USA). He holds a Ph.D. in religious ethics from the University of Virginia and has written on the role the American philosophical tradition of pragmatism plays in Christian ethics.

D. Brandon Hornsby is an attorney practicing products liability, medical malpractice, and personal injury law in Atlanta, Georgia. A member of the Georgia Bar Association, he served as assistant district attorney in Clayton County, Georgia, from 1994 until 1999. In that capacity, he was responsible for prosecuting death penalty cases. In 1998, he was selected as the Georgia Assistant District Attorney of the Year. Hornsby graduated from Florida State University and the Emory University School of Law, where he served as associate editor of the *Emory Law Journal.*

Chris Hutton teaches courses in criminal law, criminal procedure, and evidence at the University of South Dakota School of Law. A member of the bar in South Dakota and Kansas, she has written widely on capital punishment throughout her legal career. Hutton holds a J.D. from Washburn University and an LL.M. from Harvard University.

J. Michael Martinez began his career in the private practice of law. He currently works as a governmental affairs representative with a manufacturing company and teaches political science as a part-time faculty member at Kennesaw State University in Kennesaw, Georgia. In addition to publishing articles in numerous academic journals, he coedited *Ethics and Character: The Pursuit of Democratic Virtues* (Carolina Academic Press, 1998) and *Confederate Symbols in the Contemporary South* (University Press of Florida, 2000). A member of the bar in Georgia and South Carolina, Martinez earned a J.D. from Emory University and a Ph.D. in political science from Georgia State University.

John C. McAdams holds a Ph.D. from Harvard University and has been a faculty member in the Marquette University Department of Political Science in Milwaukee, Wisconsin, since 1977. His articles have appeared in the *Journal of Politics*, the *American Journal of Political Science*, the *Sociological Quarterly, Law and Contemporary Problems*, and numerous other journals. At Marquette, he teaches courses in American politics and public policy.

Robert A. Miller retired as chief justice of the South Dakota Supreme Court following a long and distinguished legal career. After earning degrees in business (1961) and law (1963) from the University of South Dakota, he served for two years as an assistant attorney general. Later, he practiced law for six years in Philip, South Dakota, and worked as state's attorney and city attorney. In 1971, Miller was appointed to the Sixth Circuit bench and eventually served as presiding judge of the circuit for ten years, beginning in 1976. In 1986, he was appointed to the state supreme court, where he won reelection in 1990 and 1998.

His colleagues on the state supreme court elected him chief justice in 1990, 1994, and 1998. In 1998, President Bill Clinton appointed him to the board of directors of the State Justice Institute.

William D. Richardson is a professor of political science, chair of the Department of Political Science, and director of the W. O. Farber Center for Civic Leadership at the University of South Dakota. He has published extensively in the areas of ethics, American politics, and politics and literature. His most recent book was *Democracy, Bureaucracy and Character: Founding Thought* (University Press of Kansas, 1997). Richardson also coedited *Ethics and Character: The Pursuit of Democratic Virtues* (Carolina Academic Press, 1998) and *Confederate Symbols in the Contemporary South* (University Press of Florida, 2000). He holds B.A., M.A., and Ph.D. degrees from the State University of New York at Buffalo.

Austin Sarat is the William Nelson Cromwell Professor of Jurisprudence and Political Science at Amherst College in Amherst, Massachusetts. A prolific scholar, Sarat has edited or authored more than thirty-five books on a wide range of topics, although he is best known for his writings in opposition to the death penalty. Admirers and critics alike have hailed his 2001 book, *When the State Kills: Capital Punishment and the American Condition*, as a landmark work in the study of American criminal justice. He holds a Ph.D. in political science from the University of Wisconsin and a J.D. from Yale Law School.

Timothy J. Schorn is an associate professor of political science and coordinator of the International Studies Program at the University of South Dakota. He holds J.D. and Ph.D. degrees from the University of Notre Dame.

Elizabeth Theiss Smith teaches at the University of South Dakota (USD) where she holds a joint appointment to the political science department and the W. O. Farber Center for Civic Leadership. Prior to joining USD, she was a visiting assistant professor in the master of public administration program at the University of Connecticut and spent two years teaching American government and politics at Clark University. Smith received her Ph.D. in political science from the University of Connecticut in 1998. She also earned a master of science in criminal justice from the University of New Haven, where she has served as an adjunct faculty member.

Glen H. Stassen is the Lewis B. Smedes Professor of Christian Ethics at Fuller Theological Seminary in Pasadena, California. A prolific scholar, he has written widely on issues such as social justice, Christian ethics, and peacemaking. In

1998, he edited and contributed to a series of essays, *Capital Punishment: A Reader*, published by Pilgrim Press. Stassen holds a B.D. from Union Theological Seminary and a Ph.D. from Duke University.

Ernest van den Haag retired as the John M. Olin Professor of Jurisprudence and Public Policy from the Fordham University School of Law in New York City. During his long and distinguished career, he taught political philosophy and law at New York University and lectured at the New School for Social Research. He also served as a Guggenheim fellow, a senior fellow of the National Endowment for the Humanities, a member of the Council on Foreign Relations, and president of the Philadelphia Society. Van den Haag is the author or coauthor of more than a dozen books and numerous articles, many of which focus on capital punishment.

Jacob J. Vellenga's 1959 seminal article in *Christianity Today*, "Is Capital Punishment Wrong?" is a classic theological defense of capital punishment. It is reprinted here as a response to the arguments advanced by Professors Douglas and Stassen.

Robert L. Young currently serves as professor and chair of the Department of Sociology and Anthropology at the University of Texas–Arlington. His areas of research include social interaction processes and public reactions to crime. Author of numerous academic articles on crime and punishment, Young also wrote *Understanding Misunderstandings* (University of Texas Press, 1999). He holds a Ph.D. in sociology from the University of Michigan.